OFFICE OF THE UNITED NATIONS
HIGH COMMISSIONER FOR HUMAN RIGHTS

# LEGISLATIVE HISTORY OF THE
# CONVENTION ON THE RIGHTS OF THE CHILD

VOLUME I

United Nations
New York and Geneva, 2007

**NOTE**

The designations employed and the presentation of the material in this publication do not imply the expression of any opinion whatsoever on the part of the Secretariat of the United Nations concerning the legal status of any country, territory, city or area, or of its authorities, or concerning the delimitation of its frontiers or boundaries.

\*

\*     \*

Material contained in this publication may be freely quoted or reprinted, provided credit is given and a copy of the publication containing the reprinted material is sent to the Office of the United Nations High Commissioner for Human Rights, 1211 Geneva 10, Switzerland.

HR/PUB/07/1

# Foreword by Louise Arbour, United Nations High Commissioner for Human Rights

The adoption of the Universal Declaration of Human Rights sixty years ago ushered in an era of prolific standard-setting in the field of international human rights law. As of 2007, universal human rights norms have been articulated in nine international human rights treaties, including the Convention on the Rights of the Child and its Optional Protocols. Since its unanimous adoption in 1989 and entry into force in 1990, the Convention has become the most widely ratified of the human rights treaties with 193 States parties, testifying to the willingness of States to embrace overarching norms that protect the rights of children, regardless of race, sex, religion, ethnic origin, ability or other status. These instruments reflect the principle of universal indivisible rights and responsibilities that are shared by all nations.

In the 21st century, our emphasis has shifted from standard-setting to implementation. The Convention on the Rights of the Child and its Optional Protocols are invaluable tools for doing just that. Through forty-four articles, the Convention outlines obligations borne by States parties, which are underpinned by the concepts of non-discrimination, the best interests of the child, the right to life, survival and development, and respect for the views of the child. Its Optional Protocols provide further tools to address the sexual exploitation of children and their involvement in armed conflict.

These volumes provide a comprehensive record of the legislative history of the Convention. I am confident that children and their advocates will find this publication to be an essential research tool. I would like to acknowledge the tireless efforts of Ms. Simone Ek of Save the Children, who was the driving force behind the preparation of this work. Many staff members of Save the Children also provided invaluable assistance. Significant support was provided by staff members of my Office.

Governments, individuals and members of the international community share an obligation to uphold the rights and freedoms of all, and to ensure that those rights are a living reality. This publication will be an important tool in achieving this goal.

Louise Arbour
United Nations High Commissioner for Human Rights

# Foreword by Rädda Barnen – Save the Children Sweden

Since the foundation of Rädda Barnen in 1919, the rights of the child have been the cornerstone of all our work. As early as 1923, the International Save the Children Union in Geneva drafted the first Geneva Declaration of the Rights of the Child, which the League of Nations adopted in 1924.

Of course, the work of Rädda Barnen has been strengthened by the adoption of the Convention on the Rights of the Child. It is the foundation underlying our work and an integral part of our statutes and of those of many other NGOs that are striving for a better world for our children. The Convention has not only given greater legitimacy to our work on the rights of the child, it has also provided us with a valuable tool to ensure the practical application of these rights. Putting the Convention into practice is ultimately a State obligation, but NGOs have a crucial role to play in persuading individual Governments that the rights of the child are a priority and that public funds should be allocated to them accordingly.

We are honoured that our initiative in compiling the proceedings that lasted a decade and led to the Convention has resulted in this *Legislative History* – the first such publication on any United Nations human rights treaty.

As an NGO, we find this historical perspective extremely valuable for interpreting the Convention in our work in Sweden and elsewhere. We also believe that this publication will help Governments, States parties, the Committee on the Rights of the Child, United Nations specialized agencies and organs, and international and national NGOs to acquire a deeper and more holistic understanding of the Convention. We expect that, by explaining the intentions of the drafters, this *Legislative History* will be useful in the interpretation of the standards, norms and principles of the Convention and in strengthening their application. Crucially, the *Legislative History* shows just how active NGOs were during the negotiation of the Convention. The cooperation between NGOs, Governments and the United Nations in this process highlights the importance of putting the best interests of the child first in all decision-making.

Finally, we hope that this *Legislative History* will also inspire research on the rights of the child at universities worldwide.

Marianne Nivert
Chair
Save the Children Sweden

Simone Ek
Former Director of International Relations
Rädda Barnen International in Geneva

# Contents

## (Volume I)

**Part three**

## (Volume II)

# Introduction by Adam Lopatka, Chairman/Rapporteur of the Working Group on a draft convention on the rights of the child

The United Nations Convention on the Rights of the Child is a universal international agreement relating to human rights and fundamental freedoms. It is one of a number of international instruments in the field of human rights whose aim is to promote and protect the rights of people who are particularly vulnerable to having their rights abused. Such groups include women, people with disabilities, those belonging to national, ethnic, religious or linguistic minorities, indigenous peoples, refugees and migrant workers and their families.

The 1959 Declaration of the Rights of the Child recognized the vulnerability of the child, who "by reason of his physical and mental immaturity needs special safeguards and care, including appropriate legal protection before as well as after birth". As set out in its article 1, the Convention on the Rights of the Child deals with the protections necessary for the child after his or her birth. Decisions as to the form and scope of legal protection of the child before birth have been left to individual States. The Convention provides protection for the rights of the child at a minimum level, below which States should not go. But the Convention provides for a higher level of protection under article 41, where those standards already exist, and the spirit of the Convention strongly encourages the further development of such standards.

## The Polish contribution

Poland was the initiator of the Convention on the Rights of the Child. At the beginning of 1978, the Polish Government submitted a draft convention to the United Nations Commission on Human Rights with a request to include the issue of a draft convention on the Commission's agenda. To date, this has been the most significant international initiative by Poland in the field of human rights. Yet it was not the only initiative. Almost at the same time, on 15 December 1978, the General Assembly built upon a Polish initiative and adopted the Declaration on the Preparation of Societies for Life in Peace. It is also worth mentioning that, following the initiative of a Pole – Ludwik Rajchman – in 1946, the United Nations General Assembly created UNICEF. Moreover, the delegates of Poland actively participated in the process of drafting the Declaration of the Rights of the Child, which was adopted by the United Nations in 1959. There was thus an international tradition of Polish engagement for the improvement of the situation of children all over the world. This tradition has its foundation in the sensitivity of Polish society to the suffering and misery of children. During the First World War and even more so during the Second World War, children in Poland experienced suffering that is hard to describe. It was caused by the wartime operations taking place on Polish territory. As a result, many children starved, were deprived of basic health care and of access to education, and were forced to perform difficult and excessive work. During the Second World War children and their parents were massively displaced from their homes and many were taken from their families in order to undergo Nazi indoctrination. Children of Jewish and Gypsy origin were victims of extermination. Few remember today that the Nazi authorities even set up a concentration camp for children in Poland where thousands of children lost their lives. These past events were a stimulus for the Polish authorities to undertake action to improve the situation of children, which – as we know – very often was and still is tragic.

In the years between the two world wars, a contemporary concept of childhood was developed. At its core is the conviction that the child is an autonomous person who has his or her own needs, interests and rights; and that he or she is not only an object of care and concern but also a subject whose interests and rights should be respected. According to that concept, the child, at a certain stage of his or her development, is capable of formulating and expressing his/her own opinions which ought to be taken into consideration. The main exponent of this new concept of childhood was Dr. Janusz Korczak – a doctor of medicine, a writer, a philosopher and an educator. He confirmed the loyalty to his vision of childhood in his own life. Although he had the opportunity to save his life, he decided to remain instead with the children he was taking care of until the very end – and died with them in a gas chamber in the Nazi concentration camp of Treblinka in 1942. When the Polish Government put forward the first draft convention on the rights of the child in 1978, it wished to popularize Dr. Korczak's concept of childhood throughout the world.

Poland also wanted to prove that – as a country at that time belonging to the system of socialist States – it was able to come up with a constructive and badly needed initiative in the field of human rights. It was a good opportunity to show that this type of initiative did not have to be a monopoly of Western States.

Poland was therefore a trustworthy initiator and promoter of the Convention. The historical pretext for Poland's initiative to draft a convention on the rights of the child came in 1978 during the preparations for the twentieth anniversary of the adoption of the Declaration of the Rights of the Child in 1979. The year 1979 was also proclaimed by the United Nations General Assembly as the International Year of the Child.

## Work is launched on the draft convention

The Polish Government expected the draft convention to be adopted within a short period of time. This was considered possible because the original draft was largely based on the text of the universally accepted Declaration of the Rights of the Child. It was also presumed that the convention project would win broad interest and support from the developing countries. In Poland, the original draft submitted to the Commission on Human Rights was worked out at the Ministry of Foreign Affairs with the assistance of a group of academicians, who were specialists in the field of law on family and guardianship relations. Before Poland officially submitted the draft convention, preliminary consultations with some members of the Commission on Human Rights had been held via diplomatic protocol. Support for the initiative had also been sought among States belonging to the socialist bloc.

The Commission approved Poland's motion requesting the inclusion of the question of a draft convention in its agenda. Following a preliminary discussion, the Commission decided to send the draft to the United Nations Member States for consideration as well as to international and non-governmental organizations which expressed an interest in the matter with a request for their comments. Many replies were received and support for a draft convention was very enthusiastic. It was suggested that work should proceed at a considerable pace to take into account the achievements of the International Year of the Child. Some were in favour of the convention including all rights of the child – civil rights, economic rights, and social and cultural rights – while maintaining an appropriate balance between them. Those who expressed this view argued that the Polish draft excessively emphasized economic, social and cultural rights. They also advised that the convention should refer specifically to the rights of children in difficult situations, such as children with disabilities, child refugees, children who had infringed the law, orphans, etc. The need to guarantee the equal rights of girls was also strongly emphasized.

The Polish Government carefully studied the large number of suggestions and recommendations and prepared a second, amended version of the draft convention. This draft was submitted to the Commission on Human Rights in 1979 and became the basis for further work on the convention.

## Initial difficulties

The Commission appointed a sessional Working Group open to all interested States to work on the draft convention. In the years 1979 and 1980 the Working Group had only a number of hours for its discussions. The sittings took place simultaneously with the meetings of the Commission and other open-ended Working Groups convened by the Commission. This fact itself held up progress on the convention. The cold war between the West and East also adversely affected the pace at which the draft took shape. Within the Commission on Human Rights itself there was tough competition between the United States and the Soviet Union. The delegates of certain countries used tactics of obstruction. For example, they submitted controversial proposals and then withdrew them when a consensus was finally reached after long and tedious discussions. Some representatives also submitted large numbers of proposals all at once which – as was clear from the outset – could not be considered in due time because they were too numerous. Although the proposals were certainly pertinent, it was necessary to find time to consider them. And indeed some of these proposals were adopted later.

During the first years, even important organizations such as UNICEF were not involved in the project. Initially, the attitude of some delegates of non-governmental organizations was not conducive to progress either. However, the efforts of the late Ms. Evi Underhill and some other NGO activists ultimately raised public awareness and increased participation in the work on the draft convention. Delegates of the Holy See also adopted a relatively positive attitude to the Idea of a convention.

The advancement of work on the draft depended on progress on other projects that were of particular importance to some Western States. They included the draft declaration on the elimination of all forms of intolerance and discrimination based on religion or belief adopted in 1981 and work on the Convention against Torture and Other Cruel, Inhuman or Degrading Treatment or Punishment adopted in 1984.

## An expanding Working Group

In 1981 the Commission allowed the Working Group to have sittings a few days before the Commission session and approved of the Group continuing its work during the session. Later the Working Group was granted the Commission's consent to hold one-week or – in the final stages – even two-week meetings before the Commission session. This significantly increased the pace of the proceedings. During the last stage of work on the draft convention, the Executive Director of UNICEF, James Grant, involved the organization, both physically and financially, in the process of completing the draft in order to finalize it before 1989, the thirtieth anniversary of the adoption of the Declaration of the Rights of the Child and the tenth anniversary of the International Year of the Child. The participation of such international organizations as the International Labour Organization, the United Nations Educational, Scientific and Cultural Organization (UNESCO), the World Health Organization (WHO) and the International Committee of the Red Cross was becoming more and more conspicuous. Non-governmental organizations cooperated effectively under the umbrella of the NGO Group, for which Defence for Children International served as the secretariat. Each year the Group submitted a number of valuable proposals, of which many were adopted by the Working Group. Non-governmental organizations also mounted an active international campaign in favour of the convention, organizing many seminars and conferences. Several events of this type took place in Yerevan in the Soviet Union, in Italy, Spain, Jordan and some other countries including Poland. Such meetings provided a good opportunity to evaluate progress on the draft and to share opinions and consider suggestions. For example, a conference in Amman, Jordan, resulted in the concept of international monitoring of compliance with the convention. It was suggested that a committee on the rights of the child should be appointed, an idea that found its place in the convention. It was also suggested that the committee should be financed from the regular budget of the United Nations, unlike the Committee under the Convention against Torture adopted in 1984.

## Working by consensus and consultation

From the very beginning, the Working Group applied the principle of adopting all Convention texts by consensus. This meant that each proposal was discussed and amended unless a veto was applied by any party to the discussion. Much assistance came from small drafting groups, usually made up of the most interested delegations, whose task was to consider a controversial proposal thoroughly and agree upon a version that the Working Group could accept.

The Working Group decided that the draft convention, once completed, would need to undergo a second reading. Following this decision, the draft convention was submitted to the Governments of all United Nations Member States and international organizations for their evaluation and comments. The Working Group also requested the opinion of the United Nations Office of Legal Affairs on the technical and legal correctness of the draft. UNICEF appointed its own special expert, Philip Alston, whose task was to evaluate the draft agreed on at first reading. A group of UNICEF officers, very effectively and discreetly headed by Victor Soler-Sala, Deputy Director of UNICEF's European office, constructively contributed to work on the draft at that time.

The evaluation of the draft by various bodies resulted in another inflow of new proposals and recommendations aimed at moulding the draft into the finest shape possible. A final two-week session of the Working Group at second reading ended with the adoption of many suggestions that improved the quality of the draft. The only matter that the Working Group and the Commission on Human Rights did not manage to settle was the means of financing the activity of the Committee on the Rights of the Child. A decision on this issue was taken later by a vote in the Third Committee of the United Nations General Assembly – only days before the Assembly adopted the Convention.

The positions taken by delegates of certain States were certainly determined by instructions from their Governments. Nevertheless, the personality and attitudes of individual delegates played its role in the discussions. Some States – particularly the United States and Australia – changed their delegates to the Working Group quite frequently. These changes tended to have a positive impact on the development of work on the draft. Some changes within delegations had no influence on the work. Occasionally, however, it could be quite problematic. Once, for example, the Government of one State sent in a delegate who submitted a set of proposals which, if adopted, would have diminished the quality of the Convention and set back its adoption. Fortunately, the delegate's proposals met with concerted criticism from other delegates and were almost all rejected. In this case, it looked as though the delegate's standpoint was based on his personal views rather than on instructions from the Government he represented.

Generally speaking, the Working Group operated throughout the period in an atmosphere of mutual understanding and respect for different opinions.

## Critical assistance

The draft convention was prepared in all six official languages of the United Nations, like all UN documents. In reality, however, it was English that played the dominant role in the drafting and misunderstandings sometimes resulted from difficulties with translations of certain texts into other languages. In this context it is appropriate to mention the valuable role played by the delegates from the United Kingdom, the United States and Canada, who effectively served as linguistic experts as well. A delegate from the United Kingdom, Michael Longford, enjoyed great respect as one such expert.

The United Nations Secretariat played an important role in documenting and organizing work on the draft. Support in this regard improved significantly when a Swedish diplomat, Jan Mårtenson, was appointed Director-General of the United Nations Office at Geneva and Head of the Centre for Human Rights. When Tom McCarthy of the Centre for Human Rights was placed in charge of the technical service and support for the Working Group, the situation improved dramatically. The Secretariat took valuable initiatives and provided perfect service to the Working Group. It is worth adding that significant expert help in the final editing of the Convention's articles was rendered by staff members of the United Nations Office in Vienna.

## The participation of children

Sometimes I was asked half seriously and even half derisively whether children – the beneficiaries of the Convention – participated in the work on the draft convention and if so what were their proposals. It is obvious that the Convention on the Rights of the Child, like any other international human rights treaty, is an accomplishment of the government representatives of all States concerned. The same procedure was followed in the case of the Convention on the Rights of the Child. When submitting proposals on the draft, the delegates of a few States referred to opinions held by children and youth organizations active in the countries they represented. Sweden was one such country. When work on the draft was about to be completed, a group of Swedish children entered the hall where the Working Group was holding its meeting and submitted a petition written on a poster one metre wide and several metres long signed by approximately twelve thousand children. The petition contained support for the Convention and especially for Sweden's proposal that children should not be called up for service in the armed forces or involved in armed conflicts. On a few occasions, schoolchildren from Canada came to listen to the debates in the Working Group. Also, representatives of several French child and youth organizations displayed an active interest in the work on the draft convention.

An hour after the Convention was adopted by the United Nations General Assembly, thousands of children from all over the world gathered at UN Headquarters in New York in celebration. Officials such as the United Nations Secretary-General, the Executive Director of UNICEF, ambassadors and other representatives of organizations working in the field of culture and science participated in the ceremony. The children gathered there were obviously delighted to join in the celebrations marking a historic moment.

## Particular points of contention

Work on many articles of the Convention proceeded relatively harmoniously. In several other cases, however, the draft text of the Convention was discussed many times over, often in a strained atmosphere. When it seemed that consensus had finally been reached on certain matters, delegates of some States or international organizations suddenly reverted to the controversial points. The definition of the child (article 1) was the most contentious of all – it caused a great deal of disagreement and argument and was discussed at length. Proponents of the view that the child's rights come into being at the moment of conception insisted on including this view in the Convention. Others claimed that the Convention's objective was to protect the child after birth. Finally, agreement was reached on inserting a sentence in the preamble to the Convention from the Declaration of the Rights of the Child to the effect that the child needs "appropriate legal protection before as well as after birth". Furthermore, the wording of article 1 was left imprecise. It states that "for the purposes of the present Convention a child means every human being below the age of 18 years".

Much time was spent on formulating articles on the right of the child to express his or her views (article 12), the right of the child to freedom of expression (article 13) and the right of the child to freedom of thought, conscience and religion (article 14). Discussions of article 17 regarding the role of the mass media were characterized by a clash between two competing approaches: one supporting a free flow of information and the other favouring protection of the child from information and material injurious to his or her well-being. In the end, the first view prevailed.

Unexpectedly for some members of the Working Group, there were serious difficulties in reaching common agreement on the content of article 21 concerning adoption. Delegates of States with an Islamic culture had problems accepting the proposed text because adoption is not recognized in those countries. Moreover, a delegate from a Latin American State kept blocking a consensus by making statements on financial gain for persons or institutions that act as brokers in intercountry adoptions.

The Working Group encountered another controversy when discussing the content of the article on the right of the child to education, especially the part referring to mandatory primary education that should be available free to all. Delegates of some States claimed that their countries were far from being able to meet this requirement. A similar note of pessimism was struck during the formulation of some other articles dealing with the social rights of the child.

Long and exhaustive negotiations also took place among delegates from Sweden and some other States as well as the representatives of Rädda Barnen and the International Committee of the Red Cross over the content of article 38 dealing with children in armed conflict. In the end, however, the Swedish delegate, Anders Rönquist, emphasized that Sweden could not accept the final text that was adopted.

## Towards universality

When the Working Group reported on its progress during a given year to the Commission on Human Rights, the opinion was occasionally expressed that the standards set in some articles of the draft convention were too low. It was said that they would not sufficiently mobilize the necessary support of States to become parties to the Convention. Yet this feature was considered by other delegates not as a weakness but as an advantage, since such standards made it possible for States with limited resources to ratify the Convention. According to this view, the Convention's range of influence would thus be broadened. Furthermore, higher standards would apply where applicable since article 41 provides that "nothing in the present Convention shall affect any provisions which are more conducive to the realization of the rights of the child and which may be contained in the law of the State Party or international law in force for that State".

Undoubtedly, the Working Group participants did not expect that in a relatively short period of time as many as 192 States – almost all Member States of the United Nations – would become parties to the Convention. Indeed the entry into force of the Convention was achieved in just a few months, which was a record for any human rights treaty. The moderately ambitious standards of some articles certainly encouraged some States to ratify the Convention. Nevertheless, the matter of the level of requirements laid down by some articles of the Convention remains very flexible. Those States that favoured more ambitious standards found their own way to realize their ideas. For States wishing to adhere to higher standards than those contained in the Convention, two important additional and optional protocols to the Convention were drafted and adopted in the framework of the Commission on Human Rights: the Optional Protocols on the involvement of children in armed conflict (adopted by the General Assembly on 25 May 2000; entered into force on 12 February 2002) and on the sale of children, child prostitution and child pornography (adopted by the General Assembly on 25 May 2000; entered into force on 18 January 2002).

Since the adoption of the Convention only one amendment has been submitted and it actually testifies to the quality of the instrument. The amendment provides for the replacement of the word "ten" by the word "eighteen" in article 43, paragraph 2. Ten is the number of experts elected to the Committee on the Rights of the Child established for the purpose of examining the progress made by States parties in achieving the realization of the obligations undertaken in the Convention. The ten-person Committee was no longer capable of considering the large numbers of reports from States parties. Hence the requirement for an increase in the number of experts. The amendment entered into force on 18 November 2002. The Convention seems to have stood the test of time.

**Impact of the Convention**

When ratifying the Convention a great number of States entered significant reservations. Notwithstanding article 51, some of the reservations are clearly incompatible with the object and purpose of the Convention, which weakens the effect of ratification. Some States also made declarations at the time of ratification expressing a specific, often limited, understanding of certain provisions of the Convention. Such reservations and declarations can be withdrawn by the State party at any time. Unfortunately, appeals for withdrawing these reservations have not so far been very successful. Both reservations and – to a lesser extent – declarations impair the efficiency of the Convention and limit the extent of its application.

Under the influence of the Convention, many States have changed their legislation, adjusting it to meet the treaty's requirements. The Convention has become the framework for all of UNICEF's programmes and activities. Moreover, provisions of the Convention are referred to by such international organizations as UNESCO, WHO and ILO. Improvement of the welfare of the child has been given priority in the activities of the United Nations and other international organizations. The binding force of the Convention has also considerably influenced the activities of both international and national non-governmental organizations focusing on the rights of the child. In many countries the Convention has given a stimulus to research on the condition of children and the enjoyment of their rights. The Convention on the Rights of the Child has also stimulated the adoption of regional conventions aimed at improving the situation of children, namely the African Charter on the Rights and Welfare of the Child of 1990 (which entered into force on 29 November 1999) and the European Convention on the Exercise of Children's Rights of 1996 (which entered into force on 1 July 2000).

Despite the above-mentioned beneficial effects of the Convention on the Rights of the Child and other conspicuous positive outcomes of its implementation, we cannot claim that the Convention has already brought about a considerable improvement in the situation of children all over the world. As recognized by the General Assembly in its resolution 44/25, the "situation of children in many parts of the world remains critical as a result of inadequate social conditions, natural disasters, armed conflicts, exploitation, illiteracy, hunger and disability". The General Assembly therefore noted that "children's rights require special protection and call for continuous improvement of the situation of children all over the world as well as for their development and education in conditions of peace and security". This led the Assembly to repeat its call for "urgent and effective national and international action".

**Conclusion**

Certainly, not even the greatest optimists could have expected that seventeen years after the adoption of the Convention all children in the world would be smiling all the time. The Convention is an international agreement intended to have a long-term impact. It has an ability to make States direct their activities towards improving the situation of children in the twenty-first century. This should constitute a source of satisfaction for all those who contributed in one way or another to the drafting of the Convention and who provided it with its deeply humanistic content. We can say that these people responded appropriately to the opportunity that fortune granted them.

As Chairman-Rapporteur of the Working Group, I would like to express my deepest gratitude for their fruitful cooperation to all those who participated in the proceedings of the Working Group, either throughout the period of work on the Convention or during parts of it. I have in mind delegates of States, representatives of international organizations and non-governmental organizations and staff of the United Nations Secretariat and UNICEF. I would also like to express my thanks to those organizations and persons who contributed to the competent compilation and efficient dissemination of documentation concerning the work of drafting the Convention. In that regard, Ms. Simone Ek of Rädda Barnen (Save the Children, Sweden) deserves special mention for her vision and persistence. It is to be hoped that the documentation will serve as a useful tool in all efforts aimed at the fullest and most universal implementation of the Convention's principles and norms.

Adam Lopatka
CHAIRMAN-RAPPORTEUR

# Interrelated articles of the Convention

*The following grouping of interrelated substantive articles is based on the guidelines adopted by the Committee on the Rights of the Child for the preparation of State party reports (CRC/C/5):*

General measures of implementation

- Implementation of rights (article 4)

- Promotion of rights and dissemination of information (article 42)

- Respect for higher standards (article 41)

Definition of a child

- Definition of a child (article 1)

General principles

- Non-discrimination (article 2)

- Best interests of the child (article 3)

- Right to life, survival and development (article 6)

- Respect for the views of the child (article 12)

Civil rights and freedoms

- Name and nationality (article 7)

- Preservation of identity (article 8)

- Freedom of expression (article 13)

- Access to appropriate information (article 17)

- Freedom of thought, conscience and religion (article 14)

- Freedom of association and peaceful assembly (article 15)

- Protection of privacy (article 16)

- Prohibition of torture and the death penalty (article 37 (a))

Family environment and alternative care

- Parental guidance and the child's evolving capacities (article 5)

- Parental responsibilities (article 18 (1) and (2))

- Separation from parents (article 9)

- Family reunification (article 10)

- Recovery of maintenance for the child (article 27 (4))

- Children deprived of a family environment (article 20)

- Adoption (article 21)

# Issues covered by the Convention's articles

**I**

**K**

**L**

**M**

**N**

**O**

# Renumbering of articles

| New | Old (before second reading) | |
| --- | --- | --- |
| 1 | 1 | (Child - age) |
| 2 | 4 | (Non-discrimination) |
| 3 | 3 | (Best interests of child) |
| 4 | 5 | (Implementation of rights recognized) |
| 5 | 5 bis | (Parental guidance) |
| 6 | 1 bis | (Right to life) |
| 7 | 2 | (Right to name and nationality) |
| 8 | 9 bis | (Preservation of identity) |
| 9 | 6 | (Parental care /non-separation from parents) |
| 10 | 6 bis | (Family reunification) |
| 11 | 6 ter | (Illicit transfer and non-return) |
| 12 | 7 | (Child's right to express opinions) |
| 13 | 7 a | (Freedom of expression and information) |
| 14 | 7 bis | (Freedom of thought, conscience and religion) |
| 15 | 7 ter | (Freedom of association) |
| 16 | 7 quater | (Privacy, honour, reputation) |
| 17 | 9 | (Mass media) |
| 18 | 8 | (Upbringing and child-rearing) |
| 19 | 8 bis | (Prevention of abuse) |
| 20 | 10 | (Parentless children) |
| 21 | 11 | (Adoption) |
| 22 | 11 bis | (Refugee child) |
| 23 | 12 | (Disabled child) |
| 24 | 12 bis | (Health) |
| 25 | 12 ter | (Periodic review of placed children) |
| 26 | 13 | (Social security) |
| 27 | 14 | (Standard of living) |
| 28 | 15 | (Education) |
| 29 | 16 | (Objectives of education) |
| 30 | 16 bis | (Cultural, religious and linguistic rights) |
| 31 | 17 | (Rest and leisure) |
| 32 | 18 | (Protection from economic exploitation) |
| 33 | 18 bis | (Protection from narcotic and psychotropic substances) |
| 34 | 18 ter | (Protection from sexual exploitation) |
| 35 | 18 quater | (Prevention of abduction, sale and traffic) |
| 36 | 18 quinto | (Protection from all other forms of exploitation) |
| 37 | 19 | (Torture / capital punishment) |
| 38 | 20 | (Armed conflicts) |
| 39 | 18 sixto | (Recovery and reintegration) |
| 40 | 19 bis | (Treatment in penal matters) |
| 41 | 21 | (Other more favourable provisions) |
| 42 | 21 ter | (Dissemination of the principles and provisions of the Convention) |
| 43 | 22 | (Establishment of the Committee) |
| 44 | 23 | (Reports from States parties) |

# Prelude

Part one

# The League of Nations and the rights of the child

Attempts to set minimum standards for the protection of children pre-date the League of Nations by more than a decade. In the late nineteenth century, NGOs had started to combat the white-slave traffic, and by 1902 their efforts were carried forward by an international conference which led to the adoption of two international conventions in 1905 and 1910 respectively. Other efforts focused on children employed in factories and mines, and in 1890 the first Conference on Workers' Protection in Berlin recommended a minimum age of 14 years for miners. Both issues were addressed in the Covenant of the League of Nations, which obliged its members to "endeavour to secure and maintain fair and humane conditions of labour for men, women and children" (art. 23 (a)) and to "entrust the League with the general supervision over the execution of agreements with regard to the traffic in women and children" (art. 23 (c)).

Several bodies and committees of the League were established to deal with the issues of working conditions of children, trafficking and stateless children. In 1924 the League also incorporated the "Association internationale pour la protection de l'enfant", which had been established in 1921 by 35 Governments.

## The Declaration of Geneva (1924)

The 1924 Declaration of the Rights of the Child, also known as the Geneva Declaration, was adopted by the Fifth Assembly of the League of Nations in 1924 and was the first international instrument explicitly acknowledging children's rights. As a declaration, however, it referred only to "men and women of all nations" without imposing obligations on States. Furthermore, the child was not yet seen as a holder of rights of its own but rather as an object of the protection that the Declaration aimed to afford.

As with the Convention on the Rights of the Child, NGOs (such as Save the Children Fund and International Council of Women) played an important role in the drafting of the Geneva Declaration. In fact the Declaration was part of the 1923 Charter of Save the Children International Union, with the introductory paragraph being added before its adoption by the Assembly.

*The following is taken from the records of the Fifth Assembly, League of Nations Official Journal, Special Supplement No. 23, p. 179.*

By the present Declaration of the Rights of the Child, commonly known as the Declaration of Geneva, men and women of all nations, recognizing that mankind owes to the child the best that it has to give, declare and accept it as their duty that, beyond and above all considerations of race, nationality or creed:

I. The child must be given the means requisite for its normal development, both materially and spiritually;

II. The child that is hungry must be fed; the child that is sick must be helped; the child that is backward must be helped; the delinquent child must be reclaimed; and the orphan and the waif must be sheltered and succoured;

III. The child must be the first to receive relief in times of distress;

IV. The child must be put in a position to earn a livelihood and must be protected against every form of exploitation;

V. The child must be brought up in the consciousness that its talents must be devoted to the service of its fellow men.

# First steps towards a convention on the rights of the child

## The Declaration of 1959

The Second World War and the events leading up to it brought international action in the field of children's rights to an almost complete standstill. After the war, the International Labour Organization (ILO) revived the question of child welfare. At the International Labour Conference held in Paris in October 1945, the ILO resolution concerning the Protection of Children and Young Workers (also known as the ILO Children's Charter) was adopted (see ILO: *Record of Proceedings of the Twenty-Seventh Session of the International Labour Conference*, Paris 1945, pp. 241, 365 and 456, reprinted in E/CN.5/111, p. 62). Although the ILO Children's Charter focused mainly on labour-related issues, it also addressed such related issues as the promotion of the physical, intellectual and moral development of children and young persons (para. 6 (d)).

The newly established United Nations concerned itself with the rights of the child from an early stage. The Temporary Social Commission discussed the question of a declaration of children's rights when certain functions of the League of Nations were transferred to the United Nations in 1946. A possible update of the Geneva Declaration was considered so that its provisions "should bind the peoples of the world today as firmly as it did in 1924" (Economic and Social Council Official Records, 1st year, 2nd session, p. 283). In 1947, the Social Commission called for "the preparation of documentation on the [...] Geneva Declaration (1924), referring in particular to any changes or additions which it may be considered necessary to make with a view to its acceptance as the United Nations Charter of the Rights of the Child" (E/578, para. 25 c (ii)). At its third session, the Social Commission recommended that, even though great weight should be given to the Geneva Declaration, the proposed Charter should nevertheless include additional principles which "would transform the document into a United Nations Charter of the Rights of the Child, embodying the main features of the newer conception of child welfare" (E/779, para. 76). The Social Commission also suggested that the Secretary-General consult with Member States and non-governmental organizations. The resulting report (E/CN.5/111) supported the Commission's view that a new instrument should be drafted. At this point it was also proposed to draw up a non-binding declaration rather than a charter. The Social Commission subsequently appointed a committee to draft such a declaration (see below, para. 57). This draft (E/CN.5/L.76), which was then amended by the Commission (E/CN.5/L.96), is reproduced below in paragraph 59.

## 1.　　Draft declaration of the rights of the child (Social Commission, 1950)

*The following is taken from document E/CN.5/221, paragraphs 55-61.*

C.　　FAMILY, YOUTH AND CHILD WELFARE

[...]

(b)　　*Draft preamble and principles of the declaration of the rights of the child (item 6 (b) of the agenda)*

55.　　The Social Commission at its fourth session instructed the Secretary-General to prepare a draft preamble and principles of a declaration of the rights of the child, taking into account the Geneva Declaration, the comments expressed by the members of the Commission, as well as comments from Member Governments and specialized agencies, the non-governmental organizations and other appropriate sources (documents E/CN.5/111, E/CN.5/111/Add.1, E/CN.5/111/Add.2, E/CN.5/111/Add.2/Corr.1 and E/CN.5/126).

56.　　Following this instruction, the Secretary-General submitted a note including a draft preamble and principles requested by the Commission (E/CN.5/199).

57.　　After discussion on the relation of the Commission on Human Rights to the subject, the Social Commission appointed a committee composed of the representatives of Australia, Brazil, France, Iraq and Yugoslavia to consider the note of the Secretary-General together with previous documentation, and to prepare a draft declaration of the rights of the child for submission to the Economic and Social Council, requesting the Council after consultation with the Commission on Human Rights to transmit the draft declaration to the General Assembly.

58.	The Commission, in considering the draft prepared by the Committee (E/CN.5/L.96) decided that the needs of the child justified an instrument in addition to the Universal Declaration of Human Rights and on vote it was decided to retain the title "Declaration of the Rights of the Child". The Commission believed that the declaration should emphasize broad principles regarding the rights of the child toward the attainment of which the peoples of the world should strive. The parallel concepts of individual rights and obligations toward society, the emphasis on protection against factors likely to foster discrimination and the implanting in the minds of children, as well as their elders, the ideals set out in the declaration, were considered of prime importance. The Commission further emphasized the need for special care of the rights of the child because of his immaturity in respect to a name, nationality, security, health, education and protection against all forms of exploitation which might prejudice his development.

59.	The Commission discussed the draft declaration as prepared by the Committee paragraph by paragraph, incorporated some amendments and finally adopted the draft declaration without dissent, 13 in favour, none against, with 3 abstentions.

DRAFT UNITED NATIONS DECLARATION OF THE RIGHTS OF THE CHILD

*Preamble*

1.	*Whereas* the United Nations have, in the Charter and in the Universal Declaration of Human Rights, reaffirmed their faith in fundamental human rights, and in the dignity and worth of the human person, and have determined to promote social progress and better standards of life in larger freedom,

2.	*Whereas* the United Nations have declared that everyone is entitled to all the rights and freedoms set forth in the Universal Declaration of Human Rights, without distinction of any kind, such as race, colour, sex, language, religion, political or other opinion, national or social origin, property, birth or other status,

3.	*Whereas* Member States have in the Universal Declaration of Human Rights proclaimed their recognition of the fundamental rights of persons,

4.	*Whereas,* as has specifically been stated since 1924 in the Geneva Declaration of the Rights of the Child, mankind owes to the child the best it has to give,

5.	*Whereas* the child needs special safeguards by reason of his physical and mental immaturity and his particular legal status,

*Now therefore*

6.	*The General Assembly recognizes and proclaims the essential Rights of the Child* to the end that he may have a happy childhood and be enabled to grow up to enjoy for his own good and for the good of society, the fundamental rights and freedoms, particularly those specified in the Universal Declaration of Human Rights, and calls upon men and women as individuals as well as through their local authorities and national Governments to recognize and strive for the observance of those rights through the application of the following principles.

*Principles*

1.	The child shall be given the means necessary to enable him to develop physically, mentally, morally, spiritually and socially in a healthy and normal manner and in conditions of freedom and dignity.

2.	The child shall be entitled from his birth to a name and a nationality.

3.      The child shall enjoy the benefits of social security. He shall be entitled even from before birth to grow and develop in health. He shall have the right to adequate nutrition, housing, recreation and free medical services.

4.      The child shall be given opportunity to grow up in economic security, in the care of his own parents whenever possible, and in a family atmosphere of affection and understanding favourable to the full and harmonious development of his personality.

5.      The child shall be given an education which will bestow upon him general culture and enable him to develop his abilities and individual judgement and to become a useful member of society. Such education shall be free.

6.      The child shall in all circumstances be amongst the first to receive protection and relief.

7.      The child shall be protected against all forms of neglect, cruelty and exploitation. He shall in no case be caused to engage in any occupation or employment which would prejudice his health or education or interfere with his development.

8.      The child shall be protected against any practice which may foster racial or national discrimination or hatred. He shall be brought up in the consciousness that he will achieve his fullest development and derive greatest satisfaction through devoting his energy and talents to the service of his fellow men, in a spirit of universal brotherhood and peace.

9.      The child who is physically, mentally or socially handicapped shall be given the special treatment, education and care required by his particular condition.

10.     The child shall enjoy all the rights set forth above, irrespective of any consideration of race, colour, sex, language, caste, religion, political or other opinion, national or social origin, property, birth, legitimacy or other status.

*The General Assembly calls upon* all Governments and peoples to make known the above principles and explain them to parents, educators, doctors, social workers and all others who deal directly with children, and to children themselves.

60.     The following resolution for transmission to the Economic and Social Council, was adopted by 10 in favour, 1 against, with 2 abstentions.

*The Social Commission*

*Having adopted* the draft declaration of the rights of the child, in which the Declaration of Geneva, the comments expressed by the members of the Commission, as well as the suggestions from Member Governments, specialized agencies and non-governmental organizations are taken into account,

*Bearing* in mind the close relationship between this draft declaration and the Universal Declaration of Human Rights,

*Transmits* this draft declaration to the Economic and Social Council with the request that, after consultation with the Commission on Human Rights, it be submitted to the General Assembly,

*Recommends* that the Economic and Social Council adopt the following resolution:

> "*The Economic and Social Council*
>
> *Noting* the close relationship between the draft Declaration of the Rights of the Child and the Universal Declaration of Human Rights;
>
> *Requests* the Commission on Human Rights to inform the Council at its thirteenth session of its observations on the Draft Declaration of the Rights of the Child, with a view to its approval by the General Assembly."

61.     The representative of Canada abstained, because he believed the phrases regarding free education and free medical services were extraneous to the subject. The representatives of China, Denmark and the United States of America reserved the rights of their respective Governments on one or another aspects of the Declaration.

## 2.     Draft declaration of the rights of the child (Commission on Human Rights, 1959)

*After the Social Commission adopted the draft declaration of the rights of the child in 1950, ECOSOC decided to refer it to the Commission on Human Rights for further consideration in 1951 (E/Res/309 C (XI)). As the Commission on Human Rights at the time was drafting the two international covenants on civil and political rights and economic, social and cultural rights, the draft declaration was considered for the first time in 1957. A new draft was sent out to Member States and non-governmental organizations and then discussed by the Commission at its 626th to 640th meetings, from 30 March to 8 April 1959.*

*The following is taken from the 1959 report of the Commission on Human Rights (E/CN.4/789, paras. 104-197).*

VII.     DRAFT DECLARATION OF THE RIGHTS OF THE CHILD

104.     In 1950 the Social Commission at its sixth session adopted a draft Declaration of the Rights of the Child. The draft Declaration was transmitted to the Economic and Social Council, which discussed it at its eleventh session. The Economic and Social Council, in resolution 309 C (XI), requested the Commission on Human Rights to consider the draft Declaration and to communicate to the Council "its observations on the principle and contents" of the draft.

105.     The draft Declaration was placed on the agenda of the Commission at its seventh session in 1951, but was considered by the Commission for the first time at its thirteenth session in 1957. After a general discussion, the Commission decided to transmit to the Governments of Member States the draft Declaration together with the record of the discussions and proceedings in the Commission on Human Rights and in the Economic and Social Council and the written statements submitted by non-governmental organizations "with a view to receiving their comments thereon by 1 December 1957 at the latest, so that the Commission might be able to take these comments into account during its further consideration of the question".

106.     On 24 July 1957 the Economic and Social Council adopted resolution 651 E (XXIV) in which it considered that "the purposes of the Commission would be fully served if Governments were given more time to prepare their comments" on the draft Declaration; and resolved that the comments of Governments on the draft Declaration may be transmitted until 1 December 1958 in order that the Secretary-General may circulate them to the members of the Commission by 31 December 1958 for consideration by the Commission at its next session thereafter.

107.     The following twenty-one Governments replied to the request for comments: Australia, Cambodia, Ceylon, Denmark, Dominican Republic, Greece, Hungary, Israel, Jordan, Laos, Luxembourg, Nepal, New Zealand, Norway, Pakistan, Philippines, Poland, Portugal, Sudan, the United Kingdom of Great Britain and Northern Ireland and the United States of America (E/CN.4/780); Finland, France, Japan, the Union of Soviet Socialist Republics and Yugoslavia (E/CN.4/780/Add.1); India, Netherlands and Turkey (E/CN.4/780/Add.2).

108.     The following two non-governmental organizations having consultative status in category B submitted written statements: the International Federation of Women Lawyers (E/CN.4/NGO/85) and the International Union for Child Welfare (E/CN.4/NGO/84).

109.     The Commission also had before it a memorandum by the Secretary-General (E/CN.4/512) containing the text of the draft Declaration of the Rights of the Child, background information and the Declaration of Geneva of 1924.

110.     The draft Declaration of the Rights of the Child was considered by the Commission at its 626th to 640th meetings, on 30 March to 8 April 1959.

111.    During the discussion many of the members of the Commission expressed themselves in favour of a brief declaration which should proclaim general principles without provisions on methods of implementation. Some members stated that they would have preferred a legally binding convention rather than a declaration, but they were prepared to support the principle of a declaration. They stressed, however, that such a declaration should not be limited to a simple proclamation of general principles but should also provide for practical measures to ensure the observance of the rights of the child proclaimed.

112.    Some members recalled that in its resolution 309 C (XI) the Council had requested the Commission to communicate "its observations on the principle and contents" of the draft Declaration and wondered whether the Commission was in a position to redraft the declaration. It was pointed out, however, that the Declaration had been proposed many years previously and that since then further comments had been requested and received from Governments. It seemed, therefore, that the Commission could submit its observations in any form that it desired. It was agreed that the Commission was not precluded from forwarding a new draft, which the Council could consider with the draft Declaration prepared by the Social Commission.

113.    The Commission proceeded to discuss the draft Declaration, particularly in the light of the amendments submitted to it by the members and taking into account the provisions of the Universal Declaration of Human Rights as suggested by the Council in its resolution 309 C (XI). The amendments and voting thereon are set out below together with the texts adopted by the Commission. The Commission, however, draws the attention of the Council to the summary records of the discussion (E/CN.4/SR.626-640) because the various, and in many cases divergent, opinions expressed by the members of the Commission cannot be indicated accurately or adequately in any concise and brief account which might be furnished in this report.

114.    The Chairman of the Commission on the Status of Women suggested to the Commission on Human Rights that it might wish to refer the text it finally adopted to the Commission on the Status of Women for study and comment.

115.    The Commission also heard the representatives of the International Labour Organization and UNESCO and the representatives of the following non-governmental organizations in consultative status: the Agudas Israel World Organization, the International Confederation of Free Trade Unions, the International Federation of Women Lawyers, the International Union for Child Welfare and the Women's International League for Peace and Freedom.

*Preamble*

116.    At its 628th and 629th meetings, on 31 March 1959, the Commission discussed the first five paragraphs of the preamble to the draft prepared by the Social Commission, the text of which read as follows:

> "1.    *Whereas* the United Nations have, in the Charter and in the Universal Declaration of Human Rights, reaffirmed their faith in fundamental human rights, and in the dignity and worth of the human person, and have determined to promote social progress and better standards of life in larger freedom,
>
> "2.    *Whereas* the United Nations have declared that everyone is entitled to all the rights and freedoms set forth in the Universal Declaration of Human Rights, without distinction of any kind, such as race, colour, sex, language, religion, political or other opinion, national or social origin, property, birth or other status,
>
> "3.    *Whereas* Member States have, in the Universal Declaration of Human Rights, proclaimed their recognition of the fundamental rights of persons,
>
> "4.    *Whereas,* as has specifically been stated since 1924 in the Geneva Declaration of the Rights of the Child, mankind owes to the child the best it has to give,
>
> "5.    *Whereas* the child needs special safeguards by reason of his physical and mental immaturity and his particular legal status."

117.    Amendments to the second and third paragraphs of the preamble were submitted by France (E/CN.4/L.524) and Israel (E/CN.4/L.525). Subsequently, France joined Israel as a sponsor of its amendments.

118.    In the absence of any objection, the Commission accepted the following text for the first paragraph:

> "*Whereas* the United Nations have, in the Charter, reaffirmed their faith in fundamental human rights and in the dignity and worth of the human person, and have determined to promote social progress and better standards of life in larger freedom,"

119.    In the absence of any objection, the Commission also adopted the following text for the second paragraph:

> "*Whereas* the United Nations have, in the Universal Declaration of Human Rights, proclaimed that everyone is entitled to all the rights and freedoms set forth therein without distinction of any kind, such as race, colour, sex, language, religion, political or other opinion, national or social origin, property, birth or other status,"

120.    In the absence of any objection, the Commission decided to delete the third paragraph of the preamble and to replace it by the text proposed by Israel, as orally revised. The text read as follows:

> "*Whereas* the child needs special safeguards, including special legal protection, by reason of its physical and mental immaturity,"

121.    A text was submitted by Israel (E/CN.4/L.525) to replace the text of the fourth paragraph of the preamble. As orally revised to incorporate suggestions by France and the United Kingdom, the text read as follows:

> "*Whereas* the need for such special safeguards has been stated in the Geneva Declaration of the Rights of the Child of 1924, and has again been recognized in article 25, paragraph 2, of the Universal Declaration of Human Rights and in the statutes of specialized agencies and international organizations concerned with the welfare of children,"

122.    This text was adopted by the Commission, without objection, to replace the fourth paragraph of the original text.

123.    In the absence of any objection, it was decided that the fifth paragraph should be replaced by the following text taken from an amendment proposed by Israel (E/CN.4/L.525):

> "*Whereas* mankind owes to the child the best it has to give,"

*Operative paragraph*

124.    The operative paragraph (paragraph 6) preceding the principles set forth in the draft prepared by the Social Commission was as follows:

> "*Now therefore*

> "6.    *The General Assembly recognizes and proclaims the essential rights of the child* to the end that he may have a happy childhood and be enabled to grow up to enjoy, for his own good and for the good of society, the fundamental rights and freedoms, particularly those specified in the Universal Declaration of Human Rights, and calls upon men and women as individuals as well as through their local authorities and national Governments to recognize and strive for the observance of these rights through the application of the following principles:"

125.    The Commission discussed this paragraph at its 630th meeting, on 1 April 1959. An amendment submitted by the USSR (E/CN.4/L.526) calling for the insertion of the words "the Governments of States as well as all" after the words "calls upon" and the deletion of the words "as individuals as well as through their local authorities and national Governments" was not pressed to a vote. The representative of the USSR reserved his right to raise the question again. The original text, with an oral amendment by India replacing the words "through their" by "upon", was adopted unanimously.

*Principles*

126.　　At its 628th meeting, on 31 March 1959, the Commission discussed an amendment proposed by Iran and the Philippines (E/CN.4/L.523) replacing the word "the" before the word "child" in all the principles by the word "every". The amendment was not adopted, the vote being 6 in favour, 6 against and 5 abstentions.

127.　　The numbers of the principles given below are those finally determined by the Commission on Human Rights; the numbers of the principles in the draft prepared by the Social Commission are indicated at the beginning of each principle. Decisions by the Commission on the numbering of certain principles are indicated.

*Principle 1*

128.　　At its 630th meeting, on 1 April 1959, the Commission decided by 11 votes to none, with 6 abstentions, on the proposal of France (E/CN.4/L.524), to include principle 10 of the draft prepared by the Social Commission as principle 1 of the new draft.

129.　　Principle 10 of the draft prepared by the Social Commission was as follows:

"The child shall enjoy the rights set forth above, irrespective of any consideration of race, colour, sex, language, caste, religion, political or other opinion, national or social origin, property, birth, legitimacy or other status."

130.　　The Commission discussed this principle at its 630th meeting, on 1 April 1959. Amendments were submitted by France (E/CN.4/L.524), Israel (E/CN.4/ L.525) and the United Kingdom (E/CN.4/L.529).

131.　　The text proposed in the Israel amendment, as orally revised, was as follows:

"The child shall enjoy all the rights set forth in this Declaration without distinction or discrimination on account of race, colour, sex, language, caste, religion, political or other opinion, national or social origin, property, birth or other status, whether of himself or of either of his parents. All children, whether born in or out of wedlock, shall enjoy these rights."

132.　　The United Kingdom amendment deleting the word "caste" was adopted by 15 votes to none, with 3 abstentions. The second sentence of the text proposed in the Israel amendment was adopted by 9 votes to 1, with 8 abstentions.

133.　　The text proposed in the Israel amendment, as amended, as a whole, was adopted by 12 votes to 1, with 5 abstentions, as principle 1 of the Declaration.

*Principle 2*

134.　　Principle 1 of the draft prepared by the Social Commission was as follows:

"The child shall be given the means necessary to enable him to develop physically, mentally, morally, spiritually and socially in a healthy and normal manner and in conditions of freedom and dignity."

135.　　The Commission discussed this principle at its 631st meeting, on 1 April 1959. The original text was adopted unanimously.

*Principle 3*

136.　　At its 639th meeting, on 7 April 1959, the Commission discussed a proposal by Poland (E/CN.4/L.527/ Add.1) for the insertion of a new principle which, as orally revised, read as follows:

"The child shall enjoy protection by law and by other means. Whenever necessary, opportunities and facilities shall be provided by law to enable him to develop in accordance with the principles of this Declaration. The best interests of the child shall be the paramount consideration in the enactment of such laws."

137.　　The words "and by other means" in the first sentence were adopted by 10 votes to 2, with 5 abstentions.

138.    The second sentence was adopted by 12 votes to 3, with 8 abstentions.

139.    An oral amendment by the Philippines replacing the words following "consideration" in the third sentence by the words "in the granting of protection, opportunities, and facilities for his development", was rejected by 11 votes to 2, with 4 abstentions. The original text of the third sentence was adopted by 12 votes to 2, with 4 abstentions.

140.    The new principle, as proposed, as a whole, was adopted by 12 votes to 2, with 4 abstentions. The Commission also decided by 14 votes to none, with 3 abstentions, on the motion of the representative of Iraq, to insert this new principle as principle 3 of the new draft.

*Principle 4*

141.    Principle 2 of the draft prepared by the Social Commission was as follows:

"The child shall be entitled from his birth to a name and a nationality."

142.    The Commission discussed this principle at its 631st meeting, on 1 April 1959, and unanimously adopted the original text. An amendment by Poland (E/CN.4/L.527) was withdrawn on the understanding that it would be submitted subsequently as a proposal for insertion as a new principle (see principle 3 above).

*Principle 5*

143.    Principle 3 of the draft prepared by the Social Commission was as follows:

"The child shall enjoy the benefits of social security. He shall be entitled even from before birth to grow and develop in health. He shall have the rights to adequate nutrition, housing, recreation and free medical services."

144.    The Commission discussed this principle at its 631st to 633rd meetings, on 1 and 2 April 1959. Amendments were submitted by the USSR (E/CN.4/L.526 and Add.1 and Add.1/Rev.1), the United Kingdom (E/CN.4/L.529), the United States (E/CN.4/L.530), the Philippines (E/CN.4/L.531) and India (E/CN.4/L.533).

145.    The Commission rejected by 9 votes to 3, with 6 abstentions, the amendment of the Soviet Union (E/CN.4/L.526/Add.1/Rev.1) calling for the insertion of the following text after the sentence ending with the words "to grow and develop in health":

"To safeguard the normal development of the child, it is recommended that States should take steps, in particular, to ensure that women workers are granted paid maternity leave both before and after confinement, that the employment of expectant and nursing mothers on work detrimental to their health is prohibited, and that such mothers are transferred, where necessary, to lighter work without any reduction in pay and are granted intervals during the working day to enable them to feed their children."

146.    The Commission rejected by 9 votes to 3, with 6 abstentions, the amendment of the Soviet Union (E/CN.4/L.526/Add.1/Rev.1) calling for the replacement of the last sentence by the following:

"The child shall have the right to proper nutrition, housing, recreation and free medical services. The State shall assure free medical care to all children and expectant and nursing mothers by establishing an adequate network of hospitals, clinics, maternity homes and other medical institutions.

"States shall also promote the balanced physical development of the rising generation and, to that end, encourage the provision of various sports facilities for children."

147.    The Commission then voted on the text proposed in the amendment of India (E/CN.4/L.533), which was as follows:

"The child shall enjoy the benefits of social security. He shall be entitled to grow and develop in health. To this end adequate prenatal and post-natal care, including social and health services (such as grant of maternity leave before and after delivery, prohibition of heavy work during such periods, and establishment of clinics and maternity homes), shall be provided to the mother. The child shall have the right to adequate nutrition, housing, recreation and medical services."

148. The Commission adopted by 10 votes to 4, with 4 abstentions, the oral amendment to the Indian amendment proposed by the United Kingdom. The amendment consisted in inserting a semi-colon after the second sentence and adding the following text to replace the third sentence:

> "to this end special care and protection shall be provided both to him and to his mother, including adequate prenatal and post-natal care".

149. The oral amendment of the Soviet Union to insert the word "free" before the words "medical services" in the last sentence of the Indian amendment was voted on by roll-call and rejected by 11 votes to 3, with 4 abstentions. The voting was as follows:

> *In favour*: Poland, Ukrainian Soviet Socialist Republic, Union of Soviet Socialist Republics.

> *Against*: Argentina, Belgium, China, France, India, Israel, Italy, Lebanon, Mexico, the United Kingdom of Great Britain and Northern Ireland, the United States of America.

> *Abstentions*: Ceylon, Iran, Iraq, Philippines.

150. The first sentence of the text proposed in the Indian amendment was adopted unanimously. The last sentence of the Indian text was adopted by 16 votes to none, with 2 abstentions.

151. The text proposed in the Indian amendment as a whole, as amended, was adopted by 15 votes to none, with 3 abstentions, in the following form:

> "The child shall enjoy the benefits of social security. He shall be entitled to grow and develop in health; to this end special care and protection shall be provided both to him and to his mother, including adequate prenatal and post-natal care. The child shall have the right to adequate nutrition, housing, recreation and medical services."

*Principle 6*

152. Principle 4 of the draft of the Social Commission was as follows:

> "The child shall be given opportunity to grow up in economic security, in the care of his own parents whenever possible, and in a family atmosphere of affection and understanding favourable to the full and harmonious development of his personality."

153. The Commission discussed this principle at its 633rd to 635th meetings, on 2 and 3 April 1959, amendments were submitted by France (E/CN.4/L.524), the USSR (E/CN.4/L.526), Poland (E/CN.4/L.527 and Add.2), the Philippines (E/CN.4/L.531) and by France and Israel (E/CN.4/L.535), which superseded the previous amendment submitted by France. The Philippines amendment was subsequently withdrawn.

154. The voting commenced with the amendment of France and Israel, which, as orally revised to incorporate a suggestion of Iran, was as follows (E/CN.4/L.535 and E/CN.4/SR.633-635):

> "For the full and harmonious development of his personality, the child needs love and understanding. He shall, save where his best interest requires otherwise, grow up in the care of his own parents, and a young child shall not, save in exceptional circumstances, be separated from his mother. In any case, opportunity shall be provided to the child to grow up in an atmosphere of affection and moral and material security."

155. An Iraqi amendment consisting in deleting the word "young" was not adopted, there being 7 votes in favour, 7 against and 4 abstentions.

156. The first sentence was adopted by 17 votes to none, with 1 abstention.

157. The phrase "He shall, save where his best interest requires otherwise, grow up in the care of his own parents" in the second sentence was adopted unanimously. The rest of the second sentence was adopted by 9 votes to 5, with 4 abstentions.

158. The third sentence was adopted by 17 votes to none, with 1 abstention.

159.     The amendment as a whole was adopted by 16 votes to none, with 2 abstentions.

160.     The Commission rejected by 10 votes to 2, with 6 abstentions, the amendment proposed by the Soviet Union (E/CN.4/L.526), consisting in the addition of the following paragraph:

> "States shall provide for the proper maintenance and upbringing in children's homes, boarding schools and other children's institutions of orphaned children and children whose parents have insufficient means for their maintenance. The payment by the State of maintenance allowances to large families is desirable."

161.     The Commission adopted by 10 votes to 5, with 3 abstentions, the revised amendment submitted by Poland (E/CN.4/L.527/Add.2) adding the following sentence at the end of the principle:

> "Society as well as public authorities shall have the duty to extend particular care to children without a family or those without adequate means of support."

162.     Principle 6, as amended, was unanimously adopted as a whole.

*Principle 7*

163.     Principle 5 of the draft of the Social Commission was as follows:

> "The child shall be given an education which will bestow upon him general culture and enable him to develop his abilities and individual judgement and to become a useful member of society. Such education shall be free."

164.     The Commission discussed this principle at its 635th to 637th meetings, on 3 and 6 April 1959. Amendments were submitted by France (E/CN.4/L.524), Israel (E/CN.4/L.525), the Soviet Union (E/CN.4/L.526 and Add.2), Italy (E/CN.4/L.528), the United Kingdom (E/CN.4/L.529), the United States of America (E/CN.4/L.530), India, Iran and Iraq (E/CN.4/L.537), China (E/CN.4/L.538). A sub-amendment to the amendment of the United Kingdom was submitted by the Soviet Union (E/CN.4/L.536) and to the amendment of India, Iran and Iraq by the Soviet Union (E/CN.4/L.539 and E/CN.4/L.539/Rev.1) and by the Ukrainian SSR (E/CN.4/L.540). The first of the amendments submitted by France (E/CN.4/L.524) and the amendment of Israel (E/CN.4/L.525), the amendment of Italy (E/CN.4/L.528), the United Kingdom (E/CN.4/L.529), the United States of America (E/CN.4/L.530) and the sub-amendment of the Ukrainian SSR (E/CN.4/L.540) were subsequently withdrawn.

165.     The Commission at its 639th meeting, on 7 April 1959, voted on the basis of the substitute text submitted by India, Iran and Iraq, which took into account the French amendment. The text was as follows (E/CN.4/L.537):

> "The child is entitled to receive free and compulsory education, at least in the elementary stages. The education of the child shall be directed to the full development of his personality and the strengthening of respect for human rights and fundamental freedoms. It shall enable him, enjoying the same opportunities as others, to develop his abilities and individual judgement and to become a useful member of society. It shall promote tolerance and understanding of his own as well as other cultures and of the principles and purposes of the United Nations."

166.     The Commission rejected by 4 votes to 3, with 9 abstentions, the amendment of the Soviet Union (E/CN.4/L.539/Rev.1) calling for the insertion of the following text after the first sentence of the joint amendment:

> "The right shall be ensured by the State through the organization of an extensive network of schools, adequately staffed, housed and equipped. States shall take all necessary steps to extend the principle of free and universal education to secondary schools as well. Every child, including minors in employment, shall have the right to education."

167.     The Commission then voted by parts on the amendment submitted by the Soviet Union (E/CN.4/L.539/Rev.1) whereby the last part of the joint amendment, beginning after the words "enjoying the same opportunities as others", was to be replaced by the following:

"... to develop his abilities and to become a responsible and useful member of society. It shall promote mutual understanding, tolerance and friendship, among all peoples and racial or religious groups, as well as understanding of the culture both of his own people and of other peoples and of the principles and purposes of the United Nations.

"States shall prohibit the dissemination of war propaganda and racial and national hatred in schools."

168.     The first sentence of the first paragraph of the amendment submitted by the Soviet Union was rejected by 6 votes to 3, with 7 abstentions. The second sentence of the first paragraph, replacing the last sentence of the joint amendment, was adopted by 5 votes to 2, with 8 abstentions. The second paragraph of the amendment was rejected by 9 votes to 3, with 4 abstentions.

169.     The Commission adopted by 11 votes to none, with 6 abstentions, the amendment submitted by France (E/CN.4/L.524) consisting in the addition of the following:

"The best interest of the child shall be the guiding principle of those responsible for his education and guidance; that responsibility lies in the first place with his parents."

170.     The first part of the sentence of the joint amendment (E/CN.4/L.537) up to the word "education" was adopted unanimously. The remaining part of the first sentence, namely, the words "at least in the elementary stages" was adopted in a roll-call vote by 14 votes to 2, with 1 abstention. The voting was as follows:

*In favour:* Argentina, Belgium, Ceylon, China, France, India, Iran, Iraq, Israel, Lebanon, Mexico, Philippines, United Kingdom of Great Britain and Northern Ireland, United States of America.

*Against:* Ukrainian Soviet Socialist Republic, Union of Soviet Socialist Republics.

*Abstaining:* Poland.

171.     The joint amendment, as a whole, as amended, was adopted by 15 votes to none, with 2 abstentions, in the following form:

"The child is entitled to receive free and compulsory education, at least in the elementary stages. The education of the child shall be directed to the full development of his personality and the strengthening of respect for human rights and fundamental freedoms; it shall enable him, enjoying the same opportunities as others, to develop his abilities and individual judgement and to become a useful member of society. It shall promote mutual understanding, tolerance and friendship among all peoples and racial or religious groups, as well as understanding of the culture both of his own people and of other peoples and of the principles and purposes of the United Nations. The best interests of the child shall be the guiding principles of those responsible for his education and guidance; that responsibility lies in the first place with his parents."

*Principle 8*

172.     Principle 6 of the draft of the Social Commission was as follows:

"The child shall in all circumstances be amongst the first to receive protection and relief."

173.     The Commission discussed this principle at its 638th meeting on 7 April 1959. It adopted by 10 votes to 2, with 5 abstentions, the amendment submitted by Israel (E/CN.4/L.525) deleting the word "amongst". The text as amended was unanimously adopted.

*Principle 9*

174.     Principle 9 of the draft of the Social Commission was as follows:

"The child who is physically, mentally or socially handicapped shall be given the special treatment, education and care required by his particular condition."

175.     This principle was discussed at the 639th meeting, on 7 April 1959. The original draft was adopted unanimously. It was also agreed without objection that this principle should be included as principle 9 of the new draft.

*Principle 10*

176.     Principle 7 of the draft of the Social Commission was as follows:

"The child shall be protected against all forms of neglect, cruelty and exploitation. He shall in no case be caused to engage in any occupation or employment which would prejudice his health or education or interfere with his development."

177.     The Commission discussed this principle at its 638th meeting, on 7 April 1959. Amendments were submitted by Israel (E/CN.4/L.525) and the USSR (E/CN.4/L.526) and orally by the United Kingdom.

178.     The Commission rejected by 9 votes to 3, with 6 abstentions, the amendment submitted by the Soviet Union (E/CN.4/L.526) calling for the insertion of the following sentence after the first sentence:

"In particular, the child shall not be subjected to corporal punishment in schools."

179.     The Commission then voted on the amendment submitted by the Soviet Union (E/CN.4/L.526) consisting in the addition of the following paragraphs at the end of the principle:

"To these ends, the States shall enact legislation prohibiting the employment of minors below a certain age-limit to be established by law, and also the employment of minors for unhealthy or hazardous work. Criminal liability shall be established for the employment of minors who have not attained the minimum age established by law, and also for the employment of minors for unhealthy or hazardous work.

"States shall take measures to ensure a shorter working day, adult wage rates and adequate paid annual leave for minors."

180.     The first sentence of the first paragraph of the amendment was rejected by 8 votes to 4, with 6 abstentions. The second sentence of the first paragraph of the amendment was rejected by 9 votes to 2, with 7 abstentions. The second paragraph of the amendment was rejected by 10 votes to 2, with 6 abstentions.

181.     The first sentence of the original text was adopted unanimously.

182.     The United Kingdom oral amendment, which consisted in adding, at the beginning of the second sentence of the original text, the phrase, "He shall not be admitted to employment before an appropriate age;" was adopted by 16 votes to none, with 2 abstentions.

183.     The amendment submitted by Israel was orally revised to add the words "or permitted," after the word "caused" and to insert the words "physical, mental or moral" before the word "development" in the second sentence. The first part of the amendment was adopted unanimously and the second part of the amendment was adopted by 16 votes to none, with 2 abstentions.

184.     The text of the principle as a whole as amended was adopted by 16 votes to none, with 2 abstentions, in the following form:

"The child shall be protected against all forms of neglect, cruelty and exploitation. He shall not be admitted to employment before an appropriate age; he shall in no case be caused or permitted to engage in any occupation or employment which would prejudice his health or education or interfere with his physical, mental or moral development."

*Principle 11*

185.     Principle 8 of the draft of the Social Commission was as follows:

"The child shall be protected against any practice which may foster racial or national discrimination or hatred. He shall be brought up in the consciousness that he will achieve his fullest development and derive greatest satisfaction through devoting his energy and talents to the service of his fellow men, in a spirit of universal brotherhood and peace."

186.　　The Commission discussed this principle at its 639th meeting, on 7 April 1959. Amendments were submitted by Israel (E/CN.4/L.525), the Soviet Union (E/CN.4/L.526), Poland (E/CN.4/L.527), the United States of America (E/CN.4/L.530), the Philippines (E/CN.4/L.531) and India, Lebanon and Mexico (E/CN.4/L.543) and a sub-amendment to the United States amendment by India, Lebanon and Mexico (E/CN.4/L.542). The Israel and Philippine amendments were subsequently withdrawn.

187.　　The Commission voted first on a revised amendment submitted by Poland calling for the insertion of the following sentence at the beginning of the principle: "The child has the right to live in peace." This amendment was rejected by 5 votes to 3, with 9 abstentions.

188.　　The amendment submitted by the United States of America, incorporating the sub-amendment of India, Lebanon and Mexico, as orally revised, was adopted by 17 votes to none, with 1 abstention, in the following form as a replacement of the first sentence:

> "The child shall be brought up in an atmosphere which will promote understanding, tolerance and friendship among peoples, and national, racial and religious groups, and aversion for all forms of national, racial or religious discrimination."

189.　　The Commission adopted by 15 votes to 1, with 2 abstentions, the amendment submitted by India, Lebanon and Mexico as orally revised to insert a new sentence after the first sentence as follows: "He shall be protected from practices based on any such discrimination."

190.　　The amendment submitted by the Soviet Union, as orally revised, which consisted in inserting in the second sentence after the words "brought up" the words "in a spirit of peace, friendship and brotherhood among nations", was adopted by 11 votes to 1, with 6 abstentions.

191.　　An oral amendment submitted by the Ukrainian SSR calling for the replacement of the words "his fellow men" by "society" was not adopted, the vote being 7 in favour, 7 against and 4 abstentions.

192.　　The amendment submitted by the Soviet Union, calling for the addition of the following sentence: "States shall prohibit the dissemination of war propaganda and racial and national hatred in schools," at the end of the principle, was rejected by 12 votes to 2, with 4 abstentions.

193.　　The principle, as a whole, as amended, was adopted by 14 votes to none, with 4 abstentions.

*Last paragraph*

194.　　The last paragraph of the draft of the Social Commission was as follows:

> "*The General Assembly calls upon* all Governments and peoples to make known the above principles and explain them to parents, educators, doctors, social workers and all others who deal directly with children and to children themselves."

195.　　The Commission discussed this paragraph at its 639th meeting, on 7 April 1959. It adopted, by 14 votes to none, with 3 abstentions, the proposal by Iraq for the deletion of the paragraph. The representative of Poland then stated that she would not press her amendment (E/CN.4/L.527) calling for the addition of another paragraph to the draft Declaration, but would reserve her right to raise the matter in the Economic and Social Council.

*Adoption of the draft Declaration and transmission of the text to the Economic and Social Council*

196.　　At the 639th meeting, on 7 April 1959, the Commission adopted by 7 votes to none, with 11 abstentions, the proposal of the representative of India that the draft Declaration as prepared by the Commission on Human Rights should be voted on as a whole. At its 642nd meeting, on 10 April 1959, the Commission adopted, by 8 votes to 2, with 6 abstentions, a proposal by the representative of Iraq that separate votes should be taken on such provisions of the draft Declaration prepared by the Commission as might be requested before voting on the draft as a whole. The voting was as follows:

    (a)    The paragraph preceding principle 1 was adopted by 16 votes to none, with 2 abstentions;

    (b)    Principle 5 was adopted by 14 votes to none, with 3 abstentions;

    (c)    It was decided, by 11 votes to 4, with 2 abstentions, to retain the word "young" in the second sentence of principle 6; and principle 6 was adopted by 15 votes to none, with 2 abstentions;

    (d)    Principle 7 was adopted by 15 votes to none, with 2 abstentions;

    (e)    Principle 10 was adopted by 15 votes to none, with 2 abstentions;

    (f)    Principle 11 was adopted by 13 votes to none, with 4 abstentions;

    (g)    The draft Declaration as a whole as prepared by the Commission was adopted unanimously.

197.    At the 639th and 640th meetings, on 7 and 8 April 1959, the Commission discussed a draft resolution submitted by Argentina, India and the Philippines, (E/CN.4/L.544 and E/CN.4/L.544/Rev.1) and adopted it unanimously. The text of the resolution adopted at the 640th meeting, on 8 April 1959, is as follows:

5 (XV). DRAFT DECLARATION OF THE RIGHTS OF THE CHILD

*The Commission on Human Rights,*

*Having considered,* in accordance with Economic and Social Council resolution 309 (XI) of 13 July 1950, the draft Declaration of the Rights of the Child prepared by the Social Commission,

*Having taken* into account the comments of Governments and non-governmental organizations submitted under Council resolution 651 E (XXIV) of 24 July 1957,

*Transmits* to the Economic and Social Council its observations in the form of a draft Declaration adopted by the Commission, together with the records and documents of its proceedings.

## TEXT OF THE COMMISSION ON HUMAN RIGHTS

*Preamble*

*Whereas* the United Nations have, in the Charter, reaffirmed their faith in fundamental human rights, and in the dignity and worth of the human person, and have determined to promote social progress and better standards of life in larger freedom,

*Whereas* the United Nations have, in the Universal Declaration of Human Rights, proclaimed that everyone is entitled to all the rights and freedoms set forth therein, without distinction of any kind, such as race, colour, sex, language, religion, political or other opinion, national or social origin, property, birth or other status,

*Whereas* the child needs special safeguards, including special legal protection by reason of his physical and mental immaturity,

*Whereas* the need for such special safeguards has been stated in the Geneva Declaration of the Rights of the Child of 1924, and has again been recognized in Article 25 (2) of the Universal Declaration of Human Rights and in the statutes of specialized agencies and international organizations concerned with the welfare of children,

## TEXT OF THE SOCIAL COMMISSION

*Preamble*

1.    *Whereas* the United Nations have, in the Charter and in the Universal Declaration of Human Rights, reaffirmed their faith in fundamental human rights, and in the dignity and worth of the human person, and have determined to promote social progress and better standards of life in larger freedom,

2.    *Whereas* the United Nations have declared that everyone is entitled to all the rights and freedoms set forth in the Universal Declaration of Human Rights, without distinction of any kind, such as race, colour, sex, language, religion, political or other opinion, national or social origin, property, birth or other status,

3.    *Whereas* Member States have, in the Universal Declaration of Human Rights, proclaimed their recognition of the fundamental rights of persons,

4.    *Whereas,* as has specifically been stated since 1924 in the Geneva Declaration of the Rights of the Child, mankind owes to the child the best it has to give,

*Whereas* mankind owes to the child the best it has to give,

*Now therefore*

*The General Assembly recognizes and proclaims the essential Rights of the Child* to the end that he may have a happy childhood and be enabled to grow up to enjoy for his own good and for the good of society, the fundamental rights and freedoms, particularly those specified in the Universal Declaration of Human Rights, and calls upon men and women as individuals as well as upon local authorities and national Governments to recognize and strive for the observance of those rights through the application of the following principles.

*Principles*

1.      The child shall enjoy all the rights set forth in this Declaration without distinction or discrimination on account of race, colour, sex, language, religion, political or other opinion, national or social origin, property, birth or other status, whether of himself or of either of his parents. All children whether born in or out of wedlock shall enjoy these rights.

2.      The child shall be given the means necessary to enable him to develop physically, mentally, morally, spiritually and socially in a healthy and normal manner and in conditions of freedom and dignity.

3.      The child shall enjoy special protection by law and by other means. Whenever necessary, opportunities and facilities shall be provided by law to enable him to develop in accordance with the principles of this Declaration. The best interests of the child shall be the paramount consideration in the enactment of such laws.

4.      The child shall be entitled from his birth to a name and a nationality.

5.      The child shall enjoy the benefits of social security. He shall be entitled to grow and develop in health; to this end special care and protection shall be provided both to him and to his mother, including adequate prenatal and post-natal care. The child shall have the right to adequate nutrition, housing, recreation and medical services.

6.      For the full and harmonious development of his personality, the child needs love and understanding. He shall, save where his best interests require otherwise, grow up in the care of his parents, and a young child shall not, save in exceptional circumstances, be separated from

5.      *Whereas* the child needs special safeguards by reason of his physical and mental immaturity and his particular legal status,

*Now therefore*

6.      *The General Assembly recognizes and proclaims the essential rights of the child* to the end that he may have a happy childhood and be enabled to grow up to enjoy, for his own good and for the good of society, the fundamental rights and freedoms, particularly those specified in the Universal Declaration of Human Rights, and calls upon men and women as individuals as well as through their local authorities and national Governments to recognize and strive for the observance of these rights through the application of the following principles:

*Principles*

10.      The child shall enjoy the rights set forth above, irrespective of any consideration of race, colour, sex, language, caste, religion, political or other opinion, national or social origin, property, birth, legitimacy or other status.

1.      The child shall be given the means necessary to enable him to develop physically, mentally, morally, spiritually and socially in a healthy and normal manner and in conditions of freedom and dignity.

*[No equivalent]*

2.      The child shall be entitled from his birth to a name and a nationality.

3.      The child shall enjoy the benefits of social security. He shall be entitled even from before birth to grow and develop in health. He shall have the rights to adequate nutrition, housing, recreation and free medical services.

4.      The child shall be given opportunity to grow up in economic security, in the care of his own parents whenever possible, and in a family atmosphere of affection and understanding favourable to the full and harmonious development of his personality.

his mother. In any case, opportunity shall be provided to the child to grow up in an atmosphere of affection and moral and material security. Society as well as public authorities shall have the duty to extend particular care to children without a family or those without adequate means of support.

7.	The child is entitled to receive free and compulsory education, at least in the elementary stages. The education of the child shall be directed to the full development of his personality and the strengthening of respect for human rights and fundamental freedoms; it shall enable him, enjoying the same opportunities as others, to develop his abilities and individual judgement and to become a useful member of society. It shall promote mutual understanding, tolerance and friendship among all peoples and racial or religious groups, as well as understanding of the culture both of his own people and of other peoples and of the principles and purposes of the United Nations.

The best interests of the child shall be the guiding principle of those responsible for his education and guidance; that responsibility lies in the first place with his parents.

8.	The child shall in all circumstances be the first to receive protection and relief.

9.	The child who is physically, mentally or socially handicapped shall be given the special treatment, education and care required by his particular condition.

10.	The child shall be protected against all forms of neglect, cruelty and exploitation. He shall not be admitted to employment before an appropriate age; he shall in no case be caused or permitted to engage in any occupation or employment which would prejudice his health or education or interfere with his physical, mental or moral development.

11.	The child shall be brought up in an atmosphere which will promote understanding, tolerance and friendship among peoples and national, racial and religious groups and aversion for all forms of national, racial or religious discrimination. He shall be protected from practices based on any such discrimination. He shall be brought up in a spirit of peace, friendship and brotherhood among nations in the consciousness that he will achieve his fullest development and derive greatest satisfaction through devoting his energy and talents to the service of his fellow men. in a spirit of universal brotherhood and peace.

5.	The child shall be given an education which will bestow upon him general culture and enable him to develop his abilities and individual judgement and to become a useful member of society. Such education shall be free.

6.	The child shall in all circumstances be amongst the first to receive protection and relief.

9.	The child who is physically, mentally or socially handicapped  shall be given the special treatment, education and care required by his particular condition.

7.	The child shall be protected against all forms of neglect, cruelty and exploitation. He shall in no case be caused to engage in any occupation or employment which would prejudice his health or education or interfere with his development.

8.	The child shall be protected against any practice which may foster racial or national discrimination or hatred. He shall be brought up in the consciousness that he will achieve his fullest development and derive greatest satisfaction through devoting his energy and talents to the service of his fellow men, in a spirit of universal brotherhood and peace.

[Deleted]

The General Assembly calls upon all Governments and peoples to make known the above principles and explain them to parents, educators, doctors, social workers and all others who deal directly with children, and to children themselves.

## 3. Economic and Social Council resolution 728 (XXVIII) C adopted on 30 July 1959

DRAFT DECLARATION OF THE RIGHTS OF THE CHILD

*The Economic and Social Council,*

*Having considered* the draft Declaration of the Rights of the Child submitted to the Council by the Commission on Human Rights in the report of the Commission on its fifteenth session,

*Decides* to transmit chapter VII of the Commission's report, relating to the Draft Declaration, together with the records of the discussion of this subject in the Council, and the other documents before the Council, to the General Assembly for consideration at its fourteenth session.

*1088th plenary meeting*

*30 July 1959*

## 4. Discussion in the General Assembly on 20 November 1959

*The draft declaration was discussed in the Third Committee at its 907th to 929th meetings, held from 25 September to 19 October 1959 (A/C.3/SR.907 to 929). Proposals included the drafting of a briefer and more concise declaration, a declaration restricted to the proclamation of principles rather than suggestions for implementation, and the adoption of a convention instead of a declaration. Amendments were introduced by Afghanistan (A/C.3/L.716, para. 8), Ecuador (A/C.3/L.761) and Israel (A/C.3/L.719), all of which were withdrawn. The following is taken from the Official Records of the General Assembly, Fourteenth session Plenary meetings (841st meeting on 20 November 1959).*

*Agenda item 64: Draft Declaration of the Rights of the Child*

*Report of the Third Committee (A/4249 and Corr.2)*

27.     Mr. CUEVAS CANCINO (Mexico), Rapporteur of the Third Committee (*translated from Spanish*): I have the honour to present the report of the Third Committee [A/4249 and Corr.2] on agenda item 64, to this plenary meeting of the General Assembly. In it representatives will find a review of the history of the draft Declaration of the Rights of the Child and of the debates on it, and also its text. These are accompanied by a draft resolution designed to ensure that the draft Declaration is given publicity. The task was originally undertaken by the Social Commission; it was then taken up by the Commission on Human Rights and it has fallen to the Third Committee to bring it to a happy conclusion.

28.     The United Nations has been in existence for nearly fifteen years, during which period not a few items have passed through its hands. It has brought its best efforts to bear upon them and has devoted to them all the political wisdom of the representatives of its Member States. To many of them the United Nations has found happy solutions, while others are on the way to a conclusion. For the most part, however, they are matters connected with the constantly changing international scene. They are like the pebbles brought by the breakers to the shore, to remain there only for an instant and to return again to the ever-moving element.

29.     From time to time, however, we have items of a different kind. These are not related to the solution of specific problems; they do not seek to reconcile opposing interests or to make some small contribution towards eliminating those vast economic problems which confront a constantly expanding world population. These exceptions are items which are identified with ourselves, with that mankind which we, however imperfectly and incompletely, represent.

30.     For a moment at least, the Assembly transforms itself into the spokesman of mankind; conscious of its innumerable limitations, it looks ahead, so to speak, to its own future. From among the multitude of details which constitute the little world or politics, it seizes upon something permanent; and it does so with full faith in its destiny. Such was the Universal Declaration of Human Rights approved by the General Assembly in 1948 [resolution 217 (III)]; such is the Declaration which it is my honour to introduce now.

31.     The draft Declaration of the Rights of the Child is a brief document. Some representatives would have liked it to be more laconic, while others tried to expand it to include details of implementation, machinery putting each and every one of its principles into effect. Although it has not been unduly reduced and even includes a few indications of how some of its principles should be put into effect, I have no hesitation in describing the document which the Assembly now has before it as brief. Its brevity conceals a fundamental purpose: that of bringing home to the hearts of men an awareness of the rights of the child.

32.     The subject of this draft Declaration is children; fundamentally, however, it is directed towards society, towards adults. Its point of departure is the undisputed principle that the child is weak and therefore requires special care and safeguards (third and fourth paragraphs of the preamble and principle 2). Hence the child is incapable of protecting himself, and this draft Declaration therefore embodies an appeal on his behalf: it calls upon the child's elders as individuals organized into family and national groups to respect and maintain the rights of every child (sixth preambular paragraph).

33.     These rights are regarded as inherent in the human being (first and second paragraphs of the preamble); a human being, that is to say, in a state of physical and moral growth. We suppose that the state of moral growth never ends. But, as in the case of a plant, it consists in a development which continues the process that begins with the germination of the seed. Hence the importance of the germinative period of childhood. They are rights which - like any other - imply obligations; however, it was thought better to stress this accompanying aspect only indirectly (sixth preambular paragraph). First of all it must be recognized that the child is entitled to these rights (principle 2) and his enjoyment of them must be guaranteed, in order that he may become, as the draft Declaration itself states, a useful member of society (principles 7 and 10).

34.     The draft Declaration dwells upon the ultimate contribution which the child will make to the human group to which he belongs. In the child we can foresee the male or female citizen, full of civic virtue and materially productive. The child is given rights so that he may become a complete and perfect human being. Obviously, so sovereign an achievement must depend upon the enjoyment of a happy childhood.

35.     It is not surprising that the draft Declaration should attach such importance to the spiritual factors which determine the development of the child. Stress is laid upon the love and understanding with which the child should be surrounded; mention is made of the atmosphere of affection and of moral and material security upon which he should be able to depend (principle 6). It is only upon this firm foundation that we then build the structure of protection to which the child should be entitled.

36.     First comes the right to subsistence; it is the child who guards our future - the future of us all - and this future must be protected. Hence his privileged position among those who in the event of danger should receive protection and relief (principle 8). The strong roots by which he is attached to the land of his birth and to the family group are set forth next: he is given the right to possess from his birth a name and nationality (principle 3), thus covering him with the mantle of a personality which distinguishes him as an individual among the other members of his species. And as we are dealing here with fundamental rights, it was the desire of those who drafted the draft Declaration that these should be granted to every child, without distinction of any kind, in an instrument which applied to all equally (second preambular paragraph and principle 1).

37.     As a being in the process of development, the child requires special protection in that process; his development must be neither impeded nor forced into anti-social directions. Mention is made therefore

of the rights to health, with particular reference to physically or mentally handicapped children (principles 4 and 5) and to social security, which extends from the person of the child to the family and even as far as State subsidies to large families (principles 4 and 6).

38.      Much consideration was devoted to the educational problem, touching on the many and varied criteria that exist on this subject. Emphasis is laid on the need for educators always to bear in mind that the interests of the child are paramount and on the need for this wide field of education to include also the play and recreation proper to childhood, which are equally important to the formation of the grown man (principle 7). The desire that education should promote his general culture is also set forth in the draft Declaration (principle 7); it was the feeling among the representatives participating that this represents the best potential means of bringing about a better world, for through an understanding of alien cultures, and through the extension of national horizons to the universal, the idea of a world federation may one day come to fruition.

39.      We have stressed the fact that the child is an immature being. The draft Declaration sets forth those rights which it regards as essential to the child's full development. It would not, however, be fulfilling its purpose if it did not cite, in the same category, the regulations which should be promulgated by States in order to protect him from a society when it is not always understanding and may on occasion be cruel. He is to be protected against neglect, cruelty and exploitation; traffic in his person is prohibited; work unsuitable to his tender years is proscribed (principle 9); and to guard him from a harm more subtle and less perceptible, and hence more dangerous, he is to be protected from practices which may foster discrimination either within a given social group or at the international level (principle 10).

40.      This draft Declaration adds something - I should be inclined to say it adds a great deal - to the Universal Declaration on Human Rights. The purpose of both is to improve the environment in which the human being develops; both seek to raise his intellectual and moral standing. The latter relates to the individual as a whole; the former concentrates on that state which is at once the most transitory and the most influential for good or ill. Thus we may say that this present draft Declaration strengthens the Declaration adopted in 1948. It concentrates upon childhood as part of the development of the individual; in so doing it does not detract from the Universal Declaration in any way. Childhood is the only privileged class which transcends societies and epochs; it extends beyond frontiers and prevails over civilizations. Representatives of the most diametrically opposed social systems find common ideals and aspirations in discussing the privileges of childhood. In focusing attention upon this very human aspiration the United Nations is contributing to the realization of the elusive but irreplaceable ideal of universal brotherhood.

41.      Childhood embraces our future; the future is the repository of our hopes. We of this generation are prepared to make sacrifices in order to improve the lot of future generations and in order to do so we, unlike the unreasoning beasts, introduce the idea of rights. We are endowing children with the rights we think they should have, in our striving for a better future for mankind, based on a greater spirit of justice. In setting forth these rights that we are now proclaiming, we start by making of childhood's privileges a new claim on behalf of equality: equality of children as children, and as the future guardians of the privileges which future generations will enjoy.

42.      Our draft Declaration has its own intrinsic value. In examining it we should not draw too fine a line between the obligations which are based on treaties and those based on less formal international instruments. Can anything be more binding than principles and rights based on mutual understanding amongst peoples? Nor is there any point in enlarging upon the dividing line between domestic and international affairs. There are Articles in the Charter on which our draft Declaration is based but its roots are planted even more deeply in the conviction that all our Governments would find in it ideas which would be a source of inspiration to them and would enable them to consolidate, reinforce, extend or improve, as the case may be, their national laws. Such a process represents an ideal fusion of the ideals of nations, and those of the international community.

43.     It would be unrealistic and dangerous to disregard the problems which our draft Declaration creates for many nations whose inadequate development affects both their present and their future generations. The fact that its principles are recognized and that it provides an incentive to their realization would be sufficient justification for the draft Declaration. But it would not be enough. In bringing the rights of the child into prominence through this draft Declaration, the General Assembly is taking upon itself the implicit obligation of helping to make these rights a reality. Hence this is only the beginning of what the United Nations will do on behalf of the child; it has broken new ground, for what has been done by UNICEF cannot be underestimated or forgotten.

44.     Another problem is clearly perceptible: that of the manifold stresses and strains to which the child is exposed in the complex and uncertain world of today. The sense of insecurity experienced by recent generations produces grievous fears among children. Our draft Declaration is a clarion call to mankind to face those fears and to redouble its efforts to fulfil its obligations to the future, for in conditions which are constantly changing it must not forget to provide a sound foundation for coming generations.

45.     That sound foundation can only be provided by a happy childhood; not happy in the empty sense of mere pampering, or of building a wall to protect the child from the realities of life, but happy in the sense that the child is given every opportunity to develop the powers with which he has been endowed and to grow into a complete human being so that he will be able to contribute to the progress of mankind. One way in which he can do that - and undoubtedly the most important and effective way - will be by making the world a united and peaceful whole.

46.     The draft declaration contains the essence of all we have endeavoured to do for the child; it is a clear and forthright affirmation that mankind owes to the child the best it has to give (fifth preambular paragraph). Taking its stand upon these words, which reflect the idealism, hopes and aspirations of our era, the Third Committee now places before the General Assembly the draft Declaration of the Rights of the Child.

47.     The PRESIDENT (*translated from Spanish*): I request the Assembly to take a decision on the recommendations of the Third Committee, contained in that Committee's report [A/4249 and Corr.2].

48.     The General Assembly will now vote on the draft Declaration of the Rights of the Child, which appears in annex I of the report.

*The draft Declaration was adopted by 78 votes to none.*

49.     The PRESIDENT (*translated from Spanish*): The draft resolution concerning the publicity to be given to the Declaration of the Rights of the Child, which appears in annex H of the report, was unanimously adopted by the Third Committee. In the absence of any objections, I shall assume that the General Assembly also adopts it unanimously.

*The draft resolution was adopted unanimously.*

## 5.     Declaration of the Rights of the Child, proclaimed by General Assembly resolution 1386 (XIV) of 20 November 1959

*Whereas* the peoples of the United Nations have, in the Charter, reaffirmed their faith in fundamental human rights and in the dignity and worth of the human person, and have determined to promote social progress and better standards of life in larger freedom,

*Whereas* the United Nations has, in the Universal Declaration of Human Rights, proclaimed that everyone is entitled to all the rights and freedoms set forth therein, without distinction of any kind, such as race, colour, sex, language, religion, political or other opinion, national or social origin, property, birth or other status,

*Whereas* the child, by reason of his physical and mental immaturity, needs special safeguards and care, including appropriate legal protection, before as well as after birth,

*Whereas* the need for such special safeguards has been stated in the Geneva Declaration of the Rights of the Child of 1924, and recognized in the Universal Declaration of Human Rights and in the statutes of specialized agencies and international organizations concerned with the welfare of children,

*Whereas* mankind owes to the child the best it has to give,

*Now therefore,*

*The General Assembly,*

*Proclaims* this Declaration of the Rights of the Child to the end that he may have a happy childhood and enjoy for his own good and for the good of society the rights and freedoms herein set forth, and calls upon parents, upon men and women as individuals, and upon voluntary organizations, local authorities and national Governments to recognize these rights and strive for their observance by legislative and other measures progressively taken in accordance with the following principles:

### Principle 1

The child shall enjoy all the rights set forth in this Declaration. Every child, without any exception whatsoever, shall be entitled to these rights, without distinction or discrimination on account of race, colour, sex, language, religion, political or other opinion, national or social origin, property, birth or other status, whether of himself or of his family.

### Principle 2

The child shall enjoy special protection, and shall be given opportunities and facilities, by law and by other means, to enable him to develop physically, mentally, morally, spiritually and socially in a healthy and normal manner and in conditions of freedom and dignity. In the enactment of laws for this purpose, the best interests of the child shall be the paramount consideration.

### Principle 3

The child shall be entitled from his birth to a name and a nationality.

### Principle 4

The child shall enjoy the benefits of social security. He shall be entitled to grow and develop in health; to this end, special care and protection shall be provided both to him and to his mother, including adequate prenatal and post-natal care. The child shall have the right to adequate nutrition, housing, recreation and medical services.

### Principle 5

The child who is physically, mentally or socially handicapped shall be given the special treatment, education and care required by his particular condition.

### Principle 6

The child, for the full and harmonious development of his personality, needs love and understanding. He shall, wherever possible, grow up in the care and under the responsibility of his parents, and, in any case, in an atmosphere of affection and of moral and material security; a child of tender years shall not, save in exceptional circumstances, be separated from his mother. Society and the public authorities shall have the duty to extend particular care to children without a family and to those without adequate means of support. Payment of State and other assistance towards the maintenance of children of large families is desirable.

### Principle 7

The child is entitled to receive education, which shall be free and compulsory, at least in the elementary stages. He shall be given an education which will promote his general culture and enable him, on a basis of equal opportunity, to develop his abilities, his individual judgement, and his sense of moral and social responsibility, and to become a useful member of society.

The best interests of the child shall be the guiding principle of those responsible for his education and guidance; that responsibility lies in the first place with his parents.

The child shall have full opportunity for play and recreation, which should be directed to the same purposes as education; society and the public authorities shall endeavour to promote the enjoyment of this right.

*Principle 8*

The child shall in all circumstances be among the first to receive protection and relief.

*Principle 9*

The child shall be protected against all forms of neglect, cruelty and exploitation. He shall not be the subject of traffic, in any form.

The child shall not be admitted to employment before an appropriate minimum age; he shall in no case be caused or permitted to engage in any occupation or employment which would prejudice his health or education, or interfere with his physical, mental or moral development.

*Principle 10*

The child shall be protected from practices which may foster racial, religious and any other form of discrimination. He shall be brought up in a spirit of understanding, tolerance, friendship among peoples, peace and universal brotherhood, and in full consciousness that his energy and talents should be devoted to the service of his fellow men.

# The question of a convention considered by the Commission on Human Rights, the Economic and Social Council and the General Assembly

# Part two

# A. 1976

## 1. General Assembly resolution 31/169 on an "International Year of the Child" adopted on 21 December 1976

*The General Assembly,*

*Having considered* the report of the Secretary-General on measures and modalities to ensure the adequate preparation, support and financing of an international year of the child, Economic and Social Council decision 178 (LXI) of 5 August 1976 on an international year of the child and the additional report of the Secretary-General prepared in the light of the discussions in the Economic and Social Council,

*Recognizing* the fundamental importance in all countries, developing and industrialized, of programmes benefiting children not only for the well-being of the children but also as part of broader efforts to accelerate economic and social progress,

*Recalling* in this connection its resolutions 2626 (XXV) of 24 October 1970 containing the International Development Strategy for the Second United Nations Development Decade, 3201 (S-VI) and 3202 (S-VI) of 1 May 1974 containing the Declaration and the Programme of Action on the Establishment of a New International Economic Order and 3362 (S-VII) of 16 September 1975 on development and international economic cooperation,

*Deeply concerned* that, in spite of all efforts, far too many children, especially in developing countries, are undernourished, are without access to adequate health services, are missing the basic educational preparation for their future and are deprived of the elementary amenities of life,

*Convinced* that an international year of the child could serve to encourage all countries to review their programmes for the promotion of the well-being of children and to mobilize support for national and local action programmes according to each country's conditions, needs and priorities,

*Affirming* that the concept of basic services for children is a vital component of social and economic development and that it should be supported and implemented by the cooperative efforts of the international and national communities,

*Bearing in mind* that the year 1979 will be the twentieth anniversary of the Declaration of the Rights of the Child and could serve as an occasion to promote further its implementation,

*Aware* that, for an international year of the child to be effective, adequate preparation and the widespread support of Governments, non-governmental organization[s] and the public will be required,

*Believing* that administrative costs for the international year should be kept to the minimum necessary,

*Taking note* of the statement made by the Executive Director of the United Nations Children's Fund before the Second Committee,

1.      *Proclaims* the year 1979 International Year of the Child;

2.      *Decides* that the International Year of the Child should have the following general objectives:

        (a)      To provide a framework for advocacy on behalf of children and for enhancing the awareness of the special needs of children on the part of decision makers and the public;

        (b)      To promote recognition of the fact that programmes for children should be an integral part of economic and social development plans with a view to achieving, in both the long term and the short term, sustained activities for the benefit of children at the national and international levels;

3.      *Urges* Governments to expand their efforts at the national and community levels to provide lasting improvements in the well-being of their children, with special attention to those in the most vulnerable and particularly disadvantaged groups;

4.    *Calls upon* the appropriate organs and organizations of the United Nations system to contribute to the preparation and implementation of the objectives of the International Year of the Child;

5.    *Designates* the United Nations Children's Fund as the lead agency of the United Nations system responsible for coordinating the activities of the International Year of the Child, and the Executive Director of the Fund to be responsible for its coordination;

6.    *Invites* non-governmental organizations and the public to participate actively in the International Year of the Child and to coordinate their programmes for the Year as fully as possible, especially at the national level;

7.    *Appeals* to Governments to make contributions or pledges for the International Year of the Child through the United Nations Children's Fund to ensure the adequate financing of activities for the preparation and carrying out of the Year;

8.    *Expresses the hope* that Governments, non-governmental organizations and the public will respond generously with contributions to attain the objectives of the International Year of the Child and, through the United Nations Children's Fund and other channels of external aid, to increase substantially the resources available for services benefiting children;

9.    *Requests* the Executive Director of the United Nations Children's Fund to report to the General Assembly at its thirty-second session, through the Economic and Social Council at its sixty-third session, on progress in preparing for the International Year of the Child, including its financing and the level of contributions pledged.

*106th plenary meeting*
*21 December 1976*

# B. 1978

## 1. Original Polish draft

*The following is taken from document E/CN.4/1284 (18 January 1978).*

Letter dated 17 January 1978 from the Permanent Representative of Poland to the United Nations Office at Geneva addressed to the Director of the Division of Human Rights

Acting upon the instruction of my Government, I have the honour to submit herewith for inclusion in the Agenda of the 34th session of the Commission on Human Rights the following item: "The question of the convention on the rights of the child". I am also enclosing herewith the Explanatory Memorandum on that question.

I would appreciate if you could, at your earliest convenience, bring this request together with the Explanatory Memorandum, in an appropriate manner, to the attention of all the Members of the Commission.

(Signed)
*Eugeniuz WYZNER*
Ambassador
*Permanent Representative*

EXPLANATORY MEMORANDUM

In 1959 on the initiative of various countries, including Poland, the General Assembly of the United Nations Organization passed the Declaration of the Rights of the Child. In the opinion of the Government of the Polish People's Republic, the principles of this Declaration have played a significant part in the assistance, care and the rights of children in the entire world as well as in shaping various forms of the international cooperation in this sphere.

The Government of the Polish People's Republic is fully convinced that today, i.e. almost twenty years after the proclamation of the principles of this Declaration by the General Assembly, the conditions to take further and more consistent steps by adopting the internationally binding instrument in the form of a convention, have been already created.

The development of the international cooperation in different areas shows that both the care of the child and its rights should not lag behind the elaboration of the international legal rules in other spheres.

The above-mentioned proposal is closely related to the United Nations General Assembly programme of the International Year of the Child. As the celebrations are planned for 1979, the Government of the Polish People's Republic proposes to consider the question of the convention on the rights of the child during the 34th session of the Commission on Human Rights.

The adoption of the above-proposed convention on the occasion of the International Year of the Child, besides just mentioned substantial reasons, would give a special meaning to these celebrations. In the opinion of the Polish Government, the convention on the rights of the child should be entirely based on the principles of the Declaration of the Rights of the Child.

## 2. Discussion in the Commission on Human Rights

*The following is taken from document E/CN.4/SR.1429 (7 February 1978).*

8.　　[...] the CHAIRMAN [Mr. N'Baye (Senegal)] said that, if there was no objection, he would take it that the Commission was prepared to adopt the provisional agenda appearing in document E/CN.4/1262, with the following amendments:

[...]

Two new items, item 21 "Rights of persons belonging to national, ethnic, religious and linguistic minorities" and item 22 "Question of a convention on the rights of the child" had been included in the agenda.

## 3.   Polish draft resolution

*The following is taken from document E/CN.4/L.1366 (7 February 1978).*

QUESTION OF A CONVENTION ON THE RIGHTS OF THE CHILD (agenda item 22)

Poland, draft resolution

*The Commission on Human Rights,*

*Recommends* to the Economic and Social Council the adoption of the following draft resolution:

"*The Economic and Social Council,*

*Having in mind* the fact that General Assembly resolution 31/169 of 21 December 1976 proclaimed 1979 as the International Year of the Child,

*Bearing in mind* that since the adoption by the General Assembly of the Declaration of the Rights of the Child 19 years have elapsed, during which period States Members of the United Nations have taken into account in the formulation of their socio-economic policies the principles of that Declaration,

*Conscious* of the need further to strengthen the comprehensive care and the well-being of children all over the world,

*Being aware* of the special need to assist children in the developing countries in a manner consistent with the goals of the new international economic order,

*Having in mind* the International Covenant on Civil and Political Rights, in particular its articles 23 and 24, as well as the International Covenant on Economic, Social and Cultural Rights, in particular its article 10,

*Resolves* to recommend to the General Assembly the adoption of an international, legally binding instrument in the form of a convention on the rights of the child on the basis of principles and provisions contained in the United Nations Declaration of the Rights of the Child.

*Draft Convention on the Rights of the Child*

*The States Parties to the present Convention,*

*Bearing in mind* that the peoples of the United Nations have, in the Charter, reaffirmed their faith in fundamental human rights and in the dignity and worth of the human person, and have determined to promote social progress and better standards of life in larger freedom,

*Recognizing* that the United Nations have, in the Universal Declaration of Human Rights and in the International Covenants on Human Rights, proclaimed and agreed that everyone is entitled to all the rights and freedoms set forth therein, without distinction of any kind, such as race, colour, sex, language, religion, political or other opinion, national or social origin, property, birth or other status,

*Recognizing also* that the child, by reason of his physical and mental immaturity, needs social safeguards and care, including appropriate legal protection, before as well as after birth,

*Having in mind* that the need for such special safeguards has been stated in the Geneva Declaration of the Rights of the Child of 1924 and in the United Nations Declaration of the Rights of the Child of 1959 and recognized in the Universal Declaration of Human Rights, in the International Covenant on Civil and Political Rights (in particular in its articles 23 and 24), in the International Covenant on Economic, Social and Cultural Rights (in particular in its article 10) and in the statutes of specialized agencies and international organizations concerned with the welfare of children,

*Proclaiming* that mankind owes to the child the best it has to give,

*Have agreed as follows:*

### Article I

Every child, without any exception whatsoever, shall be entitled to the rights set forth in this Convention, without any distinction or discrimination on account of race, colour, sex, language, religion, political and other opinion, national or social origin, property, birth or status, whether of himself or of his family.

### Article II

The child shall enjoy special protection and shall be given opportunities and facilities, by law and by other means, to enable him to develop physically, mentally, morally, spiritually and socially in a healthy and normal manner and in conditions of freedom and dignity. In the enactment of laws for this purpose, the best interests of the child shall be the paramount consideration.

### Article III

The child shall be entitled from his birth to a name and a nationality.

### Article IV

The child shall enjoy the benefits of social security. He shall be entitled to grow and develop in health; to this end, special care and protection shall be provided both to him and to his mother, including adequate prenatal and post-natal care. The child shall have the right to adequate nutrition, housing, recreation and medical services.

### Article V

The child who is physically, mentally or socially handicapped shall be given the special treatment, education and care required by his particular condition.

### Article VI

The child, for the full and harmonious development of his personality, needs love and understanding. He shall, wherever possible, grow up in the care and under the responsibility of his parents and, in any case, in an atmosphere of affection and of moral and material security; a child of tender years shall not, save in exceptional circumstances, be separated from his mother. Society and the public authorities shall have the duty to extend particular care to children without a family and to those without adequate means of support. Payment of State and other assistance towards the maintenance of children of large families is desirable.

### Article VII

1.      The child is entitled to receive education, which shall be free and compulsory, at least in the elementary stages. He shall be given an education which will promote his general culture and enable him, on a basis of equal opportunity, to develop his abilities, his individual judgements and his sense of moral and social responsibility, and to become a useful member of society.

2.      The best interests of the child shall be the guiding principle of those responsible for his education and guidance; that responsibility lies in the first place with his parents.

3.      The child shall have full opportunity for play and recreation, which should be directed to the same purposes as education; society and the public authorities shall endeavour to promote the enjoyment of this right.

*Article VIII*

The child shall in all circumstances be among the first to receive protection and relief.

*Article IX*

1.      The child shall be protected against all forms of neglect, cruelty and exploitation. He shall not be the subject of traffic, in any form.

2.      The child shall not be admitted to employment before an appropriate minimum age; he shall in no case be caused or permitted to engage in any occupation or employment which would prejudice his health or education, or interfere with his physical, mental or moral development.

*Article X*

The child shall be protected from practices which may foster racial, religious or any other form of discrimination. He shall be brought up in a spirit of understanding, tolerance, friendship among peoples, peace and universal brotherhood, and in full consciousness that his energy and talents should be devoted to the service of his fellow men.

*Article XI*

The States Parties to the present Convention agree to report on the status of implementation of this Convention to the Economic and Social Council through the Secretary-General of the United Nations one year after ratification of the Convention and thereafter once every five years.

*Article XII*

The present Convention is open for signature by all States. Any State which does not sign the Convention before its entry into force may accede to it.

*Article XIII*

1.      The present Convention is subject to ratification. Instruments of ratification shall be deposited with the Secretary-General of the United Nations.

2.      Accession shall be effective by the deposit of an instrument of accession with the Secretary-General of the United Nations.

*Article XIV*

1.      The present Convention shall enter into force six months after the date of the deposit with the Secretary-General of the Untied Nations of the fifteenth instrument of ratification or accession.

2.      For each State ratifying the present Convention or acceding to it after the deposit of the fifteenth instrument of ratification or instrument of accession, the Convention shall enter into force six months after the date of the deposit of its own instrument of ratification or instrument of accession.

*Article XV*

Any State Party may denounce the present Convention by a written notification to the Secretary-General of the United Nations. Denunciation shall take effect one year after the date of receipt of the notification by the Secretary-General.

*Article XVI*

1.      A request for the revision of the present Convention may be made at any time by any State Party by means of a notification in writing addressed to the Secretary-General of the United Nations.

2.      The General Assembly of the United Nations shall decide upon the steps, if any, to be taken in respect of such request.

*Article XVII*

The Secretary-General of the United Nations shall inform all States of the following particulars:

(a)     Signatures, ratifications and accessions under articles XII and XIII;

(b)     The date of entry into force of the present Convention under article XIV;

(c)     Denunciations under article XV;

(d)     Notifications under article XVI.

*Article XVIII*

1.     The present Convention, of which the Chinese, English, French, Russian and Spanish texts are equally authentic, shall be deposited in the archives of the United Nations.

2.     The Secretary-General of the United Nations shall transmit certified copies of the present Convention to all States.

## 4.   Revised draft resolution on the "Question of a convention on the rights of the child"

*The following is taken from document E/CN.4/L.1366/Rev.1 (14 February 1978). Only changes from document E/CN.4/L.1366 are noted.*

Austria, Bulgaria, Colombia, Jordan, Poland, Senegal and Syrian Arab Republic: draft resolution

*The Commission on Human Rights,*

*Taking into consideration* the draft convention on the rights of the child submitted by Poland on 7 February 1978 and annexed to the present resolution,

1.     *Requests* the Secretary-General to transmit the draft convention to Member States inviting them to communicate to him not later than 30 June 1978 their views, observations and suggestions on such a convention and requests him to submit a report thereon to the Economic and Social Council at its second regular session of 1978;

2.     *Requests* the Economic and Social Council to undertake at its second regular session of 1978 the consideration of the draft convention on the rights of the child, taking into account both the draft presented by Poland and the report of the Secretary-General;

[...]

"*The Economic and Social Council,*

[...]

*Resolves* to recommend to the General Assembly that it consider the drafting of a convention on the rights of the child based on the principles and provisions contained in the United Nations Declaration of the Rights of the Child as presented in the draft convention annexed to Commission on Human Rights resolution ___ (XXXIV) as well as on the views, observations and suggestions of Member States transmitted to the Secretary-General under paragraph 1 of Commission resolution ___ (XXXIV), with the hope that it will be adopted at the thirty-fourth session of the General Assembly.

## 5.   Discussion in the Commission on Human Rights

*The following is taken from document E/CN.4/SR.1438 (15 February 1978).*

QUESTION OF A CONVENTION ON THE RIGHTS OF THE CHILD (agenda item 22) (E/CN.4/L.1366 and Rev.1)

40.     Mr. Van BOVEN (Director, Division of Human Rights) said that a study of the international legislation on human rights showed that special provisions had to be drawn up for certain categories of people - refugees,

detainees, displaced persons, etc. Those provisions could be incorporated in general instruments such as covenants or in specialized instruments such as conventions, declarations, recommendations and regulations. The rights of the child were defined in articles 23 and 24 of the International Covenant on Civil and Political Rights and in article 10 of the International Covenant on Economic, Social and Cultural Rights, as also in the 1959 Declaration of the Rights of the Child. It was in commemoration of the twentieth anniversary of that Declaration that the General Assembly had decided to proclaim 1979 the International Year of the Child.

41.      Mr. LOPATKA (Poland), introducing draft resolution E/CN.4/L.1366 and Rev.1 on behalf of Austria, Bulgaria, Colombia, Jordan and Poland, appealed to all countries of the Commission to co-sponsor the draft resolution as a way of expressing their desire that better provision should be made urgently for children and of demonstrating that all countries were prepared to cooperate in that domain of human rights. He was confident that the draft resolution would be adopted unanimously, as in the case of the decision to include the question on the agenda for the thirty-fourth session of the Commission.

42.      In 1959, on the initiative of several countries, including Poland, the General Assembly had adopted the Declaration of the Rights of the Child, which had played a significant part in the assistance given to children throughout the world and in the protection of their rights, and whose principles had been drawn upon in shaping various forms of international cooperation in that sphere. Nearly 20 years had passed since the adoption of the Declaration and the time had come to take more consistent steps through the adoption of an internationally binding instrument such as a convention. Progress in legislating on the rights of the child should not lag behind that made in other spheres of international law. It would seem all the more appropriate to adopt the proposed convention in that 1979 was to be the International Year of the Child, as proclaimed by the General Assembly.

43.      The draft convention, which should be based entirely on the principles of the Declaration of the Rights of the Child, stipulated that every child, without discrimination, should enjoy special protection and should be able to develop morally and physically in a healthy and normal manner, have the benefits of social security and have the right to adequate housing, opportunities for recreation, medical services and education. The child should be protected from all forms of cruelty and exploitation and should not be employed before a certain age. Furthermore, the child should be brought up in a spirit of understanding, tolerance and friendship. The draft convention also included provisions for handicapped children. Lastly, it included provisions concerning ratification, entry into force and implementation.

44.      In the amended draft resolution (E/CN/L.1366/Rev.1), the Commission, the Secretary-General and the Economic and Social Council were requested to take the necessary steps for the adoption of the convention by all Governments.

## 6.    Written statement by non-governmental organizations

*The following is taken from document E/CN.4/NGO/225 (23 February 1978).*

*Written statement submitted by the following non-governmental organizations in consultative status: International Council of Women, International Planned Parenthood Federation (category I), All India Women's Conference, Anti-Slavery Society, International Child Bureau, International Council of Jewish Women, International Federation for Human Rights, International Federation of Business and Professional Women, International Federation of Women in Legal Careers, International Federation of Women Lawyers, International Social Service, International Union for Child Welfare, International Union of Family Organizations, St. Joan's International Alliance, World Association of Girl Guides and Girl Scouts, World Jewish Congress, World Movements of Mothers, World Union of Catholic Women's Organizations, World Union of Organizations for the Safeguard of Youth, World Young Women's Christian Association (category II), International Federation for Parent Education (roster)*

The Secretary-General has received the following statement, which is circulated in accordance with paragraphs 29 and 30 of Economic and Social Council resolution 1296 (XLIV).

[23 February 1976]

The non-governmental organizations mentioned above appreciate the proposal for the elaboration of a draft convention on the rights of the child (E/CN.4/L.1366/Rev.1), which would bring a new and complementary contribution to the promotion of the well-being of the child. The International Year of the Child is in effect an occasion well-suited to creating among Governments and the general public a greater awareness of the urgent needs of children and of the necessity to take action to meet those needs.

However, several studies, surveys and programmes concerning the rights of the child and more specifically concerning the implementation of the Declaration of the Rights of the Child and the application of other existing international pronouncements, are already planned or in progress in governmental, intergovernmental and non-governmental sectors. The value of a convention on the rights of the child would be that much greater and richer if it could take into account the results of this work.

This is why the non-governmental organizations listed above suggest that the debate on such a draft convention commence only when the results of these studies are known, i.e., in the course of the thirty-sixth session of the Commission on Human Rights in 1980.

## 7. Second revised draft resolution on the "Question of a convention on the rights of the child"

*The following is taken from document E/CN.4/L.1366/Rev.2 (1 March 1978). Only changes to document E/CN.4/L.1366/Rev.1 are noted.*

Austria, Bulgaria, Colombia, Jordan, Peru, Poland, Senegal and Syrian Arab Republic: revised draft resolution

*The Commission on Human Rights,*

*Taking into consideration* the draft convention on the rights of the child submitted by Poland on 7 February 1978,

1.        *Requests* the Secretary-General to transmit the draft convention to Member States and to competent specialized agencies, regional intergovernmental organizations and competent non-governmental organizations, inviting them to communicate to him not later than 31 October 1978 their views, observations and suggestions on such a convention and requests him to submit a report thereon to the Commission on Human Rights at its thirty-fifth session;

2.        *Decides* to continue, as a matter of priority, at its thirty-fifth session, its consideration of the draft convention on the rights of the child, taking into account both the draft convention annexed to this resolution and the report of the Secretary-General, with a view to adopting the convention at that session for transmission to the General Assembly through the Economic and Social Council;

"*The Economic and Social Council,*

[...]

*Noting* resolution ___ (XXXIV) of the Commission on Human Rights,

*Takes note with satisfaction* of the work undertaken by the Commission at its thirty-fourth session with a view to preparing a convention on the rights of the child and its decision finally to adopt such a convention at its thirty-fifth session,

*Recommends* to the General Assembly that it include in the agenda for its thirty-fourth session, as a priority matter, the question of the adoption of a convention on the rights of the child.

Draft Convention on the Rights of the Child

[...]

*Article XI*

The States Parties undertake to submit to the Economic and Social Council, through the Secretary-General, periodic reports on the implementation of this Convention. These reports shall be submitted initially, one year after entry into force of the Convention for the State concerned, and thereafter every five years.

*Article XII*

The reports submitted by the States Parties under article XI shall be considered by the Economic and Social Council which may make general observations and bring them to the attention of the General Assembly.

## 8. Discussion in the Commission on Human Rights

*The following is taken from document E/CN.4/SR.1471 (13 March 1978).*

QUESTION OF A CONVENTION ON THE RIGHTS OF THE CHILD (agenda item 22) (E/CN.4/NGO/225; E/CN.4/L.1366/Rev.2)

56.      Mr. LOPATKA (Poland) explained that the second revised version of the draft convention on the rights of the child (E/CN.4/L.1366/Rev.2) had been drafted to meet some suggestions made by members of the Secretariat and some points made in document E/CN.4/NGO/225.

57.      In the new version the Secretary-General was requested to transmit the draft resolution (E/CN.4/L.1366/Rev.2) to which the draft convention was annexed not only to Member States but also to competent specialized agencies, regional intergovernmental organizations and competent non-governmental organizations, inviting them to communicate to him their views, observations and suggestions, not by 30 June, as in the previous draft, but by 31 October 1978. It was also proposed that the draft convention should be considered, not in 1978 at the sixty-fifth session of the Economic and Social Council, but by the Commission on Human Rights at its thirty-fifth session, in 1979, with a view to the adoption of the convention at that session and its transmission to the General Assembly through the Economic and Social Council. It was also requested that the Economic and Social Council should recommend to the General Assembly the inclusion of the question of the adoption of a convention on the rights of the child in the agenda for its thirty-fourth session.

58.      It was clear from the draft resolution that the sponsors wished to request the Commission to take a direct part in the process of working out the draft convention, so that it could be adopted by the General Assembly at its thirty-fourth session, during the International Year of the Child. The draft convention made some additional recommendations concerning the procedure for reporting on its implementation, with a view to improving the international control provided for in paragraphs XI and XII.

59.      On behalf of the sponsors, he thanked all delegations, as also the Secretariat of the Division of Human Rights, who had cooperated in improving the document, and he announced that Peru had joined the sponsors. His delegation was sure that the other States members of the Commission were animated by the noble desire to contribute to improving the lot of children by adopting that international document during the International Year of the Child. To that end it urged that draft resolution E/CN.4/L.1366/Rev.2 should be adopted by consensus.

60.      Mr. ROWE (Canada) said that, when the Commission had agreed by consensus to include the question in its programme of work for the thirty-fourth session, several delegations had been under the impression that it would be desirable to adopt a resolution by consensus on the possible preparation of a draft convention on the rights of the child. His delegation, like a number of others, wondered, however, whether that initiative should be given priority in the work that the Commission was to accomplish at its thirty-fourth session and whether it was appropriate at that stage to talk about adopting the convention at

the thirty-fifth session. His delegation felt that it would be a premature assumption, since the Commission would be asked to take a decision before Governments, specialized agencies, intergovernmental and regional organizations and competent non-governmental organizations had been able to communicate their views to the Secretary-General. In document E/CN.4/NGO/225, 23 non-governmental organizations had requested that the preparation of the convention should not be undertaken too rapidly, since they wanted Governments to be able to examine their studies and proposals first.

61. His delegation therefore proposed the following amendments to document E/CN.4/L.1366/Rev.2: in operative paragraph 2, the words "continue, as a matter of priority at its thirty-fifth session, its consideration" should be replaced by "include among its priority matters, at its thirty-fifth session, further consideration" and the end of the same paragraph should be amended to read: "with a view to concluding as soon as possible a convention for transmission ...". To bring the remainder of the resolution into line with those amendments, his delegation proposed that the penultimate paragraph of the draft resolution to be recommended for adoption by the Council should be amended to read: "*Takes note with satisfaction* of the work undertaken by the Commission at its thirty-fourth session with a view to completing as soon as possible a convention on the rights of the child and to start considering this work at its thirty-fifth session." The last paragraph would be reworded to read: "*Recommends* to the General Assembly that it should consider the inclusion in the agenda for its thirty-fourth session the question of the adoption of a convention on the rights of the child".

62. He reaffirmed his delegation's strong support for the International Year of the Child. He sincerely hoped that measures acceptable to all could be adopted with regard to a convention on the rights of the child but felt that the resolution could be improved to take into account the wishes of several delegations and the important work of the non-governmental organizations. He hoped that those amendments would be accepted by the sponsors so that the Commission could adopt the resolution, as amended, by consensus.

63. Mr. LOPATKA (Poland), replying to make the proposals by the Canadian delegation, said that the sponsors would like the convention to be adopted in 1979 to mark the International Year of the Child. That would be possible if the Governments of all States Members of the United Nations showed good will; moreover, it should be remembered that the draft convention was based on declarations which were already in being concerning the rights of the child.

64. With regard to the opinions of non-governmental organizations, his country attached great importance to their views but did not think they needed several years to make their opinions known on questions which they had long had under consideration.

65. If Canada shared the Commission's desire, it would agree to withdraw its amendments, which were not in keeping with the hopes which had been expressed that the convention could be adopted during the International Year of the Child. Moreover, the amendments seemed to prejudge the outcome of the Commission's work at its thirty-fifth session, for while it might not be able to complete its consideration of the draft convention, it was premature to assert that it could not.

66. Miss SHEIKH FADLI (Syrian Arab Republic) said that the Syrian Arab Republic had joined the sponsors of draft resolution E/CN.4/L.1366/Rev.2. The protection of the child should be one of the primary objectives of social and economic development strategy. The creation of a social climate favourable to the child would perhaps eliminate some of the problems which were obstacles to the right to development. Nineteen years after the adoption by the General Assembly of the Declaration of the Rights of the Child, hundreds of children were still dying of hunger, disease or the consequences of natural disasters such as drought. Thousands of children were deprived of their most fundamental rights by the racist regimes of southern Africa, while thousands more in Palestine were deprived of their right to a nationality, the right to return to their own countries and to have proper housing. At the beginning of the session, the representative of the International Indian Treaty Council had stated that one Indian child out of three died before it was six months old because of malnutrition and the wretched living conditions of the American Indian nation.

67.     The Syrian Arab delegation considered that the rights of the child varied from one geographical region to another. The privileged children had a right to leisure and to the full development of their personality, and to be protected against violence, cruelty, exploitation, drugs and the slave trade, while the underprivileged children of developing societies had the right to life, to their daily bread, to shelter and to protection against underdevelopment. Only through international solidarity could children be properly protected. At the national level, it was essential that children should be protected against all practices leading to hatred, to segregation or to racial or religious supremacy. They must be brought up in a spirit of equality among peoples and universal brotherhood. For all those reasons, the proposed draft resolution should be able to serve as a basis for a final document.

68.     Mr. FRAMBACH (observer for the German Democratic Republic) said that the chief aim of the year 1979, which had been declared the International Year of the Child by General Assembly resolution 31/169 of 21 December 1976, would be to consolidate the fundamental rights of the child, which in many countries were still not guaranteed. The delegation of the German Democratic Republic therefore welcomed the proposal for the preparation of the convention on the rights of the child. Children continued to be the innocent victims of acts of aggression, colonialism, fascism and racism and were still exposed to discrimination because of their national or social origin, their beliefs or their sex.

69.     Two of the consequences of centuries of colonial oppression and imperialist exploitation were that children grew up illiterate and that, according to UNICEF, some 350 million children lacked the minimum necessities of life. In addition, according to the UNICEF Information Bulletin No. 14/1977 there were all the groups of children faced with special problems. His delegation therefore considered that a convention on the rights of the child could be an important basis for the adoption of measures designed to solve the problems he had mentioned and to improve the lives of millions of children. His delegation was ready to make an active contribution to the preparation of such a convention.

70.     Mr. DANELIUS (Sweden) said that the Swedish delegation felt strongly that a convention should differ in many respects from the 1959 Declaration. During the 20 years that had elapsed, considerable experience had been gained, general views on some of the questions had changed, and new States which had not participated in drafting the Declaration would be able to take part in the drafting of the convention.

71.     In 1970, the International Year of the Child, Governments would present national reports on the situation of children in their respective countries. Those reports would provide a better basis for evaluating the contents of a convention and for judging to what extent the provisions of the 1959 Declaration were being observed. His delegation therefore considered that it would be premature to aim at completing the work on a convention during the 1979 session and that it would be preferable to complete that work at a later stage after the Commission had had the opportunity to study the material which would be made available in 1979.

72.     Sir Keith UNWIN (United Kingdom) said that he did not think that the sponsors of draft resolution L.1366/Rev.2 had sufficiently demonstrated the advantages that a convention on the rights of the child would have over the 1959 Declaration of the Rights of the Child. Furthermore, the preparations for the International Year of the Child had led to a large number of studies, surveys and programmes being undertaken both by non-governmental organizations competent in the field of the rights of the child and in specialized bodies such UNEP, UNESCO and ILO. Those documents would not be available before the Commission's next session. It would therefore seem premature to push on at the present stage of the discussions to the adoption of the draft resolution in question. He therefore supported the amendments proposed by the representative of Canada.

73.     Mr. GARVALOV (Bulgaria) said that his delegation welcomed the Polish delegation's initiative in having the question of a convention on the rights of the child placed on the agenda of the present session of the Commission. That initiative had met with unanimous support in the Commission. His delegation was also glad to have been able to be a sponsor of draft resolution L.1366/Rev.2. In his opinion, it was necessary that the rights of the child should be laid down in an instrument which was mandatory and it was also important

that the preparation of the draft convention should coincide with the International Year of the Child (1979). A considerable amount of work had already been done or was being done on the subject. The draft resolution had already been amended to take account of the views expressed and its adoption would in no way prejudice the position which the Governments concerned might adopt with regard to the convention, since it was unanimously recognized that there must be an instrument of that kind. Moreover, the work of drawing up a convention would not begin until Governments had communicated their views on the draft resolution and the draft convention. While account must be taken of the views of the non-governmental organizations which had suggested (E/CN.4/NGO/225) that the discussions on such a draft convention should start during the thirty-sixth session of the Commission on Human Rights, in 1980, it must not be forgotten that the views of Member States were particularly important, since it was they which would become parties to the convention. He therefore hoped that the Commission would adopt the draft resolution without a formal vote. While fully appreciating the reasons and the concern that had prompted the amendments proposed by the Canadian delegation he considered that the text of draft resolution L.1366/Rev.2 could be accepted by the Commission.

74.     Mr. ERMACORA (Austria) said that, after hearing the comments made by the Canadian and United Kingdom delegations, his delegation found itself in a difficult position. As one of the sponsors of the draft resolution in question it could not go back on the text of the draft. Nevertheless the discussions had raised points of procedure, and the possibility of compromise on the draft resolution should be considered. As far as the convention itself was concerned, it was not certain that the Austrian Government would be able to adopt a convention at the thirty-fifth session of the Commission. Speaking on behalf of the Austrian delegation, he said that he would be able to accept a change in the wording of operative paragraph 1 of the draft resolution to take into account the amendment proposed by the Canadian delegation.

75.     Mr. DAVIS (Australia) said that he welcomed the initiative taken by the Polish delegation. In his opinion, there was room for constructive statesmanship and it would be desirable for the draft resolution to be adopted by consensus. The value of the convention, which should be a lasting instrument, would depend on its contents and not on the date on which it was adopted. As the representative of Sweden had pointed out, the reports which Governments would present in 1979 on the occasion of the International Year of the Child would be a valuable element which should influence the actual content of a convention. The Commission should therefore take its time in considering the draft resolution and not adopt a position on the subject at the present meeting.

76.     Mr. ZORIN (Union of Soviet Socialist Republics) stressed the importance of the Polish delegation's initiative for future generations, and thus for the future of the Commission's work. He had noted that no delegation had spoken against the substance of the initiative, indeed the contrary was the case. That being so, he was surprised that a number of delegations, which happened all to belong to the same geographical region, were trying to delay the accomplishment of the Commission's work on the subject. The representative of Sweden had even considered it premature to draw up a convention on the rights of the child. Yet that was a task to which no one who was concerned with human rights and the rights of future generations could object. The representative of the United Kingdom had questioned whether a convention would have any advantage over the Declaration of the Rights of the Child. A convention, however, was a binding agreement, while a declaration was a moral and political document. A convention would therefore be· particularly valuable for the rights of children, since it was children who suffered most from wars, from privileges given to others, etc. The practical difficulties did not seem to be insoluble, for the Commission would in fact have before it a year of preparatory work and a session (the thirty-sixth) before submitting the draft convention to the General Assembly.

77.     Unlike other representatives, he considered the time at which the convention would be adopted to be very important. There was a Russian proverb which said that Easter was the time for Easter eggs, and it was during the International Year of the Child that a convention on the rights of the child should be adopted. He was entirely in favour of draft resolution L.1366/Rev.2 and considered that the Commission could adopt

it without amendments. He saw no need for amendments that would have the effect of slowing down the work in a domain which was so important for peace.

78.     Mr. DANELIUS (Sweden) said he wished to explain the purport of his earlier remarks. During 1979 important new documents would become available which should be taken into consideration in drawing up the draft convention on the rights of the child. If the Commission wished to be able to take advantage of them, it could not complete its work at the next session. It would therefore be preferable to postpone the completion of the work of drawing up a draft convention until after the thirty-sixth session of the Commission.

79.     Mrs. UNDERHILL (International Union for Child Welfare), speaking at the invitation of the Chairman in accordance with rules 75 and 76 of the rules of procedure, said that the first Declaration of the Rights of the Child had been promulgated in 1923 but it had taken six years of efforts to achieve its unanimous acceptance. The United Nations Declaration of the Rights of the Child had been adopted in 1959, at a time when most countries in Africa and Asia had been colonies. Those countries had since become independent and a large number of the principles in the Declaration might not be acceptable to them. One of the major tasks of the International Year of the Child was to study the implementation, applicability and non-applicability of each of the ten principles of the Declaration. For that purpose, the International Union for Child Welfare had sent a questionnaire to its 170 members in 14 countries. Other organizations were producing studies and surveys on international legislation relating to the protection of children in armed conflicts and in peace. Some countries were for the first time translating the Declaration into their local and tribal languages. Those were promotion and education activities which needed time. It was therefore necessary to allow enough time for all organizations, Governments, communities, parents and children to investigate the real problems in the different countries and regions, and to measure the differences between the legislation on the protection of children and the reality. The final aim was to arrive at a Declaration which could be implemented by every region and every community.

80.     It was true that a convention was a binding instrument and a declaration was not. It was noteworthy, however, that the Universal Declaration of Human Rights had a persuasive value that was universally recognized. The number of countries which would be able to ratify and implement fully a covenant based on the Declaration adopted by the United Nations in 1959 might be very small. If a convention on the rights of the child were decided upon too rapidly, it might possibly exclude 80 per cent of the population of the world and deprive them of the little protection they now had. It would be better to take enough time to make a thorough study which could lead to a universally acceptable new instrument. She therefore urged the Commission to accept the amendments proposed by the representative of Canada in order to allow enough time for the drafting of a convention which could be unanimously adopted.

[...]

84.     Mr. ROWE (Canada) said that he wished to draw attention to the statement by the representative of Australia. He sincerely hoped that the draft resolution would obtain general agreement in the Commission and he therefore requested the sponsors of the draft resolution and the other participants to study the matter before the next meeting of the Commission.

*The following is taken from document E/CN.4/SR.1472 (9 March 1978).*

1.     Mr. LOPATKA (Poland), speaking on behalf of the sponsors of draft resolution E/CN.4/L.1366/Rev.2, said that the discussion had revealed general agreement that a convention on the rights of the child was necessary and that it would be useful to continue work on the draft. Not all delegations, however, had supported the proposed timetable for the work. A compromise had been reached, as a result of which he proposed the following changes: in the draft resolution for the Commission, in the [first] line of operative paragraph 2 "the" before "draft convention" should be replaced by "a" and in the [third] line of that paragraph, the phrase "with a view to adopting the convention" should be replaced by the phrase "with a view to concluding, if possible, a convention". In the draft resolution for the Economic and Social Council the two operative paragraphs should read

"*Takes note with satisfaction* of the initiative undertaken by the Commission at its thirty-fourth session with a view to concluding a convention on the rights of the child and to the adoption of this convention, if possible, by the General Assembly during the International Year of the Child;

"*Recommends* to the General Assembly that it consider including in the agenda for its thirty-fourth session, as a priority matter, the question of the adoption of a convention on the rights of the child."

2.        He hoped that the Commission would adopt the draft resolution by consensus.

3.        Mr. RIOS (Panama) said that his Government was especially interested in protecting the rights of the child and intended to enact a series of permanent measures to commemorate the International Year of the Child. The Commission's work on the convention would encourage States to enact legislation to protect children, who constituted a large and totally defenceless sector of the world population, open to every kind of abuse, even from their own parents. The United Nations must take a firm stand on the question. The Panamanian Government offered its full cooperation to ensure that during the International Year of the Child rules of conduct were established which would outlaw both the corporal and the mental punishment of children.

4.        Mr. MEZVINSKY (United States of America) said that his delegation supported the oral amendments to the draft resolutions proposed by the Polish representative. It would be premature to negotiate a convention on the rights of the child by 1979, since continued efforts were still necessary for the implementation at the national level of the Declaration on that subject. The activities which would take place in 1979 in association with the International Year of the Child would provide the necessary basis for the negotiation of a convention which it was to hoped would be implemented by national legislation.

5.        He understood that the United Nations Children's Fund (UNICEF) would report to the Economic and Social Council and to the General Assembly at its thirty-fourth session with interim recommendations, which might well include a recommendation for a convention and valuable information on which to base it. At that time the decision whether the Commission or some other United Nations body like the Commission for Social Development should conduct the necessary negotiations would be taken.

6.        He pointed out that his delegation supported only the draft resolutions in document E/CN.4/L.1366/Rev.2 and not the annexed draft convention.

7.        The CHAIRMAN [Mr. N'Baye (Senegal)] said that if there were no objections, he would take it that the Commission wished to adopt draft resolution E/CN.4/L.1366/Rev.2 as orally amended, by consensus.

8.        *It was so decided.*

9.        Mr. GROS (France) recorded his delegation's reservation on the fourth preambular paragraph of the draft resolution for the Economic and Social Council which, in a text meant to be universally applicable, referred to the new international economic order. If a vote had been taken on the draft resolution, his delegation would have abstained.

## 9.   Commission on Human Rights resolution 20 (XXXIV) on the "Question of a convention on the rights of the child" adopted on 8 March 1978

*The following is taken from document E/1978/34 (=E/CN.4/1292).*

*The Commission on Human Rights,*

*Taking into consideration* the draft convention on the rights of the child submitted by Poland on 7 February 1978,

1.        *Requests* the Secretary-General to transmit the draft convention to Member States and to the competent specialized agencies, regional intergovernmental and non-governmental organizations inviting

them to communicate to him not later than 31 October 1978 their views, observations and suggestions on such a convention and requests him to submit a report thereon to the Commission on Human Rights at its thirty-fifth session;

2.      *Decides* to continue at its thirty-fifth session, as one of its priorities, its consideration of a draft convention on the rights of the child, taking into account both the draft convention annexed to the present resolution and the report of the Secretary-General, with a view to concluding, if possible, a convention at that session for transmission to the General Assembly through the Economic and Social Council;

3.      *Recommends* that the Economic and Social Council should adopt the following draft resolution:

"*The Economic and Social Council,*

*Having in mind* the fact that General Assembly resolution 31/169 of 21 December 1976 proclaimed 1979 as the International Year of the Child,

*Bearing in mind* that since the adoption by the General Assembly of the Declaration of the Rights of the Child nineteen years have elapsed, during which period States Members of the United Nations have taken into account in the formulation of their socio-economic policies the principles of that Declaration,

*Conscious* of the need further to strengthen the comprehensive care and the well-being of children all over the world,

*Being aware* of the special need to assist children in the developing countries in a manner consistent with the goals of the new international economic order,

*Having in mind* the International Covenant on Civil and Political Rights, in particular its articles 23 and 24, as well as the International Covenant on Economic, Social and Cultural Rights, in particular its article 10,

*Noting* Commission on Human Rights resolution 20 (XXXIV),

1.      *Takes note with satisfaction* of the initiative taken by the Commission at its thirty-fourth session with a view to the conclusion of a convention on the rights of the child and to the adoption of this convention by the General Assembly, if possible during the International Year of the Child;

2.      *Recommends* to the General Assembly that it consider including in the agenda for its thirty-fourth session, as a priority matter, the question of the adoption of a convention on the rights of the child."

*Annex*

DRAFT CONVENTION ON THE RIGHTS OF THE CHILD

*The States Parties to the present Convention,*

*Bearing in mind* that the peoples of the United Nations have, in the Charter, reaffirmed their faith in fundamental human rights and in the dignity and worth of the human person, and have determined to promote social progress and better standards of life in larger freedom,

*Recognizing* that the United Nations have, in the Universal Declaration of Human Rights and in the International Covenants on Human Rights, proclaimed and agreed that everyone is entitled to all the rights and freedoms set forth therein, without distinction of any kind, such as race, colour, sex, language, religion, political or other opinion, national or social origin, property, birth or other status,

*Recognizing also* that the child, by reason of his physical and mental immaturity, needs social safeguards and care, including appropriate legal protection, before as well as after birth,

*Having in mind* that the need for such special safeguards has been stated in the Geneva Declaration of the Rights of the Child of 1924 and in the United Nations Declaration of the Rights of the Child of 1959 and recognized in the Universal Declaration of Human Rights, in the International Covenant on Civil and Political Rights (in particular in its articles 23 and 24), in the International Covenant on Economic, Social and Cultural Rights (in particular in its article 10) and in the statutes of specialized agencies and international organizations concerned with the welfare of children,

*Proclaiming* that mankind owes to the child the best it has to give,

*Have agreed as follows:*

### Article I

Every child, without any exception whatsoever, shall be entitled to the rights set forth in this Convention, without distinction or discrimination on account of race, colour, sex, language, religion, political or other opinion, national or social origin, property, birth or other status, whether of himself or of his family.

### Article II

The child shall enjoy special protection and shall be given opportunities and facilities, by law and by other means, to enable him to develop physically, mentally, morally, spiritually and socially in a healthy and normal manner and in conditions of freedom and dignity. In the enactment of laws for this purpose, the best interests of the child shall be the paramount consideration.

### Article III

The child shall be entitled from his birth to a name and a nationality.

### Article IV

The child shall enjoy the benefits of social security. He shall be entitled to grow and develop in health; to this end, special care and protection shall be provided both to him and to his mother, including adequate prenatal and post-natal care. The child shall have the right to adequate nutrition, housing, recreation and medical services.

### Article V

The child who is physically, mentally or socially handicapped shall be given the special treatment, education and care required by his particular condition.

### Article VI

The child, for the full and harmonious development of his personality, needs love and understanding. He shall, wherever possible, grow up in the care and under the responsibility of his parents and, in any case, in an atmosphere of affection and of moral and material security; a child of tender years shall not, save in exceptional circumstances, be separated from his mother. Society and the public authorities shall have the duty to extend particular care to children without a family and to those without adequate means of support. Payment of State and other assistance towards the maintenance of children of large families is desirable.

### Article VII

1.      The child is entitled to receive education, which shall be free and compulsory, at least in the elementary stages. He shall be given an education which will promote his general culture and enable him, on a basis of equal opportunity, to develop his abilities, his individual judgement and his sense of moral and social responsibility, and to become a useful member of society.

2.      The best interests of the child shall be the guiding principle of those responsible for his education and guidance; that responsibility lies in the first place with his parents.

3.      The child shall have full opportunity for play and recreation, which should be directed to the same purposes as education; society and the public authorities shall endeavour to promote the enjoyment of this right.

## Article VIII

The child shall in all circumstances be among the first to receive protection and relief.

## Article IX

1.      The child shall be protected against all forms of neglect, cruelty and exploitation. He shall not be the subject of traffic, in any form.

2.      The child shall not be admitted to employment before an appropriate minimum age; he shall in no case be caused or permitted to engage in any occupation or employment which would prejudice his health or education, or interfere with his physical, mental or moral development.

## Article X

The child shall be protected from practices which may foster racial, religious or any other form of discrimination. He shall be brought up in a spirit of understanding, tolerance, friendship among peoples, peace and universal brotherhood, and in full consciousness that his energy and talents should be devoted to the service of his fellow men.

## Article XI

The States Parties undertake to submit to the Economic and Social Council, through the Secretary-General, periodic reports on the implementation of this Convention. These reports shall be submitted initially one year after the entry into force of the Convention for the State concerned, and thereafter every five years.

## Article XII

The reports submitted by the States Parties under article XI shall be considered by the Economic and Social Council, which may make general observations and bring them to the attention of the General Assembly.

## Article XIII

The present Convention is open for signature by all States. Any State which does not sign the Convention before its entry into force may accede to it.

## Article XIV

1.      The present Convention is subject to ratification. Instruments of ratification shall be deposited with the Secretary-General of the United Nations.

2.      Accession shall be effective by the deposit of an instrument of accession with the Secretary-General of the United Nations.

## Article XV

1.      The present Convention shall enter into force six months after the date of the deposit with the Secretary-General of the Untied Nations of the fifteenth instrument of ratification or accession.

2.      For each State ratifying the present Convention or acceding to it after the deposit of the fifteenth instrument of ratification or instrument of accession, the Convention shall enter into force six months after the date of the deposit of its own instrument of ratification or instrument of accession.

## Article XVI

Any State Party may denounce the present Convention by a written notification to the Secretary-General of the United Nations. Denunciation shall take effect one year after the date of receipt of the notification by the Secretary-General.

## Article XVII

1.      A request for the revision of the present Convention may be made at any time by any State Party by means of a notification in writing addressed to the Secretary-General of the United Nations.

2.      The General Assembly of the United Nations shall decide upon the steps, if any, to be taken in respect of such request.

*Article XVIII*

The Secretary-General of the United Nations shall inform all States of the following particulars:

(a)     Signatures, ratifications and accessions under articles XIII and XIV;

(b)     The date of entry into force of the present Convention under article XV;

(c)     Denunciations under article XVI;

(d)     Notifications under article XVII.

*Article XIX*

1.      The present Convention, of which the Chinese, English, French, Russian and Spanish texts are equally authentic, shall be deposited in the archives of the United Nations.

2.      The Secretary-General of the United Nations shall transmit certified copies of the present Convention to all States.

## 10.   Economic and Social Council resolution 1978/18 on the "Question of a convention on the rights of the child" adopted on 5 May 1978

*The Economic and Social Council,*

*Having in mind* the fact that the General Assembly, by its resolution 31/169 of 21 December 1976, proclaimed the year 1979 International Year of the Child,

*Bearing in mind* that since the adoption by the General Assembly of the Declaration of the Rights of the Child nineteen years have elapsed, during which period States Members of the United Nations have taken into account in the formulation of their socio-economic policies the principles of that Declaration,

*Conscious* of the need further to strengthen the comprehensive care and the well-being of children all over the world,

*Aware* of the special need to assist children in the developing countries in a manner consistent with the goals of the new international economic order,

*Having in mind* the International Covenant on Civil and Political Rights, in particular its articles 23 and 24, as well as the International Covenant on Economic, Social and Cultural Rights, in particular its article 10,

*Taking note* of resolution 20 (XXXIV) of 8 March 1978 of the Commission on Human Rights,

1.      *Takes note with satisfaction* of the initiative taken by the Commission on Human Rights at its thirty-fourth session with a view to the conclusion of a convention on the rights of the child and to its adoption by the General Assembly, if possible during the International Year of the Child;

2.      *Recommends* to the General Assembly that it should consider including in the agenda of its thirty-fourth session, as a priority matter, the question of the adoption of a convention on the rights of the child.

*15th plenary meeting*
*5 May 1978*

## 11.   Economic and Social Council resolution 1978/40 on the "International Year of the Child" adopted on 1 August 1978

*The Economic and Social Council,*

*Having considered* the progress report of the Executive Director of the United Nations Children's Fund on the International Year of the Child, 1979,

*Convinced* of the need for all States to pay increased attention to the welfare, protection and education of children in a spirit of solidarity, equality and respect among all nations,

*Noting with satisfaction* that to date the Governments of 141 countries have indicated their intention to respond to General Assembly resolution 31/169 of 21 December 1976, by which the Assembly proclaimed the year 1979 International Year of the Child, and that 91 of those countries have already established national commissions for the Year,

*Noting with appreciation* the equally positive response from the organizations of the United Nations system and the no less positive response from non-governmental organizations,

*Bearing in mind* Council resolution 1978/18 of 5 May 1978 concerning the question of a convention on the rights of the child,

*Recalling* the relevant resolutions of the General Assembly which laid the foundations for a new international economic order, as well as other pertinent resolutions and decisions of United Nations organizations,

*Taking note* of the message sent by the Executive Board of the United Nations Children's Fund to the General Assembly at its tenth special session devoted to disarmament, which appeals to Governments to ensure that an adequate portion of any savings that may result from a reduction in expenditures on armaments is channelled through national or multinational programmes towards meeting the minimum requirements of children everywhere,

*Commending* the work of the Interagency Advisory Group for the International Year of the Child and the creation of a single Committee of Non-Governmental Organizations for the Year, which Committee is a member of the Advisory Group,

1.      *Expresses its appreciation* to the United Nations Children's Fund for the manner in which it has carried out the responsibility of lead agency entrusted to it by the General Assembly in its resolution 31/169;

2.      *Reaffirms* that the International Year of the Child is intended to be a Year for action at the national level, supported, where called for, by activities and consultations at the regional and international levels;

3.      *Expresses the strong hope* that each country will take this occasion to review the situation of its children in depth, to elaborate plans, including the setting of realistic goals, for the initiation, extension or improvement of services meeting the particular needs of its children, and to put those plans into operation in the course of 1979;

4.      *Urges*, in addition, the Governments of Member States to increase their assistance to programmes benefiting children in the developing countries, with a view to helping the Governments of those countries to ensure that all children will be provided with at least the most essential services by the end of the century;

5.      *Urges* the United Nations Children's Fund and other United Nations agencies concerned to give appropriate attention during the International Year of the Child, in their programmes to assist children, to those children who find themselves in special circumstances that might not be adequately covered in paragraphs 3 and 4 above, in particular children living under colonial rule, apartheid and foreign occupation, and requests such agencies to consult with their respective recognized representatives and other interested governmental and non-governmental bodies, in order to identify the particular problems and needs of those children and give them the necessary assistance and care;

6.      *Commends* those Governments which have made voluntary contributions towards the cost of the secretariat of the International Year of the Child and urges Governments which have not yet taken such action to do so.

*35th plenary meeting*
*1 August 1978*

## 12.  General Assembly resolution 33/166 on the "Question of a convention on the rights of the child" adopted on 20 December 1978 without a vote

*The General Assembly,*

*Having in mind* its resolution 31/169 of 21 December 1976, in which it proclaimed the year 1979 International Year of the Child,

*Recalling* its resolution 32/109 of 15 December 1977, in which it, inter alia, reaffirmed that the major focus of the International Year of the Child should be at the national level, but that this should be supported by regional and international cooperation,

*Taking note* of Commission on Human Rights resolution 20 (XXXIV) of 8 March 1978 and Economic and Social Council resolutions 1978/18 of 5 May 1978 and 1978/40 of 1 August 1978,

*Bearing in mind* that, since the adoption of the Declaration of the Rights of the Child, nineteen years have already elapsed, and that during this time the principles of the Declaration have played a significant part in the promotion of the rights of children in the entire world as well as in shaping various forms of international cooperation in this sphere,

*Considering* that during these nineteen years the conditions to take further steps by adopting a convention on the rights of the child have been created,

*Conscious* of the need to strengthen further the comprehensive care and the well-being of children all over the world,

1. *Takes note with satisfaction* of the decision of the Commission on Human Rights at its thirty-fourth session, in its resolution 20 (XXXIV), to continue at its thirty-fifth session, as one of its priorities, its consideration of a draft convention on the rights of the child;

2. *Requests* the Commission on Human Rights to organize its work on the draft convention on the rights of the child at its thirty-fifth session so that the draft of the convention may be ready for adoption if possible during the International Year of the Child;

3. *Decides* to include in the provisional agenda of its thirty-fourth session the question of a convention on the rights of the child.

*90th plenary meeting*
*20 December 1978*

# C. 1979

## 1. European Conference on the Rights of the Child in Warsaw

*The following is taken from document E/CN.4/L.1428 (23 February 1979).*

*Note by the Secretary-General*

In accordance with a request received from the Permanent Representative of Poland to the United Nations Office at Geneva, the annexed document pertaining to the European Conference on the Rights of the Child held in Warsaw from 16 to 19 January 1979 on the initiative of the International Commission of Jurists, the International Association of Democratic Lawyers and the Polish Association of Jurists is circulated as a document of the Commission on Human Rights.

WARSAW CONFERENCE ON THE LEGAL PROTECTION OF THE RIGHTS OF THE CHILD, 16-19 JANUARY

*Organized by the International Association of Democratic Lawyers, the International Commission of Jurists and the Polish Association of Jurists*

A conference on the Legal Protection of the Rights of the Child was held in Warsaw on 16-19 January 1979, organized by the International Commission of Jurists, the International Association of Democratic Lawyers and the Polish Association of Jurists.

The Polish Association of Jurists, as the host organization, generously provided conference premises in the Palace of Culture and Science, interpretation in four languages (Polish, Russian, French and English), and a most interesting series of visits for the participants, including one to the new Children's Hospital built as a memorial to the 13 million children killed in the Second World War of whom over two million came from Poland.

Apart from numerous Polish jurists, some 50 participants came from abroad, approximately half from the socialist countries of Eastern Europe (Bulgaria, Czechoslovakia, German Democratic Republic, Hungary, Romania, USSR and Yugoslavia) and half from Western Europe (Austria, Belgium, France, German Federal Republic, Ireland, Italy, Netherlands, Norway, Sweden, Switzerland and the United Kingdom as well as representatives of the United Nations Secretariat for the International Year of the Child, the United Nations Division of Human Rights and the United Nations High Commissioner for Refugees. Many of the participants were jurists of considerable eminence with experience and expertise in the field of family law.

Professor Adam Lopatka, President of the Polish Association of Jurists and Polish delegate to the United Nations Commission on Human Rights, presided at the opening session and the Polish Minister of Justice, M. Jerzy Bafia, attended both the opening and closing session of the Conference, as well as hosting a reception to the participants.

Working Papers were prepared by the three General Rapporteurs for the three Commissions of the Conference as follows:

I        The Evolution of the Concept of the Rights of the Child, by Maître Roland Weyl (France, IADL);

II        The Responsibility of the Family and of Society towards the Child, by Dr. Olive Stone (United Kingdom and Canada, ICJ);

III        State Organs Empowered to take Decisions about Children, by Dr. Marta Katona Soltez (Presidente de Chambre, Supreme Court of Hungary).

Several other very informative papers were prepared by participants describing the legislation and practice concerning the rights of the child in their own countries.

At the Closing Plenary Session presided by Mr. N. MacDermot, Secretary-General of the International Commission of Jurists, reports were received from the three Commissions and a statement of principles concerning the legal protection of the rights of the child was approved. A copy of this statement of principles is annexed together with two resolutions adopted by the Conference, one in support of the early adoption of an international convention on the rights of the child, and the other in support of the implementation of the United Nations Declaration on the Preparation of Societies for Life in Peace.

## RESOLUTION IN SUPPORT OF THE ADOPTION OF AN INTERNATIONAL CONVENTION ON THE RIGHTS OF THE CHILD

We, the participants at the International Conference on the Legal Protection of the Rights of the Child held under the auspices of the International Commission of Jurists and the International Association of Democratic Lawyers,

Having met in Warsaw, capital of a country which lost more than two million children during the Second World War,

Convinced that our organizations and all lawyers should support every initiative aimed at realizing progressive and humanist ideals in the service of greater respect for the dignity and value of man, of social progress and the creation of better conditions of life in greater freedom,

Being agreed that mankind should always give of its best to every child,

Welcome with satisfaction the initiative of the Thirty-fourth Session of the Commission on Human Rights in March 1978 contained in its resolution 20/XXXIV and confirmed in resolutions of the Economic and Social Council and the thirty-third session of the General Assembly of the United Nations, aimed at the acceptance by the United Nations, if possible in 1979, of an international convention on the rights of the child.

Every child needs care, education and the assurance that its material needs will be met. He has a right to full development. For balanced development of his personality, he needs love, understanding and a sense of security. All these can and should be assured to the child by adults. It is their duty to protect the child against neglect, cruelty and exploitation. It is also their duty to bring up the child in the spirit of peace and humanity and to provide conditions which will ensure that the rights of the child are respected and the obligations of society towards the child are carried out.

Special protection of the child requires legally guaranteed opportunities and facilities for his physical, mental, moral, spiritual and social development in freedom and dignity. This applies to all children without exception, distinction or discrimination on grounds of race, colour, sex, language, religion, political or other opinion, nationality, social origin, property, birth or for any other reason relating to the child or his family.

These duties towards the child, which are now a supreme moral imperative of society, should be reinforced by giving them the status of norms under international law in the form of an international convention on the rights of the child.

For this reason we call upon all who cherish the ideals of law and democracy to support actively the initiative for the speedy adoption of such a convention.

In common with all progressive opinion throughout the world we consider it necessary to draw attention to the need to take energetic measures for the purpose of realizing the ideals which led to the proclamation of 1979 as the International Year of the Child.

We lawyers from every part of Europe, meeting in Warsaw, consider that the adoption of an international convention on the rights of the child would be a highly significant event in the service of achieving these goals, bringing nearer the realization of the rights of childhood, the recognition and assurance of which are in the interest of all progressive States and of all humanity.

Warsaw, 19 January 1979

## STATEMENT OF PRINCIPLES ON THE LEGAL PROTECTION OF THE RIGHTS OF THE CHILD

At the final plenary session of the Conference the participants, who came from 19 countries of Eastern and Western Europe, agreed unanimously upon the following principles:

1.　　　The State has an important responsibility to secure the Rights of the Child through support to the family in need, and thus to ensure that the child will grow up happily from its birth.

2.　　　To this end, the State should set out clearly what is required of parents to ensure the welfare of the child in society, and also how the State and organizations and individuals in society propose to assist parents in the upbringing of their children.

3.　　　At the same time, both the State and parents should respect the right of the child to be consulted about its welfare whenever the child is in a position to express such opinions.

In the particular areas of the child's development which are the subject of education, health and recreation, the following more detailed conclusions were reached.

*Education*

4.　　　The duty to provide the means of education (including the training of teachers in adequate numbers) falls in the first place on the State.

5.　　　In deciding on the content and form of programmes of education, the State, parents, teachers and the children themselves, and their representative organizations, all have an important role. How the responsibility for those decisions is distributed must depend in part on the institutional and social structures and traditions of different countries, but there are dangers in placing too great a degree of responsibility on any one of the four parties to the exclusion of the others. Therefore, even where the law places that responsibility on a single organ, that organ should ensure that all the other parties are able to participate in the making of the decisions.

6.　　　So far as possible, both parents and children should benefit from improvements in methods of education by having a choice of those best suited to enable the child to develop its abilities to the full.

7.　　　Although it is desirable to provide special educational facilities for children who are exceptional either in their talents or in their handicaps, it is important that their education should, so far as possible, be integrated with that of other children.

8.　　　Where it has not yet been realized both in law and in fact, priority should be given, within the available resources, to equating education for girls and women with that of boys and men, in all fields and at all levels, including mathematics, science, engineering, economics, medicine (including all its specialities), and administration, as well as the arts, humanities and sports.

*Health*

9.　　　The obligation to provide adequate health care for all children falls primarily upon the State.

10.　　　As a child becomes older and more responsible its own views on the events which will shape its future become increasingly important. Even before it reaches the age of legal majority, it should be able to participate in any major decisions about its physical and mental health. In order that its participation should be both free and informed, the child should have access to full information and independent advice, and procedures should be made available for the resolution of differences between the views of the child and those of its parents.

11.　　　The primary responsibility for preventing a child from pursuing activities harmful to itself (such as drinking alcohol, smoking tobacco, or taking other drugs) falls upon the parents, both by education and by example. Although the State can reinforce this protection by suitable legislation and education, there is an age (not later than the age of legal majority) after which a person has the sole moral responsibility to make decisions on these matters, and accept the consequences which the laws of his country impose.

*Recreation*

12.　　　The obligation to provide means for the recreation of children falls primarily on the State.

13.	As their age increases, the choice by children of different forms of recreation should increase also. Older children should not be forced to engage in forms of recreation which they do not wish to pursue; at the same time, they should be free to pursue forms of recreation which they enjoy and which do not harm others.

*Child Labour*

14.	Further, as child labour is damaging for the development of the child in its education, its health and its recreation, we demand the end of child labour everywhere and we call for all nations to implement the provisions of Convention No. 138 of the International Labour Organization.

Accordingly, the Conference concludes that:

15.	A distinction should be drawn between the way of dealing with rights concerning children whose age entails their absolute legal incapacity, and those for whom, by reason of their greater maturity, the law can provide forms of partial legal capacity, especially in the choice of their studies, their profession and, if necessary, their residence, which will prepare them by stages for the exercise of their full legal capacity on attaining majority.

16.	Protection of the child should, in the case of interventions by public authorities, be accompanied by legal procedures which ensure judicial control, full discussion and rights of appeal, so as to ensure that the concept of the interests of the child shall be applied in the most objective way taking into account the complex realities of specific situations.

17.	In their relations with families and individuals concerning children, State institutions and social organizations should avoid as far as possible making the child an object of dispute and should act in a spirit of the widest possible cooperation, as indeed should individuals, and particularly the parents, in their relations with each other.

18.	Particular importance attaches to principle 7 of the United Nations Declaration on the Rights of the Child, since the interests of the child include the right to be prepared by an adequate education so as to be able to face the complex problems of his or her future adult life, including all that this implies in terms of the duties, efforts and constraints inherent in social life.

19.	The children of refugees and child refugees should be treated in the same way as other children and enjoy the same protection, both in their country of asylum and abroad.

20.	The same principle should be applied to the children of migrant workers.

21.	It follows also that equality of opportunity should be effectively guaranteed to children by the provision of the necessary material and cultural means. This should be done both by public facilities placed by the community and the State at the disposal of the children and of the adults responsible for them, by reason of their importance for the multilateral development of the child, as well as through social security and welfare benefits which will ensure to the families the material and cultural conditions of life to enable them to fulfil their role under truly favourable conditions. The satisfaction of these needs should become an integral part of the development plan of each country.

## 2.	General comments by Member States on the first Polish draft – annexed to Commission on Human Rights resolution 20 (XXXIV) of 8 March 1978

*Unless otherwise indicated, the following are all taken from document E/CN.4/1324 (27 December 1978).*

### (a)	Australia

The Australian Government, while it is alive to the importance of the rights of children, believes that consideration of the proposal to draft a convention on the rights of the child should be deferred until after the various activities to be mounted in connection with the International Year of the Child have afforded Member States the opportunity to examine in detail the need for such a convention.

**(b)      Austria**

1.      The substantive provisions of the present draft correspond literally to the United Nations Declaration of the Rights of the Child (1959). If clear and unequivocal obligations under international law are to be based on a convention on the rights of the child, the Austrian Federal Government feels that its wording should be much more concrete and specific than that of the Declaration.

2.      Finally, the Austrian Federal Government takes the liberty of suggesting a thorough revision of the draft. Revisers should in particular see whether the rights referred to in the draft are not already safeguarded by the International Covenants on Human Rights.

**(c)      Bahrain**

1.      The 10 principles included in the United Nations Declaration of the Rights of the Child are fundamental principles whose comprehensiveness as general principles is indisputable.

2.      What needs to be developed is the means to implement such principles at the level of the United Nations Secretariat as well as at the level of Member States, in order to have the said means adjusted to the world's changing and developing circumstances.

3.      In this regard, the United Nations Secretariat may investigate the extent to which Member States apply the aforementioned 10 principles in their legislation and in actuality, and can thus derive several facts spotlighting the real world of childhood today.

4.      The Secretariat may also translate each of these principles into several realistic and concrete proposals, so as to enable each State to ascertain, by comparing such proposed measures with actual practice therein, whether or not it applies such principles properly.

5.      Member States should not be content just with proclaiming these principles and circulating them in their original form, but should translate them into legislation and into executive as well as partial measures.

6.      Member States should also embody these principles and make them accessible to their citizens, i.e. to fathers and mothers and to children also, because children are the fathers and mothers of the future, in every possible field, particularly in the fields of education and mass media, e.g. the press, television and radio.

**(d)      Barbados**

1.      The Government of Barbados is in favour of the adoption of a convention on the rights of the child and is in general agreement with the draft convention submitted by Poland.

2.      It has been observed that no article deals directly with the adoption of children where this is desirable in their best interest. If this is to be accepted then provision should be made whereby an adoption should not take place without the consent of the parent. However such consent may be dispensed with by a competent court if the person whose consent is to be dispensed with:

   (a)      has abandoned, neglected or persistently ill-treated the infant; or

   (b)      cannot be found or is incapable of giving his consent or is withholding his consent unreasonably.

3.      The child's right to life has not been articled. How far should this right go? Does the child include the unborn child, or the foetus? Under specified circumstances, should a foetus be aborted without an offence being committed or at the relevant time was the foetus a human life? All these are questions which should be considered before the child's right to life is articled.

**(e)      Belgium**

1.      The Belgian Government welcomes any initiative likely to improve the status of the child and attaches the utmost importance to the legal aspect of the protection of the child.

2.        It notes that the preamble and substantive articles contained in the draft convention submitted by Poland are absolutely identical to the text of the Declaration of the Rights of the Child adopted by the General Assembly on 20 November 1959. The draft also provides for a system for reporting to the Economic and Social Council. Articles XIII et seq. contain the final provisions which are customary in treaty law.

3.        Clearly, the sole effect of the Polish draft is to give an existing declaration the form of a binding convention.

4.        It should be noted, however, that the Declaration was not, and was not intended to be, drafted in such a way as to be directly usable as a convention. Basically, it provides guidelines by bringing together, with specific reference to the child, a broad range of rights deriving from numerous other United Nations instruments.

5.        The Belgian Government does not consider that, under these circumstances, the mere transformation of the Declaration of the Rights of the Child into a convention constitutes a tangible contribution to the protection of the child. It would prefer the international community to endeavour to translate into terms more directly applicable in internal law such rights of the child as are not yet sufficiently covered by other binding international instruments.

6.        The Belgian Government therefore urges the Commission on Human Rights to embark on the study of a convention on the rights of the child which, although of course inspired by the Declaration of the Rights of the Child, would establish specific legal provisions supplementing existing international law.

## (f)      Bulgaria

*Taken from document E/CN.4/1324/Add.1.*

The initiative of preparing and adopting a convention on the rights of the child represents an eminently humane and progressive act which is in keeping with the policy of the People's Republic of Bulgaria in this area. The adoption of this timely international instrument in 1979, which has been proclaimed the International Year of the Child, will promote the realization of the principles set out as long ago as in 1959 in the Declaration of the Rights of the Child as well as in other international and legal instruments containing provisions regarding the rights of the child (articles 23 and 24 of the International Covenant on Civil and Political Rights, article 10 of the International Covenant on Economic, Social and Cultural Rights, etc.)

## (g)      Byelorussian Soviet Socialist Republic

*Taken from document E/CN.4/1324/Add.1.*

The draft convention on the rights of the child submitted by the Polish People's Republic to the Commission on Human Rights constitutes an excellent basis which will probably enable an international legal instrument on the subject to be prepared at the forthcoming thirty-fifth session of the Commission.

## (h)      Central African Empire

*Taken from document E/CN.4/1324/Add.1.*

The Government of the Central African Empire approves the draft convention on the rights of the child submitted by the secretariat, and wishes to point out that the provisions of this convention form part of the social legislation of the Central African Empire. Its adoption will thus simply have the effect of endorsing the existing regulations.

## (i)      Chad

The draft convention on the rights of the child annexed to resolution 20 (XXXIV) has received the careful consideration of the Ministry of Public Health, Labour and Social Affairs, which is of the view that "all aspects of the question have been taken into consideration and that the wording seems clear. It has no special observation to make".

## (j)      Colombia

*Taken from document E/CN.4/1324/Add.2*

[…]

In addition, we submit a few suggestions which might be taken into account in the convention:

1.        A permanent United Nations agency should be created to monitor implementation of the rights of the child by Member States.

2.        States Parties to the convention should undertake to ratify the Declaration of the Rights of the Child, adopted at the United Nations General Assembly held at Geneva in 1959, with any amendments or revisions which may result from its analysis and revision.

3.        Any plan or programme which a nation may adopt in relation to children should consider the child as an active and participating member of a society in general and of a family in particular, so that his actions are not dissociated from the social environment in which he lives, and so that he is not regarded as an abstract subject alien to any objective reality.

4.        The item concerning the convention should include as a topic of discussion the development of new scientific methods for the fertilization and preservation of human reproductive cells and experiments concerning their genetic structure.

5.        Steps should be taken in the States Members of the United Nations to promote solidarity with the children of developing countries.

## (k)      Cyprus

The Government of the Republic of Cyprus in general accepts the draft convention on the rights of the child. It has, however, the following suggestions to make:

1.        A provision could be included in the draft convention which would take into account the economic capabilities of the Contracting Parties as regards the implementation of the convention. Article 2, paragraph 1, of the International Covenant on Economic, Social and Cultural Rights could serve as a model for drafting this article;

2.        A provision as regards the right of the child to own property might also be considered.

## (l)      Denmark

1.        The Danish Government welcomes the initiative which the Commission on Human Rights took at its thirty-fourth session in March 1978 by adopting resolution 20 (XXXIV) recommending the conclusion of a convention on the rights of the child.

2        The objective of such a convention should be to provide a constructive contribution to strengthening the rights of the child throughout the world, and in drawing up its individual provisions the best interests of the child shall always be the paramount consideration.

3.        Such a convention must be thoroughly prepared and the areas in which there are the greatest needs to further strengthen the legal status of children through the drawing up of a convention must be carefully examined in the light of existing instruments such as the International Covenant on Civil and Political Rights, the Geneva Conventions of 12 August 1949 and the Protocols additional thereto, and relevant ILO Conventions.

4.        The 1959 Declaration on the Rights of the Child has thus already been followed up to some extent by the adoption of various treaty provisions on this subject. It would hardly be advisable, as done in the proposal contained in document E/CN.4/L.1366 of 7 February 1978, merely to elevate the Declaration into a convention. The Declaration is in the form of a manifesto, and it thus lacks the preciseness and clarity which is required in the formulation of legally binding texts.

## (m)     Dominican Republic

The Dominican Government has examined the draft convention on the rights of the child and in general supports the idea that all matters relating to the rights and the care which should be accorded to children throughout the world should be embodied in a binding legal instrument which should take the form of a convention for the signatory parties.

## (n)     Finland

The Government of Finland supports fully the objectives of the proposed convention on the rights of the child and is ready to collaborate in its further elaboration.

## (o)     France

*Taken from document E/CN.4/1324/Add.1.*

1.      The French Government has been in favour of preparing a convention on the rights of the child from the outset. It considers that the Declaration of the Rights of the Child, adopted by the United Nations in 1959, should be one of the main sources to be drawn upon in preparing the convention.

2.      However, my Government considers that the text of the Declaration cannot be reproduced as it stands in the draft convention, but needs to be re-examined carefully and amended in certain respects.

3.      This requires intensive work, which could be entrusted to a group of experts. If this is agreed upon, the French Government would like to participate in the work to be undertaken.

4.      At this juncture, the French Government wishes to make a number of comments on the draft that has been submitted:

> When drawing up the convention it would be preferable to separate the provisions that would be couched in the form of a recommendation from those that would constitute an actual commitment for States.
>
> (a) The provisions that would constitute a recommendation, such as article II, the first sentence of article VI and article X, might be included in a preliminary declaration or a recommendation annexed to the convention;
>
> (b) The commitments to be accepted by States would form part of the text of the convention itself.

## (p)     German Democratic Republic

1.      The German Democratic Republic welcomes the proposal submitted by the Polish People's Republic to make provision in international law for the legal status of the child. The German Democratic Republic views the draft convention, which was prepared on the basis of the Declaration of the Rights of the Child of 1959, as a major contribution to the International Year of the Child, 1979, as proclaimed by the United Nations. The draft meets with the German Democratic Republic's general approval.

2.      Drawing on its previous experience in this field, the German Democratic Republic should like to make the following suggestion to make the language more precise:

> "An explicit provision should be included in the convention to preclude discrimination against children of unmarried parents. On this subject, the German Democratic Republic earlier submitted to the Secretary-General of the United Nations detailed observations on the 'Draft general principles on equality and non-discrimination in respect of children born out of wedlock'."

3.      The German Democratic Republic believes that the principles set forth in the draft convention on the rights of the child, and in particular the provisions of article I on non-discrimination and the attendant right of all children to physical and spiritual development without distinction, are in accordance with one of the principal tasks facing the United Nations, i.e. to support the peoples in their struggle against colonialism, neocolonialism, racial discrimination and apartheid. It is the German Democratic Republic's understanding that in implementing the convention one should be aware of the inseparable unity of the striving for peace and détente, and the happiness, advancement and protection of children all over the world.

## (q)     Federal Republic of Germany

1.      The Federal Government is prepared to cooperate in the elaboration of a convention on the rights of the child, based on the draft submitted to the Commission on Human Rights. In order to achieve the goal of adopting a convention which takes full account of the needs of children, the existing draft, which should not be considered

as the only starting point for deliberations, should be subjected to a thorough, careful and unhurried review. In this connection, the Federal Government recommends that consideration should be given to the possibility of convening a group of experts to carry out a comprehensive and specialist review of all the questions which ought to be raised during the preparation of a convention, in particular, legal issues or questions relating to social policy. The fact that the Federal Government is proposing such a procedure demonstrates the importance it attaches to a carefully drafted convention which contains genuinely usable regulations relating to the protection of the child and which will therefore continue to prove effective after the International Year of the Child.

2.      Unlike the Declaration of the Rights of the Child (United Nations General Assembly resolution 1386 (XIV), dated 20 November 1959), on which the draft convention in question is largely based, a convention should be worded in such a way as to leave no possible doubt regarding the legal scope of each regulation. It must, in particular, draw a clear distinction between regulations representing rights of the individual and those which might simply be the subject of an undertaking on the part of States. Moreover, the provisions of the draft concerning objectives, content and methods of education should be considered separately.

3.      Without prejudice to a final assessment, we consider that articles I, III, IV (understood as the right of the child to have his needs provided for in the broadest sense), the first and second sentences of article VI, the first sentence of article VII, paragraph 1 (right to education), and the second part of article VII, paragraph 2 (primary right of parents), should be grouped together in a separate section as rights of the individual.

4.      However, this can apply only if all those provisions are retained as they stand.

5.      The Federal Government suggests that a thorough review should also be made of other provisions of the draft, in the same way as for article III, to ascertain whether it is desirable to adopt them as part of the convention on the rights of the child, in the light of the measures already taken or provided for in other international instruments.

6.      Unlike the series of measures on the rights of the individual, article II, article IV (first and second sentences), article V, article VI (fourth sentence), article VII, paragraph 1 (second sentence), article VII, paragraph 3, article IX and article X (first sentence) can be considered only as undertakings on the part of States.

7.      Conversely, the provisions of the draft relating to objectives, content and methods of education cannot be considered as either rights of the individual or undertakings on the part of States. The provisions in question are contained in the first sentence of article VI, the first part of article VII, paragraph 2, and the second sentence of article X of the draft. It is the responsibility and duty of the parents whose rights are also recognized in the draft to take binding decisions in this regard. The provisions referred to can more appropriately be made the subject of a recommendation to be incorporated in the preamble to the convention.

8.      The Federal Government also expresses reservations as to the comprehensiveness of the safeguards provided regarding efforts to ensure the protection of the child which have been undertaken elsewhere in the United Nations. This applies particularly to natural children whose status has long been the subject of consultations within the Sub-Commission on Prevention of Discrimination and Protection of Minorities of the United Nations Commission on Human Rights. This question should receive special attention. Another matter that should receive special attention in this context is whether the application of the convention to natural children is also provided for in the present draft. Admittedly, article I provides that every child shall be entitled to the rights set forth in the convention, without distinction or discrimination on account of birth or status, among other factors. Furthermore, the wording of principle 1 of the Declaration of the Rights of the Child of 20 November 1959, on which article 1 of the draft convention is based, seems to have been designed to assure natural children of the same rights as those enjoyed by legitimate children. However, the other provisions of the Declaration of 20 November 1959, and consequently of the draft convention based on it, do not take account of the situation of natural children. For instance, the second part of article VII, paragraph 2, provides that responsibility for the education and guidance of the child lies in the first place with "his parents". This provision needs to be modified to cover the situation of natural children, most of whom are brought up in the family of the mother.

9.      Reference should also be made to resolution 8 (XXVII) of the United Nations Commission on the Status of Women, dated 5 April 1978, which relates to measures for the protection of women and children against the division of families as a result of the policy of apartheid.

10.      In the view of the Federal Government, another question that should be considered is whether the draft convention should also make specific provision for the protection of adopted children and children who are brought up by foster-parents. Efforts have been in progress for a number of years within the United Nations to draft a convention or, at the very least, a declaration on adoption. In this connection, particular reference should be made to Economic and Social Council resolution 1925 (LVIII) of 6 May 1975. The present draft convention also deals with adopted children in so far as its article I prohibits any distinction in the treatment of children on account of their "status". However, as in the case of natural children, the draft contains no other provision relating specifically to adoption or to the situation of the foster-child. Consequently, it should also be made clear whether the protection of adopted children and foster-children should be dealt with separately, or whether it is preferable to treat these questions in greater detail on the basis and in the framework of the proposed convention, after they have been raised in article I of the draft. One reason why this is essential is to avoid any conflict between the different United Nations instruments on the protection of the child.

11.      The same problem arises in respect of the relationship between the proposed convention and the instruments for the protection of the child provided for under *international humanitarian law*. In this connection, reference should be made in the first instance to Economic and Social Council resolution 1687 (LII) of 2 June 1972, and to resolution 7 (XXVII) of the United Nations Commission on the Status of Women, dated 5 April 1978, concerning the "Protection of women and children in emergency and armed conflict in the struggle for peace, self-determination, national liberation and independence" and to the Protocols Additional to the Geneva Conventions of 12 August 1949, adopted in Geneva on 8 June 1977 by the Diplomatic Conference on Reaffirmation and Development of International Humanitarian Law Applicable in Armed Conflicts (cf. United Nations document A/32/144 of 15 August 1977). In this area, too, a study should be carried out and, in the light of its results, a provision drafted defining exactly the specific scope of the proposed convention.

12.      In view of the large number of questions left unresolved by the present draft convention, the Federal Republic of Germany would like to stress once again the need for a careful review of the draft. A convention can only be satisfactory over the long term if it is able to provide comprehensive protection for the rights of the child.

13.      The Federal Government considers that an essential contribution will have been made to the International Year of the Child if, in 1979, some progress can be made, along the lines set out above, towards the formulation of a convention for the protection of the child.

## (r)      Greece

The Greek Government strongly supports the resolution submitted by Poland for a convention on the rights of the child. It believes, though, that a declaration of intent is not sufficient and that Member States by signing this resolution must be ready to promote the necessary legislation and to allocate the necessary funds to translate this document into meaningful action.

## (s)      Hungary

1.      In 1959 the General Assembly of the United Nations adopted the Declaration of the Rights of the Child which was an important step in the field of ensuring and protecting the rights of the child. Nearly 20 years have passed since the adoption of the Declaration and the time has come to take further steps in this respect.

2.      The Hungarian Government welcomes and fully supports the initiative aimed at elaborating a convention on the rights of the child. It holds the view that the adoption of a convention with legally binding force under the auspices of the United Nations would be instrumental in the more effective protection and more consistent enforcement of the rights of the child.

3.      The draft convention transmitted to the Governments contains the most important rights of the child and expresses the most essential basic principles.

4.      The Hungarian Government is of the opinion that by the early adoption of a convention on the rights of the child Member States may concretely demonstrate their sincere endeavour for wide and universal guarantee of human rights.

**(t)    Madagascar**

1.    The draft convention on the rights of the child annexed to resolution 20 (XXXIV) adopted by the Commission on Human Rights on 8 March 1978 embodies, in the form of a convention, the principles contained in the Declaration of the Rights of the Child proclaimed by the United Nations General Assembly on 20 November 1959 (resolution 1386 (XIV)), which has the full and whole-hearted support of the Government of the Democratic Republic of Madagascar.

2.    In this regard, the adoption of a convention on the rights of the child during the International Year of the Child (General Assembly resolution 31/169) is a means of strengthening still further the general protection and well-being of the children of the world.

**(u)    Mauritius**

The Government of Mauritius is in total agreement with the contents of the draft convention on the rights of the child.

**(v)    Morocco**

*Taken from document E/CN.4/1324/Add.1.*

The Moroccan Government has no objections to make to the draft in question.

**(w)    Netherlands**

1.    The Netherlands Government can subscribe in principle to the idea of devoting a special convention to the rights of the child.

2.    In elaborating this idea, however, it is not considered sufficient to merely try and copy the Declaration of the Rights of the Child which dates back as early as 1959 and does not reflect the social, economic and cultural development and changes since then.

3.    Moreover, the formulation of the principles in the present draft convention is rather vague. A lot of them are already embodied in the mandates of agencies like the ILO, WHO and UNESCO, or in more appropriate juridical wordings, in instruments like the Covenants on Civil and Political and on Economic, Social and Cultural Rights. In these contexts the implementation and observance of the principles is taken care of in a far more extended and concrete manner.

4.    For these reasons the Netherlands Government seriously doubts the usefulness of a draft convention as annexed to resolution 20 (XXXIV) of the Commission on Human Rights. In its view a draft convention on the rights of the child must consist of timely, up-to-date and concrete principles, accompanied by practical guidelines for application, and supplementary to already existing instruments and activities, in order to avoid unnecessary duplication.

**(x)    Norway**

1.    Norway fully recognizes the need for greater international efforts for the protection and promotion of the rights of children, and therefore supports the main principles outlined in the draft convention. It would seem necessary, however, to complete the present draft and take account of developments and changes in social structures and States' family policies.

2.    In the opinion of Norwegian authorities, the interests of children would best be served if seen in conjunction with the interests of adults. Today the interests of children are very often overlooked in the decision-making process. Therefore, a convention on the subject of the rights of children should deal with children *as a group*. This aspect ought to be emphasized by using the noun "child" in its plural form throughout the convention. By the use of "children" and, consequently, "they", "them" and "their", the terms "he", "whom" and "his" could be avoided, and the equal status of the two sexes would appear more clearly.

3.    On this basis, the following amendments to the draft convention are suggested:

Throughout the draft convention, substitute "children" for "the child", "they" for "he", "them" for "him", and "their" for "his".

4.      It should also be considered to impose on the States Parties an obligation to establish or designate national administrative organs to be responsible for the protection and promotion of the rights of children.

## (y)     Pakistan

*Taken from document E/CN.4/1324/Add.3.*

The Government of Pakistan supports the draft convention on the rights of the child annexed to the Commission on Human Rights resolution 20 (XXXIV) entitled "Question of a convention on the rights of the child".

## (z)     Peru

The Peruvian National Institute for the Assistance and Promotion of Minors and the Family has indicated its approval of the draft convention on the rights of the child annexed to resolution 20 (XXXIV).

## (aa)    Poland

1.      As the original author of the draft convention on the rights of the child the Government of the Polish People's Republic has no additional suggestions or amendments to the text as presented by the Polish delegation during the thirty-fourth session of the Commission on Human Rights.

2.      It is the considered view of the Polish Government that no effort should be spared in order to bring about the adoption of the convention by the General Assembly at its thirty-fourth session in 1979. This would coincide with the International Year of the Child. Such a step would not only give an additional and significant stimulus and meaning to the International Year of the Child objectives but also would highlight the necessity and significance of measures envisaged by the convention itself for child's care all over the world.

3.      The adoption of the convention in 1979 can be achieved since, in particular, the principles of the United Nations Declaration of the Rights of the Child - constituting the basis for the draft convention - have been known to Governments and the world community for 20 years.

4.      The Government of the Polish People's Republic would like to suggest the need to create an open-ended working group and to entrust it with a task of drafting the convention during the thirty-fifth session of the Commission on Human Rights.

## (bb)    Portugal

1.      The draft convention on the rights of the child has the approval of the competent Portuguese authorities, which are aware of the importance of drawing up such a Convention.

2.      However, the competent Portuguese authorities are of the view that the wording of the draft could be improved. The rights of the child prior to birth could be more clearly defined.

3.      The competent Portuguese authorities consider that attention should be drawn to the fact that children must be the result of a choice freely exercised by their parents. The happiness and well-being of children should therefore be closely linked with family planning.

## (cc)    Suriname

*Taken from document E/CN.4/1324/Add.1.*

1.      The Government of the Republic of Suriname is in principle in agreement with the text of a draft convention on the rights of the child submitted by Poland on 7 February 1978, the text of which was attached to resolution 20 (XXXIV) adopted by the Commission on Human Rights at its 1472nd meeting in March 1978.

2.      In this connection the Government of the Republic of Suriname wishes to state that it attaches particular importance to the articles VI, VII sub[paragraph] 3 and IX sub[paragraphs] 1 and 2 of the above-mentioned draft convention.

## (dd)    Sweden

1.      The Swedish Government looks favourably at any international efforts aimed at strengthening the rights of the child. Since a convention dealing with this important subject could be a valuable new instrument, the Swedish Government is prepared to participate actively in its drafting.

2.      In this work it is natural to seek inspiration from the Declaration of the Rights of the Child which was adopted by the General Assembly in 1959. Consequently the provisions of that Declaration could be a starting point when drafting a new convention. It would not be desirable, however, simply to include the text of the Declaration in a convention, since the two instruments are of a different legal character and provisions which are appropriate in a declaration will not always be well suited to constitute legally binding rules. The 1959 Declaration contains certain general statements which do not have their proper place in the operative part of a convention which, being an agreement between States, should lay down concrete, mutual obligations.

3.      Another important difference between a declaration and a convention relates to the implementation aspect. While a declaration is merely a recommendation or a moral guideline, as the case may be, a convention has to be implemented if it is to become effective. In a convention on the rights of the child, special attention should therefore be given to the implementation machinery.

4.      Since the adoption of the Declaration, views on the situation of the child have developed in many parts of the world. It is clear, for instance, that in many countries, views on the family, on marriage, on the relations between children and parents and on the child as an individual having its own needs and rights have undergone important changes. Nor are the material conditions and the social structures in which children live always the same today as they were 20 years ago. This development should, in the view of the Swedish Government, affect the contents of the convention which is to be drafted at the present time.

5.      It may also be recalled that since 1959 a large number of States have been admitted as Members of the United Nations. These States - which did not participate in the drafting of the 1959 Declaration - ought to be given an opportunity to influence the drafting of the new convention.

6.      As regards the contents of the new convention, there are certain areas which, in the view of the Swedish Government, should be given particular attention. It is important, for instance, to emphasize the effects which economic and labour market conditions may have upon the situation of children. The responsibility of Governments as regards the day care of children of working parents ought to be mentioned.

7.      Finally, it is essential that a new convention on the rights of the child should be brought into line with other existing international agreements, in particular the two International Covenants on Human Rights, and with certain new instruments which are now being prepared, for instance the Convention on the Elimination of Discrimination against Women. It may prove useful also to record in the preamble to the convention or in a separate resolution certain new objectives or guidelines which are difficult to express as obligations in the operative part of the convention but which should be pursued by States in their long-term policies for the protection of children and the safeguarding of their rights.

## (ee)    Turkey

The draft convention on the rights of the child annexed to resolution 20 (XXXIV) has been studied by the competent Turkish authorities and has received a positive response. In fact, the contents of the draft convention are in conformity with the relevant Turkish legislation covering, namely, the protection, education, nutrition, accommodation of children, and in general the steps to be taken in order to enable them to become useful members of the society.

## (ff)    Ukrainian Soviet Socialist Republic

*Taken from document E/CN.4/1324/Add.1.*

1.      The Ukrainian SSR has no comments or suggestions to make on the draft convention on the rights of the child submitted by the Polish People's Republic to the Commission on Human Rights at its thirty-fourth session.

2.      The draft may serve as a basis for the preparation in the near future of a convention on this subject.

## (gg)    Union of Soviet Socialist Republics

*Taken from document E/CN.4/1324/Add.1.*

The draft convention on the rights of the child submitted to the United Nations Commission on Human Rights by the Polish People's Republic is a good basis for the elaboration of an international legal instrument on the rights of the child. It would seem that work on the draft could be completed already at the thirty-fifth session of the Commission on Human Rights.

## (hh)    United Arab Emirates

The provisions of the draft convention contradict neither the principles of Islamic law nor the provisions of the Provisional Constitution of the United Arab Emirates. The proposed draft entails the introduction of many guarantees to provide children with a better life by ensuring their physical and spiritual formation and development, the development of their abilities and judgement, their growing up in an atmosphere of love and friendship and their liberation from all forms of subjugation and exploitation, thus making them individuals fit to support the society in which they live. This affirms their psychological and social freedom, ensures their uprightness and prevents their deviation. ... We have no objection to the provisions of the aforementioned draft convention, provided that the above points are taken into consideration.

## (ii)    United Kingdom of Great Britain and Northern Ireland

The Government of the United Kingdom has the following observations to make:

1.      The Government of the United Kingdom will, in principle, support the concept of a convention on the rights of the child if it is the will of the majority of Member States that there should be one. So far as the United Kingdom is concerned, the rights of each child are well safeguarded in United Kingdom law. It will, nevertheless, be recalled that the United Kingdom reserved its position, in the Commission on Human Rights, on the need for such a convention and considered that the matter needed further study. So far, the proposal for a convention has not been adequately discussed.

2.      The present text of the draft convention, annexed to resolution 20/XXXIV of the Commission on Human Rights, is in many respects vague and open to widely differing interpretations. If there is to be a convention, there will be a need to elaborate a more precise text than the present one, which is based on the 1959 Declaration of the Rights of the Child.

3.      It would be appropriate for any decision on the need for a convention to await a full assessment of the results of activities and discussions which are to take place during 1979 in connection with the International Year of the Child. It would also be useful for non-governmental organizations to be consulted on this question and their views taken into account.

## (jj)    Zambia

1.      As a human person, the child has as much right as any other person to protection and enjoyment of the fundamental human rights proclaimed in the Universal Declaration of Human Rights and in the International Covenants on Human Rights.

2.      As a potential adult, the child is owed every right by his particular country as a future leader and potential contributor to that country's development. Indeed, in this respect, the child is a valuable investment for the future.

3.      As rightly stated in the draft convention, "the child, by reason of his physical and mental immaturity, needs special safeguards and care, including appropriate legal protection, before and after birth". Also, by virtue of his helplessness and total dependency on his parents (or other adult guardians), the child's interests and welfare are so tied up with those of his adult custodians that what happens, or does not happen, to the latter has a direct bearing on him. In practical terms this, for instance, means that as long as some parents continue to earn under-subsistence

wages and as long as such parents continue to live in substandard housing conditions, so long will the welfare of their children continue to suffer; as long as the institution of marriage is casually contracted and marriages continue to remain unstable, the interests of the children from such marriages will continue to suffer. Therefore, any measures for the safeguard and protection of the child must take into account certain factors pertaining to the interests and welfare of adults where these have a direct or indirect bearing on the interests and welfare of the child.

4.      Zambia should have no problem in endorsing and adopting the draft convention on the rights of the child since most of the provisions therein are in full accord with her own principles and philosophy on childcare.

## 3.    General comments by specialized agencies on the first Polish draft – annexed to Commission on Human Rights resolution 20 (XXXIV) of 8 March 1978

*Unless otherwise indicated, the following are all taken from document E/CN.4/1324 (27 December 1978).*

### (a)    International Labour Organization (ILO)

The provisions contained in the draft convention on the rights of the child annexed to resolution 20 (XXXIV) are in no way incompatible with those of the conventions and recommendations adopted by the International Labour Conference regarding the protection of the child.

### (b)    United Nations Educational, Scientific and Cultural Organization (UNESCO)

1.      The draft text as proposed by the United Nations does not appear to accord sufficient importance to the right of the child to cultural development by acknowledging, inter alia, broader rights to education and cultural identity. In our view, this draft should:

      (a)    Mention, in particular, the right to be different as defined in article 1, paragraph 2, of the draft declaration on race and racial prejudice to be submitted to the General Conference at its twentieth session;

      (b)    Be based more closely on the following three standard-setting instruments adopted under the auspices of UNESCO:

      The Convention against Discrimination in Education,

      The Recommendation concerning Education for International Understanding, Cooperation and Peace and Education relating to Human Rights and Fundamental Freedoms,

      The Recommendation on Participation by the People at Large in Cultural Life and Their Contribution to It;

      (c)    Mention, in this year of the thirtieth anniversary of the Universal Declaration of Human Rights, the right of the child to be educated in respect of human rights;

      (d)    Provide for the teaching of the rights of the child to adults (a similar idea has already been considered at the International Congress on the Teaching of Human Rights held in Vienna from 12 to 16 September 1978, since the recommendations made by the rapporteurs of the Congress contain a paragraph 11 which acknowledges the right of the child to receive an education in human rights and suggests the preparation of a specific programme of instruction on the rights of the child).

2.      On the basis of these various considerations, UNESCO suggests the insertion of supplementary provisions in both the preambular and operative parts of the draft convention.

### (c)    World Health Organization (WHO)

1.      A convention on the rights of the child should constitute a realistic contribution to the "comprehensive care and the well-being of children all over the world". In this respect the present draft still appears to be incomplete. Although we welcome the initiative of elaborating a legally binding instrument in addition to the Declaration of the Rights of the Child, we note that the proposed convention does not contain new ideas and concepts. It appears, on the contrary, to be weaker and less explicit than the Declaration.

2. In order to be comprehensive we would like such a convention to place the child in his various contexts, such as the family, the society, the legal context, the new international economic order. We would also welcome more detailed provisions on the obligations of parents, both as individuals and as couples, of the family and the society, particularly in relation to the promotion of child growth and development in its threefold dimensions: physical, mental and emotional. Furthermore, the role of health and social services should be clearly defined.

## 4. General comments by non-governmental organizations on the first Polish draft – annexed to Commission on Human Rights resolution 20 (XXXIV) of 8 March 1978

*Unless otherwise indicated, the following are all taken from document E/CN.4/1324 (27 December 1978).*

### (a) International Council of Women

1. The International Council of Women is a co-signatory of document E/CN.4/NGO/225. We believe that a convention, however well thought out, may be incomplete, fail to achieve its purpose and forfeit all chance of success if it is not based on studies made and experience acquired during the International Year of the Child.

2. Any other approach would overlook the important role which the Year is already playing, and will continue to play, in mobilizing world public opinion. Consequently, we maintain the position set out in document E/CN.4/NGO/225.

### (b) Women's International Democratic Federation

1. [...] WIDF strongly supports the draft convention submitted by a number of States at the thirty-fourth session of the Commission on Human Rights and expresses its satisfaction at the fact that the Commission on Human Rights, in its resolution 20 (XXXIV), recommends the conclusion of a convention on the rights of the child and its adoption by the General Assembly, if possible during the International Year of the Child (1979).

2. This convention, which, after ratification by States, will have the force of law, could make a significant contribution to the improvement of the condition (education, health, etc.) of children in many countries.

3. WIDF therefore expresses its agreement with all the articles of the draft convention on the rights of the child, which fully reflect the principles proclaimed in the Declaration of the Rights of the Child of 1959, and will make the convention an effective legal instrument for the realization of the rights of the child.

4. WIDF ventures to make one suggestion regarding this excellent text, namely to include in it an additional article whereby Governments would undertake to implement measures to ensure that their military budgets are smaller than the budgets for health, education and social infrastructure (day-care centres, kindergartens, schools, etc.) and would be requested to submit periodic reports on the progress achieved in that direction.

### (c) International Association of Youth Magistrates

1. The International Association of Youth and Family Magistrates fully endorses the draft convention. In its articles I to X the draft lays down a well-formulated catalogue of minimum conditions for the mental, physical and educational well-being of the child. By being aware of the fact that in many parts of the world, industrialized and non-industrialized, the actual situation still is far from corresponding to these conditions, they are considered most important to further, last but not least, harmony among peoples by paying due attention to the generations to come.

2. All in all, the International Association of Youth and Family Magistrates strongly advocates the United Nations efforts to arrive at a worldwide convention on the rights of the child.

### (d) International Catholic Child Bureau

*Taken from document E/CN.4/1324/Corr.1.*

[...] there is nothing which should make this convention undesirable. However, there is a danger linked with this procedure: a convention is a legal instrument which only binds those who have signed it and it is foreseeable that in the first years many countries will not immediately sign the convention and might thus consider themselves to be not at all bound by some principles concerning the rights of the child. Attention should be drawn to the fact that even if there is a convention, the Declaration of the Rights of the Child remains. The Declaration is a moral document appealing to the consciences of all individuals and of governments.

*The content of the draft convention*

Since the text of the draft convention takes up the text of the Declaration of the Rights of the Child and since this latter is a very good text which is generally appreciated, one cannot make objections to the content of the draft convention.

*Whether 1979 is the opportune time to discuss the draft convention*

Many studies and inquiries are being carried out within the framework of the IYC on the rights of the child and the Declaration and also several seminars and other working groups on the rights of the child have been organized on the occasion of the IYC. Some of the findings of these different activities might be interesting and worthy of being taken into account on the occasion of the final drafting of the convention. But these findings will only be known at the end of 1979.

Furthermore, some of the problems now under examination might be raised at the meeting of the Commission on Human Rights, or at the Economic and Social Council or at the General Assembly if the draft convention is under discussion in these different bodies during the IYC. Without the results of the IYC studies and inquiries to focus on as a basis, these debates could become very diffused and digress from the immediate concerns of IYC and the child. For these different reasons the International Catholic Child Bureau finds it extremely desirable not to have a debate on this draft convention before the end of the IYC:

1.     This will allow those who are now working on the rights of the child and the Declaration to develop and complete their activities as planned before the Year.

2.     It will further make it possible to take the findings of the ongoing activities into account when the draft of the final text of the convention is drawn up.

Only under these circumstances will it be possible to say that the draft convention is really the result of the IYC.

**(e)     International Commission of Jurists**

The International Commission of Jurists fully supports the proposal.

**(f)     International Federation of Women Lawyers**

1.     When 1979 was declared the International Year of the Child, we took it for granted that our celebration thereof required meetings and discussion during that year, the results of which would be communicated ... for use in the final drafting of such a convention. We therefore scheduled for our 20th biennial international congress to be held in October 1979 in Sante Fe, New Mexico, a broad and in-depth comparative study of laws for the protection of children. [...]. Other NGOS, we understand, will be holding similar meetings on other subjects pertaining to children.

2.     It seems to us that it would be a gross disservice to the cause of children to adopt a convention without considering the work of so many NGOs. After all, the very structure of the United Nations provides for consultative input by non-governmental organizations representing people at grass-roots levels.

3.     It is therefore respectfully requested that the adoption of a convention on the rights of the child be postponed until after the many current studies can be completed and utilized.

### (g)    International Union for Child Welfare

The IUCW has signed, together with a great number of other NGOs, the document E/CN.4/NGO/225 of 23 February 1978, asking that the convention should not enter into force until 1980. ... In particular, we should appreciate it being pointed out to all participants that the United Nations Declaration of the Rights of the Child remains an independent instrument in the same way as the Universal Declaration of Human Rights, and that it will retain all its moral force and obligation.

### (h)    World Jewish Congress

1.    My organization has already made known its views, together with several other organizations, in document E/CN.4/NGO/225 of 23 February 1978, in which support was expressed for the idea of the elaboration of a draft convention on the rights of the child in the framework of the International Year of the Child.

2.    We confirm that we favour such a development following from the principles contained in the Declaration of the Rights of the Child, and note that these principles will continue to hold validity in the form of this international instrument, establishing essential standards in the field of child protection.

### (i)    World Movement of Mothers

1.    The World Movement of Mothers, together with many other international non-governmental organizations, signed a communication which was submitted to the Commission on Human Rights at its thirty-fourth session.

2.    We considered it more urgent, during this International Year of the Child, to take stock of the progress made in each country in implementing the rights of the child as already defined.

3.    Our attitude has not changed and we suggest once again to the Commission on Human Rights that consideration of a draft convention on the rights of the child should not begin until the results of the studies now in progress are known, that is to say, at the thirty-sixth session of the Commission on Human Rights in 1980.

### (j)    World Union of Catholic Women's Organizations

1.    I wish to recall that, at the thirty-fourth session of the Commission on Human Rights, the World Union of Catholic Women's Organizations, together with 20 other non-governmental organizations, signed a communication in which it was suggested that any discussion of the subject should be postponed until the thirty-sixth session of the Commission, so as to enable the full benefit to be derived from the results of the various activities during the International Year of the Child.

2.    I wish to confirm that the position of the World Union of Catholic Women's Organizations on this question has not changed.

### (k)    World Union of Organizations for the Safeguard of Youth

With reference to the communication (E/CN.4/NGO/225) submitted to the Commission on Human Rights at its thirty-fourth session, a communication of which our organization was a signatory, WUOSY would like consideration of the draft convention to be postponed until the thirty-sixth session of the Commission on Human Rights in 1980, by which time the results of the different programmes undertaken within the framework of the International Year of the Child will be known.

### (l)    International Federation of Home Economics

This organization [...] is wholly in favour of the draft convention, but would like the actual provisions of the draft to be reviewed in the light of the work carried out during the International Year of the Child.

### (m)    International Humanist and Ethical Union

Though in general we agree with the text submitted, we would like to offer suggestions for amendment. ... Moreover, we also hope that it will be possible to include in one of the articles the phrase "every child has a right to be born a wanted child", for we feel that if the child does not get the love it needs to find its place in society among its fellow human beings, this constitute a mental or social handicap.

**(n)      International Union of Judges**

The International Union of Judges approves the draft as a whole.

# 5.    Report of the Working Group

*The following is taken from E/CN.4/L.1468 (12 March 1979).*

1.       The open-ended working group held meetings on 14, 20, 21, 22 and 26 February and 2 March 1979. At its first meeting, Mr. Adam Lopatka (Poland) was elected Chairman-Rapporteur by acclamation.

2.       The working group had before it the Secretary-General's report on the Question of a convention on the rights of the child (E/CN.4/1324 and Corr. 1 and Add. 1-4). It also had before it the report of the thirty-fourth session of the Commission on Human Rights (E/CN.4/1292), which contained the text of the draft convention on the rights of the child, as included in resolution 20 (XXXIV) of the Commission, and working papers containing amendments to the preamble and articles of the draft convention presented by Canada, France, Federal Republic of Germany, Norway, Poland, Sweden, the United Kingdom, and the United States of America.

3.       The representative of Sweden stressed that as the Swedish authorities had not prepared any specific drafting proposals before the current session, any comments or proposals put forward by Sweden in the working group must be regarded as preliminary as far as the exact wording was concerned.

4.       During the general discussion it was suggested by some representatives that consideration of the proposal to draft a convention on the rights of the child should take account of the results of the activities which were taking place during 1979 in connection with the International Year of the Child, and at that time people dealing with children's welfare and their rights and legal experts could apply their experience to make the draft convention more useful and up-to-date. However, other representatives expressed support for the idea of proceeding with the discussion and formulation of the convention immediately.

5.       A number of delegations emphasized that it could not be appropriate merely to incorporate the provisions of the Declaration of the Rights of the Child, which was drafted 20 years ago, in the convention, but that the convention must be drafted precisely and with due regard for the current problems confronting children. Those delegations emphasized that it was more important to prepare a comprehensive convention than to conclude a convention quietly. Some delegations expressed deep conviction that the draft presented by the delegation of Poland was a good and solid basis for elaboration of the convention at the current session of the Commission and appealed to all delegations to be constructive and cooperative.

6.       Several representatives stated that in the drafting of the convention, consideration should be given to such matters as the right to life of the unborn child; the question of abortion; the question of children born out of wedlock; the family and the child; the question of children in territories under foreign occupation and of children living under an apartheid regime; racial discrimination; ill-treatment of children; the age of criminal responsibility of children; child labour; the protection of foster-children; the right of the child to receive a religious education; family reunification; the rights of students to peaceful assembly, to travel and to access to information; the right of the child to be consulted in proceedings affecting his or her welfare. The convention should refer to the need to respect the rights of children of missing persons, refugees, hostages and migrant workers. Attention should also be given to the status of children in developing countries suffering from malnutrition, hunger or poverty.

7.       At the third meeting of the working group, a non-governmental organization brought to the attention of the group a document (E/CN.4/NGO/230) dealing with, inter alia, some recent developments in science and technology affecting the rights of the child.

8.      Some views were expressed as to the procedure to be followed when the text of the draft convention was discussed. It was felt that the comments submitted by Governments and international and other organizations were a most valuable contribution. The representative of the Federal Republic of Germany stated that a distinction should be drawn between the regulations on the rights of the individual and those which might be the subject of an undertaking on the part of States, as indicated in his Government's comments contained in the report of the Secretary-General. Other representatives pointed out that the Declaration of the Rights of the Child constituted a natural starting point in the working group's endeavours to draft a convention, and should be used as a guide for the group's discussions.

9.      A number of representatives expressed a preference for the title as contained in the draft convention while others felt that the convention should deal with children as a group and that this aspect ought to be emphasized by using the term "children" throughout the convention, so there would be no discrimination between sexes. The working group decided to adopt the present title of the draft convention on the understanding that it might later decide to change it.

[...]

21.      At the sixth meeting, the representatives of France and the Federal Republic of Germany reminded the working group of the recommendations of their Governments contained in the report of the Secretary-General concerning the desirability of convening a group of experts to draw up the convention.

## 6.    Articles adopted in 1979

*Preamble, first paragraph*

*Considering* that, in accordance with the principles proclaimed in the Charter of the United Nations, recognition of the inherent dignity and of the equal and inalienable right of all members of the human family is the foundation of freedom, justice and peace in the world.

*Preamble, second paragraph*

*Bearing in mind* that the people of the United Nations have, in the Charter, reaffirmed their faith in fundamental human rights and in the dignity and worth of the human person, and have determined to promote social progress and better standards of life in larger freedom.

*Preamble, third paragraph*

*Recognizing* that the United Nations have, in the Universal Declaration of Human Rights and in the International Covenants on Human Rights, proclaimed and agreed that everyone is entitled to all the rights and freedoms set forth therein, without distinction of any kind, such as race, colour, sex, language, religion, political or other opinion, national or social origin, property, birth or other status.

## 7.    Polish draft resolution on the "Question of a convention on the rights of the child"

*The following is taken from document E/CN.4/L.1465/Rev.1 (13 March 1979). Document E/CN.4/L.1465 (12 March 1979) contains only part A of the revised version below. Reference is made to documents E/CN.4/1324 and Corr. 1 and Add.1-4 in the second preambular paragraph.*

*Poland: draft resolution*

**A**

*The Commission on Human Rights,*

*Having in mind* the draft convention on the rights of the child submitted by Poland on 7 February 1978,

*Taking into account* the report of the Secretary-General on the views, observations and suggestions on the question of the convention on the rights of the child submitted by Member States, competent specialized agencies, regional intergovernmental organizations and non-governmental organizations (E/CN.4/1324 and Corr.1 and Add.1-4),

*Taking note* of the report of the working group set up at the thirty-fifth session of the Commission to draw up the convention on the rights of the child,

*Considering* that owing to lack of time it was not possible to complete work on the draft convention on the rights of the child,

*Recalling* Economic and Social Council resolution 1978/18 of 5 May 1978 and General Assembly resolution 33/166 of 20 December 1978 relating to the question of the convention on the rights of the child,

*Convinced* that it would be desirable to adopt an international convention on the rights of the child in connection with the International Year of the Child,

1.　　*Decides* to continue at its thirty-sixth session, as a matter of priority, its work on a draft convention on the rights of the child with a view to completing, if possible, the elaboration of the said convention at that session for transmission to the General Assembly through the Economic and Social Council;

2.　　*Requests* the Economic and Social Council to bring to the notice of the General Assembly at its thirty-fourth session the present resolution and the relevant chapter of the report of the Commission on Human Rights on its thirty-fifth session.

**B**

*The Commission on Human Rights,*

*Having in mind* the fact that the General Assembly in its resolution 31/169 of 21 December 1976 proclaimed 1979 as the International Year of the Child,

*Conscious* of the need further to strengthen the comprehensive care and well-being of children all over the world,

*Convinced* of the importance of international cooperation in this field,

*Desiring* to make its contribution to the observance of the International Year of the Child and to its follow-up activities,

*Invites the* Secretary-General to consider the possibility of organizing, within the framework of advisory services in the field of human rights, a two-week seminar on the rights of the child in the light of international instruments concerning human rights and questions of their implementation and progressive development.

## 8.　Discussion in the Commission on Human Rights on 14 March 1979

*No summary records were issued for the 1479th meeting of the Commission, at which the question of a convention on the rights of the child was also discussed. The following record of the 1521st meeting is taken from document E/CN.4/SR.1521 (19 March 1979).*

QUESTION OF A CONVENTION ON THE RIGHTS OF THE CHILD (agenda item 13) (E/CN.4/1324 and Corr.1 and Add.1-4; E/CN.4/L.1465/Rev.1)

61.　　Mr. LOPATKA (Poland), Chairman-Rapporteur of the Working Group set up at the Commission's thirty-fifth session to draw up the convention on the rights of the child, introduced draft resolution E/CN.4/L.1465/Rev.1 on that matter. First of all, he reminded the Commission that in 1979 the international community was observing the International Year of the Child, and that a programme of national and international measures had been adopted to improve the lot of children all over the world. That was why, at the preceding session, the Polish Government had proposed the consideration of a new item entitled "Question of a convention on the rights of the child". In its resolution 20 (XXXIV), of which he quoted operative paragraph 2, the Commission had planned to conclude the draft convention at its thirty-fifth session for transmission to the General Assembly through the Economic and Social Council; a certain degree of urgency had also been stressed by the Economic and Social Council and by the General Assembly itself in resolution 33/166. However, the preparation of a convention was a lengthy process: the timetable had had to be extended and in draft resolution E/CN.4/L.1465/Rev.1 it was proposed that the Commission should decide "to continue at its thirty-sixth session, as a matter of priority, its work on a draft convention on the rights of the child with a view to completing, if possible, the elaboration of the said convention at that session for transmission to the General Assembly through the Economic and Social Council". To that end, the Working Group established at the thirty-fifth session must be re-established at the thirty-sixth, and more time allotted to it. In the light of General Assembly resolution 33/166, the Economic and Social Council was requested, in paragraph 2 of draft resolution E/CN.4/L.1465/Rev.1, "to bring to the notice of the General Assembly at its thirty-fourth session the present resolution and the relevant chapter of the report of the Commission on Human Rights on its thirty-fifth session".

62.      With regard to the idea of organizing a seminar put forward in part B of that draft resolution, he considered that that would be an excellent contribution to the observance of the International Year of the Child and that the results of the work of the specialists from different countries who would participate in such a seminar would be of great value in the drafting of a convention. That idea had been put forward by the delegations of the Federal Republic of Germany and France, among others. He hoped that all Governments would be united in the desire to help the children of the world, especially those of developing countries, and that draft resolution E/CN.4/L.1465/Rev.1 would be adopted by consensus.

## 9.    Commission on Human Rights resolution 19 (XXXV) on the "Question of a convention on the rights of the child" adopted on 14 March 1979

### A

*The Commission on Human Rights,*

*Having in mind* the draft convention on the rights of the child submitted by Poland on 7 February 1978,

*Taking into account* the report of the Secretary-General on the views, observations and suggestions on the question of the convention on the rights of the child submitted by Member States, competent specialized agencies, regional intergovernmental organizations and non-governmental organizations,

*Taking note* of the report of the working group set up at the thirty-fifth session of the Commission to draw up the convention on the rights of the child,

*Considering* that owing to lack of time it was not possible to complete work on the draft convention on the rights of the child,

*Recalling* Economic and Social Council resolution 1978/18 of 5 May 1978 and General Assembly resolution 33/166 of 20 December 1978 relating to the question of the convention on the rights of the child,

*Convinced* that it would be desirable to adopt an international convention on the rights of the child in connection with the International Year of the Child,

1.      *Decides* to continue at its thirty-sixth session, as a matter of priority, its work on a draft convention on the rights of the child with a view to completing, if possible, the elaboration of the said convention at that session for transmission to the General Assembly through the Economic and Social Council;

2.      *Requests* the Economic and Social Council to bring to the notice of the General Assembly at its thirty-fourth session the present resolution and the relevant chapter of the report of the Commission on Human Rights on its thirty-fifth session.

**B**

*The Commission on Human Rights,*

*Having in mind* the fact that the General Assembly in its resolution 31/169 of 21 December 1976 proclaimed 1979 as the International Year of the Child,

*Conscious* of the need further to strengthen the comprehensive care and well-being of children all over the world,

*Convinced* of the importance of international cooperation in this field,

*Desiring* to make its contribution to the observance of the International Year of the Child and to its follow-up activities,

*Invites the* Secretary-General to consider the possibility of organizing, within the framework of advisory services in the field of human rights, a two-week seminar on the rights of the child in the light of international instruments concerning human rights and questions of their implementation and progressive development.

*No Economic and Social Council resolution concerning the convention on the rights of the child was adopted in 1979.*

## 10. General Assembly resolution 34/4 on the "International Year of the Child" adopted on 18 October 1979

*The General Assembly,*

*Recalling* its resolutions 2626 (XXV) of 24 October 1970, containing the International Development Strategy for the Second United Nations Development Decade, 3201 (S-VI) and 3202 (S-VI) of 1 May 1974, containing the Declaration and the Programme of Action on the Establishment of a New International Economic Order, 3281 (XXIX) of 12 December 1974, containing the Charter of Economic Rights and Duties of States, and 3362 (S-VII) of 16 September 1975 on development and international economic cooperation,

*Recalling also* its resolution 31/169 of 21 December 1976, in which it proclaimed the year 1979 International Year of the Child and laid down the general objectives of the Year,

*Recalling further* its resolution 33/83 of 15 December 1978 and the resolutions referred to therein, and also Economic and Social Council resolution 1979/57 of 3 August 1979,

*Mindful* of the fact that 1979 is also the twentieth anniversary of the adoption by the United Nations of the Declaration of the Rights of the Child, contained in General Assembly resolution 1386 (XIV) of 20 November 1959,

*Mindful also* of its resolution 33/166 of 20 December 1978 entitled "Question of a convention on the rights of the child",

*Aware* that adequate maternity care is an important contribution to the creation of a total environment which would ensure equal opportunity at birth to every child for its harmonious development and preparation for life,

*Mindful* of the vital link between programmes benefiting children and the observance of their rights, and the broader and more comprehensive framework of overall economic and social development in conditions of peace,

*Recognizing* in this regard that the observance of the Year has contributed towards the reaffirmation of the goals of a new international economic order,

*Recognizing also* that the situation of children in the developing countries depends on the economic and social development of those countries and consequently on the establishment of a new international economic order,

*Deeply gratified* by the worldwide response of the international community in observing the Year as a first essential step towards achieving the longer-range objectives of the Year, while also highlighting the international cooperative efforts towards the improvement of the well-being of children and the attainment of the harmonious development of their personalities,

*Bearing in mind* the conclusions and recommendations of the International Seminar on Children under Apartheid, held in Paris from 18 to 20 June 1979 at the headquarters of the United Nations Educational, Scientific and Cultural Organization, in observance of the Year,

*Noting* that the approach adopted by the United Nations in organizing the Year contributed to its success,

*Convinced* that the fresh and necessary impetus to activities, generated by the Year, should be maintained and that the new perspectives it has created should be followed by appropriate action in the years to come,

*Having considered* the report of the Executive Director of the United Nations Children's Fund on the International Year of the Child,

1.     *Expresses its deep satisfaction* to all Governments which elaborated national programmes for the implementation of the aims of the International Year of the Child and to those among them which became initiators of major regional and other international events;

2.     *Expresses also its deep appreciation* to the United Nations Children's Fund, the lead agency, and to the Executive Director of the Fund and his Special Representative for the International Year of the Child and her staff, and commends the efforts of other concerned organizations of the United Nations system and the contributions made by non-governmental organizations;

3.     *Urges* Governments to make every effort to consolidate and to build further on the results of the Year in order to achieve lastingly increased benefits for children by such measures, where appropriate, as:

     (a)     Planning for programmes and services benefiting children, including integrated mother and child health care, in their national planning for social and economic development;

     (b)     Further identifying, defining and documenting the situation of children;

     (c)     Setting specific national targets and goals for meeting the needs of children, inter alia, in the fields of health and education and for the development of their intellectual and cultural abilities;

     (d)     Increasing budgetary provision for programmes benefiting children by reviewing and/or revising present priorities;

4.     *Recognizes* the importance of assisting and protecting the family as a basic unit of society and the natural environment for the development and welfare of all its members, especially the children;

5.     *Requests* Governments and organizations to develop special programmes of assistance to the children oppressed by the inhuman policy of apartheid;

6.     *Urges* Governments and organizations providing assistance to developing countries through the United Nations Children's Fund and other channels to review their policies, in order to give more recognition to programmes benefiting children, and to increase the flow of such assistance;

7.     *Stresses* the importance of following up the experience and activities of the Year through long-term plans and action to improve the situation of children in the world, particularly in the developing countries;

8.     *Designates* the United Nations Children's Fund as the lead agency of the United Nations system responsible for coordinating the development aspects of the follow-up activities of the Year, in consultation with the Director-General for Development and International Economic Cooperation, within their respective spheres of competence;

9.     *Notes* that the Executive Board of the United Nations Children's Fund will consider the scope of the Fund's cooperation with countries as a follow-up to the Year;

10.     *Requests* Governments and organs and organizations of the United Nations system to evaluate and follow up the impact of the Year on their activities, and to inform the Secretary-General, who will report thereon to the General Assembly at its thirty-fifth session;

11.     *Invites* non-governmental organizations to continue and expand their programmes related to children in order to maintain the momentum generated by the Year;

12.      *Requests* the Preparatory Committee for the New International Development Strategy, in elaborating its goals and objectives, to take into account the importance of the interests of children and of meeting their needs.

*39th plenary meeting*
*18 October 1979*

## 11.   Revised Polish draft resolution on the "Question of a convention on the rights of the child"

*The following is taken from document E/CN.4/1349 (10 October 1979). However, this document had to be reissued for technical reasons. The version which appears here is the original.*

*Note verbale dated 5 October 1979 addressed to the Division of Human Rights by the Permanent Representation of the Polish People's Republic to the United Nations in Geneva*

The Permanent Representation of the Polish People's Republic to the Office of the Untied Nations in Geneva presents its compliments to the Human Rights Division of the Office of the United Nations in Geneva and has the honour to enclose herewith a new draft convention of the rights of the child for circulation among all the Governments of the countries represented in the Commission on Human Rights.

We hope that the enclosed draft will be helpful and will make it possible for the Commission to complete the work on the convention in time for its forthcoming session early next year.

Revised draft convention on the rights of the child

*The States Parties to the Convention*

*Considering* that in accordance with the principles proclaimed in the Charter of the United Nations, recognition of the inherent dignity and of the equal and inalienable rights of all members of the human family is the foundation of freedom, justice and peace in the world,

*Bearing in mind* that the peoples of the United Nations have, in the Charter, reaffirmed their faith in fundamental human rights and in the dignity and worth of the human person, and have determined to promote social progress and better standards of life in larger freedom,

*Recognizing* that the United Nations have, in the Universal Declaration of Human Rights and in the International Covenants on Human Rights, proclaimed and agreed that everyone is entitled to all the rights and freedoms set forth therein, without distinction of any kind, such as race, colour, sex, language, religion, political or other opinion, national or social origin, property, birth or other status,

*Convinced* that the family, as the basic unit of society and the natural environment for the growth and well-being of all its members and particularly children, should be afforded the necessary protection and assistance so that it can fully assume its responsibilities within the community,

*Recognizing* that the child due to the needs of his physical and mental development requires particular care and assistance with regard to health, physical, mental, moral and social development as well as legal protection in conditions of freedom, dignity and security,

*Recognizing* that the child, for the full and harmonious development of his personality, should grow up in family environment, in an atmosphere of love and understanding,

*Bearing in mind* that the need for extending particular care to the child has been stated in the Geneva Declaration on the Rights of the Child of 1924 and in the Declaration on the Rights of the Child adopted by the United Nations in 1959 and recognized in the Universal Declaration of Human Rights, in the International Covenant on Civil and Political Rights (in particular in the articles 2 and 24), in the International Covenant on Economic, Social and Cultural Rights (in particular in its article 10) and in the statutes of specialized agencies and international organizations concerned with the welfare of children,

*Considering* that the child should be fully prepared to live an individual life in society, and brought up in the spirit of the ideals proclaimed in the Charter of the United Nations, and in particular in the spirit of peace, dignity, tolerance, freedom and brotherhood, and guarantee working mothers a paid leave or a leave granting adequate social security benefits,

*Have agreed as follows:*

## Article 1

According to the present Convention a child is every human being from the moment of his birth to the age of 18 years unless, under the law of his State, he has attained his age of majority earlier.

## Article 2

1.      The child shall have the right from his birth to a name and a nationality.

2.      The States Parties to the present Convention undertake to introduce into their legislation the principle according to which a child shall acquire the nationality of the State in the territory of which he has been born if, at the time of the child's birth, the application of the proper national law would not grant him any nationality whatever.

## Article 3

1.      In all actions concerning children, whether undertaken by their parents, guardians, social or State institutions, and in particular by courts of law and administrative authorities, the best interest of the child shall be the paramount consideration.

2.      The States Parties to the present Convention undertake to ensure the child such protection and care as his status requires, taking due account of the various stages of his development in family environment and in social relations, and, to this end, shall take necessary legislative measures.

3.      The States Parties to the present Convention shall create special organs called upon to supervise persons and institutions directly responsible for the care of children.

## Article 4

1.      The States Parties to the present Convention shall respect and extend all the rights set forth in this Convention to all children in their territories, irrespective of these children's race, colour, sex, religion, political and other opinion, social origin, property, birth in lawful wedlock or out of wedlock or any other distinction whatever.

2.      The States Parties to the present Convention shall undertake appropriate measures individually and within the framework of international cooperation, particularly in the areas of economy, health and education for the implementation of the rights recognized in this Convention.

## Article 5

The States Parties to the present Convention recognize the right of alien children staying in their territories to enjoy the rights provided for in this Convention.

## Article 6

The parents shall have the right to specify the place of the child's residence unless, guided by his best interests, a competent State organ is authorized, in accordance with national law, to decide in this matter.

## Article 7

The States Parties to the present Convention shall enable the child who is capable of forming his own views the right to express his opinion in matters concerning his own person, and in particular, marriage, choice of occupation, medical treatment, education and recreation.

## Article 8

1.    The duty of bringing up the child shall lie equally with both the parents, who, in any case, should be guided by his best interests and, in keeping with their own beliefs and in compliance with the stipulations of article 7, shall prepare him for an individual life.

2.    The States Parties to the present Convention shall render all necessary assistance to parents and guardians in the performance of their educational function, and shall undertake measures to organize and ensure the development of institutions of children's care.

3.    Children of working mothers shall have the right to frequent the institutions of day care of children until they have completed school age.

## Article 9

Parents, guardians, State organs and social organizations shall protect the child against any harmful influence that mass media, and in particular the radio, film, television, printed materials and exhibitions, on account of their contents, may exert on his mental and moral development.

## Article 10

A child of preschool age shall not be separated from his parents, with the exception for cases when such separation is necessary for the child's benefit.

## Article 11

1.    A child deprived of parental care shall be entitled to the protection and assistance provided by the State.

2.    The States Parties to the present Convention shall be obliged to provide appropriate educational environment to a child who is deprived of his natural family environment or, on account of his well-being, cannot be brought up in such environment.

3.    The States Parties to the present Convention shall undertake measures so as to facilitate adoption of children and create favourable conditions for establishing foster-families.

## Article 12

1.    The States Parties to the present Convention recognize the right of a mentally or physically disabled child to special protection and care, appropriate to his condition and the circumstances of his parents or guardians, and undertake to extend adequate assistance to any such child.

2.    A disabled child shall grow up and receive education in conditions possibly most similar to those provided to all other children, aiming at social integration of such a child.

## Article 13

1.    It is recognized that the child shall be entitled to benefit from the highest attainable standard of health care for his physical, mental and moral development, and also, in the case of need, from medical and rehabilitation facilities.

2.    The States Parties to the present Convention shall pursue full implementation of this right, and, in particular, shall:

    (a)    take measures to lower the mortality index of babies,

    (b)    provide a generally accessible system of health protection,

    (c)    develop the system of health protection so that medical assistance and care shall be open to all children,

    (d)    extend particular care to expectant mothers for a reasonable period of time before and after confinement.

*Article 14*

The States Parties to the present Convention recognize that every child shall have the right to social security benefits, and undertake to introduce appropriate legal and organizational measures for the implementation of this right.

*Article 15*

1.      The States Parties to the present Convention recognize the right of every child to a standard of living adequate for his healthy and normal physical, mental and moral development in every phase of the child's development.

2.      The parents shall, within their financial possibilities and powers, secure conditions of living necessary for a normal growth of the child.

3.      The States Parties to the present Convention shall take appropriate measures to implement this right, particularly with regard to nutrition, clothing and housing, and shall extend the necessary material assistance to parents and other persons bringing up children, with special attention paid to incomplete families and children lacking parental care.

*Article 16*

1.      The child shall have the right to education which shall be free and compulsory, at least at elementary school level. The parents and the State shall guarantee the child ample conditions for the realization of this right.

2.      The States Parties to the present Convention shall develop various forms of secondary general and vocational education systems, and shall pursue gradual introduction of free education at this level, so as to enable all children to develop their talents and interests on a basis of equal opportunity.

*Article 17*

1.      The States Parties to the present Convention recognize that the bringing up and education of the child should promote the full development of his personality, his respect for human rights and fundamental freedoms.

2.      The child shall be prepared for an individual life in a free society, in the spirit of understanding, tolerance and friendship among all peoples, ethnic and religious groups and educated in harmony with the principles of peace proclaimed by the United Nations.

*Article 18*

The child shall have full opportunity for recreation and amusement appropriate to his age. The parents and other persons responsible for the care of the child, educational institutions and State organs shall be obliged to implement this right.

*Article 19*

1.      The child shall be protected against all forms of discrimination, social exploitation and degradation of his dignity. He shall not be the subject of traffic and exploitation in any form.

2.      The States Parties to the present Convention recognize that the child shall not be employed in any form of work harmful to his health or his moral development, or in work dangerous to his life or which would interfere with his normal growth, and undertake to subject to legal punishment persons violating this law.

3.      The States Parties to the present Convention shall comply with the law prohibiting the employment of children before the age of fifteen years.

*Article 20*

1.      The child undergoing penal procedure shall have the right to special treatment and privileges.

2.      The child shall not be liable to capital punishment. Any other punishment shall be adequate to the particular phase of his development.

3. The penitentiary system shall be aimed at re-education and re-socialization of the sentenced child. It should enable the child to serve the sentence of deprivation or limitation of freedom in a special manner, and in particular, in separation from adult offenders.

### Article 21

The States Parties to the present Convention shall submit periodical reports on the implementation of this Convention to the Economic and Social Council through the Secretary-General of the United Nations. The first such report shall be submitted three years after its entry into force, and thereafter every five years.

### Article 22

The reports submitted by the States Parties to the present Convention under article 21 shall be considered by the Economic and Social Council, which may bring its observations and suggestions to the attention of the General Assembly of the United Nations.

### Article 23

The present Convention is open for signature by all States until...

### Article 24

The present Convention is subject to ratification. Instruments of ratification shall be deposited with the Secretary-General of the United Nations.

### Article 25

The present Convention shall remain open for accession by any State. Instruments of accession shall be deposited with the Secretary-General of the United Nations.

### Article 26

1. The present Convention shall enter into force six months after the date of deposit of the fifteenth instrument of ratification or accession.

2. For each State ratifying or acceding to the present Convention after the deposit of the fifteenth instrument of ratification or accession, the Convention shall enter into force on the.................. day after the deposit by such State of its instrument of ratification or accession.

### Article 27

As depository of the present Convention the Secretary-General of the United Nations shall inform all States:

(a) of signatures, ratifications and accessions under articles 23, 24 and 25,

(b) of the date of the entry into force of the present Convention under the article 26.

### Article 28

1. The original of the present Convention, of which the Chinese, English, French, Russian and Spanish texts are equally authentic, shall be deposited with the Secretary-General of the United Nations, who shall send certified copies thereof to all States.

# D. 1980

## 1.   Report of the Working Group

*The following is taken from document E/CN.4/L.1542 (10 March 1980).*

1.      The open-ended Working Group held meetings on 22, 25, 26, 27, 28 and 29 February and 7 March 1980. At its first meeting, Mr. Adam Lopatka (Poland) was elected Chairman-Rapporteur by acclamation. The Working Group adopted this report at its last meeting, held on 7 March 1980. By consensus decision of the Working Group, that meeting was chaired by Mr. Andrzej Olszowka (Poland).

2.      The Working Group had before it the text of a draft convention on the rights of the child annexed to Commission resolution 20 (XXXIV) of 8 March 1978 and the report of the Secretary-General on the views, observations and suggestions on the question submitted by Member States, competent specialized agencies, regional intergovernmental organizations and non-governmental organizations (E/CN.4/1324 and Corr.1 and Add.1-5). In addition, the Working Group had before it the text of a revised draft convention submitted by Poland on 5 October 1979 (E/CN.4/1349). The Working Group also had before it a number of Sub-Commission documents relating to the exploitation of child labour which the Sub-Commission, by operative paragraph 4 of resolution 7 B (XXXII), had recommended be taken into account in drafting the appropriate articles of the convention (E/CN.4/Sub.2/433; E/CN.4/Sub.2/434; E/CN.4/Sub.2/SR.853 and 836). Two non-governmental organizations in consultative status also submitted written statements for consideration by the Commission (E/CN.4/NGO/265 and 276).

3.      At its first meeting, following the proposal of the Chairman, the Working Group took up the revised draft convention contained in document E/CN.4/1349, which incorporated the four preambular paragraphs adopted by the Working Group the previous year, as its basic working document.

4.      In the course of the general discussion at that meeting, some representatives suggested that the term "child" should be clearly defined, and perhaps replaced by a more precise term with greater juridical significance, such as "minor", before proceeding with the adoption of further paragraphs. It was also pointed out that, at the previous session, the Working Group had adopted the title of the convention on the understanding that it might later decide to change it. However, other representatives expressed support for the idea of proceeding with the discussion and formulation of the rest of the preamble immediately. It was therefore decided to postpone the discussion of the definition until the Working Group considered article 1 of the draft convention.

[...]

45.      Several delegations expressed the view that the Working Group should ask the Commission to request the Economic and Social Council to authorize the Working Group to meet for one week prior to the next session of the Commission in order to facilitate completion of the work on the draft convention. Several other delegations, however, opposed this view.

## 2.   Articles adopted in 1980

*Preambular paragraphs 4-9*

*Recalling* that in the Universal Declaration of Human Rights, the United Nations had proclaimed that childhood is entitled to special care and assistance,

*Convinced* that the family, as the basic unit of society and the natural environment for the growth and well-being of all its members and particularly children, should be afforded the necessary protection and assistance so that it can fully assume its responsibilities within the community,

*Recognizing* that, as indicated in the Declaration on the Rights of the Child adopted in 1959, the child due to the needs of his physical and mental development requires particular care and assistance with regard to health, physical, mental, moral and social development, and requires legal protection in conditions of freedom, dignity and security,

*Recognizing* that the child, for the full and harmonious development of his personality, should grow up in family environment, in an atmosphere of happiness, love and understanding,

*Bearing in mind* that the need for extending particular care to the child has been stated in the Geneva Declaration on the Rights of the Child of 1924 and in the Declaration on the Rights of the Child adopted by the United Nations in 1959 and recognized in the Universal Declaration of Human Rights, in the International Covenant on Civil and Political Rights (in particular in the articles 23 and 24), in the International Covenant on Economic, Social and Cultural Rights (in particular in its article 10) and in the statutes of specialized agencies and international organizations concerned with the welfare of children,

*Considering* that the child should be fully prepared to live an individual life in society, and brought up in the spirit of the ideals proclaimed in the Charter of the United Nations, and in particular in the spirit of peace, dignity, tolerance, freedom and brotherhood,

*Have agreed as follows:*

*Article I*

According to the present Convention a child is every human being to the age of 18 years unless, under the law of his State, he has attained his age of majority earlier.

*Article II*

1.          The child shall have the right from his birth to a name and to acquire a nationality.

## 3.    Discussion in the Commission on Human Rights

*The Commission discussed the "Question of a convention on the rights of the child" at its 1526th meeting, the summary records of which have not been distributed.*

## 4.    Commission on Human Rights resolution 36 (XXXVI) on the "Question of a convention on the rights of the child" adopted on 12 March 1980

*The Commission on Human Rights,*

*Having in mind* the draft convention on the rights of the child submitted by Poland on 7 February 1978 and the new amended version of the draft submitted on 5 October 1979,

*Taking into account* the report of the Secretary-General on the views, observations and suggestions on the question of the convention on the rights of the child submitted by Member States, competent specialized agencies, regional intergovernmental organizations and non-governmental organizations, which served as a basis for the amended draft convention,

*Noting* the progress in the further elaboration of the final draft of the convention on the rights of the child made by the Working Group set up at the thirty-sixth session of the Commission on Human Rights,

*Recalling* Economic and Social Council resolution 1978/18 of 5 May 1978 and General Assembly resolution 33/166 of 20 December 1978, as well as General Assembly resolution 34/4 of 18 October 1979 by which the Assembly had borne in mind the question of a convention on the rights of the child,

*Convinced* that, in connection with the International Year of the Child which was celebrated during the year 1979, it would be desirable to adopt an international convention on the rights of the child,

1.          *Decides* to continue at its thirty-seventh session, as a matter of priority, its work on a draft convention on the rights of the child with a view to completing the elaboration of the convention at that session for transmission to the General Assembly through the Economic and Social Council;

2.      *Requests* the Economic and Social Council to authorize a one-week session of an open-ended working group prior to the thirty-seventh session of the Commission on Human Rights to facilitate completion of the work on a draft convention on the rights of the child.

## 5.    Economic and Social Council decision 1980/138 of 2 May 1980

At its 22nd plenary meeting, on 2 May 1980, the Council, noting Commission on Human Rights resolution 36 (XXXVI) of 12 March 1980, decided to authorize a one-week session of an open-ended working group prior to the thirty-seventh session of the Commission to facilitate the completion of the work on a draft convention on the rights of the child.

## 6.    General Assembly resolution 35/131 on the "Question of a convention on the rights of the child" adopted on 11 December 1980 without a vote

*The General Assembly,*

*Recalling* its resolutions 33/166 of 20 December 1978, entitled "Question of a convention on the rights of the child", and 34/4 of 18 October 1979, entitled "International Year of the Child",

*Bearing in mind* Commission on Human Rights resolutions 20 (XXXIV) of 8 March 1978, 19 (XXXV) of 14 March 1979 and 36 (XXXVI) of 12 March 1980, as well as Economic and Social Council resolutions 1978/18 of 5 May 1978 and 1978/40 of 1 August 1978 and Council decision 1980/138 of 2 May 1980,

*Aware* of the widespread interest during the International Year of the Child in working out an international convention on the rights of the child and of the important role the United Nations Educational, Scientific and Cultural Organization and the United Nations Children's Fund have to play in the subject matter concerned,

*Noting* further progress in discussions on and in the elaboration of such a draft convention by the Commission on Human Rights,

1.      *Takes note with satisfaction of* the work so far accomplished and the spirit of cooperation in elaborating a convention on the rights of the child,

2.      *Welcomes* Economic and Social Council decision 1980/138 by which the Council authorized an open-ended working group of the Commission on Human Rights to meet for a period of one week prior to the thirty-seventh session of the Commission to complete the work on the draft convention;

3.      *Requests* the Commission on Human Rights, at its thirty-seventh session, to continue to give high priority to the question of completing the draft convention on the rights of the child;

4.      *Decides* to include in the provisional agenda of its thirty-sixth session the item entitled "Question of a convention on the rights of the child".

*92nd plenary meeting*
*11 December 1980*

# E. 1981

## 1. Report of the Working Group

*The following is taken from document E/CN.4/L.1575 (17 February 1981).*

INTRODUCTION

1.　　In resolution 36 (XXXVI) of 12 March 1980, the Commission on Human Rights resolved to continue its work on the draft convention on the rights of the child as a matter of priority. By decision 1980/138 of 2 May 1960, the Economic and Social Council authorized an open-ended Working Group to meet for one week prior to the Commission's thirty-seventh session to facilitate the completion of the work on the draft convention. At its thirty-fifth session, the General Assembly, by resolution 35/131 of 11 December 1980, welcomed Council decision 1980/138 and requested the Commission, at its thirty-seventh session, to continue to give high priority to the question of completing the draft convention.

2.　　At its 1583rd meeting on 3 February 1981, the Commission on Human Rights by decision 1 (XXXVII) decided that a sessional open-ended Working Group should be established for the consideration of item 14 on its agenda concerning the drafting of a convention on the rights of the child.

3.　　The 1981 pre-sessional Working Group held 10 meetings from 26 January 1981 to 30 January 1981, at which it discussed paragraph 2 of article 2 and articles 3, 4, 5, 6, 7 and 8 of the revised draft convention (E/CN.4/1349). The sessional Working Group had discussions on articles 6, 8 and 9 during meetings held on 2 and 3 February 1981. At its meetings on 25, 26 and 27 February 1981, the Working Group adopted its report as contained in the present document.

ELECTIONS

4.　　At the first meeting of the pre-sessional Working Group, on 26 January 1981, Mr. Adam Lopatka (Poland) was elected by acclamation Chairman-Rapporteur. Mr. Lopatka continued as Chairman-Rapporteur of the Working Group established by the Commission on Human Rights at its thirty-seventh session to continue the work of the pre-sessional Working Group.

PARTICIPATION

5.　　The meetings of the pre-sessional and the sessional Working Groups, which were open to all members of the Commission on Human Rights, were attended by representatives of the following States: Argentina, Australia, Brazil, Bulgaria, Byelorussian Soviet Socialist Republic, Canada, Cuba, Denmark, France, the Federal Republic of Germany, India, the Netherlands, Pakistan, the Philippines, Poland, Portugal, the Union of Soviet Socialist Republics, the United Kingdom of Great Britain and Northern Ireland, the United States of America, Yugoslavia and Zaire.

6.　　The following States, non-members of the Commission on Human Rights, were represented at the Working Group by observers: Egypt, Holy See, Ireland, Italy, Norway and Turkey.

7.　　The International Labour Organization was represented at the Working Group by an observer.

8.　　The International Catholic Child Bureau, the International Association of Penal Law, the International Union for Child Welfare and the World Association for the School as an Instrument of Peace sent observers to the Working Group.

DOCUMENTS

9.　　The Working Group had before it a number of relevant documents including the Revised draft convention on the rights of the child (E/CN.4/1349), the report of the Secretary-General on the views, observations and suggestions on the question submitted by Member States, competent specialized agencies, regional intergovernmental organizations and non-governmental organizations (E/CN.4/1324 and Corr.1 and

Add.1-5), the reports of the 1979 and 1980 Working Groups (E/CN.4/L.1468 and E/CN.4/L.1542) and a written statement by the International Labour Office concerning the employment of children (E/CN.4/WG.1/WP.1). Non-governmental organizations in consultative status also submitted written statements for consideration by the Commission (E/CN.4/NGO/230, 234, 244, 265, 276, 291 and 295).

10.      As in 1980, the basic working document for the discussions in the Working Group was the revised draft convention submitted by Poland (E/CN.4/1349), which incorporated the four preambular paragraphs adopted by the Working Group in 1979. It will be recalled that the five further preambular paragraphs as well as article 1 and paragraph 1 of article 2 of this draft were adopted and annexed to the report of the Working Group of 1980 (E/CN.4/L.1542).

[...]

PROCEDURAL QUESTIONS

126.      The view was expressed by several delegations that the Working Group should ask the Commission on Human Rights to request the Economic and Social Council to authorize the Working Group to meet for one week prior to the next session of the Commission in order to facilitate completion of the work on the draft convention. Several other delegations did not fully share this view in that the matter had financial implications which must be considered by Governments and that the question was entirely for the plenary of the Commission to resolve in dealing with the forthcoming draft resolution on the convention.

## 2.   Articles adopted in 1981

*Article 2, paragraph 2*

2.      The States Parties to the present Convention shall ensure that their legislation recognizes the principle according to which a child shall acquire the nationality of the State in the territory of which he has been born if, at the time of the child's birth, he is not granted nationality by any other State in accordance with its laws.

*Article 3*

1.      In all actions concerning children, whether undertaken by public or private social welfare institutions, courts of law, or administrative authorities, the best interests of the child shall be a primary consideration.

2.      In all judicial or administrative proceedings affecting a child that is capable of forming his own views, an opportunity shall be provided for the views of the child to be heard, either directly or indirectly through a representative, as a party to the proceedings, and those views shall be taken into consideration by the competent authorities, in a manner consistent with the procedures followed in the State Party for the application of its legislation.

3.      The States Parties to the present Convention undertake to ensure the child such protection and care as is necessary for his well-being, taking into account the rights and duties of his parents, legal guardians, or other individuals legally responsible for him, and, to this end, shall take appropriate legislative and administrative measures.

4.      The States Parties to the present Convention shall ensure competent supervision of officials and personnel of institutions directly responsible for the care of children.

*Article 4*

1.      The States Parties to the present Convention shall respect and extend all the rights set forth in this Convention to each child in their territories without distinction of any kind, irrespective of the child's or his parents' or legal guardians' race, colour, sex, language, religion, political or other opinion, national or social origin, family status, ethnic origin, cultural beliefs or practices, property, educational attainment, birth, or any other basis whatever.

2.      States Parties to the present Convention shall take all appropriate measures to ensure that the child is protected against all forms of discrimination or punishment on the basis of the status, activities, expressed opinions, or beliefs of the child's parents, legal guardians, or other family members.

*Article 5*

The States Parties to the present Convention shall undertake all appropriate administrative and legislative measures, in accordance with their available resources, and, where needed, within the framework of international cooperation, for the implementation of the rights recognized in this Convention.

*Article 7*

The States Parties to the present Convention shall assure to the child who is capable of forming his own views the right to express his opinion freely in all matters, the wishes of the child being given due weight in accordance with his age and maturity.

*Article 8*

1. Parents or, as the case may be, guardians, have the primary responsibility for the upbringing and development of the child. The best interests of the child will be their basic concern. States Parties shall use their best efforts to ensure recognition of the principle that both parents have common and similar responsibilities for the upbringing and development of the child.

2. For the purpose of guaranteeing and promoting the rights set forth in this Convention, the States Parties to the present Convention shall render appropriate assistance to parents and guardians in the performance of the child rearing responsibilities and shall ensure the development of institutions for the care of children.

3. States Parties shall take all appropriate measures to ensure that children of working parents have the right to benefit from childcare services and facilities for which they are eligible.

4. The institutions, services and facilities referred to in paragraphs 2 and 3 of this article shall conform with the standards established by competent authorities, particularly in the areas of safety, health, and in the number and suitability of their staff.

# 3. Polish draft resolution

*The following is taken from document E/CN.4/L.1573 (2 March 1981). The original document is in English, but the United Nations issued only the French version.*

Pologne: projet de résolution

*La Commission des droits de l'homme,*

*Ayant présents à l'esprit* le projet de convention sur les droits de l'enfant que la Pologne a présenté le 7 février 1978 et la version modifiée du projet présentée le 5 octobre 1979,

*Rappelant* les résolutions de l'Assemblée générale 33/166 du 20 décembre 1978 et 34/4 du 18 octobre 1979, ainsi que la résolution 35/151, en date du 11 décembre 1980, par laquelle l'Assemblée a prié la Commission des droits de l'homme de continuer d'accorder une haute priorité à la question de l'achèvement d'un projet de convention relative aux droits de l'enfant,

*Rappelant* aussi ses résolutions 20 (XXXIV) du 8 mars 1978, 19 (XXXV) du 14 mars 1979 et 36 (XXXVI) du 12 mars 1980, ainsi que les résolutions du Conseil économique et social 1978/18 du 5 mai 1978 et 1978/40 du 1er août 1978 et la décision 1980/138 du Conseil en date du 2 mai 1980,

*Notant avec satisfaction* les progrès considérables accomplis par le Groupe de travail, de composition non limitée, au cours de la semaine de négociation qu'il a tenue avant la trente-septième session de la Commission,

*Notant également* l'existence d'un intérêt général pour l'élaboration d'une convention internationale complète et détaillée sur les droits de l'enfant, manifesté jusqu'à présent par les représentants de nombreux pays et organisations internationales,

1.		*Décide* de poursuivre à sa trente-huitième session, à titre prioritaire, ses travaux sur un projet de convention relative aux droits de l'enfant en vue d'achever l'élaboration de la convention à ladite session, pour transmission à l'Assemblée générale, par l'intermédiaire du Conseil économique et social;

2.		*Prie* le Conseil économique et social d'autoriser un groupe de travail de composition non limité à tenir une session d'une semaine avant la trente-huitième session de la Commission des droits de l'homme, pour faciliter l'achèvement des travaux sur un projet de convention relative aux droits de l'enfant.

## 4.	Administrative and financial implications

*The following is taken from document E/CN.4/L.1580 (5 March 1981).*

*Administrative and financial implications of the draft resolution contained in document E/CN.4/L.1573: Statement submitted by the Secretary-General in accordance with rule 28 of the rules of procedure of the functional commissions of the Economic and Social Council*

1.		In paragraph 2 of draft resolution E/CN.4/L.1573, the Commission would request the Economic and Social Council to authorize a one-week session of an open-ended working group prior to the thirty-eighth session of the Commission on Human Rights to facilitate completion of the work on a draft convention on the rights of the child.

2.		The relating conference servicing costs which would be incurred in 1982 are calculated on a full-cost basis at $35,408 under Section 29 B, Conference Services, Geneva.

## 5.	Discussion in the Commission on Human Rights on 10 March 1981

*The following is taken from document E/CN.4/SR.1635 (13 March 1981).*

QUESTION OF A CONVENTION ON THE RIGHTS OF THE CHILD (agenda item 14) (E/CN.4/L.1573; E/CN.4/L.1575; E/CN.4/L.1580)

50.		Mr. LOPATKA (Chairman-Rapporteur, Working Group on a draft convention on the rights of the child) said that the report of the Working Group (E/CN.4/L.1575) reflected the results of negotiations held in the course of one week prior to the thirty-seventh session of the Commission and at the Group's meetings on 2 and 3 February 1981. The Working Group had reached agreement on articles 3, 4, 5, 7 and 8 and on paragraph 2 of article 2 of the draft convention on the rights of the child. Owing to lack of time, it had not been possible to examine the proposals and amendments submitted in connection with the other articles. The provisions of the draft convention as agreed by the Working Group were set forth in the annex to the report. Lastly, he expressed appreciation for the atmosphere of compromise which had prevailed throughout the negotiations.

51.		Mr. KALINOWSKI (Poland), introducing draft resolution E/CN.4/L.1573, said that in the course of the preparations for the International Year of the Child, his country had taken the initiative of submitting a draft convention on the rights of the child. It was essential to improve the lot of children throughout the world, for 600 million lived in or on the verge of starvation and 50 million were subjected to slavery. Moreover, the rights of the child had not hitherto been adequately protected by the instruments of international law.

52.		The first draft convention proposed by Poland, which was based on the United Nations Declaration of the Rights of the Child, had been submitted to the Member States of the United Nations and to international organizations for consideration. Twenty-six Member States, and the competent specialized agencies and non-governmental organizations, had formulated observations and suggestions which had served as the basis for the amended version of the draft convention that was now before the Commission. The preamble to draft resolution E/CN.4/L.1573 recalled those facts and the resolutions adopted by the General Assembly in that connection, in particular resolution 35/131, which had been sponsored by 52 Member States. The fourth preambular paragraph referred to the considerable progress achieved by the Working Group before the thirty-seventh session of the Commission. The progress made during the one week of negotiations and the views expressed in the General Assembly, the Economic and Social Council, the Commission on Human Rights and other United Nations bodies showed that the idea of a convention on the rights of the child enjoyed universal support because of its humanitarian nature. The last preambular paragraph noted that widespread interest. His delegation therefore proposed that the Commission should decide to continue its work on the draft convention at its thirty-eighth session as a matter of priority, and should request the Economic and Social Council to authorize another open-ended working group to meet for one week prior to the Commission's next session. He hoped that, given its humanitarian character, the draft resolution would be adopted by consensus.

53.     Mr. SILVA y SILVA (Peru) said that his delegation had become a sponsor of draft resolution E/CN.4/ L.1573, which it hoped would be adopted by consensus.

54.     Mr. BEAULNE (Canada) said he considered it a little premature for the Commission to take a decision on paragraph 2 of draft resolution E/CN.4/L.1573 straight away, since it was first necessary to know how many working groups would meet before the Commission's thirty-eighth session, how much time would be available to the Commission and what was the fairest way of dividing up that time. It would therefore be preferable to wait until the next meeting or even the last day of the session before taking a decision.

55.     The CHAIRMAN [Mr. Calero RODRIGUEZ (Brazil)] said that, in the circumstances, it would be preferable not to take an immediate decision on draft resolution E/CN.4/L.1573 as a whole. There were in fact several proposals before the Commission for working groups to meet prior to the next session.

56.     Mr. van BOVEN (Director, Division of Human Rights) said that it was not possible to service the meetings of more than four working groups at the same time. The Commission had already decided that the Working Group on the Implementation of the International Convention on the Suppression and Punishment of the Crime of Apartheid and the Working Group set up under Economic and Social Council resolution 1503 (XLVIII) should meet prior to its next session. The Commission also had before it three other proposals relating to the Working Group on a draft convention on the rights of the child, the Working Group on a Draft Convention against Torture and the Working Group on the Right to Development. The work of the sessional working groups also had to be borne in mind. For the present session, the Commission had been provided with three additional hours of conference services each day and it was essential to have the same amount in 1982.

57.     Mr. MAKSIMOV (Byelorussian Soviet Socialist Republic) said that his delegation attached a great deal of importance to the question of a convention on the rights of the child. It considered that the open-ended Working Group appointed to consider the matter should have the opportunity to meet again for one week prior to the Commission's thirty-eighth session, since its work was a guarantee of success. His country was therefore in favour of the proposal set forth in draft resolution E/CN.4/L.1573.

58.     Mr. GUTSENKO (Union of Soviet Socialist Republics) said that he was in favour of the draft resolution submitted by Poland, and in particular operative paragraph 2. He had no doubts as to the importance of the topics studied by the other Working Groups but considered that the draft convention on the rights of the child was a crucial matter. It was three years since the original version of the draft had been presented, but the Working Group had only reached article 8, and 28 articles still had to be dealt with. His delegation therefore trusted that the Commission would authorize the Working Group to meet prior to its next session and that it would accept draft resolution E/CN.4/L.1573 as it stood.

59.     Mr. LAMB (Australia) said that the draft resolution submitted by Poland raised no substantive difficulties. It would be regrettable, however, if the Commission had to proceed immediately to a vote on the draft resolution, which should be adopted by consensus. It would therefore seem better to wait until the next meeting before taking a decision.

60.     Mr. KALINOWSKI (Poland) agreed that a decision on draft resolution E/CN.4/L.1573 could be taken at the next meeting.

61. The CHAIRMAN [Mr. Calero RODRIGUEZ (Brazil)] said that, if there was no objection, he would take it that the Commission wished to take a decision at its next meeting on draft resolution E/CN.4/L.1573.

62. It was so decided.

*The following is taken from document E/CN.4/SR.1636 (16 March 1981)*

93. Mr. Lopatka (Poland), Chairman-Rapporteur of the Working Group on a draft convention on the rights of the child, drew attention to the Working Group's report (E/CN.4/L.1575) and commended draft resolution E/CN.4/L.1573 to the Commission for adoption.

94. Draft resolution E/CN.4/L.1573 was adopted by consensus.

## 6. Commission on Human Rights resolution 26 (XXXVII) on the "Question of a convention on the rights of the child" adopted on 10 March 1981

*The Commission on Human Rights,*

*Having in mind* the draft convention on the rights of the child submitted by Poland on 7 February 1978 and the amended version of the draft submitted on 5 October 1979,

*Recalling* General Assembly resolutions 33/166 of 20 December 1978 and 34/4 of 18 October 1979, as well as resolution 35/131 of 11 December 1980, by which the Assembly requested the Commission on Human Rights to continue to give high priority to the question of completing the draft convention on the rights of the child,

*Recalling also* its resolutions 20 (XXXIV) of 8 March 1978, 19 (XXXV) of 14 March 1979 and 36 (XXXVI) of 12 March 1980, as well as Economic and Social Council resolutions 1978/18 of 5 May 1978 and 1978/40 of 1 August 1978 and Council decision 1980/138 of 2 May 1980,

*Noting with satisfaction* the considerable progress made by the open-ended working group during its one week of negotiations prior to the thirty-seventh session of the Commission,

*Noting also* a widespread interest in working out a truly comprehensive international convention on the rights of the child, displayed so far by the representatives of numerous countries and international organizations,

1. *Decides* to continue at its thirty-eighth session, as a matter of priority, its work on a draft convention on the rights of the child with a view to completing the elaboration of the convention at that session for transmission to the General Assembly through the Economic and Social Council;

2. *Requests* the Economic and Social Council to authorize a one-week session of an open-ended working group prior to the thirty-eighth session of the Commission on Human Rights to facilitate completion of the work on a draft convention on the rights of the child.

## 7. Economic and Social Council decision 1981/144 of 8 May 1981

At its 18th plenary meeting, on 8 May 1981, the Council took note of resolution 26 (XXXVII) of 10 March 1981 of the Commission on Human Rights, and decided to authorize a one-week session of an open-ended working group prior to the thirty-eighth session of the Commission to facilitate completion of the work on a draft convention on the rights of the child.

## 8. General Assembly, Third Committee, status of draft convention

*The following is taken from A/C.3/36/6 (7 October 1981).*

QUESTION OF A CONVENTION ON THE RIGHTS OF THE CHILD (agenda item 86)

Document submitted by Poland

STATUS OF A DRAFT CONVENTION ON THE RIGHTS OF THE CHILD

I. *Articles agreed upon in the Commission on Human Rights*

*The States Parties to the Convention,*

*Considering* that, in accordance with the principles proclaimed in the Charter of the United Nations, recognition of the inherent dignity and of the equal and inalienable rights of all members of the human family is the foundation of freedom, justice and peace in the world,

*Bearing in mind* that the peoples of the United Nations have, in the Charter, reaffirmed their faith in fundamental human rights and in the dignity and worth of the human person, and have determined to promote social progress and better standards of life in larger freedom,

*Recognizing* that the United Nations have, in the Universal Declaration of Human Rights and in the International Covenants on Human Rights, proclaimed and agreed that everyone is entitled to all the rights and freedoms set forth therein, without distinction of any kind, such as race, colour, sex, language, religion, political or other opinion, national or social origin, property, birth or other status,

*Recalling* that in the Universal Declaration of Human Rights, the United Nations had proclaimed that childhood is entitled to special care and assistance,

*Convinced* that the family, as the basic unit of society and the natural environment for the growth and well-being of all its members and particularly children, should be afforded the necessary protection and assistance so that it can fully assume its responsibilities within the community,

*Recognizing* that, as indicated in the Declaration on the Rights of the Child adopted in 1959, the child due to the needs of his physical and mental development requires particular care and assistance with regard to health, physical, mental, moral and social development, and requires legal protection in conditions of freedom, dignity and security,

*Recognizing* that the child, for the full and harmonious development of his personality, should grow up in family environment, in an atmosphere of happiness, love and understanding,

*Bearing in mind* that the need for extending particular care to the child has been stated in the Geneva Declaration on the Rights of the Child of 1924 and in the Declaration on the Rights of the Child adopted by the United Nations in 1959 and recognized in the Universal Declaration of Human Rights, in the International Covenant on Civil and Political Rights (in particular in the articles 23 and 24), in the International Covenant on Economic, Social and Cultural Rights (in particular in its article 10) and in the statutes of specialized agencies and international organizations concerned with the welfare of children,

*Considering* that the child should be fully prepared to live an individual life in society, and brought up in the spirit of the ideals proclaimed in the Charter of the United Nations, and in particular in the spirit of peace, dignity, tolerance, freedom and brotherhood,

*Have agreed as follows:*

### Article 1

According to the present Convention a child is every human being to the age of 18 years unless, under the law of his State, he has attained his age of maturity earlier.

### Article 2

1.      The child shall have the right from his birth to a name and to acquire a nationality.

2.      The States Parties to the present Convention shall ensure that their legislation recognizes the principle according to which a child shall acquire the nationality of the State in the territory of which he has been born if, at the time of the child's birth, he is not granted nationality by any other State in accordance with its laws.

### Article 3

1.      In all actions concerning children, whether undertaken by public or private social welfare institutions, courts of law, or administrative authorities, the best interests of the child shall be a primary consideration.

2.	In all judicial or administrative proceedings affecting a child that is capable of forming his own views, an opportunity shall be provided for the views of the child to be heard, either directly or indirectly through a representative, as a party to the proceedings, and those views shall be taken into consideration by the competent authorities, in a manner consistent with the procedures followed in the State Party for the application of its legislation.

3.	The States Parties to the present Convention undertake to ensure the child such protection and care as is necessary for his well-being, taking into account the rights and duties of his parents, legal guardians, or other individuals legally responsible for him, and, to this end, shall take all appropriate legislative and administrative measures.

4.	The States Parties to the present Convention shall ensure competent supervision of officials and personnel of institutions directly responsible for the care of children.

## Article 4

1.	The States Parties to the present Convention shall respect and extend all the rights set forth in this Convention to each child in their territories without distinction of any kind, irrespective of the child's or his parents' or legal guardians' race, colour, sex, language, religion, political or other opinion, national or social origin, family status, ethnic origin, cultural beliefs or practices, property, educational attainment, birth, or any other basis whatever.

2.	States Parties to the present Convention shall take all appropriate measures to ensure that the child is protected against all forms of discrimination or punishment on the basis of the status, activities, expressed opinions, or beliefs of the child's parents, legal guardians, or other family members.

## Article 5

The States Parties to the present Convention shall undertake all appropriate administrative and legislative measures, in accordance with their available resources, and, where needed, within the framework of international cooperation, for the implementation of the rights recognized in this Convention.

## Article 7

The States Parties to the present Convention shall assure to the child who is capable of forming his own views the right to express his opinion freely in all matters, the wishes of the child being given due weight in accordance with his age and maturity.

## Article 8

1.	Parents or, as the case may be, guardians, have the primary responsibility for the upbringing and development of the child. The best interests of the child will be their basic concern. States Parties shall use their best efforts to ensure recognition of the principle that both parents have common and similar responsibilities for the upbringing and development of the child.

2.	For the purpose of guaranteeing and promoting the rights set forth in this Convention, the States Parties to the present Convention shall render appropriate assistance to parents and guardians in the performance of the child rearing responsibilities and shall ensure the development of institutions for the care of children.

3.	States Parties shall take all appropriate measures to ensure that children of working parents have the right to benefit from childcare services and facilities for which they are eligible.

4.	The institutions, services and facilities referred to in paragraphs 2 and 3 of this article shall conform with the standards established by competent authorities, particularly in the areas of safety, health, and in the number and suitability of their staff.

*Revised text of remaining draft articles being submitted to facilitate the drafting process*

### Article 6

The States Parties to the present Convention shall recognize the right of the child to have his residence to be determined by his parents. If the place of residence specified by the parents is likely to be detrimental to the child's well-being, or in the case of disagreement between the parents, a competent public organ, guided by the child's well-being, shall determine his place of residence.

### Article 9

1.     The States Parties to the present Convention shall encourage opinion-making quarters to disseminate information which promotes the upbringing of children in the spirit of the principles as laid down in article 16.

2.     The States Parties shall also encourage parents and guardians to provide their children with appropriate protection if, on account of its contents, the disseminated information might negatively affect the physical and moral development of the child.

### Article 10

1.     A child deprived of parental care shall be entitled to special protection and assistance provided by the State.

2.     The States Parties to the present Convention shall provide appropriate environment for the upbringing of a child who is deprived of his natural family environment or who, on account of his well-being, cannot be brought up in such an environment.

3.     The States Parties to the present Convention shall take measures, where appropriate, to facilitate adoption of children, and shall provide favourable conditions for establishing foster-families.

4.     The provisions of the preceding paragraphs apply accordingly, if the parents or one of them cannot provide the child with appropriate care because of imprisonment or another similar judicial or administrative sanction.

### Article 11

1.     The States Parties to the present Convention recognize the right of a mentally or physically disabled child to special protection and care, commensurate with his condition and those of his parents or guardians, and shall extend appropriate assistance to such a child.

2.     A disabled child shall grow up and receive education in conditions designed to achieve his fullest possible social integration. His special educational needs shall be cared for free of charge; aids and appliances shall be provided to ensure equal opportunity and access to the care services and facilities for which he is eligible.

### Article 12

1.     The States Parties to the present Convention shall ensure the child with health-care facilities and, in case of need, rehabilitation facilities of the highest attainable standard.

2.     In particular, States Parties to the present Convention shall undertake measures with a view to:

    (a)     lowering the infant mortality rate,

    (b)     ensuring medical assistance and health care to all children,

    (c)     providing expectant mothers with appropriate health-care services and ensuring working mothers a paid leave or a leave granting adequate social security benefits for a reasonable period of time, before and after confinement.

*Article 13*

The States Parties to the present Convention shall ensure to every child the right to social security benefits for which he is eligible on account of the situation of his parents or legal guardians or another situation and shall take appropriate legal and administrative measures in order to guarantee the implementation of this right.

*Article 14*

1.　　The States Parties to the present Convention recognize the right of every child to a standard of living which guarantees his normal physical, mental and moral development.

2.　　The parents shall, within their powers and financial possibilities, secure conditions of living indispensable for a normal development of the child.

3.　　The States Parties to the present Convention shall take appropriate measures to implement this right, particularly with regard to feeding, clothing and housing, and, within their means, shall extend the necessary material assistance to parents and other persons bringing up children, special regard to be given to incomplete families and children deprived of parental care.

*Article 15*

1.　　The States Parties to the present Convention shall guarantee all children compulsory and free education, at least at an elementary school level.

2.　　The States Parties to the present Convention shall develop various forms of secondary, general and vocational education, aiming at a gradual introduction at this level of free education, so as to enable all children to develop their talents and interests in conditions of equal opportunity.

*Article 16*

1.　　The States Parties to the present Convention recognize that raising up and educating the child should promote development of his personality and intensify his respect for human rights and fundamental freedoms.

2.　　The States Parties to the present Convention shall ensure that the child be prepared for independent life in a free society, in the spirit of understanding, tolerance and friendship among all peoples, ethnic and religious groups and educated in harmony with the principles of peace established by the United Nations.

*Article 17*

The States Parties to the present Convention undertake to ensure to all children opportunities for leisure and recreation commensurate with their age. Parents and other persons responsible for children, educational institutions and State organs shall supervise the practical implementation of the foregoing provision.

*Article 18*

1.　　The States Parties to the present Convention undertake to protect the child against all forms of discrimination, social exploitation or degradation of his dignity. The child shall not be subject of traffic in any form.

2.　　The States Parties to the present Convention shall ensure that the child be not employed in any form at work harmful to his health or development nor dangerous to his life, and they undertake to sue persons acting to the contrary.

3.　　The States Parties to the present Convention shall comply with the law prohibiting employment of children below the age of fourteen years, in accordance with the ILO Convention No. 5 of 13 June 1921.

*Article 19*

1.　　The child undergoing penal procedure shall have the right to special treatment and privileges.

2.　　The child shall not be liable to capital punishment. Any other punishment shall be adequate to the subsequent phase of his development.

3.      The penitentiary system shall be aimed at re-education and re-socialization of the sentenced child. It shall enable the child to serve the sentence of deprivation or limitation of freedom under special circumstances and, in particular, in separation from adult offenders.

*Article 20*

The States Parties to the present Convention every three years shall submit periodical reports on the implementation of the present Convention to the Economic and Social Council through the Secretary-General of the United Nations.

*Article 21*

The reports submitted by the States Parties to the present Convention under article 20 shall be considered by the Economic and Social Council, which may bring its observations and suggestions to the attention of the General Assembly of the United Nations.

*Article 22*

The present Convention is open for signature by all States.

*Article 23*

The present Convention is subject to ratification. Instruments of ratification shall be deposited with the Secretary-General of the United Nations.

*Article 24*

The present Convention shall remain open for accession by any State. Instruments of accession shall be deposited with the Secretary-General of the United Nations.

*Article 25*

1.      The present Convention shall enter into force six months after the date of deposit of the fifteenth instrument of ratification or accession.

2.      For each State ratifying or acceding to the present Convention after the deposit of the fifteenth instrument of ratification or accession.

3.      For each State ratifying or acceding to the present Convention after the deposit of the fifteenth instrument of ratification or accession, the Convention shall enter into force on the day after the deposit by such State of its instrument of ratification or accession.

*Article 26*

As depositary of the present Convention, the Secretary-General of the United Nations shall inform all States of:

   (a)      signatures, ratifications and accessions under articles 22, 23 and 24,

   (b)      the date of the entry into force of the present Convention under article 25.

*Article 27*

The original of the present Convention, of which the Chinese, English, French, Russian and Spanish texts are equally authentic, shall be deposited with the Secretary-General of the United Nations, who shall send certified copies thereof to all States.

## 9.   General Assembly resolution 36/57 on the "Question of a convention on the rights of the child" adopted on 25 November 1981 without a vote

*The General Assembly,*

*Recalling* its resolutions 33/166 of 20 December 1978, 34/4 of 18 October 1979 and 35/131 of 11 December 1980,

*Mindful* of the vital link between programmes benefiting children and the observance of their rights, and a broader and more comprehensive framework of overall economic and social development in conditions of peace,

*Convinced* that the fresh and necessary impetus to activities generated by the International Year of the Child should be maintained and that the new perspectives it has created should be followed by appropriate action in the years to come,

*Reaffirming* the important role that the United Nations Children's Fund has to play in the subject matter concerned,

*Aware* of the importance of an international convention on the rights of the child for the protection of children's rights and improvement in their situation,

*Having in mind* Commission on Human Rights resolutions 20 (XXXIV) of 8 March 1978, 19 (XXXV) of 14 March 1979, 36 (XXXVI) of 12 March 1980 and 26 (XXXVII) of 10 March 1981, as well as Economic and Social Council resolutions 1978/18 of 5 May 1978 and 1978/40 of 1 August 1978 and Council decisions 1980/138 of 2 May 1980 and 1981/144 of 8 May 1981,

*Noting with appreciation* the further progress made in the elaboration of a draft convention on the rights of the child by the Commission on Human Rights prior to and during its thirty-seventh session,

1.      *Welcomes* Economic and Social Council decision 1981/144 by which the Council authorized an open-ended working group of the Commission on Human Rights to meet for a period of one week prior to the thirty-eighth session of the Commission to facilitate completion of the work on the draft convention on the rights of the child;

2.      *Requests* the Commission on Human Rights to give the highest priority to the question of completing the draft convention;

3.      *Requests* the Secretary-General to provide all necessary assistance to the working group in order to ensure its smooth and efficient work;

4.      *Decides* to include in the provisional agenda of its thirty-seventh session the item entitled "Question of a convention on the rights of the child".

*73rd plenary meeting*
*25 November 1981*

# F. 1982

## 1. Report of the Working Group

*The following is taken from document E/CN.4/1982/L.41 (8 March 1982) (reproduced from documents E/1982/12/ Add.1 and E/CN.4/1982/30/Add.1).*

INTRODUCTION

1.　　　By resolution 26 (XXXVII) of 10 March 1981, the Commission on Human Rights decided to continue at its thirty-eighth session as a matter of priority, its work on a draft convention on the rights of the child with a view to completing the elaboration of the convention at that session for transmission to the General Assembly through the Economic and Social Council. By decision 1981/144 of 8 May 1981, the Economic and Social Council noted resolution 26 (XXXVII) of the Commission on Human Rights, and decided to authorize a one-week session of an open-ended working group prior to the thirty-eighth session of the Commission to facilitate completion of the work on a draft convention of the rights of the child. At its thirty-sixth session, the General Assembly, by resolution 36/57 of 25 November 1981, welcomed Economic and Social Council decision 1981/144 and requested the Commission on Human Rights to give the highest priority to the question of completing the draft convention.

2.　　　At its fourth meeting on 2 February 1982, the Commission on Human Rights by decision 101/1982 decided that a sessional open-ended Working Group should be established for the consideration of item 13 on its agenda concerning the drafting of a convention on the rights of the child.

3.　　　The 1982 pre-sessional Working Group held 10 meetings from 25 January to 29 January 1982, at which it discussed articles 6, 9, 10 and 11 of the revised draft convention (E/CN.4/1349). The sessional Working Group had discussions on articles 6, 11 and 12 during meetings held on 2, 3, 4, 8 and 9 February 1982. At its meeting on 5 March 1982, the Working Group considered article 12 and adopted its report.

ELECTIONS

4.　　　At the first meeting of the pre-sessional Working Group, on 25 January 1982, Mr. Adam Lopatka (Poland) was elected Chairman-Rapporteur by acclamation. Mr. Lopatka continued as Chairman-Rapporteur of the Working Group established by the Commission on Human Rights at its thirty-eighth session to continue the work of the pre-sessional Working Group.

PARTICIPATION

5.　　　The meetings of the pre-sessional and the sessional Working Groups, which were open to all members of the Commission on Human Rights, were attended by representatives of the following States: Argentina, Australia, Brazil, Bulgaria, the Byelorussian SSR, Canada, China, Cuba, Denmark, France, Germany, Federal Republic of, India, Italy, Japan, Netherlands, Philippines, Poland, Senegal, the Union of Soviet Socialist Republics, the United Kingdom of Great Britain and Northern Ireland, the United States of America and Yugoslavia.

The following States, non-members of the Commission on Human Rights, were represented at the meetings of the Working Group by observers: Colombia, the German Democratic Republic, Holy See, Norway, Sweden and Switzerland.

The International Labour Organization, United Nations High Commissioner for Refugees and United Nations Children's fund, as well as a number of non-governmental organizations, were represented at the Working Group by observers.

The Associated Country Women of the World, the International Association of Juvenile and Family Court Magistrates, the International Federation of Women in Legal Careers, the International Association of Penal Law, the International Catholic Child Bureau, the International Commission of Jurists, the International Council on Social Welfare, the International Federation of Women Lawyers, the International Union for Child Welfare, the Minority Rights Group, the World Movement of Mothers and Rädda Barnen's Rikförbund sent observers to the Working Group.

DOCUMENTS

6.      The Working Group had before it a number of documents including the Revised draft convention on the rights of the child (E/CN.4/1349), the document submitted by Poland on the status of a draft convention on the rights of the child (A/C.3/36/6), the report of the Secretary-General on the views, observations and suggestions on the question submitted by Member States, competent specialized agencies, regional intergovernmental organizations and non-governmental organizations (E/CN.4/1324 and Corr.1 and Add.1-5), the reports of the 1979, 1980 and 1981 Working Groups (E/CN.4/L.1463, E/CN.4/L.1542 and E/CN.4/L.1575), the reports of the Working Group on Slavery on its fifth, sixth and seventh sessions (E/CN.4/Sub.2/434, E/CN.4/Sub.2/447, E/CN.4/Sub.2/486 and Corr.1), the Study on the Exploitation of Child Labour (E/CN.4/Sub.2/479), and summary records of the debates referring to child labour during the thirty-fourth session of the Sub-Commission (E/CN.4/Sub.2/SR.908-911, and 921-922). Non-governmental organizations in consultative status also submitted the following written statements: E/CN.4/NGO/230, 234, 244, 265, 276 and E/CN.4/1982/WG.1/WP.1. This latter statement was sponsored by the Afro-Asian People's Solidarity Organization, the All India Women's Conference, Arab Lawyers Union, Associated Country Women of the World, International Alliance of Women, International Association of Democratic Lawyers, International Association of Juvenile and Family Court Magistrates, International Catholic Union of the Press, International Council of Jewish Women, International Federation of Business and Professional Women, International Federation of Women Lawyers, Rädda Barnen's Rikförbund, Soroptimist International (subject to reservation on article 20 of the draft convention proposed in E/CN.4/1982/WG.1/WP.1), Women's International League for Peace and Freedom, World Association of Girl Guides and Girl Scouts, World Confederation of Organizations of the Teaching Profession and Zonta International, in addition to the non-governmental organizations indicated in document E/CN.4/1982/WG.1/WP.1.

7.      As in 1981, the basic working document for the discussions in the Working Group was the revised draft convention submitted by Poland (E/CN.4/1349). It will be recalled that the preamble as well as articles 1 to 5 and 7 and 8 as adopted, were annexed to the report of the Working Group of 1981 (E/CN.4/L.1575).

[...]

116.    At its final meeting on 5 March 1982, the Working Group adopted its report by consensus.

117.    At the close of its series of meetings, the Working Group expressed the view that its work constituted an important contribution to the next phase of the elaboration of the draft convention on the rights of the child. The representative of the Union of Soviet Socialist Republics, supported by the representative of the Byelorussian SSR, stated that the report of the Chairman-Rapporteur did not fully reflect the situation that had prevailed in the Working Group with respect to those members who had favoured the elaboration of the draft convention and those who had done everything in order to hamper the work and even to prevent the elaboration of this important international instrument. The other delegations disagreed with this statement.

## 2.   Articles adopted in 1982

*The following is taken from document E/CN.4/1982/301/Add.1.*

*Article 6*

1.      The States Parties to the present Convention recognize that the child should enjoy parental care and should have his place of residence determined by his parent(s), except as provided herein.

2.      States Parties shall ensure that a child shall not be separated from his parents against their will, except when competent authorities subject to judicial review determine, in accordance with applicable law and procedures, that such separation is necessary for the best interests of the child. Such a determination may be necessary in a particular case such as one involving abuse or neglect of the child by the parents, or one

where the parents are living separately and a decision must be made as to the child's place of residence. Such determinations shall not be made until all interested parties have been given an opportunity to participate in the proceedings and to make their views known. Such views shall be taken into account by the competent authorities in making their determination.

## Article 10

1. A child permanently or temporarily deprived of his family environment for any reason shall be entitled to special protection and assistance provided by the State.

2. The States Parties to the present Convention shall ensure that a child who is parentless, or who is temporarily or permanently deprived of his family environment, or who in his best interests cannot be brought up or be allowed to remain in that environment shall be provided with alternative family care which could include, inter alia, adoption, foster placement, or placement in suitable institutions for the care of children.

## Article 11

1. The States Parties to the present Convention shall undertake measures, where appropriate, to facilitate the process of adoption of the child. Adoption of a child shall be authorized only by competent authorities who determine, in accordance with applicable law and procedures and on the basis of all pertinent and reliable information, that the adoption is permissible in view of the child's status concerning parents, relatives and guardians and that, if required, the appropriate persons concerned have given their informed consent to the adoption on the basis of such counselling as may be necessary.

2. The States Parties to the present Convention shall take all appropriate measures to secure the best interests of the child who is the subject of intercountry adoption. States Parties shall ensure that placements are made by authorized agencies or appropriate persons under the adequate supervision of competent authorities, providing the same safeguards and standards that are applied in exclusively domestic adoptions. The competent authorities shall make every possible effort to ensure the legal validity of the adoption in the countries involved. States Parties shall endeavour, where appropriate, to promote these objectives by entering into bilateral or multilateral agreements.

## Article 11 bis

The States Parties to the present Convention shall take appropriate measures to ensure that a child who is seeking refugee status or who is considered a refugee in accordance with applicable international or domestic law and procedures shall, whether unaccompanied or accompanied by his parents, legal guardians or close relatives, receive appropriate protection and humanitarian assistance in the enjoyment of applicable rights set forth in this Convention and other international human rights or humanitarian instruments to which the said States are Parties. In view of the important functions performed in refugee protection and assistance matters by the United Nations and other competent intergovernmental and non-governmental organizations, the States Parties to the present Convention shall provide appropriate cooperation in any efforts by these organizations to protect and assist such a child and to trace the parents or other close relatives of an unaccompanied refugee child in order to obtain information necessary for reunification with his family. In cases where no parents, legal guardians or close relatives can be found, the child shall be accorded the same protection as any other child permanently or temporarily deprived of his family environment for any reason, as set forth in the present Convention.

## Article 12, paragraph 1

The States Parties to the present Convention recognize that a mentally or physically disabled child should enjoy a full and decent life in conditions which ensure his dignity, promote his self-reliance, and facilitate his active participation in the community.

# 3. Draft resolution on the "Question of a convention on the rights of the child"

*The following is taken from document E/CN.4/1982/L.35 (26 February 1982).*

Argentina, Byelorussian Soviet Socialist Republic, Canada, Costa Rica, France, India, Panama, Peru, Poland and Senegal: draft resolution

*The Commission on Human Rights,*

*Having in mind* the draft convention on the rights of the child submitted by Poland on 7 February 1978, the amended version of the draft submitted on 5 October 1979 and the document submitted by Poland on 7 October 1981,

*Recalling* General Assembly resolutions 33/166 of 20 December 1978, 34/4 of 18 October 1979 and 35/131 of 11 December 1980, as well as resolution 36/57 of 25 November 1981, by which the Assembly requested the Commission on Human Rights to continue to give the highest priority to the question of completing the draft convention on the rights of the child,

*Recalling also* its resolutions 20 (XXXIV) of 8 March 1978, 19 (XXXV) of 14 March 1979, 36 (XXXVI) of 12 March 1980 and 26 (XXXVII) of 10 March 1981, as well as Economic and Social Council resolutions 1978/18 of 5 May 1978 and 1978/40 of 1 August 1978, Council decisions 1980/138 of 2 May 1980 and 1981/144 of 8 May 1981,

*Noting with satisfaction* the considerable progress made by the open-ended working group during its one week of negotiations prior to the thirty-eighth session of the Commission and during this session,

*Noting also* the widespread interest in working out a truly comprehensive international convention on the rights of the child displayed so far by the representatives of numerous countries and international organizations,

1.      *Decides* to continue at its thirty-ninth session, as a matter of high priority, its work on a draft convention on the rights of the child with a view to completing the elaboration of the convention at that session for transmission to the General Assembly through the Economic and Social Council;

2.      *Requests* the Economic and Social Council to authorize a one-week session of an open-ended working group prior to the thirty-ninth session of the Commission on Human Rights to facilitate completion of the work on a draft convention on the rights of the child;

3.      *Recommends* that the Economic and Social Council should adopt the following resolution:

"*The Economic and Social Council,*

*Recalling* General Assembly resolutions 33/166 of 20 December 1978, 34/4 of 18 October 1979 and 35/131 of 11 December 1980, as well as resolution 36/57 of 25 November 1981 by which the Assembly requested the Commission on Human Rights to continue to give the highest priority to the question of completing the draft convention on the rights of the child, and Economic and Social Council resolutions 1978/18 of 5 May 1978 and 1978/40 of 1 August 1978 as well as Council decisions 1980/138 of 2 May 1980 and 1981/144 of 8 May 1981, by which the Economic and Social Council authorized a meeting of an open-ended working group of the Commission on Human Rights for a period of one week prior to the thirty-eighth session of the Commission in order to complete the work on a draft convention on the rights of the child,

*Considering* that it was not found possible to complete the work on this convention during the thirty-eighth session of the Commission,

*Taking note* of Commission on Human Rights resolution ... of ... March 1982,

1.      *Authorizes* a meeting of an open-ended working group for a period of one week prior to the thirty-ninth session of the Commission on Human Rights to facilitate the completion of the work on a draft convention on the rights of the child;

2. *Requests* the Secretary-General to transmit to the Commission on Human Rights at its thirty-ninth session all relevant material relating to the draft convention on the rights of the child.

## 4. Administrative and financial implications

*The following is taken from document E/CN.4/1982/L.47 (5 March 1982).*

QUESTION OF A CONVENTION ON THE RIGHTS OF THE CHILD (agenda item 13)

Administrative and financial implications of the draft resolution contained in document E/CN.4/1982/L.35

Statement submitted by the Secretary-General in accordance with rule 2 of the rules of procedure of the functional commissions of the Economic and Social Council

1. By paragraph 2 of draft resolution E/CN.4/1982/L.35 the Commission would request the Economic and Social Council to authorize a one-week session of an open-ended working group prior to the thirty-ninth session of the Commission on Human Rights to facilitate completion of the work on a draft convention on the rights of the child.

2. On the basis of the foregoing the relevant costs under Section 29 B, Conference Services Geneva, are estimated on a full-cost basis at $42,600 for 1983.

## 5. Discussion in the Commission on Human Rights on 11 March 1982

*The following is taken from document E/CN.4/1982/SR.60 (26 March 1982). The Commission had previously decided, at its fourth meeting on 3 February 1982, to set up an informal open-ended working group for the consideration of the question of a convention on the rights of the child (decision 1982/101: Organization of work).*

QUESTION OF A CONVENTION ON THE RIGHTS OF THE CHILD (agenda item 13) *(continued)* (E/CN.4/1982/L.35, L.41 and L.47)

72. Mr. LOPATKA (Poland), speaking as Chairman-Rapporteur of the Working Group on a draft convention on the rights of the child, introduced its report (E/CN.4/1982/L.41). He thanked the participants and the Secretariat for their cooperation. Turning to draft resolution E/CN.4/1982/L.35, he announced that Australia and Cuba had joined the sponsors. The draft resolution was a procedural resolution which would enable the Economic and Social Council to authorize the Commission to continue to give priority to the work on the draft convention, in accordance with General Assembly resolution 36/57.

73. The CHAIRMAN announced that Greece had joined the sponsors of the draft resolution and drew attention to the statement of its financial implications contained in document E/CN.4/1982/L.47.

74. Mr. JOHNSON (United States of America) commended the Secretariat for the drafting of the report, which reflected lengthy and complicated discussions. It would represent a contribution to the legislative history of the convention.

75. Mrs. HERRAN (observer for Colombia) associated herself with the comments of the United States representative and announced that her delegation wished to become a sponsor of the draft resolution.

76. The Commission took note of the report of the Working Group (E/CN.4/1982/L.41).

77. The Commission adopted draft resolution E/CN.4/1982/L.35 without a vote.

## 6. Commission on Human Rights resolution 1982/39 on the "Question of a convention on the rights of the child" adopted on 11 March 1982

*The Commission on Human Rights,*

*Having in mind* the draft convention on the rights of the child submitted by Poland on 7 February 1978, the amended version of the draft submitted on 5 October 1979 and the document submitted by Poland on 7 October 1981,

*Recalling* General Assembly resolutions 33/166 of 20 December 1978, 34/4 of 18 October 1979 and 35/131 of 11 December 1980, as well as resolution 36/57 of 25 November 1981, by which the Assembly requested the Commission on Human Rights to continue to give the highest priority to the question of completing the draft convention on the rights of the child,

*Recalling also* its resolutions 20 (XXXIV) of 8 March 1978, 19 (XXXV) of 14 March 1979, 36 (XXXVI) of 12 March 1980 and 26 (XXXVII) of 10 March 1981, as well as Economic and Social Council resolutions 1978/18 of 5 May 1978 and 1978/40 of 1 August 1978, and Council decision 1980/138 of 2 May 1980 and 1981/144 of 8 May 1981,

*Noting with satisfaction* the considerable progress made by the open-ended working group during its one week of negotiations prior to the thirty-eighth session of the Commission and during the present session,

*Noting also* the widespread interest in working out a truly comprehensive international convention on the rights of the child displayed so far by the representatives of numerous countries and international organizations,

1.      *Decides* to continue at its thirty-ninth session, as a matter of high priority, its work on a draft convention on the rights of the child with a view to completing the elaboration of the convention at that session for transmission to the General Assembly through the Economic and Social Council;

2.      *Requests* the Economic and Social Council to authorize a one-week session of an open-ended working group prior to the thirty-ninth session of the Commission on Human Rights to facilitate completion of the work on a draft convention on the rights of the child;

3.      *Recommends* that the Economic and Social Council should adopt the following resolution:

"*The Economic and Social Council,*

*Recalling* General Assembly resolutions 33/166 of 20 December 1978, 34/4 of 18 October 1979 and 35/131 of 11 December 1980, as well as resolution 36/57 of 25 November 1981 by which the Assembly requested the Commission on Human Rights to continue to give the highest priority to the question of completing the draft convention on the rights of the child, and Economic and Social Council resolutions 1978/18 of 5 May 1978 and 1978/40 of 1 August 1978 as well as Council decisions 1980/138 of 2 May 1980 and 1981/144 of 8 May 1981, by which the Economic and Social Council authorized a meeting of an open-ended working group of the Commission on Human Rights for a period of one week prior to the thirty-eighth session of the Commission in order to complete the work on a draft convention on the rights of the child,

*Considering* that it was not found possible to complete the work on this convention during the thirty-eighth session of the Commission,

*Taking note* of Commission on Human Rights resolution 1982/39 of 11 March 1982,

1.      *Authorizes* a meeting of an open-ended working group for a period of one week prior to the thirty-ninth session of the Commission on Human Rights to facilitate the completion of the work on a draft convention on the rights of the child;

2.      *Requests* the Secretary-General to transmit to the Commission on Human Rights at its thirty-ninth session all relevant material relating to the draft convention on the rights of the child."

## 7.   Economic and Social Council resolution 1982/37 on the "Question of a convention on the rights of the child" adopted on 7 May 1982

*The Economic and Social Council,*

*Recalling* General Assembly resolutions 33/166 of 20 December 1978, 34/4 of 18 October 1979 and 35/131 of 11 December 1980, as well as resolution 36/57 of 25 November 1981, by which the Assembly requested the Commission on Human Rights to continue to give the highest priority to the question of completing the draft convention on the rights of the child, and Economic and Social Council resolutions 1978/18 of 5 May 1978 and 1978/40 of 1 August 1978 and decisions 1980/138 of 2 May 1980 and 1981/144 of 8 May 1981, by which the Council authorized a one-week session of an open-ended working group prior to the thirty-eighth session of the Commission to facilitate completion of the work on a draft convention on the rights of the child,

*Considering* that it was not found possible to complete the work on the draft convention during the thirty-eighth session of the Commission on Human Rights,

*Taking note* of resolution 1982/39 of 11 March 1982 of the Commission on Human Rights,

1.      *Authorizes* a meeting of an open-ended working group for a period of one week prior to the thirty-ninth session of the Commission on Human Rights to facilitate the completion of the work on a draft convention on the rights of the child;

2.      *Requests* the Secretary-General to transmit to the Commission on Human Rights at its thirty-ninth session all relevant material relating to the draft convention on the rights of the child.

*28th plenary meeting*
*7 May 1982*

## 8.  Economic and Social Council resolution 1982/39 on the "Protection of the rights of children and parents in cases of removal or retention of children" adopted on 7 May 1982

*The Economic and Social Council,*

*Bearing in mind* the Declaration of the Rights of the Child proclaimed by the General Assembly in its resolution 1386 (XIV) of 20 November 1959,

*Recalling* that, under the terms of principle 2 of that Declaration, the child shall enjoy special protection, and shall be given opportunities and facilities, by law and by other means, to enable him to develop physically, mentally, morally, spiritually and socially in a healthy and normal manner and in conditions of freedom and dignity,

*Concerned* about the proliferation of conflicts between couples of different nationalities and at the consequences which result therefrom for children, concerned particularly by their removal from the country of one spouse to the country of the other without the consent of one of the two spouses, and without or in violation of a judicial or administrative decision, and, lastly, concerned about the cases of child retention in which such situations sometimes end,

*Noting* the existence of a common interest in the elaboration of a full and detailed international convention on the rights of the child, as already evinced by the representatives of many countries and international organizations,

*Recalling* that the universally acknowledged standards and principles in the field of human rights impose on States the obligation to protect all individuals under their jurisdiction from infringements of their freedom and dignity by any private person,

1.      *Calls the attention* of States to the proliferation of cases of removal and retention of children and invites them to cooperate actively with a view to preventing the occurrence of such cases and to solving them speedily, out of concern for the interest of the child;

2.      *Invites* States to organize such cooperation through the conclusion of bilateral arrangements or through accession to regional conventions or international conventions such as the Hague Convention on the Civil Aspects of International Child Abduction of 25 October 1980, which is open to all States;

3.      *Invites* the Commission on Human Rights, when drafting the convention on the rights of the child, to take into consideration the protection of the rights of the child in cases of unauthorized international removal;

4.      *Requests* the Secretary-General to consult with Governments on this problem and to report to the Commission on Human Rights at its thirty-ninth session under the agenda item entitled "Question of a convention on the rights of the child".

*28th plenary meeting*
*7 May 1982*

## 9. General Assembly resolution 37/190 on the "Question of a convention on the rights of the child" adopted on 18 December 1982

*The General Assembly,*

*Recalling* its resolutions 33/166 of 20 December 1978, 34/4 of 18 October 1979, 35/131 of 11 December 1980 and 36/57 of 25 November 1981,

*Recalling also* Commission on Human Rights resolutions 20 (XXXIV) of 8 March 1978, 19 (XXXV) of 14 March 1979, 36 (XXXVI) of 12 March 1980, 26 (XXXVII) of 10 March 1981 and 1982/39 of 11 March 1982 as well as Economic and Social Council resolutions 1978/18 of 5 May 1978, 1978/40 of 1 August 1978 and 1982/37 of 7 May 1982 and Council decisions 1980/138 of 2 May 1980 and 1981/144 of 8 May 1981,

*Conscious* of the importance of its task to contribute to the improvement of the situation of children in the world and to ensure their development and education in conditions of peace,

*Bearing in mind* the need to pursue effective action with a view to generating an international record of accomplishment such as that of the International Year of the Child,

*Noting again* the important role of the United Nations Children's Fund and the specialized agencies in promoting the well-being of children and their development,

*Aware* of the importance of an international convention on the rights of the child for more effective protection of children's rights,

*Noting with appreciation* that further progress has been made in the elaboration of a draft convention on the rights of the child prior to and during the thirty-eighth session of the Commission on Human Rights,

1.	*Welcomes* Economic and Social Council resolution 1982/37, by which the Council authorized a meeting of an open-ended working group of the Commission on Human Rights for a period of one week prior to the thirty-ninth session of the Commission in order to facilitate completion of the work on a draft convention on the rights of the child;

2.	*Invites* all Member States to offer their effective contribution to the elaboration of a draft convention;

3.	*Requests* the Commission on Human Rights to give the highest priority at its thirty-ninth session to the question of completing a draft convention;

4.	*Requests* the Secretary-General to provide all necessary assistance to the working group in order to ensure its smooth and efficient work;

5.	*Decides* to include in the provisional agenda of its thirty-eighth session the item entitled "Question of a convention on the rights of the child".

*111th plenary meeting*
*18 December 1982*

# G. 1982/83

## 1. General comments by Member States, competent specialized agencies, regional intergovernmental organizations and non-governmental organizations on Economic and Social Council resolution 1982/39

*The following is, unless noted otherwise, taken from document E/CN.4/1983/32 and Add.1-5 (21 December 1982; 12 January - 4 March 1983).*

I INTRODUCTION

1.      In its resolution 1982/39, the Economic and Social Council, inter alia, called the attention of States to the proliferation of cases of removal and retention of children and invited them to cooperate actively with a view to preventing the occurrence of such cases and to solving them speedily, out of concern for the interest of the child. In this connection, it invited the Commission on Human Rights, when drafting the convention on the rights of the child, to take into consideration the protection of the rights of the child in cases of unauthorized international removal. It further requested the Secretary-General to consult with Governments on this problem and to report to the Commission on Human Rights at its thirty-ninth session, under the agenda item entitled "Question of a convention on the rights of the child".

2.      Notes verbale relating to this question were sent to all Member States of the United Nations. The present report contains summaries of replies received from Governments as of 21 December 1982 on action taken pursuant to the above-mentioned resolution. Any additional replies will be reproduced as addenda to the present document.

### (a)    Austria

The Government refers to the Hague Convention on the Civil Aspects of International Child Abduction of 25 October 1980 and makes observations on a number of points including, in particular, the enforcement of decisions concerning custody of children, measures guaranteeing the expeditious return of children in cases of removal, grounds for refusing the return of a child, and the question of the costs incurred through recourse to the assistance of a lawyer.

### (b)    Barbados

The Government of Barbados states that the retention of children, removal or abduction of children from a country by a parent in defiance of a custody order is becoming an increasing problem in Barbados.

This issue has been discussed at several Commonwealth Law Ministers meetings since 1977 and an attempt is being made by members of the Commonwealth to draft a convention along similar lines as the Hague Convention.

The broad aim of this convention would be to recognize and enforce custody orders made within Commonwealth countries and to ensure that an application to vary or modify a custody order would only be done in the child's country of residence. There is, however, general consensus that in order to alleviate this problem, there must be (a) an intergovernmental agreement and (b) subsequent legislative changes.

The Government has already implemented some initial legislative changes. In the Family Law Bill of 1981 foreign custody orders can be registered and are recognized. A limit is placed on the right of the court in Barbados to exercise jurisdiction on the matter unless (a) each person having rights in the original order consents to the proceedings or (b) the welfare of the child will be adversely affected by non-action. There is also provision for the transmission of Barbadian custody orders to overseas countries.

The inclusion of the rights of the child in cases of unauthorized removal in the draft convention on the rights of the child would ensure that countries become more aware of the size and scope of the problem and safeguard the right of a child to a stable and secure environment.

## (c) Colombia

The Government of Colombia reports that chapter 8 of Administrative Decision No. 0773 of 1981 refers expressly to permits to leave Colombia and prescribes the requirements concerning minors.

1.          When both parents agree to the minor's departure: In this case, a statement of intent that has been signed by both parents and authenticated shall be submitted in writing to the Ministry of External Relations so that a passport may be issued to the minor or minors concerned.

2.          When there is disagreement between the parents regarding the minor's departure from Colombia, the official having competence to settle the dispute is the Minors' Judge.

3.          When the domicile of one of the parents or legal representatives is unknown, the Minors' Counsel shall, in administrative proceedings, allow or refuse to allow the minor or minors concerned to leave Colombia, as appropriate.

All these decisions must be complied with by the immigration authorities.

In addition to such cases, somewhat irregular de facto situations occur when one of the parents manages, by resorting to bribes, forging signatures or travelling by land to the borders with Ecuador, Brazil, Venezuela, Panama, etc., unlawfully to obtain a visa for other countries from the competent officials.

In view of the foregoing, we consider it advisable, important and urgent that international agreements should be concluded on such matters and that the Commission on Human Rights should draft agreements on the rights of children which take account of the protection of their rights in cases of unauthorized and unlawful international travel.

It is extremely important that such agreements should deal not only with the protection of minors, but also provide for machinery to pave the way for, facilitate and make possible the repatriation of a minor or minors unlawfully removed from Colombia.

## (d) Cyprus

The Government states that it supports Economic and Social Council resolution 1982/39 and that it is also considering the ratification of the European Convention on Recognition and Enforcement of Decisions concerning Custody of Children and on Restoration of Custody of Children, of 20 May 1980.

## (e) Denmark

The Government states that it is considering whether to accede to the European Convention on Recognition and Enforcement of Decisions concerning Custody of Children and on Restoration of Custody of Children, drafted within the framework of the Council of Europe, or to the Hague Convention on the Civil Aspects of International Child Abduction of 25 October 1980.

## (f) Ethiopia

The Government expresses its full support for Economic and Social Council resolution 1982/39 and declares that States should organize some form of cooperation for preventing the occurrence of cases such as those referred to in the resolution. The Government further notes that it is in favour of the elaboration of an international convention on the question.

## (g) Federal Republic of Germany

The Government states that it welcomes Economic and Social Council resolution 1982/39. It further states that it is willing to cooperate with other States on the basis of the Hague Convention on the Civil Aspects of International Child Abduction of 25 October 1980, and that it therefore intends to ratify the Hague Convention.

## (h) Greece

The Government states that it attaches great importance to the inclusion, in drafting the convention on the rights of the child, of sufficient and effective safeguards for the prevention of unauthorized removals from State to State.

The efforts being made to construct a complete and up-to-date system for the protection of the child against unauthorized removal across frontiers, may find inspiration in the European Convention on Recognition and Enforcement of Decisions concerning Custody of Children and on Restoration of Custody of Children, of 20 May 1980, which Greece has already signed and intends to ratify shortly.

### (i)  Kuwait

The Government states that its legislation fully safeguards the right of the child to live undisturbed under the protection of the person legally responsible for his welfare, irrespective of whether that person is the child's guardian, trustee or any other individual in whose custody the child has been placed. According to articles 178 to 184 of the Penal Code, it is absolutely forbidden to remove a child under 21 years of age from his environment or from the place in which he normally lives if such removal would entail the severance of the child's links with his family, who are responsible for his welfare.

The State of Kuwait intends to cooperate with other State Members of the United Nations with a view to the adoption of measures and rules to prevent the removal or retention of children.

### (j)  Additional reply from Kuwait

The Government states that Kuwaiti legislation contains numerous provisions under the Personal Status Act to protect the child's individuality, development and maintenance. Chapter II of the Constitution stipulates that the family is the foundation of society and is based on religion, morality and patriotism. The law shall safeguard the family and strengthen its bonds, thereby ensuring the protection of mothers and children.

Article 10 of the Constitution stipulates that: "The State shall provide for the welfare of the younger generation, protect it from exploitation, and preserve it from moral, physical and spiritual neglect."

In the event of a conflict between spouses, the customary practice followed by the courts in the State of Kuwait is to grant child custody to the mother, since she is regarded as the person most likely to show concern for the welfare of the child during the early stages of his life. The child remains in the custody of his mother, or whoever replaces her, until he comes of age as prescribed in the Islamic sharia.

The Nationality Act No. 15 of 1959 ensures extensive protection for mothers and children.

### (k)  Netherlands

The Government notes that it intends to ratify the two recently concluded international instruments which deal with the problem of preventing the occurrence of cases of removal of children, namely: the Hague Convention on the Civil Aspects of International Child Abduction, and the European Convention on Recognition and Enforcement of Decisions concerning Custody of Children and on Restoration of Custody of Children. Interested States should organize cooperation in this field by acceding to one or both Conventions. Furthermore, if the Commission on Human Rights intends to include in the draft convention on the rights of the child provisions concerning the removal of children, it should pay due attention to existing instruments in order to ensure the effective prevention of the unauthorized removal of children.

### (l)  Norway

It is the Government's view that the question of the unauthorized removal of children should be taken into consideration when drafting a convention on the rights of the child. At the same time, the need for coordination with the work already done by other international organizations should also be taken into account. The Government is, in principle, in favour of adhering to one or both Conventions on the subject, namely, the Hague Convention and the Convention elaborated by the Council of Europe.

### (m)  Pakistan

The Government states that it does not permit the removal or retention of children from their parents' family by other persons. The family courts decide on custody in cases arising out of divorce. The Government supports the proposal that all countries should cooperate closely through accession to the Hague Convention on the Civil Aspects of International Child Abduction of 25 October 1980, which is open to all States.

## (n)      Qatar

The Government states that it endorses Economic and Social Council resolution 1982/39. Islamic law recognizes the need to protect children. The Government proposes that one of the aspects of the question which should be considered is the importance of ensuring adequate services for the fundamental needs of children suffering from the problem of removal.

## (o)      Singapore

The Government states that there are adequate laws in Singapore to cover the protection of the rights of children and young persons, namely, the Laws of Children and Young Persons Act, the Women's Charter and the Penal Code. In addition to these laws, the Ministry of Social Affairs of Singapore contains two divisions - the Counselling and Advice Division and the Protection and Welfare of Children and Young Persons Division - which deal with all problems connected with children and young persons. Any parent who is aggrieved by the unauthorized removal of a child by one spouse can have recourse to the Courts, provided he or she is a Singapore citizen or has resided in Singapore continuously for a period of no less than six months. There is provision for an expedited order where the Court is satisfied that there is imminent danger of the child being taken out of the country. The Court is also empowered to order a child to be kept at a place of safety to await a decision. The Penal Code also has a provision which safeguards a child against kidnapping from lawful guardianship.

## (p)      Spain

The Government states that it shares the concern underlying the text of Economic and Social Council resolution 1982/39 in view of the increasing number of cases of Spanish nationals becoming involved in situations of this type, usually as a result of marriages with aliens. Noting that it had played an active part in the preparation of the Hague Convention on the Civil Aspects of International Child Abduction to which it intends to accede, the Government adds that it would be very opportune if, at its thirty-ninth session, the Commission on Human Rights completes its work on the elaboration of that convention on the rights of the child with a view to achieving the speedy solution of the cases referred to in the Council's resolution 1982/39.

## (q)      Sudan

The Government states that it fully supports Economic and Social Council resolution 1982/39. Although cases of retention and international removal of children rarely occur because of the existence of strong social and family ties, Sudan welcomes international cooperation and the exchange of experience in the field of the rights of the child.

The Constitution and other legislative acts clearly indicate the importance of moral, spiritual, mental, physical and social values for the development of the child.

## (r)      Switzerland

The Government states that it has taken the necessary steps for the ratification, in the near future, of the Hague Convention on the Civil Aspects of International Child Abduction, of 25 October 1980, as well as of the European Convention on Recognition and Enforcement of Decisions concerning Custody of Children and on Restoration of Custody of Children, of 20 May 1980. The Swiss Government also proposes to begin negotiations with certain States not intending to become parties to either of the above-mentioned conventions, with a view to examining the possibility of concluding bilateral agreements with those States for mutual aid in the event of international child abduction by a parent or close relative.

Within the framework of the draft convention on the rights of the child, Switzerland supports the proposal to grant to a child having parents of different nationalities who are separated the right to maintain personal relations with both.

## (s) Thailand

The Government states that the protection of children and of youth is the responsibility of various governmental organizations. The services provided to disadvantaged children include family assistance, protection measures, adoption arrangements and the promotion of voluntary child welfare institutions.

## (t) Additional reply from Thailand

The Government states that cases of unauthorized removal and retention of children in Thailand are not only the result of conflicts arising between couples of different nationalities, but also of an increasing demand for children for adoption abroad.

It is the Government's view that national legislative measures are not sufficient for control on infringements of the rights and benefits of such children. It therefore suggests that the Commission on Human Rights should take up this problem when drafting the convention on the rights of the child. At the same time, the public should be made aware that a child given for adoption should be provided with the facilities to develop in conditions of freedom and dignity.

## (u) Yugoslavia

According to Yugoslav law parents shall exercise the parental right together and by mutual consent, and in case of disagreement the guardianship authority shall decide. If parents are separated, the parental right shall be exercised by the parent with whom the child lives; in the case of parental disagreement a decision shall be reached by the guardianship authority or in specified cases by the court. Furthermore, if, in case of the separation of parents, dissolution or annulment of their marriage, the child has been entrusted by a court decision or by the decision of any other competent authority to the care and upbringing of one of the parents, that parent shall exercise the parental right.

In exceptional cases Yugoslav laws provide that a child may be removed from a parent by a decision of the guardianship authority, if the child's proper upbringing is seriously threatened. The act of removal of the child in such cases does not imply that any other rights and duties of parents have ceased. Anyone who removes or retains a child not entrusted to him/her would be subject to civil and criminal liability. The penal laws of the Republics and autonomous provinces provide for a specific type of offence (removal of a minor) for which, in cases of unauthorized removal of a minor by a natural parent, adoptive parent, guardian or any other person, the offender may be punished with imprisonment.

# H. 1983

## 1. Report of the Working Group

*The following is taken from document E/CN.4/1983/62 (25 March 1983) (reproduced from documents E/CN.4/1983/L.1 (8 March 1983) and Add.1 (10 March 1983)).*

INTRODUCTION

1.    By resolution 1982/39 of 11 March 1982, the Commission on Human Rights decided to continue at its thirty-ninth session, as a matter of high priority, its work on a draft convention on the rights of the child, with a view to completing the elaboration of the convention at that session for transmission to the General Assembly through the Economic and Social Council. By resolution 1982/37 of 7 May 1982, the Economic and Social Council took note of resolution 1982/39 of the Commission on Human Rights, and authorized the meeting of an open-ended working group for a period of one week prior to the thirty-ninth session of the Commission to facilitate the completion of the work on a draft convention on the rights of the child. At its thirty-seventh session, the General Assembly, by resolution 37/190 of 18 December 1982, welcomed Economic and Social Council resolution 1982/37 and requested the Commission on Human Rights to give the highest priority at its thirty-ninth session to the question of completing the draft convention.

2.    The Working Group held 11 meetings from 24 to 28 January 1983, and on ..... it adopted article 6, paragraphs 3 and 4, part of article 6 bis, 6 ter and article 12, paragraphs 2, 3 and 4. Article 6 quater and 7 bis were considered but not yet adopted. In this connection, it should be recalled that the open-ended working group established prior to previous sessions of the Commission had adopted a number of articles. The text of the articles adopted so far may be found in annex I of the present report.

3.    The proposals submitted at the present session but not considered by the Group may be found in document E/CN.4/WG.1/WP.2, WP.3, WP.4, WP.9, WP.21, WP.26, WP.27, WP.29 and WP.30.

4.    The draft convention submitted by Poland in 1979 (E/CN.4/1349) continued to be used as the basis for the discussions.

5.    At its first meeting on 21 January 1983, Mr. Adam Lopatka was elected Chairman-Rapporteur of the Working Group.

5a.    The meetings of the Working Group, which were open to all members of the Commission on Human Rights, were attended by representatives of the following States: Argentina, Australia, Bangladesh, Brazil, Canada, China, Costa Rica, Cuba, Finland, France, Germany, Federal Republic of, India, Italy, Japan, Netherlands, Nicaragua, Pakistan, Poland, Senegal, the Ukrainian Soviet Socialist Republic, the United Kingdom of Great Britain and Northern Ireland, the Union of Soviet Socialist Republics, the United States of America and Yugoslavia.

The following States, non-members of the Commission on Human Rights, were represented at the meetings of the Working Group by observers: Algeria, Belgium, Denmark, Holy See, the Islamic Republic of Iran, Morocco, Norway, Peru, Sweden, Switzerland and Venezuela.

The United Nations High Commissioner for Refugees and the United Nations Children's Fund, as well as a number of non-governmental organizations, were represented at the Working Group by observers. Amnesty International, the Anti-Slavery Society, the Associated Country Women of the World, the Baha'i International Community, the International Association of Juvenile and Family Court Magistrates, the International Catholic Child Bureau, the International Commission of Jurists, the International Federation of Women in Legal Careers, the International Union for Child Welfare, the Minority Rights Group, Rädda Barnen Sweden and Zonta International sent observers to the Working Group.

DOCUMENTS

6.    The Working Group had before it the following documents:

(a)     E/CN.4/1983/32 and Add.1-4 containing the replies received from Governments with regard to Economic and Social Council resolution 1982/39 of 7 May 1982 entitled "Protection of the rights of children and parents in cases of removal and retention of children". In its resolution the Council, inter alia, invited the Commission on Human Rights, when drafting the convention on the rights of the child, to take into consideration the protection of the rights of the child in cases of unauthorized international removal. It further requested the Secretary-General to consult with Governments on this problem and to report to the Commission on Human Rights at its thirty-ninth session.

(b)     E/CN.4/1982/WG.1/WP.1. Question of a convention on the rights of the child; proposals submitted by non-governmental organizations.

(c)     E/CN.4/1349. Revised draft convention on the rights of the child, submitted by Poland.

(d)     A/C.3/36/6. Status of a draft convention on the rights of the child. Document submitted by Poland.

(e)     E/1982/12/Add.1. Part C. Report of the Commission on Human Rights on its thirty-eighth session.

(f)     E/CN.4/1983/NGO/3. Written statement submitted by the Baha'i International Community, a non-governmental organization in consultative status (category II).

7.     A list of the working papers submitted to the Working Group at the present session may be found in annex [II] to the report.

## 2.   Articles adopted in 1983

*The following is taken from document E/CN.4/1983/62, annex I.*

*Article 6, paragraphs 3 and 4*

3.     A child who is separated from one or both parents has the right to maintain personal relations and direct contacts with both parents on a regular basis, save in exceptional circumstances.

4.     Where such separation results from any action initiated by a State Party, such as the detention, imprisonment, exile, deportation or death (including death arising from any cause while the person is in the custody of the State) of one or both parents or of the child, that State Party shall, upon request, provide the parents, the child or, if appropriate, another member of the family with essential information concerning the whereabouts of the absent member(s) of the family unless the provision of the information would be detrimental to the well-being of the child. States Parties shall further ensure that the submission of such a request shall of itself entail no adverse consequences for the person(s) concerned.

*Article 6 bis*

2.     In accordance with the obligation of States Parties under article 6 (2), applications by a child or his parents to enter or leave a State Party for the purpose of family reunification shall be dealt with by States Parties in a positive, humane and expeditious manner.

3.     A child whose parents reside in different States shall have the right to maintain on a regular basis save in exceptional circumstances personal relations and direct contacts with both parents.

*Article 6 ter*

1.     The States Parties to the present Convention shall take appropriate measures to combat the illicit transfer and non-return of children abroad.

2.     To this end, the States Parties shall promote the conclusion of bilateral or multilateral agreements or accession to existing agreements, as well as the introduction of periodic consultations between the competent national authorities.

2.      The States Parties to the present Convention recognize the right of the disabled child to special care and shall encourage and ensure the extension, subject to available resources, to the eligible child and those responsible for his care, of assistance for which application is made and which is appropriate to the child's condition and to the circumstances of the parents or others caring for the child.

3.      Recognizing the special needs of a disabled child, assistance extended in accordance with para. 2 shall be provided free of charge, whenever possible, taking into account the financial resources of the parents or others caring for the child, and shall be designed to ensure that the disabled child has effective access to and receives education, training, health-care services, rehabilitation services, preparation for employment and recreation opportunities in a manner conducive to the child's achieving the fullest possible social integration and individual development, including his cultural and spiritual development.

4.      States Parties shall promote in the spirit of international cooperation the exchange of appropriate information in the field of preventive health care and of medical, psychological and functional treatment of disabled children, including dissemination of and access to information concerning methods of rehabilitation, education and vocational services, with the aim of enabling States Parties to improve their capabilities and skills and to widen their experience in these areas. In this regard, particular account shall be taken of the needs of developing countries.

## 3.      Draft resolution on the "Question of a convention on the rights of the child"

*The following is taken from document E/CN.4/1983/L.51 (25 February 1983).*

Argentina, Australia, Bangladesh, Bulgaria, Byelorussian SSR, Canada, China, Cuba, Czechoslovakia, France, Ghana, Islamic Republic of Iran, Italy, Libyan Arab Jamahiriya, Netherlands, Mexico, Mozambique, Nicaragua, Peru, Philippines, Poland, Syrian Arab Republic, Ukrainian SSR, USSR, Yugoslavia, Zimbabwe: draft resolution

*The Commission on Human Rights,*

*Bearing in mind* the draft convention on the rights of the child submitted by Poland on 7 February 1978, the amended version of the draft submitted on 5 October 1979 to the Commission on Human Rights and the document (A/C.3/36/6) submitted on 7 October by Poland to the General Assembly at its thirty-sixth session,

*Recalling* General Assembly resolutions 33/166 of 20 December 1978, 34/4 of 18 October 1979, 35/131 of 11 December 1980, 36/57 of 25 November 1981 and 37/190 of 18 December 1982, by which the Assembly requested the Commission on Human rights to continue to give the highest priority to the question of completing the draft convention on the rights of the child,

*Recalling also* its resolutions 20 (XXXIV) of 8 March 1978, 19 (XXXV) of 14 March 1979, 36 (XXXVI) of 12 March 1980, 26 (XXXVII) of 10 March and 1982/39 of 11 March 1982, Economic and Social Council decisions 180/138 of 2 May 1980 and 1981/144 of 8 May 1981 as well as Council resolutions 1978/18 of 5 May 1978, 1978/40 of 1 August 1978 and 1982/37 of 7 May 1982, by which it authorized a meeting of an open-ended working group for a period of one week prior to the thirty-ninth session of the Commission to facilitate the completion of the work on the draft convention on the rights of the child,

*Noting* further progress made by the open-ended working group during its one-week meeting prior to the thirty-ninth session of the Commission,

*Noting also* the widespread interest in working out a comprehensive international convention on the rights of the child displayed by numerous Governments and international organizations,

1.        *Decides* to continue at its fortieth session, as a matter of the highest priority, its work on the elaboration of the convention on the rights of the child, with a view to completing its draft at that session for transmission, through the Economic and Social Council, to the General Assembly;

2.        *Requests* the Economic and Social Council to authorize a one-week session of an open-ended working group prior to the fortieth session of the Commission on Human Rights to facilitate and speed up completion of the work on a draft convention on the rights of the child;

3.        *Recommends* that the Economic and Social Council adopt the following resolution:

"*The Economic and Social Council,*

*Recalling* General Assembly resolution 37/190 of 18 December 1982, by which the General Assembly requested the Commission on Human Rights to continue to give the highest priority at its thirty-ninth session to the question of completing the draft convention on the rights of the child and Economic and Social Council resolution 1982/37 of 7 May 1982, by which it authorized a meeting of an open-ended working group for a period of one week prior to the thirty-ninth session of the Commission to facilitate the completion of the work on the draft convention on the rights of the child,

*Considering* that it was not found possible to complete the work on drafting the convention during the thirty-ninth session of the Commission,

*Taking* note of the Commission on Human Rights resolution 1983/.. of... March 1983,

1.        *Authorizes* a meeting of an open-ended working group for a period of one week prior to the fortieth session of the Commission on Human Rights to facilitate and speed up the completion of the work on a draft convention on the rights of the child;

2.        *Requests* the Secretary-General to transmit documents relating to the draft convention on the rights of the child to the Commission on Human Rights at its fortieth session and to extend all the facilities to the open-ended working group during its meeting prior to the fortieth session of the Commission.

## 4.    Administrative and budget implications

*The following is taken from document E/CN.4/1983/L.52 (28 February 1983).*

QUESTION OF A CONVENTION ON THE RIGHTS OF THE CHILD (agenda item 13)

*Administrative and programme budget implications of the draft resolution contained in document E/CN.4/1983/L.51*

Statement submitted by the Secretary-General in accordance with rule 28 of the rules of procedure of the functional commissions of the Economic and Social Council

1.        By paragraph 1 of the draft resolution contained in document E/CN.4/1983/L.51 the Commission would recommend the Economic and Social Council to authorize a one-week session of an open-ended working group prior to the fortieth session of the Commission on Human Rights to facilitate and speed up completion of the work on a draft convention on the rights of the child.

2.        The relevant conference servicing requirements in 1984 under section 29B (Conference Services, Geneva) are estimated on a full-cost basis at $57,700.

## 5.    Discussion in the Commission on Human Rights on 10 and 11 March 1983

*The following is taken from document E/CN.4/1983/SR.56 (16 March 1983).*

QUESTION OF A CONVENTION ON THE RIGHTS OF THE CHILD (agenda item 13) (E/CN.4/1983/L.51, L.52)

64.     Mr. KALINOWSKI (Poland), speaking on behalf of the 26 sponsors, introduced draft resolution E/CN.4/1983/L.51, concerning the question of a convention on the rights of the child. The preamble referred to the action taken so far by the Commission, the Economic and Social Council and the General Assembly, more particularly resolution 37/190, in which the Assembly had requested the Commission to continue to give the highest priority to the question of completing the draft convention. The preambular part also noted the progress made by the open-ended Working Group during its one-week meeting prior to the thirty-ninth session of the Commission and the widespread interest displayed by numerous Governments and international organizations.

65.     In the operative part, the Commission decided to continue at its fortieth session the work on the elaboration of the convention and requested the Economic and Social Council to authorize a one-week session of the open-ended Working Group beforehand. For that reason, a draft recommendation intended for the Economic and Social Council was attached to the draft resolution.

66.     There was no longer any need to underscore the importance of elaborating a convention on the rights of the child, but he did wish to point out that, in a report entitled "The State of the World's Children 1982-83", the Executive Director of UNICEF noted a slowdown in progress towards protecting the lives of children.

67.     Convinced that an international instrument such as the convention on the rights of the child could considerably foster the political will so necessary for better protection of such a vulnerable group, his delegation found it extremely gratifying that the initiative commanded increasing support from the members of the Commission and from other organs of the United Nations; proof of that lay in the lengthy list of delegations acting as sponsors of draft resolution E/CN.4/1983/L.51, since they were from all geographical regions and represented very different social and political systems. It was to be hoped that the Commission would adopt the draft resolution by consensus.

68.     The CHAIRMAN [Mr. OTUNNU (Uganda)] announced that the delegations of Bolivia, Colombia, India, Senegal and Togo had become sponsors of draft resolution E/CN.4/1983/L.51.

69.     Mr. COLLIARD (France) expressed the great satisfaction with which his delegation had welcomed Economic and Social Council resolution 1982/32 on protection of the rights of children in cases of removal or retention of children, a situation which involved dramatic human aspects. It was gratifying to see the considerable progress achieved in the course of the present session by the open-ended Working Group on the elaboration of the convention on the rights of the child, and he paid tribute to the Polish delegation, which had played such an important role in that work.

70.     It should be noted that consideration of the international aspects of the interests of children, an innovative idea in the draft convention, would be effective only when States engaged in cooperation by means of international conventions.

71.     Again, his delegation took the view that special attention should be paid to the reports on the exploitation of child labour prepared by Mr. Bouhdiba; the dangers of the exploitation of children could not be minimized and involved problems that were often dramatic, something the Commission had acknowledged when, at its thirty-eighth session, it had adopted resolution 82/21 without a vote.

72.     Draft resolution E/CN.4/1983/L.51 was adopted without a vote.

73.     In reply to a question by Mr. CALERO RODRIGUES (Brazil), Mr. NYAMEKYE (Deputy Director, Centre for Human Rights) said that the services provided by the Conference Services Division did not differ according to whether working groups met before or during the Commission's sessions, for which reason the costs indicated for the meetings of the Working Group on Minorities, which would be meeting during the next session, were identical to those of the meetings of the Working Group on the elaboration of a convention on the rights of a child. which would be held before the session.

*The following is taken from document E/CN.4/1983/SR.58 (21 March 1983).*

QUESTION OF A CONVENTION ON THE RIGHTS OF THE CHILD (agenda item 13) (continued) (E/CN.4/1983/L.1 and Add.1)

1.        Mr. THWAITES (Australia) thanked the Working Group on the question of a convention on the rights of the child for its report (E/CN.4/1983/L.1 and Add.1), which the Chairman-Rapporteur was unfortunately not able to introduce at the meeting.

2.        He had some reservations concerning the way in which the report had been prepared. Firstly, the separate presentation of the summary of the discussions and of the proposals was in practice a source of repetition and confusions and reduced the report's usefulness. Secondly, the document, was unduly brief; it would be preferable to model the next report on the report of the Working Group on a draft convention against torture (E/CN.4/1983/L.2), which was closer to meeting the requirements. He was sure that, at its next session, the Commission would be provided with an even better report on the question concerned.

3.        Mr. PACE (Secretary of the Commission) said that some errors had unfortunately crept into the text of the report. In particular two paragraphs were missing from article 12 in certain languages. The document would be issued in final form at a later date and the current imperfections would be corrected at that time.

4.        The CHAIRMAN [Mr. OTUNNU (Uganda)] suggested that the Commission should take note of the report of the Working Group on the question of a convention on the rights of the child (E/CN.4/1983/L.1 and Add.1).

5.        It was so decided.


## 6.    Commission on Human Rights resolution 1983/52 on the "Question of a convention on the rights of the child" adopted on 10 March 1983

*The Commission on Human Rights,*

*Bearing in mind* the draft convention on the rights of the child submitted by Poland on 7 February 1978, the amended version of the draft submitted on 5 October 1979 to the Commission on Human Rights and the document submitted on 7 October 1981 by Poland to the General Assembly at its thirty-sixth session,

*Recalling* General Assembly resolutions 33/166 of 20 December 1978, 34/4 of 18 October 1979, 35/131 of 11 December 1980, 36/57 of 25 November 1981 and 37/190 of 18 December 1982, by which the Assembly requested the Commission on Human Rights to continue to give the highest priority to the question of completing the draft convention on the rights of the child,

*Recalling also* its resolutions 20 (XXXIV) of 8 March 1978, 19 (XXXV) of 14 March 1979, 36 (XXXVI) of 12 March 1980, 26 (XXXVII) of 10 March 1981 and 1982/39 of 11 March 1982, and Economic and Social Council decisions 1980/138 of 2 May 1980 and 1981/144 of 8 May 1981 and resolutions 1978/18 of 5 May 1978, 1978/40 of 1 August 1978 and 1982/37 of 7 May 1982, by which it authorized a meeting of an open-ended working group for a period of one week prior to the thirty-ninth session of the Commission to facilitate the completion of the work on the draft convention on the rights of the child,

*Noting* the further progress made by the open-ended working group during its one-week meeting prior to the thirty-ninth session of the Commission,

*Noting also* the widespread interest in working out a comprehensive international convention on the rights of the child displayed by numerous Governments and international organizations,

1.        *Decides* to continue at its fortieth session, as a matter of the highest priority, its work on the elaboration of the draft convention on the rights of the child, with a view to completing the draft at that session for transmission, through the Economic and Social Council, to the General Assembly;

2.    *Requests* the Economic and Social Council to authorize a one-week session of an open-ended working group prior to the fortieth session of the Commission on Human Rights to facilitate and speed up completion of the work on a draft convention on the rights of the child;

3.    *Recommends* the following draft resolution to the Economic and Social Council for adoption:

"*The Economic and Social Council*,

*Recalling* General Assembly resolution 37/190 of 18 December 1982, by which the General Assembly requested the Commission on Human Rights to continue to give the highest priority at its thirty-ninth session to the question of completing the draft convention on the rights of the child, and Economic and Social Council resolution 1982/37 of 7 May 1982, by which the Council authorized a meeting of an open-ended working group for a period of one week prior to the thirty-ninth session of the Commission to facilitate the completion of the work on the draft convention on the rights of the child,

*Considering* that it was not found possible to complete the work on drafting the convention during the thirty-ninth session of the Commission,

*Taking note* of the Commission on Human Rights resolution 1983/52 of 10 March 1983,

1.    *Authorizes* a meeting of an open-ended working group for a period of one week prior to the fortieth session of the Commission on Human Rights to facilitate and speed up the completion of the work on a draft convention on the rights of the child;

2.    *Requests* the Secretary-General to transmit documents relating to the draft convention on the rights of the child to the Commission on Human Rights at its fortieth session and to extend all facilities to the open-ended working group during its meeting prior to the fortieth session of the Commission.

## 7.    Economic and Social Council resolution 1983/39 on the "Question of a convention on the rights of the child" adopted on 27 May 1983

*The Economic and Social Council*,

*Recalling* General Assembly resolution 37/190 of 18 December 1982, by which the Assembly requested the Commission on Human Rights to continue to give the highest priority at its thirty-ninth session to the question of completing the draft convention on the rights of the child, and Economic and Social Council resolution 1982/37 of 7 May 1982, by which the Council authorized a meeting of an open-ended working group for a period of one week prior to the thirty-ninth session of the Commission to facilitate the completion of the work on the draft convention on the rights of the child,

*Considering* that it was not found possible to complete the work on the draft convention during the thirty-ninth session of the Commission,

*Taking note* of Commission on Human Rights resolution 1983/52 of 10 March 1983,

1.    *Authorizes* a meeting of an open-ended working group for a period of one week prior to the fortieth session of the Commission on Human Rights to facilitate and speed up the completion of the work on a draft convention on the rights of the child;

2.    *Requests* the Secretary-General to transmit documents relating to the draft convention on the rights of the child to the Commission on Human Rights at its fortieth session and to extend all facilities to the open-ended working group during its meeting prior to the fortieth session of the Commission.

*15th plenary meeting*
*27 May 1983*

## 8. General Assembly resolution 38/114 on the "Question of a convention on the rights of the child" adopted on 16 December 1983

*The General Assembly,*

*Recalling* its resolutions 33/166 or 20 December 1978, 34/4 of 18 October 1979, 35/131 or I I December 1980, 36/57 of 25 November 1981 and 37/190 of 18 December 1982,

*Recalling* also Commission on Human Rights resolutions 20 (XXXIV) of 8 March 1978, 19 (XXXV) of 14 March 1979, 36 (XXXVI) of 12 March 1980, 26 (XXXVII) of 10 March 1981, 1982/39 of 11 March 1982 and 1983/52 of 10 March 1983 as well as Economic and Social Council resolutions 1978/18 of 5 May 1978, 1978/40 of 1 August 1978, 1982/37 of 7 May 1982 and 1983/39 of 27 May 1983 and Council decisions 1980/138 of 2 May 1980 and 1981/144 of 8 May 1981,

*Bearing in mind* that children's rights are basic human rights and call for continuous improvement of the situation of children all over the world, as well as their development and education in conditions of peace,

*Mindful* of the need to keep up the momentum of positive action for the sake of children generated by the International Year of the Child,

*Noting* the important role of the United Nations Children's Fund and the United Nations in promoting the well-being of children and their development,

*Aware* of the importance of an international convention on the rights of the child for a more effective protection of children's rights, as well as of the widespread interest in the elaboration of such an international instrument displayed by a growing number of Governments and international organizations,

*Considering* that the year 1984 will mark the twenty-fifth anniversary of the Declaration of the Rights of the Child,

*Reaffirming* that mankind owes to the child the best it has to give,

*Noting with appreciation* that further progress was made in the elaboration of a draft convention on the rights of the child prior to and during the thirty-ninth session of the Commission on Human Rights,

1.      *Welcomes* Economic and Social Council resolution 1983/39, in which the Council authorized a meeting of an open-ended working group of the Commission on Human Rights for a period of one week prior to the fortieth session of the Commission to facilitate and speed up the completion of the work on a draft convention on the rights of the child;

2.      *Requests* the Commission on Human Rights to give the highest priority at its fortieth session to the question of completing the draft convention and to make every effort to submit it, through the Economic and Social Council, to the General Assembly at its thirty-ninth session, as the Commission's tangible contribution to the commemoration of the twenty-fifth anniversary of the Declaration of the Rights of the Child;

3.      *Invites* all Member States to offer their effective contribution to the completion without delay of the draft convention on the rights of the child;

4.      *Requests* the Secretary-General to provide all necessary assistance to the working group to ensure its smooth and efficient work;

5.      *Decides* to include in the provisional agenda of its thirty-ninth session the item entitled "Question of a convention on the rights of the child".

*100th plenary meeting*
*16 December 1983*

# I. 1984

## 1. Report of the Working Group

*The following is taken from document E/CN.4/1984/71 (23 February 1984) (reproduced from document E/CN.4/1984/L.1).*

INTRODUCTION

1.      The Commission on Human Rights, by resolution 1983/52 of 10 March 1983, decided to continue its work on the elaboration of a draft convention on the rights of the child at its fortieth session, as a matter of the highest priority. The Commission also requested the Economic and Social Council to authorize a one-week session of a open-ended working group prior to the fortieth session of the Commission to facilitate and speed up the completion of the work on a draft convention on the rights of the child. This request was approved by Economic and Social Council resolution 1983/39 of 27 May 1983. At its thirty-eighth session, the General Assembly, by resolution 38/114 of 16 December 1983, requested the Commission on Human Rights to give the highest priority at its fortieth session to the question of completing the draft convention and to make every effort to submit it, through the Economic and Social Council, to the General Assembly at its thirty-ninth session, as the Commission's tangible contribution to the commemoration of the twenty-fifth anniversary of the Declaration of the Rights of the Child.

2.      The Working Group held 11 meetings from 30 January to 3 February, and on 2 March 1984. It adopted articles 7 bis, 8 bis, 9 and 13. In this connection, it should be recalled that the open-ended working group established prior to and during previous sessions of the Commission had adopted a number of articles. The text of the articles adopted so far may be found in annex I to the present report. During the session, representatives of States proposed draft articles and amendments which were not discussed by the Working Group for lack of time, and which appear in annex II to the present report.

ELECTIONS

3.      At the first meeting of the pre-sessional working group, on 30 January 1983, Professor Adam Lopatka (Poland) was elected Chairman-Rapporteur by acclamation.

PARTICIPATION

4.      The meetings of the Working Group, which were open to all members of the Commission on Human Rights, were attended by representatives of the following States: Argentina, Brazil, Bulgaria, Canada, China, Cuba, Cyprus, Finland, France, German Democratic Republic, Germany, Federal Republic of, India, Italy, Japan, Netherlands, Spain, the Ukrainian Soviet Socialist Republic, the Union of Soviet Socialist Republics, the United Kingdom of Great Britain and Northern Ireland and the United States of America.

5.      The following States, non-members of the Commission on Human Rights, were represented at the meetings of the Working Group by observers: Australia, Denmark, Greece, Holy See, the Islamic Republic of Iran, Lebanon, Morocco, Norway, Peru, Poland, Switzerland and Venezuela.

6.      The International Labour Office and the United Nations Children's Fund were represented at the Working Group by observers.

7.      The following, non-governmental organizations sent observers to the Working Group: Amnesty International, Baha'i International Community, Defence for Children International Movement, Friends World Committee for Consultation, Human Rights Internet, International Association of Juvenile and Family Court Magistrates, International Catholic Child Bureau, International Commission of Jurists, International Federation of Women in Legal Careers, International Social Service, International Union for Child Welfare, Minority Rights Group, Rädda Barnen International and Zonta International.

DOCUMENTS

8.      The Working Group had before it a number of documents including the report of the working group on a draft convention on the rights of the child to the Commission on Human Rights at its thirty-ninth session

(E/CN.4/1983/62), the document submitted by Poland on the status of a draft convention on the rights of the child (A/C.3/36/6), amendments submitted by the delegation of the United States of America (E/CN.4/1983/WG.1/WP.3, WP.4 and WP.8), a proposal by the Union of Soviet Socialist Republics (E/CN.4/1983/WG.1/WP.7), a proposal submitted by Canada (E/CN.4/1983/WG.1/WP.9), a proposal submitted by Poland (E/CN.4/1983/WG.1/WP.10), a proposal submitted by Belgium (E/CN.4/1983/WG.1/WP.21), new proposals presented by Canada (E/CN.4/1983/WG.1/WP.26), and proposals by Algeria (E/CN.4/1983/WG.1/WP.27).

GENERAL CONSIDERATIONS

9.      The representative of the United Kingdom stated that, even as a State participating in the work of the open-ended Working Group, his delegation continued to have difficulties with some of the articles already adopted (e.g. articles 2, paragraph 1, 3, paragraph 1, 4, paragraph 1, 6 and 8, paragraphs 1 and 2). Article 2, paragraphs 1 and 2, caused difficulties in relation to United Kingdom nationality law. Article 6, paragraph 1, as currently drafted was not compatible with United Kingdom immigration legislation because the parents of a child who did not have rights of residence in the United Kingdom could not determine that he should live there unless he qualified for residence under United Kingdom immigration rules. In addition, draft articles 3, paragraph 1, 4, paragraph 1, 6, paragraphs 2 and 3, 6 bis, paragraphs 2 and 3, and 8, paragraphs 1 and 2, all posed problems in relation to United Kingdom immigration law. Certain of those draft provisions were difficult or even impossible to reconcile with his country's law and practice. Nevertheless, his delegation had joined the consensus at the Working Group in recognition of the efforts made by other delegations to get an acceptable draft completed and available for comment by Member States with as little delay as possible. However, the United Kingdom thought it important that all States, including those which had not participated in the Working Group, should have an opportunity to consider and comment on those articles after the current drafting exercise was concluded. If, after the drafting was completed and notwithstanding that certain parts of the text remained substantially as they were now, the United Kingdom authorities were nevertheless to consider that they could proceed to signature and ratification, his delegation foresaw that there would be a need to enter reservations and declarations, in particular to deal with the aforementioned difficulties over immigration and nationality.

10.      The Netherlands delegation believed that a convention on the rights of the child would only be effective if it were broadly acceptable to a large number of States. It was therefore considered important that all States should have an opportunity to comment on the Working Group's draft before it was submitted to the Commission on Human Rights for finalization. Accordingly, the Netherlands delegation supported the United Kingdom's proposal to that end.

11.      The representative of the Federal Republic of Germany stated that his delegation shared the concerns of the United Kingdom delegation particularly with regard to article 2, paragraph 2, and article 6, paragraphs 1 and 2. Article 2, paragraph 2, posed problems with regard to his country's nationality law. As in the case of the United Kingdom, the provisions of draft article 6, paragraphs 1 and 2, were not compatible with the Federal Republic's immigration legislation. Should article 2, paragraph 2, and article 6, paragraphs 1 and 2, be retained in their present form during the forthcoming deliberations in spite of the concerns of some delegations, and should the draft convention be opened for signature and ratification in that form, his Government might feel obliged to enter reservations to both articles. The representative of the Federal Republic of Germany also expressed his support for the United Kingdom proposal that all States be given an opportunity to comment on the Working Group's completed draft before its submission to the Commission on Human Rights.

12.      The Japanese delegation asked whether, for the purposes of article 1 of the draft convention, an 18-year-old human being was to be considered a child.

## 2.  Articles adopted in 1984

*The following is taken from document E/CN.4/1984/71, annex I.*

*Article 7 bis*

1.      The States Parties to the present Convention shall respect the right of the child to freedom of thought, conscience and religion.

2.      This right shall include in particular the freedom to have or to adopt a religion or whatsoever belief of his choice and freedom, either individually or in community with others and in public or private, to manifest his religion or belief, subject only to such limitations as are prescribed by law and are necessary to protect public safety, order, health and morals, and the right to have access to education in the matter of religion or belief.

3.      The States Parties shall respect the rights and duties of the parents and, where applicable, legal guardians, to provide direction to the child in the exercise of his right in a manner consistent with the evolving capacities of the child.

4.      The States Parties shall equally respect the liberty of the child and his parents and, where applicable, legal guardians, to ensure the religious and moral education of the child in conformity with convictions of their choice.

*Article 8 bis*

1.      The States Parties to the present Convention shall take all appropriate legislative, administrative, social and educational measures to protect the child from all forms of physical or mental injury or abuse, neglect or negligent treatment, maltreatment or exploitation including sexual abuse, while in the care of parents, legal guardians or any other person who has the care of the child.

2.      Such protective measures should, as appropriate, include effective procedures for the establishment of social programmes to provide necessary support for the child and for those who have the care of the child, as well as for other forms of prevention and for identification, reporting, referral, investigation, treatment, and follow-up of instances of child maltreatment described heretofore, and, as appropriate, for judicial involvement.

*Article 9*

The States Parties to the present Convention recognize the important function performed by the mass media and shall ensure that the child has access to information and material from a diversity of national and international sources, including those aimed at the promoting of his social, spiritual and moral well-being and physical and mental health. To this end the States Parties shall:

(a)      Encourage the mass media agencies to disseminate information and material of social and cultural benefit to the child and in accordance with the spirit of article 16;

(b)      Encourage international cooperation in the production, exchange and dissemination of such information and material from a diversity of cultural, national and international sources;

(c)      Encourage the mass media agencies to have particular regard to the linguistic needs of the child who belongs to a minority group or an indigenous population;

(d)      Encourage the development of appropriate guidelines for the protection of the child from information and material potentially injurious to his well-being bearing in mind the provisions of article 8.

*Article 13*

1.      The States Parties to the present Convention shall, in a manner appropriate to national conditions, recognize for every child the right to benefit from social security and shall take the necessary measures to achieve the full realization of this right.

2.      The benefits should, where appropriate, be granted taking into account the national resources available and the resources and the circumstances of the child and persons having responsibility for the maintenance of the child as well as any other consideration relevant to an application for benefits made by or on behalf of the child.

## 3.   Draft resolution on the "Question of a convention on the rights of the child"

*The following is taken from document E/CN.4/1984/L.68 (6 March 1984).*

Afghanistan, Algeria, Argentina, Bangladesh, Bulgaria, Byelorussian Soviet Socialist Republic, Cameroon, China, Colombia, Congo, Costa Rica, Cuba, Cyprus, Czechoslovakia, Ecuador, Egypt, Hungary, France, Gambia, German Democratic Republic, India, Iran, Islamic Republic of, Iraq, Jordan, Libyan Arab Jamahiriya, Mauritania, Mexico, Mongolia, Mozambique, New Zealand, Nicaragua, Nigeria, Pakistan, Peru, Philippines, Poland, Rwanda, Senegal, Spain, Sri Lanka, Sudan, Syrian Arab Republic, Togo, Ukrainian Soviet Socialist Republic, Union of Soviet Socialist Republics, United Republic of Tanzania, Uruguay, Venezuela, Viet Nam, Yugoslavia, Zaire and Zimbabwe: draft resolution

*The Commission on Human Rights,*

*Bearing in mind* the draft convention on the rights of the child submitted by Poland on 7 February 1978, the amended version of the draft submitted on 5 October 1979 to the Commission on Human Rights and the document submitted on 7 October 1981 by Poland to the General Assembly at its thirty-sixth session,

*Recalling* General Assembly resolutions 33/166 of 20 December 1978, 34/4 of 18 October 1979, 35/131 of 11 December 1980, 36/57 of 25 November 1981, 37/190 of 18 December 1982 and 38/114 of 16 December 1983, by which the Assembly requested the Commission on Human Rights to give the highest priority to the question of completing the draft convention on the rights of the child,

*Recalling also* its resolutions 20 (XXXIV) of 8 March 1978, 19 (XXXV) of 14 March 1979, 36 (XXXVI) of 12 March 1980, 26 (XXXVII) of 10 March 1981, 1982/39 of 11 March 1982 and 1983/52 of 10 March 1983, and Economic and Social Council decisions 1980/138 of 2 May 1980 and 1981/144 of 8 May 1981 and resolutions 1978/18 of 5 May 1978, 1978/40 of 1 August 1978, 1982/37 of 7 May 1982 and 1983/39 of 27 May 1983, by which it authorized a meeting of an open-ended working group for a period of one week prior to the fortieth session of the Commission to facilitate completion of the work on the draft convention on the rights of the child,

*Mindful* of the General Assembly's request that the highest priority be given to the question of completing the draft convention at the Commissions's fortieth session and that every effort be made to submit it, through the Economic and Social Council, to the General Assembly at its thirty-ninth session, as the Commission's tangible contribution to the commemoration of the twenty-fifth anniversary of the Declaration of the Rights of the Child,

*Aware* that children's rights are basic human rights and call for continuous improvement of the situation of children all over the world as well as their development and education in conditions of peace and security,

*Welcoming* with appreciation the report entitled "The State of the World's Children, 1984" by the Executive Director of the United Nations Children's Fund and his idea of a revolution for children, with a view to promoting and protecting children's rights, life and health,

*Noting* the further progress made by the open-ended working group during its one-week meeting prior to the fortieth session of the Commission,

*Noting also* the growing interest in, and the need to work out, a comprehensive international convention on the rights of the child displayed by numerous Governments and international organization,

1.      *Decides* to continue at its forty-first session, as a matter of the highest priority, its work on the elaboration of the draft convention on the rights of the child, with a view to completing the draft at that session for transmission, through the Economic and Social Council, to the General Assembly;

2.      *Requests* the Economic and Social Council to authorize a one-week session of an open-ended working group prior to the forty-first session of the Commission on Human Rights to facilitate and speed up completion of the work on a draft convention on the rights of the child;

3.      *Recommends* the following draft resolution to the Economic and Social Council for adoption:

"*The Economic and Social Council,*

*Recalling* General Assembly resolution 38/114 of 16 December 1983, by which the General Assembly requested the Commission on Human Rights to give the highest priority at its fortieth session to the question of completing the draft convention on the rights of the child, and Economic and Social Council resolution 1983/39 of 27 May 1983, by which the Council authorized a meeting of an open-ended working group for a period of one week prior to the fortieth session of the Commission to facilitate and speed up the completion of the work on a draft convention on the rights of the child,

*Considering* that it was not found possible to complete the work on the draft convention during the fortieth session of the Commission,

*Taking note* of the Commission on Human Rights resolution 1984/... of ... March 1984,

1.      *Authorizes* a meeting of an open-ended working group for a period of one week prior to the forty-first session of the Commission on Human Rights to facilitate and speed up the completion of the work on a draft convention on the rights of the child;

2.      *Requests* the Secretary-General to transmit documents relating to the draft convention on the rights of the child to the Commission on Human Rights at its forty-first session and to extend all facilities to the open-ended working group during its meeting prior to the forty-first session of the Commission."

## 4.  Administrative and programme budget implications

*The following is taken from document E/CN.4/1984/L.75 (7 March 1984).*

QUESTION OF A CONVENTION ON THE RIGHTS OF THE CHILD (agenda item 13)

*Administrative and programme budget implications of the draft resolution contained in document E/CN.4/1984/L.68*

Statement submitted by the Secretary-General in accordance with rule 28 of the rules of procedure of the functional commissions of the Economic and Social Council

1.      By operative paragraph 3 of the draft resolution contained in document E/CN.4/1984/L.68 the Commission would recommend a draft resolution to the Economic and Social Council in operative paragraph 1 of which the Council would authorize a one-week session of an open-ended working group prior to the forty-first session of the Commission on Human Rights to facilitate and speed up the completion of the work on a draft convention on the rights of the child.

2.      The relevant conference servicing requirements in 1985 under section 29 B, Conference Services Division, Geneva are estimated on a full-cost basis at $59,300.

## 5.  Discussion in the Commission on Human Rights on 8 March 1984

*The following is taken from document E/CN.4/1984/SR.46 (16 March 1984).*

QUESTION OF A CONVENTION ON THE RIGHTS OF THE CHILD (agenda item 13) (E/CN.4/1984/L.1; L.68; L.75)

1.      Mr. LOPATKA (Poland), Chairman-Rapporteur of the Working Group, introducing the report of the Working Group on a convention on the rights of the child (E/CN.4/1984/L.1), said that the Group had met

from 30 January to 3 February, and on 2 March 1984. Although it had unfortunately not been able to complete its work on the draft convention, considerable progress had been made and the Group had adopted articles 7 bis, 8 bis, 9 and 13, which had created difficulties the previous year, by consensus. Despite some divergencies of view, a spirit of understanding and cooperation had enabled the Group to accomplish fruitful work, the results of which were contained in the report.

2.      Mr. KHMEL (Ukrainian Soviet Socialist Republic), speaking on behalf of the sponsors. introduced draft resolution E/CN.4/1984/L.68 on the question of a convention on the rights of the child.

3.      The Working Group had done a great deal of work and had succeeded in making considerable progress in preparing an important document that would lay down international standards designed to promote the welfare of the child. The problem to which draft resolution E/CN.4/1984/L.68 was directed was how to speed up the completion of the work on the convention. He expressed the hope that the draft resolution would be adopted by consensus.

4.      Mr. THWAITES (Australia) said that his delegation endorsed the Working Group's report and also supported draft resolution E/CN.4/1984/L.68. As in previous years, his delegation had participated actively in the work of the Group, in which a most constructive atmosphere had prevailed, enabling it to adopt several important articles of the draft convention. His delegation would continue to approach the Commission's work on the subject with all seriousness and was confident that it could be brought to a successful conclusion in due course.

5.      Mr. COLLIARD (France) said that his delegation welcomed the work done by the Working Group and appreciated the spirit of cooperation which had prevailed.

6.      Miss CAMBY (France), continuing the French delegation's statement, said that France had always been keenly interested in the deliberations of the Working Group and considered that the Group had achieved fruitful results.

7.      At the current session, her delegation had drawn particular attention to the serious problem of transferring children from one place to another and the need to ensure effective protection in that field. The subjects considered by the Group in 1984 - the right to freedom of religion and freedom of information, and the right to receive social benefits and protection against maltreatment - were of primary importance. Her delegation was pleased to note that progress had been made to those areas and welcomed the fact that the discussions had made it possible to bring the views of delegations closer, thus enabling States to define the minimum common principles which would place them in a better position in the future to ensure respect for the rights of the child. By giving those rights the character of fundamental principles and by placing them in an international framework, the future convention should promote cooperation among States, without which protection of the rights of the child could not be fully effective. To that end, her delegation endorsed the general recommendation in the draft convention that States should conclude international conventions on the subject.

8.      Mr. BUCKINGHAM (Canada) said that his delegation would support draft resolution E/CN.4/1984/L.68. He expressed his delegation's appreciation of the excellent quality of the Working Group's report.

9.      Mr. ADAMS (United Kingdom) noted that several important articles had been adopted by the Working Group and said that a major reason was probably the spirit of cooperation and compromise which had prevailed. His delegation welcomed the report of the Working Group and assured the Commission of its continued interest in the subject. It looked forward to participating in the work of the Group in 1985.

10.      Mr. KUMAR (India) congratulated the Working Group on the considerable progress it had made towards the completion of work on the draft convention, and urged all delegations to make every effort to finalize the text. India supported draft resolution E/CN.4/1984/L.68.

11.      Mr. RICHTER (German Democratic Republic) said that his delegation joined others which had stressed the successful results achieved by the Working Group. It endorsed the Working Group's report and hoped that draft resolution E/CN.4/1984/L.68 would be adopted by consensus.

12.     The CHAIRMAN [Mr. KOOIJMANS (Netherlands)] said that if there was no objection, he would take it that the Commission wished to adopt draft resolution E/CN.4/1984/L.68 without a vote.

13.     *It was so decided.*

## 6.   Commission on Human Rights resolution 1984/24 on the "Question of a convention on the rights of the child" adopted without a vote on 8 March 1984

*The Commission on Human Rights,*

*Bearing in mind* the draft convention on the rights of the child submitted by Poland to the Commission on Human Rights on 7 February 1978, the amended version of the draft submitted to the Commission on 5 October 1979 and the document submitted by Poland to the General Assembly at its thirty-sixth session. on 7 October 1981,

*Recalling* General Assembly resolutions 33/166 of 2 December 1978, 34/4 of 18 October 1979, 35/131 of 11 December 1980, 36/57 of 25 November 1981, 37/190 of 18 December 1982 and 38/114 of 16 December 1983, by which the Assembly requested the Commission on Human Rights to give the highest priority to the question of completing the draft convention on the rights of the child,

*Recalling also* its resolutions 20 (XXXIV) of 8 March 1978, 19 (XXXV) of 14 March 1979, 36 (XXXVI) of 12 March 1980, 26 (XXXVII) of 10 March 1981, 1982/39 of 11 March 1982 and 1983/52 of 10 March 1983, and Economic and Social Council decisions 1980/138 of 2 May 1980 and 1981/144 of 8 May 1981 and resolutions 1978/18 of 5 May 1978, 1978/40 of 1 August 1978, 1982/37 of 7 May 1982 and 1983/39 of 27 May 1983, by which it authorized a meeting of an open-ended working group for a period of one week prior to the fortieth session of the Commission to facilitate the completion of the work on the draft convention on the rights of the child,

*Mindful* of the General Assembly's request that the highest priority be given to the question of completing the draft convention at the Commission's fortieth session and that every effort be made to submit it, through the Economic and Social Council, to the General Assembly at its thirty-ninth session, as the Commission's tangible contribution to the commemoration of the twenty-fifth anniversary of the Declaration of the Rights of the Child,

*Aware* that children's rights are basic human rights and call for continuous improvement of the situation of children all over the world as well as their development and education in conditions of peace and security,

*Welcoming with appreciation* the report entitled *The State of the World's Children - 1984* by the Executive Director of the United Nations Children's Fund and his idea of a revolution for children, with a view to promoting and protecting children's rights, life and health,

*Noting* the further progress made by the open-ended working group during its one-week meeting prior to the fortieth session of the Commission,

*Noting also* the growing interest in, and the need to work out, a comprehensive international convention on the rights of the child displayed by numerous Governments and international organizations,

1.     *Decides* to continue at its forty-first session, as a matter of the highest priority, its work on the elaboration of the draft convention on the rights of the child, with a view to completing the draft at that session for transmission, through the Economic and Social Council, to the General Assembly;

2.     *Requests* the Economic and Social Council to authorize a one-week session of an open-ended working group prior to the forty-first session of the Commission on Human Rights to facilitate and speed up completion of the work on a draft convention on the rights of the child;

3.     *Recommends* the following draft resolution to the Economic and Social Council for adoption:

"*The Economic and Social Council,*

*Recalling* General Assembly resolution 38/114 of 16 December 1983, by which the General Assembly requested the Commission on Human Rights to give the highest priority at its fortieth session to the question of completing the draft convention on the rights of the child, and Economic and Social Council resolution 1983/39 of 27 May 1983, by which the Council authorized a meeting of an open-ended working group for a period of one week prior to the fortieth session of the Commission to facilitate and speed up the completion of the work on a draft convention on the rights of the child,

*Considering* that it was not found possible to complete the work on the draft convention during the fortieth session of the Commission,

*Taking note* of Commission on Human Rights resolution 1984/24 of 8 March 1984,

1.      *Authorizes* a meeting of an open-ended working group for a period of one week prior to the forty-first session of the Commission on Human Rights to facilitate and speed up the completion of the work on a draft convention on the rights of the child;

2.      *Requests* the Secretary-General to transmit documents relating to the draft convention on the rights of the child to the Commission on Human Rights at its forty-first session and to extend all facilities to the open-ended working group during its meeting prior to the forty-first session of the Commission."

## 7.     Economic and Social Council resolution 1984/25 on the "Question of a convention on the rights of the child" adopted on 24 May 1984

*The Economic and Social Council,*

*Recalling* General Assembly resolution 38/114 of 16 December 1983, by which the General Assembly requested the Commission on Human Rights to give the highest priority at its fortieth session to the question of completing the draft convention on the rights of the child, and Economic and Social Council resolution 1983/39 of 27 May 1983, by which the Council authorized a meeting of an open-ended working group for a period of one week prior to the fortieth session of the Commission to facilitate and speed up the completion of the work on a draft convention on the rights of the child,

*Considering* that it was not found possible to complete the work on the draft convention during the fortieth session of the Commission,

*Taking note* of Commission on Human Rights resolution 1984/24 of 8 March 1984,

1.      *Authorizes* a meeting of an open-ended working group for a period of one week prior to the forty-first session of the Commission on Human Rights to facilitate and speed up the completion or the work on a draft convention on the rights of the child;

2.      *Requests* the Secretary-General to transmit documents relating to the draft convention on the rights of the child to the Commission an Human Rights at its forty-first session and to extend all facilities to the open-ended working group during the meeting to be held prior to the forty-first session of the Commission.

*20th plenary meeting*
*24 May 1984*

## 8.     General Assembly resolution 39/135 on the "Question of a convention on the rights of the child" adopted on 14 December 1984

*The General Assembly,*

*Recalling* its resolutions 33/166 of 20 December 1978, 34/4 of 18 October 1979, 35/131 of 11 December 1980, 36/57 of 25 November 1981, 37/190 of 18 December 1982 and 38/114 of 16 December 1983,

*Recalling also* Commission on Human Rights resolutions 20 (XXXIV) of 8 March 1978, 19 (XXXV) of 14 March 1979, 36 (XXXVI) of 12 March 1980, 26 (XXXVII) of 10 March 1981, 1982/39 of 11 March 1982, 1983/52 of 10 March 1983 and 1984/24 of 8 March 1984, as well as Economic and Social Council resolutions 1978/18 of 5 May 1978, 1978/40 of 1 August 1978, 1982/37 of 7 May 1982, 1983/39 of 27 May 1983 and 1984/25 of 24 May 1984 and Council decisions 1980/138 of 2 May 1980 and 1981/144 of 8 May 1981,

*Reaffirming* that children's rights are basic human rights and call for continuous improvement of the situation of children all over the world, as well as their development and education in conditions of peace and security,

*Recalling* that the year 1984 marks the twenty-fifth anniversary of the adoption of the Declaration of the Rights of the Child which was proclaimed to the end that the child might have a happy childhood and enjoy for his own good and for the good of society the rights and freedoms set forth therein and be, in all circumstances, among the first to receive protection and relief,

*Aware* of the fact that, twenty-five years after the adoption of the Declaration of the Rights of the Child, the situation of children in many parts of the world still continues to be far from satisfactory,

*Stressing again* the need to keep up the momentum of positive action for the sake of children, generated by the International Year of the Child,

*Mindful* of the important role of the United Nations Children's Fund and the United Nations in promoting the well-being of children and their development,

*Convinced* of the significance of an international convention on the rights of the child as a standard-setting accomplishment of the United Nations, in the fields of social development and human rights, for protecting children's rights and ensuring their well-being,

*Noting with satisfaction* the widespread interest in the elaboration of an international convention on the rights of the child displayed by a great number of Member States, representing all geographical regions and socio-political systems, as well as by international organizations,

*Noting with appreciation* that further progress was made in the elaboration of a draft convention on the rights of the child during the fortieth session of the Commission on Human Rights,

1.      *Stresses* the significance of the twenty-fifth anniversary of the Declaration of the Rights of the Child which has directly stimulated the idea of elaborating an international convention on the rights of the child;

2.      *Welcomes* Economic and Social Council resolution 1984/25, in which the Council authorized a meeting of an open-ended working group of the Commission on Human Rights for a period of one week prior to the forty-first session of the Commission to facilitate and speed up the completion of the work on a draft convention on the rights of the child;

3.      *Requests* the Commission on Human Rights to give the highest priority to this question and to make every effort at its forty-first session to complete the draft convention and to submit it, through the Economic and Social Council, to the General Assembly at its fortieth session;

4.      *Invites* all Member States to offer their effective contribution to the completion of the draft convention on the rights of the child at the forty-first session of the Commission on Human Rights;

5.      *Requests* the Secretary-General to provide all necessary assistance to the working group to ensure its smooth and efficient work in the fulfilment of this important task;

6.      *Decides* to include in the provisional agenda of its fortieth session the item entitled "Question of a convention on the rights of the child".

*101st plenary meeting*
*14 December 1984*

# J. 1985

## 1. Report of the Working Group

*The following is taken from document E/CN.4/1985/64 (reproduced from document E/CN.4/1985/L.1).*

INTRODUCTION

1.        The Commission on Human Rights, by resolution 1984/24 of 8 March, decided to continue at its forty-first session, as a matter of the highest priority, its work on the elaboration of the draft convention on the rights of the child, with a view to completing the draft at that session for transmission, through the Economic and Social Council, to the General Assembly. By resolution 1984/25 of 24 May 1984, the Economic and Social authorized the open-ended working group to meet for a period of one week prior to the Commission's forty-first session to facilitate and speed up the completion of the work on the draft convention. At its thirty-ninth session, the General Assembly, by resolution 39/135 of 14 December 1984, requested the Commission on Human Rights to give the highest priority and undertake every effort at its forty-first session to complete the draft convention and to submit it to the General Assembly at its fortieth session through the Economic and Social Council.

2.        The Working Group held its meetings from 28 January to 1 February, and on 8 March 1985. It adopted articles 12 bis, 14, 15, 16 and 17. In this connection, it should be recalled that the open-ended working group established prior to and during previous sessions of the Commission had adopted a number of articles. The text of the articles adopted so far may be found in annex I to the present report. During the sessions, representatives of States proposed draft articles and amendments which were not discussed by the Working Group for lack of time, and which appear in annex II to the present report.

ELECTIONS

3.        At the first meeting of the pre-sessional working group, on 28 January 1985, Professor Adam Lopatka (Poland) was elected Chairman-Rapporteur by acclamation.

PARTICIPATION

4.        The meetings of the Working Group, which were open to all members of the Commission on Human Rights, were attended by representatives of the following States: Argentina, Australia, Austria, Bangladesh, Brazil, Bulgaria, China, Finland, France, German Democratic Republic, Germany, Federal Republic of, India, Japan, Liberia, Mexico, Netherlands, Nicaragua, Peru, Senegal, Spain, Sri Lanka, the Ukrainian Soviet Socialist Republic, the Union of Soviet Socialist Republics, the United Kingdom of Great Britain and Northern Ireland and the United States of America.

5.        The following States, non-members of the Commission on Human Rights, were represented at the meetings of the Working Group by observers: Algeria, Belgium, Bolivia, Canada, Cuba, Denmark, Egypt, Gabon, Guinea, Haiti, Holy See, Iraq, Italy, Morocco, New Zealand, Norway, Pakistan, Panama, Poland, Sweden, Turkey and Switzerland.

6.        The International Labour Office and the United Nations Children's Fund were represented at the Working Group by observers.

7.        The following non-governmental organizations sent observers to the Working Group: Amnesty International, Baha'i International Community, Defence for Children International Movement, Four Directions Council, Friends World Committee for Consultation, Human Rights Internet, International Abolitionist Federation, International Association of Juvenile and Family Court Magistrates, International Catholic Child Bureau, International Commission of Jurists, International Committee of the Red Cross, International Council of Jewish Women, International Council of Women, International Federation of Women in Legal Careers, International Social Service, International Union for Child Welfare, Rädda Barnen International and Zonta International.

DOCUMENTS

8.　　The Working Group had before it a number of documents including the report of the working group on a draft convention on the rights of the child to the Commission on Human Rights at its fortieth session (E/CN.4/1984/71), comments submitted by the International Labour Office on 30 August 1983 (E/CN.4/1984/WG.1/WP.1), the provisional agenda prepared by the Secretary-General (E/CN.4/1985/WG.1/L.1), and an article-by-article compilation of outstanding proposals by Governments and non-governmental organizations, prepared by the Secretariat (E/CN.4/1985/WG.1/WP.1).

GENERAL CONSIDERATIONS

9.　　The representative of Argentina introduced a new article for consideration by the Working Group at its next session to be held in 1986. He stated that such an article constituted a safeguard to preserve personal, legal and family identity of children throughout the world. The representative of the Netherlands also drew the Working Group's attention to a proposed article relating to children in armed conflicts submitted by the delegations of the Netherlands, Belgium, Finland, Peru, Senegal and Sweden, in order that Governments might review this proposal for discussion at the Group's next session.

10.　　The delegation of Australia indicated that the article-by-article compilation of proposals submitted by Governments and non-governmental organizations, prepared by the Secretariat, had proved very helpful to all delegations, and therefore requested that a similar document be issued in time for delegations to prepare for the next session of the Working Group. The Australian delegation also noted the usefulness of providing, together with the article-by-article compilation of proposals, relevant provisions of other international instruments. These comments were supported by a number of delegations.

## 2.　Articles adopted in 1985

*The following is taken from document E/CN.4/1985/64, annex I.*

*Article 12 bis*

1.　　The States Parties to the present Convention recognize the right of the child to the enjoyment of the highest attainable standard of health and to medical and rehabilitation facilities. The States Parties shall strive to ensure that no child is deprived for financial reasons of his right of access to such health-care services.

2.　　The States Parties to the present Convention shall pursue full implementation of this right and in particular, shall take appropriate measures to:

　　(a)　　Diminish infant and child mortality,

　　(b)　　Ensure the provision of necessary medical assistance and health care to all children with emphasis on the development of primary health care,

　　(c)　　Ensure appropriate health care for expectant mothers,

　　(d)　　Encourage the provision of full and accurate information regarding methods of infant nutrition, including the advantages of breastfeeding,

　　(e)　　Ensure the provision of information and training for parents and children in basic health care, sanitation and prevention of accidents,

　　(f)　　Develop preventive health care and family planning education and services.

3.　　States Parties to the present Convention undertake to promote and encourage international cooperation with a view to achieving progressively the full realization of the right recognized in this article. In this regard, particular account shall be taken of the needs of developing countries.

*Article 13*

1.        The States Parties to the present Convention shall, in a manner appropriate to national conditions, recognize for every child the right to benefit from social security and shall take the necessary measures to achieve the full realization of this right.

2.        The benefits should, where appropriate, be granted taking into account the national resources available and the resources and the circumstances of the child and persons having responsibility for the maintenance of the child as well as any other consideration relevant to an application for benefits made by or on behalf of the child.

*Article 14*

1.        The States Parties to the present Convention recognize the right of every child to a standard of living adequate for the child's physical, mental, spiritual, moral and social development.

2.        The parent(s) or others responsible for the child have the primary responsibility to secure, within their abilities and financial capacities, the conditions of living necessary for the child's development.

3.        The States Parties to the present Convention, in accordance with national conditions and within their means, shall take appropriate measures to assist parents and others responsible for the child to implement this right and shall in case of need provide material assistance and support programmes, particularly with regard to nutrition, clothing and housing.

*Article 15*

1.        The States Parties to the present Convention recognize the right of the child to education and, with a view to achieving the full realization of this right on the basis of equal opportunity, they shall, in particular:

(a)        Make primary education free and compulsory as early as possible,

(b)        Encourage the development of different forms of secondary education systems, both general and vocational, to make them available and accessible to all children, and take appropriate measures such as the introduction of free education and offering financial assistance in case of need,

(c)        Make higher education equally accessible to all on the basis of capacity by every means.

*Article 16*

1.        The States Parties to the present Convention agree that the education of the child shall be directed to:

(a)        The promotion of the development of the child's personality, talents and mental and physical abilities to their fullest potential and the fostering of respect for all human rights and fundamental freedoms.

(b)        The preparation of the child for responsible life in a free society, in the spirit of understanding, peace, tolerance and friendship among all peoples, ethnic and religious groups.

(c)        The development of respect for the natural environment and for the principles of the Charter of the United Nations.

2.        No part of paragraph 1 of this article shall be construed so as to interfere with the liberty of individuals and bodies to establish and direct educational institutions, subject always to the observance of the principles set forth in paragraph 1 and to the requirement that the education given in such institutions shall conform to such minimum standards as may be laid down by the State.

*Article 17*

1. States Parties to the present Convention recognize the right of the child to rest and leisure, to engage in play and recreational activities appropriate to the age of the child and to participate freely in cultural life and the arts.

2. The States Parties to the present Convention shall respect and promote the right of the child to fully participate in cultural and artistic life and shall encourage the provision of appropriate and equal opportunities for cultural, artistic, recreational and leisure activity.

## 3. Draft resolution on the "Question of a convention on the rights of the child"

*The following is taken from document E/CN.4/1985/L.74 (7 March 1985).*

Afghanistan, Algeria, Angola, Argentina, Australia, Bangladesh, Bolivia, Bulgaria, Byelorussian Soviet Socialist Republic, Cameroon, Canada, China, Colombia, Congo, Costa Rica, Cuba, Cyprus, Czechoslovakia, Democratic Yemen, Egypt, Ethiopia, Finland, France, Gabon, Gambia, German Democratic Republic, Hungary, India, Iran, Islamic Republic of, Jordan, Lesotho, Liberia, Libyan Arab Jamahiriya, Mexico, Mongolia, Morocco, Nicaragua, Pakistan, Panama, Peru, Philippines, Poland, Senegal, Spain, Somalia, Sri Lanka, Sudan, Syrian Arab Republic, Tunisia, Ukrainian Soviet Socialist Republic, Union of Soviet Socialist Republics, United Republic of Tanzania, United States of America, Viet Nam and Yugoslavia: draft resolution

*The Commission on Human Rights,*

*Bearing in mind* the draft convention on the rights of the child submitted by Poland to the Commission on Human Rights on 7 February 1978, the amended version of the draft submitted to the Commission on 5 October 1979 and the document submitted by Poland to the General Assembly at its thirty-sixth session, on 7 October 1981,

*Recalling* General Assembly resolutions 33/166 of 20 December 1978, 34/4 of 18 October 1979, 35/131 of 11 December 1980, 36/57 of 25 November 1981, 37/190 of 18 December 1982, 38/114 of 16 December 1985 and 39/135 of 14 December 1984 by which the Assembly requested the Commission on Human Rights to give the highest priority and to make every effort at its forty-first session to complete the draft convention and submit it, through the Economic and Social Council, to the General Assembly at its fortieth session,

*Recalling also* its resolutions 20 (XXXIV) of 8 March 1978, 19 (XXXV) of 14 March 1979, 36 (XXXVI) of 12 March 1980, 26 (XXXVII) of 10 March 1981, 1982/39 of 11 March 1982, 1983/52 of 10 March 1983 and 1984/24 of 8 March 1984, and Economic and Social Council decisions 1980/138 of 2 May 1980 and 1981/144 of 8 May 1981 and resolutions 1978/18 of 5 May 1978, 1978/40 of 1 August 1978, 1982/37 of 7 May 1982, 1983/39 of 27 May 1983 and 1984/25 of 24 May 1984, by which it authorized a meeting of an open-ended working group for a period of one week prior to the forty-first session of the Commission to facilitate and speed up the completion of the work on the draft convention on the rights of the child,

*Aware* of the fact that 25 years after the adoption of the Declaration of the Rights of the Child, the situation of children in many parts of the world still continues to be far from satisfactory, and that the full enjoyment by children of human rights calls for continuous improvement of the situation of children as well as their development and education in conditions of peace and security,

*Stressing* the importance of an international convention on the rights of the child for the effective improvement of the situation of children all over the world,

*Welcoming* the efforts made by the United Nations Children's Fund with a view to promoting and protecting children's rights, life and well-being,

*Noting* the further progress made by the open-ended working group during its one-week meeting prior to the forty-first session of the Commission,

*Noting also* the growing interest in elaborating a comprehensive international convention on the rights of the child displayed by numerous Governments and international organizations,

1.　　*Decides* to continue at its forty-second session, as a matter of the highest priority, its work on the elaboration of the draft convention on the rights of the child, with a view to completing the draft at that session for transmission, through the Economic and Social Council, to the General Assembly;

2.　　*Requests* the Economic and Social Council to authorize a one-week session of an open-ended working group prior to the forty-second session of the Commission on Human Rights with a view to completing the work on the draft convention on the rights of the child at that session;

3.　　*Recommends* the following draft resolution to the Economic and Social Council for adoption:

"*The Economic and Social Council*,

*Recalling* General Assembly resolution 39/135 of 14 December 1984, by which the General Assembly requested the Commission on Human Rights to give the highest priority and to make every effort at its forty-first session to complete the draft convention and to submit it, through the Economic and Social Council, to the General Assembly at its fortieth session,

*Considering* that it was not found possible to complete the work on the draft convention during the forty-first session of the Commission on Human Rights,

*Taking note* of Commission on Human Rights resolution ... of ... March 1985,

1.　　*Authorizes* a meeting of an open-ended working group for a period of one week prior to the forty-second session of the Commission on Human Rights with a view to completing the work on the draft convention on the rights of the child at that session;

2.　　*Requests* the Secretary-General to extend all facilities to the working group for its meeting prior to and during the forty-second session of the Commission to enable it to fulfil its task successfully, and notes the usefulness of providing the working group, in advance of its session, with such working documents as a compilation of all amendments and new proposals and relevant provisions of other international instruments."

## 4.　Administrative and programme budget implications

*The following is taken from document E/CN.4/1985/L.86 (11 March 1985).*

QUESTION OF A CONVENTION ON THE RIGHTS OF THE CHILD (agenda item 13)

*Administrative and programme budget implication of the draft resolution contained in document E/CN.4/1985/L.74*

Statement submitted by the Secretary-General in accordance with rule 28 of the rules of procedure of the functional commissions of the Economic and Social Council

A.　　Request contained in the draft resolution

1.　　By operative paragraph 3 of the draft resolution contained in document E/CN.4/1985/L.74 the Commission would recommend a draft resolution to the Economic and Social Council in operative paragraph 1 of which the Council would authorize a meeting of an open-ended working group for a period of one week prior to the forty-second session of the Commission with a view to completing the work on the draft convention on the rights of the child at that session.

B.　　Relationship of the proposed request to current legislative mandates

2.　　The activities referred to above would fall under chapter 6, II. programme: Centre for Human Rights, subprogramme 2 - Elimination and prevention of discrimination and protection of minorities and vulnerable groups, the objective of and the strategy for which are described in paragraphs 6.25 and 6.27 of the medium-term plan for the period 1984-1989 (A/37/6).

3.      The following programme element of section 23, Human rights, of the programme budget proposed for 1986-1987 would be directly affected by the activities referred to in the draft resolution:

Programme element 2.1 Elimination and prevention of discrimination and protection of minorities and vulnerable groups

Output: (vii) Substantive servicing of the Working Group of the Commission on Human Rights engaged in drafting a convention on the rights of the child.

C.      Activities by which the proposed request would be implemented

4.      In order to determine the financial implications of the decision, it has been noted that the travel expenses of the members concerned will be covered under the normal provision for the attendance of members of the Commission.

D.      Modifications required in the programme of work proposed for 1986-1987

5.      No modifications are required in the approved programme of work for 1986-1987 since the activity appears under programme element 2.1.

E.      Additional requirements at full cost

6.      Conference servicing costs to be financed under section 29B, Conference Services Division, Geneva, calculated on a full cost basis, are estimated at $54,900 for 1986.

## 5.  Discussion in the Commission on Human Rights on 12, 13 and 14 March 1985

*The following is taken from document E/CN.4/1985/SR.53/Add.1 (26 March 1985).*

QUESTION OF A CONVENTION ON THE RIGHTS OF THE CHILD (agenda item 13) (E/CN.4/1985/NGO/24, 41 and 48; E/CN.4/1985/L.1, L.74 and L.86).

108.      Mr. HERNDL (Assistant Secretary-General for Human Rights) introducing the item, recalled that, in opening the session of the Working Group on a draft convention on the rights of the child on 28 January 1985, he had expressed the hope that the commencement of International Youth Year would inspire greater efforts to promote and protect the rights of young people; that inspiring cause must naturally begin with the child. The Declaration of the Rights of the Child, adopted in 1959, had proclaimed that "The child shall enjoy special protection, and shall be given opportunities and facilities, by law and by other means, to enable him to develop physically, mentally, morally, spiritually and socially in a healthy and normal manner and in conditions of freedom and dignity". Since 1978, the Commission had been engaged in drafting a convention on the rights of the child with a view to developing the Declaration and concluding a universal instrument containing binding obligations for States. The Working Group had met for a week prior to the present session and held some meetings during the session. Its report was contained in document E/CN.4/1985/L.1.

109.      The CHAIRMAN [Mr. CHOWDHURY (Bangladesh)] said that Mr. Lopatka, Chairman-Rapporteur of the Working Group on a draft convention on the rights of the child, was respected for the high offices he held in his own country and for the admirable way in which he conducted the deliberations of the Working Group. He invited Mr. Lopatka to introduce the report of the Working Group.

110.      Mr. LOPATKA (Chairman-Rapporteur of the Working Group on a draft convention on the rights of the child) said that, by resolution 1984/24, the Commission had decided to continue, as a matter of the highest priority, its work on the draft convention on the rights of the child. By resolution 1984/25, the Economic and Social Council had authorized the establishment of an informal open-ended Working Group to meet for one week prior to the Commission's forty-first session. The Group had held 10 meetings between 30 January and 8 March 1985, when it had unanimously adopted its report (E/CN.4/1985/L.1).

111.      Unfortunately, the Group had not been able to complete the draft convention. It had adopted five new articles concerning: the right of the child to enjoy the best possible health; the right of all children to an

adequate standard of living; the right of the child to education; the basic goals of the education of children; and the right of the child to rest and leisure. To date, the preamble and 23 articles of the draft convention had been adopted by the Group. A few articles of the operative part remained to be agreed upon; the adoption by the Commission of draft resolution (E/CN.4/1985/L.74) would help the Group carry out its tasks both prior to and during the forty-second session of the Commission.

112.     A spirit of objective cooperation had prevailed in the Working Group, in which all decisions had been taken by consensus. He proposed that the Commission should adopt the Working Group's report without a vote.

113.     Mr. KONATE (Senegal) said that a lengthy period had elapsed between the adoption of the Declaration of the Rights of the Child and the international community's manifestation of a desire to translate the principles contained in the Declaration into legal obligations. The fact that the Working Group had spent several years, trying to draft a convention was admittedly due to certain difficulties. Firstly, the limited number of participating delegations, despite the fact that the Group was open-ended, meant that some of the concerns of most of the countries interested in the issue might be neglected. Secondly, it was difficult to grant rights to a legal category of persons - children - without taking all necessary precautions, namely, by drawing on the traditional and cultural values of the subject's milieu. In the African countries, for example, at what age did one cease to be a child? For that reason, his delegation considered that in relation to article 1 of the draft convention, the age-limit for childhood should be left to national legislation.

114.     The convention must take account of the economic, social and cultural environment of each country; the legal situation of children in developing countries, for example, could not be approached without taking into consideration their wretched living conditions. They were the children of famine, malnutrition and illiteracy, the children of millions of refugees, victims of armed conflict and concentration-camp inmates who were counting on international solidarity to help them out of their desperate situation. The convention was a difficult exercise since it could not satisfactorily reflect the concerns and legislation of every country; but as a common denominator, it should pay particular attention to the millions of children of the Third World and reflect in clear terms the aspirations and tragic situation of the children of armed conflict, the fear of refugees, and the food and sanitary conditions of the unfortunate children in developing countries. Account must also be taken of children in certain developed countries who had become the "new poor" or the "Fourth World". Those disadvantaged children too, were counting on the understanding and aid of the international community.

115.     The crucial question for the peoples of the Third World was what were the rights of the child for developing countries? First of all, what was the significance of the right to leisure to a starving and sick child? The draft convention must specifically affirm the right to life and contain provisions concerning the right of the child to health and to adequate food. Assuming that parents and the community in which the child lived were primarily responsible for him, the drastic economic situation of the developing countries could not be avoided. That would undoubtedly be a source of inspiration for the drafters of the convention, who should consider the need for international solidarity and cooperation to help those countries implement health programmes and overcome their food shortage, estimated at 6 million tons of cereals. The tragedy of Africa was illustrative in that respect. Furthermore, if the objective of the convention was to establish a universal legal framework, that search for universality should take account of the objective condition of the developing countries and their contractual capacity to give effect to the convention.

116.     Secondly, what child could develop while being tormented by the horrors of war? International humanitarian law required the drafters of the convention unequivocally to affirm the child's right not only to enjoy special assistance and protection, but to live in peace.

117.     Thirdly, the convention must at the very least offer child refugees the hope of returning to their families by guaranteeing them adequate assistance. Principle 8 of the Declaration of the Rights of the Child stated that "The child shall in all circumstances be among the first to receive protection and relief"; that was

especially important in cases of mass exodus, periods of emergency, armed conflicts and natural disasters. The convention would certainly be based upon the Geneva Conventions, and especially the Additional Protocols of 1977, stressing the obligation of the parties to conflicts to give aid to children.

118.    A final difficulty concerned politics. Since it was generally admitted, in all systems of education, that children did not engage in politics, the rights granted to them should be less politicized. It was that appeal which Senegal wished to make to the international community and to the Working Group in particular.

119.    Ms. PEARCE (Australia) reiterated her delegation's priority commitment to the satisfactory conclusion of a draft convention on the rights of the child which would recognize the individuality of the child and the prerogatives of the family when establishing standards for national policies and legislation. It was particularly encouraged by the progress made during the latest session of the Working Group, when five articles had been adopted. It was also pleased to note the wider participation of member States in that session, and appreciated and wished to encourage the involvement of non-governmental organizations and specialized agencies in the Group.

120.    The preparation by the Secretariat for the 1985 session of a list of proposed articles to be considered by the Working Group had been greatly appreciated by all parties involved, and her delegation noted the usefulness of such procedural assistance. Her Government would continue its active participation in the Working Group. In particular, at the following session, it would propose the removal of all sexist language from the current draft of the convention - a reflection of her delegation's concern that the rights incorporated should apply equally to every child in every society.

121.    Mr. CLEMENT (France) said that his country had always attached great importance to the Working Group's task of preparing a draft convention on the rights of the child. A spirit of seriousness and cooperation had once again prevailed among the participating delegations and a particularly constructive role had been played by the representatives of Poland and Canada, who had submitted proposals and draft articles. The participation of many non-governmental organizations had also enhanced the debates.

122.    The five articles adopted on first reading touched upon essential aspects of the promotion of the rights of the child. The right to medical services, the right to a standard of living adequate for a child's physical, spiritual and social development, and the right to education and leisure all provided an environment capable of guaranteeing the development of the child, towards which States as well as parents and guardians must strive.

123.    Children were frequently the first victims of the sometimes brutal reality of relationships within the community of nations. In that respect, the fate of children shared between two parents who were separated by a frontier was particularly distressing. Geographical separation drove to despair both children, who needed material and paternal stability, and parents, who were prevented from performing their role. Unfortunately, the current international situation provided tragic examples of that situation, to which the Governments concerned should give serious attention.

124.    His delegation hoped that the efforts of the Working Group to complete the draft convention would soon be successful. In that connection, it had listened with great attention to the statement by the representative of Senegal, who had touched upon some essential issues. His delegation hoped that the Economic and Social Council would authorize the Working Group to continue its work for one week prior to the forty-second session of the Commission, and wished to assure the Group of its continuing active cooperation.

125.    Mrs. KSENTINI (observer for Algeria) noted that the Working Group had made considerable progress and that many articles had already been adopted on first reading. Her delegation, however, was concerned that the main provisions adopted so far in relation to the economic and cultural rights of the child were severely weakened by considerations linked to "availability of resources". Moreover, the provisions of the draft convention were in some respects much weaker than those of other international human rights instruments. Her delegation had on a previous occasion criticized the dichotomy between "rights inherent

in the individual", which by their nature enjoyed privileged protection, and so-called economic rights, which would only be applied "progressively", taking account of available resources. It hoped for a more fruitful and constructive approach in the final text of the convention.

126.     The completion of an international instrument taking into account the interests, needs and basic rights of children in general and those of the developing countries in particular would be a key contribution to the protection of children and the establishment of equal opportunities for future generations.

127.     At a decisive stage in its development, Algeria was showing a marked interest in young people and children, who were one of the crucial sectors of the population. Article 65 of the Algerian Constitution defined the family as the basic unit of society and provided for State protection of motherhood, children, young people and old people. Article 66 established the right of all citizens to free education, and article 67 provided that all citizens had the right to protection of their health. Those provisions were reflected in a development policy which ensured social and economic progress, and the welfare of the population and especially of the most disadvantaged and vulnerable sectors.

128.     Nearly 45 per cent of the Algerian population was under 15 years of age. The number of children of school age was increasing at an annual rate of 4.2 per cent and would reach 9 million by the year 2000. The rate of school attendance had risen from 20 per cent immediately following independence to 44 per cent in 1966 and 81.2 per cent in 1982. In September 1984, all children six years of age had been in school. The efforts made by Algeria in the area of education could be appreciated by considering the fact that Algeria's 5 million children represented one fourth of its population, and that the infrastructure necessary for meeting the immediate needs of that age group required the opening of 5,000 classrooms, 100 basic polytechnical schools and 40 high schools every year. Furthermore, broad social activities were undertaken with a view to encouraging studies, for example in the areas of scholarships, aid to families, etc.

129.     Algeria strove to promote quality education which would meet the requirements of modern society and allow Algerian children access to the scientific and technical knowledge necessary for their future as citizens of a country oriented towards development and progress. Algeria's achievements in the area of education came within its global development objective for all sectors of economic, social and cultural life and reflected its efforts constantly to improve the standard of living of its citizens in general and children in particular. The protection of children and the promotion of their rights demanded true commitment at the national and international levels.

130.     Turning to the situation of children of separated or divorced couples, particularly those of mixed marriages, she said the Algerian authorities had given constant attention to that distressing problem, which arose in many countries. Sensitive to the human dimension of the situation, the authorities examined individual cases with parents. Such situations required speedy bilateral negotiations between the authorities concerned, who must ensure that the interests of the child were met and that the rights, culture and national values of all the parties involved were respected.

131.     Mr. YAKOVLEV (Union of Soviet Socialist Republics) expressed gratitude to Mr. Lopatka for his efforts to ensure the completion of the drafting of a very important new international instrument, the convention on the rights of the child. He noted that Mr. Lopatka's Government had been one of the sponsors of the Declaration of the Rights of the Child 25 years before. He joined previous speakers in stressing the importance of the problem and recalled that enormous steps had been taken in that area in Poland 40 years before, after Hitler's armies had virtually destroyed that country.

132.     General Assembly resolution 39/135 provided for completion of the convention; however, obstacles created artificially by certain representatives had hindered the fulfilment of that mandate. He hoped that the efforts of the Working Group would ensure the successful completion of the text and its submission to the Commission at the following session. His delegation supported the observations on the text made by previous delegations, especially those of Senegal and Algeria, and the proposal for the extension of the mandate of the Special Rapporteur.

133. Ms. MARTIN (observer for Canada) said that her delegation had taken an active part in the Working Group and had been particularly pleased at the widespread participation in the Group at the current session. The successful adoption by consensus of five articles constituted considerable progress towards completion of the substantive articles of the draft convention. Of note was the introduction of an article that aimed at protecting children in situations of armed conflict. The particular vulnerability of children in such situations warranted the Commission's urgent consideration.

134. As her delegation had stated in the Third Committee of the General Assembly, children were the future of mankind, but they were more than that abstract expression suggested. They were individuals, persons with rights civil, political, economic, social and cultural rights that merited careful elaboration in the form of legal standards. There was a tendency to subsume the rights of children in the rights of their parents. While it was true that certain rights of children were inevitably dependent on the parent for their enjoyment, they were not thereby rights accruing only to the parent.

135. It was a complex task to translate those concepts into carefully drafted principles that took into account the respective roles of parents and the State in the implementation of the rights of the child, while at the same time respecting the privacy of the family. A further complication was the fact that a child's ability to exercise his or her rights naturally increased as the child matured. That notion had been addressed by the Working Group the year before in the context of the child's freedom of religion.

136. Because those concepts were not easily expressed in the language of an international instrument, the drafting process was understandably proceeding at a measured pace. Her delegation hoped that the convention would be completed as quickly as possible, but it should be a carefully worded and internally consistent document which addressed some of the difficult questions surrounding the rights of the child. The convention should also be consistent with existing rights that children enjoyed under other basic human rights instruments which included children through their use of the term "everyone".

137. Her delegation was concerned at the increasing number of qualifications linking the progressive implementation of certain rights with national conditions or available resources. It was equally concerned that inconsistencies might arise in the text when such different terms were used to convey the notion of progressive implementation. It had suggested in the Working Group that those qualifying references might be eliminated during the second reading of the convention and replaced by a single article such as article 2 (1) of the International Covenant on Economic, Social and Cultural Rights. It hoped that such an article would meet the concern of some countries about the feasibility of the immediate implementation of some of the rights embodied in the draft convention. It was important not to draft in 1985 a convention that provided fewer rights for children than conventions drafted 20 years before.

138. Maximum progress on the draft convention could be achieved only if delegations participating in the Working Group had access to all the necessary information. Certain documents should be provided well in advance of the Working Group's session. Those documents should include: a consolidated list of proposals for amendments or new articles submitted to date; an analysis of articles in international instruments relating to the article of the draft which remained to be considered; and an analysis of final clauses. For its part, her delegation intended to make as constructive a contribution as possible to the drafting of the convention.

*The following is taken from document E/CN.4/1985/SR.54 (21 March 1985).*

1. Mr. CERDA (Argentina) expressed appreciation for the work done by the Working Group on a draft convention on the rights of the child. His delegation hoped that a draft convention acceptable to all States would shortly be agreed on in accordance with General Assembly resolution 39/135.

2. A particular form of violation of the rights of the child had occurred recently in Argentina; some children had been abducted with their parents, and others had been born in prison; in both cases they had subsequently disappeared. The identity of the children concerned had been falsified by registering them as the children of third parties or of the abductors themselves. His Government had taken measures to identify such children and return them to their families. At the most recent session of the Working Group, his

delegation had proposed the addition to the draft convention of a new article (reproduced in document E/CN.4/1985/WG.1/L.2/Add.3). The proposed text laid down the inalienable right of the child to retain his true and genuine personal, legal and family identity and the obligation of the State to give him special protection and assistance, and to restore him to his blood relations to be brought up.

3.      A particular problem arose when parents of different nationalities were separated or divorced, since it was often difficult for both parents to have access to the child or to supervise his education. States should redouble their efforts to establish bilateral contacts in order to achieve a satisfactory legal solution to the problem in the child's best interests.

4.      Ms. ROMERO (International Federation of Human Rights) said that every year, more than 600 children from broken families were abducted by one or the other parent. In 97 per cent of cases, it was the mother who was denied her rights vis-à-vis her children. There were often delays of six to seven years before cases were heard, especially in the Maghreb countries. Another subtle obstacle was the failure of some countries, including some EEC and Nordic countries, to ratify international conventions. There has then further delay in the implementation of conventions once they had been ratified. For children who had been abducted and for their mothers the result was an interminable wait and many wasted years which could never be replaced. A child snatched from his familiar environment and deprived of his relationship with his mother often suffered irreparable damage. Mothers were exhausted by fruitless procedures without the protection which all persons were entitled to expect from their own country. The Commission should adopt a resolution requesting the States concerned in the matter to collaborate closely so as to prevent further violations, for otherwise many more desperate parents were liable to take the law into their own hands.

5.      Mr. GAY (Pax Romana) paid tribute to the Working Group on a draft convention on the rights of the child, which would supplement the provisions of the Declaration of the Rights of the Child of November 1950. His organization supported the substance of documents E/CN.4/1985/NGO/41 and E/CN.4/1985/L.86.

6.      He agreed with the representative of Senegal that the human rights of the child were indeed the same as those of all other persons, but violations of the rights of the child were even less pardonable, since a child was more vulnerable than an adult.

7.      Children of divorced parents were often used as a means of blackmail or arbitrarily deprived of contact with one parent. The problem was particularly acute in the case of mixed-nationality or mixed-religion marriages, where each parent tried to ensure that legal jurisdiction was exercised in his or her country. The problem had been discussed at a congress held in November 1984 in Strasbourg on the subject of "The right of families to live in dignity".

8.      Children, the weakest members of the family, needed special protection, and there was an urgent need for States to ratify conventions like that signed on 20 May 1980 in Luxembourg under the aegis of the Council of Europe and the Hague Convention of 25 October 1980. Many States had made efforts to solve the problem. His organization offered its full cooperation to the Working Group in its future activities.

*The following is taken from document E/CN.4/1985/SR.57 (21 March 1985).*

Draft resolution E/CN.4/1985/L.74

55.      Mr. LEBAKINE (Ukrainian Soviet Socialist Republic) introduced draft resolution E/CN.4/1985/L.74 on behalf of its sponsors.

56.      Like the other tests on the question submitted to the Commission at its earlier sessions, the draft resolution under consideration was mainly procedural in character. It concerned a one-week session of an open-ended working group prior to the forty-second session of the Commission, with a view to completing the work on the draft convention on the rights of the child. The task was an essential one, since, 25 years after the adoption of the Declaration of the Rights of the Child, the situation of children in many parts of the world still continued to be far from satisfactory and an international convention would make an

important contribution to a genuine improvement in the situation of children all over the world. Numerous Governments and international, intergovernmental and non-governmental organizations were showing an increasing interest in such a convention.

57.　　His delegation wished to point out that, when preparing the draft resolution, the sponsors had taken account of certain procedural and organizational proposals made by other delegations, mainly concerning the length of the working group session in 1986, but had not thought it necessary to retain the proposals relating to substantive matters, namely, the situation of children throughout the world, since they would have changed the purely procedural character of the text and would have complicated the adoption of a decision.

58.　　It should be noted that the draft resolution had a very large number of sponsors.

59.　　The administrative and programme budget implications of the draft resolution were published in document E/CN.4/1985/L.86.

60.　　The CHAIRMAN [Mr. CHOWDHURY (Bangladesh)] announced that Italy, Greece, New Zealand, Mozambique and Venezuela had become sponsors of the draft resolution.

61.　　Draft resolution E/CN.4/1985/L.86 was adopted without a vote.

62.　　Mrs. KRAMARCZYK (German Democratic Republic) noted that the newly adopted text quite rightly alluded to the further progress made by the working group. In effect, it had been possible to adopt five new extensive articles.

63.　　Her delegation, which had participated actively in the working group, had noted that a growing number of States and non-governmental organizations were awaiting the final version of the draft convention on the rights of the child. Consequently, at its next session, the Commission should give priority attention to tackling that task. Her delegation was ready to make its contribution to that end.

64.　　Finally, her delegation wished to congratulate Mr. Lopatka on his outstanding work.

## 6.　Commission on Human Rights resolution 1985/50 on the "Question of a convention on the rights of the child" adopted on 14 March 1985

*The Commission on Human Rights,*

*Bearing in mind* the draft convention on the rights of the child submitted by Poland to the Commission on Human Rights on 7 February 1978, the amended version of the draft submitted to the Commission on 5 October 1979 and the document submitted by Poland to the General Assembly at its thirty-sixth session, on 7 October 1981,

*Recalling* General Assembly resolutions 33/166 of 20 December 1978, 34/4 of 18 October 1979, 35/131 of 11 December 1980, 36/57 of 25 November 1981, 37/190 of 18 December 1982, 38/114 of 16 December 1983 and 39/135 of 14 December 1984 by which the Assembly requested the Commission on Human Rights to give the highest priority and to make every effort at its forty-first session to complete the draft convention and submit it, through the Economic and Social Council, to the General Assembly at its fortieth session,

*Recalling also* its resolutions 20 (XXXIV) of 8 March 1978, 19 (XXXV) of 14 March 1979, 36 (XXXVI) of 12 March 1980, 26 (XXXVII) of 10 March 1981, 1982/39 of 11 March 1982, 1983/52 of 10 March 1983 and 1984/24 of 8 March 1984, and Economic and Social Council decisions 1980/138 of 2 May 1980 and 1981/144 of 8 May 1981 and resolutions 1978/18 of 5 May 1978, 1978/40 of 1 August 1978, 1982/37 of 7 May 1982, 1983/39 of 27 May 1983 and 1984/25 of 24 May 1984, by which it authorized a meeting of an open-ended working group for a period of one week prior to the forty-first session of the Commission to facilitate and speed up the completion of the work on the draft convention on the rights of the child,

*Aware* of the fact that 25 years after the adoption of the Declaration of the Rights of the Child, the situation of children in many parts of the world still continues to be far from satisfactory, and that the full enjoyment by children of human rights calls for continuous improvement of the situation of children as well as their development and education in conditions of peace and security,

*Stressing* the importance of an international convention on the rights of the child for the effective improvement of the situation of children all over the world,

*Welcoming* the efforts made by the United Nations Children's Fund with a view to promoting and protecting children's rights, life and well-being,

*Noting* the further progress made by the open-ended working group during its one-week meeting prior to the forty-first session of the Commission,

*Noting also* the growing interest in elaborating a comprehensive international convention on the rights of the child displayed by numerous Governments and international organizations,

1       *Decides* to continue at its forty-second session, as a matter of the highest priority, its work on the elaboration of the draft convention on the rights of the child, with a view to completing the draft at that session for transmission, through the Economic and Social Council, to the General Assembly;

2.      *Requests* the Economic and Social Council to authorize a one-week session of an open-ended working group prior to the forty-second session of the Commission on Human Rights with a view to completing the work on the draft convention on the rights of the child at that session;

3.      *Recommends* the following draft resolution to the Economic and Social Council for adoption:

"*The Economic and Social Council,*

*Recalling* General Assembly resolution 39/135 of 14 December 1984, by which the General Assembly requested the Commission on Human Rights to give the highest priority to and to make every effort at its forty-first session to complete the draft convention and to submit it, through the Economic and Social Council, to the General Assembly at its fortieth session,

*Considering* that it was not found possible to complete the work on the draft convention during the forty-first session of the Commission on Human Rights,

*Taking note* of Commission on Human Rights resolution 1985/50 of 14 March 1985,

1.      *Authorizes* a meeting of an open-ended working group for a period of one week prior to the forty-second session of the Commission on Human Rights, with a view to completing the work on the draft convention on the rights of the child at that session;

2.      *Requests* the Secretary-General to extend all facilities to the working group for its meeting prior to and during the forty-second session of the Commission to enable it to fulfil its task successfully, and notes the usefulness of providing the working group, in advance of its session, with such working documents as a compilation of all amendments and new proposals, and relevant provisions of other international instruments."

## 7.      Economic and Social Council resolution 1985/42 on the "Question of a convention on the rights of the child" adopted on 30 May 1985

*The Economic and Social Council,*

*Recalling* General Assembly resolution 39/135 of 14 December 1984, by which the Assembly requested the Commission on Human Rights to give the highest priority to and to make every effort at its forty-first session to complete the draft convention on the rights of the child and to submit it, through the Economic and Social Council, to the General Assembly at its fortieth session,

*Considering* that it was not found possible to complete the work on the draft convention during the forty-first session of the Commission on Human Rights,

*Taking note* of Commission on Human Rights resolution 1985/50 of 14 March 1985,

1.      *Authorizes* a meeting of an open-ended working group for a period of one week prior to the forty-second session of the Commission on Human Rights, with a view to completing the work an the draft convention on the rights of the child at that session;

2.      *Requests* the Secretary-General to extend all facilities to the working group for its meeting prior to and during the forty-second session of the Commission to enable it to fulfil its task successfully, and notes the usefulness of providing the working group, in advance of its session, with such working documents as a compilation of all amendments and new proposals, and relevant provisions of other international instruments.

*25th plenary meeting*
*30 May 1985*

## 8.    General Assembly resolution 40/113 on the "Question of a convention on the rights of the child" adopted on 13 December 1985

*The General Assembly,*

*Recalling* its resolutions 33/166 of 20 December 1973, 34/4 of 18 October 1979, 35/131 of 11 December 1980, 36/57 of 25 November 1981, 37/190 of 18 December 1982, 38/114 of 16 December 1983 and 39/135 of 14 December 1984,

*Recalling also* Commission on Human Rights resolutions 20 (XXXIV) of 8 March 1978, 19 (XXXV) of 14 March 1979, 36 (XXXVI) of 12 March 1980, 26 (XXXVII) of 10 March 1981, 1982/39 of 11 March 1982, 1983/52 of 10 March 1983, 1984/24 of 8 March 1984 and 1985/50 of 14 March 1985, as well as Economic and Social Council resolutions 1978/18 of 5 May 1978, 1978/40 of 1 August 1978, 1982/37 of 7 May 1982, 1983/39 of 27 May 1983, 1984/25 of 24 May 1984 and 1985/42 of 30 May 1985 and Council decisions 1980/138 of 2 May 1980 and 1981/144 of 8 May 1981,

*Reaffirming,* on the fortieth anniversary of the United Nations, that children's rights require special protection and call for continuous improvement of the situation of children all over the world, as well as their development and education in conditions of peace and security,

*Profoundly concerned* that the situation of children in many parts of the world remains critical as a result of unsatisfactory social conditions, natural disasters, armed conflicts, exploitation, hunger and disability, and convinced that urgent and effective national and international action is called for,

*Mindful* of the important role of the United Nations Children's Fund and the United Nations in promoting the well-being of children and their development,

*Convinced* that an international convention an the rights or the child would make a positive contribution to ensuring the protection of children's rights and their well-being,

*Welcoming* the growing interest in the elaboration of an international convention on the rights of the child displayed by a great number of Member States representing all geographical regions and socio-political systems, as well as by governmental and non-governmental international organizations,

*Noting with appreciation* that further progress was made during the forty-first session of the Commission on Human Rights in the elaboration of a draft convention on the rights of the child,

*Noting* the document entitled "Status of elaboration of draft convention on the rights of the child", submitted by Poland,

1.      *Welcomes* Economic and Social Council resolution 1985/42, in which the Council authorized a meeting of an open-ended working group of the Commission on Human Rights for a period of one week prior to the forty-second session of the Commission with a view to completing the work on a draft convention on the rights of the child;

2.      *Requests* the Commission on Human Rights to give the highest priority to, and to make every effort at its forty-second session to complete, the draft convention and to submit it, through the Economic and Social Council, to the General Assembly at its forty-first session;

3.      *Invites* all Member States to offer their active contribution to the completion of the draft convention on the rights of the child at the forty-second session of the Commission on Human Rights;

4.      *Requests* the Secretary-General to provide all necessary assistance to the working group in order to ensure its smooth and efficient work in the fulfilment of its important task;

5.      *Decides* to include in the provisional agenda of its forty-first session the item entitled "Question of a convention on the rights or the child".

*116th plenary meeting*
*13 December 1985*

# K. 1986

## 1. Report of the Working Group

*The following is taken from document E/CN.4/1986/39 (13 March 1986).*

INTRODUCTION

1.      The Commission on Human Rights, by resolution 1985/50 of 14 March 1985, decided to continue at its forty-second session, as a matter of the highest priority, its work on the elaboration of the draft convention on the rights of the child, with a view to completing the draft at that session for transmission, through the Economic and Social Council, to the General Assembly. By resolution 1985/42 of 30 May 1985, the Economic and Social Council authorized the open-ended working group to meet for a period of one week prior to the Commission's forty-second session, in order to facilitate completion of the work on the draft convention. At its fortieth session, the General Assembly, resolution 40/113 of 13 December 1985, requested the Commission on Human Rights to give the highest priority to, and to make every effort at its forty-second session to complete the draft convention and to submit it, through the Economic and Social Council, to the General Assembly at its forty-first session. The General Assembly also invited all Member States to offer their active contribution to the completion of the draft convention on the rights of the child at the forty-second session of the Commission.

2.      The Working Group held 11 meetings from 27 to 31 January 1986, and on 11 March 1986. It adopted articles 9 bis, 12 ter, 18, 18 bis, 19, 20 and 21. In that connection, it should be recalled that the open-ended working group established prior to and during previous sessions of the Commission had adopted a number of articles. The text of the articles adopted so far may be found in annex I to this report. Annex II to this report contains proposals that have been discussed by the Working Group but remain pending for further consideration by the group. During the session, and at previous sessions, representatives of States proposed draft articles and amendments which were not discussed by the Working Group for lack of time, and which appear in annex III to this report. Annex IV to this report contains a paper relating to the draft convention which was submitted by the Permanent Representative of Bangladesh with the request that it be annexed as a document to the report of the Working Group on its current session.

ELECTIONS

3.      At the first meeting of the pre-sessional Working Group, on 27 January 1986, Mr. Adam Lopatka (Poland) was elected Chairman-Rapporteur by acclamation.

PARTICIPATION

4.      The meetings of the Working Group, which were open to all members of the Commission on Human Rights, were attended by representatives of the following States: Algeria, Argentina, Australia, Austria, Bangladesh, Belgium, Brazil, Bulgaria, Byelorussian Soviet Socialist Republic, China, Cyprus, Ethiopia, France, German Democratic Republic, India, Japan, Mexico, Norway, Peru, Senegal, Sri Lanka, Union of Soviet Socialist Republics, United Kingdom of Great Britain and Northern Ireland, United States of America and Venezuela.

5.      The following States, non-members of the Commission on Human Rights, were represented by observers at the meetings of the Working Groups: Canada, Cuba, Denmark, Finland, Holy See, Iraq, Morocco, Netherlands, New Zealand, Poland, Sweden and Switzerland.

6.      The International Labour Organization and the United Nations Children's Fund were represented at the Working Group by observers.

7.      The following non-governmental organizations sent observers to the Working Group: Amnesty International, Associated Country Women of the World, Baha'i International Community, Defence for Children International Movement, Four Directions Council, Human Rights Internet, International Abolitionist Federation, International Catholic Child Bureau, International Commission of Jurists, International Committee of the Red

Cross, International Council of Jewish Women, International Council of Women, International Federation of Women in Legal Careers, International Federation of Women Lawyers, International Social Service, Rädda Barnen International, Save the Children Fund, World Association for the School as an Instrument of Peace, World Organization for Early Childhood Education and Zonta International.


## DOCUMENTS

8.      The Working Group had before it a number of documents including the provisional agenda prepared by the Secretary-General (E/CN.4/1986/WG.1/L.1), the report of the Working Group on a draft convention on the rights of the child to the forty-first session of the Commission on Human Rights (E/CN.4/1985/64), a compilation of proposed articles and amendments and related provisions in international instruments regarding the draft convention elaborated by the Secretariat (E/CN.4/1986/WG.1/WP.1), the report of the Working Group on Slavery on its eleventh session (E/CN.4/Sub.2/1985/25 and Corr.1), and the final report by Mr. Bouhdiba on exploitation of child labour (E/CN.4/Sub.2/479/Rev.1).

## GENERAL CONSIDERATIONS

9.      One new article was submitted to the Working Group by the representatives of France and the Netherlands, and another by the representatives of the Netherlands, the United Kingdom and the United States of America, for consideration by the Group at its 1987 session. The first one was a proposal for an article 18 ter which read as follows:

> "The States Parties to this Convention undertake to protect the child against all forms of exploitation, particularly sexual exploitation, as well as against all degrading treatment and all acts prejudicial to the moral, spiritual, mental or physical integrity of the child."

The second one was a proposal for an article 21 bis to read:

> "Nothing in this Convention shall be interpreted as legitimizing any alien's illegal entry into and presence in a State, nor shall any provision be interpreted as restricting the right of any State to promulgate laws and regulations concerning the entry of aliens and the terms and conditions of their stay, or to establish differences between nationals and aliens. However, such laws and regulations shall not be incompatible with the international legal obligations of that State, including those in the field of human rights."

10.      At the first meeting of the Working Group, Mr. V. Tarzie Vittachi, Deputy Executive Director for External Relations of UNICEF, made a statement to the Group.

11.      The representative of the United Kingdom said how useful he had found the paper prepared by the Secretariat (E/CN.4/1986/WG.1/WP.1) and expressed the hope that, for future meetings, the Working Group would have an annual update of that paper which provided a very helpful overview of the matters to be discussed.

12.      The representative of the United States withdrew the proposal put forward by her delegation in 1985 for a new paragraph in article 11 concerning legislative and administrative measures which States Parties might take to safeguard the confidentiality of adoption records. She explained to the Working Group that since the relevant provision adopted by the Group was neutral on the subject and did not require the disclosure of adoption records, the amendment had been withdrawn on the understanding that her delegation might return to it if any later amendment to the convention made it necessary.

*The following is taken from document E/CN.4/1986/39, annex IV (13 March 1986).*

*Paper submitted by the Permanent Representative of Bangladesh*

The Permanent Representative of Bangladesh to the United Nations Office in Geneva has submitted the following paper in connection with the draft convention on the rights of the child with the request that it be annexed to the report.

General:

While Bangladesh fully supports the successive General Assembly resolutions calling for the early settling of the Draft convention on the rights of the child, she believes with other States that such a convention would only be effective if it is broadly acceptable to the largest number of States. It is, therefore, considered that maximum opportunity to consult with all States and to afford them an opportunity to comment on the Working Group draft in its entirety before submission to the Commission on Human Rights is essential to attract such broad support.

These considerations are reinforced by the very nature of the subject, viz., the rights of the child. Conceptions of the rights of the child are heavily conditioned by conceptions of family law in differing legal systems. Moreover, the conception of the family itself varies in various legal systems and in different cultures. The Muslim countries representing one of the most important legal systems obtaining in the modern world, viz., Islamic Law have their own conceptions of the nuclear family, the extended family and the rights of the child within the framework of those conceptions. It is considered essential that the draft convention should be acceptable to the Islamic countries who constitute one of the largest groups of States in the international community. These States also account for a very large and significant number of children in the world population.

In addition, it is felt that since the vast majority of the world's children are actually resident in developing countries including the Islamic countries, it would help to attract broad support in the developing countries, if the standards imposed for the treatment of children are not so onerous that even their attempted application becomes meaningless and indeed absurd. Standards developed in market economies or in centrally planned economies do not correspond to the existing realities in the developing countries including the realities in Bangladesh.

## 2. Articles adopted in 1986

*The following is taken from document E/CN.4/1986/39, annex I.*

### Article 9 bis

1.        The State Parties to the present Convention undertake to respect the right of the child to preserve his or her identity (nationality, name, family relations as recognized by law) without unlawful interference.

2.        Where a child is illegally deprived of some or all of the elements of his or her identity, the States Parties shall provide appropriate assistance and protection, with a view to speedily re-establishing his or her identity.

### Articles 12 ter

States Parties to the present Convention recognize the right of a child who has been placed by the competent authorities for the purposes of care, protection, or treatment of his or her physical or mental health, to a periodic review of the treatment provided to the child and all other circumstances relevant to his or her placement.

### Article 18

1.        The States Parties to the present Convention recognize the right of the child to be protected from economic exploitation and from performing any work that is likely to be hazardous or to interfere with the child's education, or to be harmful to the child's health or physical, mental, spiritual, moral or social development.

2.        The States Parties to the present Convention shall take legislative and administrative measures to ensure the implementation of this article. To this end, and having regard to the relevant provisions of other international instruments, the States Parties shall in particular:

        (a)        provide for a minimum age or minimum ages for admission to employment;

(b)     provide for appropriate regulation of the hours and conditions of employment; and

(c)     provide for appropriate penalties or other sanctions to ensure the effective enforcement of this article.

*Article 18 bis*

The States Parties to the present Convention shall take all appropriate measures, including legislative, social and educational measures, to protect children from the illegal use of narcotic and psychotropic substances as defined in the relevant international treaties, and to prevent the use of children in the illegal production and trafficking of such substances.

*Article 19*

1.     States Parties to the present Convention recognize the right of children who are accused or recognized as having infringed the penal law to be treated in a manner which is consistent with promoting their sense of dignity and worth and intensifying their respect for the human rights and fundamental freedoms of others, and which takes into account their age and the desirability of promoting their rehabilitation.

2.     To this end, and having regard to the relevant provisions of international instruments, the States Parties to the present Convention shall, in particular, ensure that:

(a)     no child is arbitrarily detained or imprisoned or subjected to torture, cruel, inhuman or degrading treatment or punishment;

(b)     capital punishment or life imprisonment without possibility of release is not imposed for crimes committed by persons below 18 years of age;

(c)     children accused of infringing the penal law

(i)     are presumed innocent until proven guilty according to law;

(ii)     are informed promptly of the charges against them and, as of the time of being accused, have legal or other appropriate assistance in the preparation and presentation of their defence;

(iii)     have the matter determined according to law in a fair hearing within a reasonable period of time by an independent and impartial tribunal and

(iv)      if found guilty are entitled to have their conviction and sentence reviewed by a higher tribunal according to law.

3.     An essential aim of treatment of children found guilty of infringing the penal law shall be their reformation and social rehabilitation. A variety of dispositions, including programmes of education and vocational training and alternatives to institutional care shall be available to ensure that children are dealt with in a manner appropriate and proportionate both to their circumstances and the offence.

4.     All children deprived of their liberty shall be treated with humanity and respect for the inherent dignity of the human person, and shall in particular:

(a)     be brought as speedily as possible for adjudication

(b)     be separated from adults accused or convicted of having committed an offence unless it is considered in the child's best interest not to do so, or it is unnecessary for the protection of the child and

(c)     have the right to maintain contact with their family through correspondence and visits, save in exceptional circumstances.

*Article 20*

1.　　The States Parties to the present Convention undertake to respect and to ensure respect for rules of international humanitarian law applicable to them in armed conflicts which are relevant to the child.

2.　　States Parties to the present Convention shall take all feasible measures to ensure that no child takes a direct part in hostilities and they shall refrain in particular from recruiting any child who has not attained the age of 15 years into their armed forces.

3.　　In accordance with their obligations under international humanitarian law to protect the civilian population in armed conflicts, States Parties to this Convention shall take all feasible measures to ensure protection and care of children who are affected by an armed conflict.

*Article 21*

Nothing in this Convention shall affect any provisions that are more conducive to the realization of the rights of the child and that may be contained in:

(a)　　The law of a State Party; or

(b)　　Any other international convention, treaty or agreement in force for that State.

## 3.　Draft resolution on the "Question of a convention on the rights of the child"

*The following is taken from document E/CN.4/1986/L.70 (10 March 1986).*

Afghanistan, Algeria, Angola, Argentina, Australia, Austria, Bangladesh, Bolivia, Bulgaria, Byelorussian Soviet Socialist Republic, Cameroon, Canada, China, Colombia, Congo, Costa Rica, Cuba, Cyprus, Czechoslovakia, Denmark, Ethiopia, Egypt, Finland, France, Gabon, Gambia, German Democratic Republic, Greece, Hungary, India, Iran (Islamic Republic of), Italy, Jordan, Kenya, Lebanon, Lesotho, Liberia, Libyan Arab Jamahiriya, Madagascar, Mauritania, Mexico, Mongolia, Morocco, Mozambique, New Zealand, Nicaragua, Norway, Pakistan, Peru, Philippines, Poland, Senegal, Somalia, Spain, Sri Lanka, Sudan, Syrian Arab Republic, Ukrainian Soviet Socialist Republic, Union of Soviet Socialist Republics, United Republic of Tanzania, United States of America, Venezuela, Viet Nam and Yugoslavia : draft resolution

*The Commission on Human Rights,*

*Bearing in mind* the draft convention on the rights of the child submitted by Poland to the Commission on Human Rights on 7 February 1978, the amended version of the draft submitted to the Commission on 5 October 1979, and the documents submitted by Poland to the General Assembly at its thirty-sixth session, on 7 October 1981 and at its fortieth session, on 7 October 1985,

*Recalling* General Assembly resolutions 33/166 of 20 December 1978, 34/4 of 18 October 1979, 35/131 of 11 December 1980, 36/57 of 25 November 1981, 37/190 of 18 December 1982, 38/114 of 16 December 1983, 39/135 of 14 December 1984 and 40/113 of 13 December 1985, by which the Assembly requested the Commission on Human Rights to give the highest priority to, and to make every effort at its forty-second session to complete the draft convention and submit it, through the Economic and Social Council, to the General Assembly at its forty-first session,

*Recalling* also its resolutions 20 (XXXIV) of 8 March 1978, 19 (XXXV) of 14 March 1979, 36 (XXXVI) of 12 March 1980, 26 (XXXVII) of 10 March 1981, 1982/39 of 11 March 1982, 1983/52 of 10 March 1983, 1984/24 of 8 March 1984 and 1985/50 of 14 March 1985, and Economic and Social Council decisions 1980/138 of 2 May 1980 and 1981/144 of 8 May 1981 and resolutions 1978/18 of 5 May 1978, 1978/40 of 1 August 1978, 1982/37 of 7 May 1982, 1983/39 of 27 May 1983, 1984/25 of 24 May 1984 and 1985/42 of 30 May 1985, by which it authorized a meeting of an open-ended working group for a period of one week prior to the forty-second session of the Commission, with a view to completing the work on the draft convention on the rights of the child,

*Aware* of the fact that 26 years after the adoption of the Declaration of the Rights of the Child, the situation of children in many parts of the world still continues to be far from satisfactory, and that the full enjoyment by children of human rights calls for continuous improvement of the situation of children as well as their development and education in conditions of peace and security,

*Stressing* the importance of an international convention on the rights of the child for the effective improvement of the situation of children all over the world,

*Welcoming* the efforts made by the United Nations Children's Fund with a view to promoting and protecting children's rights, life and well-being,

*Noting* the further progress made by the open-ended working group during its one-week meeting prior to the forty-second session of the Commission,

*Noting also* the growing interest in elaborating a comprehensive international convention on the rights of the child displayed by numerous Governments and international organizations,

1.    *Decides* to continue at its forty-third session, as a matter of the highest priority, its work on the elaboration of the draft convention on the rights of the child, with a view to completing the draft at that session for transmission, through the Economic and Social Council, to the General Assembly;

2.    *Requests* the Economic and Social Council to authorize a one-week session of an open-ended working group prior to the forty-third session of the Commission on Human Rights, with a view to completing the work on the draft convention on the rights of the child at that session;

3.    *Recommends* the following draft resolution to the Economic and Social Council for adoption:

   "*The Economic and Social Council,*

   *Recalling* General Assembly resolution 40/113 of 13 December 1985, by which the General Assembly requested the Commission on Human Rights to give the highest priority to, and to make every effort at its forty-second session to complete the draft convention and to submit it, through the Economic and Social Council, to the General Assembly at its forty-first session,

   *Considering* that it was not found possible to complete the work on the draft convention during the forty-second session of the Commission on Human Rights,

   *Taking note* of Commission on Human Rights resolution 1986/... of ... March 1986,

   1.    *Authorizes* a meeting of an open-ended working group for a period of one week prior to the forty-third session of the Commission on Human Rights with a view to completing the work on the draft convention on the rights of the child at that session;

   2.    *Requests* the Secretary-General to extend all facilities to the working group for its meeting prior to and during the forty-third session of the Commission to enable it to fulfil its task successfully, and notes the usefulness of providing the working group, in advance of its session, with such working documents as a compilation of all amendments and new proposals and relevant provisions of other international instruments."

## 4.    Administrative and programme budget implications

*The following is taken from document E/CN.4/1986/L.90 (10 March 1986).*

QUESTION OF A CONVENTION ON THE RIGHTS OF THE CHILD (agenda item 13)

*Administrative and programme budget implications of the draft resolution contained in document E/CN.4/1986/L.70*

Statement submitted by the Secretary-General in accordance with rule 28 of the rules of procedure of the functional commissions of the Economic and Social Council

A.      Requests contained in the draft resolution

1.      By operative paragraph 1 of the draft resolution recommended by the Commission for adoption by the Economic and Social Council under draft resolution E/CN.4/1986/L.70, the Council would authorize a meeting of an open-ended working group for a period of one week prior to the forty-third session of the Commission with a view to completing the work on the draft convention on the rights of the child at that session.

B.      Relationship of proposed request to current legislative mandates

2.      The activities referred to above would fall under chapter 6, section II, "Programme: Centre for Human Rights", subprogramme 2, "Elimination and prevention of discrimination and protection of minorities and vulnerable groups", the objective of and the strategy for which are described in paragraphs 6.25 and 6.27 of the medium-term plan for the period 1984-1989 (A/37/6).

3.      The following programme element of section 23 (Human Rights) of the proposed programme budget for 1986-1987 would be directly affected by the activities referred to in draft resolutions:

Programme element 2.1 - Elimination and prevention of discrimination and protection of minorities and vulnerable groups

Output: (XV) Substantive servicing of the Working Group of the Commission on Human Rights engaged in drafting a convention on the rights of the child.

C.      Activities by which the requests would be implemented

4.      In order to determine the financial implications of the decision, it has been noted that the travel expenses of the members concerned would be covered under the normal provision for the attendance of members of the commission.

D.      Modification required in the programme of work

5.      No modifications are required in the programme of work proposed for 1986-1987 since the activity appears under programme element 2.1.

E.      Additional requirements at full cost

6.      Conference servicing costs to be financed under section 29 B (Conference Services Division, Geneva), calculated on a full-cost basis, are estimated at $53,900 for 1987.

## 5.   Discussion in the Commission on Human Rights on 13 March 1986

*The following is taken from document E/CN.4/1986/SR.56/Add.2 (14 April 1986).*

*Draft resolution E/CN.4/1986/L.70*

7.      Mr. OGOURTSOV (Byelorussian Soviet Socialist Republic), introducing draft resolution E/CN.4/1986/L.70 on behalf of its numerous sponsors, which included all the members of the Commission, said that, notwithstanding the adoption of the Declaration of the Rights of the Child 26 years previously, the situation of children in some parts of the world was still far from satisfactory. The sponsors were convinced, therefore, that children needed help in order to fully enjoy their rights and to be able to develop and obtain education in conditions of peace and security. It should be possible to finalize the convention on the rights of the child at the next session of the Commission. The sponsors were confident that their draft resolution would be adopted by consensus.

8.      Mr. LOPATKA (observer for Poland), Chairman of the Working Group on the question of a convention on the rights of the child, said that in that capacity he also wished to make some remarks in introduction of draft resolution E/CN.4/1986/L.70. He recalled that the Commission had decided, in its resolution 1985/50, to continue its work on the draft convention as a matter of high priority and that the Economic and Social Council, in its resolution 1985/42, had authorized a meeting of an informal open-ended working group for one

week before the forty-second session of the Commission. That group had adopted its report (E/CN.4/1986/WG.1/WP.7) unanimously on 11 March 1986.

9.      Although the Working Group had not been able to finalize the draft convention, it had nevertheless approved seven new articles concerning the right of the child to preserve his or her identity, the right of the child to a periodic review of all the circumstances relating to his or her treatment, protection of the child against economic exploitation, protection against the use of narcotic and psychotropic substances, treatment of the child that infringed the penal law, and the special protection of children in armed conflicts. The Group had also approved an article calling for the application of rules that were more advantageous to the child in cases where particular provisions of the text of the convention did not offer the same safeguards as other international or national instruments.

10.     The preamble and the substantive operative part of the draft convention had already been approved by the Group and the proposals on which no agreement had yet been reached were of secondary importance and without a direct bearing on the specific needs of the child. The Working Group had yet to approve the operative provisions concerning the machinery for implementing the convention, but it hoped to be able to complete its work during the course of the year. The Group believed, however, that consideration of the draft in second reading would be necessary. The adoption of draft resolution E/CN.4/1986/L.70 should further the Group's work before and during the forty-third session of the Commission.

11.     He welcomed the spirit of cooperation and objectivity that had characterized the Group's debates and also its decisions, all of which had been adopted by consensus. He thanked the international organizations, especially UNICEF and ILO, and the representatives of non-governmental organizations for their active participation in the work of the Group and for the extensive publicity given to the draft convention, particularly by UNICEF. For example, the draft had been considered at two meetings organized by UNICEF in 1985 and at the International Conference in Warsaw which had been organized in February 1986 by the Polish Committee for Children. He also thanked members of the secretariat and proposed that the Commission should adopt the draft resolution without a vote.

12.     Mr. VITTACHI (Deputy Executive Director of UNICEF) said that the presence at his side of Mr. Thedin, a veteran member of the Executive Board of UNICEF and of the Swedish Save the Children organization (Rädda Barnen) which was the originator of the concept of children as a neutral zone of peace, together with Canon Moerman, Chairman of the UNICEF NGO Committee and the moving force behind the International Year of the Child, clearly showed UNICEF's determination to assist in every way it could in the drafting and implementation of the convention on the rights of the child. Being especially interested in the implementation of the practical provisions of that instrument and in the moral foundation of adult obligations, UNICEF seemed to possess the vigour and credibility needed to help countries to put the convention into practical effect by, inter alia, providing them with the technical and material assistance required at the national level. However, since experience had proved that, without dynamic social mobilization, even the worthiest bill of rights could not transcend the stage of good intentions, UNICEF would also be employing all its acquired expertise and energies to help create conditions favourable to the implementation of the convention.

13.     Such social mobilization to protect the rights of the child would only be achieved by making it unconscionable for any country to let children die when their death could be prevented, allow them to be disabled and stunted when their bodies could be whole, leave them imprisoned in illiteracy when the means of education were available or allow them to be neglected, exploited, abused and threatened with annihilation before they had barely begun to live. Such mobilization was the key to many problems of preventable ill-health, ignorance and sociopathy and, in that way, the convention could become a living testimony to the progress of civilization.

14.     Mr. CHOWDHURY (Bangladesh) congratulated the Working Group on its tenacity and its determination to establish principles that could help to improve the lot of countless children, particularly in the developing countries, who were suffering not only from lack of food, clothing and shelter but also, more generally, from a lack of opportunity to prepare themselves for life. Furthermore, from a very early age,

many were exploited like virtual slaves and, under those circumstances, had no means of developing their personality and frequently died young.

15. The purpose of the draft convention was to formulate principles and standards of behaviour that would make it possible to alleviate the sufferings of children and protect them from exploitation. Bangladesh, which had played a modest but active role in the work of the Group, hoped that the convention on the rights of the child would be adopted as soon as possible and regretted that the Working Group did not have sufficient time to devote to the draft so that it could be finalized in the very near future.

16. Mrs. ULLOA DE DUQUE (Colombia) said that, in the opinion of her delegation, the effectiveness of international law depended more on the qualitative than on the quantitative aspect and, in general, the application of rules was more important than their promulgation. To be effective, international standards should be viewed in a universal perspective that took into account not only political pluralism but also the cultural diversity, particularities and traditions of peoples. Flexibility, respect for others, imagination and the rejection of all dogmatism were indispensable in that respect.

17. Those considerations were particularly important as far as the elaboration of a convention on the rights of the child was concerned, since that was not a question that could be dealt with in isolation. The safeguarding of those rights and the elimination of situations that constituted a violation thereof necessitated closely interrelated direct and indirect measures. The problem of children was linked to that of development and was indissociable from policies designed to remedy poverty, inequalities and underdevelopment by reforms in employment, agriculture, social security, education, vocational training, demography, wages and the family. It was important never to lose sight of the equilibrium that must be maintained between international standards and the role of national legislation in order to avoid a further increase in the exploitation and sufferings of children, by clandestine employment for example.

18. The democratically elected Colombian Government was taking a dynamic approach to the various aspects of the rights of the child. The protection of children against excessive work was a well-established practice in Colombia, where a ministerial department had special responsibility for the protection of children. The labour legislation made provision for maternity leave and breastfeeding periods without loss of pay, prohibited the dismissal of pregnant women and regulated conditions of employment and social security schemes, granting working mothers special protection. The Ministry of Health, which was particularly concerned with child health, had organized vaccination campaigns, involving three quarters of the national population, with the help of the Colombian Red Cross, UNICEF, UNDP and WHO. That Ministry and the Family and Welfare Institute were making great efforts to organize nurseries. Legal penalties had also been prescribed for parents who abandoned their families. Particular attention was being given to primary education, and a large-scale campaign for the eradication of illiteracy had achieved highly encouraging results. Within the context of an integrated development strategy, progress was being maintained in the fields of employment policy, agrarian reform, internal migration and educational infrastructure, and every effort was being made to place man at the hub of development and to bear constantly in mind that the child of today was the adult of tomorrow.

19. Miss BOUAMRANE (Algeria) said that her delegation had noted with satisfaction that the Working Group had adopted new articles in the draft convention in first reading. She expressed the hope that States would manifest adequate political will for the early adoption of that convention, taking into consideration the special requirements of the developing countries, which were facing numerous problems, and stressing the need for international cooperation in that respect.

20. The National Charter recently adopted by the Algerian people acknowledged youth to be the nation's most important social force and since independence Algeria had assigned priority to the sectors of education and training. The Charter proclaimed that a coherent and harmonious policy for youth must be based on sectoral strategies in education, training, health and social protection, cultural and leisure activities, all of which formed part of the development plans implemented by Algeria.

21.     The number of States that had sponsored the draft resolution - 64 in all - was indicative of the concern aroused by the problems of children and of the support that the draft convention had attracted. That should give fresh impetus to the Working Group's activities.

22.     Mr. GRIEGER (German Democratic Republic) said that his delegation, which had played an active role in the meetings of the Working Group, was able to confirm the progress the Group had made by adopting seven important new articles, and he drew attention to the mounting interest sparked off by the elaboration of an international convention whose impact was undeniable. The representatives of States and NGOs working in a constructive manner towards that end had steadily increased in number.

23.     To enable the requests contained in the draft resolution to be granted and the Working Group to complete the draft convention, all delegations should refrain from proposing further articles that were only distantly related to the main objective of the draft convention. The eminent Professor Lopatka, Minister of the Government of the Polish People's Republic, deserved credit in his capacity as Chairman of the Working Group, for the skill, circumspection and expertise with which he had supervised the elaboration of a complex instrument. His own delegation would work actively with a view to finalizing the text of the draft convention, and it recommended that draft resolution E/CN.4/1986/L.70 should be adopted by consensus.

24.     Mr. FAIRWEATHER (Canada) said that his delegation welcomed the progress made on the draft convention and the adoption of seven new articles by the Working Group. It had noted that the Working Group's productivity had been greatly enhanced by the preparation of a revised version of the draft convention by the Polish delegation. In addition, the presentation of various proposals in document A/AC.3/40/3, distributed during the General Assembly's fortieth session in the autumn of 1985, had enabled delegations to be better prepared for the consideration of the text of the draft. Two compilations of related international instruments and of draft articles and amendments submitted by UNICEF and the United Nations Secretariat respectively had also greatly simplified the task of everyone. Finally, timely suggestions by the Chairman of the Group had made it possible to resolve the most difficult issues that had arisen in the Group.

25.     If the Working Group could have equally helpful documents in the same time frames and continued able chairmanship at its future meetings, it should be able to move a considerable distance towards completing a first reading of the draft convention, and begin consideration of the articles concerned with implementation of the convention. A number of Governments, together with UNICEF and several NGOs, had already circulated preliminary ideas, and it would be interesting to see how they would be elaborated.

26.     Drafting a convention on the rights of the child was not an easy task; it posed difficult problems, such as the balance to be struck between a child's rights and its need for protection, the rights of children and those of parents, or the protection of children and undue interference by the State with the family, and so on. It was important that the Group should be able to begin a second reading of the draft convention in a session that might last longer than had been envisaged hitherto, in order to be able to clarify certain issues and ensure consistency in terminology.

27.     His delegation intended to take an active part in the Working Group's next session, and encouraged other delegations to do the same.

28.     Mr. RAVENNA (Argentina) congratulated the Working Group and the Secretariat on their efficiency. He was particularly satisfied with the deliberations on article 9 bis of the draft convention which, inter alia, had repercussions on the identification of children (and consequently on the possibility of restitution to their family) by means of blood tests. His delegation was particularly concerned with the issues relating to cases of the kidnapping and disappearance of children raised in the Commission a few days earlier. It hoped that the Working Group would be able to complete its consideration of the draft convention at its next session. Needless to say, to enable them to be applied with effect, the rules to be formulated would have to take account of the individual needs of the various countries.

29.     His delegation would spare no effort in support of the activities of the Working Group.

30.     Sir Anthony WILLIAMS (United Kingdom) recalled that his delegation, which had been awaiting the opinion of its experts, had made certain reservations when the report of the Working Group had been adopted. Those reservations, which might have been mentioned in the final version of the report, not yet published, continued to stand, and the Chairman of the Working Group had been requested to note that fact.

31.     He also drew the attention of the representative of the Byelorussian SSR to the fact that six members of the Commission, including the United Kingdom, were not sponsors of the draft resolution.

32.     Mr. KOLBY (Norway) said that his delegation, like that of the United Kingdom and several other delegations, had found it necessary to make certain reservations on the report of the Working Group, since its experts had not been able to carry out an in-depth study of the document. Those reservations continued to stand, although his delegation generally endorsed the report. His delegation wished to express its gratitude to the Chairman and members of the Working Group, in which it had been happy to work.

33.     The CHAIRMAN [Mr. CHARRY SAMPER (Colombia)] said that if there was no objection, he would take it that the Commission wished to adopt the draft resolution by consensus.

34.     Draft resolution E/CN.4/1986/L.70 was adopted without a vote.

## 6.    Commission on Human Rights resolution 1986/59 on the "Question of a convention on the rights of the child" adopted without a vote on 13 March 1986

*The Commission on Human Rights,*

*Bearing in mind* the draft convention on the rights of the child submitted by Poland to the Commission on Human Rights on 7 February 1978, the amended version of the draft submitted to the Commission on 5 October 1979, and the documents submitted by Poland to the General Assembly at its thirty-sixth session, on 7 October 1981 and at its fortieth session, on 7 October 1985,

*Recalling* General Assembly resolutions 33/166 of 20 December 1978, 34/4 of 18 October 1979, 35/131 of 11 December 1980, 36/57 of 25 November 1981, 37/190 of 18 December 1982, 38/114 of 16 December 1983, 39/135 of 14 December 1984 and 40/113 of 13 December 1985, by which the Assembly requested the Commission on Human Rights to give the highest priority to, and to make every effort at its forty-second session to complete, the draft convention and to submit it, through the Economic and Social Council, to the General Assembly at its forty-first session,

*Recalling also* its resolutions 20 (XXXIV) of 8 March 1978, 19 (XXXV) of 14 March 1979, 36 (XXXVI) of 12 March 1980, 26 (XXXVII) of 10 March 1981, 1982/39 of 11 March 1982, 1983/52 of 10 March 1983, 1984/24 of 8 March 1984, 1985/50 of 14 March 1985 and Economic and Social Council decisions 1980/138 of 2 May 1980 and 1981/144 of 8 May 1981 and resolutions 1978/18 of 5 May 1978, 1978/40 of 1 August 1978, 1982/37 of 7 May 1982, 1983/39 of 27 May 1983, 1984/25 of 24 May 1984 and 1985/42 of 30 May 1985, by which it authorized a meeting of an open-ended working group for a period of one week prior to the forty-second session of the Commission with a view to completing the work on the draft convention on the rights of the child,

*Aware* of the fact that 26 years after the adoption of the Declaration of the Rights of the Child, the situation of children in many parts of the world still continues to be far from satisfactory, and that the full enjoyment by children of human rights calls for continuous improvement of the situation of children as well as their development and education in conditions of peace and security,

*Stressing* the importance of an international convention on the rights of the child for the effective improvement of the situation of children all over the world,

*Welcoming* the efforts made by the United Nations Children's Fund with a view to promoting and protecting children's rights, life and well-being,

*Noting* the further progress made by the open-ended working group during its one-week meeting prior to the forty-second session of the Commission,

*Noting also* the growing interest in elaborating a comprehensive international convention on the rights of the child displayed by numerous Governments and international organizations,

1.      *Decides* to continue at its forty-third session, as a matter of the highest priority, its work on the elaboration of the draft convention on the rights of the child, with a view to completing the draft at that session for transmission, through the Economic and Social Council, to the General Assembly;

2.      *Requests* the Economic and Social Council to authorize a one-week session of an open-ended working group prior to the forty-third session of the Commission on Human Rights, with a view to completing the work on the draft convention on the rights of the child at that session;

3.      *Recommends* the following draft resolution to the Economic and Social Council for adoption:

"*The Economic and Social Council,*

*Recalling* General Assembly resolution 40/113 of 13 December 1985, by which the General Assembly requested the Commission on Human Rights to give the highest priority to, and to make every effort at its forty-second session to complete, the draft convention and to submit it, through the Economic and Social Council, to the General Assembly at its forty-first session,

*Considering* that it was not found possible to complete the work on the draft convention during the forty-second session of the Commission on Human Rights,

*Taking note* of Commission on Human Rights resolution 1986/59 of 13 March 1986,

1.      *Authorizes* a meeting of an open-ended working group for a period of one week prior to the forty-third session of the Commission on Human Rights with a view to completing the work on the draft convention on the rights of the child at that session;

2.      *Requests* the Secretary-General to extend all facilities to the working group for its meeting prior to and during the forty-third session of the Commission to enable it to fulfil its task successfully, and notes the usefulness of providing the working group, in advance of its session, with such working documents as a compilation of all amendments and new proposals and relevant provisions of other international instruments."

## 7.    Economic and Social Council resolution 1986/40 on the "Question of a convention on the rights of the child" adopted on 23 May 1986

*The Economic and Social Council,*

*Recalling* General Assembly resolution 40/113 of 13 December 1985, by which the Assembly requested the Commission on Human Rights to give the highest priority to, and to make every effort at its forty-second session to complete, the draft convention on the rights of the child and to submit it, through the Economic and Social Council, to the General Assembly at its forty-first session,

*Considering* that it was not found possible to complete the work on the draft convention during the forty-second session of the Commission on Human Rights,

*Taking note* of Commission on Human Rights resolution 1986/59 of 13 March 1986,

1.      *Authorizes* a meeting of an open-ended working group for a period of one week prior to the forty-third session of the Commission on Human Rights, with a view to completing the work on the draft convention on the rights of the child at that session;

2.      *Requests* the Secretary-General to extend all facilities to the working group for its meeting prior to and during the forty-third session of the Commission to enable it to fulfil its task successfully, and notes the usefulness

of providing the working group, in advance of its session, with such working documents as a compilation of all amendments and new proposals, and relevant provisions of other international instruments.

*19th plenary meeting*
*23 May 1986*

## 8. General Assembly resolution 41/116 on the "Question of a convention on the rights of the child" adopted on 4 December 1986

*The General Assembly,*

*Recalling* its resolutions 33/166 of 20 December 1978, 34/4 of 18 October 1979, 35/131 of 11 December 1980, 36/57 of 25 November 1981, 37/190 of 18 December 1982, 38/114 of 16 December 1983, 39/135 of 14 December 1984 and 40/113 of 13 December 1985,

*Recalling also* Commission on Human Rights resolutions 20 (XXXIV) of 8 March 1978, 19 (XXXV) of 14 March 1979, 36 (XXXVI) of 12 March 1980, 26 (XXXVII) of 10 March 1981, 1982/39 of 11 March 1982, 1983/52 of 10 March 1983, 1984/24 of 8 March 1984, 1985/50 of 14 March 1985 and 1986/59 of 13 March 1986, as well as Economic and Social Council resolutions 1978/18 of 5 May 1978, 1978/40 of 1 August 1978, 1982/37 of 7 May 1982, 1983/39 of 27 May 1983, 1984/25 of 24 May 1984, 1985/42 of 30 May 1985 and 1986/40 of 23 May 1986 and Council decisions 1980/138 of 2 May 1980 and 1981/144 of 8 May 1981,

*Reaffirming* that children's rights require special protection and call for continuous improvement of the situation of children all over the world, as well as their development and education in conditions of peace and security,

*Profoundly concerned* that the situation of children in many parts of the world remains critical as a result of unsatisfactory social conditions, natural disasters, armed conflicts, exploitation, hunger and disability, and convinced that urgent and effective national and international action is called for,

*Mindful* of the important role of the United Nations Children's Fund and the United Nations in promoting the well-being of children and their development,

*Convinced* of the positive contribution which an international convention on the rights of the child, as a standard-setting accomplishment of the United Nations in the field of human rights, would make to protecting children's rights and ensuring their well-being,

*Noting with satisfaction* the widespread interest in the elaboration of an international convention on the rights of the child displayed by a great number of Member States representing all geographical regions and socio-political systems, as well as by international governmental and non-governmental organizations,

*Noting with appreciation* that further progress was made during the forty-second session of the Commission on Human Rights in the elaboration of a draft convention on the rights of the child,

1.      *Welcomes* Economic and Social Council resolution 1986/40, in which the Council authorized a meeting of an open-ended working group of the Commission on Human Rights for a period of one week prior to the forty-third session of the Commission in order to facilitate completion of the work on a draft convention on the rights of the child;

2.      *Requests* the Commission on Human Rights to give the highest priority to, and to make every effort at its forty-third session to complete, the draft convention and to submit it, through the Economic and Social Council, to the General Assembly at its forty-second session;

3.      *Invites* all Member States to offer their active contribution to the completion of the draft convention on the rights of the child at the forty-third session of the Commission on Human Rights;

4.      *Requests* the Secretary-General to provide all necessary assistance to the working group in order to ensure its smooth and efficient work in the fulfilment of its important task;

5.      *Decides* to include in the provisional agenda of its forty-second session the item entitled "Question of a convention on the rights of the child".

# L. 1987

## 1. Report of the Working Group

*The following is taken from document E/CN.4/1987/25 (9 March 1987).*

INTRODUCTION

1.      The Commission on Human Rights decided, at its forty-second session, by resolution 1986/59, to continue its work on the elaboration of the draft convention on the rights of the child as a matter of the highest priority, and requested the Economic and Social Council to authorize a one-week session of an open-ended working group prior to the forty-third session of the Commission, with a view to completing the work on the draft convention. The Council so decided by its resolution 1986/40 of 23 May 1986.

2.      The Working Group held 11 meetings from 26 to 30 January 1987 and on 6 March 1987. It adopted articles 6 bis, additional sentences to paragraphs 1 and 2; 9, new subparagraph (c); 10, additional sentence to paragraph 2; 12 bis, paragraph 3; 16, paragraph 1, subparagraph (d); 16 bis; 18 ter; 18 quater; 18 quinto; and 21 ter. The annex to this report contains proposals by delegations of States, other than those appearing in the body of the report not yet considered by the Working Group. By a note verbale of 30 January 1987, the Permanent Mission of Morocco asked that their observations on the draft convention be brought to the attention of the Working Group; those observations were contained in E/CN.4/1987/WG.1/WP.35.

ELECTIONS

3.      At the first meeting of the pre-sessional working Group, on 26 January 1987, Mr. Adam Lopatka (Poland) was elected Chairman-Rapporteur by acclamation.

QUESTION OF NEW PROPOSALS

4.      A number of delegations noted that at each session a number of new proposals for articles or amendments were submitted to the Working Group and expressed concern that the Group would not be able to complete its work in due time. Suggestions were made that a deadline be set for the submission of new proposals.

PARTICIPATION

5.      The meetings of the Working Group, which were open to all members of the Commission on Human Rights, were attended by representatives of the following States: Algeria, Argentina, Australia, Austria, Bangladesh, Belgium, Brazil, Bulgaria, China, Colombia, Cyprus, France, German Democratic Republic, Germany, Federal Republic of, India, Iraq, Italy, Japan, Mexico, Norway, Pakistan, Peru, Senegal, Union of Soviet Socialist Republics, United Kingdom of Great Britain and Northern Ireland, United States of America, Venezuela and Yugoslavia.

6.      The following States, non-members of the Commission on Human Rights, were represented by observers at the meetings of the Working Group: Canada, Denmark, Finland, Holy See, Iran, Islamic Republic of, Morocco, Netherlands, New Zealand, Poland, Sweden, Switzerland and Yemen Arab Republic.

7.      The International Labour Organization, the United Nations Children's Fund and the United Nations High Commissioner for Refugees were represented at the Working Group by observers.

8.      The following non-governmental organizations sent observers to the Working Group: Amnesty International, Anti-Slavery Society for the Protection of Human Rights, Associated Country Women of the World, Baha'i International Community, Defence for Children International Movement, Four Directions Council, Human Rights Internet, International Abolitionist Federation, International Association of Democratic Lawyers, International Association of Juvenile and Family Court Magistrates, International Catholic Child Bureau, International Commission of Jurists, International Committee of the Red Cross, International Council of Jewish Women, International Council of Women, International Council on Social Welfare, International

Federation of Women in Legal Careers, International Federation of Women Lawyers, International Movement ATD Fourth World, International Movement for Fraternal Union among Races and Peoples, Rädda Barnen International, Save the Children Fund, World Association for the School as an Instrument of Peace, World Organization for Early Childhood Education, Zonta International.

## 2. Articles adopted in 1987

*Article 6 bis, second sentence of paragraph 1*

States Parties shall further ensure that the submission of such a request shall entail no adverse consequences for the applicants and for the members of their family.

*Article 6 bis, second and third sentences of paragraph 2*

Towards that end and in accordance with the obligation of States Parties under article 6, paragraph 2, States Parties shall respect the right of the child and his parents to leave any country, including their own, and to enter their own country. The right to leave any country shall be subject only to such restrictions as are prescribed by law and which are necessary to protect the national security, public order (*ordre public*), public health or morals or the rights and freedoms of others and are consistent with the other rights recognized in the present Convention.

*Article 9, new subparagraph (c)*

Encourage the production and dissemination of children's books.

*Article 10, additional sentence to paragraph 2*

When considering alternative family care for the child and the best interest of the child, due regard shall be paid to the desirability of continuity in a child's upbringing and to the child's ethnic, religious or linguistic background.

*Article 12 bis, paragraph 3*

The State Parties to the present Convention shall seek to take all effective and appropriate measures with a view to abolishing traditional practices prejudicial to the health of children.

*Article 16, additional subparagraph (d) to paragraph 1*

The development of respect for the child's own cultural identity and values, for the national values of the country in which the child is living, for civilizations different from its own, and for human rights and fundamental freedoms.

*Article 16 bis*

In those States in which ethnic, religious or linguistic minorities or indigenous populations exist, a child belonging to such minorities or population shall not be denied the right, in community with other members of its group, to enjoy its own culture, to profess and practise its own religion, or to use its own language.

*Article 18 ter*

The State Parties to the present Convention undertake to protect the child from all forms of sexual exploitation and sexual abuse. For these purposes the States Parties shall in particular take all appropriate national, bilateral and multilateral measures to prevent:

(a)     The inducement or coercion of a child to engage in any unlawful sexual activity;

(b)     The exploitative use of children in prostitution or other unlawful sexual practices;

(c)     The exploitative use of children in pornographic performances and materials.

*Article 18 quater*

The States Parties to the present Convention shall take all appopriate national, bilateral and multilateral measures to prevent the abduction, the sale of or traffic in children for any purpose or in any form.

*Article 18 quinto*

The State Parties to the present Convention shall protect the child against all other forms of exploitation prejudicial to any aspects of the child's welfare.

*Article 21 ter*

The States Parties to the present Convention undertake to make the principles and provisions of the Convention widely known, by appropriate and active means, to adults and children alike.

## 3. Draft resolution on the "Question of a convention on the rights of the child"

*The following is taken from document E/CN.4/1987/L.57 (5 March 1987).*

Afghanistan, Algeria, Angola, Argentina, Australia, Austria, Bangladesh, Bhutan, Bolivia, Bulgaria, Byelorussian Soviet Socialist Republic, Cameroon, Canada, China, Colombia, Congo, Costa Rica, Côte d'Ivoire, Cuba, Cyprus, Czechoslovakia, Democratic Yemen, Denmark, Egypt, Ethiopia, Finland, France, Gabon, Gambia, German Democratic Republic, Ghana, Greece, Hungary, India, Iran (Islamic Republic of), Iraq, Italy, Jordan, Kenya, Lebanon, Libyan Arab Jamahiriya, Madagascar, Mexico, Mongolia, Morocco, Mozambique, Nepal, Netherlands, New Zealand, Nicaragua, Nigeria, Norway, Pakistan, Panama, Peru, Philippines, Poland, Portugal, Romania, Rwanda, Senegal, Somalia, Spain, Sri Lanka, Syrian Arab Republic, Togo, Tunisia, Ukrainian Soviet Socialist Republic, Union of Soviet Socialist Republics, United Republic of Tanzania, Uruguay, Venezuela, Viet Nam, Yemen, Zaire and Zimbabwe: draft resolution

*The Commission on Human Rights,*

*Bearing in mind* the draft convention on the rights of the child submitted by Poland to the Commission on Human Rights on 7 February 1978, the amended version of the draft submitted to the Commission on 5 October 1979, and the amended documents submitted by Poland to the General Assembly at its thirty-sixth session, on 7 October 1981, and at its fortieth session, on 7 October 1985,

*Recalling* General Assembly resolutions 33/166 of 20 December 1978, 34/4 of 18 October 1979, 35/131 of 11 December 1980, 36/57 of 25 November 1981, 37/190 of 18 December 1982, 38/114 of 16 December 1983, 39/135 of 14 December 1984, 40/113 of 13 December 1985 and 41/116 of 4 December 1986, by which the Assembly requested the Commission on Human Rights to give the highest priority to, and to make every effort at its forty-third session to complete, the draft convention and to submit it, through the Economic and Social Council, to the General Assembly at its forty-second session,

*Recalling also* its resolutions 20 (XXXIV) of 8 March 1978, 19 (XXXV) of 14 March 1979, 36 (XXXVI) of 12 March 1980, 26 (XXXVII) of 10 March 1981, 1982/39 of 11 March 1982, 1983/52 of 10 March 1983, 1984/24 of 8 March 1984, 1985/50 of 14 March 1985 and 1986/59 of 13 March 1986, and Economic and Social Council decisions 1980/138 of 2 May 1980 and 1981/144 of 8 May 1981 and resolutions 1978/18 of 5 May 1978, 1978/40 of 1 August 1978, 1982/37 of 7 May 1982, 1983/39 of 27 May 1983, 1984/25 of 24 May 1984, 1985/42 of 30 May 1985 and 1986/40 of 23 May 1986, by which it authorized a meeting of an open-ended working group for a period of one week prior to the forty-third session of the Commission, with a view to completing the work on the draft convention on the rights of the child,

*Aware* of the fact that 27 years after the adoption of the Declaration of the Rights of the Child, the situation of children in many parts of the world still continues to be far from satisfactory, and that the full enjoyment by children of human rights calls for continuous improvement of the situation of children as well as their development and education in conditions of peace and security.

*Stressing* the importance of an international convention on the rights of the child for the effective improvement of the situation of children all over the world,

*Welcoming* the efforts made by the United Nations Children's Fund with a view to promoting and protecting children's rights, life and well-being,

*Noting* the further progress made by the open-ended working group during its one-week meeting prior to the forty-third session of the Commission,

*Noting also* the growing interest in elaborating a comprehensive international convention on the rights of the child displayed by numerous Governments and international organizations,

1.    *Decides* to continue at its forty-fourth session, as a matter of the highest priority, its work on the elaboration of the draft convention on the rights of the child, with a view to completing the draft at that session for transmission, through the Economic and Social Council, to the General Assembly;

2.    *Requests* the Economic and Social Council to authorize a one-week session of an open-ended working group prior to the forty-fourth session of the Commission on Human Rights, with a view to completing the work on the draft convention on the rights of the child at that session;

3.    *Recommends* the following draft resolution to the Economic and Social Council for adoption:

"*The Economic and Social Council,*

*Recalling* General Assembly resolution 41/116 of 4 December 1986, by which the General Assembly requested the Commission on Human Rights to give the highest priority to, and to make every effort at its forty-third session to complete, the draft convention and to submit it, through the Economic and Social Council, to the General Assembly at its forty-second session,

*Considering* that it was not found possible to complete the work on the draft convention during the forty-third session of the Commission on Human Rights,

*Taking note* of Commission on Human Rights resolution 1987/... of ... March 1987,

1.    *Authorizes* a meeting of an open-ended working group for a period of one week prior to the forty-fourth session of the Commission on Human Rights with a view to completing the work on the draft convention on the rights of the child at that session;

2.    *Requests* the Secretary-General to extend all facilities to the working group for its meeting prior to and during the forty-fourth session of the Commission to enable it to fulfil its task successfully, and notes the usefulness of providing the working group, in advance of its session, with such working documents as a compilation of all amendments and new proposals and relevant provisions of other international instruments."

## 4.    Administrative and programme budget implications

*The following is taken from document E/CN.4/1987/L.82 (6 March 1987).*

QUESTION OF A CONVENTION ON THE RIGHTS OF THE CHILD (agenda item 13)

*Administrative and programme budget implications of the draft resolution contained in document E/CN.4/1987/L.57*

Statement submitted by the Secretary-General in accordance with rule 28 of the rules of procedure of the functional commissions of the Economic and Social Council

A.    Requests contained in the draft resolution

1.    By operative paragraph 1 of draft resolution E/CN.4/1987/L.57 recommended by the Commission for adoption by the Economic and Social Council, the Council would authorize a meeting of an open-ended working group for a period of one week prior to the forty-fourth session of the Commission with a view to completing the work on the draft convention on the rights of the child at that session.

B.    Relationship of request to proposed programme of work

2.      The activities referred to above would fall under chapter 6, section II, "Programme: Centre for Human Rights", subprogramme 4, "Standard-setting, research and studies", the objective of and the strategy for which are described in paragraphs 6.38 and 6.40 of the medium-term plan for the period 1984-1989 (A/37/6).

3.      The following programme element of section 23 (Human Rights) of the proposed programme budget for 1988-1989 would be directly affected by the activities referred to in the draft resolution:

Programme element 4.1 - Standard-setting

Output: (ii) Substantive servicing of the pre-sessional Working Group of the Commission on Human Rights engaged in drafting a convention on the rights of the child.

C.      Activities by which the proposed request would be implemented

4.      In order to determine the financial implications of the draft resolution it has been noted that the travel expenses of the members concerned would be covered under the normal provision for the attendance of members of the Commission.

D.      Modifications required in the proposed programme of work for 1988-1989

5.      No modifications are required in the proposed programme of work for 1988-1989 since the activity appears under programme element 4.1.

E.      Additional requirements at full cost

6.      Conference servicing costs to be financed under section 29 B (Conference Services Division, Geneva), calculated on a full-cost basis, are estimated at $73,700 for 1988.

## 5.    Discussion in the Commission on Human Rights on 11 March 1987

*The following is taken from document E/CN.4/1987/SR.55 (16 March 1987).*

QUESTION OF A CONVENTION ON THE RIGHTS OF THE CHILD (agenda item 13) (continued) (E/CN.4/1987/WG.1/CRP.1, E/CN.4/1987/L.57 and L.82)

1.      Mr. LOPATKA (Poland), speaking as Chairman-Rapporteur of the Working Group on the question of a convention on the rights of the child, presented the Group's report (E/CN.4/1987/WG.1/CRP.1). He recalled that the Group, which was informal and open-ended, had been established by Economic and Social Council resolution 1986/40. It had met from 26 to 30 January 1987 and had held 10 meetings, after which its report had been adopted unanimously. Unfortunately, it had not been able to complete the draft convention, but it had adopted five new articles: on the rights of the child belonging to an ethnic, religious or linguistic minority, on the protection of the child from all forms of sexual exploitation, on the protection of the child from all other forms of exploitation, of whatever nature, and on the prevention of the abduction of, or trafficking in, children. It had also adopted an article on the widest possible dissemination of the text of the convention. It had completed the drafting of five other articles, namely, articles 6 bis, 9, 10, 12 bis and 16.

2.      A number of proposals, which had been thoroughly discussed, had not achieved a consensus and other substantive proposals would be considered during the following year. The Group had held an in-depth discussion on the most appropriate mechanism for monitoring the implementation of the convention, and a joint text had been prepared. The discussion of that mechanism would be continued in 1988.

3.      To sum up, the results achieved by the Group were positive and encouraging, since it had adopted the preamble and 35 articles of the draft convention. It would probably not be possible to complete the first drafting of the entire text of the convention by 1988. If the Commission adopted draft resolution E/CN.4/1987/L.57, it would facilitate the task of the Group, which would meet again before the forty-fourth session in order to help the Commission to conclude its work.

4.      He emphasized that all the decisions had been taken by consensus as a result of the participants' willingness to cooperate. He thanked, in particular, those international organizations such as UNICEF, the Red

Cross and ILO, as well as non-governmental organizations, which, in addition to participating actively in the Group's work, had given extensive publicity to the draft convention. For example, the text had been studied at an international conference in Yerevan, the capital of the Armenian SSR, in September 1986, under the auspices of the Soviet youth organizations, international youth organizations and UNICEF. In conclusion, he proposed that the Commission should adopt the report of the Working Group without a vote.

5.      Mr. COLLIARD (France) said that his delegation welcomed the further progress that had been achieved during the year by the Working Group on the question of a convention on the rights of the child (E/CN.4/1987/WG.1/CRP.1), as a result of which several articles had been adopted. The aim of the draft convention was to promote consideration of the interests of the child and to give that fundamental principle an international dimension. In fact, children were frequently the first victims of the sometimes brutal reality of relations among nations.

6.      In that respect, the fate of children torn between two parents separated by a frontier was particularly distressing. Geographical distance often led to despair on the part of mothers and fathers hoping to fulfil their role as parents and educators. Distance was also heart-rending to children, who needed both a maternal and a paternal stabilizing influence and who were entitled not only to the affection of their fathers and mothers and their paternal and maternal families, but also to the benefits of two distinct cultures. With the possible exception of special cases, those children also had a right to freedom of movement between the two countries.

7.      Unfortunately, recent events throughout the world offered tragic examples of split families of that kind. In that connection, there was a need to establish or enhance bilateral cooperation between the States concerned, in a spirit of mutual respect for their traditions and cultures. That approach, which was being pursued by the French authorities, was in keeping with that adopted by the Working Group at its most recent session, during which it had considered article 16 of the draft convention.

8.      A group of divorced or separated mothers had recently come to Geneva to express their distress and suffering; his delegation wished to assure them that a bilateral convention was currently being negotiated between Algeria and France. In order to give special consideration to the human dimension in each case, it would be helpful to have a flexible and pragmatic procedure that would make it easier to take actual family situations into account. The mothers who had come could also appeal to a mediatory body composed of two eminent persons recently designated pursuant to an accord concluded between the Prime Ministers of Algeria and France in the autumn of 1986.

9.      In conclusion, he expressed the hope that the Economic and Social Council would authorize the Working Group to continue its work during the week preceding the forty-fourth session of the Commission. He assured the Group of his country's continuing interest in the text currently nearing completion and of its active cooperation.

10.      Sir Anthony WILLIAMS (United Kingdom) endorsed the sentiments expressed by the representative of France on the question of child abduction. That was a distressing problem which had recently been highlighted by the march organized by the Collective for Solidarity with the Mothers of Abducted Children. It was heartening to learn that some of the mothers who had travelled to Geneva had been temporarily reunited with their children in Strasbourg and had agreed informally with their estranged husbands on future arrangements for access to their children.

11.      In general, his Government felt that the international community should encourage the widest possible use of arrangements that had the force of law. Although ad hoc agreements were useful, they could break down very easily. In 1986, the United Kingdom had ratified the Hague Conventions on the recognition and enforcement of decisions concerning the custody of children and on the restoration of the custody of children. Even if those two Conventions did not always offer a remedy, as the courts in individual States might not always recognize an order made in another contracting State, they were a step in the right direction. His delegation hoped that they would have a deterrent effect and help to provide a solution to that growing

international problem. It also hoped that other States which had not acceded to those Conventions would recognize their value and become parties to them.

12.	Mrs. KSENTINI (Algeria) said the fact that the Working Group had not yet finalized the draft convention or begun the second reading of the articles provisionally adopted (E/CN.4/1987/WG.1/CRP.1) was solely due to the meticulous manner in which the convention was being drafted and the participants' desire to take the various aspects of the rights of the child into consideration. In fact, a convention that was intended to be universal could not confine itself to a blinkered view of the rights of the child. The Group had made a special effort to take into account the interests of children in the Third World and the special problems they were facing. She welcomed that constructive approach and urged the Group to persevere in that course of action.

13.	Her delegation wished to emphasize that, when dealing with questions relating to the status of the child, it was extremely important to pay due regard to the various legal and cultural traditions that existed in different parts of the world. In that respect, her delegation felt that the convention should take account of the practice of kafalah, for example. The second reading of the draft articles would provide an appropriate opportunity to rectify that omission and to reformulate the relevant provisions in a manner consistent with the declaration adopted by the General Assembly at its forty-first session (resolution A/41/85), entitled "Declaration on Social and Legal Principles relating to the Protection and Welfare of Children, with Special Reference to Foster Placement and Adoption Nationally and Internationally". In the preamble to that text, the General Assembly recognized that, in the principal legal systems of the world, various valuable alternative institutions existed, such as the kafalah in Islamic law, which provided substitute care for children who could not be cared for by their own parents. Her delegation hoped that the Working Group would give due consideration to the provisions of that Declaration and draw inspiration from it. Her delegation wished to take the opportunity to reaffirm the capital importance of drafting an international instrument to ensure respect for the interests, needs and rights of future generations.

14.	It also wished to refer to the case of the children of estranged mixed couples, whose situation was particularly distressing when the trauma of separation was aggravated by parental conflicts which were hardly mitigated by the differing cultural and geographical backgrounds of the spouses. The tragic situation of those children was not specific to a particular country or region. The distressing plight of those innocent child victims made it necessary to devise means that would enable a settlement to be reached in each case, in such a way as to safeguard the interests of the child while respecting the rights of both parents.

15.	Algeria had shown that it was fully conscious of the humanitarian aspect of the problem and had adopted an extremely open-minded approach with a view to furthering the interests of the child and promoting dialogue and harmony as illustrated by the negotiation of a legal convention which, through bilateral agreement, would govern legal assistance between France and Algeria. Pending the conclusion of such a convention, the competent Algerian authorities were carefully examining the cases submitted for their consideration. For obvious reasons, an Algerian magistrate could not recognize the *exequatur* of foreign judgements that failed to make recognition of the mother's right of custody conditional on the granting of visiting rights to the father, or confined those visiting rights to the territory in which the judgement had been delivered, which in practice was often tantamount to a denial of the father's visiting rights. However, it should be noted that, of the 300 applications submitted for consideration by the Algerian authorities, more than 100 cases had been settled.

16.	Algeria had always stressed the need to organize the exercise of international visiting rights with a legal guarantee of return, and it was still willing to take action to that effect, possibly through an exchange of letters between Governments. It had also consistently advocated the settlement of problems on a case-by-case basis through parental conciliation. To that end, it had appointed a mediator whose mandate had recently been renewed. Accordingly, her country welcomed the parental agreements recently concluded at Strasbourg, and was willing to guarantee their execution.

17.    In conclusion, she recognized that the Commission was not the appropriate forum to discuss the cases of children of estranged mixed couples, since the real dispute was between the parents as individuals. However, her country wished to indicate that it was aware of the humanitarian dimension of those cases and repeated its willingness to promote solutions that attached primary importance to the interests of the children, preserved their links with both parents and safeguarded the rights of the father as well as the mother. With regard to legal assistance, the bilateral negotiations between the Governments concerned remained the best way to find means of regulating such assistance on an equal and reciprocal basis conducive to respect for the values inherent in each society.

18.    Mr. AL-KHADI (Iraq) said that the promotion of human rights began with a proper upbringing of the child within the framework of the ideals of peace, dignity and freedom as set forth in the Charter. The need to give special attention to children had been affirmed in most international instruments and by the bodies concerned with the well-being of children. His delegation believed that, when drafting an international convention on the rights of the child, it was necessary to take into consideration the different laws relating to personal status and their attitudes to the family and the child, in order to produce a universally acceptable convention.

19.    However, that was not sufficient in itself: a spirit of international cooperation was also essential in order to put an end to the carnage of wars and disturbances in which children also faced death, starvation and disease. Cooperation among nations was a prerequisite for the establishment of the international economic conditions needed to help the developing countries to overcome the economic crisis and, consequently, for the development of children, who must be prepared for the effective enjoyment of their rights as stipulated in the convention. The specialized agencies and organizations particularly concerned with children could play a very significant humanitarian role in that connection.

20.    His Government shared the view expressed by States and organizations that had participated in the Working Group's consideration of draft article 20, which would remain inadequate unless efforts were made to put an end to the serious armed conflicts that were taking a deadly toll throughout the world (see paras. 159-164 of document E/CN.4/1987/WG.1/CRP.1). His Government could speak from sad experience since, for a long time, it had been embroiled in a war that had been forced on it. Furthermore, for seven years, it had witnessed the tragic fate of thousands of Iranian children whom the Government in Teheran had thrown into the battlefield as cannon fodder. Hundreds who had survived, often barely 12 years of age, were now in prisoner-of-war camps. In order to alleviate their plight, Iraq had assembled them in a special camp where they enjoyed humanitarian treatment in keeping with their age. Those children were receiving an education under an agreement concluded with Terre des Hommes, which was supervising the teaching and vocational training programme available in the camp.

21.    His delegation believed that the situation of children thrown into battle should be considered by the drafting committee working on the text of the convention, so that such occurrences could be prohibited in future. Countries should endeavour to ensure the dignity of all in a spirit of peace and understanding, failing which future generations would continue to fall victim to the hazards of war.

22.    Mr. LOMEIKO (Union of Soviet Socialist Republics) recalled that the Soviet Union had always fully supported the initiative taken by Poland with a view to the formulation and adoption of a convention on the rights of the child. His delegation was very grateful to the Working Group and, in particular, to its Chairman for the efforts they had made during the meeting held prior to the present session of the Commission. It was regrettable that the pace of the activities in which the open-ended Working Group had been engaged for many years had not been more rapid. The delays that had occurred were attributable partly to the numerous discussions that took place every year concerning the wording of provisions on which agreement had already been reached, and partly to the fact that some delegations were constantly submitting new proposals, a process that could continue indefinitely. It was essential to achieve results, particularly in view of the fact that, even in developed countries, many rights of children were still being violated and a large number of the scourges threatening children, such as slavery, sale, abduction and exploitation for various purposes

had still not been eliminated. In fact, there was even a growing number of child prostitutes, alcoholics and drug addicts, who were frequently the indirect victims of unemployment, of the inadequacy or total lack of medical services, or of a defective educational system. If, as the French author Saint-Exupéry had written, every dead child might have been another assassinated Mozart, it must be acknowledged that the situation of child victims of war was a particularly shameful phenomenon. He also noted the frequency of suicides among young people, who left letters saying that they were taking their own lives for fear of entering the war-torn world of adults and living under the threat of monstrous weapons. Adults had obligations towards children; they should respect their right to a future in a world of peace, equity and security.

23.      His delegation was convinced that a common desire and effort on the part of all would make it possible to draw up a satisfactory instrument. It would welcome an agreement to the effect that the countries participating in the Working Group would refrain from submitting new proposals. Delegations that had already distributed the texts of proposals should examine them with a critical eye and not press for their discussion by the Working Group. That applied in particular to proposals which merely repeated provisions that already existed in other international instruments, such as those relating to human rights. Those provisions had been proclaimed by the United Nations with a view to their implementation and not their constant reaffirmation. At all events, duplication should be avoided. Accordingly, the work could be speeded up and steps could be taken to ensure that, at its next session, the Working Group would be in a position to settle the questions concerning implementation machinery and to submit an agreed draft text to the Commission at its forty-fourth session. His delegation endorsed the proposals made by Mr. Lopatka and hoped that other delegations would also support them.

24.      Mr. BOSSUYT (Belgium) shared the concern expressed by the delegations of France and the United Kingdom concerning the freedom of movement of children of estranged mixed couples. In that connection, he had noted with interest the statement by the Algerian delegation.

25.      Mr. PACE (Secretary of the Commission) announced that Honduras had joined the sponsors of draft resolution E/CN.4/1987/L.57.

26.      The CHAIRMAN [Mr. EVMENOV (Byelorussian Soviet Socialist Republic)] invited the representative of the Byelorussian Soviet Socialist Republic to introduce draft resolution E/CN.4/1987/L.57.

27.      Mr. OGURTSOV (Byelorussian Soviet Socialist Republic) welcomed the extensive support that had been given to Poland's initiative, as could be seen from the fact that the draft resolution had been sponsored by almost 80 countries from virtually every part of the world. Although all those who had taken part in the sessions of the Working Group had contributed many valuable ideas, which had enhanced both the form and the substance of the draft convention, the most significant contribution had been made by Poland. Twenty-seven years after the adoption of the Declaration on the Rights of the Child, the situation of children was still far from satisfactory and must be improved. There was a need to ensure the development of children in a peaceful and secure environment. The future convention would be extremely useful since it would fill the gap in the present system of international human rights instruments, in which very inadequate consideration was given to children, who nevertheless constituted the most vulnerable human group.

28.      He referred to the principal points in the operative paragraphs of the draft resolution and expressed the hope that the text would be adopted by consensus.

29.      The CHAIRMAN [Mr. EVMENOV (Byelorussian Soviet Socialist Republic)] drew the attention of the members of the Commission to the statement of the draft resolution's financial implications, as set forth in document E/CN.4/1987/L.82.

30.      He suggested that, if there was no objection, the Commission should adopt draft resolution E/CN.4/1987/L.57 by consensus.

31.      *It was so decided.*

## 6. Commission on Human Rights resolution 1987/48 on the "Question of a convention on the rights of the child" adopted without a vote on 11 March 1987

*The Commission on Human Rights,*

*Bearing in mind* the draft convention on the rights of the child submitted by Poland to the Commission on Human Rights on 7 February 1978, the amended version of the draft submitted to the Commission on 5 October 1979, and the documents submitted by Poland to the General Assembly at its thirty-sixth session, on 7 October 1981, and at its fortieth session, on 7 October 1985,

*Recalling* General Assembly resolutions 33/166 of 20 December 1978, 34/4 of 18 October 1979, 35/131 of 11 December 1980, 36/57 of 25 November 1981, 37/190 of 18 December 1982, 38/114 of 16 December 1983, 39/135 of 14 December 1984, 40/113 of 13 December 1985 and 41/116 of 4 December 1986, by which the Assembly requested the Commission on Human Rights to give the highest priority to, and to make every effort at its forty-third session to complete, the draft convention and to submit it, through the Economic and Social Council, to the General Assembly at its forty-second session,

*Recalling also* its resolutions 20 (XXXIV) of 8 March 1978, 19 (XXXV) of 14 March 1979, 36 (XXXVI) of 12 March 1980, 26 (XXXVII) of 10 March 1981, 1982/39 of 11 March 1982, 1983/52 of 10 March 1983, 1984/24 of 8 March 1984, 1985/50 of 14 March 1985 and 1986/59 of 13 March 1986, and Economic and Social Council decisions 1980/138 of 2 May 1980 and 1981/144 of 8 May 1981 and resolutions 1978/18 of 5 May 1978, 1978/40 of 1 August 1978, 1982/37 of 7 May 1982, 1983/39 of 27 May 1983, 1984/25 of 24 May 1984, 1985/142 of 30 May 1985 and 1986/40 of 23 May 1986, by which it authorized a meeting of an open-ended working group for a period of one week prior to the forty-third session of the Commission with a view to completing the work on the draft convention on the rights of the child,

*Aware* of the fact that twenty-seven years after the adoption of the Declaration of the Rights of the Child, the situation of children in many parts of the world still continues to be far from satisfactory, and that the full enjoyment by children of human rights calls for continuous improvement of the situation of children as well as their development and education in conditions of peace and security,

*Stressing* the importance of an international convention on the rights of the child for the effective improvement of the situation of children all over the world,

*Welcoming* the efforts made by the United Nations Children's Fund with a view to promoting and protecting children's rights, life and well-being,

*Noting* the further progress made by the open-ended working group during its one-week meeting prior to the forty-third session of the Commission,

*Noting also* the growing interest in elaborating a comprehensive international convention on the rights of the child displayed by numerous Governments and international organizations,

1.      *Decides* to continue at its forty-fourth session, as a matter of the highest priority, its work on the elaboration of the draft convention on the rights of the child, with a view to completing the draft at that session for transmission, through the Economic and Social Council, to the General Assembly;

2.      *Requests* the Economic and Social Council to authorize a one-week session of an open-ended working group prior to the forty-fourth session of the Commission on Human Rights, with a view to completing the work on the draft convention on the rights of the child at that session;

3.      *Recommends* the following draft resolution to the Economic and Social Council for adoption:

"*The Economic and Social Council,*

*Recalling* General Assembly resolution 41/116 of 4 December 1986, by which the Assembly requested the Commission on Human Rights to give the highest priority to, and to make every effort at its forty-third session to complete, the draft convention and to submit it, through the Economic and Social Council, to the General Assembly at its forty-second session,

*Considering* that it was not found possible to complete the work on the draft convention during the forty-third session of the Commission on Human Rights,

*Taking note* of Commission on Human Rights resolution 1987/48 of 11 March 1987,

1.      *Authorizes* a meeting of an open-ended working group for a period of one week prior to the forty-fourth session of the Commission on Human Rights with a view to completing the work on the draft convention on the rights of the child at that session;

2.      *Requests* the Secretary-General to extend all facilities to the working group for its meeting prior to and during the forty-fourth session of the Commission to enable it to fulfil its task successfully, and notes the usefulness of providing the working group, in advance of its session, with such working documents as a compilation of all amendments and new proposals and relevant provisions of other international instruments."

## 7.   Economic and Social Council resolution 1987/58 on the "Question of a convention on the rights of the child" adopted on 29 May 1987

*The Economic and Social Council,*

*Recalling* General Assembly resolution 41/116 of 4 December 1986, by which the Assembly requested the Commission on Human Rights to give the highest priority to, and to make every effort at its forty-third session to complete, the draft convention on the rights of the child and to submit it, through the Economic and Social Council, to the General Assembly at its forty-second session,

*Considering* that it was not found possible to complete the work on the draft convention during the forty-third session of the Commission on Human Rights,

*Taking note* of Commission on Human Rights resolution 1987/48 of 11 March 1987,

1.      *Authorizes* a meeting of an open-ended working group for a period of one week prior to the forty-fourth session of the Commission on Human Rights, with a view to completing the work on the draft convention on the rights of the child at that session;

2.      *Requests* the Secretary-General to extend all facilities to the working group for its meeting prior to and during the forty-fourth session of the Commission to enable it to fulfil its task successfully, and notes the usefulness of providing the working group, in advance of its session, with such working documents as a compilation of all amendments and new proposals and relevant provisions of other international instruments;

3.      *Draws attention* to the need for new proposals to be submitted early in the session of the working group.

*18th plenary meeting*
*29 May 1987*

## 8.   General Assembly resolution 42/101 on the "Question of a convention on the rights of the child" adopted on 7 December 1987

*The General Assembly,*

*Recalling* its resolutions 33/166 of 20 December 1978, 34/4 of 18 October 1979, 35/131 of 11 December 1980, 36/57 of 25 November 1981, 37/190 of 18 December 1982, 38/114 of 16 December 1983, 39/135 of 14 December 1984, 40/113 of 13 December 1985 and 41/116 of 4 December 1986,

*Recalling also* Commission on Human Rights resolutions 20 (XXXIV) of 8 March 1978, 19 (XXXV) of 14 March 1979, 36 (XXXVI) of 12 March 1980, 26 (XXXVII) of 10 March 1981, 1982/39 of 11 March 1982, 1983/52 of 10 March 1983, 1984/24 of 8 March 1984, 1985/50 of 14 March 1985, 1986/59 of 13 March 1986 and 1987/48 of 11 March 1987, as well as Economic and Social Council resolutions 1978/18 of 5 May 1978, 1978/40 of 1 August 1978, 1982/37 of 7 May 1982, 1983/39 of 27 May 1983, 1984/25 of 24 May 1984, 1985/42 of 30 May 1985, 1986/40 of 23 May 1986 and 1987/58 of 29 May 1987 and Council decisions 1980/138 of 2 May 1980 and 1981/144 of 8 May 1981,

*Reaffirming* that children's rights require special protection and call for continuous improvement of the situation of children all over the world, as well as their development and education in conditions of peace and security,

*Profoundly concerned* that the situation of children in many parts of the world remains critical as a result of unsatisfactory social conditions, natural disasters, armed conflicts, exploitation, hunger and disability and convinced that urgent and effective national and international action is called for,

*Mindful* of the important role of the United Nations Children's Fund and the United Nations in promoting the well-being of children and their development,

*Convinced* of the positive contribution which an international convention on the rights of the child, as a standard-setting accomplishment of the United Nations in the field of human rights, would make to protecting children's rights and ensuring their well-being,

*Noting with appreciation* that further progress was made during the forty-third session of the Commission on Human Rights in the elaboration of a draft convention on the rights of the child,

*Bearing in mind* that 1989 marks the thirtieth anniversary of the Declaration on the Rights of the Child and of the tenth anniversary of the International Year of the Child,

*Considering* that these anniversaries could constitute an appropriate target date for completion of the work on a draft convention on the rights of the child and for its adoption by the General Assembly at its forty-fourth session in 1989,

1.      *Welcomes* Economic and Social Council resolution 1987/58, in which the Council authorized a meeting of an open-ended working group of the Commission on Human Rights for a period of one week prior to the forty-fourth session of the Commission in order to facilitate completion of the work on a draft convention on the rights of the child;

2.      *Requests* the Secretary-General to authorize convening, if necessary and within existing resources, the open-ended working group of the Commission on Human Rights for an additional week at its January 1988 session in order to complete a draft convention so as to facilitate its conclusion in 1989, the year of the thirtieth anniversary of the Declaration on the Rights of the Child and of the tenth anniversary of the International Year of the Child;

3.      *Requests* the Commission on Human Rights to give the highest priority to, and to make every effort at its sessions in 1988 and in 1989 to complete, a draft convention on the rights of the child and to submit it, through the Economic and Social Council, to the General Assembly at its forty-fourth session;

4.      *Invites* all Member States to offer their active support to the completion of a draft convention on the rights of the child in 1989;

5.      *Requests* the Secretary-General to provide all necessary assistance to the working group in order to ensure its smooth and efficient work in the fulfilment of its important task;

6.      *Decides* to include in the provisional agenda of its forty-third session the item entitled "Question of a convention on the rights of the child".

*93rd plenary meeting*
*7 December 1987*

# M. 1988

## 1.  Report of the Working Group

*The following is taken from document E/CN.4/1988/28 (6 April 1988).*

INTRODUCTION

1.          The Commission on Human Rights decided, at its forty-third session, by resolution 1987/48, to continue its work on the elaboration of the draft convention on the rights of the child as a matter of the highest priority, and requested the Economic and Social Council to authorize a one-week session of an open-ended working group prior to the forty-fourth session of the Commission, with a view to completing the work on the draft convention. The Council so decided at its first regular session of 1987 by its resolution 1987/58. The General Assembly, by its resolution 42/101, inter alia, requested the Secretary-General to authorize the convening of the open-ended working group of the Commission for an additional week at its January 1988 session, if necessary and within existing resources, in order to complete the draft convention so as to facilitate its conclusion in 1989.

2.          The working group held 22 meetings from 25 January to 5 February 1988 and on 7 and 10 March 1988. It adopted an additional paragraph of the preamble, articles 1 bis, 5 bis, 7a, 7 ter, 7 quater, 12 bis (revised), paragraph 4 of article 14, article 18 sixt, an additional sentence to paragraph 2 of article 20, as well as articles 22 through 31 inclusive. The text of the draft convention as adopted by the working group is contained in document E/CN.4/1988/WG.1/WP.1/Rev.2.

ELECTIONS

3.          At the first meeting of the pre-sessional working group on 25 January 1988, Mr. Adam Lopatka (Poland) was elected Chairman-Rapporteur by acclamation.

QUESTION OF NEW PROPOSALS

4.          At the beginning of the session, the working group established a deadline of 29 January 1988 for the submission of new proposals.

PARTICIPATION

5.          The meetings of the working group, which were open to all members of the Commission on Human Rights, were attended by representatives of the following States: Algeria, Argentina, Bangladesh, Belgium, Brazil, Bulgaria, China, Colombia, Cyprus, France, German Democratic Republic, Germany, Federal Republic of, India, Iraq, Italy, Japan, Mexico, Nigeria, Norway, Pakistan, Peru, Philippines, Portugal, Senegal, Spain, United Kingdom of Great Britain and Northern Ireland, United States of America, Union of Soviet Socialist Republics, Venezuela, Yugoslavia.

6.          The following States, non-members of the Commission on Human Rights, were represented by observers at the meetings of the working group: Australia, Austria, Canada, Cuba, Czechoslovakia, Egypt, Finland, Holy See, Jordan, Kenya, Morocco, Netherlands, Poland, New Zealand, Sweden, Switzerland, Yemen, Zimbabwe.

7.          The United Nations Children's Fund, the United Nations High Commissioner for Refugees, the International Labour Organization, and the Inter-American Children's Institute of the Organization of American States were represented at the working group as observers.

8.          The following non-governmental organizations sent observers to the working group: Amnesty International, Associated Country Women of the World, Baha'i International Community, Caritas Internationalis, Defence for Children International Movement, Friends World Committee for Consultation, Human Rights Internet, Indian Council of South America, International Abolitionist Federation, International Association of Democratic Lawyers, International Association of Juvenile and Family Court Magistrates, International Association of Penal Law, International Catholic Child Bureau, International Committee of the Red Cross,

International Council of Jewish Women, International Council on Social Welfare, International Federation of Human Rights, International Federation of Women in Legal Careers, International Movement ATD Fourth World, International Right to Life Federation, Rädda Barnen International, Save the Children Alliance, Save the Children Fund (UK), World Association for the School as an Instrument of Peace, World Federation of Democratic Youth, World Federation of Methodist Women, Zonta International.

[...]

III.     OTHER QUESTIONS

A.       Numbering of the articles in the draft convention

236.     At the request of the Chairman, the representative of Norway submitted a proposal for the renumbering of the articles of the draft convention (E/CN.4/1988/WG.1/WP.30). Some speakers stated that they hesitated to renumber the articles at that stage, because the work had not arrived at a point where a final renumbering could be done. In the meantime, it was better to keep the old numbering of the articles for easy reference of the members during the second reading. Otherwise, it would be necessary to refer to the new and the old numbers. which will not facilitate the discussion. The Chairman of the working group stated that he thought it would be useful to make some progress in the renumbering, but he agreed to postpone the question until the second reading.

B.       Technical review of the draft convention

237.     The question of a technical review of the draft convention was discussed on the basis of a proposal submitted by Australia (E/CN.4/1988/WG.1/WP.20). In the course of the discussion the members of the working group expressed their views on the main aspects to be considered when undertaking a technical review of the text.

238.     Several speakers stated that they understood that in a technical review the text of the convention would be examined and its provisions would be compared with those contained in other international instruments in order to ensure that they met, as a minimum, the standards of other instruments of international human rights and humanitarian law. They did not agree with including in the review an assessment of whether the provisions were such as to be realistically attainable immediately by all States. That was considered to be a matter that each individual State would decide when ratifying the convention.

239.     One participant stated that the convention encompassed two categories of rights: those which could be immediately implemented and were therefore obligatory for the States parties and those which, though applicable, were to be fully realized progressively. It was their view that, in the technical review, those rights which, on the basis of existing international norms, were considered to be fully applicable immediately should be identified.

240.     As the proposal mentioned the checking of the internal consistency of the articles of the convention, some delegations hesitated to support that formulation, which they found too vague. They stated that the internal logic of the convention should not be reviewed because all its articles were the result of a very difficult compromise and long discussion. In that regard, some speakers wished to confine the review to strictly technical aspects, the substantive ones being excluded as well as the areas of political controversy.

241.     The observer for Egypt stated that the members of the working group were not bound by the review or by any document issued as a consequence of the review; a report would be submitted to the working group and it would be discussed at the working group's next session.

242.     In connection with internal consistency, some speakers wished to have a list of definitions of terms used in the convention, which would be of great help for a correct understanding of the legal and practical effects of its provisions. For example, there was no definition of the concept of "parents" or "legal guardians". Were only biological parents concerned, or were other persons also entitled to be considered parents for some purposes, with equal responsibilities in relation to the child or children concerned? There was an analysis of definitions prepared by a non-governmental organization which could be of some help when

preparing such a list for the convention. This should be considered during the quality control exercise so that the issue could be resolved at second reading.

243.     The linguistic aspects of the review were discussed in detail. One speaker proposed revising the language used in the draft convention when it was unnecessarily complicated. Another warned that a linguistic revision could bring about a change in meaning and there was a risk in effecting changes that went beyond the mere technical aspects. According to some speakers, no one intended to change the approach and to reopen the substantive debate, but in some cases, words could be improved to reflect better the intentions of the working group. The language should not be so simple that it lacked precision; it was necessary to find the most adequate words. It was also necessary to pay attention to the internal logic of the sentences and of each one of the articles and to take care that the language utilized did not imply any kind of discrimination, as certain forms of expression that could, in English, exclude women from the provisions of the draft convention.

244.     Some delegations pointed out that the linguistic review should cover all the languages into which the convention would be translated.

245.     All members agreed that overlap and repetition between and within draft articles should be identified.

246.     In order to ensure that those who would conduct the review had a correct interpretation of the intentions of the members of the working group in drafting each of the articles, it was suggested that the reports of the different sessions of the working group could be made available to the persons in charge of the review.

247.     An exchange of ideas took place as to who would be charged with the review. One speaker suggested that it should be carried out by an independent body, either the Centre for Human Rights or the Office of Legal Affairs of the United Nations. His view was shared by most of the delegations. One participant suggested that an independent interdisciplinary group should carry out the review. The need to have the review presented with the minimum delay possible was stressed by one speaker and supported by others.

248.     The members of the group agreed that the Chairman on behalf of the group, should address a letter to the Secretary-General requesting a technical review of the draft in accordance with United Nations technical standards and practices regarding that kind of international instrument in which the points agreed upon in previous discussions should be underlined. A new text was drafted and adopted which reads as follows:

> Attached is the completed draft of the first reading of the convention on the rights of the child. The working group has proposed that this draft be circulated to all Member States so that their comments on it can be taken into account when the group conducts its second reading of the draft.
>
> The working group has also proposed that the draft as it stands be the subject of a technical review taking account of accepted United Nations technical standards and practices regarding multilateral human rights treaties and treaties of international humanitarian law. In the view of the working group such a review, which would best be carried out by the United Nations Secretariat in advance of the second reading, might:
>
> -        identify overlap and repetition between and within draft articles;
>
> -        check for consistency in the text, including the use of key terms and the use of gender-neutral language, and between the different language versions;
>
> -        compare the standards established with those in other widely accepted human rights instruments, particularly the two International Covenants; and
>
> -        make textual and editorial suggestions and recommendations as to how any overlaps or inconsistencies identified might be corrected in the second reading, including through the consolidation and relocation of articles.

The working group has asked me to draw to your attention and to that of those who conduct the review, the report of the working group on its discussion of this issue. This will make clear the nature of the review envisaged. In particular, it was the firm view of the working group that the technical review should not enter into areas of substantive or political controversy but should be confined to technical issues.

In order for the technical review to be of full benefit to the working group, I would hope it could be completed by 31 August 1988.

Signed:


Adam LOPATKA,

<small>CHAIRMAN OF THE WORKING GROUP ON THE DRAFT CONVENTION ON THE RIGHTS OF THE CHILD</small>

IV.     ADOPTION OF THE REPORT

250.      The representative of Japan stated that since his delegation had not participated in the working group from the beginning of its work, he had not been able to comment on some of the articles of the draft convention. For this reason, he wished to reserve the right to make further comments during the second reading on various articles already adopted.

251.      The Chairman noted that during the second reading all delegations would be invited to comment on the text of the draft convention which had already been adopted by the working group.

252.      While drawing attention to the importance Senegal attached to the adoption of a convention on the rights of the child, the Senegalese representative nevertheless stated that the drafting exercise had failed to take account of the concerns of the developing countries and he expressed his concern over the imbalance of the draft, which did not reflect the universality that was desired. He felt therefore compelled to enter his delegation's reservations on the report, which, he stated, did not reflect the work of the working group and which was characterized by a selectivity of the delegations that had taken part in the drafting exercise, the consequence of which was an imbalance in the proposed text. He also indicated his misgivings concerning the future work of the working group if concerns and needs of the developing countries were not borne in mind at all times. He urged the working group to be more responsive to those countries in the course of the second reading of the draft convention so that there would be more chance of universal recognition of the future convention. By way of example, he stated that there continued to be many differences of opinion with respect to the definitions reserved for terms such as "guardianship", "adoption", "filiation", "legal situation of legitimate and illegitimate children", "protection of the child before birth", "custody of children", etc. This statement was supported by the delegations of Egypt and Morocco.

253.      In this regard, the Chairman noted that participants from a wide range of developing and developed countries had taken part in the work of the group and that, through their declarations and suggestions, they had made significant and positive contributions to the draft convention which he felt reflected universal concerns. He stated that limits imposed by the General Assembly on the length of documents required the working group to adopt a style of report which did not permit a full account of each participant's statement. It was only possible to provide a summary of the main ideas. Thus, reference was made in the report to specific delegations only when a direct proposal had been made by that delegation, or the delegation had expressly asked that a reservation be included in the report.

254.      The representative of Venezuela expressed the view that the first reading of the draft convention had not been completed. She hoped that this would be done at the working group's next meeting or, in any event, before the second reading began.

255.    At the 22nd meeting of its tenth session, on 10 March 1988, the working group adopted the present report.

## 2.    Articles adopted in 1988

*Preamble, eighth paragraph*

*Recognizes* that, in rich as well as in poor countries, there are children living in exceptionally difficult conditions, and that such children need special consideration.

*Article 1 bis*

1.    The State Parties to the present Convention recognize that every child has the inherent right to life.

2.    States Parties shall ensure, to the maximum extent possible, the survival and development of the child.

*Article 5 bis*

The States Parties to the present Convention shall respect the responsibilities, rights, and duties of parents or, where applicable, legal guardians or other individuals legally responsible for the child, to provide, in a manner consistent with the evolving capacities of the child, appropriate direction and guidance in the exercise by the child of the rights recognized in the present Convention.

*Article 7a*

1.    The child shall have the right to freedom of expression; this right shall include freedom to seek, receive and impart information and ideas of all kinds, regardless of frontiers, either orally, in writing or in print, in the form of art, of through any other media of the child's choice.

2.    The exercise of this right may be subject to certain restrictions, but these shall only be such as are provided by law and are necessary:

(a)    For respect of the rights and reputations of others; or

(b)    For the protection of national security or of public order (*ordre public*), or of public health and morals.

*Article 7 ter*

1.    The States Parties to the present Convention recognize the rights of the child to freedom of association and to freedom of peaceful assembly.

2.    No restrictions may be placed on the exercise of these rights other than those imposed in conformity with the law and which are necessary in a democratic society in the interests of national security or public safety, public order (*ordre public*), the protection of public health or morals or the protections of the rights and freedoms of others.

*Article 7 quater*

1.    The States Parties to the present Convention recognize the right of the child not be subjected to arbitrary or unlawful interference with his or her privacy, family, home or correspondence, nor to unlawful attack on his or her honour and reputation.

2.    The child has the right to the protection of the law against such interference or attacks.

*Article 12 bis, revision*

1.    The States Parties to the present Convention recognize the right of the child to the enjoyment of the highest attainable standard of health and to medical and rehabilitation facilities. The States Parties shall strive to ensure that no child is deprived for financial reasons of his right of access to such health-care services.

2.    The States Parties to the present Convention shall pursue full implementation of this right and, in particular, shall take appropriate measures:

(a)    To diminish infant and child mortality;

(b)    To ensure the provision of necessary medical assistance and health care to all children with emphasis on the development of primary health care;

(c)    To combat disease and malnutrition within the framework of primary health care, through the application of readily available technology and through the provision of adequate nutritious foods and clean drinking water;

(d)    To ensure appropriate health care for expectant mothers;

(e)    To ensure that all segments of society, in particular parents and children, are informed, and supported in the use, of basic knowledge of child health and nutrition, the advantages of breastfeeding, hygiene and environmental sanitation and the prevention of accidents;

(f)    To develop preventive health care and family planning education and services.

3.    The States Parties to the present Convention shall seek to take all effective and appropriate measures with a view to abolishing traditional practices prejudicial to the health of children.

4.    States Parties to the present Convention undertake to promote and encourage international cooperation with a view to achieving progressively the full realization of the right recognized in this article. In this regard, particular account shall be taken of the needs of developing countries.

*Article 14, paragraph 4*

4.    States Parties to the present Convention shall take all appropriate measures to secure the recovery of maintenance for the child from the parents or other persons having financial responsibility for the child, both within the State Party and from abroad. In particular, where the person having financial responsibility for the child lives in a different State from the child, States Parties shall promote the accession to international agreements or the conclusion of such agreements as well as the making of other appropriate arrangements.

*Article 18 sixt*

The States Parties to the present Convention shall take all appropriate measures to ensure the physical and psychological recovery and social reintegration of a child victim of: any form of neglect, exploitation, or abuse; torture or any other form of cruel, inhuman, or degrading treatment or punishment. Such recovery and reintegration shall take place in an environment which fosters the health, self-respect and dignity of the child.

*Article 20, additional sentence to paragraph 2*

In recruiting among those persons who have attained the age of fifteen years but who have not attained the age of eighteen years, the States Parties to the present Convention shall endeavour to give priority to those who are oldest.

*Article 22*

1.    For the purpose of examining the progress made by States Parties in achieving the realization of the obligations undertaken in the present Convention, there shall be established a Committee on the rights of the child, which shall carry out the functions hereinafter provided.

2.    The Committee shall consist of 10 experts of high moral standing and recognized competence in the field covered by this Convention. The members of the Committee shall be elected by the States Parties from among their nationals and shall serve in their personal capacity, consideration being given to equitable geographical distribution as well as to the principal legal systems.

3.    The members of the Committee shall be elected by secret ballot from a list of persons nominated by States Parties. Each State Party may nominate one person from among its own nationals.

4.    The initial election to the Committee shall be held no later than six months after the date of the entry into force of the present Convention and thereafter every second year. At least four months before the date of each election, the Secretary-General of the United Nations shall address a letter to the States Parties inviting them to submit their nominations within two months. The Secretary-General shall subsequently prepare a list in alphabetical order of all persons thus nominated, indicating the States Parties which have nominated them, and shall submit it to the States Parties to the present Convention.

5.      The elections shall be held at meetings of the States Parties convened by the Secretary-General at United Nations Headquarters. At those meetings, for which two thirds of the States Parties shall constitute a quorum, the persons elected to the Committee shall be those who obtain the largest number of votes and an absolute majority of the votes of the representatives of States Parties present and voting.

6.      The members of the Committee shall be elected for a term of four years. They shall be eligible for re-election if renominated. The term of five of the members elected at the first election shall expire at the end of two years; immediately after the first election the names of these five members shall be chosen by lot by the Chairman of the meeting.

7.      If a member of the Committee dies or resigns or for any other cause can no longer perform the duties of the Committee, the State Party which nominated the member shall appoint another expert from among its nationals to serve for the remainder of the term, subject to the approval of the Committee.

8.      The Committee shall establish its own rules of procedure.

9.      The Committee shall elect its officers for a period of two years.

10.     The meetings of the Committee shall normally be held at the United Nations Headquarters or at any other convenient place as determined by the Committee. The Committee shall normally meet annually. The duration of the meetings of the Committee shall be determined, and reviewed, if necessary, by a meeting of the States Parties to the present Convention, subject to the approval of the General Assembly.

10. bis    The Secretary-General of the United Nations shall provide the necessary staff and facilities for the effective performance of the functions of the Committee under the present Convention.

11.     [With the approval of the General Assembly, the members of the Committee established under the present Convention shall receive emoluments from United Nations resources on such terms and conditions as the Assembly may decide.]

or

11.     [States Parties shall be responsible for the expenses of the members of the Committee while they are in performance of Committee duties.]

[12.     The State Parties shall be responsible for expenses incurred in connection with the holding of meetings of the States Parties and of the Committee, including reimbursement to the United Nations of any expenses, such as the cost of staff and facilities, incurred by the United Nations pursuant to paragraph 10 of this article.]

*Article 23*

1.      State Parties to the present Convention undertake to submit to the Committee, through the Secretary-General of the United Nations, reports on the measures they have adopted which give effect to the rights recognized herein and on the progress made on the enjoyment of those rights:

        (a)     Within two years of the entry into force of the Convention for the State Party concerned,

        (b)     Thereafter every five years.

2.      Reports made under this article shall indicate factors and difficulties, if any, affecting the degree of fulfilment of the obligations under the present Convention. Reports shall also contain sufficient information to provide the Committee with a comprehensive understanding of the implementation of the Convention in that country.

3.      A State Party which has submitted a comprehensive initial report to the Committee need not in its subsequent reports submitted in accordance with paragraph 1 (b) repeat basic information previously provided.

4.      The Committee may request from the State Parties further information relevant to the implementation of the Convention.

5.      The Committee shall submit to the General Assembly of the United Nations through the Economic and Social Council, every two years, reports on its activities.

6.      The States Parties shall make their reports widely available to the public in their own countries.

*Article 24*

In order to foster the effective implementation of the Convention and to encourage international cooperation in the field covered by the Convention:

(a)    The specialized agencies and UNICEF shall be entitled to be represented at the consideration of the implementation of such provisions of the present Convention as fall within the scope of their mandate. The Committee may invite the specialized agencies, UNICEF and other competent bodies as it may consider appropriate to provide expert advice on the implementation of the Convention in areas falling within the scope of their respective mandates. The Committee may invite the specialized agencies and UNICEF to submit reports on the implementation of the Convention in areas falling within the scope of their activities.

(b)    The Committee shall transmit, as it may consider appropriate, to the specialized agencies, UNICEF and other competent bodies, any reports from States Parties that contain a request, or indicate a need, for technical advice or assistance along with the Committee's observations and suggestions, if any, on these requests or indications.

(c)    The Committee may recommend to the General Assembly to request the Secretary-General to undertake on its behalf studies on specific issues relating to the rights of the child.

(d)    The Committee may make suggestions and general recommendations based on information received pursuant to articles 23 and 24 of this Convention. Such suggestions and general recommendations shall be transmitted to any State Party concerned and reported to the General Assembly, together with comments, if any, from States Parties.

*Article 25*

1.    The present Convention shall be open for signature by all States.

2.    The Secretary-General of the United Nations is designated as the depositary of the present Convention.

3.    The present Convention is subject to ratification. Instruments of ratification shall be deposited with the Secretary-General of the United Nations.

4.    The present Convention shall be open to accession by all States. Accession shall be effected by the deposit of an instrument of accession with the Secretary-General of the United Nations.

*Article 26 (Amendments)*

1.    Any State Party to the present Convention may propose an amendment and file it with the Secretary-General of the United Nations. The Secretary-General shall thereupon communicate the proposed amendment to the States Parties to the present Convention with a request that they indicate whether they favour a conference of States Parties for the purpose of considering and voting upon the proposals. In the event that within four months from the date of such communication at least one third of the States Parties favour such a conference, the Secretary-General shall convene the conference under the auspices of the United Nations. Any amendment adopted by a majority of the States Parties present and voting at the conference shall be submitted to the General Assembly of the United Nations for approval.

2.    An amendment adopted in accordance with paragraph 1 of this article shall enter into force when it has been approved by the General Assembly of the United Nations and accepted by a two-thirds majority of the States Parties to this Convention.

3.    When an amendment enters into force, it shall be binding on those States Parties which have accepted it, other States Parties still being bound by the provisions of this Convention and any earlier amendments which they have accepted.

*Article 27*

1.    The present Convention shall enter into force on the thirtieth day after the date of deposit with the Secretary-General of the United Nations of the twentieth instrument of ratification or accession.

2.	For each State ratifying the present Convention or acceding to it after the deposit of the twentieth instrument of ratification or accession, the Convention shall enter Into force on the thirtieth day after the date of the deposit of its own instrument of ratification or accession.

*Article 28*

1.	The Secretary-General of the United Nations shall receive and circulate to all States the text of reservations made by States at the time of ratification or accession.

2.	A reservation incompatible with the object and purpose of the present Convention shall not be permitted.

3.	Reservations may be withdrawn at any time by notification to this effect addressed to the Secretary-General of the United Nations, who shall then inform all States thereof. Such notification shall take effect on the date on which it is received.

*Article 29*

A State Party may denounce this Convention by written notification to the Secretary-General of the United Nations. Denunciation becomes effective one year after the date of receipt of the notification by the Secretary-General.

*Article 30*

The Secretary-General of the United Nations shall inform all States Members of the United Nations and all States which have signed this Convention or acceded to it of the following:

(a)	Signatures, ratifications and accessions;

(b)	The date of entry into force of this Convention and the date of the entry into force of any amendments;

(c)	Denunciations.

*Article 31*

1.	This Convention, of which the Arabic, Chinese, English, French, Russian and Spanish texts are equally authentic, shall be deposited with the Secretary-General of the United Nations.

2.	The Secretary-General of the United Nations shall transmit certified copies of this Convention to all States.

## 3.	Draft resolution on the "Question of a convention on the rights of the child"

*The following is taken from document E/CN.4/1988/L.86 (3 March 1988). The original document is in English but only the French version has been issued.*

Afghanistan, Angola, Australie, Bangladesh, Bulgarie, Canada, Costa Rica, Côte d'Ivoire, Finlande, France, Grèce, Hongrie, Inde, Liban, Mexique, Mozambique, Népal, Norvège, Panama, Pérou, Pologne, Roumanie, Somalie, Suède, Uruguay, République démocratique allemande, République socialiste soviétique de Biélorussie et Zimbabwe: projet de résolution

*La Commission des droits de l'homme,*

*Ayant présents à l'esprit* le projet de convention relative aux droits de l'enfant que la Pologne a présenté à la Commission des droits de l'homme le 7 février 1978 et qui est annexé à la résolution 20 (XXXIV) adoptée par la Commission le 8 mars 1978, la version amendée du projet présentée à la Commission le 5 octobre 1979 (E/CN.4/1349) et les documents que la Pologne a présentés à l'Assemblée générale à sa trente-sixième session, le 7 octobre 1981 (A/C.3/36/6), et à sa quarantième session, le 7 octobre 1985 (A/C.3/40/3 et Corr.1),

*Rappelant* les résolutions de l'Assemblée générale 33/166 du 20 décembre 1978, 34/4 du 18 octobre 1979, 35/131 du 11 décembre 1980, 36/57 du 25 novembre 1981, 37/190 du 18 décembre 1982, 38/114 du 16 décembre 1983, 39/135 du 14 décembre 1984, 40/113 du 13 décembre 1985, 41/116 du 4 décembre 1986 et la résolution

42/101 du 7 décembre 1987, par laquelle l'Assemblée a prié la Commission des droits de l'homme d'accorder le rang de priorité le plus élevé au projet de convention relative aux droits de l'enfant et de n'épargner aucun effort pour l'achever, à ses quarante-quatrième et quarante-cinquième sessions, et de lui présenter ce projet à sa quarante-quatrième session, par l'intermédiaire du Conseil économique et social,

*Rappelant aussi* ses résolutions antérieures, en particulier la résolution 1987/48 du 11 mars 1987, et les résolutions pertinentes du Conseil économique et social, en particulier la résolution 1987/58 du 29 mai 1987,

*Notant* que 1989 sera l'année du trentième anniversaire de la Déclaration des droits de l'enfant et du dixième anniversaire de l'Année internationale de l'enfant,

*Reconnaissant* que, comme cela est indiqué dans la résolution 42/101 de l'Assemblée générale, ces anniversaires pourraient offrir l'occasion voulue pour achever l'élaboration du projet de convention relative aux droits de l'enfant qui serait adoptée par l'Assemblée générale,

*Consciente* de ce que, vingt-huit ans après l'adoption de la Déclaration des droits de l'enfant, la situation des enfants dans l'ensemble du monde laisse encore beaucoup à désirer, et que la pleine jouissance par les enfants de leurs droits fondamentaux exige une amélioration constante de la condition des enfants ainsi que leur épanouissement et leur éducation dans un climat de paix et de sécurité,

*Constatant avec satisfaction* les efforts déployés par le Fonds des Nations Unies pour l'enfance en vue de protéger et d'aider les enfants dans l'ensemble du monde,

*Soulignant* l'importance d'une convention internationale relative aux droits de l'enfant pour l'amélioration effective de la condition des enfants dans le monde entier,

*Notant également* que l'achèvement des travaux sur l'élaboration d'une convention internationale détaillée relative aux droits de l'enfant suscite un intérêt croissant de la part d'un grand nombre de gouvernements et d'organisations internationales,

*Considérant* que la convention doit tenir dûment compte du milieu culturel et des besoins des enfants de tous les pays, y compris les pays en développement, pour que les droits qui y sont énoncés soient universellement reconnus,

1.      *Note avec satisfaction* que le Groupe de travail à composition non limitée de la Commission des droits de l'homme a achevé la première lecture d'un projet de convention détaillée relative aux droits de l'enfant;

2.      *Décide* de poursuivre, à titre hautement prioritaire, ses travaux sur l'élaboration du projet de convention relative aux droits de l'enfant;

3.      *Prie* le Conseil économique et social d'autoriser, dans les limites des ressources existantes, le Groupe de travail à composition non limitée a se réunir pendant une période ne dépassant pas deux semaines en novembre/décembre 1988, en vue d'achever la deuxième lecture du projet de convention relative aux droits de l'enfant avant la quarante-cinquième session de la Commission et de soumettre le texte à l'Assemblée générale à sa quarante-quatrième session, par l'intermédiaire du Conseil économique et social;

4.      *Prie* le Secrétaire général de faire distribuer le rapport du Groupe de travail sur sa dixième session (E/CN.4/1988/28) et le texte du projet de convention tel qu'il a été adopté en première lecture à tous les Etats en vue de faciliter leur participation, à l'échelle internationale, à la deuxième lecture;

5.      *Prie en outre* le Secrétaire général de prévoir les ressources nécessaires pour l'examen technique du texte issu de la première lecture du projet de convention, comme le Groupe de travail l'a demandé, de façon à ce que cet examen technique puisse être achevé au 31 août 1988 et ses résultats communiqués à tous les Etats bien avant que la deuxième lecture ne soit entamée;

6.      *Encourage* tous les pays, en particulier les pays en développement, à participer activement à la deuxième lecture de façon à ce que la convention exprime les besoins des enfants de tous les pays;

7.    *Recommande* au Conseil économique et social d'adopter le projet de résolution suivant:

"*Le Conseil économique et social,*

*Rappelant* la résolution 42/101 de l'Assemblée générale du 7 décembre 1987 par laquelle l'Assemblée a prié la Commission des droits de l'homme d'accorder le rang de priorité le plus élevé au projet de convention relative aux droits de l'enfant et de n'épargner aucun effort pour l'achever à ses quarante-quatrième et quarante-cinquième sessions, et de lui présenter ce projet à sa quarante-quatrième session, en 1989, par l'intermédiaire du Conseil économique et social,

*Considérant* qu'il n'a pas été possible d'achever les travaux sur le projet de convention pendant la quarante-quatrième session de la Commission,

*Prenant note* de la résolution 1988/ ... de la Commission des droits de l'homme du ... mars 1988.

1.    *Autorise*, dans les limites des ressources existantes, le Groupe de travail à composition non limitée à se réunir pendant une période ne dépassant pas deux semaines en novembre-décembre 1988 en vue d'achever la deuxième lecture du projet de convention relative aux droits de l'enfant avant la quarante-cinquième session de la Commission des droits de l'homme et de soumettre le texte à l'Assemblée générale à sa quarante-quatrième session, par l'intermédiaire du Conseil économique et social;

2.    *Prie* le Secrétaire général de continuer à fournir au Groupe de travail tout l'appui et les services nécessaires pour qu'il puisse mener sa tâche à bien et, en particulier, de faire distribuer le rapport du Groupe de travail (E/CN.4/1988/28) et le projet de convention tel qu'il a été adopté en première lecture à tous les Etats ainsi que de prévoir les ressources nécessaires pour l'examen technique demandé par le Groupe de travail et pour la prochaine session du Groupe de travail en novembre-décembre 1988."

## 4.    Administrative and programme budget implications

*The following is taken from document E/CN.4/1988/L.91 (7 March 1988). The original document is in English but only the French version has been issued.*

Incidences administratives et incidences sur le budget-programme du projet de résolution publié sous la cote E/CN.4/1988/L.86

Etat présenté par le Secrétaire général conformément à l'article 28 du règlement intérieur des commissions techniques du Conseil économique et social

A.    Demande contenue dans le projet de résolution

1.    Aux termes du paragraphe 1 du projet de résolution recommandé au Conseil économique et social pour adoption par la Commission dans son projet de résolution E/CN.4/1988/L.86, le Conseil autoriserait, dans les limites des ressources existantes, le Groupe de travail à composition non limitée à se réunir pendant une période ne dépassant pas deux semaines en novembre-décembre 1988, en vue d'achever la deuxième lecture du projet de convention relative aux droits de l'enfant à cette session.

B.    Relation entre la demande et le programme de travail proposé

2.    Les activités mentionnées ci-dessus entrent dans le cadre du chapitre 6, section II, "Programme: Centre pour les droits de l'homme", sous-programme 4, "Etablissement de normes, recherches et études", dont les objectifs et la stratégie sont décrits aux paragraphes 6.38 et 6.40 du plan à moyen terme pour la période 1984-1989 (A/37/6).

3.    Les activités prévues dans le projet de résolution affecteraient directement l'élément de programme ci-après du chapitre 23 (Droits de l'homme) du budget-programme pour 1988-1989:

Elément de programme 4.1 - Etablissement de normes

Produit : ii) Services fonctionnels nécessaires pour le Groupe de travail préliminaire de la Commission des droits de l'homme chargé de l'élaboration d'une convention relative aux droits de l'enfant.

C.      Activités à entreprendre pour donner suite à la demande

4.      Pour déterminer les incidences financières du projet de résolution, il a été noté que les frais de voyage des membres concernés seraient couverts par les crédits normalement ouverts au titre de la participation des membres de la session de la Commission.

D.      Modifications à apporter au programme de travail proposé

5.      Il n'y aurait pas de modification à apporter au programme de travail pour 1988-1989, l'activité considérée étant prévue au titre de l'élément de programme 4.1.

E.      Crédits supplémentaires sur la base du coût intégral

6.      Le coût des services de conférence à imputer sur le chapitre 29 B [Division des services de conférence (Genève)], calculé sur la base du coût intégral, est estimé à 166 400 dollars pour 1988.

F.      Possibilité d'absorption

7.      Conformément à la pratique établie, le coût des services de conférence susmentionnés a été calculé pour information sur la base du coût intégral. Cependant, ainsi qu'il est indiqué au paragraphe 29.6 du budget-programme (A/42/6), les crédits prévus dans les estimations du Secrétaire général pour le personnel temporaire de réunion ont été calculés sur la base de la moyenne quinquennale des crédits ouverts et des dépenses réelles effectuées durant la période 1982-1986. Autrement dit, il a été tenu compte dans le budget-programme non seulement des réunions prévues au moment de l'élaboration du budget mais également des réunions qui seraient ultérieurement autorisées, le nombre et la répartition des réunions et conférences durant la période biennale en cours devant être cependant conformes à l'expérience des cinq dernières années. On estime, sur cette base, qu'aucune ouverture de crédit supplémentaire ne serait nécessaire au titre du chapitre 29 du budget-programme pour la période biennale 1988-1989 à la suite de l'adoption du projet de résolution de la Commission des droits de l'homme en question.

## 5.   Discussion in the Commission on Human Rights on 10 March 1988

*The following is taken from document E/CN.4/1988/SR.56 (11 April 1988).*

QUESTION OF A CONVENTION ON THE RIGHTS OF THE CHILD (agenda item 13) (*continued*) (E/CN.4/1988/28, E/CN.4/1988/L.86, E/CN.4/1988/L.91)

8.      Mr. TOWPIK (observer for Poland), speaking on behalf of the sponsors of draft resolution E/CN.4/1988/L.86, who had been joined by Austria, China, Colombia, Cyprus, Cuba, Democratic Yemen, and Yemen, Ghana, Italy, Luxembourg, Netherlands, New Zealand, Portugal, Syrian Arab Republic, said that the draft resolution acknowledged the considerable progress made towards the completion of the work on a draft convention on the rights of the child, particularly at the last session of the open-ended working group, and took into account the growing interest in that work, as expressed, in particular, in General Assembly resolution 42/101, which requested the Commission to make every effort to complete the draft convention and submit it to the Assembly in 1989. The draft resolution also recognized the need to take due account of the cultural values and needs of the children of all countries, including developing countries. He then proceeded to read the text of the operative part of the draft resolution.

9.      Following the consultations that had taken place among a large number of delegations during the preparation of that text, and in the course of which a number of suggestions had been made, he stated that the last preambular paragraph had been revised to read:

> "Bearing in mind the necessity to take due account in the convention of the cultural values and needs of the children of all countries, in particular developing countries, in order to achieve universal recognition of the rights contained therein".

10.     His delegation hoped that the draft resolution, as thus revised, would be adopted by consensus.

11.     Mr. LEBAKINE (observer for the Ukrainian Soviet Socialist Republic) and Mr. ZORIGTBAATAR (observer for Mongolia) stated that their delegations wished to become sponsors of draft resolution E/CN.4/1988/L.86.

12.     Mr. TAYLHARDAT (Venezuela) said that his delegation, which endorsed the spirit and the objectives of draft resolution E/CN.4/1988/L.86, welcomed in particular the General Assembly's decision to request the Commission to give the highest priority to the draft convention on the rights of the child, so that the draft could be submitted to the Assembly in 1989 through the Economic and Social Council and be ready for adoption in time for the anniversary of the Declaration of the Rights of the Child (1959) and the International Year of the Child (1979). Venezuela, which wished to join the sponsors of the draft, had the greatest respect for the mission and activities of UNICEF. Indeed, it had been a member of the Executive Council of UNICEF virtually since its inception.

13.     Nevertheless, in his delegation's view, priority should not amount to undue haste and the right of every State to reflect on the impact of the draft convention in question should not be ignored. His delegation was not satisfied with the manner in which the working group had endeavoured to complete its work at any price, and regretted the fact that a certain measure of disinformation should have spread the belief that one delegation was making reservations tantamount to obstruction with regard to certain elements of the draft convention. It was unbelievable that a subsidiary body of the Commission such as the working group should refuse to allow a delegation the necessary time to consider a draft of such importance. During the session of the working group, moreover, the suggestion by his delegation that certain elements of the text should be placed between square brackets had been rejected on the pretext that those square brackets did not form the subject of a consensus, thereby implying that there was consensus on the remainder of the text. There was no precedent for such a procedure. His delegation would of course continue to participate in the work of the working group, but it felt bound to make that clarification.

14.     Mr. TOWPIK (observer for Poland), speaking on behalf of the Chairman of the working group who had had to leave Geneva, recalled that the Commission had decided, by its resolution 1987/48, to continue, as a matter of the highest priority, its work on the elaboration of a draft convention on the rights of the child. By its resolution 1987/58, the Economic and Social Council had authorized a meeting up of an open-ended working group for a period of one week prior to the forty-forth session of the Commission. The General Assembly, by its resolution 42/101 had requested the Secretary-General to authorize, if necessary and within existing resources, the convening of an open-ended working group for an additional week at the 1988 session of the Commission in order to complete the draft convention and so as to facilitate its final adoption in 1989.

15.     The working group, which had held 20 meetings from 25 January to 5 February 1988, had adopted its report unanimously and had completed, in principle, the elaboration of the text of a draft convention (see documents E/CN.4/1988/WG.1/CRP.1 and E/CN.4/1988/WG.1/WP.1/Rev.1 respectively). The working group had proposed to the Secretary-General that the text be distributed to all Member States so that their observations could be taken into consideration at the second reading and so that a technical review of the draft in its existing form, could be carried out in order to bring it into line with United Nations practices and standards with regard to multilateral treaties on human rights and treaties on international humanitarian law. That review, which should preferably be conducted by the United Nations Secretariat before the second reading, should be completed in time for the group to benefit from it. To sum up, the working group had obtained encouraging results and it would certainly be possible to complete, at the forty-fifth session of the Commission, work on the final text of the convention. The adoption of draft resolution E/CN.4/1988/ L.86 would enable the working group to complete its task and would provide an opportunity for the General Assembly to adopt the convention in 1989, the year that would mark the thirtieth anniversary of the Declaration on the Rights of the Child and the tenth anniversary of the International Year of the Child.

16.     The Chairman of the working group had made a point of stressing the spirit of cooperation and compromise which had prevailed in the group, whose decisions had, as usual, been taken by consensus. The work on the preparation of the convention had elicited a growing interest on the part of public opinion and of eminent persons such as a group of Nobel Prize winners, who had addressed a letter of support to the working group, and of Ms. Ullman, an actress of world renown who had attended the discussions of the Group. The Chairman would also have wished to have thanked personally the representatives of Governments, the observers and the representatives of UNICEF, the Red Cross, ILO and of the non-governmental organizations that had participated in the work of the group and given extensive publicity to the draft convention, for example at Linguano-Sabbiadoro (Italy) in September 1987 at a conference organized by the Italian Committee for UNICEF and the ad hoc group of non-governmental organizations, with the participation of Mrs. Mubarak, Vice-President of the Arab Council for Children and Development. Thanks were also due to the Secretary-General of the United Nations who had provided the group with all the necessary services and facilities, as well as to the officials of the Secretariat. The working group hoped that the Commission would adopt its report (E/CN.4/1988/WG.1/CRP.1) without a vote.

17.     Mr. KONATE (Senegal) expressed his appreciation to the Chairman of the working group, Mr. Lopatka, for the dedication and wisdom with which he had performed his duties.

18.     In 1983, the Senegalese delegation had warned against the temptation to adopt a uniform pattern for the children of the whole world and had drawn the Commission's attention to the need for the future convention to take into account the cultural dimensions and realities of the developing countries. In his delegation's view, efforts to promote universality should take into consideration the economic, social, cultural and religious diversity of the various regions and various legal systems of the world. That aim could be achieved by adopting a flexible approach that would allow for all those dimensions in the search for a common denominator for the various concerns being manifested throughout the world. There was reason to fear that, if the future convention were effective, it would give pride of place to assimilation rather than to participation. Enactments which ignored reality, however, were destined to become a dead letter, sacrificed on the altar of legal monuments. The Commission had to take up that challenge.

19.     The working group's report had proved difficult to adopt, because of the reservations and concerns of a number of delegations. Without wishing to complicate the Commission's work still further, his delegation proposed, on behalf of the delegations of Algeria, Angola, Bangladesh, Egypt, Ethiopia, Gambia, Iraq, Morocco, Mozambique, Nigeria, Peru, Rwanda, Sao Tome and Principe, Somalia, Senegal and Togo, that the last preambular paragraph of draft resolution E/CN.4/1988/L.86 be amended to read:

> "Bearing in mind the necessity of taking due account of the cultural values and needs of developing countries in the second reading of the draft convention, in order to achieve the universal recognition of the rights contained in the future convention on the rights of the child."

20.     The purpose of that amendment was to stress the importance of the universal acceptance of the convention at a time when the work of the Working Group was reaching a crucial stage. His delegation hoped that its proposal would benefit from the spirit of cooperation and understanding which had always prevailed when draft resolutions relating to the agenda item under consideration were being adopted.

21.     Mr. LEPRETTE (France) said that his delegation had welcomed the plan, submitted by Poland in 1978 within the framework of the International Year of the Child, to prepare a convention on the rights of the child. That initiative had been designed to fill a gap in the international system of human rights protection and to break a long chain of unjust causalities and to bring about a genuine change in the relations between adults and children.

22.     For its part, France had, since the nineteenth century, progressively enacted legislative measures to protect children, particularly in the realm of civil and criminal law and in that of labour legislation. The task was, however, a long-term one for any State, since it required action by political leaders and by public and private associations. It was significant that, among the first recipients of the prize recently created by the

French Secretary of State in charge of human rights there was the Association "La voix de l'enfant" ("The voice of the child") which campaigned for the rights of minors.

23.      The existence of a United Nations convention in the area under consideration would undoubtedly make a decisive contribution to the mobilization and development of the law and the facts in a progressive way. His delegation, which had participated very actively from the outset in the activities of the working group, warmly welcomed the completion of the first reading of the text after 10 years of work. It hoped that the draft of the convention would be finally and rapidly settled before the Commission's forty-fifth session and had decided, as in the previous year, to co-sponsor the draft resolution submitted on the matter by Poland.

24.      The comparative slowness of the process was due in the first place to the decision to opt for the more ambitious exercise, namely the elaboration of a full-fledged convention instead of an additional protocol to the Covenant; the latter approach might have been adopted, in particular to ward off the danger that the "categorization" of rights in that manner might detract from the security and universality of the rights recognized in an absolute and general manner by the two Covenants. That slowness was also attributable to the diversity of legal systems represented in the working group, a diversity which it had been possible to overcome in a spirit of compromise, and to the depth and thoroughness of the debates, which had been in keeping with the stakes involved. The high quality and constructive character of the contributions of the many non-governmental organizations which participated had also to be commended.

25.      It could be asserted, in conclusion, that the first ambition of the draft convention was to enshrine at the international level the recognition of the interests of the child. That concern was also one of the priorities for his Government, at both the social and legal levels. On the proposal of the Secretariat of State for Human Rights, his Government had ensured the enactment in the previous year of legislation aimed at favouring the joint exercise of parental authority by divorced or unmarried parents. In the case of divorce, the aim had been to ensure for the child the continuity of the parental couple in such a way that both parents could jointly exercise authority over their children by continuing to take together all important decisions concerning them. In the case of children born out of wedlock, the aim had been to ensure the exercise of parental authority by enabling the father and the mother to shoulder their responsibilities jointly.

26.      Lastly, mention should be made of the difficult question of the children of separated couples of different nationalities, who were sometimes taken illegally to the country of which one of the parents was a citizen. The solution of that problem, which arose from historical, legal, social and individual factors, should be sought in the resort to appropriate mechanisms, some of a temporary character but others of a more enduring kind, such as conventions for reciprocal assistance in the administration of justice. A convention of that kind required very lengthy negotiations, however, before it could be effectively applied in the two countries concerned. That was precisely the approach being adopted by his Government in its relations with other concerned Governments and, more particularly, at that stage, with the Government of Algeria. Two days previously, the Commission had agreed to receive a delegation of the Collective for Solidarity with Mothers of Abducted Children who had come to express their concerns and their hopes. His delegation, which had met those women, had informed them that it was proposed to establish, with the consent of the Algerian authorities, a mixed joint commission for the settlement of individual cases.

27.      Mr. BOSSUYT (Belgium) said that his delegation wished to associate itself with the statements that had just been made on the problems pertaining to the fate of children divided between two parents who were separated by a national border. Such a separation could cause genuine tragedies for the parents but above all for the children, whose interests must take precedence over all other considerations. His delegation had been pleased to note the previous year that the States most concerned were in the process of working out solutions. Those efforts must be intensified so that appropriate humanitarian solutions could be found, perhaps through the establishment of joint standing commissions. His Government would support any productive initiative that might facilitate the settlement of such family disputes.

28.     Mr. STEEL (United Kingdom) said that, like the delegations of France and Belgium, his own held that child abduction, for whatever motive and whatever the circumstances, was a tragedy, and everyone must sympathize with those, whether children or their parents, who were victims of such actions. His delegation had had some interesting talks, at the current session and the previous year, with members of the Collective for Solidarity with Mothers of Abducted Children. Although it was encouraging to note that many of the mothers who had come to Geneva in 1987 had been briefly reunited with their children during the summer and even in some cases at Christmas, other mothers had not been so fortunate. The event demonstrated that ad hoc private arrangements were of necessity fragile. It was for that reason that his Government attached so much importance to the establishment of arrangements that were backed up by the force of law, such as the Hague Convention on the Civil Aspects of International Child Abduction and the Council of Europe Convention on the recognition and enforcement of custody decisions. A number of countries had become parties to one or both of those Conventions, like the United Kingdom, which had enacted legislation specifically to enable it to ratify and implement those instruments (the Child Abduction and Custody Act, 1985). He wished also to mention the Child Abduction Act of 1984, which had made child abduction a criminal offence in the United Kingdom.

29.     His Government was convinced that the drafting of multilateral international agreements implemented by a network of effective national legislation offered the best hope both of deterring those who might be tempted to resort to child abduction, and of undoing the effects of such actions as quickly as possible. All States that were in a position to do so should become parties to the relevant conventions and should introduce the necessary domestic laws and machinery.

30.     Mr. BEZABIH (Ethiopia) said that the rights of the child constituted an issue which deserved utmost priority in the Commission's efforts to uphold and promote the basic principles underlying respect for human rights throughout the world. Children were, after all, the most vulnerable members of society, especially in areas of the world which had been or still were subjected to colonialism, racism and foreign domination. In some countries, children were deprived even of the right to a name and a nationality and were subjected to forced labour, which constituted a threat to their health, their psychological development and their education. Sexual exploitation, prostitution and the sale and abduction of children were in some countries an undeniable reality which made the adoption of measures designed to ensure the protection of minors all the more necessary.

31.     As early as 1924, the League of Nations had endorsed the Geneva Declaration of the Rights of the Child, the first attempt to codify in a single instrument the fundamental conditions to which all children in the world had a right. In 1948, that document, revised and amplified, had become the 10-point Declaration of the Rights of the Child, later adopted unanimously by the General Assembly of the United Nations on 20 November 1959, which stressed the fact that the rights of the child were an integral part of the human rights set forth in the Universal Declaration. The submission by Poland of a draft convention on the rights of the child in 1979, which had been proclaimed the International Year of the Child, had provided an opportunity to define more clearly, within the framework of a binding international instrument, the human rights standards that should apply to children everywhere in the world.

32.     Before the popular revolution in his country, most Ethiopian children had lived in extremely disadvantaged conditions. After the revolution, special measures had been introduced by the Government to improve the lot of the children, who accounted for nearly 45 per cent of the country's population. The establishment of nurseries, kindergartens, childcare centres and children's recreation centres had become a priority programme for the Government and for the country's popular organizations. To cite but one example, in the 10 years which had elapsed since the pre-revolutionary period, the number of kindergartens had grown from 77 to 610. Furthermore, in order to encourage, coordinate and supervise the nationwide efforts to improve the overall development of the child, a children's commission had been established in 1981. Despite the country's poverty, efforts were also being made to ensure that disabled children could realize their rights as Ethiopian citizens. The right of the child to citizenship was guaranteed in the newly

adopted constitution, which provided that any person with at least one parent having Ethiopian citizenship was an Ethiopian.

33.    The draft convention on the rights of the child prepared by the working group established by the Commission on Human Rights in 1979 would set universally agreed standards for the protection of the rights of children and provide an extremely useful framework for the elaboration of future programmes aimed at continuously improving the situation of children in the world. His delegation hoped that the final draft would be completed, as scheduled, in 1989 - a symbolic year for children everywhere, since it marked the tenth anniversary of the International Year of the Child and the thirtieth anniversary of the historic Declaration of the Rights of the Child.

34.    Mr. MEZZALAMA (Italy) took the Chair.

35.    Mr. FATHALLAH (observer for Egypt) said that, in his country, the child was regarded as the nucleus of the family, itself the basic cell of society. For that reason if for no other, children must be given every guarantee of enjoying all their rights. The first right of the child was to have two natural and acknowledged parents, so that he could grow up in a psychological environment that was conducive to his all-round development. The Egyptian delegation viewed that right as being more important than the right to name and nationality, which formed the subject of article 2 of the draft convention and which was incompatible with the principles of the social, legal and religious systems in many countries. That was why his delegation was in favour of removing that provision from the draft convention and introducing the notion of the right to natural and acknowledged parents. If it was desirable that the convention be universal in nature, it was precisely so that it might have a positive impact on cooperation and consultation among States and on international relations in general, especially in the political and economic spheres. After all, the fate of an entire generation was to be determined, and that was a heavy responsibility.

36.    His delegation had contributed to the efforts of the working group and supported its recommendations. It welcomed the stress that had been placed on the need to transmit to Governments the results of the first reading of the draft convention, before 31 August 1988, in order to facilitate the second reading. The fact that the first reading had been completed did not, however, mean that no further amendments could be made to the text and, in that connection, his delegation endorsed the initiative of the Senegalese and other delegations which had submitted an amendment to the eighth preambular paragraph of draft resolution E/CN.4/1988/L.86.

37.    While welcoming the efforts made by the working group, his delegation deplored the procedure by which the group's report had been prepared, for the reasons it had expounded during the adoption of the report. As for the draft convention itself, his delegation considered that the provisions of article 2, paragraph 2, were at variance with the legislation of the many countries which did not automatically grant nationality to children born in their territory. It also had reservations regarding article 12, the provisions of which were incompatible with Muslim law, and should be deleted. Finally, its support for the general agreement that had been reached on a particular portion of article 20 did not mean that it had gone back on its original position, which was that a distinction must be made between the compulsory enlistment of children in the armed forces and voluntary admission of children to military schools to follow a course of training additional to ordinary education. Under no circumstances, however, should children participate in military operations. In view of the extent of that phenomenon, his delegation had, in 1968, submitted a draft declaration on the protection of women and children in situations of armed conflict and thought that the international community should devote special attention to the matter.

38.    His delegation supported the idea of establishing an ad hoc committee, to be financed out of the regular budget of the United Nations, with the mandate of monitoring the implementation of the convention. In view of the existence of regional conventions on the protection of the rights of the child, it was essential that regional machinery be set up to facilitate the task of the ad hoc committee. Regional and international activities in the area should be complementary and not mutually contradictory. In that

connection, his delegation understood the expression "other competent bodies" in article 24 (b) to apply to regional institutions such as the Arab Council for Children and Development.

39.    In conclusion, his delegation thanked UNESCO for having organized, in January 1988, the informal meetings which had facilitated the task of the working group.

40.    Mrs. SEIMANE-BOUAMRANE (Algeria) said that her delegation welcomed the spirit of cooperation that had prevailed within the working group responsible for preparing a draft convention on the rights of the child. The group had made good progress and had been able to complete the consideration in first reading of a large portion of the draft. Like other delegations, her own endorsed the General Assembly's recommendation that the drafting of the convention should be completed in 1989. She hoped, however, that, during the second reading, a number of elements linked to cultures and civilizations and the particular needs of the developing countries would be taken into account so that the convention might be universally acceptable.

41.    With regard to the issue of children of separated couples of different nationalities, it must be stressed that the traumatic situation of those innocent victims was not specific to a single country or region, and that there was a rich body of international case law on the subject. That delicate problem called for a solution to be found that would above all preserve the interests of the child and also respect the rights of the parents. Her Government had always tried to work towards such a solution, with the emphasis on dialogue and the seeking of compromise. Accordingly, it had been involved in the negotiation of a legally binding convention that would, through bilateral agreements, regulate mutual legal assistance on the basis of equality, reciprocity and respect for the fundamental values of every society. Pending the conclusion of that convention, the Algerian authorities gave careful consideration to each case submitted to them. It was essential to guarantee a cross-frontier visiting right, with the agreement of the two parents confirmed by a judicial decision, the State [in whose territory] the visit took place undertaking to ensure the child's actual return. The agreements between the Algerian and French authorities in that area had yielded some conclusive results, since a good many cross-frontier visits had recently taken place.

42.    Her delegation reaffirmed its Government's desire to facilitate a settlement of the problem first and foremost in the interest of the child, on the understanding that its links with both parents must certainly be preserved, and the rights of both mother and father guaranteed.

43.    Mr. CERDA (Argentina) said that his delegation welcomed the progress made by the working group at its most recent session: the first reading of the draft convention had been completed in accordance with the provisions of General Assembly resolution 42/101.

44.    At the end of the meeting organized at UNICEF's initiative in late 1987, non-governmental organizations dealing with the rights of the child had made some recommendations concerning the draft convention being prepared, and he hoped those recommendations would be taken into account during the second reading of the draft.

45.    Like the delegation of Senegal, he believed that only an instrument that emerged from broad-based consultations and in-depth negotiations would be effective in protecting the rights of the child. Finally, he wished to thank the Chairman of the working group for his personal contribution to the progress it had made.

46.    Miss CHAHABI (observer for the Syrian Arab Republic) said that, ever since its establishment, the United Nations had been devoting particular attention to the question of children and their rights. UNICEF efforts had culminated in the adoption of the 1959 Declaration of the Rights of the Child and yet, thirty years later, the mortality rate varied from 50 to 230 per 1,000 live births in the most underprivileged, or developing, countries, and a large proportion of children did not reach one year of age for lack of care and malnutrition. In some countries, large numbers of children were exploited, ill-treated and sexually abused. In the wake of armed conflicts and natural disasters, millions of children found themselves in refugee camps, where their lives were constantly threatened by military attacks. Lastly, and more generally, children were the first victims

of the armed conflicts that were raging in many countries for, even if they did not perish, they were often traumatized for life.

47.     Thus, in the territories occupied by the Israelis, the Zionist entity was violating the rights of children by denying them food and medication when it did not go as far as committing more barbarous crimes. In early February 1988 alone, 30 children under 12 years of age had been abducted on the West Bank, and Israeli colonists had fired upon demonstrators in a village, killing a child. That was but one example, for innocent victims were falling every day under the bullets of the occupying force. That policy of oppression constituted a crime against humanity and a threat to international peace and security. It was high time that the United States stopped supporting the Zionist entity against the Palestinians and the Pretoria regime against the indigenous populations of South Africa.

48.     Her delegation urged the Commission to do everything in its power to ensure the protection of the children suffering throughout the world and to give them hope of a better life. It thanked the working group for its efforts and hoped that it would complete its consideration of the draft convention on the rights of the child in the near future. Finally, it also wished to thank all the organizations, such as UNICEF, WHO, UNHCR and UNRWA, that provided assistance to children.

49.     Mr. MARKHUS (observer for the Libyan Arab Jamahiriya) said that, in terms of the protection of children from birth onwards, international instruments such as the Universal Declaration of Human Rights and the Declaration of the Rights of the Child had merely repeated age-old principles that had nevertheless been formulated more precisely in the nineteenth century.

50.     The United Nations and UNICEF were to be thanked for their efforts to help children, particularly in the most underprivileged countries. The deterioration in the world economic system and the effect thereof on the developing world had worsened the sufferings of children. Moreover, in the developing countries, official child protection schemes were virtually non-existent, and were rendered all the more difficult to apply by the economic situation of those countries. His delegation thanked the working group for what it had done: its activities had enabled the States that were members of the Commission to submit new proposals aimed, inter alia, at ensuring that the projected convention was of a universal nature. All the members of the international community must work together at the regional, bilateral and international levels to improve the lot of all underprivileged children, whether they had been disabled, orphaned, made refugees or rendered homeless by an armed conflict, were victims of exploitation or racial discrimination, or were deprived of health care and proper nourishment. The international community must make it possible for the future generations to grow up under normal living conditions and in an atmosphere of peace and harmony.

51.     The CHAIRMAN [Mr. MEZZALAMA (Italy)] recalled, in connection with draft resolution E/CN.4/1988/L.86, the amendment to the last preambular paragraph read out by the representative of Senegal and said that, if he heard no objection, he would take it that the Commission wished to adopt the draft resolution E/CN.4/1988/L.86, as amended, without a vote.

52.     Draft resolution E/CN.4/1988/L.86, as amended, was adopted.

53.     Mr. KONATE (Senegal), Mr. FATHALLAH (observer for Egypt), Mr. HACENE (Algeria), Mr. GOSHU (Ethiopia), Mr. SECKA (Gambia), Mr. CERDA (Argentina), Mr. OKONJI (Nigeria), Mrs. CASCO (Nicaragua) and Mr. OMAR (observer for the Libyan Arab Jamahiriya) said that, as the Senegalese amendment had been adopted, their respective countries wished to become sponsors of draft resolution E/CN.4/1988/L.86, as amended, which the Commission had just adopted.

54.     The CHAIRMAN [Mr. MEZZALAMA (Italy)] read out a draft decision on prevention of the disappearance of children:

"The Commission on Human Rights,

Noting the expression of deep concern by the Sub-Commission on Prevention of Discrimination and Protection of Minorities in its decision 1987/107 of 3 September 1987 over reports concerning the critical situation of children who had disappeared in Argentina and who have recently been located in Paraguay,

*Sharing* the Sub-Commission's desire to facilitate family reunion and prevent any new risk of disappearance of those children and bearing in mind the lessons of the unfortunate cases which have occurred in the past in similar situations,

1.      *Approves* the Sub-Commission's request to its Chairman to appoint one or several members to establish urgently and maintain contact with the competent authorities and institutions, including humanitarian organizations, which would report to him on the situation and ensure that there are no further risks of disappearance;

2.      *Requests* the authorities concerned to facilitate the implementation of the present resolution;

3.      *Authorizes* the Secretary-General to provide all the assistance necessary for the implementation of the present resolution."

55.      If he heard no objection, he would take it that the Commission wished to adopt the draft decision without a vote.

56.      *The draft decision was adopted.*

## 6.    Commission on Human Rights resolution 1988/75 on the "Question of a convention on the rights of the child" adopted without a vote on 10 March 1988

*The Commission on Human Rights,*

*Bearing in mind* the draft convention on the rights of the child submitted by Poland to the Commission on Human Rights on 7 February 1978 and annexed to Commission resolution 20 (XXXIV) of 8 March 1978, the amended version of the draft submitted to the Commission on 5 October 1979 (E/CN.4/1349), and the documents submitted by Poland to the General Assembly at its thirty-sixth session, on 7 October 1981 (A/C.3/36/6), and at its fortieth session, on 7 October 1985 (A/C.3/40/3 and Corr.1),

*Recalling* General Assembly resolutions 33/166 of 20 December 1978, 34/4 of 18 October 1979, 35/131 of 11 December 1980, 36/57 of 25 November 1981, 37/190 of 18 December 1982, 38/114 of 16 December 1983, 39/135 of 14 December 1984, 40/113 of 13 December 1985, 41/116 of 4 December 1986 and 42/101 of 7 December 1987, by which the Assembly requested the Commission on Human Rights to give the highest priority to, and to make every effort at its forty-fourth and forty-fifth sessions to complete, a draft convention on the rights of the child and to submit it, through the Economic and Social Council, to the General Assembly at its forty-fourth session,

*Recalling also* its prior resolutions, in particular resolution 1987/48 of 11 March 1987, and pertinent Economic and Social Council resolutions, in particular resolution 1987/48 of 29 May 1987,

*Noting* that 1989 will be the year of the thirtieth anniversary of the Declaration of the Rights of the Child and the tenth anniversary of the International Year of the Child,

*Recognizing*, as stated in General Assembly resolution 42/101, that these anniversaries could constitute an appropriate target date for completion of the work on a draft convention on the rights of the child and for its adoption by the General Assembly,

*Aware* that, twenty-eight years after the adoption of the Declaration of the Rights of the Child, the situation of children throughout the world still continues to be far from satisfactory, and that the full enjoyment by children of human rights calls for continuous improvement of the situation of children as well as their development and education in conditions of peace and security,

*Welcoming* the efforts made by the United Nations Children's Fund with a view to protecting and assisting children throughout the world,

*Stressing* the importance of an international convention on the rights of the child for the effective improvement of the situation of children all over the world,

*Noting* the growing interest in successful completion of the work on a comprehensive international convention on the rights of the child displayed by numerous Governments and international organizations,

*Bearing in mind* the necessity of taking due account of the cultural values and needs of developing countries in the second reading of the draft convention, in order to achieve the universal recognition of the rights in the future convention on the rights of the child,

1.      *Notes with appreciation* that the first reading of a comprehensive draft convention on the rights of the child has been completed by the open-ended working group of the Commission on Human Rights;

2.      *Decides* to continue, as a matter of the highest priority, its work on the elaboration of the draft convention on the rights of the child;

3.      *Requests* the Economic and Social Council to authorize, within existing resources, the convening of an open-ended working group for a period of up to two weeks in November-December 1988, with a view to completing the second reading of the draft convention on the rights of the child prior to the forty-fifth session of the Commission for transmission, through the Economic and Social Council, to the General Assembly at its forty-fourth session;

4.      *Requests* the Secretary-General to circulate the report of the working group on its tenth session (E/CN.4/1988/28) and the text of the draft convention, as adopted during its first reading, to all States with a view to facilitating their participation, on a universal basis, in the second reading of the convention;

5.      *Further requests* the Secretary-General to provide the resources necessary for the technical review of the first reading of the convention, as requested by the working group, so that the technical review may be completed by 31 August 1988 and its results sent to all States well in advance of the second reading;

6.      *Encourages* all countries, especially developing countries, to take an active part in the second reading so that the convention will reflect the needs of the children of all countries;

7.      *Recommends* the following draft resolution to the Economic and Social Council for adoption:

"*The Economic and Social Council,*

*Recalling* General Assembly resolution 42/101 of 7 December 1987, by which the General Assembly requested the Commission on Human Rights to give the highest priority to, and to make every effort at its forty-fourth and forty-fifth sessions to complete, a draft convention on the rights of the child and to submit it, through the Economic and Social Council, to the General Assembly at its forty-fourth session, in 1989,

*Considering* that it was not found possible to complete the work on the draft convention during the forty-fourth session of the Commission on Human Rights,

*Taking note* of Commission on Human Rights resolution 1988/75 of 10 March 1988,

1.      *Authorizes,* within existing resources, a meeting of the open-ended working group for a period of up to two weeks in November-December 1988, with a view to completing the second reading of the draft convention on the rights of the child prior to the forty-fifth session of the Commission on Human Rights for transmission, through the Economic and Social Council, to the General Assembly at its forty-fourth session;

2.      *Requests* the Secretary-General to continue to provide to the working group all the support and facilities necessary for the successful completion of its tasks and, in particular, to circulate the report of the working group (E/CN.4/1988/28) and the draft convention as adopted during its first reading to all States, and to provide the resources necessary for the technical review requested by the working group and for the working group's session in November-December 1988."

## 7. Economic and Social Council resolution 1988/40 on the "Question of a convention on the rights of the child" adopted on 27 May 1988

*The Economic and Social Council,*

*Taking note* of General Assembly resolution 42/101 of 7 December 1987, in which the Assembly requested the Commission on Human Rights to give the highest priority to the elaboration of a draft convention on the rights of the child, to make every effort at its forty-fourth and forty-fifth sessions to complete it, and to submit it, through the Economic and Social Council, to the Assembly at its forty-fourth session, in 1989,

*Considering* that it was not found possible to complete the work on the draft convention at the forty-fourth session of the Commission,

*Taking note* of Commission on Human Rights resolution 1988/75 of 10 March 1988,

1.	*Authorizes,* within existing resources, the open-ended working group of the Commission on Human Rights to meet for a period of up to two weeks in November-December 1988, with a view to completing the second reading of the draft convention on the rights of the child prior to the forty-fifth session of the Commission so that it may be submitted, through the Economic and Social Council, to the General Assembly at its forty-fourth session;

2.	*Requests* the Secretary-General to continue to provide to the working group all the support and facilities necessary for the successful completion of its task, to circulate to all States the report of the working group and the text of the draft convention as adopted during its first reading, and to provide the resources necessary for the technical review requested by the working group and for the meeting of the working group in November-December 1988.

*16th plenary meeting*
*27 May 1988*

## 8. General Assembly resolution 43/112 on the "Question of a convention on the rights of the child" adopted on 8 December 1988

*The General Assembly,*

*Recalling* its previous resolutions, as well as Commission on Human Rights and Economic and Social Council resolutions, on the question of a convention on the rights of the child,

*Reaffirming* that children's rights require special protection and call for continuous improvement of the situation of children all over the world, as well as their development and education in conditions of peace and security,

*Profoundly concerned* that the situation of children in many parts of the world remains critical as a result of unsatisfactory social conditions, natural disasters, armed conflicts, exploitation, illiteracy, hunger and disability and convinced that urgent and effective national and international action is called for,

*Mindful* of the important role of the United Nations Children's Fund and the United Nations in promoting the well-being of children and their development,

*Convinced* of the positive contribution that an international convention on the rights of the child, as a standard-setting accomplishment of the United Nations in the field of human rights, would make to protecting children's rights and ensuring their well-being,

*Noting with appreciation* that the first reading of a full text of a draft convention on the rights of the child has been completed by the open-ended working group of the Commission on Human Rights,

*Bearing in mind* that 1989 marks the thirtieth anniversary of the Declaration on the Rights of the Child and the tenth anniversary of the International Year of the Child,

*Considering* that these anniversaries could constitute an appropriate target date for completion of the work on a draft convention on the rights of the child and for its adoption by the General Assembly at its forty-fourth session, in 1989,

*Bearing in mind* the necessity of taking due account of the cultural values and needs of developing countries in the second reading of the draft convention on the rights of the child, in order to achieve the universal recognition of those rights in the future convention,

1.      *Welcomes* Economic and Social Council resolution 1988/40 of 27 May 1988, in which the Council authorized a meeting of the open-ended working group of the Commission on Human Rights for a period of up to two weeks in November-December 1988, with a view to completing the second reading of the draft convention on the rights of the child prior to the forty-fifth session of the Commission;

2.      *Requests* the Commission on Human Rights to give the highest priority to the draft convention on the rights of the child and to make every effort at its session in 1989 to complete it and to submit it, through the Economic and Social Council, to the General Assembly at its forty-fourth session;

3.      *Invites* all Member States to offer their active support to the completion of the draft convention on the rights of the child in 1989, the year of the thirtieth anniversary of the Declaration on the Rights of the Child and of the tenth anniversary of the International Year of the Child;

4.      *Requests* the Secretary-General to provide all the support and facilities necessary for the successful completion and adoption of the draft convention on the rights of the child;

5.      *Decides* to include in the provisional agenda of its forty-fourth session an item entitled "Adoption of the convention on the rights of the child".

*75th plenary meeting*
*8 December 1988*

## 9.    General comments in the technical review

*The following is taken from document E/CN.4/1989/WG.1/CRP.1 (15 October 1988).*

INTRODUCTION

1.      The Working Group of the Commission on Human Rights on the draft convention on the rights of the child at its last session held in January 1988 prior to the forty-fourth session of the Commission decided that a technical review of the text of the draft convention should be carried out in accordance with United Nations technical standards and practices regarding that kind of international instrument. The terms of the technical review were set out in a letter adopted by the Working Group and read as follows:

> "The working group has also proposed that the draft as it stands be the subject of a technical review taking account of accepted United Nations technical standards and practices regarding multilateral human rights treaties and treaties of international humanitarian law. In the view of the working group such a review, which would best be carried out by the United Nations Secretariat in advance of the second reading, might:
>
> -      identify overlap and repetition between and within draft articles;
>
> -      check for consistency in the text, including the use of key terms and the use of gender-neutral language, and between the different language versions;
>
> -      compare the standards established with those in other widely accepted human rights instruments, particularly the two International Covenants; and
>
> -      make textual and editorial suggestions and recommendations as to how any overlaps or inconsistencies identified might be corrected in the second reading, including through the consolidation and relocation of articles.
>
> The working group has asked me to draw to your attention and to that of those who conduct the review, the report of the working group on its discussion of this issue. This will make clear the nature of the review envisaged. In particular, it was the firm view of the working group that the technical

review should not enter into areas of substantive or political controversy but should be confined to technical issues."

2.      Pursuant to this request, the Secretary-General requested the comments on matters within their respective mandates of the Office of Legal Affairs, the Centre for Social Development and Humanitarian Affairs, the United Nations Children's Fund, the United Nations High Commissioner for Refugees, the International Labour Organization, the United Nations Educational, Scientific and Cultural Organization, the Food and Agriculture Organization, the World Health Organization and the International Committee of the Red Cross for matters relating to the Geneva Conventions. The Department of Conference Services at United Nations Headquarters was asked to review the text of the draft convention from the point of view of the linguistic issues raised by the working group. In addition, the Centre for Human Rights carried out its own internal review.

3.      The present document reflects the comments received from the Office of Legal Affairs, the Social Development Division and the Branch for the Advancement of Women at the Centre for Social Development and Humanitarian Affairs, the United Nations Children's Fund, the United Nations High Commissioner for Refugees, the International Labour Organization, the United Nations Educational, Scientific and Cultural Organization, the Food and Agriculture Organization, the World Health Organization and the International Committee of the Red Cross.

4.      For its part, the Department of Conference Services revised the Arabic, Chinese, French, Russian and Spanish versions of the draft to ensure standardization within each language and consistency between them and the English text. The revised versions will be made available separately.

1.      GENERAL COMMENTS

## (a)    Language

1.      *Gender-neutral language*

*Comment by UNESCO* (page 1)

Insufficient attention has as yet been accorded in this text to the need for gender-neutral language.

UNESCO's experience in this question shows that, although the English language does not lend itself as readily as others to such problems, simple solutions of drafting can indeed be found in every case. We are at your entire disposal if you require our assistance in this matter.

*Comment by UNICEF* (pages 5-6)

There are four different techniques which may be applied in order to avoid exclusive use of the masculine singular pronoun "his" and ensure gender neutrality:

        1.      Use of both the masculine and feminine pronouns

        2.      Use of the plural

        3.      Omission of the pronouns

        4.      Repetition of the noun

One additional technique would be the usage of the impersonal pronoun "its" (as in draft articles 16 and 16 bis). But, it is grammatically incorrect to use an impersonal pronoun to refer to something possessed by a person as opposed to a thing. In addition, it is not common usage, not commonly used in legislative drafting, and, arguably, is demeaning or even dehumanizing. For these reasons, it is suggested that one of the other techniques be used in place of this one. A possible reformulation will be offered, on an article-by-article basis, wherever appropriate.

*Other comments*

Use of gender-neutral language was also recommended by the ILO and FAO.

2.      *Reference to "The States Parties to the present Convention"*

*Comment by the Legal Counsel* (paragraph B-1)

There should be consistency in use of the term "The States Parties to the present Convention". This is not so with regard to articles 1, 4, 6, 12, 12 bis, 14, 15, 16 bis, 17, 19, and 20.

3.      *Final editorial and drafting review*

*Comment by the Legal Counsel* (paragraph 2)

A final drafting and editorial review of the provisions of the draft convention, and the concordance of the various language versions (which could best be achieved in a drafting committee with the assistance of the United Nations Language Service) is considered necessary.

**(b)      Organization of the text of the draft convention and the order of articles**

*Comment by the Legal Counsel* (paragraph B-1)

Consideration should be given to an eventual division of the draft convention into parts or sections (like the two Covenants).

| e.g.: | Articles 1-19: | Substantive provisions. |
|---|---|---|
| | Articles 22-24: | Deal with the establishment, reports and methods of work of the Committee on the Rights of the Child. |
| | Articles 25-31: | Final provisions. |

Consequently, the various parts or sections of the draft convention should be given separate titles (as in the supplementary Convention on the Abolition of Slavery). The same should be done for various articles (as in the Convention relating to Stateless Persons).

This would give greater clarity to the text and facilitate ease of reference.

*Comment by UNESCO* (page 1)

This draft text still needs considerable work, and not only in respect of education. There is too much repetition, hidden to some extent by the lack of logical sequencing and linking of items dealing with the same or similar matters. For example:

Article 9 bis seems to belong with article 2;

Article 5 belongs with article 20;

Article 8 bis belongs with article 18 ter;

Article 17 belongs with article 7a; etc.

*Comment by UNICEF* (page 8)

In order to conform to the general practice with respect to international human rights treaties, consideration might be given to the following reordering of the first few articles:

| Article 1 | Definition of the child |
|---|---|
| Article 4 | Obligations clause dealing with non-discrimination |
| Article 5 | General obligations clause |
| Article 5 bis | General qualification clause |
| Article 1 bis | And so on - substantive rights provisions |

**(c)      Article on settlement of disputes**

*Comment by the Legal Counsel* (para. 5)

The draft convention should include an article on the settlement of disputes. Such a provision would be very useful, for such a new subject as this one.

**(d)    Administrative and financial implications of meetings of States parties and the Committee**

*Comment by the Legal Counsel* (para. 1)

A report on the administrative and financial implications of articles 22, 23 and 24 which provide for the servicing of meetings of States Parties and the Committee on the Rights of the Child, would, of course, be necessary under Financial Regulation XIII and the related Financial Rules.

*Comment by the ILO* (page 3)

With regard to the system of States Parties meeting the expenses of supervision, it is recalled that ILO supervision operates on the principle of participation and contribution to expenses by the whole membership. It would appear desirable that the principle should apply to instruments on human rights such as the draft convention on the rights of the child. Such an approach would appear consistent with the aims set by the world community in adopting the instruments in question.

**(e)    Equality of men and women: discrimination against female children**

*Comment by the Branch for the Advancement of Women* (paragraphs 2-3)

The draft convention covers most of the sensitive points closely related to women's role and discrimination against them. The draft convention no doubt reflects a concern widely expressed regarding the child, and his or her physical and mental development in a changing society where his/her rights had not been specified and the status of the family had to evolve within a general socio-economic crisis affecting equally developed and developing countries.

Among the points deserving some thought we found, along with some initial comments made early at the beginning of the discussion of the draft convention, that emphasis should be placed on the principle of "equal rights of men and women" as it appears in the second paragraph of the United Nations Charter. This suggestion finds its own justification from the impact of the effects in practice of certain legislation which does not grant both parents equal responsibility vis-à-vis the child, when the parent, by his or her behaviour implicitly rejects such responsibility. Whenever possible legislation and practice should be confronted in the course of the final discussion of the relevant articles and paragraphs dealing with parental responsibilities and the rights of the child.

*Comment by FAO* (page 1)

The convention should include provisions to prevent discrimination against female children as far as food and education are concerned.

*Comment by UNESCO*

See also comment of UNESCO relating to the preamble.

**(f)    Education**

See below the UNESCO comments relating to the preamble.

**(g)    Food**

*Comment by FAO* (pages 1-4)

The document appears to fulfil General Assembly resolution 4/120 which calls for consistency between standards being developed in new international instruments and those already existing.

The Food and Agriculture Organization's development policy lays stress on the continuing ever-growing importance of the small farmer and the family as a production unit in the world's food supply. This policy implicitly recognizes the importance of all family inputs into production. It may be necessary to include certain caveats included in the FAO's policy statements regarding productive activity by children on small family farm enterprises.

The convention should include provisions to prevent discrimination against female children as far as food and education are concerned.

In the present text, there are only two marginal references to the right to food (article 12 bis and article 14(3)).

The convention on the rights of the child offers an excellent opportunity to implement one of the recommendations proposed by Mr. Asbjorn Eide in his "Report on the Right to Adequate Food as a Human Right". He suggests that it is not sufficient to recognize the right to food, but consideration should also be given to the identification of its corresponding obligations.

There should be a full article on the right to food as one of the fundamental rights of the child. This article could be included in the convention after article 1 (bis) (right to life, child's survival and development) or before article 12 bis (health and access to care).

Three aspects should be considered in the definition of the child's right to food. The State Parties should:

(a)     Recognize the children's right to food and the significance of food culture as part of a wider cultural identity (national obligation to respect the right to food).

(b)     Prevent distortion of positive nutritional aspects of existing food patterns and develop national legislation and administrative mechanisms and procedures to protect and facilitate a valid food procurement for all children (national obligation to protect the right to food).

(c)     Incorporate nutritional considerations into relevant development activities and formulate and execute policies, plans and programmes to facilitate and assist children in obtaining viable food procurement (national obligation to fulfil the right to food).

Among the many rights referred to in the draft the ones related to what might be called *"Basic needs"* or *"Material conditions of life"* seem to have been given little stress or have not been considered at all.

The right to eat enough, both in quantity and quality from early life (perhaps even from the mother's womb) has never had enough support. In many countries some specific points are presently being discussed, such as:

(a)     The right to be breastfed from birth.

(b)     The right to a suitable diet (breastfeeding plus weaning foods) from the third month of age.

(c)     The right to clean, nutritious food and water.

(d)     The right to live free of insects, parasites and heavy contamination.

Perhaps food and health should come first because without these many of the other rights would be worthless.

## (h)     Health: role of WHO

*Comment by WHO (page 1)*

The draft convention is quite comprehensive and provides for a variety of rights for the child, with some detailed aspects thereof. A number of articles in the draft convention, and also some preambular paragraphs are of direct relevance to the World Health Organization's areas of competence. However, apart from general references to the specialized agencies and international cooperation (e.g. articles 12 and 24) no particular role has been given to the World Health Organization in the draft convention, nor is it mentioned by name.

**(i)     Other matters**

A suggestion was made during the 1988 session of the Working Group on Slavery that the concept of "mutilation" should be included as one of the practices that ought to be specifically forbidden and that an express prohibition of the use of children for medical experimentation should also be included in the draft convention.

# 10.   Additional comments in the technical review

*The following is taken from document E/CN.4/1989/WG.1/CRP.1/Add.1 (14 November 1988).*

INTRODUCTION

1.        The present document contains additional elements for the technical review. In preparing them, attention was given to the request of the General Assembly in resolution 41/120 that new instruments in the field of human rights should "be consistent with the existing body of international human rights law". When new texts are suggested they are underlined.

1. GENERAL COMMENTS

**(a)     Gender-neutral language**

2.        With regard to the use of gender-neutral language in the English text, it would appear that the use of both the masculine and feminine pronouns is best suited to achieve this purpose as it raises the least questions of substantive and language changes. The Working Group has already used this approach in several draft articles and may wish to continue it for reasons of consistency. It is therefore proposed that the words "he", "him", or "his", wherever they appear in the text, be immediately followed by the words *"or she"*, or *"or her"*, as appropriate. Similarly, the word "its" may be replaced by *"his or her".*

3.        When the word "brotherhood" appears in the tenth preambular paragraph, it has been suggested by UNESCO in document E/CN.4/1989/WG.1/CRP.1 to use instead the words *"equality and solidarity".*

4.        For the other language versions, technical services may be requested to make the appropriate suggestions once the text has been adopted on second reading.

**(b)     Reference to "The States Parties to the present Convention"**

5.        The Legal Counsel (document E/CN.4/1989/WG.1/CRP.1) urges consistency in the use of the term "The States Parties to the present Convention". It may then be proposed that the term "The States Parties to the present Convention" be employed in full on the first occasion of its use in the draft convention and that thereafter the term *"States Parties"* be employed. In addition to being the shortest expression, it follows an example set by such instruments as the International Convention on the Elimination of All Forms of Racial Discrimination and Convention on the Elimination of All Forms of Discrimination Against Women.

**(c)     Use of the word "appropriate"**

6.        Attention may be drawn to the frequent use of the word "appropriate" in the draft convention. In one article, article 11 for example, the word appears five times. The use of this word may unnecessarily weaken the draft convention. The Working Group may therefore wish, as it examines the individual articles, to look into the possibility of either deleting the word or replacing it with stronger adjectives.

# N. 1989

## 1. Meeting of Central American parliamentarians on the rights of the child

*The following is taken from document E/CN.4/1989/54 (19 January 1989).*

*Note by the Secretariat*

The attention of the Commission is drawn to the attached concerning the Conclusions and Recommendations of the meeting of parliamentarians from Central America on the subject "Rights of the child, towards peace and development in Central America", organized by the Congress of Guatemala in cooperation with UNICEF and sponsored by the Inter-Parliamentary Union.

Annex I

MEETING OF PARLIAMENTARIANS ON THE RIGHTS OF THE CHILD

(Guatemala City, I - 3 December 1988)

A Workshop on the subject "Rights of the child towards peace and development in Central America" was held in Guatemala City from I to 3 December 1988. The Workshop was organized by the Congress of Guatemala in cooperation with UNICEF and was sponsored by the Inter-Parliamentary Union. Members of Parliament from Costa Rica, El Salvador, Guatemala, Honduras and Nicaragua took part.

His Excellency Roberto Carpio Nicolle, Vice-President of the Republic of Guatemala, solemnly opened the Workshop and Mrs. Raquel Blandón de Cerezo, First Lady of the Republic, spoke at the inaugural meeting. For three days, parliamentarians from the five Central American countries worked with UNICEF experts and observers from international organizations to draft the following text which was adopted unanimously:

CONCLUSIONS AND RECOMMENDATIONS

We, parliamentarians from Costa Rica, El Salvador, Guatemala, Honduras and Nicaragua, participants of the Meeting of Central American Parliamentarians on the Rights of the Child, held in Guatemala City between 1 and 3 December 1988, have agreed on the following conclusions and recommendations.

*General considerations:*

Considering that the situation of the child in Central America is a reflection of the social, economic and political conditions prevailing in this region and that children's conditions of health, education and development have thus been particularly affected,

Concerned with the infant mortality rates in Central America which continue to be unacceptably high, causing the death of 100,000 children per year in the region from preventable causes such as malnutrition, diarrhoea, measles, whooping cough and tuberculosis,

Also deeply concerned that over 50 per cent of the children who survive the first 5 years, live in extreme poverty, without having their basic needs met (food, housing, clothes) and without having any access to public services such as health, education, sanitation and other basic services which, in addition to the consequences of armed violence, constitute an inadmissible waste of valuable resources which will not be available in the future for the peaceful development of the region,

Concerned by the fact that armed violence affects mostly and increasingly women and children,

Recognizing the important role of Central American women in ensuring the child's survival and health, and the fact that their education and health are, thus, directly linked with the child's well-being,

Aware that peace is the essential condition for the survival and the full development of children, who are in turn the bridge for peace in Central America,

Reaffirm the need for an effective implementation of the Esquipulas II Agreement, which grants high priority to the problems of children, as a means of achieving a firm and long-lasting peace as well as development in Central America,

Recognize the initiative undertaken by the Central American First Ladies, who met in Costa Rica in September 1988, in the Central American Conference on Care of Children Affected by Violence, and are happy to note its recommendations, in particular the creation of a Central American Commission for the Care of Children Affected by Armed Violence,

Also take due note of the interest expressed by the international community with regard to the region's problems and are aware that its support and solidarity are absolutely essential to achieve its goals,

Further recognize the urgent need for the important programmes for the child, particularly the global awareness campaign of the United Nations Fund for the Child (UNICEF), in confronting the "silent emergency" of 15 million avoidable child deaths each year,

Consider that this Meeting of parliamentarians is proof that the parliamentarians of the region are willing and able to meet and accomplish fruitful work, as well as of the need for an appropriate forum, such as a Central American Parliament, where problems of the region and matters relating to its economic and social development could be debated, and also consider that such a Parliament would be the ideal forum for evaluating the follow-up of this meeting and encouraging future action,

Conscious that as parliamentarians, representatives of the people, promoters of legal protection, and guardians of national Constitutions, we have a special responsibility to support family and community efforts in protecting our children.

*Plan of action:*

In view of the above, the participants recommend the following Plan of Action:

1.      To create, within the legal framework of each country, a parliamentary body - a committee, a sub-committee or any other entity - for child protection, with the commitment that such a body would be operational within a year;

2.      To review present national legislation and adopt new legal measures aimed at ensuring a better and more widespread protection of children, especially those in particularly difficult circumstances;

3      To expand the curriculum of primary and secondary education so as to include health education and, in particular, the basic elements of child survival;

4.      To promote educational projects aimed at peace and respect of human rights;

5      To encourage each of the Central American countries to develop and/or to continue developing an effective programme primarily aimed at health care which would include operational aspects such as:

-       Universal immunization aimed at reaching the target set for 1990;

-       Oral rehydration therapy;

-       Maternal breastfeeding;

-       Growth and development monitoring (establishing the use of control records);

6.      To promote action aimed at literacy training and functional education for women (instruction related to diseases);

7.      To promote health measures for women such as: pregnancy check-ups and improved nutrition, (reduction of anemia, etc.), as well as other measures aimed at improving their emotional well-being;

8.      To take measures to improve the laws and, if necessary, promote adequate action to prevent children from being victims of exploitation, especially in processes of adoption;

9      To appeal to the member States of the United Nations promptly to finalize the preliminary draft convention on the rights of the child, work for its adoption by the United Nations General Assembly in 1989 and speed up its subsequent ratification by each Central American country;

10.     To expedite the ratification process of the two Additional Protocols of 1977 to the 1949 Geneva Conventions concerning the protection of victims of international and non-international armed conflicts;

11. To promote, within Central America, the concept of "Children as a Zone of Peace", to receive special protection from all parties engaged in armed conflicts;

12. To ensure that the budgetary resources for health, education, nutrition, drinking water provision and sanitation be maintained or increased in relation to other non-productive expenses;

13. To guarantee that the economic, political and social adjustment measures imply an adjustment with a human face and guide development, according to the internal and external possibilities of each country;

14. To call upon the donor communities to support these initiatives at regional, national and local levels;

15. To support the creation of a "Central American Fund for Technical and Financial Cooperation for Care of Children Affected by Armed Violence", and to call upon the international community to help with its funding and implementation, and in particular, Spain, to play the role of an intermediary;

16. To increase efforts to speed up, with the support of competent international organizations, the repatriation of war-displaced children and their families to their country or place of origin, under conditions of absolute respect for their fundamental rights;

17. To give priority to preventive aspects regarding street children;

18. To promote, especially through massive and permanent campaigns, more humane treatment of street children;

19. To ensure better living conditions for street children and young single mothers, providing them with better access to health, food, housing and educational services;

20. To promote and support the efforts of public and private institutions and associations dedicated to dealing with street children's problems;

21. To ensure the respect of culture and traditions of youngsters of indigenous communities and peoples as an indispensable element for their adequate development;

22. To promote the creation of a national and Central American "Grand Alliance", including all sectors of the society, in order to turn them into promoters and defenders of children, as well as into collaborators in all programmes benefiting children.

*Follow-up measures*:

We, the participating members of the Central American Parliaments, commit ourselves to:

1. Submit the conclusions of this Meeting to our respective Parliaments and to actively promote their effective implementation;

2. Give wide publicity, in each of our countries, to these conclusions and channel them to the media, as well as to the official institutions, non-governmental organizations and charitable child protection associations;

3. Facilitate contacts between our Parliaments and UNICEF representatives in order to promote the implementation of the recommendations adopted;

4. Further develop the contacts established in this Meeting, exchanging, through National IPU Groups, information regarding steps taken and results obtained, and also transmit this information to UNICEF and the Office of the Secretary General of the Inter-Parliamentary Union;

5. Promote, among Central American countries, the development of the exchange of information, experience, specialized knowledge, and material resources which would allow better care and development of children in Central America.

## 2. Report of the Working Group

*The following is taken from document E/CN.4/1989/48 (2 March 1989). For the text of the draft convention as adopted by the General Assembly, see annex I.*

I.      INTRODUCTION

1.      The Commission on Human Rights, at its forty-fourth session, decided in resolution 1988/75, to continue its work on the elaboration of the draft convention on the rights of the child as a matter of the highest priority, and requested the Economic and Social Council to authorize, within existing resources, the convening of an open-ended working group for a period of up to two weeks in November-December 1988, with a view to completing the second reading of the draft convention prior to the forty-fifth session of the Commission. The Council authorized that meeting in its resolution 1988/40 of 27 May 1988.

2.      The working group held 23 meetings from 28 November to 9 December 1988 and on 21, 22 and 23 February 1989. Two fully serviced meetings of the Working Group were held on Saturday 3 December 1988 thanks to the financial support of UNICEF. During the sessions, 16 informal drafting groups were established with regard to different articles of the draft convention; these drafting groups met prior to and after the plenary meeting of the Working Group.

3.      The text of the draft convention as adopted by the Working Group at the second reading is contained in document E/CN.4/1989/29.

*(a)     Elections*

4.      At the first meeting of the Working Group on 28 November 1988, Mr. Adam Lopatka (Poland) was elected Chairman-Rapporteur by acclamation and Mr. Anders Röhnquist (Sweden) was elected acting chairman for the three meetings during which the Chairman was absent.

*(b)     Participation*

5.      The meetings of the Working Group, which were open to all members of the Commission on Human Rights, were attended by representatives of the following States: Algeria, Argentina, Bangladesh, Belgium, Brazil, Bulgaria, China, Colombia, Cyprus, Ethiopia, France, German Democratic Republic, Germany, Federal Republic of, India, Iraq, Ireland, Italy, Japan, Mexico, Mozambique, Nicaragua, Norway, Pakistan, Peru, Philippines, Portugal, Senegal, Spain, United Kingdom of Great Britain and Northern Ireland, United States of America, Union of Soviet Socialist Republics, Venezuela, Yugoslavia.

6.      The following States, non-members of the Commission on Human Rights, were represented by observers at the meetings of the Working Group: Angola, Australia, Austria, Bahrain, Bhutan, Canada, Cuba, Czechoslovakia, Denmark, Egypt, Finland, Holy See, Honduras, Jordan, Kuwait, Lebanon, Libyan Arab Jamahiriya, Malta, Morocco, Nepal, Netherlands, New Zealand, Oman, Panama, Poland, Romania, Sweden, Switzerland, Tunisia, Turkey, Ukrainian Soviet Socialist Republics, Yemen.

7.      The Centre for Social Development and Humanitarian Affairs of the United Nations Secretariat, the United Nations Children's Fund, the United Nations High Commissioner for Refugees, the International Labour Organization, the United Nations Educational, Scientific and Cultural Organization, the World Health Organization, the League of Arab States and the Inter-American Children's Institute of the Organization of American States were represented at the Working Group by observers.

8.      The following non-governmental organizations in consultative status with the Economic and Social Council were represented by observers at the meetings of the Working Group: Amnesty International, Associated Country Women of the World, Baha'i International Community, Co-ordinating Board of Jewish Organizations, Defence for Children International Movement, Foster Parents Plan International, Grand Council of the Crees of Quebec, Human Rights Internet, Indian Council of South America, International Association of Juvenile and Family Court Magistrates, International Association of Penal Law, International Catholic Child Bureau, International Committee of the Red Cross, International Council of Jewish Women, International

Council on Jewish Social and Welfare Organizations, International Council of Women, International Federation of Women in Legal Careers, International Movement ATD Fourth World, Inter-Parliamentary Union, International Right to Life Federation, International Social Service, Rädda Barnen International, Save the Children Fund - UK, World Association of Girl Guides and Girl Scouts, World Association for the School as an Instrument of Peace, World Council of Indigenous Peoples, the World Federation of Methodist Women, World Jewish Congress, Zonta International.

*(c)    Documents*

9.      The Working Group had before it the text of the technical review of the draft convention as requested by the Working Group at its tenth session (E/CN.4/1989/WG.1/CRP.1 and Corrs.1 and 2, and Adds.1 and 2) and a working paper submitted by the Chairman containing the text of the draft convention as adopted at first reading in which was incorporated the revisions suggested in the technical review (E/CN.4/1989/WG.1/WP.2). It also had before it revisions to the Arabic, Chinese, French, Russian and Spanish language versions of the convention contained respectively in documents E/CN.4/1989/WG.1/CRP.2 through 6. In addition, the Government of Argentina submitted a document containing the report of a Latin American meeting of non-governmental organizations held in Buenos Aires in support of the United Nations draft convention on the rights of the child (E/CN.4/1989/WG.1/WP.1). Finally, a further 67 working papers were submitted by delegations dealing with specific aspects or articles of the draft convention and they are referred to as appropriate in the body of the report.

[...]

*(d)    General debate*

11.     The session was opened by the Under-Secretary-General for Human Rights who underlined the importance of the task assigned to the Working Group and reaffirmed his and the Secretariat's full support for those efforts. The Chairman in his opening statement made, inter alia, a general reference to the substance of the documents at the disposal of the Working Group for its consideration during the session.

12.     In the general debate, the representative of Senegal stated that, during the second reading of the draft convention which was about to begin, account should be taken of the concerns of the developing countries to ensure that the draft convention reflected the desired universality. The concerns and needs - including cultural needs - of all countries, but particularly of the developing countries, to express their aspirations and to make their contributions to the draft convention should be taken into account. Noting that the same concerns had been expressed at previous sessions of the Working Group, he expressed the hope that the current session would see reflected in the draft convention the cultural diversity of the various nations and that universality which was so much desired.

13.     The representative of Senegal also drew the attention of the Working Group to the results of the West African seminar on the draft convention, held in Senegal in November 1988. The seminar, which had been a success, had adopted the *"Declaration of Dakar"*, which stressed the need to take account of the cultural values of Africa and expressed the support of the participants for the drafting of the convention on the rights of the child. The text of the *"Declaration of Dakar"* was brought to the attention of the Working Group.

14.     The observer for Australia said that the technical review exercise had demonstrated its value although that did not mean that there were no problems concerning the draft convention apart from those that had come up in the technical review. Nonetheless, the priority for his Government was to complete the second reading of the draft convention at the current session and he believed this could be accomplished without in any way compromising the quality of the instrument in preparation, if the Working Group made full use of the suggestions in the technical review as a basis for its work.

15.     The representative of Argentina mentioned the Latin American meeting in support of the draft convention on the rights of the child which had taken place at Buenos Aires in September-October 1988,

with particular reference to the suggested amendments to the text of the draft convention which were put forward by that Latin American meeting (contained in document E/CN.4/1989/WG.1/WP.1) and asked the Working Group to take them into consideration in the course of its debates. He also drew the attention of the Working Group to the first draft elaborated by the above-mentioned meeting of a Latin American Charter on the Rights of the Child.

16.       The observer for Egypt referred to the seminar on the rights of the child that had been held at Alexandria in November 1988, stating that its main recommendations were: (a) that the United Nations Working Group on the Rights of the Child should bear in mind during the second reading the fact that articles 7 bis and 11 were incompatible with the legal systems of several countries and should take the concern of those countries into account; (b) that the Working Group should give closer attention in the draft convention to encouraging the mental and spiritual education of the child; (c) that the Egyptian Ministry of Justice should be requested to revise the country's laws - if and where necessary - to bring them into line with the future convention on the rights of the child.

17.       The representative of Portugal stated that in September 1988, the Portuguese-speaking countries had met at Lisbon under the auspices of UNICEF to study the draft convention on the rights of the child. At that meeting, there had been an exchange of experience and the solutions adopted by the various countries represented were described. Giving a general account of the conclusions reached, she emphasized that the child should be considered from a dual perspective: as an object of protection and as a possessor of rights. The need to ensure the active participation of the State, of society, of parents and other persons legally responsible for the child was recognized and stress was laid on the fundamental role that the national community could play in ensuring the realization of the rights of the child. Special attention was paid to the situation of children that suffer the painful consequences of armed conflicts. The participants also decided that they should hold regular meetings in view of the fact that, as they were well aware, the need for the protection of children would not disappear once the convention was adopted.

18.       The representative of Rädda Barnen International informed the Working Group of a seminar on the convention on the rights of the child which had taken place in Stockholm in October 1988, organized by the Swedish National Committee of UNICEF and Rädda Barnen. Among the issues considered at the aforementioned seminar were article 20 of the draft convention concerning children in armed conflicts, UNICEF-sponsored regional seminars and their recommendations, a comparison between Swedish legislation and the draft convention, implementation of the future convention and its dissemination.

19.       The representative of Venezuela regretted the fact that there had been no Latin American regional meeting for consultation of Governments like those held in Dakar, Egypt and Portugal, especially since the Latin American region had a tradition in the area of minors' rights dating back to the late 1930s and there was considerable specialization by Latin American jurists and lawyers in that branch of law.

*(e)       Statements after the adoption of the convention*

20.       Following the adoption of the draft convention some delegations made statements of a general character.

21.       The representative of the United Kingdom of Great Britain and Northern Ireland stated that nothing in this convention may be interpreted as affecting in any way the operation of the United Kingdom immigration or nationality legislation in so far as it relates to the entry of aliens and the terms and conditions of their stay in the United Kingdom, and to the acquisition and possession of citizenship. In the absence of the advice from Legal Counsel on the Chairman's statement regarding paragraph 6 (new paragraph 9) of the Preamble, the United Kingdom also stated that their Government might have to lodge a reservation with regard to article 1 and 1 bis at the time of ratification.

22.       The representative of Japan expressed the reservation of his Government with regard to the legal nature of the declaration that the Chairman of the Working Group should make on article 6 bis to the effect that this article was not intended to affect the immigration laws of States Parties. Doubts were also expressed

as to the consequences for the national immigration laws of some other provisions of the convention, namely of article 6, paragraphs 2 and 4, and of article 11 bis. The representative of Japan further stated that a number of other newly adopted proposals and articles of the draft convention would be *ad referendum* to his Government which will express its formal view on them at an appropriate opportunity.

23.    The observer for New Zealand stated that the text of the draft convention, with particular reference to its preamble, is *ad referendum* to his Government which may have further views to express and positions to adopt on the text at a later stage.

24.    Statements to this effect were also made by the representatives of India, the United Kingdom of Great Britain and Northern Ireland and Venezuela.

[...]

IV.    STATEMENTS MADE DURING THE ADOPTION OF THE REPORT

*Statements of a general nature*

719.    In connection with the consideration and adoption of the report (22nd, 23rd and 24th meetings) statements of a general nature for the record were made by several delegations.

720.    The delegation of the Federal Republic of Germany stated that it could accept the text of the draft convention as adopted. Although it had no strong feelings concerning the deadline of 1989 for the final adoption of the text, it held the view that the draft was ripe for adoption by the General Assembly at its forthcoming session. The Federal Republic of Germany had several hesitations concerning the text of various articles. Nevertheless, it felt that further discussions on substantive articles would not necessarily lead to an improvement of the convention as a whole. Taking that into account, the delegation felt that there was nevertheless some reasoning in keeping the deadline of 1989.

721.    The delegation of the Federal Republic of Germany stated its desire that the discussion on substantive articles of the draft convention not be reopened. However, it expressed its disappointment that nothing more could be done for the protection of an extremely weak group of children, the children born out of wedlock. In January 1988 it had tabled a detailed proposal on this issue which unfortunately had to be withdrawn but which it would have to present once again if the discussion of the substance of the draft is reopened again. The representative of the Federal Republic of Germany further asked that the following declarations be entered in the report:

(a)    Nothing in the convention on the rights of the child shall be interpreted as legitimizing the illegal entry and presence on the territory of the Federal Republic of Germany of any alien, nor shall any provision be interpreted as restricting the right of the Federal Republic of Germany to promulgate laws and regulations concerning the entry of aliens and the conditions of their stay or to establish differences between nationals and aliens.

(b)    Concerning article 26, paragraph 1 (the numbering follows document E/CN.4/1989/29) the Government of the Federal Republic of Germany understands that it is consistent with this provision of the convention that national law recognizes entitlement to social insurance benefits of children within the meaning of this convention only in so far as they are either insured together with one parent in their capacity as dependents or surviving dependents or insured together with another person entitled to bring up the child or if, as a result of employment or apprenticeship admissible under article 32 of this convention they have a social insurance coverage of their own.

(c)    Concerning article 32, paragraph 2, the Government of the Federal Republic of Germany understands that the provisions of the international conventions mentioned in this paragraph relate only to such provisions as are binding upon the respective contracting parties of this convention.

(d)    Concerning article 32, paragraph 2 *lita* the Government of the Federal Republic of Germany understands that within the framework of this provision it is admissible to provide in their national legislation the children having not yet attained the stipulated minimum age can be given specified easy work to the extent that such work does not meet the criteria stated in paragraph 1 of this article.

722.    The representative of Japan drew the attention of the Working Group to the Chairman's declaration contained in paragraph 203 of the report stating that article 6 of the convention (present article 9) was intended to apply to separations that arise in domestic situations and also that article 6 bis (present article 10) was not intended to affect the general right of States to establish and regulate their respective immigration laws in accordance with their international obligations. His delegation accepted articles 9 and 10 provided that the Chairman's declaration was maintained. In this connection, the Japanese delegation understood that "their own countries" which appears in the 6th and 7th lines of paragraph 2 of article 10 means the countries of which they are nationals. As to article 22, the delegation of Japan accepted article 22 on the understanding that this provision was not intended to request the States to take further measures in addition to the present procedures for the recognition of refugees in accordance with their international obligations and their national laws on refugees. As to article 28, the delegation accepted article 28 on the understanding that "primary education" in paragraph 1 (a) does not include education in kindergartens.

723.    As to article 37, subparagraph (c), the representative of Japan said that, according to article 81 of the Japanese Criminal Procedure Law, the court is allowed to restrict the contact of the child deprived of his or her liberty with his or her family, in case the court shall have reason to believe that the child may escape, or destroy evidence. The Japanese delegation understood that situations such as the possibility of escape or the possibility of destruction of evidence fell within the "exceptional circumstances" in the end of that subparagraph. Concerning the "right to prompt access to legal and other appropriate assistance" of subparagraph (d), the delegation accepts that subparagraph on the understanding that it confirmed the right to assistance of defence counsel for the child placed under physical restraint and that it did not oblige the State to assign a defence counsel on behalf of the child when the child is unable to secure it.

724.    As to article 40, the Japanese delegation understood that "every child alleged as or accused of having infringed the penal law" in 2 (b)(ii) means such child who is deprived of his or her liberty in the criminal procedure. Concerning 2 (b)(iv) of the same article, his delegation understood that in Japan that provision of 2 (b)(iv) is applicable only to the criminal procedure at the criminal court and not to the procedure at the family court which has for purpose protective measures for the wholesome rearing of juveniles. Concerning 2 (b)(vi), his delegation understood that this provision was intended to guarantee that the defendant who could not understand the language used in the court exercise sufficient defensive activities in the court, and therefore it is not prohibited that the whole or part of the costs be charged to the accused when he is found guilty.

725.    The delegation of Portugal emphasized the importance it attached to the fact that, after lengthy analysis and exchanges of experience, it had been possible to complete a standard-setting exercise in the United Nations. A range of children's rights had been gathered together in a single text so as to ensure the protection of children in various fields and their active participation in society. It was in that spirit that Portugal viewed the convention and had participated in the Working Group, taking into consideration, inter alia, two criteria for action: firstly, an openness to consensus; and, secondly, the need to take account of the provisions of other international instruments concerning human rights, particularly those adopted by the United Nations. There would certainly be articles where a different wording could have been desired and others where it would have been desirable to go further - that was the price that inevitably had to be paid to obtain a convention of universal scope. However, there were other instances where the draft convention did not measure up to the level of protection ensured by other legal instruments adopted by the international community. That was the case of article 38, and Portugal deeply regretted the fact. The delegation of Portugal added that, for the purposes of implementing that article, Portugal would also take account of article 41 of the draft convention, which invited States to take into consideration more favourable provisions applicable in their country.

726.     Lastly, the delegation of Portugal expressed certain misgivings about the statements made by some delegations concerning the content of several provisions of the text, at the very moment when the Working Group was completing the preparation of the draft convention. The delegation of Portugal said it was sure that, at the time of ratifying that convention and in the event that the formulation of reservations proved justified, those delegations would take into account the applicable principles of international law, and in particular article 51 of the draft convention.

727.     The representative of Venezuela said that her delegation was able to concur in the adoption of the draft convention *ad referendum*. The limited time available for the second reading of the draft convention had meant that some of its articles had been adopted without her delegation being able to consult its Government properly. The Venezuelan authorities were studying the draft convention as expeditiously as they could in the absence of final documents. Accordingly, the delegation of Venezuela would feel bound to make some substantive comments concerning the draft convention during the discussion of item 13 in March. Nevertheless, the delegation of Venezuela reiterated its support for all efforts to secure the final adoption of the draft convention during the present year, at the next session of the United Nations General Assembly.

728.     The delegation of Venezuela took the view that an article such as article 21, dealing with adoption, which had only been studied in its existing form by the plenary Group for a few minutes at its last meeting without the participants being able to consult experts or theory on the subject, or their respective capitals, could only lead to serious confusion. The representative of Venezuela said that, while it was true that that article was largely based on articles 17 and 20 of the 1986 United Nations Declaration on Social and Legal Principles relating to the Protection and Welfare of Children, with Special Reference to Foster Placement and Adoption Nationally and Internationally, her delegation did not consider that enough: recent events reported in the press and analysed by the Working Group on Contemporary Forms of Slavery of the Sub-Commission on Prevention of Discrimination and Protection of Minorities, which clearly demonstrated the existence of a market for and traffic in children for adoption, especially intercountry adoption, in many parts of the world, had highlighted the need to combat such practices by all possible national and international forms of action. Therefore, it was a matter for concern that intercountry adoption should be established as an alternative for a child who "cannot in any suitable manner be cared for in the child's country of origin", as stated in article 21, paragraph (b). Adoption created ties of *patria potestas* going far beyond mere care for children which, in the case of children deprived of a family and as appropriate, was the responsibility of foster homes properly chosen by the competent authorities in other words, the system of family placement in its various forms. The representative of Venezuela stated that the confusion in that article between two legal institutions, namely adoption and family placement, could only create problems for the children who were the potential victims of such confusion.

729.     The representative of Venezuela said that her delegation also had difficulty with article 21, paragraph (d), since it was not possible to combat a market for children which obviously existed in the world and at the same time to institutionalize that market by permitting persons dealing with intercountry adoption to make "financial gain". The Venezuelan delegation urged Governments to reflect on the implications of those two paragraphs in article 21 with a view to deleting them or devising an appropriate wording. Should that not be possible, Venezuela reserved its position concerning the paragraphs concerned.

730.     The delegation of Venezuela stated that, as already announced during the discussion on article 30, Venezuela also had difficulty with that text, which referred to ethnic, religious or linguistic minorities. There was no doubt that the purpose of including such a provision had been to ensure to the fullest possible extent that children belonging to those minorities were guaranteed the rights stipulated in the convention. However, the Venezuelan delegation believed that the fact of including a separate or special provision on "minorities" gave the impression that children belonging to them were different from other children in their own country or elsewhere in the world, particularly as article 2 of the draft convention contained basic rules for ensuring that States respected and applied the rights set forth in the convention without discrimination of any kind. In the view of the Venezuelan delegation, the provision concerned was likely to give rise to discriminatory situations.

*Statements regarding specific articles*

731.     The representative of the United Kingdom in connection with the adoption of paragraph 43 of the report, said that the United Kingdom understood that the reference to article 1 in the Chairman's statement in that paragraph included a reference to article 1 bis. The representative of Ireland stated that he had no recollection of such a statement having been made at the time that the text of preambular paragraph 6 was adopted. He therefore questioned the appropriateness of its inclusion in the official report of the Working Group.

732.     During the meeting at which the report of the Working Group was adopted, with regard to the first sentence of paragraph 612 above, the representatives of Argentina, Bahrain, Egypt, the Federal Republic of Germany, Ireland, Morocco, Pakistan, Senegal, the Union of Soviet Socialist Republics, the United Kingdom of Great Britain and Northern Ireland, and the United States of America declared that paragraph 2 of article 20 had been adopted by consensus in the Working Group in the same manner as all other provisions in the draft convention. Other representatives confirmed that they had not been able to join the consensus on that paragraph.

733.     The observer for Austria stated that the wording of paragraphs 612, 613 and 732 as adopted fairly reflected the unsatisfactory situation they were confronted with before and after the "adoption" of article 38 (former article 20) during the Group's session of December 1988. The Austrian delegation therefore reserved its position on the consequences of what was stated in the report.

734.     The observer for Switzerland stated that his delegation had joined the consensus on paragraphs 612, 613 and 732 of the report relating to the adoption of article 38 (former article 20) of the convention. His delegation, however, referred to the speed and confusion which characterized the meeting during which article 38 (former article 20) was adopted and asked that the transcript of that meeting be annexed to the report.

735.     The Chairman, in light of the discussion concerning the Swiss proposal, stated that the transcript would be made available at the Secretariat upon request.

736.     At the end of the last meeting of the Working Group the Chairman expressed thanks to all those involved in the drafting of the convention, in particular to the delegations, the international organizations, the Secretariat and the non-governmental organizations.

V.     ADOPTION OF THE REPORT

737.     At the 23rd meeting of its eleventh session, on 23 February 1989, the Working Group adopted the present report.

## 3.     Draft resolution on the "Question of a convention on the rights of the child"

*The following is taken from document E/CN.4/1989/L.88 (3 March 1989).*

Afghanistan, Argentina, Australia, Bangladesh, Botswana, Bulgaria, Byelorussian Soviet Socialist Republic, Canada, China, Costa Rica, Cyprus, Denmark, Egypt, Ethiopia, Finland, France, German Democratic Republic, Greece, Hungary, Ireland, Lebanon, Libyan Arab Jamahiriya, Madagascar, Mexico, Mongolia, Morocco, New Zealand, Norway, Philippines, Poland, Portugal, Romania, Senegal, Syrian Arab Republic, Sweden and Yugoslavia: draft resolution

*Question of a convention on the rights of the child*

*The Commission on Human Rights,*

*Bearing in mind* the draft convention on the rights of the child submitted by Poland to the Commission on Human Rights on 7 February 1978 and annexed to Commission resolution 20 (XXXIV) of 8 March 1978, in which it decided to continue, as one of its priorities, its consideration of a draft convention on the rights of the child,

*Recalling* Economic and Social Council resolution 1978/18 of 5 May 1978, in which the Council took note with satisfaction of the initiative taken by the Commission with a view to the conclusion of a convention on the rights of the child,

*Recalling* General Assembly resolution 33/166 of 20 December 1978,

*Bearing in mind* all subsequent pertinent resolutions of the Commission on Human Rights, the Economic and Social Council and the General Assembly and in particular General Assembly resolution 43/112 of 8 December 1988, in which it requested the Commission on Human Rights to give the highest priority to a draft convention on the rights of the child and to make every effort at its forty-fifth session to complete a draft and to submit it, through the Economic and Social Council, to the General Assembly at its forty-fourth session, and invited all Member States to offer their active support to the completion of a draft convention on the rights of the child in 1989, the year of the thirtieth anniversary of the Declaration of the Rights of the Child and of the tenth anniversary of the International Year of the Child,

*Having examined* the report of the open-ended working group of the Commission on Human Rights on a draft convention on the rights of the child concerning its meeting to complete the second reading of the draft convention (E/CN.4/1989/48),

*Having also examined* the text of the draft convention as adopted by the open-ended working group (E/CN.4/1989/29 and Corr.1),

1.    *Expresses its appreciation* for the work achieved by the open-ended working group;

2.    *Decides* to adopt the draft convention on the rights of the child, as submitted by the open-ended working group;

3.    *Decides also* to transmit to the General Assembly, through the Economic and Social Council, the draft convention as submitted by the open-ended working group as well as the report of the working group;

4.    *Recommends* the following draft resolution for adoption by the Economic and Social Council:

"*The Economic and Social Council,*

*Recalling* the General Assembly resolutions related to the question of a convention on the rights of the child and, in particular, resolution 43/112 of 8 December 1988, in which it requested the Commission on Human Rights to submit a draft convention on the rights of the child, through the Economic and Social Council, to the General Assembly at its forty-fourth session,

*Expressing its appreciation* to the Commission on Human Rights for having concluded the elaboration of a draft convention on the rights of the child,

*Decides* to submit the draft convention on the rights of the child and the report of the working group to the General Assembly for consideration, with a view to the adoption of the convention by the Assembly at its forty-fourth session."

## 4.    Administrative and programme budget implications

*The following is taken from document E/CN.4/1989/L.102 (8 March 1989).*

QUESTION OF A CONVENTION ON THE RIGHTS OF THE CHILD (agenda item 13)

*Administrative and programme budget implications of the draft resolution contained in document E/CN.4/1989/L.88*

Statement submitted by the Secretary-General in accordance with rule 28 of the rules of procedure of the functional commissions of the Economic and Social Council

A.        Requests contained in the draft resolution

1.        By operative paragraph 4 of the draft resolution E/CN.4/1989/L.88, the Commission on Human Rights would recommend for adoption by the Economic and Social Council a draft resolution recalling General Assembly resolutions related to the question of a convention on the rights of the child and, in particular, resolution 43/112 of 8 December 1988 in which the Assembly requested the Commission to submit a draft convention on the rights of the child, through the Economic and Social Council, to the General Assembly at its forty-fourth session.

B.        Relationship of requests to programme of work

2.        The activities proposed in the draft resolution would fall under chapter 6, section II, "Programme: Centre for Human Rights", subprogramme 1, "Implementation of international standards, instruments and procedures", the objectives of and strategy for which are outlined in paragraphs 6.20 to 6.24 of the medium-term plan for the period 1984-1989 (A/37/6 and Corr.1) as extended through 1991.

3.        The activities are particularly relevant to section 23 (Human rights) of the proposed programme budget for the biennium 1990-1991, programme element 1.1: "Implementing regular supervisory procedures", of subprogramme 1, which constitutes the highest priority element in the human rights programme.

C.        Activities by which the requests would be implemented

4.        Should the recommendations contained in the draft resolution be adopted, the following activities would have to be envisaged upon the entry into force of the convention in accordance with article 49; (a) meeting of States parties to the convention: first meeting six months after entry into force, thereafter every two years; (b) sessions of the committee on the rights of the child: normally the committee will meet annually; (c) processing of reports submitted to the committee.

        (a)        Meeting of the States parties to the convention

5.        The first meeting of the States parties to elect members of the committee on the rights of the child would be convened by the Secretary-General at United Nations Headquarters for one day (two meetings) in 1991. In accordance with article 43 of the convention, subsequent meetings of the States parties would be convened by the Secretary-General at biennial intervals.

        (b)        Sessions of the Committee on the Rights of the Child

6.        In accordance with article 43, the committee on the rights of the child would meet annually. The Secretary-General, subject to the entry into force of the convention and the election of committee members, would convene the first regular session of the committee at the United Nations Office at Geneva for a period of three weeks during the first half of 1991. The committee at its first regular session would be expected, inter alia, to consider and adopt its rules of procedures in accordance with article 43 of the convention, draft approved guidelines for the submission of reports and take decisions on matters relating to the organization of its future work and preparation of its annual report to the General Assembly.

7.        Article 43, paragraph 11, of the draft convention, if accepted by the General Assembly, would provide for members of the committee to receive emoluments from United Nations resources on such terms and conditions as the Assembly might decide.

        (c)        Processing of reports submitted to the committee and substantive servicing of meetings of States parties and sessions of the committee on the rights of the child

8.        Under article 44 of the convention, States parties would undertake to submit reports through the Secretary-General of the United Nations, within two years of the entry into force of the convention and thereafter every five years. Article 45 would also provide, subject to the decision of the committee, for other reports to be submitted to the committee.

9.        Under article 44, the committee would submit a report on its activities every two years to the General Assembly through the Economic and Social Council.

10.    Under the terms of article 43, "The Secretary-General of the United Nations shall provide the necessary staff and facilities for the effective performance of the functions of the Committee under the present Convention". Without prejudice to decisions which may be taken regarding emoluments - the appropriate financial implications being submitted in connection with any specific proposals - or with regard to the manner of financing the operation of the convention, the Secretary-General estimates that the following expenses would be incurred in connection with the implementation of the convention as described above.

D.    Modifications required in the proposed programme of work

11.    Three new outputs would have to be added to the text of section 23 (Human rights) of the proposed programme budget for the biennium 1990-1991, as follows:

Subprogramme

1.    Implementation of international standards, instruments and procedures

1.1.    Implementing regular supervisory procedures

Output:

(xxix)    Substantive servicing of one meeting of States parties to the convention on the rights of the child;

(xxx)    Substantive servicing of two sessions of the committee on the rights of the child;

(xxxi)    Preparation of one report of the committee on the rights of the child to be submitted to the General Assembly.

E.    Additional requirements at full cost

12.    It is envisaged that the Secretary-General would convene the first regular session of the committee on the rights of the child at the United Nations Office at Geneva for a period of three weeks during the first half of 1991.

(a)    Travel and subsistence of experts

Travel and subsistence of 10 members of the committee for one session of three-weeks' duration

55 000    (US dollars; calculated on a notional basis)

(b)    Conference services requirements

13.    With regard to the requirements for meeting services and documentation which will arise for the first meeting of States parties to the convention to be held in New York in 1991 and the first session of the committee on the rights of the child to be held in Geneva in the first half of 1991, the following costs have been estimated:

|  |  | US$ |
|---|---|---|
| (i) | Meeting of States parties | 108 800 |
| (ii) | Committee on the rights of the child | 1 058 400 |
| Total |  | 1 167 200 |

(c)    Staffing requirements

14.    The extra staffing resources that would be required will depend upon the programme of work adopted by the committee and the extent to which the committee would require substantive and technical assistance from the staff of the Centre for Human Rights. It is estimated, however, that initially at least two professionals and one General Service staff member would be required to deal with the preparatory work

and servicing of meetings of the States parties to the convention and the sessions of the committee on the rights of the child. The extra staff costs are estimated as follows (calculated on a yearly basis):

|  | US$ |
|---|---|
| Twelve work-months at P-4 level | 98 200 |
| Twelve work-months at P-2 level | 66 600 |
| Twelve work-months at General Service level | 55 100 |
| Total | 219 900 |

15.     The requirements listed above include $274,900 under section 23 (Human rights) and conference servicing requirements under section 29 (Conference Services) estimated at $1,167,200 for 1991.

## 5.    Discussion in the Commission on Human Rights on 6 and 8 March 1989

*The following is taken from document E/CN.4/1989/SR.50 (13 June 1989).*

ORGANIZATION OF WORK (*continued*)

1.      Following a proposal made by the officers and introduced by the CHAIRMAN [Mr. QIAN Jiadong (China)] to the effect that the Commission should confine itself to making decisions and giving explanations of vote on the draft resolutions and decisions submitted on certain individual agenda items, Mr. TAYLHARDAT (Venezuela) objected that such a procedure would not be appropriate for agenda item 13, "Question of a convention on the rights of the child". In resolution 43/112, the General Assembly had requested the Commission to give the highest priority to a draft convention on the rights of the child. The Commission could not adopt the draft convention without a discussion, especially since delegations had not yet received the text of the draft (E/CN.4/1989/29), or the report of the open-ended Working Group dealing with the question (E/CN.4/1989/48).

2.      Mrs. DOS SANTOS PAIS (Portugal) said that she too would like a substantive discussion on the draft convention on the rights of the child.

3.      Mr. CERDA (Argentina) agreed with the two previous speakers, and pointed out that a debate on the question had been scheduled for the afternoon of Tuesday, 7 March.

4.      Mr. JOHNSON (United States of America) said that he could appreciate the arguments adduced by the representatives of Venezuela, Portugal and Argentina, but thought that, in view of the number of draft resolutions to be dealt with, the officers had little choice; the proposal transmitted by the Chairman seemed to be the only possible method to follow. The United States delegation would confine itself to an explanation of vote before the decision was made on the draft convention on the rights of the child.

5.      Mr. WHITAKER SALLES (Brazil), Mr. RONQUIST (Sweden), Mr. BRANCO (Sao Tome and Principe) and Mrs. LUETTGEN DE LECHUGA (Cuba) endorsed the views of the delegations of Venezuela, Portugal and Argentina.

6.      The CHAIRMAN [Mr. QIAN Jiadong (China)] said that in the light of the opinions expressed by a number of delegations, the officers would review their proposal concerning agenda item 13, and then notify the Commission.

*The following is taken from document E/CN. 4/1989/SR.54 (15 June 1989).*

QUESTION OF A CONVENTION ON THE RIGHTS OF THE CHILD (agenda item 13) (E/CN.4/1989/29 and Corr.1 and E/CN.4/1989/48, E/CN.4/1989/L.88)

1.      Mr. MARTENSON (Under-Secretary-General for Human Rights) said that the decisions to be taken under agenda item 13 would have a major long-term impact. The convention on the rights of the child prepared by the Commission's Working Group recognized the dignity and rights of all children, whom it

sought to protect by facilitating their transition to adulthood. The convention also contained important measures of implementation. The 10 years of efforts by the Commission in that field were reflected in the reports of the Working Group, whose Chairman-Rapporteur, Mr. Lopatka, would personally introduce the report of the last session.

2.		The drafting of the convention had been supported by the Secretary-General of the United Nations and by himself, and he had made it his own personal concern to ensure that, even during the current period of budgetary restrictions, the maximum resources available were placed at the disposal of the Working Group. He was confident that the outcome of the discussion on the draft would be fruitful.

3.		Mr. LOPATKA (Chairman-Rapporteur of the Working Group on the question of a convention on the rights of the child) said that the Working Group had completed the elaboration of the draft convention on the rights of the child, which was contained in document E/CN.4/1989/29 and Corr. 1. In accordance with Commission resolution 1988/75 and Economic and Social Council resolution 1988/40, the Working Group had, during its last session held from 28 November to 9 December 1988, completed the second reading of the draft. The Group had also met on 21, 22 and 23 February to adopt the report on its last session (E/CN.4/1989/48). Accordingly, the Commission could, as the General Assembly had requested in its resolution 43/112, present the draft convention to the General Assembly, through the Economic and Social Council, at its forty-fourth session.

4.		The initial draft of the convention had been submitted to the Commission in 1978 by Poland. After 11 years of intensive work, the present text had been finalized thanks to the cooperation of all sides, and even the proposals which had not been included had played a useful role in the discussion. Attention should be drawn to the contributions made by UNICEF, UNESCO, ILO, the Office of the United Nations High Commissioner for Refugees, ICRC and also the numerous non-governmental organizations which had worked to promote and gain worldwide acceptance of the principle of such a convention.

5.		It had been necessary to reconcile numerous differences relating to traditions, cultures, religions, levels of economic development, legal systems and, indeed, political attitudes. The proposed text represented a broad consensus on what should be the obligations of the family, society and the international community towards children. On certain issues the text could be regarded as realistic, and some people might perhaps have wished it to be more ambitious. As it stood, however, it codified and even developed the international norms applicable to children without weakening already existing obligations. Article 41 of the draft text explicitly stated that nothing in the convention should affect "any provisions that are more conducive to the realization of the rights of the child" and that might be contained in the law of a State party or in international law in force for that State. The draft was necessarily a compromise, which reflected not a weakness but the spirit of mutual understanding that had prevailed in the Group's work. In article 1, for example, the members of the Group had been able to reach agreement on an upper age-limit for the definition of a child but not on a lower age-limit, i.e. on the inclusion into, or exclusion from, that definition of children before birth. Considering the fundamental divergence of views on that issue, the Working Group had preferred not to prejudge the solution that each State party to the convention might adopt.

6.		Even if not all the provisions of the text fully satisfied all States, the draft did represent a coherent and balanced whole. It would therefore be desirable, in view of the risk that a challenge of certain provisions by one State might entail the challenging of other provisions by other States, for the Commission to adopt the draft at the current stage without any modification. States wishing to make changes would have the opportunity to do so during the consideration of the text by the General Assembly.

7.		The Group had unanimously agreed to take no decision with regard to the financing of the Committee on the Rights of the Child. Article 43, paragraphs 11 and 12, which contained alternative solutions, therefore remained in square brackets. The general opinion in the Group was that the matter should be referred to the General Assembly for a decision.

8.      The draft convention had been devised mainly for the benefit of children living in normal conditions but also in the interests of those in extremely difficult situations, such as children living in war zones, children of refugees, children deprived of their parents, handicapped children or children who were abused. It also took into account the interests of children from minority groups and of children from developing countries where economic systems were weak. The text was the product of cooperation between countries from East and West, South and North, and the very process of its preparation had contributed to the improvement of mutual understanding in a so often controversial domain of human rights. The draft was neither too optimistic nor too pessimistic, but quite simply realistic. It was to be noted that States which for various reasons had not taken part in the elaboration of other important human rights instruments had associated themselves with the work, a fact that augured well for universal ratification of the convention. The adoption of that instrument by the General Assembly in 1989 would be the best way of celebrating the thirtieth anniversary of the Declaration of the Rights of the Child and the tenth anniversary of the International Year of the Child.

9.      He wished to thank all the delegations which had taken part in the elaboration of the draft, the representatives of international organizations, in particular UNICEF, and the representatives of non-governmental organizations, which he was sure would continue to play a role in the propagation of the convention and in the promotion of its ratification. In addition, he wished to express his appreciation to the Secretariat and also to Mr. van Boven, a long-serving Director of the United Nations Division of Human Rights, to Mr. Herndl, Assistant Secretary-General and former Director of the Centre for Human Rights, and especially to Mr. Martenson, the present Under-Secretary-General for Human Rights.

10.     Mrs. SAULLE (Italy) expressed her thanks to the Chairman of the Working Group, who had greatly contributed to enabling the Group to prepare a definitive draft text at its last session. She also wished to thank all the delegations which had participated in the endeavour, and the Secretariat of the United Nations and non-governmental organizations which had joined in that effort. Her delegation for its part, had tried to promote the consensus and the finalization of the draft.

11.     Even if the draft text, as it stood, was able to assure a good standard of rights and quality of life for children, it was nevertheless regrettable that a consensus had not emerged on a number of proposals concerning in particular the possibility of assuring a life "as normal as possible" to disabled children. Her delegation also wished to recall its position regarding the participation of children in armed conflicts, as set out in the last report of the Working Group. It was to be hoped that the safeguard clause in article 41 of the draft would be applied in order to improve the plight of children involved in armed conflicts. Efforts aimed at eliminating discrimination against the disabled, including a revision of Additional Protocol I of 1977 to the Geneva Conventions of 1949 in connection with article 41 of the draft convention, could make it possible to improve significantly the protection of such children. Although Italian law was in some respects more favourable to children than the Working Group's draft, her delegation was ready to support that draft in order to meet the wide expectations of the international community.

12.     Mr. SENE (Senegal) said that after 10 years of painstaking efforts the Working Group had succeeded, largely thanks to Mr. Lopatka, in completing the second reading of the draft convention on the rights of the child. The Group had been able not only to measure the difficulties to be overcome in building a universal legal framework, but also to test the limits of international action for the protection of children. It was a well-established fact that the value attributed to a concept depended on the end it was to serve and on the cultural context of each society. The elaboration of a legal framework for the protection of the child could not avoid that requirement. Since the proposed draft represented a careful compromise between different values, it could be expected that each provision would reflect the spirit and the letter of each State's domestic legislation. However, the purpose of the convention - as, indeed, of any international standard - was to harmonize differences and contradictions and to provide a common response to the problems of children.

13.     The Working Group had also had to reflect in a single instrument a multiplicity of different standards not endorsed by all the States which had participated in the elaboration of the future convention. Regarding

the protection of children in armed conflicts, for example, the attempts which had been made had not succeeded in giving full force to the humanitarian law covered by the 1977 Additional Protocols to the Geneva Conventions. However, agreement had been reached on a minimum standard as a realistic solution. Given the diversity of views on that point, as well as on a number of other matters, it had been necessary to find a "common denominator". Several years had been needed simply to agree on the concept of the child and even so there was still some uncertainty in interpreting the applicability of that concept.

14.       Child protection was a moral requirement of any civilized society which went beyond whatever legal mechanisms might be provided, but there was nevertheless a need to envisage legal protection for the child. Child protection was a prerequisite for the survival of future generations and, since children were the first victims of any upheaval in human society, preventive legislation was needed to provide them with a suitable environment. It was within that perspective, and in large part thanks to the efforts of non-governmental organizations and agencies such as UNICEF, that the United Nations had been able to create a new international consciousness regarding the protection of the child and of the family as its natural environment. However, the search for the universal did not mean standardization of the child's world. That world was not the same everywhere and it was necessary to respect its specific features and the economic, social and cultural realities that were themselves a function of the needs and resources of each region, each country and each civilization.

15.       His delegation had joined in the consensus which had appeared to emerge from the efforts of the Working Group because it had appreciated the fact that agreement had been reached at least on four essential principles. First, the objective of the future convention was to ensure special legal protection of children in view of their vulnerability. It was not, therefore, a matter of introducing standards that would impose a further burden on the body of international law relating to human rights. Second, all the rights and obligations set out in the future convention should be considered and applied in the interest of the child, and that interest should be determined not only in relation to the object and purpose of the convention, as stated in article 51, but also taking due account of the traditions and cultural values of each people, as stated in the twelfth preambular paragraph. That requirement should not be neglected by any legal system, since it was the basis of the legitimacy of the future convention. Third, the limitations or lacunae of the future convention could be overcome through the provisions of laws that were "more conducive to the realization of the rights of the child', as indicated in article 41 of the draft. Fourth, the difficulties involved in the realization of the rights covered by the future convention could be surmounted through an effort of international solidarity aimed at complementing national actions. In view of those principles, his delegation had not insisted on a number of elements which it regarded as fundamental but which were unfortunately absent from the draft. In deciding to join in the general agreement, it had sought to show pragmatism and avoid, as it were, opening Pandora's box.

16.       It was essential to avoid stifling the hopes that had already been raised among the future generation by the drafting of the convention, even though there was of course room for improvement of the draft. As celebrations were being held for the thirtieth anniversary of the adoption of the Declaration of the Rights of the Child, Senegal hoped that 1989 would be the year of the signing of the convention. The development of the child was the best indicator of the stability of a nation. Moreover, as UNICEF stated in its 1989 report on the state of the world's children, the protection of children today was also the most profitable of all investments.

17.       Mrs. ZELNER GONCALVES (Brazil) said she wished to congratulate Mr. Lopatka. He had noted that the draft convention, as adopted in second reading by the Working Group, represented a consensus between countries with different traditions and cultures. Brazil, which had already supported the draft convention adopted in first reading, thought that the revised text was considerably improved and refined. It hoped that the draft would be approved by the Commission and adopted by the General Assembly at the end of 1989, a year which would mark the thirtieth anniversary of the Declaration of the Rights of the Child and the tenth anniversary of the International Year of the Child.

18.      Brazil, whose total population of some 145 million comprised nearly 60 million children, had always given priority to the protection of children's rights, and article 227 of the Brazilian Constitution itself set out the rights and needs of children, as well as the duties and responsibilities of families, the Government and society towards them. It was in that spirit that Brazil had for 10 years regularly participated in the sessions of the Working Group, where it had sought to promote a broad social and legislative consensus on the way in which children should be considered and treated.

19.      Her delegation had frequently stressed the relationship that existed between the situation of children and the question of development in general. According to the UNICEF report for 1989, at least half a million young children had died in the 12 months as a result of the slowing-down or reversal of progress in the developing world. In other words, the report concluded, it was children who had been bearing the heaviest burden of debt and recession in the 1980s. As a developing country, Brazil would have liked the proposed text to emphasize those considerations, as well as the idea of the progressive application of the economic, social and cultural rights of children taking into consideration the difficulties of developing countries. The text should also have highlighted the vital role of international cooperation in implementing the future convention and consolidating the achievements of developing countries during the past decade in regard to the protection of children.

20.      With respect to the one issue still unresolved in the present draft, namely the expenses of the Committee on the Rights of the Child, Brazil felt that the implementation mechanism provided for in the convention should be financed from United Nations resources on such conditions as the General Assembly might decide in accordance with article 43, paragraph 11, of the draft.

21.      Brazil welcomed the designation of UNICEF as a focal point for the convention since that agency had actively participated in the efforts of the Working Group, inter alia by organizing a governmental meeting of Portuguese-speaking countries in Lisbon to focus on problems related to the implementation of the future convention. A tribute should also be paid to the non-governmental organizations, which had contributed greatly to the drafting of the convention and had helped to stimulate awareness of children's rights in both industrialized and developing countries. In the statement he had made at the opening of the current session, the Under-Secretary-General for Human Rights had emphasized that the convention, encompassing a wide range of basic human rights, would be a landmark in the field of standard-setting.

22.      Her delegation was convinced that the final text of the convention would not constitute a mere compilation of rights but would consider all human rights from the very specific perspective of children, taking into account all their legitimate interests. The convention could make a substantial contribution to improving the situation of the 2 billion children living in the world today.

23.      Mr. PALACIOS (Spain) said that the adoption of the draft convention - for which a special tribute was due to Mr. Lopatka - would contribute to reinforcing the safeguards set out in other international instruments, in particular the Declaration of the Rights of the Child adopted by the General Assembly in 1959. The right of all children to a standard and quality of life conducive to their physical, mental and social development, particularly in the event of separation of parents, could thus be better guaranteed.

24.      With regard to the practice of adoption, a measure considered in Spanish law as a last solution when the child could not remain in his original environment, in accordance with the Declaration on Social and Legal Principles relating to the Protection and Welfare of Children, the Spanish Government was particularly concerned with the possible implications of that measure in cases where the child had to leave his country. His delegation considered that the measures provided in article 21 (b) could be applied only on an exceptional basis, in other words when all other possibilities of placement or adoption in the child's country of origin had been exhausted. Furthermore, the provisions of article 21 (d) should be interpreted as restrictively as possible, since any financial exchange between the parties must be strictly limited to the reimbursement of legitimate costs. That, indeed, was the understanding of Mr. Lopatka himself.

25.      The question of children alleged as, accused of, or recognized as having infringed the penal law, which was the subject of article 40, deserved particular attention since the provisions contained therein

meant that countries would have to ensure that their legal systems were consistent with the United Nations Standard Minimum Rules for the Administration of Juvenile Justice ("The Beijing Rules") adopted by the General Assembly on 29 November 1985 in its resolution 40/33. His delegation considered, moreover, that the concessions which had had to be made in the interests of consensus ought not to prevent the adoption of the draft, since the provisions of article 41 allowed each State the freedom to set higher standards in certain areas, as would be desirable for implementation of the provisions of article 38. Furthermore, at the time of ratification or accession, States could make reservations, although it would be desirable for such reservations to be kept to a minimum in order not to jeopardize the universal character of the convention.

26.     His delegation approved the idea of setting up a Committee on the Rights of the Child as an independent and impartial body to examine how far States parties were complying with their obligations. In that regard, he believed that the financial question must not be an obstacle and that the work of the Committee should, therefore, be financed from the United Nations budget on such terms as might be decided by the General Assembly.

27.     His delegation hoped that the Commission would be able to approve the draft text.

28.     Mr. DESPOUY (Argentina) said that his delegation approved the draft convention on the rights of the child, although it considered that some articles could be drafted in more categorical terms.

29.     His delegation welcomed the inclusion, in the preamble, of a paragraph which read:

"Bearing in mind that, as indicated in the Declaration of the Rights of the Child adopted by the General Assembly of the United Nations on 20 November 1959, 'the child, by reason of his physical and mental immaturity, needs special safeguards and care, including appropriate legal protection, before as well as after birth'."

30.     His delegation also wished to stress the importance of the provisions of article 8 (concerning preservation of the child's identity), which were of particular significance for his country in view of the tragic situations it had experienced at the time of the military dictatorship. His delegation wished also, in that regard, to draw the Commission's attention to document E/CN.4/1989/66, which contained extracts from the annual report of the Inter-American Commission on Human Rights. In that context, Argentina had taken note of the statement made by the Paraguayan delegation, under agenda item 12, concerning the situation of missing Argentine children and had recently learned with satisfaction that the Supreme Court of Paraguay had taken a favourable decision in that regard.

31.     His delegation particularly welcomed the provisions of article 21 of the draft, aimed at preserving as far as possible the cultural identity of the child and in particular at avoiding fraudulent adoption, which often involved trafficking in children. Concerning article 38, his delegation would have preferred an outright prohibition of the recruitment and use of children in armed conflicts and, in that regard, it hoped that the provisions of article 41 would be applied in order to guarantee effective protection consistent with the standards in force in international humanitarian law.

32.     His delegation fully approved article 43 of the draft concerning the establishment of a Committee on the Rights of the Child and it welcomed in particular the final draft of paragraph 7 of that article. On the financial question, his delegation felt that the Committee should be funded from the regular budget of the United Nations and it would therefore speak, at the General Assembly, in favour of retaining the first sentence of paragraph 11, which for the time being was between square brackets.

33.     Countries must now envisage prompt ratification of the future convention. In that context, the non-governmental organizations were already playing a very important role, particularly in Latin America, where they had also undertaken the elaboration of a regional instrument concerning the rights of the child to supplement the provisions of the international convention. It was to be hoped that, as in the past, UNICEF would play a leading role in that regard. At the national level, his Government attached great importance to the draft convention, which was being given due consideration in the elaboration of a new code concerning minors.

34. His Government welcomed the initiative taken by the Polish delegation more than 10 years previously. As a co-sponsor of draft resolution E/CN.4/1989/L.88, it hoped that all countries would approve the draft and that the General Assembly, at its forty-fourth session, would be able to adopt the international convention on the rights of the child.

35. Mrs. dos SANTOS PAIS (Portugal) said that the draft convention, which was largely inspired by the international instruments already adopted in the field of human rights, unequivocally proclaimed the dual principle of the child as being both entitled to basic rights and freedoms and as being the object of special protection to ensure the harmonious development of his personality and enable him to play a constructive role in society. The draft, moreover, introduced a number of innovations. For example, in the area of family placement and adoption, the principles set out in the Declaration approved in 1986 had been very closely followed and for the first time were echoed in a binding legislative instrument.

36. Her delegation attached great importance to articles 2, 3 and 4 of the draft, which concerned non-discrimination and the fundamental role that States would have to play, taking into consideration the best interests of the child, in the adoption of legislative, administrative and other measures necessary for the respect and exercise of the rights set out in the convention. At the international level, the experts of the Committee on the Rights of the Child (whose mandate was governed by innovative provisions) would play a decisive role, and the dialogue undertaken by them would be essential in cooperative efforts aimed at improving the well-being and ensuring respect of the rights of children in all countries.

37. Considering the importance of the task that would be entrusted to the Committee, her delegation felt that it would be preferable for the costs of its meetings to be met from the general budget of the United Nations. The unfortunate example of the Committee on the Elimination of Racial Discrimination was particularly instructive in that regard. It was also important that the experts appointed should enjoy complete independence and not be subject to the availability of resources, still less, even indirectly, to the political will of States. Her delegation's view was borne out by the conclusions of the meeting of chairpersons of human rights treaty bodies.

38. In the opinion of her delegation, the importance of non-participation of children in armed conflicts and their protection in such situations had not been sufficiently emphasized in the draft. Under article 38, for example, the indirect participation of children under the age of 15 years in such conflicts was not prohibited and the discretionary powers granted to States weakened the absolute character of the protection to be afforded to children. In that regard, her delegation regretted the fact that it had been impossible to set standards that were at least identical to those existing in international humanitarian law and that the definition contained in article 1 of the draft, namely that "a child means every human being below the age of 18 years" had not served as the basis for drafting article 38. Nonetheless, States parties could be guided by the provisions of article 41, as would Portugal itself, in order to apply provisions that were more conducive to the respect of children's rights. The draft should not be considered in that regard, as well as in other respects, only as a compilation of minimum standards for the protection of children. Nor should States parties take measures aimed at restricting or undermining the application of the principles set out in the convention.

39. The Commission must now take action to ensure that the draft text could be approved by the General Assembly, if possible at its forty-fourth session.

40. Mr. RONQUIST (Sweden), speaking on behalf of the delegations of the five Nordic countries - Denmark, Finland, Iceland, Norway and Sweden - expressed those delegations' gratitude to Poland and to Professor Lopatka. He recalled that the purpose of drafting a convention on the rights of the child had been to supplement the International Bill of Human Rights, in which the rights of the child had not been taken sufficiently into consideration. Children today, in many parts of the world, were victims of hunger, armed conflicts, social injustice and economic or sexual exploitation. The Nordic countries welcomed the fact that the draft convention contained provisions aired specifically at protecting children from certain practices and at ensuring their protection in penal matters.

41.     The delegations of the Nordic countries attached particular importance to the question of the protection of children in cases of armed conflict. In that regard, they felt that the text of article 38 of the draft did not reflect the concerns expressed by a majority within the Working Group. They regretted the fact that the draft convention contained no provisions aimed at ensuring better protection than was afforded in international humanitarian law. It was therefore all the more important, in their view, that the convention should in no respect fall short of existing standards in humanitarian law. The Nordic countries welcomed those provisions aimed at making the convention widely known to adults and children, and they also attached great importance to the role assigned to UNICEF and other United Nations bodies in regard to the implementation of the convention. The importance of non-governmental organizations had also been duly recognized.

42.     As far as the financing of the activities of the Committee on the Rights of the Child was concerned, the delegations of the Nordic countries felt that the experience of other bodies whose work had been financed partly or entirely by States parties gave pause for thought and they firmly believed, therefore, that the work of the Committee should be financed from the regular budget of the United Nations.

43.     Concerning the reservations that some countries intended to make under certain articles, the delegations of the Nordic countries wished to emphasize that it was of the utmost importance for implementation of the convention that every State that wished to ratify the instrument should undertake a careful review of its legislation and practices regarding children's rights.

44.     The delegations of the Nordic countries wished to express their appreciation to a number of non-governmental organizations for the valuable cooperation they had extended to the Working Group during the elaboration of the draft convention. Lastly, they wished to point out that the adoption of the convention by the General Assembly at its forty-fourth session would not mean that the Commission had completed its work. On the contrary, in the years to come the Commission would have to examine very closely the information provided on the protection of children's rights and cooperate fully with Governments, United Nations bodies and non-governmental organizations in the implementation of all the provisions of the convention.

45.     Mr. RIETJENS (Belgium) recalled that his country had often expressed its scepticism about the elaboration of instruments aimed at establishing specific human rights for certain categories of persons. However, Belgium had encouraged the Commission to elaborate an instrument concerning the rights of the child. In its view, the convention must draw its inspiration from the Declaration of the Rights of the Child but also lay down concrete rules of law to supplement existing international law. It was in that spirit that Belgium had taken part in the work of the Group, which, under the competent and firm guidance of Professor Lopatka, had completed the draft convention now before the Commission.

46.     That draft was an honourable compromise and contained a good number of highly valuable articles but it was not entirely satisfactory, especially in so far as some of its provisions, such as articles 14 and 38, represented a step backwards compared with other binding international instruments. His delegation failed to see how the convention, whose primary aim should be to afford special protection for the child, could meet that objective if it fell short of existing, universally recognized international standards. That situation would have to be remedied.

47.     On the other hand, his delegation welcomed the fact that certain basic principles of the 1959 Declaration, such as the recognition of the need for special protection for the child both before and after birth, had eventually been included in the draft convention. Such a reaffirmation was necessary if all the other provisions were not to remain a dead letter.

48.     At the same time, his delegation noted with satisfaction that article 11 of the draft convention required States parties to promote the conclusion of bilateral or multilateral agreements or accession to existing agreements "to combat the illicit transfer and non-return of children abroad". In that regard, Belgium welcomed the fact that in June 1988 two countries particularly concerned by the problem of children shared between parents separated by a border had concluded a bilateral convention aimed at enabling the

free movement of children between those two countries and at putting an end to abductions of children between disunited couples. His delegation was convinced that those States would take the necessary follow-up measures for implementation of the convention and it remained open-minded towards any positive experience in that context.

49.     Mrs. KRAMARCZYK (German Democratic Republic) said she wished first of all to pay a tribute to Professor Lopatka for the way in which over a period of 10 years he had guided the efforts of the Working Group in its task of drafting a convention on the rights of the child. Her delegation, like many others, felt that the new convention not only entailed obligations for States parties to protect children against violations of their human rights but also made it incumbent upon the parties to create conditions which would facilitate active and creative participation by children and young adults in the social and political life of their countries.

50.     The wording of some articles of the draft nevertheless presented certain problems, in her delegation's view, because of the fact that some of the provisions incorporated from other legal instruments, such as the International Covenants on Human Rights, had not been properly adapted to the specific legal situation of children, and her delegation therefore could not fully subscribe to that wording. It was to be regretted, in particular, that article 13 of the draft convention did not expressly refer, among the restrictions applicable to children's right to information, to ideas which constituted racist or fascist propaganda, the glorification of violence and terror and incitement to hatred among peoples. She reserved her delegation's right to submit the official views of the Government of the German Democratic Republic on certain articles at a later stage. Apart from those few difficulties, her country welcomed the fact that the draft convention on the rights of the child would be submitted to the General Assembly in the year of the thirtieth anniversary of the adoption of the Declaration of the Rights of the Child. Lastly, she wished to thank Poland once again for the initiative it had taken 10 years earlier.

51.     Mrs. ZHANG (China) said that the adoption of the draft convention on the rights of the child after years of untiring effort, especially by the Working Group and its Chairman, would fill the existing gap in international law concerning the protection of children and would undoubtedly have a positive effect on the development of standards relating to human rights in general. The completion of the draft was also the most concrete way of celebrating the thirtieth anniversary of the Declaration of the Rights of the Child and the tenth anniversary of the International Year of the Child.

52.     Her Government had always attached great importance to the well-being of children, who represented the future of mankind and the hope of society. It was implementing various programmes to provide for the moral, intellectual and physical development of children and had taken a number of measures for pregnant women in order to guarantee the healthy development of the foetus.

53.     In spite of the difficulties it had encountered during its work because of the diverging legal, religious and social views between countries, the Working Group had been able to draw up a compromise text which should in principle be acceptable to all sides. It was precisely for that reason that the draft, as it now stood, was not perfect and her delegation had reservations to make on some of its provisions. It felt, for example, that the word "child" should be taken to mean children from birth to the age of 18 and that the convention should not include the foetus within its sphere of application. It was the responsibility of each different country to adopt appropriate measures regarding the foetus in accordance with its own legal system. Her Government would study further the provisions of the draft convention. However, it could already agree to the suggestion that the draft should be submitted for consideration by the Economic and Social Council and by the General Assembly.

54.     Miss WALKER (United Kingdom) said that concluding work on the draft convention on the rights of the child was no mean achievement given that the document covered many complicated and sensitive subjects on which there was a considerable divergence of views, a fact that had rendered the Working Group's task extremely difficult. It was to be hoped that the consensus which had ultimately been reached on the

text of the draft would be maintained so that the Commission could adopt it. Her delegation urged the Commission to submit the draft to the General Assembly as it stood, since the financing of the Committee on the Rights of the Child (see art. 43) was a matter for the General Assembly to decide. Her delegation expressed the hope that, once the convention was open for signature, as many Governments as possible would join her Government in signing and ratifying that instrument.

55.     Her delegation wished to draw the Commission's attention in particular to the problem of child abduction and the distress it caused to the children and families concerned. In an effort to resolve that problem, her Government had passed two Acts in 1984 and 1985 on the question, which had enabled it to ratify, in 1986, The Hague Convention on the Civil Aspects of International Child Abduction and the European Convention on Recognition and Enforcement of Decisions concerning Custody of Children and on Restoration of Custody of Children. Her delegation hoped that those two Conventions would contribute towards solving what was a major international problem and that other Governments would recognize their benefits and adhere to them. In that regard, bilateral agreements were helpful only when both parties had the will and ability to implement them, and ad hoc agreements were all too easily broken. For those reasons, her Government was in favour of concluding multilateral conventions which had the force of international law. In any event, the welfare of the child was of paramount importance and it was on that principle that her Government's position, as already explained to the Commission by Sir Geoffrey Howe, Secretary of State for Foreign and Commonwealth Affairs of the United Kingdom, was founded. Her delegation wished to thank once again Mr. Adam Lopatka, the Working Group and the Secretariat.

56.     Mrs. AVELINE (France) said that her country, which had taken an active part from the very beginning in the meetings of the Working Group of the Commission, presided over by Mr. Lopatka, entrusted with the elaboration of a convention on the rights of the child, warmly welcomed the completion of the second reading of the text after 10 years of work, even though it would have liked to see the text go further on some points. The draft represented a coherent instrument of protection both because it reaffirmed the fundamental rights guaranteed in the two Covenants, rightly including a reference to the civil rights of children, and because of the specific provisions it contained, which her delegation regarded as essential. France hoped that the draft would be adopted by the General Assembly at its next session and it would cooperate actively in the work of the Committee on the Rights of the Child appointed to monitor implementation of the convention.

57.     France was particularly concerned by the distressing question of children from separated mixed couples who were abducted by one of the parents. It had addressed that complex problem by trying, on the one hand, to protect the legitimate interests and feelings of children and their mothers and, on the other hand, to address the problem in a spirit of cooperation and confidence. It had therefore concluded with Algeria, which also had the same concerns, the Convention of 21 June 1988 [to] permit the settlement of future disputes. To deal with existing disputes, a joint commission (a most interesting feature of the Convention) had been set up. That commission had already met on seven occasions since August 1988 and had given opinions making it possible to settle a large number of outstanding cases. By the end of February 1989, 31 children in all had been reunited with their mothers. Attention should also be drawn to the "deterrent" effect of that Convention since, following its signature, only two new cases had been reported to the French authorities. The cases pending had not all been settled, of course, and many difficulties remained, especially procedural ones. It was to be hoped that the new contacts made with mothers who had come in a delegation to Geneva on 27 February to explain their situation would permit a better understanding of what needed to be done to facilitate implementation of the Convention of 21 June. The work carried out by Algeria and France in that area might also help other countries in resolving similar disputes.

58.     Mr. HOLMES (Canada) said that, in his delegation's view, the approval by the General Assembly and the eventual entry into force of the convention on the rights of the child would represent important steps in the development of international standards for the promotion and protection of basic human rights. While the new convention would not immediately relieve all the suffering inflicted on children throughout the world, it at least had the merit of offering a sufficiently flexible basis on which it would be possible

to develop more satisfactory means of addressing and resolving the problems relating to children's rights. The Committee on the Rights of the Child to be set up under the convention would be required to play a unique and important role since because of the hybrid nature of the convention, which combined civil and political rights with those of an economic, social and cultural nature, it could draw extensively upon the deliberations and views of other implementing bodies and thus would be able to devote more of its efforts to the establishment of cooperative relations with States, intergovernmental bodies and non-governmental organizations. To achieve that objective, it was essential that the Committee should be composed of experts in some of the most important areas covered by the convention, such as the treatment of juvenile delinquents or child labour laws, and that those experts should be independent, thus avoiding any politicization of their work, something that would be absolutely inadmissible. All the suggestions made regarding how the Committee should function would be for nought until the vital question of financing for the Committee had been resolved. The view of his delegation was that the United Nations itself should be responsible for the financing of the Committee given the obvious importance that must be attached to the effective functioning of bodies established to enhance the protection of human rights. That form of financing should, moreover, be extended to all implementing bodies.

59.     His delegation wished to pay a tribute to all those without whom there would have been no convention on the rights of the child: first of all, the Government of Poland, which had initiated the endeavour; then Mr. Lopatka, Chairman-Rapporteur of the Working Group, for his devotion, which had been recognized in December 1988 when he had received the United Nations prize for human rights; and, lastly, all the States and United Nations bodies, in particular UNICEF, and all the non-governmental organizations which had participated in and actively contributed to the drafting of the convention.

60.     In conclusion, his delegation urged all States, all regional organizations and all intergovernmental and non-governmental bodies to support the convention on the rights of the child and to assist the United Nations system in continuing its task of protecting and promoting the rights of the child throughout the world.

61.     Mr. BENHIMA (Morocco) said that children were the heart and arteries of all societies, and every society attached special importance to them as it placed in children all its hopes for a better future. Morocco was especially conscious of that fact since children below the age of 15 years represented 42.1 per cent of his country's population. The Government of Morocco therefore considered that its overriding duty was to provide for the education, nutrition, social welfare and training of young people, a goal which called for the adoption of a well-defined policy to meet the needs of mothers and children. For that reason, priority was given to children in all social programmes implemented by the Government and all legislative texts, such as the Labour Code and the Penal Code, contained provisions aimed at protecting children - in accordance with the principles set out in the international human rights instruments and in the conventions of the International Labour Organization - against all practices which might threaten their physical and mental development. Social welfare included the availability of free primary education and vocational training, as well as the provision of special services to disabled, abandoned or orphaned children through social centres.

62.     Morocco therefore welcomed the fact that after so many years of effort the Working Group had been able to complete the second reading of the draft convention on the rights of the child under the able chairmanship of Professor Lopatka and thanks to the assistance provided by the Centre for Human Rights, which had done everything possible to facilitate that task, and by other bodies and agencies, in particular UNICEF, as well as by various non-governmental organizations.

63.     It was difficult to elaborate fundamental texts on the rights of the child since those rights varied between legal systems and religious and family traditions. In Muslim society, the place of the child was defined according to precise criteria. For that reason, Morocco had closely followed the elaboration of the draft convention and had in particular feared the negative effects of provisions which might not take into account the sacred nature of the family and of tradition in Muslim society.

64.     Fortunately, the text presented by the Working Group was a balanced one. It should be recalled that it had been adopted in the Working Group by consensus, thus signifying that concessions had been made on all sides. The text attached due importance to children's economic, social and cultural rights and to health care, education, culture and other essential safeguards.

65.     Looking to the future, good international cooperation would be necessary to ensure that the convention afforded children the desired protection. The proposed text rightly provided for a procedure of monitoring by a committee of experts. It also provided that States parties should undertake to submit periodic reports on implementation of the convention. The draft also referred to the assistance which the committee of experts would receive from UNICEF in its work.

66.     The financial questions, however, still had to be resolved. His delegation believed that the expenses of the committee of experts should be met from the regular budget of the United Nations. Lastly, he hoped that the draft convention, once transmitted by the Economic and Social Council to the General Assembly, would be adopted as soon as possible.

67.     Mr. TAYLHARDAT (Venezuela) said it was symbolic that the discussion on the draft convention on the rights of the child coincided with International Women's Day. In many parts of the world, the situation of children was critical in many respects. The adoption of a convention aimed at protecting their rights was therefore of particular importance, and in that regard his delegation wished to express its gratitude to the Working Group and to its Chairman-Rapporteur, Mr. Lopatka. He also wished to pay a tribute to Mr. Lopatka's country of origin, Poland, and to UNICEF for the role played by that organization in the protection of children's rights.

68.     The Working Group entrusted with the task of elaborating the draft convention had pursued its work for 10 years, greatly accelerating the pace of its activities towards the end of that period. It had thus been able to complete the task allotted to it by the General Assembly, and the draft should now be adopted at the next session of the Assembly. It was important to underline the difficulties with which the Working Group had had to contend. Even now, some gaps remained in its text and it would be desirable for States to make further efforts to fill those gaps before its adoption by the General Assembly.

69.     The draft resolution on the question (E/CN.4/1989/L.88) called upon the Commission on Human Rights to "adopt" the draft convention on the rights of the child. He was not certain whether that was the role of the Commission. The General Assembly had simply requested the Commission to complete the convention and transmit the text to it. The adoption of the text was a matter for the Assembly, which had included an item in its agenda for that purpose. Nevertheless, his delegation would not oppose the adoption of draft resolution E/CN.4/1989/L.88 by consensus.

70.     Mr. BELSEY (World Health Organization) said that his organization was proud to join with the other specialized agencies, the non-governmental organizations and the many representatives who had expressed their support for the draft convention on the rights of the child (E/CN.4/1989/29). In a sense that text complemented the definition in the Constitution of WHO that health was a state of complete physical, mental and social well-being and not merely the absence of disease or infirmity. The convention would contribute to strengthening the inherent rights of children to enjoy the benefits of national health programmes.

71.     Article 24 of the draft underlined the importance of primary health care, information, technologies and programmes for mothers and children. It summarized the conclusions from the vast body of scientific evidence linking the health of children to their access to health services, to the knowledge and actions of parents, to the health of the mother and to the need for family planning. Other articles also gave expression to the direct health needs of children - especially article 23, which set out the rights of disabled children - and WHO particularly noted paragraph 4 of that article, which especially concerned WHO. His organization was also attributed a special role in article 24, paragraph 4, in facilitating the exchange of information and in strengthening national health capacities.

72.	Children in vulnerable and difficult situations had special health needs. In the case of street children, for example, the creative energies of normal development were diverted to harmful behaviour (drug abuse, prostitution or other criminal activity). Impaired growth also resulted when children worked at too young an age. In those areas WHO had programme activities and technical materials that member States and non-governmental organizations could draw upon in giving effect to the convention on the rights of the child. From that point of view, it felt that articles 9 and 18 of the draft convention, which related to circumstances affecting the growth and development of children, article 32 on child labour, article 33 on substance abuse and article 34 on sexual exploitation were of particular importance. WHO also expressed its support for those articles of the text dealing with education and information, especially articles 28 and 29.

73.	The prospects of a healthy transition to adulthood were better in societies that made a commitment to social justice and provided for an appropriate distribution of resources for health and social development. In that regard, bearing in mind the effects of urbanization, economic crises and natural or man-made disasters, WHO saw the adoption of the draft convention as being an essential component of the strategies of health for all by the year 2000. It was ready to cooperate with member States, United Nations bodies and non-governmental organizations in implementing the convention once it had been adopted by the General Assembly.

74.	Mr. JAEGER (Federal Republic of Germany) said that, following the establishment of the Working Group in 1979, the elaboration of the convention on the rights of the child had begun slowly without attracting much public attention. In the past few years, however, the situation had changed, at least in the Federal Republic of Germany. He wished to express his thanks to the Working Group, and in particular to its Chairman-Rapporteur, Mr. Lopatka.

75.	It was self-evident that children should enjoy the rights which applied to all human beings. In formulating those rights, however, an exception had to be made in the case of children, particularly as the process of growing up today was a more complex one than ever before. In many parts of the world, that process was taking place in a dramatic situation; he was thinking in particular of the children mobilized by Iran, those condemned to die of hunger or those who did not even live to the day of their birth for having become the victims of adult interference.

76.	On the latter question, he noted that the draft convention, as it now stood, no longer gave the impression of abandoning the principle enshrined in the 1959 Declaration of the Rights of the Child, under which the child must be protected even prior to its birth. Bearing in mind the provision of article 31 of the Vienna Convention on the Law of Treaties of 23 May 1969, which stated that a treaty should be interpreted in good faith and in the light of its object and purpose, the ninth preambular paragraph of the draft appeared as a great success. It was the first time that the right to life of the unborn child had been recognized in an international convention. That provision, it should be noted, was in conformity with article 1 of the Basic Law of the Federal Republic of Germany and with the long-standing tradition of that country dating back to the Prussian laws of 1794 (Preussisches Allgemeines Landrecht), which stipulated that: "the general rights of humanity also apply to children unborn, even prior to the moment of their conception".

77.	Article 2, paragraph 1 of the draft convention prohibited any discrimination against a child born out of wedlock. That was also in harmony with the objective of his Government, which desired within the limits of the possible to grant equal opportunities to all children, whether born in or out of wedlock.

78.	At the same time, his delegation felt that the wording of article 5, dealing with the responsibilities, rights and duties of parents, was too vague. Account should have been taken of possible conflicts between the rights of children and those of parents. Conflicts of that kind could arise, for example, over giving children access to presentations of the electronic media, a matter which would be covered by article 13.

79.	His country generally welcomed the provision regarding family reunification contained in article 10. It was particularly satisfied that paragraph 2 of that article affirmed the right of the child and that of its parents to leave any country, including their own, and to return to their own country. The Federal Republic of Germany, in its human rights policy, had always given emphasis to family reunification and freedom of movement. However, the application of article 10 should not undermine legislation concerning aliens. The Federal Republic of Germany was not an immigration country and reserved the right to take its own decisions concerning the reunification of families of aliens living in its territory. In conclusion, he hoped that the convention on the rights of the child would be adopted and enter into force in the near future and he gave an assurance that his country would do its utmost to ensure its implementation.

80.        Mr. PERERA (Sri Lanka) said he also wished to stress the symbolic nature of the fact that the discussion on the draft convention on the rights of the child coincided with the celebration of International Women's Day. The rights of children were already covered in international instruments such as the Universal Declaration and the two Covenants, as well as in resolutions of the General Assembly. The advantage of the draft convention presented by the Working Group was that a whole body of rights were now consolidated in a single document. Some aspects might require further clarification, however, in so far as disabled children, health, nutrition, etc. were concerned.

81.        The proposed draft (E/CN.4/1989/29) took due account of several basic concepts. First of all, there was the notion of the best interest of the child. That was a well-known concept which had long been recognized by Sri Lanka; in particular, its courts were guided by the best interests of the child in cases involving the granting of custody, even if that meant departing from certain traditional notions which emphasized the rights of the father. At the same time, the draft also took due account of the various traditions of countries and peoples, as well as of the ethical, religious, cultural and linguistic context. From that point of view, the text was well balanced. It also took into consideration the interests of developing countries and the need for international cooperation. Some ideas, however, had been overemphasized: in his delegation's view, there was no need to enter into questions of litigation or to adopt provisions which duplicated other texts.

82.        A seminar on the rights of the child had recently been held in Sri Lanka with the cooperation of UNICEF and with the participation of jurists, doctors and child health workers. Sri Lanka had long-established laws for the protection of children, particularly in the area of education, where certain measures dated back to the 1940s. Since that time, child protection had been further enhanced in the country and in the field of education, for example, Sri Lanka went beyond the provisions of the draft convention since secondary as well as primary education was free and compulsory and higher education, although not compulsory, was also free. In conclusion, he was convinced that the adoption of the draft convention would enhance the legal status of the child throughout the world.

*The following is taken from document E/CN.4/1989/SR.55 (20 March 1989)*

19.        Ms. RADIC (Yugoslavia) said that her delegation had been actively involved for a number of years in the preparation of the draft convention. When adopted, it would become part of a remarkable collection of human rights instruments.

20.        Her delegation treated as a priority the issue of ethnic, national, linguistic and religious minorities, and considered that insufficient account had been taken of some of its proposals in that regard. She was referring, not only to the rights of children belonging to minorities, but also to those of children of migrant workers. While it was clear that delegations had a wide range of priorities and interests, she was convinced that more specific provision should have been made for the enjoyment of such rights. In Yugoslavia, the children of national minorities were treated in the same way as other children in all fields. In particular, they could be educated in their mother tongue and practise their own religion.

21.        Secondly, she expressed dissatisfaction with the way in which the deliberations of the last session of the Working Group on a draft convention on the rights of the child had been reflected in the report (E/CN.4/1989/48). Referring, in particular, to article 30 (former article 16 bis), concerning cultural, religious and linguistic rights, she said that the wording could have been more positive, having the effect of granting such rights. It should have been possible to go beyond the formulation "shall not be denied the right".

22.     Mr. HOSSAIN (Bangladesh) said he was pleased that the task of preparing the draft convention had been successfully concluded. The text before the Commission was the result of long and strenuous efforts on the part of the Working Group over the course of a decade.

23.     The leaders of the seven countries belonging to the South Asian Association for Regional Cooperation (SAARC) had called for the early conclusion and adoption of the draft convention by the General Assembly. His own delegation had contributed to the efforts to achieve a consensus on items which had, until the second reading, presented serious problems for a large number of countries, mostly in the developing world because their social and cultural conditions and legal arrangements governing matters such as inheritance, foster care and adoption, had made it difficult for them to accept certain provisions.

24.     In common with other international standards laid down for a wide range of peoples of different backgrounds and traditions and with different levels of economic development, the draft convention had to be realistic rather than utopian in kind. A delicate balance had been achieved through a spirit of understanding and compromise on the part of all those concerned. He hoped that the Commission would be able to adopt the draft by consensus, so that it could be adopted by the General Assembly at its forty-fourth session.

25.     Mrs. EZZ (observer for Egypt) said she wished to emphasize the important part played by the United Nations Children's Fund (UNICEF) during the second reading of the draft, when difficulties concerning provisions conflicting with domestic legislation had been resolved. After groups had been set up within the Working Group to deal with articles of a particularly sensitive nature, it had proved possible to complete the task successfully. The final text was sensitively balanced and reflected a spirit of compromise. She referred, in particular, to articles 7 (right to name and nationality), 14 (freedom of thought, conscience and religion), 21 (adoption) and 38 (armed conflicts). With regard to the question of expenses (article 43), her delegation considered that the committee should be funded by the United Nations, and that it was not, in any case, for the Commission to settle the matter which would be dealt with by the General Assembly.

26.     It was important not to disturb the delicate balance achieved in the text after several years of work. The convention was universal in scope, covering the range of needs and seeking to protect children from all forms of exploitation. She emphasized, in particular, the importance of international cooperation, referred to in the last preambular paragraph, and the need for an effective follow-up mechanism to monitor implementation (articles 43 and 44). Adoption of the convention was in the interest of all the children of the world.

27.     Mrs. TEEKAMP (observer for the Netherlands) said that her delegation had taken an active part in the preparation of the draft convention and regretted, therefore, that it was unable to join the sponsors of the draft resolution. Among other things, it had reservations with regard to the formulation of article 14 (freedom of thought, conscience and religion) since it thought that article 18 of the International Covenant on Civil and Political Rights provided a higher standard of protection. Furthermore, her Government did not consider that a consensus had been reached on the content of article 38 (armed conflicts).

28.     Mr. ADJABI (observer for Algeria) said that the question of codifying children's rights had long been a matter of major concern to the international community. Since the beginning of the century, it had been drawing up legal standards in order to protect and promote them.

29.     The text before the Commission was the outcome of a long standard-setting process involving intense negotiations during which it had not always been easy to reach a consensus. The draft was a worthy attempt to take account of a range of concerns and of different cultural and socio-economic backgrounds.

30.     Algeria, which had a very young population, welcomed the completion of the draft in a year commemorating both the thirtieth anniversary of the adoption of the Declaration on the Rights of the Child and the tenth anniversary of the International Year of the Child.

31.     Referring to the question of children of mixed marriages that had ended in separation or divorce, he said that their distress was intensified by the complications that arose from the involvement of different legal systems. The Convention signed by Algeria and France in June 1988 represented an important step forward

in that regard, being widely regarded as a model to be followed by other countries experiencing similar problems. It would be some time, however, before it took full effect, partly because it was a new type of instrument and partly because it involved slow legal procedures. Although a number of obstacles remained to be overcome, particularly those of a psychological nature, a number of cases had already been resolved satisfactorily.

32.    Mr. KARL (observer for Austria) emphasized the importance of the draft convention as a comprehensive legal framework for the welfare of children in generations to come. Children in many parts of the world were economically exploited, sexually abused, bought and sold or recruited to fight in wars. Such abhorrent practices and more common phenomena such as neglect and deprivation of basic rights, such as the right to food and education, must be addressed and provisions adopted to remedy the situation.

33.    It had not been easy to draft a convention intended to serve as a common standard for a range of political, socio-economic and cultural systems. The United Nations Children's Fund (UNICEF) and other international bodies had provided expertise and non-governmental organizations had made valuable contributions.

34.    His delegation's own participation had been guided by the principle of improving upon or, at very least, preserving the standards set by existing human rights instruments. Although in some cases a higher level of protection could have been achieved, the draft convention generally satisfied requirements. His delegation had expected, however, that there would be time for a substantive discussion within the Commission of a few selected issues on which no genuine consensus had been reached.

35.    That applied, in particular, to the question of armed conflicts (article 38) and to that of the financial arrangements (article 43). In both cases the Commission should have endeavoured to provide the General Assembly with a draft acceptable to all delegations.

36.    With regard to article 38, the age-limit of 15 might be consistent with Geneva Protocol I, but more protection was afforded by Protocol II and his delegation could not accept lower standards. In any case, only an age-limit of 18 would satisfy humanitarian requirements. Allowing anybody below the age of 18 to become involved in armed conflicts was strictly inconsistent with the overall objectives of the draft convention, and it was deplorable that there should be so little concern for the physical and mental well-being of children forced to go to war.

37.    With regard to the expenses of the Committee (article 22) (former article 43), his delegation preferred financing by the United Nations, rather than by the States parties to the convention, it being the duty of the international community to promote and ensure the effective protection of universally recognized human rights.

*Draft resolution E/CN.4/1989/L.88*

38.    Mr. TOWPIK (observer for Poland), introducing the draft resolution, said he was pleased that the Commission had completed its work on the draft convention, which had been initiated by a draft resolution proposed by his delegation 11 years previously.

39.    The idea behind the convention was that children were an especially vulnerable group requiring particular care and attention. Furthermore, if children were better cared for, better understood and better educated, future societies would be more evolved and more open to contact and cooperation. Making children the centre of concern could be of decisive importance with regard to the development of civilization and the solving of current and future problems.

40.    A convention on the rights of the child could not be a panacea for all child-related problems. Being aware that its role and importance would depend upon its effective implementation, his Government hoped, however, that it would represent a significant step forward in the development of national and international law concerning children, play a mobilizing and educational role, lead to further action at the national and

international levels, and make an important contribution to the development and promotion of human rights in general.

41.     The proposed resolution was mainly procedural in kind and its content self-explanatory. Among other things, it provided for the adoption by the Commission of the draft in the form submitted by the Working Group, and the transmission of that draft to the General Assembly with a view to its adoption at the forty-fourth session. There were 36 sponsors representing different regions, degrees of economic development and social systems. He expressed gratitude to those delegations that had overcome their doubts in a spirit of mutual understanding, and had decided not to oppose the draft resolution. He hoped that it would be adopted by consensus.

42.     Mr. Bossuyt (Belgium) took the Chair.

43.     Mrs. MARKHUS (observer for the Libyan Arab Jamahiriya) said that her delegation paid tribute to the Working Group on a draft convention on the rights of the child. In the course of the second reading of the draft, there had been protracted and difficult discussions, but a number of gaps had been filled and the imbalance noted during the first reading had been removed. The number and the geographical and political diversity of the sponsors reflected the worldwide importance attached to the adoption of a convention; it was clear that, once it had been adopted, the protection of children's rights throughout the world would be greatly enhanced. Her delegation had contributed to the drafting work reflected in document E/CN.4/1989/WG.1/WP.3, thus showing the continuing interest it attached to the task involved.

44.     In the Libyan Arab Jamahiriya, children enjoyed the right to full educational, health, cultural and other services, as set out in the document on human rights established by the People's Councils, particularly in articles 13, 14 and 20, which upheld inter alia the right of the child to a secure home life and choice of future career.

45.     While the draft embodied in the Working Group's report (E/CN.4/1989/48) did not contain everything her Government would have wished, it did nevertheless reflect the Declaration on the Rights of the Child and a more balanced approach. In the current world situation, children were often in dire need of protection. That fact should spur everyone to do everything possible to ensure that the General Assembly would be in a position to adopt the draft convention by the end of 1989, the tenth anniversary of the International Year of the Child.

46.     Mr. BEN MALEK (observer for Tunisia) said that the draft convention on the rights of the child, adoption of which would reinforce existing international legal instruments to protect and promote human rights, reflected the world community's commitment to protecting the rights of children, who were society's weakest link. His delegation was pleased that the text of the draft took account of the world's social and cultural diversity, and thanked the specialized agencies and the non-governmental organizations for their contributions.

47.     Since 7 November 1987, his Government had been carrying out a broad programme for the further promotion of human rights, not least in relation to children, whose rights were covered by the 1957 Code of Personal Status and subsequent legislation to protect the family and deal with matters such as trusteeship, guardianship, visiting rights, adoption and fostering.

48.     A number of further measures had been adopted, such as the establishment, on 21 May 1988, of a Higher Council for Childhood to help develop general policy in respect of the child. The work of the National Institute for the Protection of Children was being reviewed also. Particular attention was being given to children without families and to the establishment of special facilities to deal with abandoned and handicapped children. It had also been decided to group, under the Ministry of Social Affairs, all children's institutions, such as children's villages, and to update the legal system for the protection of children.

49.     Measures were also being considered, including pilot leisure centres, to improve the urban environment as part of the efforts to combat child delinquency. A number of measures had also been adopted to assist the handicapped, such as encouraging businesses to recruit handicapped youths and raising funds to

provide free hospital and health treatment for the handicapped. In addition, existing provisions in areas such as education, adoption, rehabilitation of delinquents, fostering and the protection of handicapped minors were being improved. The economic and social safeguards for children also covered such aspects as children's work, property and physical and moral integrity.

50.     It was sad to note, at a time when a draft convention was about to be adopted and a broad range of human rights instruments already existed, that children's rights to education, legal safeguards and humane treatment continued to be violated and denied to children in the territories occupied by Israel and in Southern Africa. In addition to the numbers of children and young persons who had fallen victims to Israel's repression, there were those still imprisoned in inhuman conditions, or still deprived of their fundamental right to education due to the closure of educational establishments.

51.     Mr. ANDRES (observer for Switzerland) said that his Government had always been in favour of the elaboration of international standards to improve the protection of certain groups of the most vulnerable persons, in particular persons deprived of liberty, refugees, women and children. His delegation had therefore participated as an observer in the meetings of the Working Group, which had resulted in a draft convention on the rights of the child.

52.     Instead of a general convention dealing with virtually all the rights of the child, his delegation would have preferred to supplement the set of multilateral international instruments concerned with specific aspects of the protection of children that had already been concluded. Those conventions were effective in that they regulated in detail the specific issues affecting children, such as adoption, children born outside wedlock, children of separated parents, children at work, sexual exploitation, and traffic in children.

53.     While the draft convention contained some good provisions in that regard, it also had a number of articles which merely reiterated the human rights already covered by general conventions and, in particular, by the International Covenants on Human Rights. The draft convention also contained provisions which were not in keeping with the guidelines set forth in General Assembly resolution 41/120 on setting international standards in the field of human rights and which were thus not sufficiently precise to enable the resulting rights and obligations to be defined and implemented. Moreover, a few provisions of the draft were weaker than the general body of international human rights law. That was the case with article 14, on freedom of thought, conscience and religion and, in particular, article 38 on the situation of children in armed conflicts.

54.     His delegation had always stressed the need for a provision such as that in article 38 to set the protection of children in armed conflicts at a level at least equal to that in existing law, namely the 1949 Geneva Conventions and the Additional Protocols of 1977. The formula decided on by the Working Group was not satisfactory in that regard. It did not limit the participation of children in hostilities to the same extent as the corresponding provisions of the two Additional Protocols and the formulation of the protection of children against the effects of hostilities wad expressed in a much less binding way than in existing law. The time remaining before the next session of the General Assembly should be used to improve that provision.

55.     With regard to article 43, paragraphs 11 and 12, on the financing of the committee on the rights of the child, his Government's position was quite clear: it was in favour of including the expenses of the committee in the regular budget of the United Nations. Experience with the 1984 Convention against Torture, which made the States parties to the Convention responsible for the expenses of the Committee against Torture, demonstrated that only financing through the regular budget of the United Nations would make it possible to provide the committee on the rights of the child with the resources needed for its proper functioning.

56.     The draft convention enjoyed wide international support, including that of his Government. Once it had been adopted, it would have an undoubted effect on public opinion and promote increased awareness of the need for the protection of children.

57.     Ms. BRYCE (observer for Australia) said that the Australian Human Rights and Equal Opportunity Commission, of which she was a member, had taken an active interest in the process of preparing the draft

convention on the rights of the child and supported an early adoption of the convention and its ratification by Australia.

58.     Her delegation recognized and had some sympathy with the concerns expressed in the discussion about both the text and the concept of the draft convention. In particular, it shared the disappointment of those who would have liked to see article 38 increase the level of protection of children in armed conflicts under international humanitarian law and regretted the loss of the opportunity to achieve that.

59.     Her delegation also understood the concern of some delegations about the possible effects of the convention on the relationship between the parent and the child. However, it felt that such concern was misplaced since the draft convention made abundantly clear the primary responsibility of parents for their children and the right of parents to provide guidance and bring up their children according to their beliefs and customs. The text as a whole, and article 5 in particular, made that very clear and would require States parties to respect the role of parents in regard to all the rights recognized in the convention.

60.     It should also be recalled that the draft convention sought to protect those who did not receive protection of their rights through the family. Unfortunately, not all children grew up in a stable society with a secure family environment to protect them. Many children were born into such poverty that their families could not provide them with the nutrition, the essential health care or the basic education they required. Some children were not protected by their families from exploitation, some were subjected to abuse or neglect, and some never knew their parents or were rejected by their family.

61.     The Australian Human Rights and Equal Opportunity Commission had recently completed a thorough investigation of child homelessness in her society and had found that children throughout the country were exposed to exploitation and vulnerable to denial of basic rights. Children in all those situations needed a statement of their rights, a statement endorsed by the entire international community which would emphasize the responsibility of Governments to act.

62.     In conclusion, she said that children in need of the protection of the draft convention were to be found in all countries, rich and poor, industrial and developing, socialist and free-market, and she urged all members of the Commission to support the draft convention.

63.     Mrs. PACHECO EGEA (observer for Uruguay) said that her country was a party to international and regional instruments concerned with the rights of the child. When it was considered that hundreds of millions of dollars were spent on armaments while many thousands of infants died throughout the world for lack of care, it was impossible not to doubt the value of so-called "progress". Her Government therefore urged all countries to continue to seek better solutions to ensure protection of the rights of the child.

64.     Ever since the turn of the century, Uruguay had been in the forefront of efforts to protect children. It had signed a number of international instruments regulating the rights of children, including the American Convention on Human Rights. In July 1981, Uruguay and Argentina had signed one of the first Latin American agreements on the international protection of children. Moreover, in November 1987, the Prime Minister of Spain and the President of Uruguay had signed an agreement on conflicts of law in judicial procedures relating to minors. An inter-American conference on international private law, which was to be held shortly at Montevideo, would include in its agenda items concerning children, such as kidnapping and the provisions of funds for children's health-care services.

65.     Mr. DAO (International Labour Organization) said that the main aspects of the rights of the child which came under the mandate of the ILO had been incorporated in the draft convention. Moreover, the safeguard clause, as contained in draft article 41, should serve to ensure that other international standards, relating to the specific aspects of the various rights defined in the text, were respected.

66.     One of the most serious issues under the draft convention concerned child labour, in particular the exploitation of children without any concern for minimum age standards and frequently in inhumane working conditions. ILO had a special mandate for the protection of children with regard to employment and work.

Many conventions had been worked out in that area, underpinned by a programme of practical research and activity.

67.     His organization cooperated actively with the other organizations of the United Nations system, as well as with other bodies and non-governmental organizations, in joint action for the protection of the child. In that regard, it welcomed the fact that article 45 of the draft convention made provisions for the participation of the specialized agencies and other competent organs in the work of the future committee on the rights of the child.

68.     Mr. DEMIRALP (observer for Turkey) said that, as a result of endeavours to secure a consensus, the text of the draft convention contained some imperfections and was not completely satisfactory. The statements made by his delegation in respect of some articles during the meeting of the Working Group were reflected in its report (E/CN.4/1989/48).

69.     Subparagraph (d) of new article 17 referred to terms on which there was no agreed definition. Consequently, States parties would be obliged to interpret those terms in accordance with national legislation. Such a reservation might have to be made when the draft convention was opened for signature. He wished to place on record that his delegation continued to hold the views which it had expressed on other provisions of the draft convention and which were reflected in the report of the Working Group.

70.     Mrs. BEYELER (International Movement ATD Fourth World) said that, while it was owing to concern for the most disadvantaged children that work had been started on the draft convention at all, it was not at all certain that they would themselves benefit from the progress made and the resources made available. Experience seemed to teach that, in all countries, the poor were largely excluded from the development process.

71.     The poverty in which such people lived caused a break in the ties which bound them to their original community and, whether they were families living in the slums of the industrial countries, in backward rural areas of the developing countries, or the shanty towns on the edges of Third-World cities, they were alone, misunderstood and despised. To bring up their children, they could rely only on their own reserves of day-to-day courage and resourcefulness.

72.     Throughout his life, Father Joseph Wresinski had tried to break that lonely circle in which families found themselves by enlisting all the forces of the community. He had always given priority to infants and, when ATD Fourth World was being established, his first act had been to found a kindergarten for the very young. He had hoped that the draft convention would specifically stress the importance of helping infants living in poverty and of ensuring the most effective protection for their families.

73.     By its resolution on human rights and extreme poverty (E/CN.4/1989/L.12), the Commission had allied itself with the poorest families throughout the world. The convention on the rights of the child could be a valuable tool for implementing that alliance and for sustaining the courage and the hopes of such families. If decisive progress were to be made, it was necessary that those millions of impoverished children should become the Commission's constant concern.

74.     Through the regular assessment of the advances made in all the areas of the convention, it should be possible to measure the progress effectively made with regard to those children. That was why Father Joseph had hoped that the periodic reports of each State party would make specific reference to such progress. The same was true with regard to the periodic assessments made by intergovernmental and non-governmental organizations at national and regional seminars as well as at meetings of expert committees.

75.     Mrs. BECK (World Movement of Mothers) said that many universally recognized rights of the child were violated in a number of countries. Her organization denounced the poverty, beatings, abandonment and prostitution to which children were subjected. To make a positive contribution to the solution of those problems, her organization had concerned itself in particular with the plight of abandoned children. It had held a symposium on adoption at Geneva in May 1988 and had approved a programme of action in which emphasis was placed on the right of the child to a family.

76.     After recalling the rights of the child as defined in the Declaration of the Rights of the Child and other instruments, the programme declared that, from its conception, the child needed careful protection and a recognition that its interests were of prime importance. All necessary aid for the development of the child must be given to its natural family.

77.     Every child had the right to belong to a family which cherished it and, where the natural family was non-existent or defective, an endeavour should be made to find a foster or adoptive family for the child. The placing of children in institutions should be utilized only for exceptional cases or as a temporary measure. It was essential to facilitate and simplify adoption procedures and to combat any traffic in children.

78.     It was also necessary to develop a world policy on adoption and, to that end, an international centre responsible for collecting data on the situation of abandoned children should be established. Lastly, it was essential to ensure that the adopted child was recognized as a fully fledged citizen.

79.     Mrs. PARHI (International Council of Jewish Women) said that her delegation was most disappointed that article 14 relating to freedom of thought, conscience and religion had been voided of all substance. As had been pointed out, the existence of provisions enshrining the principle of freedom of religion or belief did not in itself constitute an absolute guarantee of respect for that principle. Article 14 did not confer on the child, even as an adolescent, a right to choose his religion or belief. Article 18 of the Universal Declaration on Human Rights was quite clear in that respect as was article 18 of the International Covenant on Civil and Political Rights, and it was most surprising that neither of those provisions was reflected in the draft convention on the rights of the child.

80.     The 1981 Declaration on the Elimination on All Forms of Intolerance and of Discrimination Based on Religion or Belief not only reproduced the provisions of the Universal Declaration and the International Covenant on Civil and Political Rights but also added seven articles designed to provide specific and improved guarantees for the right to freedom of conscience.

81.     The final document recently adopted at Vienna by the Conference on Security and Cooperation in Europe (CSCE) stipulated that States parties had to respect the right of every person to give and to receive religious education in the language of his choice, but there was not a single word in the draft convention concerning the right to religious education. A child's right to information was, however, firmly established in article 17 of the draft. It was significant that States which enlisted children of 15 years of age as soldiers were for the most part the same ones which refused them independence of thought when it was a question of religion or belief.

82.     It might be argued that article 41 of the draft convention constituted a safeguard clause but, if that were so, she was unable to understand why the guarantees in question could not be spelt out clearly in the text itself.

83.     In conclusion, she stressed the importance which her delegation attached to the draft convention and hoped that, before its final adoption by the General Assembly, the necessary amendments would be made to ensure that it was a truly effective legal instrument.

84.     Ms. EK (Rädda Barnen International) said that her organization was greatly concerned about article 38 of the draft convention, which the International Committee of the Red Cross interpreted as weakening the rule of the two Additional Protocols of 1977 to the Geneva Conventions. During the deliberations of the Working Group there had been overwhelming support by Governments to strengthen the provision, as could be seen in the report of the Working Group (E/CN.4/1989/48), but unfortunately, that was not reflected in resolution E/CN.4/1989/L.88. A crucial standard providing for States parties to the convention to take all feasible measures to ensure that no child took a direct part in hostilities - which had twice been adopted by the Commission by consensus - had disappeared from the current text. The non-governmental organizations were seriously concerned about the problem of child soldiers. Most of the children recruited for combat service would not be covered by article 38, which concerned only children below the age of 15 years.

85.     In her delegation's opinion, there was still a possibility of reaching a consensus on the article and she therefore urged Governments to improve the protection for children in armed conflicts prior to the adoption of the draft convention by the General Assembly at its forthcoming session.

86.     Mr. YELLOWHAIR (Four Directions Council) said that he was speaking on behalf of the Lakota Treaty Council, the Grand Council of the Crees of Quebec and the Indian Council of South America, as well as on behalf of his own organization.

87.     The list of particularly vulnerable groups referred to by the Chairman of the Working Group on a draft convention on the rights of the child must clearly include indigenous peoples. For those peoples, children were an absolute priority and, if they were unable to teach them their languages, cultures and religions, those peoples would disappear. The rights of the child thus constituted for them a question of survival.

88.     Governments had constantly tried to convince those peoples to give up their beliefs, but they had always resisted. When they resisted, their children were taken away on the pretext that it was in their best interest to grow up as non-indigenous people. In many countries of the Americas, that practice was continuing and indigenous children were even being exported to Western Europe. He was appalled at the fact that the draft convention condoned the practice of arranging for the adoption of Indian children in foreign countries.

89.     The indigenous peoples had been fighting for many years against the idea that it was in the best interest of indigenous children to be removed from their own cultures and communities. In particular, they had urged the Working Group to recognize the importance of strengthening families and communities. They had explained that, in their cultures and in most parts of the world, children spent a great part of their time with relatives other than their parents and that those extended family relationships should be recognized and protected.

90.     As a result of those efforts, some articles of the draft convention referred to the importance of continuity in a child's upbringing and to the importance of families. There was no clear recognition of extended families, however, nor was there any requirement that States should take into account the actual social and family structure prevailing in the communities in which children lived. That was strange, since a [number] of seminars and conferences had stressed the importance of respecting and strengthening existing patterns of family life.

91.     His greatest disappointment, however, was that the Working Group did not listen to the children themselves. The delegation of his organization to the January 1988 meeting of the Working Group had included two Indian high-school students, who had explained their concerns about protecting indigenous families and cultures. They had made some specific proposals, but the Working Group had not considered them.

92.     His delegation supported the text of the draft convention, however, and urged the future committee on the rights of the child, UNICEF, and the Centre for Human Rights to give priority to examining the cultural dimensions of the concept of the "best interests of the child" and the significance of respecting different patterns of family life, for the protection and welfare of children.

93.     Mr. SHERWIN (International Right to Life Federation) said that his delegation was particularly pleased that the ninth preambular paragraph (former preambular paragraph 6) of the draft convention on the rights of the child contained a reference to the appropriate legal protection of the child "before as well as after birth". However, paragraph 46 of the report of the Working Group (E/CN.4/1989/48) mentioned that the Chairman had, after the adoption of that preambular paragraph read into the record the statement that was contained in paragraph 43 of the report. The precise meaning or relevance of that statement, which had been made "on behalf of the entire Working Group", was unclear to his delegation which wondered what effect, if any, it could have on the proposed convention as a whole.

94.     It appeared from paragraphs 44 and 47 that one delegation had been particularly concerned that the domestic legislation of some States might be found to contradict the spirit and the effect of the ninth preambular paragraph (preambular paragraph 6), in particular with respect to article 1 and article 6 (former article 1 bis). It was possible that the statement had been inserted to allay such concerns on the part of that delegation and any others which felt that domestic legislation might not permit them to accept fully the effect of the ninth preambular paragraph on the articles of the draft convention. His delegation was at a loss to understand how the ninth preambular paragraph (preambular paragraph 6) could influence the interpretation of either article 1 or article 6 (former article 1 bis) in such a way as to make some States uneasy about their ability to comply with them.

95.     His delegation thus suggested that the reference to the statement contained in paragraph 43 should be removed from the Working Group's report or, if that was not possible, that a reference be inserted at the end of paragraph 46 to show that there had not been a consensus regarding its insertion or its effect.

96.     Ms. TOM (Caritas Internationalis) said that her organization appreciated the enormous amount of work that had been put into the preparation of the draft convention on the rights of the child. The text before the Commission went a long way towards defining the rights of the child and the protection it should enjoy. It also alerted people to many of the dangers which the child might encounter on its way to maturity. In times of war, strife and violence, family life was severely disturbed, and the most defenceless were the children.

97.     Unfortunately, it was precisely in areas of military or civil conflict that humanitarian efforts to assist children were often hampered - or at least not fully supported - by the local authorities. When faced with a situation in which it was prevented from rendering assistance, Caritas, like the other humanitarian organizations, had been forced to abandon hundreds of thousands of human beings crying out for help. Regrettably, that was currently the case in many countries.

98.     In its resolution 43/131, the General Assembly invited all States in need of humanitarian assistance to facilitate the work of intergovernmental and non-governmental organizations in implementing humanitarian assistance, in particular the supply of food, medicines and health care, for which access to victims was essential. Further, the Assembly urged States to facilitate, to the extent possible, the transit of humanitarian assistance.

99.     In its resolution 43/112, the General Assembly had expressed its profound concern that the situation of children in many parts of the world remained critical as a result, inter alia, of natural disasters and armed conflicts. Caritas believed that, when the survival of a child was at stake, States had the moral obligation to come to its assistance.

100.    Mr. HARDER (International Save the Children Alliance) said that the best investment which the international community could make was in its children. States should foster the right conditions to facilitate the advancement of children, and a collective approach to improving health care, small-scale enterprise development, education, agriculture, appropriate technologies and training would help children and their families to achieve self-reliance. Since its approach encompassed that broader spectrum of community-based, integrated and participatory development as well as advocacy for children's rights and social welfare, the Save the Children Alliance believed that its activities were in conformity with the draft convention on the rights of the child.

101.    The draft convention provided the International Save the Children Alliance with an opportunity to reaffirm its principles, and established a new juridical framework for children's rights as a set of standards against which the Alliance could measure itself. The entire international community - national Governments, multilateral agencies, non-governmental organizations, civic groups and many others - should endeavour to live up to those standards.

102.    Ms. UNDERHILL (International Institute of Higher Studies in Criminal Sciences) said that, in 1979 and 1980, the International Association of Penal Law had held two seminars on the control of experimentation

on human beings at the International Institute of Higher Studies in Criminal Sciences. The Association had drawn up, in English and French, a draft convention for the prevention and suppression of unlawful human experimentation, draft principles for the international regulation of human experimentation and draft guidelines for national legislation concerning human experimentation. However, the drafts did not cover unlawful experimentation on children which, it had been assumed, would be dealt with in the convention on the rights of the child.

103.    The Working Group had discussed the problem of unlawful experimentation on children, and a text had been proposed by a number of its members. Regrettably, however that text had not been adopted. Her delegation thus hoped that another international organization would study the problem in depth and find a solution to protect children from adverse and unlawful experimentation.

104.    Mr. MacPHERSON (Friends World Committee for Consultation) said that, while his organization welcomed the draft convention on the rights of the child, it believed that the draft convention was deficient in one major aspect. Draft article 38 referred to the recruitment of children into the armed forces and the participation of children in hostilities. Although it was clear from the debates which had been held in the Working Group (E/CN.4/1989/48, paras. 602-616), that many delegations believed that draft article 38 did not provide adequate protection to children, there had unfortunately been no consensus on the wording of paragraph 2 of the article. His organization was unable to accept the argument put forward by one delegation that the draft convention should merely restate an existing principle of humanitarian law. It was essential to have strong and unambiguous norms, and his delegation hoped that draft article 38 would be revised before the General Assembly adopted the draft convention later in the year.

105.    Mr. BANDIER (International Association of Educators for World Peace) said that the future of the world's children was threatened by increasing poverty, hunger, malnutrition, chronic unemployment, the external debt of developing countries, the population explosion, traffic in narcotic drugs and the forced labour and prostitution of minors. If the international community did not take immediate measures to halt the world's declining economic and social situation, the future of mankind in general and of children in particular, would remain precarious.

106.    It was essential to teach children, from an early age, about their duties towards their families, friends, schoolmates and superiors, while ensuring that children had the right to require the latter to perform their own duties. Such duties should be clearly and precisely defined in a declaration on the responsibilities of every individual with respect to his society. Without such an instrument, the Universal Declaration of Human Rights could not be fully implemented. Children would be taught about such duties first by their parents and later by educators. Within one generation, a new form of society would arise, which would be able to satisfy the legitimate aspirations of its citizens.

107.    Mr. CANTWELL (Defence for Children International), speaking on behalf of 35 non-governmental organizations in consultative status with the Economic and Social Council, said that, in addition to their participation in the drafting of the convention on the rights of the child, the non-governmental organizations had been major contributors, both as a group and individually, to the public awareness and support from which the future convention was benefiting. Scores of successful international, regional, national and local initiatives focusing on the draft convention had been undertaken or supported by the non-governmental organizations and Governments had, invariably, expressed their appreciation of such efforts.

108.    The non-governmental organizations had grave misgivings, however, about parts of the draft convention, such as the limited recognition given to the actual or potential primary role of extended family members in caring for and bringing up children. The absence of a specific reference to protection from medical experimentation was also a cause for concern and considerable disappointment, particularly in view of the worldwide consensus on the issue.

109.    All non-governmental organizations were disturbed at the amazingly low level of protection that certain Governments seemed prepared to afford to children in armed conflicts, especially with regard to

the direct participation of children in hostilities. Those few Governments which had forced a consensus on such low standards should examine the practical implications of their stance and should revise their position before the General Assembly adopted the draft convention later in the year.

110.　　The non-governmental organizations were also concerned at the revisions which had been made to the article on freedom of thought, conscience and religion, which represented a clear diminution of the standards contained in the existing international instruments. However, if the current draft reflected the standards of child welfare and protection which the governmental representatives of the world's population believed to be just and feasible, the non-governmental organizations he represented would support the adoption of the draft convention, albeit with certain misgivings.

*The following is taken from document E/CN.4/1989/SR.55/Add.1 (26 June 1989).*

*Draft resolution E/CN.4/1989/L.88* (continued)

1.　　Mr. van WEISEN (International Youth and Student Movement for the United Nations) congratulated the Working Group, specialized agencies and non-governmental organizations on their work in connection with the draft convention on the rights of the child. His organization was confident that any remaining differences would soon be settled.

2.　　In the context of its cooperation with the specialized agencies, ISMUN had recently decided to undertake a European campaign on the rights of the child, to make young people aware of the urgent need for a convention, and to mobilize their support for its early adoption and rapid ratification by Governments. The campaign would involve close cooperation with other NGOs and would be followed by actions by youth and student NGOs in other regions of the world. He expressed sincere gratitude to UNICEF for its support of that initiative.

3.　　Mrs. TOLEDO (Latin American Federation of Associations of Relatives of Disappeared Detainees) expressed concern at the fact that the draft convention addressed obliquely, if at all, many issues which her organization considered to be of crucial importance.

4.　　For instance, the rights of the child in situations of political repression had not been broached. During the military dictatorships in Argentina, Chile and Uruguay, the practice of enforced disappearance was also applied to children, who were abducted together with their parents. Most of those children disappeared while others were summarily executed together with their parents. Many disappeared children, including children born in captivity, had been taken from their mothers and often adopted by the agents of repression themselves.

5.　　In other countries with constitutionally elected Governments, such as Guatemala, El Salvador and Peru, the children of disappeared and murdered persons were defenceless and violations of their rights had increased. Efforts by churches, non-governmental organizations and in some cases State agencies were insufficient to deal with the repercussions of the political repression experienced by those children.

6.　　In addition to political instability, the economic crisis had led to the phenomenon of "street children" in varying numbers in Latin American countries. Such children were often exploited and forced to beg, steal and prostitute themselves. In many cases they incurred police repression rather than the protection and rehabilitation measures they needed.

7.　　Based on Argentina's experience, the system of genetic banks should be internationalized. The adoption laws should be seriously revised to prevent trafficking in children, especially disappeared children or children born in captivity, and extradition laws and agreements should be concluded between countries to facilitate the return of the children to their families.

8.　　Mr. GONZALES (International Indian Treaty Council) said that the prevalent attitude towards children must be changed, beginning at the international level, for institutional change to be effected at the domestic level.

9.	One of the most important aspects of indigenous sovereignty was the right of Indian nations to determine how their children were raised and educated and which children were members of their nations, to keep their children within the sacred circles of their families, clans and nations and to protect their land, culture and religion, for the sake of their children and future generations. As mentioned in his organization's previous statement, in Alaska Public Law 92-203 did not recognize as indigenous children born after December 1971. The Law excluded future generations from land rights in violation of articles 15 (10) and (2) of the Universal Declaration of Human Rights and article 8 of the draft convention on the rights of the child.

10.	In North America, the rights of children to adequate nutrition, health care, education, including bilingual education, and provisions for children in vocational and labour laws were always in jeopardy. Children of farmworker families living in the United States were often exposed to deadly chemicals sprayed in the fields. In California, communities such as McFarland, Delano and Fowler had a much higher rate of cancer among children than the national average due to contaminated table water in those areas. Recent studies showed an alarming association between pesticide exposure and leukemia and brain cancer in children. The poisoning of the children must be stopped and the cancer cluster cities in California must be contained.

11.	Mrs. KRILL (International Committee of the Red Cross) said that children urgently needed protection and assistance in wartime. Under the provisions of international humanitarian law, children were entitled to general protection. In the 1949 Geneva Conventions and the 1977 Additional Protocols, 25 articles afforded children special protection. That being the case, one might wonder why a provision on children in armed conflict should be introduced into the draft convention.

12.	The presence of far too many adolescents on the world's battlefields had led many States to call for the minimum age of combatants to be raised from 15 to 18 years, and the ICRC had repeatedly expressed its support for such a measure while stressing that none of the advances made over the years should be reversed. Unfortunately, one could only conclude that article 38 of the draft convention did not constitute a development of international humanitarian law but instead weakened it. First, Additional Protocol II of 1977 relating to non-[international] conflicts offered better protection for the child than article 38, paragraph 2, because it prohibited both direct and indirect participation by children under 15 years of age. Second, the wording "all feasible measures" in article 38, paragraph 4, created a serious risk of weakening international humanitarian law. Many provisions in the Conventions and Protocols designed to protect civilians in general and children in particular laid down absolute obligations and thus provided more effective protection than anything covered by the words "feasible measures".

13.	The International Committee of the Red Cross believed that a simple undertaking to respect and ensure respect for the rules of international humanitarian law, such as that already contained in article 38, paragraph 1, was the most reasonable solution. It had the twofold advantage of removing any ambiguity and avoiding the creation of two standards of conduct. It also eliminated the risk of overlooking the more than 25 specific provisions for the protection of children in armed conflict that already existed in international humanitarian law.

14.	Mr. NYAMEKYE (Deputy Director, United Nations Centre for Human Rights), drew attention to the administrative and programme budget implications of draft resolution E/CN.4/1989/L.88, stressing that his comments were without prejudice to decisions to be taken by the General Assembly on the financing of the convention.

15.	If the recommendations contained in the draft resolution were adopted, the following activities would have to be envisaged following the entry into force of the convention: (a) meeting of States parties, the first six months after entry into force of the convention and thereafter every two years; (b) annual sessions of the Committee on the Rights of the Child; (c) processing of reports submitted to the Committee.

16.	The first meeting of States parties to elect the members of the Committee on the Rights of the Child would be convened by the Secretary-General at United Nations Headquarters in 1991. In accordance with new article 43 of the draft convention, subsequent meetings of the State parties would be convened by the Secretary-General every two years. Subject to the entry into force of the convention and the election of the Committee members, the Secretary-General would convene the first regular session of the Committee in Geneva for a three-week period during the first half of 1991. At its first regular session, the Committee would be expected in particular to consider and adopt its rules of procedure, to draft approved guidelines for the submission of reports and to take decisions on matters relating to the organization of its future work and preparation of its annual report to the General Assembly.

17.      If accepted by the General Assembly, article 43, paragraph 11, would provide for members of the Committee to receive emoluments from United Nations resources on the terms and conditions to be decided by the General Assembly.

18.      Under article 44, States parties would undertake to submit reports through the Secretary-General, within two years of the entry into force of the convention and thereafter every five years. Article 45 also provided, subject to the decision of the Committee, for other reports to be submitted. In accordance with article 44, the Committee would submit a report on its activities every two years to the General Assembly, through the Economic and Social Council.

19.      Under the terms of article 43, the Secretary-General would provide the necessary staff and facilities for the effective performance of the functions of the Committee.

20.      The estimated costs of the first meeting of States parties to the convention to be held in New York in 1991 were US$ 108,800, and for the first session of the Committee on the Rights of the Child to be held in Geneva in the first half of 1991, US$ 1,058,400.

21.      Additional staffing would depend on the programme of work adopted by the Committee and the extent to which the latter would require substantive and technical assistance from the staff of the Centre for Human Rights. It was estimated, however, that initially at least two Professionals and one General Service staff member would be required to deal with the preparatory work and servicing of meetings of the States parties to the convention and the sessions of the Committee on the Rights of the Child. The extra staff costs, calculated on the basis of 12 work-months, were estimated at US$ 98,200 for one P-4 level post, US$ 66,600 for one P-2 level post and US$ 55,100 for one General Service post.

22.      The requirements he had just mentioned included $274,900 under section 23 (Human Rights) and conference servicing requirements under section 29 (Conference Services), estimated at $1,167,200 for 1991.

23.      The CHAIRMAN [Mr. BOSSUYT (Belgium)] said that the Ukrainian Soviet Socialist Republic, Bolivia, Spain, Nicaragua, Yemen, Peru, Kenya, Democratic Yemen, Cuba, Czechoslovakia, Somalia and Gambia wished to become co-sponsors of draft resolution E/CN.4/1989/L.88.

24.      He invited the members of the Commission to make statements in explanation of vote before the vote.

25.      Mr. JOHNSON (United States of America) said that he was pleased to affirm his delegation's support for the draft resolution as it stood, and for the adoption by consensus of the draft convention which was the outcome of many years of hard work by members of the Commission, observers and non-governmental organizations.

26.      Since his Government had been active at every stage of the process, he could agree with those speakers who had noted an evolution since its inception in 1978. Like other delegations, his had felt the draft convention to be a symbolic exercise in conjunction with the International Year of the Child rather than a broad-based perceived need. His delegation noted that the final version of the text included many important topics not addressed in the original draft and corrected its tendency to read more like a declaration than a convention. Further, the Working Group had over the years corrected the systematic bias in the original draft in favour of assuming centralized governmental control over matters concerning children and the corresponding disregard of the private sector. In that connection, it had ensured that the draft convention recognized parents' rights vis-à-vis government intervention as well as the civil and political rights of the children themselves.

27.     There had been positive changes in the composition of the Working Group over the years and progress in the Group's ability to strike a balance between legal, technical and diplomatic expertise.

28.     Despite its willingness to join the consensus, his delegation was, however disappointed with certain of the convention's provisions, which it had already specified in the Working Group. With regard to article 38, his Government considered that the General Assembly and the Commission were not appropriate forums for revising existing international humanitarian law. If the reasonable suggestion made by the representative of the International Committee of the Red Cross had been taken up at the outset, many difficulties might have been avoided.

29.     In conclusion, he expressed appreciation to the delegation of Poland for its initiative and its sustained interest and involvement in the draft convention over a 10-year period, to the Chairman of the Working Group for his dedication, determination and unlimited patience, and to the Centre for Human Rights for its excellent handling of the large volume of documentation connected with the draft resolution.

30.     Mr. FUJITA (Japan) said his delegation appreciated the efforts of the Working Group and was ready to join the consensus in adopting the draft resolution. However, it would like to make some reservations or state its understanding on a number of articles in the draft convention.

31.     In respect of articles 9 and 10, his delegation drew attention to the Chairman's declaration in paragraph 203 of the report of the Working Group (E/CN.4/1989/48) to the effect that article 6 of the convention (present article 9) was intended to apply to separations that arose in domestic situations and also that article 6 bis was not intended to affect the general right of States to establish and regulate their respective immigration laws in accordance with their international obligations. His delegation was ready to accept articles 9 and 10 provided that the Chairman's declaration was maintained.

32.     In addition, it was his delegation's understanding that "their own countries" in article 10, paragraph 2, meant the countries of which they were nationals.

33.     With regard to article 21, article 788 of the Japanese Civil Code provided that "in order to adopt a child, the permission of the Family Court must be obtained, except in the case where a person adopts any of his or her lineal descendants or those of the spouse". In that exceptional case, article 21 of the convention was inconsistent with the Civil Code, and his delegation would therefore like to reserve its position.

34.     His delegation understood that article 22 was not intended to request States to take measures in addition to the present procedures concerning the recognition of refugees in accordance with their international obligations and their national laws on refugees.

35.     It was his delegation's understanding that "primary education" in paragraph 1 (a) of article 28 did not include education in kindergartens and that the reference in subparagraph 1 (b) of article 28 to free education should be interpreted as an example of the measures which State parties should take in case of need.

36.     Further, it was his delegation's understanding that the term 'spiritual' in article 32 did not require such policies to be against the principle of the separation of religion and politics.

37.     His delegation's interpretation of article 37 was that situations such as the possibility of escape or the possibility of destruction of evidence, which were prescribed in article 81 of the Japanese Criminal Procedure Law, fell within the "exceptional circumstances" of article 37, subparagraph (c).

38.     As for the "right to prompt access to legal and other appropriate assistance" of subparagraph (d), it confirmed the right to the assistance of counsel for a child placed under physical restraint and did not oblige the State to assign a counsel to defend a child unable to secure such counsel.

39.     Concerning article 40, his delegation's understanding of "every child alleged as or accused of having infringed the penal law" in subparagraph 2 (b) (ii) was that such a child was deprived of his or her freedom. In addition, the meaning of "a fair hearing" of subparagraph 2 (b) (iii) did not imply a public trial and did not necessarily require the provision of legal assistance by the State.

40.    As for subparagraph 2 (b) (iv), in view of article 40 of the draft convention, in Japan that subparagraph applied only to criminal procedure in the criminal court and not to family court procedure, which purported to provide protective measures for juveniles.

41.    Subparagraph 2 (b) (vi) was intended to guarantee that a defendant unable to understand the language used in court would be able to have a sufficient and proper defence and that all or part of the costs might therefore be payable by the accused if he was found guilty.

42.    The CHAIRMAN [Mr. BOSSUYT (Belgium)] said that if there was no objection, he would take it that draft resolution E/CN.4/1989/L.88 was adopted without a vote.

43.    *It was so decided.*

## 6.    Commission on Human Rights resolution 1989/57 on the "Question of a convention on the rights of the child" adopted without a vote on 8 March 1989

*The Commission on Human Rights,*

*Bearing in mind* the draft convention on the rights of the child submitted by Poland to the Commission on Human Rights on 7 February 1978 and annexed to Commission resolution 20 (XXXIV) of 8 March 1978, in which it decided to continue, as one of its priorities, its consideration of a draft convention on the rights of the child,

*Recalling* Economic and Social Council resolution 1978/18 of 5 May 1978, in which the Council took note with satisfaction of the initiative taken by the Commission with a view to the conclusion of a convention on the rights of the child,

*Recalling* General Assembly resolution 33/166 of 20 December 1978,

*Bearing in mind* all subsequent pertinent resolutions of the Commission on Human Rights, the Economic and Social Council and the General Assembly, in particular General Assembly resolution 43/112 of 8 December 1988, in which the Assembly requested the Commission on Human Rights to give the highest priority to a draft convention on the rights of the child and to make every effort at its forty-fifth session to complete a draft and to submit it, through the Economic and Social Council, to the General Assembly at its forty-fourth session, and invited all Member States to offer their active support to the completion of a draft convention on the rights of the child in 1989, the year of the thirtieth anniversary of the Declaration of the Rights of the Child and of the tenth anniversary of the International Year of the Child,

*Having examined* the report of the open-ended working group of the Commission on Human Rights on a draft convention on the rights of the child concerning its meeting to complete the second reading of the draft convention (E/CN.4/1989/48),

*Having also examined* the text of the draft convention as adopted by the open-ended working group (E/CN.4/1989/29 and Corr.1),

1.    *Expresses its appreciation* for the work achieved by the open-ended working group;

2.    *Decides* to adopt the draft convention on the rights of the child, as submitted by the open-ended working group;

3.    *Decides also* to transmit to the General Assembly, through the Economic and Social Council, the draft convention as submitted by the open-ended working group as well as the report of the group;

4.    *Recommends* the following draft resolution to the Economic and Social Council for adoption:

"*The Economic and Social Council,*

*Recalling* the General Assembly resolutions related to the question of a convention on the rights of the child, in particular resolution 43/112 of 8 December 1988, in which the Assembly requested the Commission on Human Rights to submit a draft convention on the rights of the child, through the Economic and Social Council, to the General Assembly at its forty-fourth session,

*Expressing its appreciation* to the Commission on Human Rights for having concluded the elaboration of a draft convention on the rights of the child,

*Decides* to submit the draft convention on the rights of the child (E/CN.4/1989/29 and Corr. 1) and the report of the Commission's working group (E/CN.4/1989/48) to the General Assembly for consideration, with a view to the adoption of the convention by the Assembly at its forty-fourth session."

## 7. Economic and Social Council resolution 1989/79 on the "Question of a convention on the rights of the child" adopted on 24 May 1989

*The Economic and Social Council,*

*Recalling* General Assembly resolutions on the question of a convention on the rights of the child, in particular resolution 43/112 or 8 December 1988, in which the Assembly requested the Commission on Human Rights to submit a draft convention on the rights of the child, through the Council, to the Assembly at its forty-fourth session,

*Expressing its appreciation* to the Commission for having concluded the elaboration of a draft convention on the rights of the child,

*Decides* to submit the draft convention on the rights of the child and the report of the working group of the Commission on Human Rights to the General Assembly at its forty-fourth session, with a view to the adoption of the draft convention.

*16th plenary meeting*
*24 May 1989*

## 8. Draft resolution on the "Adoption of a convention on the rights of the child"

*The following is taken from document A/C.3/44/L.44 (10 November 1989).*

Argentina, Australia, Austria, Bolivia, Bulgaria, Burkina Faso, Byelorussian Soviet Socialist Republic, Canada, China, Colombia, Costa Rica, Côte d'Ivoire, Cyprus, Czechoslovakia, Ecuador, Egypt, El Salvador, Ethiopia, Finland, France, German Democratic Republic, Germany, Federal Republic of, Greece, Guatemala, Hungary, India, Indonesia, Italy, Jordan, Luxembourg, Madagascar, Malta, Mexico, Mongolia, Morocco, Nepal, New Zealand, Nicaragua, Norway, Panama, Peru, Philippines, Poland, Portugal, Romania, Senegal, Spain, Tunisia, Ukrainian Soviet Socialist Republic, Union of Soviet Socialist Republics, Venezuela, Viet Nam and Yugoslavia: draft resolution

*Adoption of a convention on the rights of the child*

*The General Assembly,*

*Recalling* its previous resolutions, especially resolutions 33/166 of 20 December 1978 and 43/112 of 8 December 1988, as well as Commission on Human Rights and Economic and Social Council resolutions related to the question of a convention on the rights of the child,

*Noting in particular* Commission on Human Rights resolution 1989/57 of 8 March 1989, by which the Commission decided to transmit a draft convention on the rights of the child, through the Economic and Social Council, to the General Assembly, as well as Economic and Social Council resolution 1989/79 of 24 May 1989,

*Reaffirming* that children's rights require special protection and call for continuous improvement of the situation of children all over the world, as well as their development and education in conditions of peace and security,

*Profoundly concerned* that the situation of children in many parts of the world remains critical as a result of inadequate social conditions, natural disasters, armed conflicts, exploitation, illiteracy, hunger and disability, and convinced that urgent and effective national and international action is called for,

*Mindful* of the important role of the United Nations Children's Fund and the United Nations in promoting the well-being of children and their development,

*Convinced* of the positive contribution that an international convention on the rights of the child, as a standard-setting accomplishment of the United Nations in the field of human rights, would make to protecting children's rights and ensuring their well-being,

*Bearing in mind* that 1989 marks the thirtieth anniversary of the Declaration on the Rights of the Child and the tenth anniversary of the International Year of the Child,

1.      *Expresses its appreciation* to the Commission on Human Rights for having concluded the elaboration of a draft convention on the rights of the child;

2.      *Adopts and opens for signature, ratification and accession* the Convention on the Rights of the Child contained in the annex to the present resolution;

3.      *Calls upon* all Member States to consider signing and ratifying or acceding to the Convention as a matter of priority and expresses the hope that it will come into force at an early date;

4.      *Requests* the Secretary-General to provide all the facilities and assistance necessary for dissemination of information on the Convention;

5.      *Invites* United Nations agencies and organizations as well as intergovernmental and non-governmental organizations to intensify their efforts with a view to disseminating information on the Convention and promote its understanding;

6.      *Requests* the Secretary-General to submit to the General Assembly at its forty-fifth session a report on the status of the Convention on the Rights of the Child;

7.      *Decides* to consider the report of the Secretary-General at its forty-fifth session under an item entitled "Implementation of the Convention on the Rights of the Child".

ANNEX

[...]

## 9.   Polish draft decision on the "Adoption of a convention on the rights of the child"

*The following is taken from A/C.3/44/L.45 (13 November 1989).*

*Poland: draft decision*

*Adoption of a convention on the rights of the child*

The Third Committee decides, with respect to article 43 of the draft convention on the rights of the child, that:

(a)      Paragraph 10 bis should be renumbered paragraph 11;

(b)      Paragraph 11 should be renumbered paragraph 12, and the brackets round the following text should be removed:

> "With the approval of the General Assembly, the members of the Committee established under the present Convention shall receive emoluments from United Nations resources on such terms and conditions as the Assembly may decide;"

(c)      In the same paragraph the following text should be deleted:

> "or

"[States Parties shall be responsible for the expenses of the members of the Committee while they are in performance of Committee duties.];"

(d)     Former paragraph 12 should be deleted.

# 10.  Proposed programme budget for 1990-1991

*The following is taken from document A/C.3/44/L.47 (14 November 1989).*

PROPOSED PROGRAMME BUDGET FOR THE BIENNIUM 1990-1991

*Adoption of a convention on the rights of the child*

*Programme budget implications of draft-decision A/C.3/44/L.45*

Statement submitted by the Secretary-General in accordance with rule 153 of the rules of procedure of the General Assembly

A.      Requests contained in the draft decision

1.      Under the provisions of draft decision A/C.3/44/L.45, the Third Committee would decide with respect to article 43 of the draft convention on the rights of the child that:

(a)     Paragraph 10 bis of the draft convention as contained in the annex to A/44/616 would be renumbered paragraph 11 and would read as follows: "The Secretary-General of the United Nations should provide the necessary staff and facilities for the effective performance of the functions of the Committee under the present Convention";

(b)     Paragraph 11 would be renumbered paragraph 12, and the brackets on the following text removed: "With the approval of the General Assembly, the members of the Committee established under the present Convention shall receive emoluments from the United Nations resources on such terms and conditions as the Assembly may decide".

2.      In addition, the two texts in brackets following new paragraph 12 would be deleted.

3.      It is the Secretary-General's understanding that these paragraphs, as renumbered and modified, would indicate that the costs associated with the implementation of the convention should be met from the regular budget of the Organization. Consequently, the present statement outlines what the implications of the convention as a whole would be for the regular budget.

B.      Relationship of the requests to the proposed programme of work

4.      The activities that would be called for under the convention fall under chapter 6, section II, "Programme: Centre for Human Rights", subprogramme 1, "Implementation of international standards, instruments and procedures", the objectives and strategy for which are outlined in paragraphs 6.20 to 6.23 of the medium-term plan for the period 1984-1989, as extended through 1991.

5.      The activities are particularly relevant to section 23 (Human rights) of the proposed programme budget for the biennium 1990-1991, programme element 1.1 "Implementing regular supervisory procedures", of subprogramme 1, which is proposed for highest priority in the human rights programme, in the proposed programme budget for the biennium 1990-1991.

C.      Activities by which the requests would be implemented

6.      Should the texts contained in the draft decision be adopted, various activities that would be required upon the entry into force of the convention in accordance with article 49, as described below, would need to be financed from the regular budget of the Organization.

7.      The first meeting of the States parties to the convention would be convened by the Secretary-General at United Nations Headquarters for one day in 1991 to elect members of the Committee on the

Rights of the Child. Subsequent meetings of the States parties would be convened by the Secretary-General at biennial intervals.

8.      In accordance with article 43, the Committee on the Rights of the Child would consist of 10 experts and would meet annually at United Nations Headquarters or at any other convenient place as determined by the Committee. The Secretary-General, subject to the entry into force of the convention and the election of Committee members, intends to convene the first regular session of the Committee for a period of three weeks during the first half of 1991 at the United Nations Office at Geneva, the headquarters of the Committee's substantive secretariat. Travel and subsistence costs would be required to be paid for the 10 members.

9.      At its first regular session, the Committee would be expected, inter alia, to consider and adopt its rules of procedure in accordance with article 43 of the convention, draft approved guidelines for the submission of reports and take decisions on matters relating to the organization of its future work and the preparation of its annual report to the General Assembly. It should be noted, however, that even though article 43 states that the Committee may determine its place of meeting, the Secretary-General believes that the principles embodied in General Assembly resolution 40/243 of 18 December 1985 should be observed and that, consequently, the Committee should meet at the headquarters of its substantive secretariat, i.e., Geneva, and this should be reflected in the calendar of conferences for future biennia.

10.      Under article 44 of the convention, States parties would undertake to submit reports through the Secretary-General of the United Nations within two years of the entry into force of the convention and thereafter every five years. The Committee would also submit a report on its activities every two years to the General Assembly through the Economic and Social Council.

11.      The adequate provision to the States parties and to the Committee of the necessary reports and of substantive services for the meetings of States parties and sessions of the Committee cannot be ensured without additional staffing resources being made available to the Centre for Human Rights. In view of the fact that the convention is not expected to enter into force until 1991, and in the absence of a programme of work which the Committee for the Rights of the Child would have to establish, the extent of support and assistance which the Centre for Human Rights would be expected to provide cannot be accurately ascertained. Under the circumstances, it is proposed, initially, to provide for an amount of $119,000 under temporary assistance in 1991 equivalent to 12 work-months at the Professional level (6 at P-4 and 6 at P-2) and 6 work-months at the General Service level. The long-term workload requirements will be established at a later stage, in the light of actual experience and will be presented to the General Assembly in the context of a subsequent proposed programme budget. By way of comparison, it should be noted that, in order to implement the supervisory procedures in respect of the Convention against Torture, three posts (1 P-4, 1 P-2 and 1 General Service) have been provided to the Centre for Human Rights, on a full-time basis.

12.      Under article 43, new paragraph 12, with the approval of the General Assembly, the members of the Committee established under the present convention would receive emoluments from the United Nations resources on such terms and conditions as the Assembly may decide. In determining the level of such emoluments and the related terms and conditions, the Assembly may wish to be guided by General Assembly resolution 35/218 of 17 December 1980. Under the terms of that resolution, an amount of $5,000 per year is provided to the Chairman and $3,000 per year to each of the members of the Human Rights Committee, which would appear to have been entrusted with functions similar to those that this Convention would entrust to the Committee on the Rights of the Child. Pending a decision by the Assembly, these amounts have been provisionally included in the current statement of programme budget implications.

D.      Modifications required in the proposed programme of work for 1990-1991

13.      In connection with the new activities proposed above to be undertaken with the adoption of the convention, three new outputs have already been included in section 23 (Human rights) of the proposed programme budget for the biennium 1990-1991, in anticipation of the adoption of the convention, as follows:

Subprogramme

1.	Implementation of international standards, instruments and procedures

1.1.	Implementing regular supervisory procedures

Output

(xxix)	Substantive servicing of one meeting of States parties to the convention on the rights of the child (first quarter, 1991);

(xxx)	Substantive servicing of one session of the Committee on the Rights of the Child (second quarter, 1991);

(xxxi)	Preparation of one report of the Committee on the Rights of the Child to be submitted to the General Assembly (third quarter, 1991).

E.	Additional requirements at full cost

14.	The full cost of requirements to undertake the activities contained in section C above would be as follows:

1991

(a)	Conference-servicing costs

| | (i) | Meeting of States parties | 97 600 |
| | (ii) | Committee on the Rights of the Child | 886 900 |

Total	(a)	984 500

(b)	Other costs

| | (i) | Travel and subsistence of 10 members for one session of 3 weeks | 55 000 |
| | (ii) | Emoluments for 10 members | 32 000 |
| | (iii) | General temporary assistance | 119 000 |

Total	(b)	206 000

F.	Potential for absorption

*Conference-servicing costs*

15.	The meetings of States parties and the Committee on the Rights of the Child have not yet been included in the draft calendar of conferences. However, the estimates of conference-servicing costs indicated in paragraph 14 above are based on the theoretical assumption that no part of the conference-servicing requirements would be met from within the permanent conference-servicing capacity under section 29 of the proposed programme budget, and that additional resources would be required for temporary assistance for meetings. The extent to which the Organization's permanent capacity needs to be supplemented by temporary assistance resources can be determined only in the light of the proposed calendar of conferences for 1990-1991. However, as indicated in paragraph 29.5 of the proposed programme budget, the 1990-1991 level of resources for temporary assistance for meetings was estimated on the basis of previous experience to accommodate not only for meetings known at the time of the budget preparations but also for meetings that would be authorized subsequently, provided that the number and distribution of meetings and conferences in the biennium 1990-1991 was consistent with the pattern of meetings in past years. On that basis, it is estimated that no additional resources would be required under section 29 of the proposed programme budget for the biennium 1990-1991 as a result of the adoption of draft decision A/C.3/44/L.45.

*Other costs*

16.        As regards the costs involved for the travel and subsistence of the 10 members of the Committee, the emoluments for the members and general temporary assistance for the Centre for Human Rights, it may be recalled that section 23 of the proposed programme budget for the biennium 1990-1991 (table 23.6 (vii)) contains provisions in the amount of $1,685,300 for activities in the field of human rights, which may be mandated by the Economic and Social Council during its regular sessions.

17.        It is the view of the Secretary-General that the estimated amount of $206,000 required for the implementation of supervisory procedures for the convention on the rights of the child should be provided for from the total amount included in the programme budget under the provision for potential mandates from the Economic and Social Council, thus making it unnecessary to request an additional appropriation or to have recourse to the contingency fund.

18.        In conclusion, therefore, should it be decided that the costs associated with the implementation of the convention be met from the regular budget of the Organization, no additional appropriations would be required under either section 23, for the reasons explained in paragraphs 16 and 17 above, or section 29 for the reasons explained in paragraph 15 above.

19.        An additional appropriation of $22,700 would, however, be required under section 31 (Staff assessment) of the proposed programme budget for the biennium 1990-1991, which would be offset by an increase of the same magnitude in the estimates of income under income section 1 (Income from staff assessment).

Annex I

Estimated cost of conference servicing of the meetings of States parties to the convention on the rights of the child

*1991*

| | | | |
|---|---|---|---:|
| I. | Pre-session documentation | | 51 500 |
| | (50 pages, 5 documents: ACEFRS) | | |
| II. | Meeting servicing | | 8 400 |
| | (Interpretation, 2 meetings: ACEFRS) | | |
| III. | Post-session documentation | | 10 300 |
| | (10 pages, 1 document: ACEFRS) | | |
| IV. | Summary records | | 26 300 |
| | (2 meetings: ACEFRS) | | |
| V. | Requirements of the Office of General Services | | 1 100 |
| | Total | | 97 600 |

Annex II

Estimated cost of conference servicing of the Committee on the Rights of the Child

*1991*

| | | | |
|---|---|---|---:|
| I. | Pre-session documentation | | 257 600 |
| | (300 pages, 30 documents: ACEFRS) | | |
| II. | Meeting servicing | | 152 000 |
| | (Interpretation, 30 meetings: ACEFRS) | | |

| | | |
|---|---|---:|
| III. | In-session documentation | 53 900 |
| | (100 pages, 10 documents: ACEFRS) | |
| IV. | Post-session documentation | 80 800 |
| | (100 pages, 1 document: ACEFRS) | |
| V. | Summary records | 326 100 |
| | (30 meetings: ACEFRS) | |
| VI. | Requirements of the Office of General Services | 16 500 |
| Total | | 886 900 |

# 11. Discussion in the Third Committee of the General Assembly from 8 to 10 and from 13 to 16 November 1989

*The following is taken from document A/C.3/44/SR.36 (27 November 1989). As eight agenda items were under discussion at the time, only statements concerning agenda item 108, "Adoption of the Convention on the Rights of the Child", are included in the following text.*

ADOPTION OF A CONVENTION ON THE RIGHTS OF THE CHILD (agenda item 108) (A/44/240, 306, 393 and 616; A/C.3/44/7)

[...]

2.      Mr. MARTENSON (Under-Secretary-General for Human Rights)

[...]

6.      The Commission on Human Rights had been dealing with agenda item 108, "Adoption of a convention on the rights of the child" for 10 years and, in its work on the convention, had encouraged all countries to take an active part in elaborating the text so that it would reflect the needs of children the world over.

7.      The draft convention recognized the child's right to an identity from the moment of birth, in other words, the right to a name, a nationality and to be cared for by his or her parents and maintain relations with them in case of separation. It also protected the child from, inter alia, dangers to which he or she was particularly exposed, such as all forms of physical or mental violence or abuse; any form of exploitation; work likely to be harmful to his or her physical or mental health or to interfere with the child's education; and the illicit use of narcotic drugs or psychotropic substances.

8.      The draft convention provided for the establishment of a Committee on the Rights of the Child which would review the progress made by States parties in fulfilling their obligations under the convention. The Committee would have a broad mandate and could, inter alia, invite specialized agencies and other competent bodies to provide expert advice on the implementation of the convention. In view of the negative consequences which unreliable financial mechanisms had had on the functioning of some treaty bodies, the Committee must have reliable and viable financing procedures.

9.      The year 1989 marked the thirtieth anniversary of the Declaration of the Rights of the Child, which should inspire everyone to greater efforts for the promotion and protection of children's rights. With the adoption of the draft convention on the rights of the child, it would be possible to offer every child in the world the necessary conditions that would enable him or her to grow up healthy and to realize his or her full potential in freedom and dignity.

[...]

23.      Mr. BONNECORSE (France) [...].

24.     The draft convention on the rights of the child, which was the result of 10 years of hard work, provided a protective mechanism that was based on the fundamental rights guaranteed in the two International Covenants on Human Rights, particularly regarding the civil rights of the child, and on a set of provisions which had not appeared to date in any other international legal instrument. Consequently, the Twelve [members of the European Community] believed that it was feasible to adopt the convention without a vote although some members of the European Community had noted some inadequacies in the process of negotiating the draft.

[...]

40.     Mr. MORA (Spain) supported the statement by France on behalf of the European Community. His delegation fully supported the adoption of the convention on the rights of the child. Although some points in the draft could be improved, he believed that reopening the debate on any particular article could endanger the adoption of the convention and would be a useless exercise. He hoped that the convention would be adopted by consensus. [...]

41.     Mr. KRENKEL (Austria) said that, despite the 1959 Declaration of the Rights of the Child and other international instruments in force, there was still a wide gap between the proclamations of the principle and their actual realization. Among the issues addressed during the International Year of the Child in 1979, the proposal of Poland to elaborate an international convention on the rights of the child had shown tangible results. The importance of such a comprehensive legal framework for the welfare of children was undisputed, above all in the light of the large number of children subject to economic exploitation, sexual abuse, trading or recruitment for wars, in addition to the even more common phenomenon of neglect or deprivation of basic rights, such as the right to food and education.

42.     The draft convention was the result of 10 years' continuous effort by the Working Group under the chairmanship of Mr. Lopatka, with the help of various intergovernmental organizations, in particular the United Nations Children's Fund (UNICEF), and non-governmental organizations. It had not been easy to draft a convention which would be a common standard for countries with different social systems. Austria, as a member of the Working Group, had been guided by the principle of improving or at least preserving the standards already set by existing human rights instruments. The drafting of new international instruments was mostly the result of prolonged negotiations between parties representing different political, economic, cultural or religious backgrounds. The convention on the rights of the child was no exception and its adoption by consensus would be of particular importance as a clear signal by Member States of their commitment on the issue.

43.     Austria was disappointed that article 38, on the protection of children in armed conflicts, fell below the standards contained in the 1977 Second Additional Protocol to the 1949 Geneva Conventions. Article 38 as it now stood provided that children under the age of 15 should not take a direct part in hostilities. The 1977 First Additional Protocol contained the same prohibition in respect of international armed conflicts, but also contained an absolute prohibition of the direct or indirect use of children under the age of 15 in non-international armed conflicts. Austria considered that only an age-limit of 18 years for participation in armed conflicts could satisfy humanitarian concern, and consequently the fundamental objectives of the convention were not adequately reflected in article 38.

44.     The draft convention contained various alternatives for financing the activities of the committee to be established under article 43. In view of the responsibility of Member States by virtue of the preamble to the Universal Declaration of Human Rights, Austria preferred the first alternative, contained in paragraph 10 bis of article 43, which provided that the activities of the committee should be financed by the United Nations.

*The following is taken from document A/C.3/44/SR.37 (15 November 1989).*

1.      Miss CASTAÑO (Colombia), speaking on agenda item 108, said that the draft convention on the rights of the child was ready for adoption. In monitoring the implementation of the convention, due account

should be taken of the differences between developed and developing countries. The latter were undergoing a dynamic development process and experiencing social, economic and political changes. They sought to improve the situation of children who were victims, directly or indirectly, of poverty, economic dependence, an unjust economic order and the consequences of the international traffic in arms and narcotic drugs. In those countries, the problems of children had structural economic and social causes. The Family Welfare Institute of Colombia had drawn up a code on minors, which would be brought into line with the provisions of the convention when it entered into force.

[...]

9.      Mr. STOLTENBERG (Norway), speaking on behalf of the Nordic countries on agenda item 108, said that the draft convention on the rights of the child covered the basic rights of the child and recognized the need for special protection for certain categories of children.

10.      The international community was united in supporting measures to protect children in view of their special needs. Furthermore, human rights provisions relating specifically to children were scattered over a range of treaties and international instruments. The draft convention consolidated those provisions in a single document establishing new standards for child protection and recognizing that children had inalienable rights.

11.      One of the most important features of the draft convention was that it recognized the child as an independent individual. The Nordic countries noted with satisfaction that it contained undertakings to prevent abuses such as economic and sexual exploitation, and sale of and traffic in children. They also welcomed the provisions aimed at ensuring enjoyment of the highest attainable standards of health and facilities for the treatment of illness and were pleased to note the improvement in the provisions concerning protection of children in penal matters.

12.      The Nordic countries attached special importance to the protection of children in armed conflict and were disturbed at reports of children being killed in armed conflicts or disabled physically and mentally. It was regrettable that article 38 of the draft convention did not deal adequately with those concerns and, in fact, represented no progress at all. The convention should offer children better protection than that offered by existing instruments and should be interpreted as a reinforcement of existing standards. In that connection he referred to the unambiguous provision in article 41 to the effect that nothing in the convention should affect any provision in national or international law which established higher standards than those defined in the convention.

13.      The Nordic countries were also disturbed by the number of delegations in the Working Group that had made reservations concerning certain articles. They would find a convention based on the lowest common denominator of national legislation unacceptable. It was essential for the convention to represent progress and to obligate every State to review its legislation and practices before it could ratify it.

14.      The Nordic countries welcomed the provisions concerning implementation of the draft convention and the role of the Committee on the Rights of the Child in coordinating international action. They attached great importance to the role of the United Nations Children's Fund (UNICEF) and other United Nations organizations, whose technical advice and assistance were essential for States parties having the will but lacking the resources for implementation. The role of non-governmental organizations had also been recognized. In the context of article 42, which provided that States Parties should make the principles and provisions of the convention widely known, the convention could be seen as a new and powerful tool for disseminating and promoting the concept and understanding of human rights.

15.      It was important that financial considerations should not prevent countries from acceding to the convention and that lack of financial resources should not hamper the functioning of the Committee on the Rights of the Child. The Nordic countries considered that the costs of the Committee should be borne by the regular budget of the United Nations.

16.      Mrs. LIZIN (Belgium) said that Belgium was especially interested in the problem of children with parents of different nationalities, particularly where the parents were separated. Kidnapping, for example, was an act of violence against parent - often the mother - and child. In that connection, the anticipated opening of frontiers in the European Community in 1992 was important. Each member State of the European Community had its own legislation on the right to custody and visitation of children, and with parents in different countries children were often brutally deprived of regular contact with one or the other parent. It was essential, when the frontiers were opened, to maintain the fundamental right of every child to have regular contact with both its parents and with the other members of its family.

17.      The subject of child custody was dealt with not only in the draft convention but also in two existing multilateral instruments: the European Convention of Luxembourg of 20 May 1989 concerning custody of children and The Hague Convention of 25 October 1980 on international kidnapping. She urged speedy ratification of those Conventions.

18.      At a time when the European Community was pursuing policies protecting the freedom of movement of persons, it was paradoxical that the children of parents in different countries could not move freely. Belgium therefore proposed the establishment of a body to act as ombudsman in dealing with such problems by negotiating with parents. She welcomed the provisions of article 9 of the draft convention.

19.      Mrs. WARZAZI (Morocco) [...]

21.      Speaking on agenda item 108, she recalled that in 1946 the United Nations Children's Fund (UNICEF) had been made responsible for children and adolescents who were the victims of aggression, and its mandate and activities had been strengthened when the General Assembly recognized the immensity of children's sufferings, particularly in the developing countries and in countries ravaged by war and other scourges. It was thanks to UNICEF, the International Labour Organization and numerous international non-governmental organizations that the world had come to realize the conditions to which millions of young children were subjected - economic exploitation, debt bondage, international traffic in persons, prostitution, torture, violence and delinquency, a life of poverty and abandonment by their parents. The physical and psychological health of millions of girls were threatened by traditional practices which Governments should do everything possible to eliminate.

22.      The tragic situation of children had led the international community to adopt a Declaration on the Rights of the Child in 1959. It had taken 10 years of study, negotiation, thought and compromise to produce the draft convention now before the Committee. The Moroccan delegation in Geneva had played an active part in the Working Group, contributing to the adoption of the draft convention by consensus in the Commission on Human Rights.

*The following is taken from document A/C.3/44/SR.38 (20 November 1989).*

1.      Mr. LOPATKA (Poland) said that the adoption and entry into force of the convention on the rights of the child would be an important step in the development of international standards for the promotion and protection of human rights and fundamental freedoms. Indeed, the very process of drafting the convention had contributed to a better understanding of children's rights and of human rights in general. He wished to pay tribute to the States, United Nations bodies and non-governmental organizations that had contributed to the drafting process.

2.      The drafters of the convention had had to find a way of harmonizing the varied and sometimes contradictory values and interests of the world's societies. The convention's main objective was to ensure special legal protection for children and, in so doing, it reinforced certain safeguards set forth in other international instruments, in particular the Declaration of the Rights of the Child, and also provided some new ones. By setting new standards in the field, the convention would promote a quality of life for children which was conducive to their political, mental and social development, irrespective of the particular features of their environment. In addition, it would play an important role in mobilizing international efforts to assist national governments in overcoming any difficulties encountered in implementing its provisions. Lastly, it

would be an important contribution to the development and promotion of human rights from the specific perspective of children.

3.    The draft convention did not simply list minimum standards for the protection of children but also made it incumbent upon States parties to create conditions facilitating active participation by children in the social and political life of their countries. Furthermore, States parties would be guided by article 41 to implement child protection measures that went beyond the provisions of the convention.

4.    As it stood, the draft convention was not perfect but provided a solid basis for seeking even more effective measures for the protection of children. Several countries felt that article 38, concerning protection of children in cases of armed conflict, did not reflect their concerns fully and fell short of the protection afforded by international humanitarian law. In that connection too, it was to be hoped that the application of article 41 would result in improved protection for children in such situations. Some States had also called for stronger provisions concerning the rights of the child before and after birth and for provisions that would better reflect the legal, religious and social differences among countries. The draft convention was meant to be a compromise, however, and to be universal in character. In the interest of pragmatism, it would be best not to jeopardize that compromise.

5.    His delegation hoped that the consensus that had already been reached on the draft convention would be maintained and that as many States as possible would join his own in signing and ratifying the instrument at the earliest possible date.

6.    Close and effective international cooperation would be needed in the future to ensure that the convention afforded children the desired protection. The establishment of a Committee on the Rights of the Child, as provided for under article 43, which would be assisted by international agencies, would promote cooperation among States, intergovernmental bodies and non-governmental organizations in that effort. Considering the importance of the task to be entrusted to that committee and the unfortunate experience of other committees which were dependent on States for their resources, his delegation believed that the Committee on the Rights of the Child should be funded from the United Nations regular budget. It was therefore in favour of retaining, and removing the square brackets from, the first sentence of article 43, paragraph 11, and of deleting the remaining text of that paragraph and the entire text of paragraph 12. Current paragraph 10 bis would then become paragraph 11 and paragraph 11, as amended, would become paragraph 12.

7.    While the need for international cooperation and the special needs of developing countries with respect to children were given due consideration in the convention, those issues could be further enhanced through the proclamation of an international year of the family. Lastly, draft adoption of the convention would help to ensure the necessary protection for disabled, abandoned or orphaned children and would be the best way to celebrate the thirtieth anniversary of the Declaration of the Rights of the Child and the tenth anniversary of the International Year of the Child.

[...]

13.    Mr. LIKHANOV (Union of Soviet Socialist Republics) called upon all delegations to adopt the draft convention on the rights of the child by consensus at the current session of the General Assembly. He represented the Soviet Children's Fund, which provided assistance to children living in poverty. The Fund attached particular importance to the draft provisions relating to parentless, mentally and physically disabled and refugee children. There were currently more than 1 million orphans in the Soviet Union and, among its activities, the Fund arranged for families to act as guardians and adopt orphans.

14.    Involving children in military operations was inadmissible and amoral. He therefore shared the position of a number of delegations and non-governmental organizations that the minimum age for service in the armed forces should be raised. The Soviet Union had established the minimum draft age at 18, a higher age than that provided for under the draft convention.

15.      The Soviet Children's Fund had taken measures to improve the health care and living conditions of children in Soviet Central Asia, and was particularly concerned at the effect of the Chernobyl disaster on the health of children living in the affected areas. Accordingly, he called upon the world community, particularly scientists in the United States, Japan, the Federal Republic of Germany and other countries, to establish an international children's medical radiology centre in the disaster area. Speedy implementation of projects of that kind would be the best way to pursue the goals of the draft convention.

16.      He was confident that the USSR Supreme Soviet would ratify the convention and bring domestic legislation into line with its provisions. The Soviet Children's Fund sought to promote the adoption of a law on the rights of the child, which would supplement existing legislation with the obligations laid down in the convention. The proposed Committee on the Rights of the Child would play a paramount role in ensuring the implementation of the convention.

17.      Ms. HALONEN (Finland) said that while the final adoption of the convention on the rights of the child would be a landmark event, it was ultimately up to national legislatures to give full effect to the convention's principles and norms. The draft convention was a remarkable instrument for a variety of reasons. First, it affirmed the human rights of the child as an independent person and not just as a member of a family or a group. Secondly, it contained a balanced combination of ideas derived from the major cultural traditions of the world. Rather than seeking to universalize any one approach, it built upon what was common to all cultures while leaving ample room for specific traditions. Thirdly, it avoided ideological conflict by giving equal consideration to civil and political rights and to economic, social and cultural rights. While it fully acknowledged the child as an independent person with a set of given rights, the convention also recognized that without a proper environment, in the broadest sense of the word, those rights lost a great deal of their meaning. In fact, owing to its strong emphasis on protecting children from the effects of negative social environments, whatever their causes, the convention was important to both developed and developing States.

18.      While social welfare was given high priority in Europe, many existing agreements did not give a prominent place to the rights of children. As a consequence, the convention would undoubtedly have an impact on legislation and practice in the industrialized countries. The new dangers threatening children in those countries, including mechanization, the pressures of commercialization, and increasing isolation, made the aims of the convention even more relevant.

19.      The convention contained many provisions that had never been set forth in a binding international instrument. Among them, she wished to stress article 3, which affirmed that in all actions concerning children, the best interests of the child should be a primary consideration; article 10, which provided that States parties should deal with applications for family reunification in a positive, humane and expeditious manner; and article 23, which requested States to pay special attention to the needs of and ensure the dignity of mentally and physically disabled children.

20.      The draft convention was not without ambiguities and compromises. Certain provisions, in particular those relating to the definition of the child, the use of children in armed conflict, children's freedom of thought, conscience and religion, and children of minorities, might have gone further. Despite those flaws, however, the convention represented a very important step towards the universal promotion of human rights. Some had questioned the need for a new convention, arguing that its contents merely repeated those of existing international conventions. While it was true that many of its provisions already appeared in other instruments, the convention was not and never had been superfluous. Not only did it go significantly beyond other international instruments in certain areas, but it also established new rights for children. Furthermore, article 41 ensured that no State could use the convention as a justification to avoid obligations laid down in other international instruments to which that State was a party.

21.      Criticism had also been levelled at the programmatic nature of the convention's provisions. Many instruments of similar format had provided countries with social goals, however, and had stimulated them to enact relevant legislation. Among the most notable of those instruments was the International Covenant on

Economic, Social and Cultural Rights, which had had an important effect on national social welfare legislation in her own country.

22.     Finland had recently introduced a number of reforms in the interests of children and was thus already in compliance with many of the provisions of the draft convention. At the same time, much remained to be done and the convention could provide the impetus for policies in her country aimed at expanded protection for children.

23.     While it might have wished for a set of provisions with a more immediate effect, her delegation was not discouraged by the second part of the convention. In particular, it welcomed the fact that United Nations specialized agencies and bodies would be able to be represented at meetings of the Committee on the Rights of the Child to be established under the convention. It also assumed that the United Nations, with the specialized agencies, particularly UNICEF would take the measures required by the implementation of the convention, for instance, the organization of meetings at various levels. Finland would support such measures actively. Lastly, her Government wished to express its firm preference for financing the committee's meetings from the regular United Nations budget, the most effective means of guaranteeing the proper functioning of the implementation machinery.

24.     Mr. SMITH (United States of America) said that his country had participated actively in the drafting of the convention on the rights of the child and believed that it marked a notable step forward in the protection of the rights of children. His delegation hoped that the General Assembly would adopt the draft as it now stood. Having introduced the initial draft over 10 years previously, the Polish Government deserved much of the credit for the conclusion of the convention and, in that connection, he wished to pay tribute to Mr. Lopatka for his work as Chairman of the working group on the draft convention. He wished also to acknowledge the valuable contribution to the drafting process made by non-governmental organizations, which had encouraged the setting of high standards in the convention.

25.     The draft convention dealt with many difficult issues and was the result of compromise and concessions. Like many others, his Government was not completely satisfied with some of those compromises. Given the importance of the convention's early adoption, however, it did not wish to reopen negotiation on any part of the text.

26.     His Government supported fully the inclusion in the preamble of the draft convention of language from the 1959 Declaration of the Rights of the Child, to the effect that the child, by reason of his physical and mental immaturity, needed special safeguards and care before as well as after birth. The positive effects for both mothers and infants of basic maternal, prenatal and neonatal care were only just being fully recognized in his country. In that connection, the United States Agency for International Development had launched a new project for maternal and neonatal health and nutrition in developing countries.

27.     His Government endorsed the convention's reaffirmation of the right of the child to freedom of thought, conscience and religion. At the same time, it would have preferred an even stronger reaffirmation of freedom of religion. In particular, it would have been desirable for the convention to include specific references, as did other international instruments, to such supplementary rights for children as the freedom to have or change a religion, the right to worship according to their beliefs alone or with others, and the right to teach, learn and practise their religion in public and in private.

28.     His Government firmly believed that the expenses of the Committee on the Rights of the Child, to be established by the convention, should be borne exclusively by the States ratifying it. That committee was to be an instrument of the States parties to the convention; they alone had the right to nominate and elect its members and were bound to submit reports to it. Furthermore, since the convention would enter into force once it had been ratified by 20 States, it was inappropriate for the entire United Nations membership to fund a body created to serve what would initially be a very small number of States. Financing by States parties would be more likely to preserve the independence of the committee, leaving it completely free to decide how to use its funds.

29. His Government was particularly concerned about family reunification and therefore welcomed the provision requesting States parties to deal with reunification applications in a positive, humane and expeditious manner.

30. The prevention of physical and mental abuse of children demanded constant vigilance, against a background of moral and ethical awareness at all levels of society. Child abuse, in all its forms, was all too prevalent throughout the world. Governments must be committed to providing legal and administrative protection to children and to supporting social and educational programmes that could prevent abuse.

31. With the active encouragement of its President, his country had promoted child adoption measures within the framework of legal safeguards and competent adoption agencies. President Bush was scheduled to sign into law a bill designating the last week of November as National Adoption Week in the United States. That initiative would increase public awareness of the rewards of adoption for children and parents alike, promote legal adoption and encourage the adoption of children with mental and physical handicaps. His Government was keenly aware of the latter group of children and fully supported the convention's appeal for a full and decent life for them. He hoped that Governments would make a strong commitment to that particular goal and ensure full social integration for children with special needs.

32. Mr. OUEDRAOGO (Burkina Faso) said that his country had long wanted to devote itself to the consideration of children's and women's concerns. In that connection with the support of UNICEF and national and international non-governmental organizations, it had hosted a meeting on the rights of the child in April 1989. His Government was committed to respecting human rights and fundamental freedoms for all and considered the rights of the child to be an integral part of human rights in general. In order to ensure the survival, development, protection and participation of children, their parents had to be guaranteed the same rights. It was in that context that his country endorsed the draft convention on the rights of the child.

33. In the face of such problems as environmental degradation, drug abuse and reverse financial flows, many delegations were concerned about the future which the world's children would inherit. Regional conflicts, especially those in Palestine and Southern Africa, created devastating, intolerable living conditions for children. His country viewed articles 2 and 3 of the draft convention as being particularly relevant to those concerns and as representing the cornerstone of the entire convention. The best interests of the child meant creating conditions for his or her full growth and development to adulthood. That in turn required the settlement of regional conflicts, a goal to which the entire international community should contribute actively.

34. Ms. NINH (Viet Nam) said that concern for the well-being and happiness of children was an integral part of her country's traditions and its current social policies. During the International Year of the Child, her Government had adopted a law on the protection, care and education of children, which laid down the fundamental rights of the child and defined the shared responsibility of the family, State and society in that regard. Viet Nam had recently decided to allocate funds and encourage contributions to upgrade and build schools, hospitals and other facilities to meet children's needs. Under an agreement between Viet Nam and the United States of America, over 27,000 Amerasian children and their relatives had been resettled in the United States. Thus, practical action was being taken to improve the lot of those unfortunate children.

35. The draft convention on the rights of the child was comprehensive in scope, fairly concrete and action-oriented. While her delegation appreciated the importance of articles which were protective or deterrent in nature, it attached particular importance to the need for affirmative action to create the best possible conditions for the development of children. In draft article 34 (b) and (c), she proposed the deletion of the word "exploitative" since retaining that word might imply that there could be non-exploitative use of children in prostitution and pornography. With regard to the financing of the proposed Committee on the Rights of the Child, Viet Nam supported the first version of article 43, paragraph 11, and believed that the United Nations as a whole should be responsible for the expenses involved. Although the draft text could perhaps be further refined, it was preferable to have a legal instrument that enjoyed universal support and

could be more easily enforced. Lastly, she expressed satisfaction at the very important contribution made by UNICEF and hoped that the draft convention could be adopted by consensus at the current session of the General Assembly.

36.	Mr. GALAL (Egypt) said that the first six years of school were free and compulsory in Egypt. [...]

[...]

38.	For the past decade, his delegation had been actively involved in the open-ended working group of the Commission on Human Rights on a draft convention on the rights of the child. The Egyptian delegation had coordinated the position of the Muslim group at Geneva during the second reading of the draft convention and had worked hard to arrive at a compromise language. Egypt had participated in a League of Arab States seminar, held in Tunisia, which had recommended adoption of the draft convention. It had also sponsored, at the summit meeting of the organization of African Unity held at Addis Ababa in July 1989, a draft resolution calling for the adoption of the convention and the proclamation of a decade of the African child.

39.	Many provisions of the draft convention had already been implemented in Egypt. A seminar to study the draft convention had been held at Alexandria in 1988, with the participation of national experts and the Executive Director of the United Nations Children's Fund (UNICEF). At the seminar, a number of suggestions had been put forward concerning the second reading of the draft convention and the President of Egypt had declared 1989-1999 the decade of Egyptian children. The objective of the decade would be to afford children full educational and psychological protection. Lastly, at a meeting of Arab countries held at Cairo in July 1989, a draft resolution on the rights of the child, sponsored by Egypt, had been adopted.

[...]

45.	Mrs. JOSHI (Nepal) said that many children, particularly in the developing and least developed countries, lacked even the most basic necessities, without which intellectual and social development were impossible. Poverty in the developing world was responsible for child labour, as well as for inadequate health care and education. Her own country suffered from high infant mortality and low school attendance rates. The Government had therefore instituted policies designed to promote the physical well-being of children even before birth through prenatal care, to provide free primary education, to discourage school dropouts, to rehabilitate disabled children and to protect children from unlawful exploitation. It had also prohibited child marriages and was providing care for homeless children and orphans. The country's community health programme, which included the provision of maternity services, midwives and health workers, was expected to reduce infant mortality to 45 per thousand by the year 2000. A vast network of child health-care services would make maternal health care, immunization, oral rehydration therapy and health education available throughout the country. Environmental health units would be established to protect drinking water and food from contamination.

46.	The Government's child welfare efforts were being supplemented by those of a number of non-governmental organizations under royal patronage and by the South Asian Association for Regional Cooperation (SAARC), a regional organization active in formulating plans and programmes to improve the conditions of children in South Asia. SAARC stressed the importance of taking the special needs of children into account in national development planning and the concept that human resources development should focus on the well-being of children. SAARC had also called for the adoption of the draft convention on the rights of the child.

47.	UNICEF had also been playing a vital role, particularly in immunization and oral rehydration therapy, and had helped to save millions of children from death and from crippling diseases. Its efforts in such areas as primary health care, nutrition and food security, joint nutrition support programmes, poverty alleviation and childhood disability prevention programmes, as well as emergency relief to children in cases of national disasters, had helped children everywhere. UNICEF and WHO had established health goals that would save the lives of 100 million children and protect many others from crippling diseases by the end of the century.

48.     In that context, the draft convention on the rights of the child was an important international instrument that would provide a framework for the coordination of national efforts to promote child survival, protection and development. Its ratification would not only lead to achieving national, regional and global child welfare objectives but would also make the world community realize that the rights of children were not a matter of charity but an integral component of human rights.

49.     Miss MORALES (Costa Rica) said that the convention on the rights of the child was an innovative instrument which more clearly defined and harmonized international norms protecting a particularly vulnerable and dependent group of human beings. In Costa Rica, the National Child Welfare Board, an autonomous institution, was responsible for enforcing the rights of the child and, in 1987, the position of children's advocate had been created as an additional guarantee in that regard.

50.     In the interest of adopting the convention by consensus, particularly on the occasion of the anniversary of the Declaration of the Rights of the Child, her delegation had refrained from proposing certain changes in the text. It did, however, believe that article 9, as currently worded, legitimized an abnormal situation by allowing the State to withhold information on the whereabouts of a child's parents if such information was deemed detrimental to the child. Her delegation was concerned that the provision on the right of access to international jurisdiction could be violated by the State of which the injured party was a national. Diplomatic immunity should not be invoked in such cases.

51.     While her delegation respected the wording of article 38 (3) on the recruitment age for military service, it strongly supported raising the age-limit and welcomed the efforts initially made by Angola, Austria, India, Mozambique, and the Nordic countries, to that end. Although the same principle was embodied in Protocols I and II of 1977 to the Geneva Conventions, the convention on the rights of the child should have been used to take more forceful action to prevent the participation of children in armed conflicts.

52.     Her delegation agreed with the representatives of Austria and Viet Nam that paragraph 10 bis should be incorporated in article 43. Lastly, the use of terminology from adult penal law in the article on the anti-social or delinquent conduct of minors stigmatized children. Instead, emphasis should have been placed on preventive programmes for those sectors of the child population who were most likely to commit crimes.

53.     Mr. BRÄUTIGAM (Federal Republic of Germany) said that his delegation supported fully the statement made on behalf of the 12 States members of the European Community at the beginning of the debate on the International Covenants on Human Rights, on the rights of the child and on torture. [...]

[...]

55.     Mrs. BLANDON de CEREZO (Guatemala) described an unprecedented demonstration in August 1989, in which Guatemalan children from all parts of the country had delivered a petition to the President of the Republic in favour of the convention on the rights of the child. In full solidarity with those children, her delegation supported the adoption of the convention and appealed to all delegations to join in the consensus. The convention was consistent with the spirit of the Guatemalan Constitution, in which the State guaranteed and protected human life from the moment of conception.

56.     The convention had aroused great interest at both the national and the regional level in Central America. The third meeting of Central American First Ladies, held at San Salvador in September, had adopted a resolution supporting the convention and urging its adoption by the General Assembly. Another resolution adopted at the meeting called on every Central American country to accede to, ratify and implement the convention.

57.     In Guatemala, an ad hoc commission, chaired by the President of the Republic, would hold its first national seminar on the convention on the rights of the child at the end of November. UNICEF, too, had done much to publicize the contents of the draft convention and, together with other governmental and non-governmental organizations, was doing extremely important work for the children of Central America.

[...]

60.     Mr. FORTIER (Canada) said that the world's failure adequately to promote the well-being of children had made it urgently necessary for the international community to supplement existing instruments for the protection of children with a convention on the rights of the child. The convention had been carefully drafted to promote the survival of children by considering their basic health needs and civil rights and the need to protect them against exploitation. The convention was vital, because children needed special protections above and beyond those provided in other instruments. It stated that the best interests of the child should be the criterion for State intervention to protect the rights of the child, and it recognized that economic, social and cultural rights must be implemented in a different manner from civil and political rights.

61.     The draft convention reflected the important contributions of many States, international agencies and non-governmental organizations. Once adopted, Canada would work for its ratification, within the framework of its own political processes, and he was optimistic that ratification would be prompt.

62.     His delegation regretted, nevertheless, that no way had been found to improve the standards set forth in article 38, on children in armed conflicts. The wording of that article should not be interpreted as lowering the standards set forth in the 1977 Geneva Protocols. Article 14, on freedom of thought, conscience and religion, must be read in the light of the provision of the International Covenant on Civil and Political Rights on which it was based. The fact that the convention had been drafted with a view to accommodating diversity should not hinder its implementation. The proposed Committee on the Rights of the Child must be the instrument through which the implementation of the convention was enhanced, and it must therefore have the moral and financial support of the United Nations. The Committee's members must be elected for their independence and qualifications.

63.     His delegation attached great importance to the effective implementation of standards in the human rights field. Before any new standard-setting initiatives were attempted, careful attention must be paid to such questions as the financing of United Nations monitoring bodies, the reporting obligations of States and the role and nature of existing and future monitoring bodies. His delegation welcomed in that connection the impending release of the Secretary-General's note on effective implementation. States parties to fundamental human rights instruments should also make every effort to encourage non-parties to ratify them, and compliance with reporting obligations must be improved.

[...]

*The following is taken from document A/C.3/44/SR.39 (20 November 1989).*

5.     Mrs. SAULLE (Italy) welcomed the consensus that had been reached on the draft convention on the rights of the child (A/44/616), although she believed that children would have been better served if the convention had set at 18 years the age at which children could be recruited for military service and take part in hostilities and had done more to protect disabled children.

6.     Her delegation nevertheless supported the agreed text because it set important, binding standards, provided adequate machinery for monitoring its implementation, and contained a safeguard clause in the form of article 41, under which States could set standards even higher than the minimum standard set by the convention. She also welcomed the provision in the convention for a system of amendment. Her delegation therefore hoped that the Committee would adopt the convention by consensus.

7.     Mrs. AIZPURUA (Panama) [...]

8.     The convention on the rights of the child (A/44/616) was an important instrument for protecting children, who in many parts of the world lacked the most basic necessities. Governments must take their responsibilities under the convention very seriously.

9.     The right to education was crucial to the future of children and could be realized only when such problems as hunger, desertification and disease were tackled. The convention and International Literacy Year were thus important stages in guaranteeing the all-round development of children who represented their countries' future.

10.	Drawing attention to the seventh preambular paragraph of the convention, she said that Panama faced the problem of protecting its children against the dangers posed by foreign military presence in its territory. It hoped that the international community would help free it from the foreign interference and pressure that kept Panamanian children from enjoying fully the rights set forth in the convention. A proper future could be assured for Panama's children only if agreements were honoured, regardless of the political situations of signatory Governments.

11.	Mr. CENKO (Albania) said that in a world in which 312 million children lived in poverty, 150 million children under the age of 15 worked in mines and 200 million children had no access to basic education, it was of paramount importance to create social and economic conditions that would prevent human rights laws designed to protect children from becoming a dead letter. In Albania, mothers and children were guaranteed all the financial, medical and educational support required to make the rights of the child a reality.

12.	Job training was an essential factor in preparing children for life, and vocational training and physical work had been made an integral part of the school curriculum in Albania with a view to teaching children the value of work.

13.	In Albania, children were taught an awareness of economic and social problems and, through their own organizations, learned to think and act independently. Radio and television broadcasts also provided a medium for children to voice their opinions. One priority remained the steady improvement of child protection laws to keep pace with the country's social development. The fact that Albania's population had tripled in 40 years and that its average age was 27 years was a tribute to the care devoted to children and their rights.

14.	Mrs. KHOURY (observer, Palestine Liberation Organization) said that the draft convention on the rights of the child was an important document intended to safeguard the rights of all children without exception and, above all, children born into exceptional circumstances. Among the latter category, the children of Palestine and South Africa were in urgent need of the protection which would be provided by the convention. Not only were they denied any of the privileges enjoyed by children in developed countries and, to a lesser extent, in developing countries, but they were also subjected to oppression, exploitation, imprisonment and killings.

15.	Palestinian children were exposed to Israeli practices of terrorism, brutality and exploitation in the occupied Palestinian territories and elsewhere. Palestinian children living in refugee camps in Arab countries, particularly Lebanon, had been victims of Israeli military raids, invasions and massacres, which had left thousands of children dead, maimed or disfigured.

16.	Palestinian children in the West Bank and Gaza had been living under Israeli military occupation for 22 years, during which time they and their parents had been physically and emotionally traumatized. Since the beginning of the intifada, Israeli violence against Palestinian children had reached new heights. Many youngsters had died or been severely injured as a result of brutal beatings which were officially condoned by the Israeli Government. The excessive and improper use of tear gas by Israeli occupation forces had been responsible for the deaths of many adults and children and had also caused numerous miscarriages among pregnant women. More than 40,000 people had been detained in the past two years, of whom an estimated 75 per cent were young people under the age of 18 who, like all Palestinian political prisoners, were severely tortured. Testimony by children themselves indicated that they had been subjected to physical and psychological brutality and had been denied basic necessities.

17.	Palestinian schools had been systematically attacked throughout the years of Israeli occupation. They had been repeatedly closed, refused permission to expand and denied adequate supplies. Students and staff had been harassed, beaten, detained and even killed. During the intifada, the war against the Palestinian educational system had escalated. Thousands of students and teachers had been detained and the entire system had been shut down, in violation of international law.

18.     The combination of abuse and denial of education would undoubtedly cause long-term psychological and social problems for Palestinian children. That population had enormous educational, physical and psychological needs which must be addressed by the international community. In order for those needs to be met, Israel must withdraw from the occupied territories. That could best be achieved by the convening of an international peace conference under United Nations auspices, with the participation of the five permanent members of the Security Council and all the parties to the conflict, including the Palestine Liberation Organization, on an equal footing.

19.     Mr. YOSSIFOV (Bulgaria) [...]

[...]

21.     The draft convention on the rights of the child not only was a positive step towards establishing a legal basis for international cooperation in the field of human rights but also raised the minimum human rights standards applicable to children. While it would not bring about an automatic improvement in children's living conditions, the convention would draw international attention to their situation and promote efforts aimed at serving their best interests. The adoption, entry into force and implementation of the draft convention was only the first step in that process. It was in that context that his delegation hoped that the convention, as it now stood, would be adopted without a vote by the General Assembly.

[...]

32.     Mr. ITO (Japan) [...]

33.     Referring to the draft convention on the rights of the child, he stressed the importance of reviewing all the circumstances in which children live and grow in the light of the emerging concept of the rights of the child. While the main purpose of the convention was to protect children after they were born, his Government respected the spirit of the ninth preambular paragraph, which stated that the child needed special safeguards and care before as well as after birth. In connection with article 43, his delegation believed that, as a matter of principle, the Committee on the Rights of the Child should be financed by the States parties to the convention. Funding from the regular budget of the United Nations would not be conducive to ensuring the true objective of the convention and would place yet another financial burden on the Organization.

34.     He hoped that the new concept of the rights of the child would be fully understood and taken into account in national policies. The adoption of the draft convention was only the beginning of a long process. The convention must be acceded to by as many Member States as possible and must be implemented through concrete measures by individual countries. Lastly, international cooperation in that area must take into account the specific situation of children in each country.

35.     Archbishop MARTINO (observer for the Holy See) said that defending the rights of the child was a central obligation for the Church. It was very significant that the draft convention on the rights of the child recognized clearly the right to life of the unborn child. Although the Holy See would have preferred to see further elaboration of that right in the articles of the draft convention, it was confident that the ninth preambular paragraph would serve as a guide for interpreting the rest of the convention. He agreed with the delegations that had proposed that the age of recruitment for military service should be raised to 18 years. The right of parents to provide for the religious and moral education of their children should also have been formulated more specifically. States should guarantee the freedom of parents to educate their children according to their own religious convictions and to provide for their religious instruction. Despite those flaws, his delegation believed that the convention, if adopted, would mark significant gains for the world's children and for the cause of human rights. The Holy See therefore urged the Committee to adopt the draft convention in its present form.

[...]

41.     Mr. WON (observer for the Republic of Korea) [...]

[...]

43.     His country was a staunch supporter of United Nations efforts to promote the welfare of children throughout the world and favoured the adoption of the draft convention on the rights of the child at the current session of the General Assembly.

44.     Mr. LOPATKA (Poland), introducing draft decision A/C.3/44/L.45 on the adoption of a convention on the rights of the child, said that it was designed to ensure that the expenses of members of the Committee on the Rights of the Child were covered from the regular budget of the United Nations. Since many delegations favoured that approach, he hoped that the Committee would support the draft decision.

*The following is taken from document A/C.3/44/SR.40 (27 November 1989).*

1.     Mr. CABRAL (Guinea-Bissau) [...]

2.     Turning to agenda item 108, he welcomed the completion of the draft convention on the rights of the child. That convention represented a systematization of standards of child protection which in many cases had been embodied in various international legal instruments but had not yet been gathered into a single instrument. In view of the fundamental nature of the convention his delegation urged the General Assembly to adopt it by consensus.

3.     After mentioning the work being carried out for children in his country by UNICEF and the World Health Organization, he noted that his country had just proclaimed 12 September, the birthday of the liberator and human rights champion Amilcar Cabral, National Children's Day. That was an indication of the importance Guinea-Bissau attached to protecting the fundamental rights of the child.

4.     Mr. WILENSKI (Australia) said that in the 41 years since adoption of the Universal Declaration of Human Rights, the international community had developed a substantial body of human rights law, most of it within the framework of the United Nations. That legal structure was a remarkable achievement, not least because it represented a fundamental departure from previous approaches to international relations and international law. All member States should seek to strengthen that framework, extending it where appropriate and ensuring its effective implementation. For that reason, his delegation welcomed the submission of two new draft instruments at the current session of the General Assembly and looked forward to their adoption.

5.     There was much scope for more effective implementation of existing human rights standards. One important contribution to that would be the accession of more States to the human rights instruments, particularly the two Covenants. His Government urged member States which had not yet acceded to those instruments to do so in order better to protect human rights in all countries. A valuable feature of the framework of human rights instruments was that it encouraged States to regard the observance of human rights standards as a global task which could be approached in a non-confrontational manner. The examination by expert committees of States parties' reports under the various treaty provisions was a means of steadily encouraging improved performance. It also demonstrated that observance of human rights standards in individual countries was an appropriate subject for international consideration and comment.

6.     Turning to agenda item 108, he said that his Government would warmly welcome adoption of the convention on the rights of the child as the culmination of many years' painstaking work. The draft did not entirely respond to all the concerns of all Governments, but Australia considered the compromise solutions that had been adopted acceptable. His delegation would therefore not support any reopening of any provision of the draft.

7.     One problem left for the General Assembly to resolve was that of funding the implementation of the convention. His Government had already expressed its concern about relying on funding from the general budget of the United Nations. In the absence of measures to obtain funding from other sources, the use of the regular budget would probably lead to a decrease in the Organization's human rights activities in other areas. Nevertheless, his delegation would not oppose the wishes of the majority if it was decided that the regular budget should be used to finance the implementation of the convention.

[...]

11.		Mr. BUZO (Byelorussian Soviet Socialist Republic), referring to agenda item 108, said that his delegation welcomed the introduction of the draft convention on the rights of the child, which represented the careful work of many United Nations bodies, specialized agencies and non-governmental organizations. The draft convention marked a significant step forward in international cooperation in humanitarian matters. His delegation supported the draft convention on the rights of the child, and hoped that it would be approved during the current session of the General Assembly. His country also held the view that the new Committee on the Rights of the Child should be financed from the regular budget of the United Nations.

[...]

13.		Mrs. TASKINUD-DIN (Pakistan) [...]

[...]

15.		Her delegation believed that all human rights were indivisible and interrelated and as such economic and social rights were just as important as civil and political rights. Unfortunately, poverty and underdevelopment still affected millions of people in the developing countries, in what amounted to the most serious and gross violation of the right to life and well-being. The primary victims were small children; according to UNICEF, more than 14 million children under the age of five died each year in the developing countries because of deprivation. In that context, the examination and approval of the draft convention on the rights of the child was envisaged for the current session of the General Assembly. The proposed convention would be a useful supplement to the existing instruments in the area of human rights, many of which referred implicitly or explicitly to the rights of the child. Her delegation was proud of being actively associated in the elaboration of the draft convention and trusted that it would be approved.

[...]

19.		Mr. SIRIRATH (Democratic Kampuchea) [...]

[...]

25.		In conclusion, his delegation reiterated its full commitment to United Nations human rights activities, especially those relating to the imminent adoption of the draft convention on the rights of the child.

[...]

29.		Mr. VOICU (Romania) [...]

30.		Referring to the draft convention on the rights of the child, whose final text was contained in document A/44/616, he recalled that his delegation was among the sponsors of the resolution relating to the draft convention, even though the text was not perfect. He commented in particular on article 28 of the draft convention dealing with the right of the child to education, which laid down the obligation of States Parties to make available compulsory and free primary education, as well as to encourage the development of different forms of secondary education, including general and vocational education, and to take appropriate measures such as the introduction of free education and offering financial assistance in case of need. He also stressed the importance of article 29, paragraph 1 (d), which specified that States parties agreed that the education of the child should be directed, inter alia, to the preparation of the child for responsible life in the spirit of understanding, peace, tolerance and friendship among all peoples. His country believed that the adoption of the convention on the rights of the child would give new impetus to the efforts to implement fully the provisions of the Guidelines for further planning and suitable follow-up in the field of youth.

[...]

32.		Mr. PIBULSONGGRAM (Thailand) recalled that 1989 marked the thirtieth anniversary of the Declaration of the Rights of the Child as well as the tenth anniversary of the International Year of the Child, and referred to the imminent adoption by the General Assembly of a convention on the rights of the child. More than one third of the population of his country was under 16 years of age. In the draft convention, children's rights were grouped under three headings: survival, development and protection.

33.      Regarding survival, primary health care was available in nearly 90 per cent of villages, which had contributed to the overall improvement in the health and welfare of children. In 1988, the mortality rate of children under the age of five declined to 51 per 1,000 live births from a previous figure of 149 per thousand in 1965. Over 80 per cent of children had been fully immunized, and all children were expected to be immunized by 1990.

34.      The right to development encompassed access to information, education, cultural activities, including the right to freedom of thought, conscience and religion. Ninety-seven per cent of Thai children were in school by the time they were seven and many began school much earlier. In 1987, there was one school for every two villages in Thailand; in 1988, 94 per cent of the male population and 88 per cent of the female population were literate. Information on children's rights continued to be incorporated into the school curriculum nationwide.

35.      Regarding the protection of children, in Thailand only one child in five was working at the age of 14, and the minimum working age had been increased from 12 to 13 years.

36.      Thailand would soon host the World Conference on Education for All, organized jointly by UNICEF, UNESCO, UNDP and the World Bank, to be held from 5 to 9 March 1990.

[...]

52.      Mr. ENGO (Cameroon), speaking on agenda item 108, said that the rights of the child were especially important from the point of view of the responsibility of the current generation to equip children with the tools needed to make their way in the modern world. The presentation of the draft convention on the rights of the child could not have been more timely, given that 1989 was the thirtieth anniversary of the General Assembly's adoption of the Declaration of the Rights of the Child. His Government supported the draft convention and was satisfied with its contents, especially article 28, which emphasized children's right to education, article 23, which outlined children's right to assistance from the State in case of physical or mental handicap, and article 21, which extended international legal protection to adopted children, particularly in cases of intercountry adoption.

53.      In Cameroon, a child came of age at 21. But his country was prepared to accept that the age of majority should be 18, as stipulated in article 1 of the draft convention. However, article 38 in its current form allowed children to be sent into combat from the age of 15. That would violate principles of Cameroonian legislation intended to protect children. Cameroon thought that the convention should stipulate that children under the age of 18 should not be conscripted or exposed to combat.

54.      His delegation welcomed the provisions of the draft convention which would direct public authorities to protect children from the effect of such social problems as extreme poverty. However, his delegation would have liked to see more emphasis put on the relationship between extreme poverty and problems with the mental and physical development of children. Throughout Africa and much of Latin America, the deterioration in the economic situation was having very adverse effects on the living conditions of children. In the 37 poorest countries, spending on health had been reduced by 50 per cent per head and on education by 25 per cent per head over the past few years. In almost half of the 103 developing countries for which recent information was available, the number of children enrolled in primary schools was falling. The worsening of the situation in those countries was also responsible for the fact that half a million young children had died there within the last 12 months. His delegation hoped that adoption of the convention would give further impetus to the launching of a real development pact between the industrialized and the developing countries. The noble objectives embodied in the convention would never be fully implemented if the current economic stagnation that affected so many countries was not overcome by the adoption of global measures.

55.      Cameroon was in favour of the convention entering into force quickly. That would encourage its wider ratification by States. His Government also leaned strongly towards the option of financing implementation of the convention through the regular budget of the United Nations.

56.      Miss DIEGUEZ (Mexico) said that the draft convention on the rights of the child was being submitted for consideration and adoption by the General Assembly at a time when the thirtieth anniversary of the Declaration of the Rights of the Child was being celebrated. The text of the draft convention represented 10 years of hard work, which had produced a broad document containing provisions on human rights in general, as well as special rules aimed at protecting the particular interests of children, the most vulnerable segment of the world's population. Although it was not perfect, the draft convention was the international community's greatest achievement on the subject to date. Its adoption would be a most important step, because it would mean recognizing adult society's responsibility for the survival, development and protection of children. They were the first to suffer in crisis situation; as UNICEF had revealed, the debt problem and recession of the 1980s had hit children particularly hard, and half a million of them had died in the past year as a result of the stagnation of development.

57.      Her delegation believed one of the most important provisions of the draft convention to be the one on the obligations of States to guarantee that every child enjoyed his or her rights without discrimination. In addition, torture and inhuman treatment were prohibited; in that connection, it was truly alarming to discover how far the children of Namibia and South Africa were from having their fundamental rights recognized. The draft convention also took account of very special situations which could only involve children, such as adoption, guardianship, the right to an identity or the treatment of minors, as well as other situations of more general nature, such as conscription or refugee status. The last was particularly important because the United Nations High Commissioner for Refugees had reported that about half of the world's refugees were children under 18 year of age. The draft convention also sought special protection for children who were victims of the drug problem.

58.      Mexico had one of the biggest populations of children, in Latin America and the Caribbean at least. Despite the current economic crisis, the Mexican authorities had made great efforts to continue allocating resources to the education and health sectors. Being convinced that it was necessary to have an international legal framework containing broad provisions on the rights of the child, Mexico had taken an active part in preparing the draft convention and had already begun legal studies to integrate it into the country's domestic legislation. Her delegation appealed for the spirit of consensus that had enabled the draft convention to be adopted by the Commission on Human Rights to be maintained in the General Assembly.

59.      Miss BACHTOBJI (Tunisia) said that the draft convention on the rights of the child provided a suitable legal framework for the international community to undertake to guarantee the well-being and protection of its most precious resources.

60.      In Tunisia, children and adolescents under 15 years of age represented 39 per cent of the total population. The beginning of a new era in the country had brought with it the political will to promote the rights of that sector of the population. Her delegation noted with interest that the provisions in the draft convention were consistent with the political stance of her Government, and trusted that it would be adopted by consensus despite its shortcomings, on which Tunisia would make known its reservations.

61.      In view of the interest aroused by the draft convention on the rights of the child among the member countries of the Arab Maghreb Union, her Government, in collaboration with UNICEF, had organized a Maghreb seminar on the subject in June 1989. The work undertaken by the participants in the seminar had culminated in the adoption of the Tunis Declaration, which contained a number of recommendations concerning the protection of children in rural areas, the protection of disabled children, the role of information in improving children's living conditions in the Maghreb and in Arab countries, and the establishment of a high-level Maghreb council on children. The participants in the seminar had recommended in the Tunis Declaration that the draft convention on the rights of the child should be adopted in accordance with the observations made by member countries of the Arab Maghreb Union.

[...]

*The following is taken from A/C.3/44/SR.41 (20 November 1989).*

1.      Mr. AYALA-LASSO (Ecuador) said that his county placed great emphasis on the plight of children. To improve society, primary attention must be given to the child.

2.    Given the existence of major philosophical, religious, social and cultural differences, flexibility had been needed to arrive at the text of the draft convention on the rights of child. While it should not be considered a definitive instrument, it was acceptable to his country because it contained provisions that protected the basic rights of the child and provided an adequate international system for guaranteeing the protection of those rights.

3.    Ecuador was especially pleased with the ninth preambular paragraph of the draft convention, which pointed to the need to protect the unborn child, and believed that that paragraph should be borne in mind in interpreting all the articles of the convention, particularly article 24. While the minimum age set in article 38 was, in its view, too low, his delegation did not wish to endanger the chances for the convention's adoption by consensus and therefore would not propose any amendment to the text.

4.    The convention had taken 10 years to draft and should be adopted quickly. Ecuador had decided to be among the first countries to sign it and would also take immediate legislative action for its ratification. Given the importance of the convention, financial arguments should not be invoked which broke the consensus. The United Nations should be proud to finance the monitoring of the convention's implementation. As some delegations had rightly pointed out, experience had shown that it was counterproductive to have only the States parties to a treaty fund its implementation.

[...]

24.    Mr. SUTRESNA (Indonesia) said that the healthy development of children, society's most vulnerable members, represented not only an investment in the future but also the fulfilment of a moral obligation. Even though the rights of the child were protected in other international human rights instruments, a convention on the rights of the child was still necessary because children were increasingly falling victim to preventable and tragic suffering as a result of a deteriorating world economic situation in which adjustment policies had meant reduced spending on the health and social sectors. While objections would inevitably be raised over certain aspects of the convention, they should not give rise to conflict over its interpretation or implementation and his delegation hoped that it would be adopted by consensus.

25.    His own country had already begun to implement many of the convention's provisions, which were compatible with its national development plans and its attitude towards children. Children in his country were being educated as to their rights and responsibilities as members of their family and of society. Indonesia would continue to work for the well-being of children at home and abroad. In that connection, he reaffirmed his country's commitment to ending apartheid which, with its attendant abuses and atrocities, so adversely affected the lives of children in South Africa. His country welcomed the adoption of the Declaration on the Elimination of All Forms of Intolerance and of Discrimination Based on Religion or Belief, because freedom of conscience and religion were essential to human dignity and to securing the most fundamental human rights. Indonesia was a land of great ethnic and religious diversity, and respect for different creeds and practices brought harmony to its society. Religious freedom in his country was guaranteed under the Constitution and he hoped that it would become universal.

26.    Lastly, he hoped that the improved international political climate would bring about a shift in the use of the world's resources from destructive to constructive ends, for instance, towards providing better health care for the world's children and relieving poverty in general.

27.    Mrs. SEMAMBO-KALEMA (Uganda) said that children were the most vulnerable and dependent sector of society and required a special legal instrument to protect them from abuse. The draft convention on the rights of the child not only enumerated the rights of the child but also obliged the State and the family to see that they were protected. It provided a basis for Governments to enact child protection laws and to remedy violations through the judicial process. Since national laws were limited in scope and existing international instruments were not binding, the convention was designed to supplement them and would be of universal application. It provided agreed standards for the protection of children everywhere without discrimination, while showing due regard for the local, religious and cultural values of the child's community.

28.      The inherent right of every child to life, provided for under article 6, of the convention, was perhaps the most fundamental right of all since it ensured the initial survival of the child. While infant mortality rates were low in developed countries, in some developing countries they were rising with alarming speed. It was estimated that by the end of the century, Africa would account for over 40 per cent of infant deaths worldwide. The situation was worse in Southern Africa, particularly in Namibia, Angola and Mozambique. That region, where armed conflict had directly or indirectly caused the deaths of thousands, had the highest infant mortality rate in the world.

29.      As a result of economic crises, Governments in developing countries had been forced to cut back severely on public spending, thereby depriving the poorest segments of the population, including children, of basic necessities. Faced with just such a situation, her Government had demonstrated its commitment to child survival by providing, in close cooperation with UNICEF, a number of health and education programmes for children. As a result of an accelerated programme of immunization and oral rehydration therapy, the infant mortality rate for the period 1984-1988 had declined and was expected to decrease further.

30.      Her delegation commanded the efforts of UNICEF, WHO and UNESCO to ensure the survival, protection and development of children. It looked forward to continued cooperation with those organizations under the convention, which was comprehensive enough to cover child protection needs in both developed and developing countries.

31.      In view of the difficulties experienced by other committees that were financed by contributions from States parties, her delegation favoured funding the Committee on the Rights of the Child from the regular budget of the United Nations. Such an arrangement would ensure better implementation of the convention.

32.      She hoped that there would be universal support for the convention and that as many States as possible would take steps to sign and ratify it so that it might enter into force at an early date. She hoped also that the convention's provisions would be implemented effectively by Governments. Lastly, she welcomed the proposal for a world summit meeting on children.

[...]

37.      Mr. KALITA (Ukrainian Soviet Socialist Republic) [...]

[...]

40.      [...] Lastly, his delegation supported the call for the adoption by consensus of the draft convention on the rights of the child.

41.      Mr. MOLINA-ARAMBARRI (Argentina) said that his delegation was proud to have participated actively in the working group on the draft convention on the rights of the child and thanked its Chairman and all those involved for their efforts.

42.      While not perfect, the draft convention was satisfactory in that it established different categories of rights which could be incorporated into the various legal and social systems of individual Member States. Moreover, since it contained a minimum set of standards for the protection of children, its adoption should not be delayed further.

43.      The first special meeting of lawmakers on the rights of the child, held in Argentina in October 1989, had adopted the La Plata Declaration, which had been issued as an official United Nations document. The Declaration proposed that, upon adoption of the convention by the General Assembly, the National Congress should take the necessary steps for its speedy adoption and ratification by Argentina and provincial legislatures should amend their legislation to conform to the convention's provisions.

44.      His delegation was pleased that the preamble to the convention included the affirmation that children needed special safeguards before as well as after birth. Such an emphasis would ensure that equal attention was paid to biological and social development, thus contributing to the optimum development of the child. His delegation had provided the impetus for article 8, concerning the identity of the child, and

had played an important role in the drafting of article 21, relating to intercountry adoption. With regard to article 38, it would have preferred a much stronger provision on the prohibition of the recruitment and use of children in armed conflicts. It endorsed the establishment of a Committee on the Rights of the Child and believed that it should be funded from the regular budget of the United Nations. The first sentence of article 43, paragraph 11, should therefore be retained and its square brackets removed. The purpose of the convention fully justified the requirement that all Member States contribute to the costs of the proposed committee.

45. He hoped that the adoption of the convention was imminent and urged all States to do their utmost to ratify it as soon as possible.

46. Ms. GAO Yianping (China) said that the draft convention on the rights of the child expressed the common desire of the international community and conformed to the principles and spirit of the relevant international human rights instruments. Because of the variety of social systems and cultural traditions in the world, the convention could not have satisfied everyone. Although her delegation, like others, had reservations concerning some of the convention's provisions, such as its definition of the child, that would not prevent it from supporting its adoption. With respect to funding for the Committee on the Rights of the Child, her Government understood the economic difficulties facing many countries and hoped that the United Nations could provide financial support for the Committee's work.

[...]

49. Ms. ILIC (Yugoslavia) [...]

[...]

51. Her Government fully supported the adoption by consensus of the convention on the rights of the child. The convention was designed to elevate to the status of international law States' obligations to protect children. Although it was based on existing standards, the convention went beyond them and even contained new provisions which were relevant to the needs of children in the contemporary world. It combined ideas from different cultural, political and economic systems leaving ample room for specific traditions. Above all, it contained some universally accepted basic rights that were essential for the full development of every child.

52. Certain provisions did not reflect fully the views of all the States that had participated in the drafting of the convention. For example, article 30 was incomplete since it did not mention the children of national minorities and migrant workers. Furthermore, as it stood, the article had a negative connotation and would have benefited from a more positive formulation.

53. Her delegation favoured funding from the United Nations regular budget for the Committee on the Rights of the Child to be established under the convention, and welcomed the possibility that United Nations specialized agencies might be represented at the committee's meetings. She wished also to express her appreciation to UNICEF for the support it had given the working group, and to the Government of Poland and Mr. Lopatka for their untiring efforts to complete the draft convention.

[...]

56. Miss AIOUAZE (Algeria) said that every effort must be made to ensure that the draft convention on the rights of the child constituted real progress in the field of human rights. Universal acceptance of the convention would depend to a large extent on its ability to meet the special needs of all the world's children. The draft convention was the result of a long and often difficult process of compromise, which explained its limitations. The need for consensus seemed to have obscured the original intent in a manner which was not always in the interests of children. In view of the many specific problems affecting children, an effort should have been made to establish new rights rather than reiterate existing ones, so that the convention not only made existing standards binding but also increased the protections afforded to children.

57.      It was alarming to note that the system of international human rights guarantees did not apply to millions of children throughout the world. It was unfortunate that the draft convention did not place sufficient emphasis on economic, social and cultural rights. Children were the first victims on the altar of the current international economic system. Of the 28 people who died each minute from hunger and malnutrition in the world, 21 were young children. The economic crisis had resulted in the deaths of half a million children in the Third World in 1988 alone. According to population projections, the total number of infant and child deaths would remain abnormally high in developing countries, particularly in Africa, throughout the rest of the century.

58.      The draft convention made no reference to children subjected to repressive and discriminatory laws. The report of the Special Committee against apartheid described the acts of brutality and violence suffered daily by South African children. The Special Committee to Investigate Israeli Practices affecting the Human Rights of the Population of the Occupied Territories likewise described the harassment and physical abuse to which Palestinian children were subjected. It had been amply demonstrated that children were all too often the first victims of such situations. The scope of the draft convention should have been broadened to provide special protection and care to all children, particularly the most vulnerable: those living under foreign or colonial occupation and the inhuman apartheid system and those who were being deprived of their basic rights by the unjust world economic system.

[...]

*The following is taken from document A/C.3/44/SR.42 (27 November 1989).*

1.      Mr. THAN (Myanmar) said that the typical Myanmar family consisted of three generations living under one roof - grandparents, parents and children - and the children received love from all the adults. Respect for the rights of the child was rooted in the nation's culture and tradition. Furthermore, the rights of the child were reinforced by the Children's Act and the 1974 Constitution. Children's welfare was provided for to the extent permitted by the resources of a developing country such as Myanmar. Primary education was free, and had been compulsory since the country had gained independence more than 40 years earlier; a nationwide literacy campaign among adults and children had been successful. Under the national health programme, no efforts were being spared to attain the objective of health for all by the year 2000. In 1986, Myanmar had received the Sasakawa Award from the World Health Organization for the successful implementation of its primary health care programme, which had decreased the child mortality rate and eradicated or substantially reduced, epidemic diseases.

2.      His delegation believed that the draft convention on the rights of the child would enable the world community to fulfil its moral obligation to protect the vulnerable and the powerless. The draft convention, which incorporated provisions of other existing legal instruments and supplemented them with new concepts and norms, had the full support of his country, and he hoped that it would be adopted by consensus.

3.      Mrs. SANTOS PAIS (Portugal), endorsing the comments made by the representative of France on behalf of the 12 States members of the European Community concerning the cluster of items under consideration, said she had a few points to make.

[...]

5.      The General Assembly should take a position on two new legal instruments: the draft second optional protocol to the International Covenant on Civil and Political Rights, aiming at the abolition of the death penalty, and the draft convention on the rights of the child.

[...]

7.      The draft convention approached the question of the rights of the child from two angles: the child's entitlement to fundamental rights and freedoms, and the child's need for special protection to foster the harmonious development of his or her personality. Certain provisions of the draft convention were not in keeping with the ideal promoted by her delegation, for example, the provision relating to the participation

of children in armed conflicts; her delegation hoped that the definition of the child in article 1 of the draft convention would prevail. At the same time, the instrument had very interesting aspects which should be preserved, particularly the role of the Committee on the Rights of the Child, which would be responsible for overseeing the implementation of the convention. Her delegation was in favour of the adoption of the draft convention.

[...]

9.        Mr. TANKOANO (Niger) [...]

[...]

14.        Regarding the rights of the child, he said that a cause of great concern for the Governments of developing countries, particularly those of Africa, was the effects of the economic crisis as reflected in the situation of children, despite the priority placed on their welfare. As part of the activities carried out in Africa to promote the adoption of the draft convention on the rights of the child, the Government of Senegal, in cooperation with UNICEF, had organized a seminar in late 1988 attended by representatives of the Economic Community of West African States (ECOWAS). The seminar had concluded that clear advances had been made in West Africa with regard to the protection of children, above all in the legal field. In March 1989 a pan-African symposium had been held in Bamako on the children of the continent. The participants, including artists and intellectuals, had focused on the question of community participation in health care and in various aspects of development. The interesting thing about that symposium was that it had attracted the attention of the heads of State of the Organization of African Unity (OAU), who had adopted several resolutions concerning the child. Several recommendations had been formulated at the Bamako symposium with a view to improving the situation of African children, whose health, education and development conditions had been particularly affected by the debt problem, economic recession, environmental degradation and armed conflict. The Secretary-General of OAU had reaffirmed its commitment to carry out a comprehensive study on a charter of the African child.

15.        In 1985, children under the age of five had accounted for 19.4 per cent of the population of the Niger. The Government, aware that children were particularly vulnerable during the first five years of life, had organized an immunization programme, which was being implemented through a system of health centres and mobile teams. In the Niger, persons under the age of 18 were considered children and enjoyed social protection. It was illegal to employ children younger than 12. Among the measures that the Government had adopted to protect children were the establishment of new maternal and child health centres, the expansion of the immunization programme, the efforts to enrol as many children as possible in school and to tailor education to the real needs of society, and the drafting of a family code which would give particular consideration to the rights of women and children. Referring to the draft convention on the rights of the child, he said that on 10 October 1989 the Minister of Foreign Affairs and Cooperation had reaffirmed to the General Assembly the strong support of the Niger for its adoption.

[...]

17.        Mr. MALAGA (Peru) referred to the imminent adoption of the draft convention on the rights of the child, and emphasized the importance of the UNICEF studies on the impact of the prolonged economic crisis in certain developing countries and the implementation of structural adjustment policies, which had imposed enormous restrictions on social welfare programmes for children. Unless primary health care programmes were greatly strengthened, by the year 2000 about 1 million children under the age of one would die in Peru. His Government was deeply concerned by the silent death of thousands of children in the Andean region, the cause of death being for the most part avoidable: malnutrition, disease, economic barriers which prevented them from completing primary school, exploitation in the workplace, and sexual abuse. On 22 May 1988, Peru had passed pioneering legislation for the protection of children, which defined as national priorities the reduction of the infant and maternal mortality rate, the increase in immunization levels and total health care, nutrition and early education. His Government also had made great efforts to achieve a minimum standard of care for urban children at risk. Those children were affected by the scourge of drug trafficking. At the

forty-third session of the General Assembly, Peru had introduced an initiative to sensitize the international community to the use of children by drug traffickers. Once again it urged all Member States to impose exemplary penalties on drug traffickers who involved children in their criminal activities.

18.      He praised UNICEF's work in Peru, and said that his country had actively participated in the meeting of the Andean Parliament held at Quito, Ecuador, from 27 February to 4 March 1989. Its agenda had given priority to the issue of the rights of the child. His delegation strongly supported draft resolution A/C.3/44/ L.45 regarding the financing of the Committee on the Rights of the Child from United Nations resources. The Peruvian legislature had organized a working group to expedite the procedure for prompt ratification of the convention on the rights of the child.

[...]

23.      Mr. KOZUBEK (Czechoslovakia) [...]

[...]

25.      On the subject of item 108, Czechoslovakia believed that international protection of the child was a major priority at the current time. The convention on the rights of the child had the great merit of applying universally recognized rights to children; the General Assembly should therefore adopt the draft convention by consensus at the current session. Moreover, the verification machinery should be financed from the regular budget.

[...]

32.      Ms. TUKAN (Jordan) [...]

33.      Jordan had participated with interest in the debate on the preparation of the draft convention on the rights of the child, which was a very important instrument. Children represented the most important population segment in society. Jordan therefore wholeheartedly supported the draft convention and urged Member States to adopt it by consensus.

[...]

36.      Ms. GEBRE-EGZIABHER (Ethiopia), referring to item 108, said that the promotion of the welfare of the child was one of her Government's priority objectives. Society's prosperity and progress depended on the proper upbringing of children. Ethiopia spared no effort to provide children with education and health care of the highest quality possible and to fulfil all their other needs. The draft convention on the rights of the child was a reaffirmation of the international community's firm commitment to ensure the well-being of the world's children. It guaranteed the fundamental rights of the child and would serve as a useful framework for Governments' activities for the benefit of children. Ethiopia therefore endorsed the draft convention and urged all countries to support its adoption.

[...]

39.      Mrs. QUISUMBING (Philippines) [...]

[...]

43.      Her delegation welcomed the submission to the General Assembly of a draft convention on the rights of the child. Because they had no political power, children needed special protection. They did not vote and were therefore totally dependent on their parents or guardians to protect their rights. The draft convention provided universally accepted standards for the protection of children and an invaluable framework for advocacy on behalf of children worldwide. Her delegation welcomed the fact that the preamble to the convention recognized that the child, by reason of his physical and mental immaturity, needed special safeguards and care, including appropriate legal protection, before as well as after birth. Nevertheless, the protection of the unborn child referred to in the preamble should have been elaborated further in the substantive articles, in particular article 6. In addition to the measures enumerated in paragraph 2 of article 32, concerning child labour, provision should have been made so that working children could

have access to health, nutrition and other basic social services. Her delegation believed that the Committee on the Rights of the Child should be financed from the regular budget of the United Nations. In view of the fundamental nature of the convention on the rights of the child, her country urged countries to adopt it by consensus.

44.     Mr. DLAMINI (Swaziland) pledged his delegation's support for the convention the rights of the child and recalled that, in his address to the General Assembly at its current session, the King of Swaziland had declared that full respect for human rights and the dignity of all citizens were fundamental to the goals of his people.

45.     It was not so long ago that children in the West had lived through the very difficult conditions of the Industrial Revolution. Today's children were subject to equally serious physical and emotional abuse by adult society. His delegation was confident that the adoption of the convention would usher in a new era of parent-child relationships and with it a new binding international jurisprudence on the rights of the child. There was no doubt that the common future of mankind depended as much on cooperation and international relations as it did on the well-being of children. The only proper and humane investment that a rational society could make was to spend much of society's wealth for the best interests of the child.

46.     His delegation acknowledged with regret that many countries, including Swaziland, lacked the means to live up to the ideals of the convention. That instrument described the rights of the child in a balanced and objective manner, avoiding elevation of the status of the child above that of its parents. His delegation also found nothing particularly objectionable in the articles of the convention.

47.     While the convention defined a child as a human being under the age of 18 years, some countries, such as his own, set the age of majority at 21 years. The convention should generate an active dialogue in favour of 18 years as the age of majority. He wished to emphasize, however, that accepting the age of 18 as the dividing line between childhood and adulthood should not prejudice the interests of the child in terms of whatever assistance parents and society might otherwise be willing to provide beyond that age. His delegation had no objections to article 1 and noted that the term "child" did not apply solely to "legitimate" children, as was the case in many common law systems.

48.     Care should be taken to ensure that the protection against punishment provided for under article 2 did not go so far as to undermine the very objective of the article; in other words, the child should not be allowed to hold and propagate the very opinions and beliefs that the article sought to proscribe.

49.     With respect to article 3, the concept of the "best interests of the child" was already present in many jurisdictions in the areas of child adoption and custody. However, not all children were the subject of individually determined adoption or custody. Furthermore, the concept was often misconstrued as being directed only at the court as the highest guardian of the child. Parents and other individuals concerned with the well-being of children did not immediately acknowledge that they too were equally obligated to take the child's best interests into account. The convention would contribute to the greater socialization and internalization of the concept so that it was not viewed purely as a judicial concept. That did not, of course, mean that societies must restructure themselves to make room for children, but that their attitude to children must undergo a profound change.

50.     Article 6 referred to the child's "inherent right to life". His delegation believed that it was not necessary for the convention to indicate exactly when life began. The adoption and enforcement of the convention were not necessarily or critically dependent on clear articulation of the point at which responsibility under the convention began. Article 24 could be invoked in support of that position.

51.     With respect to article 11, his delegation believed strongly that the illicit transfer of children should be considered a crime under international law which urgently required greater cooperation among States with a view to punishing offenders.

52.      In his delegation's view, article 12 should underscore the dignity and humanity of the child, who was entitled to a fair hearing not only in judicial and administrative proceedings affecting it but in all situations having a direct or indirect bearing on its well-being.

53.      With regard to article 13, some of the problems associated with youth could be attributed to the refusal of adult society to listen to children. Genuine effort should be made to seek out the positive aspects of youthful expression and channel it to useful ends. Healthy children were not usually wantonly destructive. As far as the rights of disabled children were concerned, many parents, particularly in developing countries, lacked the means to provide for the livelihood of disabled children. Where children traditionally had to go out early in life to provide for themselves and their families, the disabled child was a double burden, to himself and his family. Governments and humanitarian organizations must redouble their efforts to alleviate the plight of those children and their parents. Sending disabled children to institutions was not the best answer, however, even though it might provide the best technical supports for those children. In most cases the home or family environment was still the best to ensure the dignity and promote the self-reliance of the disabled child and facilitate his active participation in the community.

54.      He hoped that the criticisms made of the convention would not prevent its adoption and wide acceptance. Dissatisfaction with some parts of the convention should not deprive the child of the overall benefits likely to accrue from its acceptance. The benefits would still be real and effective, even where national laws already made adequate provision for the best interests of children in the various areas covered by the convention.

55.      His delegation was confident that the convention would go a long way towards achieving a sane society which could only be the product of a healthy generation of children. It was the totality of the rights under the convention, not a specific set of those rights, that would bring about the overall improvement of the situation of children and the quality of the child's personality everywhere.

56.      Mr. PAPPALARDO (Paraguay) welcomed the fact that the draft convention on the rights of the child took account of a number of aspects of life which had for years governed human actions and were for the first time included in an instrument on the rights of children. He particularly welcomed the decision that in all actions concerning legal, administrative or social welfare matters a primary consideration should be the best interests of the child. As far as the right to life was concerned, in Paraguay, where 80 per cent of the population were below 30 years of age, abortion was not permitted except in cases of extreme emergency, such as therapeutic abortion.

57.      Turning to article 38 of the draft convention, concerning the participation of children in armed conflicts, he recalled the battle of Acosta Nu of 16 August 1869, a very important battle in his country's history, in which almost 1,500 men and 3,500 children between the ages of 9 and 15 had been killed. Every year on 16 August, the Day of the Child, Paraguay commemorated those children who had died for their country. It would be overjoyed if children were no longer exposed to any kind of aggression, least of all armed conflict.

58.      He attached particular importance to the articles of the draft convention concerning sexual exploitation, abduction and torture, issues which were covered in Paraguay's Criminal Code and in the recently promulgated Children's Code. Paraguay had signed the Convention against Torture and Other Cruel, Inhuman or Degrading Treatment or Punishment on 23 October and had launched a national campaign to eradicate any elements of torture existing on Paraguayan soil. The judiciary had also admitted a number of requests for the punishment of torturers and their accomplices and accessories.

[...]

*The following is taken from document A/C.3/44/SR.43 (20 November 1989).*

1.      Mr. MAVROMMATIS (Cyprus) [...]

2.      His delegation fully supported the adoption of the draft convention on the rights of the child. While it was the result of compromise and did not necessarily reflect the views of every State, the convention was

nonetheless a remarkable achievement in that it affirmed the human rights of the child as an individual and not merely as a member of a family or larger grouping. In general, the draft convention constituted significant progress towards the overall improvement of the situation of children in both developing and developed countries.

[...]

7.      Mr. AGUILAR (Venezuela) [...]

[...]

10.      Venezuela had always attached great importance to protecting the rights of children. Although it had revised its laws governing the situation of minors, much remained to be done and the social impact of the country's foreign debt was making it more difficult to carry out measures in that field. Venezuela believed that an international instrument was needed that supplemented existing human rights norms and defined the rights of the child exclusively in terms of the child's best interests.

11.      Venezuela felt that the draft convention could have provided broader protection for the rights of children, and had particular difficulties with the provisions of article 21 (c) and (d), given the clear evidence of trafficking in children for adoption. He trusted that individual Governments would adopt additional measures to prevent such trafficking. Further protection should also have been provided by establishing at 18 years the minimum age for participation in armed conflicts. Nevertheless, his delegation fully supported the draft convention in the belief that, as a universal instrument, it would make an invaluable contribution to present and future generations. Once the convention was adopted, his Government would take immediate steps to ratify it.

[...]

13.      Mr. ALLAFI (Libyan Arab Jamahiriya) [...]

[...]

16.      On the occasion of the thirtieth anniversary of the Declaration of the Rights of the Child, his delegation believed that the most appropriate gift that could be made to the world's children would be the adoption of the draft convention on the rights of the child as a new instrument establishing international standards for the protection of children and providing a general framework for the promotion of programmes to improve their situation. As a participant in the sessions of the open-ended working group on a draft convention on the rights of the child, his delegation had already had the opportunity to voice its comments. Although, in its present form, the draft convention was not all that his country might desire, the Libyan Arab Jamahiriya was nevertheless pleased that it had ultimately been possible to achieve an agreed text. It was convinced of the need for the adoption of such a convention and, in the drafting of any international instrument, it was not possible to achieve perfection in the light of the multiplicity and diversity of the concerns of States. His delegation wished to reaffirm its commitment to the Tunis Declaration adopted by the representatives of the States members of the Arab Maghreb Union in June 1989, as well as to the resolution adopted by the Council of the League of Arab States in the same connection.

[...]

*The following is taken from document A/C.3/44/SR.44 (4 December 1989).*

*Action on draft decision A/C.3/44/L.45 and programme budget implications in document A/C.3/44/L.47*

50.      The CHAIRMAN [Mr. KABORE (Burkina Faso)] invited the Committee to resume consideration of agenda item 108 and drew its attention to draft decision A/C.3/44/L.45, introduced by the representative of Poland at the thirty-ninth meeting, and the corresponding statement of programme budget implications (A/C.3/44/L.47).

51.      Mr. BOLTON (United States of America) requested a recorded vote on the draft decision.

52.      *Draft decision A/C.3/44/L.45 was adopted by 137 votes to 1, with 1 abstention.*

53. Mr. BOLTON (United States of America), speaking in explanation of vote after the vote, said that his delegation had voted against the decision to fund the Committee on the Rights of the Child from the regular budget of the United Nations. The United States had made it clear many times that it believed that only States parties to the convention on the rights of the child should bear the costs of the Committee. Since the convention would enter into force with only 20 ratifications, the decision of the Third Committee would require 139 Member States to share the costs of a Committee with which they had no involvement. Moreover, there was a recent precedent, that of the Convention against Torture and other Cruel, Inhuman or Degrading Treatment or Punishment, where only the States parties were sharing the cost of the corresponding Committee. Although those States parties had not paid the entirety of their assessments to that Committee, that was to be explained by the budgetary priorities of certain countries and did not require the United Nations to take on the financing of future treaty bodies. Despite its position on the question of financing, his country favoured the substantive provisions of the convention on the rights of the child, and hoped that the Committee and the General Assembly would adopt it without change and without a vote.

54. Mr. ITO (Japan) said that his delegation had abstained in the vote on draft decision A/C.3/44/L.45 because, as a matter of principle, an intergovernmental body to be established after the entry into force of an international agreement from which it derived should be financed by the States parties to that agreement. His delegation feared that the decision just taken would set a precedent and believed that it was not the proper means to achieve the real objectives of an international agreement. It also felt that the decision had not taken into account the current budgetary constraints of the United Nations or the efforts being made to increase the efficiency of the Organization's activities. However, Japan wished to reiterate its support for the basic objective of the convention, which was to promote and ensure the full protection of the rights of the child.

*Introduction of and action on draft resolution A/C.3/44/L.44*

55. The CHAIRMAN [Mr. KABORE (Burkina Faso)] invited the Committee to consider draft resolution A/C.3/44/L.44 on the adoption of a convention on the rights of child and explained that article 43 (11) and (12) of the draft convention in the annex to the draft resolution contained the texts that the Committee had adopted in decision A/C.3/44/L.45*. He wished, therefore, to inform the Committee that the statement of programme budget implications submitted by the Secretary-General in connection with draft decision A/C.3/44/L.45* applied also to draft resolution A/C.3/44/L.44.

56. Mr. LOPATKA (Poland) introduced draft resolution A/C.3/44/L.44 on behalf of the sponsors listed in that document as well as Bangladesh, the Congo, Cuba, Denmark, the Dominican Republic, Iceland, the Libyan Arab Jamahiriya, Mali, Mauritania, Nigeria, Pakistan, Samoa, Sri Lanka, Sweden, Suriname and Uruguay, which were later joined by Cameroon, Chile, Guinea-Bissau and Honduras. He commended the United Nations efforts to promote the rights of children and recalled in particular the adoption of the Declaration of the Rights of the Child in 1959, the proclamation of the International Year of the Child in 1979 and the initiation in 1978 of the negotiations on a convention on the rights of the child.

57. The convention, if adopted, would be a significant step forward in setting human rights standards for children and would constitute the most comprehensive instrument on the question, filling in many gaps in current legislation. The draft resolution called upon all Member States to consider signing and ratifying the convention as a matter of priority and expressed the hope that it would come into force at an early date. It expressed appreciation to the Commission on Human Rights for having concluded the elaboration of a draft convention on the rights the child, and invited the Secretary-General, United Nations agencies and organizations, and intergovernmental and non-governmental organizations to disseminate information on the convention and promote its understanding. He hoped that the draft resolution would be adopted by consensus.

58. Mr. ENGFELDT (Sweden) said that the importance his Government attached to the draft convention and its conviction that the international community had to do its utmost to protect children, especially in

armed conflicts, had been brought out in the statement of the Nordic countries. Furthermore, his Government intended to continue its efforts to improve current standards with regard to the protection of children in armed conflicts and to support United Nations activities in the field. He underscored the contributions that non-governmental organizations had made and reiterated his Government's support for the adoption of the draft resolution.

59.    Mr. CABRAL (Guinea-Bissau) said that he wished to join the sponsors of the draft resolution.

60.    Mr. COVARRUBIAS (Chile) observed that the principle enunciated in the ninth preambular paragraph of the draft convention was crucial for the preservation of life. With reference to article 1, his country believed that the child came into being at the very moment of conception and that fertilization marked the beginning of the development of the individual. His delegation would have preferred, in article 8, an explicit reference to paternity, not so much in factual terms but as a value which the international community must make every effort to realize. Furthermore, concurring with the Chilean Church authorities, his Government believed that, throughout, the draft convention did not sufficiently emphasize the family as natural mediator between the child and the State. Nevertheless, his delegation expressed its firm support for the draft convention.

61.    Mr. PALMA (Honduras) thanked the delegations which had elaborated the draft convention and said that he was joining the sponsors.

62.    The CHAIRMAN [Mr. KABORE (Burkina Faso)] said that, if he heard no objection, he would take it that the Committee wished to adopt the draft resolution without a vote.

63.    *It was so decided.*

64.    Miss FUNDAFUNDA (Zambia), speaking in explanation of position on behalf of front-line States, stressed the importance which they attached to the plight of black children under the apartheid system, which had deteriorated since the imposition of the state of emergency in 1986. The convention would be enriched by the inclusion of specific provisions reflecting the situation of children under the system of apartheid and would then become more relevant for a greater part of the international community.

65.    Mr. van WULFFTEN PALTHE (Netherlands), said that his delegation, which was aware of the importance of the convention on the rights of the child, had not wished to break the consensus in favour of its adoption. The process of elaborating the convention had been far from easy and had required more than 10 years of work. It had been necessary to adopt many solutions based on compromise in order to make the convention acceptable to all, and in that spirit of compromise the Netherlands had been actively involved in the work of preparing the convention.

66.    One article of the convention established a norm which was particularly open to question. Article 38, which stipulated the rights of the child in relation to armed conflicts, should not have been worded in such a way as to permit participation by children between the ages of 15 and 17 years in hostilities. The new convention should have protected children with regard to participation in hostilities at least up to the age of 18 years. States should not be allowed to involve children, directly or indirectly, in armed conflicts. Unfortunately, that prohibition, which was laid down in additional Protocol II to the Geneva Conventions of 1949, had not been incorporated in the new convention. Neither had it been possible to raise the minimum age for recruiting children into the armed forces. The Netherlands, together with other countries, had made proposals to modify those two points which, unfortunately, had not been adopted.

67.    Mr. WHITAKER SALLES (Brazil) said that his delegation had supported draft resolution A/C.3/44/L.44 containing the convention on the rights of the child. Its adoption was the culmination of the efforts by many countries and organizations that had worked hard in order to make that possible.

68.    The solution provided in article 43 of the convention to the problem of financing the Committee on the Rights of the Child was very positive. The text of the convention was not and could not be perfect since it had been necessary to find compromise solutions to a number of problems created by cultural, political and other differences between countries. It seemed that there were discrepancies between a number of

articles in the convention. For example, the definition of a child in article 1 differed from the definition that was inferred from the contents of article 38, according to which children below the age of 18 years could take part in armed conflicts. Article 13 allowed unjustified interference by the State in questions which should be solely the responsibility of the family, as was set forth in article 5. Article 37 seemed to give the impression that the torture of adults was not as condemnable as that of children. Lastly, article 30, on children belonging to minorities, could be interpreted as being incompatible with the provisions of the Constitution of Brazil. In view of those considerations, his Government reserved its position on a number of norms in the convention, which it had to consider further before signing that instrument.

69.     Ms. MIGNOTT (Jamaica) said that her delegation had joined the consensus which had led to the adoption of the important convention on the rights of the child. She wished, however, to take that opportunity to comment on a particular provision of the convention. Article 1 defined the child as a human being below the age of 18 years, although it provided for the possibility of exceptions to that general rule. It appeared that an armed conflict was one such exception since article 38 provided that States parties should take all feasible measures to ensure that persons who had not attained the age of 15 years did not take a direct part in hostilities. That article implied that the obligation did not apply to persons over the age of 15 years. The article also provided that States parties should refrain from recruiting any person who had not attained the age of 15 years into their armed forces. It seemed that the general provision in article 1 did not apply there either.

70.     Her delegation recognized that article 38 of the convention reflected, broadly speaking, the provisions of article 77 (2) of the 1977 Additional Protocol I to the Geneva Conventions of 1949 and that some 90 countries were parties to that Protocol. However, there were situations where one should be guided more by considerations of principle than precedent. The case in question should have been one such occasion. The age at which children could be recruited into the armed forces or sent into combat should be the age of attainment of majority, namely 18 years. The relevant provisions of Additional Protocol I to the Geneva Conventions of 1949 should therefore be amended. Since the Third Committee was not competent to undertake that initiative, her delegation urged the States parties to the Protocol to amend it in that way in order to facilitate the subsequent similar amendment of the convention.

71.     Ms. ALHAMANI (Yemen) said that article 14 of the convention, which provided, inter alia, that States parties should respect the right of the child to freedom of thought, conscience and religion, and under which children would have the right to change their religion, was contrary to Islamic law, which did not permit Muslims to change their religion. Under the laws of Yemen, a Muslim child must retain his or her Muslim religion. For that reason, Yemen reserved its position on the article in question.

72.     Mrs. WARZAZI (Morocco) said that the adoption of the convention on the rights of the child was cause for particular joy for her, as a representative of Morocco, and for the representative of Costa Rica since they had both participated in 1959 in the elaboration of the Declaration on the Rights of the Child.

73.     Mr. ZIADA (Iraq) said that his delegation would have preferred the convention on the rights of the child to deal with the situation of children under occupation and the resulting economic consequences. Furthermore, his delegation had reservations about article 14 (1) of the convention, since freedom of religion was incompatible with Islamic law and Iraqi legislation.

74.     Ms. TUKAN (Jordan) said that her delegation interpreted the provisions of article 14 of the convention to mean that the child had the freedom to practise his or her religion, not to change it. Jordan interpreted articles 20 and 21 to mean that their provisions were not binding on States which, like Jordan, in accordance with Islamic law did not approve of adoption of children. If the provisions of those three articles were interpreted otherwise, the delegation of Jordan expressed its reservations.

75.     Mr. ITO (Japan) expressed his delegation's views on some of the articles. Article 7 (2) did not require States to give their nationality to any persons who were born or had become stateless in their territory. With regard to articles 9 and 10, he pointed out that the right of the child to maintain personal relations and

direct contact with parents on a regular basis could not always be guaranteed in cases where the child was separated from one or both parents; it was also his delegation's understanding that article 10 did not affect in any way the sovereign right of States to enact their respective immigration laws in accordance with their international agreements and that the expression "their own country" in article 10 (2) referred to the country of which the child or his or her parents were nationals. Furthermore, the provision in article 37 (c) concerning the separation from adults of every child deprived of liberty should be as flexible as possible so as to take into account the specific circumstances in different countries. Furthermore, the provision in article 37 (d) did not oblige the State to assign a defence counsel for a child who was under detention by court order. Referring to the various subparagraphs of article 40 (2), his delegation felt that subparagraph (b) referred to every child deprived of his or her liberty. Subparagraph 2 (b) (ii) referred to article 37 (d). The expression "a fair hearing" in subparagraph 2 (b) (iii) did not necessarily imply a public hearing and did not require the provision of legal assistance. The provision in subparagraph 2 (b) (iv) applied in Japan only to criminal proceedings. Lastly, subparagraph 2 (b) (vi) did not prevent the accused from having to assume the costs of the trial when found guilty.

76.     Mr. BARNEA (Israel) said that, although his delegation had joined the consensus on the convention, it would have to give in-depth consideration to all the details of the instrument before deciding whether to sign and ratify it.

*The following is taken from document A/C.3/44/SR.45 (1 December 1989).*

1.     The CHAIRMAN [Mr. KABORE (Burkina Faso)] recalled that at the 44th meeting the day before, the Committee had, at the request of the United States representative, held a recorded vote on draft decision A/C.3/44/L.45. He had just been informed that, for technical reasons, the electronic system had not duly recorded the results of that vote. The Secretariat regretted that technical incident, completely beyond its control, which prevented it from giving a detailed tally of the results in its report to the General Assembly. The Chairman suggested that the vote on draft decision A/C.3/44/L.45 should, if there were no objections, be considered a non-recorded vote and the results of the vote given in the summary record of the 44th meeting should be approved.

2.     *It was so decided.*

## 12.   Discussion in General Assembly Plenary Session on 20 November 1989

*The following is taken from document A/44/PV.61 (28 November 1989).*

The PRESIDENT [Mr. GARBA (Nigeria)]: I call upon the Rapporteur of the Third Committee, Mr. Wilfried Grolig of the Federal Republic of Germany, to introduce the report of the Third Committee.

Mr. GROLIG (Federal Republic of Germany), Rapporteur of the Third Committee: I have the honour to present the report of the Third Committee on agenda item 108, entitled "Adoption of a convention on the rights of the child", allocated to the Third Committee for consideration by the General Assembly.

I should like to draw attention to paragraph 12 of the report for a technical remark. In that paragraph Zimbabwe should be included among those countries on whose behalf the delegation of Zambia gave an explanation of vote.

The Third Committee recommends the adoption of the draft resolution in paragraph 13 of its report.

The PRESIDENT: If there is no proposal under rule 66 of the rules of procedure, I shall take it that the General Assembly decides not to discuss the report of the Third Committee now before the Assembly.

*It was so decided.*

The PRESIDENT [Mr. GARBA (Nigeria)]: Statements will therefore be limited to explanations of vote.

The positions of delegations regarding the various recommendations of the Third Committee have been made clear in the Committee and are reflected in the relevant official records.

[...]

May I remind members that, under paragraph 7 of decision 34/401, the General Assembly agreed that

> "When the same draft resolution is considered in a Main Committee and in plenary meeting, a delegation should, as far as possible, explain its vote only once, i.e., either in the Committee or in plenary meeting unless that delegation's vote in plenary meeting is different from its vote in the Committee."

The Assembly will now take a decision on the draft resolution recommended by the Third Committee in paragraph 13 of its report (A/44/736). The report of the Fifth Committee on the programme budget implications of this draft resolution is contained in document A/44/743.

The Third Committee adopted the draft resolution without a vote. May I take it that the Assembly wishes to do the same?

*The draft resolution was adopted* (resolution 44/25).

The PRESIDENT [Mr. GARBA (Nigeria)]: Before calling on members to explain their position, may I remind delegations that in accordance with General Assembly decision 34/401 such explanations are limited to 10 minutes and should be made by delegations from their seats.

Mr. ABOUL HASSANI (Islamic Republic of Iran): Although my delegation attaches great importance to the Convention on the Rights of the Child, I should like to place on record our reservation on any article that would contradict Islamic beliefs and values.

Mr. AL-MUKHAINI (Oman) (interpretation from Arabic): In spite of the fact that my country endorsed the Convention we have some reservations, which we shall announce later.

Mr. HAMADNEH (Jordan) (interpretation from Arabic): We are pleased at the adoption by consensus of the Convention on the Rights of the Child, and we extend our thanks and appreciation to the Commission on Human Rights and to the working group for the efforts made over 10 years to prepare the draft convention.

We should like to place on record our interpretation of three of the articles of the Convention.

First, our understanding of article 14, particularly where it deals with the right of the child to freedom of religion, is that it means that the child has the right to practise his religion, not to choose the religion or the belief. If the intention of the article is in contradiction with our understanding we would like our reservations to be placed on record.

Secondly, our understanding of the provisions of articles 20 and 21 is that they are not mandatory for countries that do not legalize the system of adoption *tabanni*. Therefore, my country, whose system legalizes only the system of bond - *kafalah* - in consonance with the Islamic sharia, does not feel obliged to act in conformity with the adoption provisions with regard to our children, whether inside or outside the country. If the intention of these two articles is in contradiction with this understanding, we should like to record our reservations.

Mr. DJOUDI (Algeria) (interpretation from French): My delegation is delighted at the adoption of the Convention on the Rights of the Child on this very symbolic day, which is the thirtieth anniversary of the Declaration of the Rights of the Child and the tenth anniversary of the International Year of the Child. However, my delegation wishes to make an interpretative statement about some of its provisions to explain why it went along with the consensus adoption of the Convention.

With regard to the fifth paragraph of the preamble, which refers to the concept of the family, we interpret this in the light of the definition of the family as established in our code on the family, article 2 of which provides as follows:

> "The family is the basis cell of society and is composed of persons united by ties of marriage and kinship."

With regard to article 1 of the Convention, which relates to the age of a child, my delegation interprets this provision in accordance with paragraph 2 of article 40 of the Algerian civil code, which fixes the age of majority at 19 years.

We interpret paragraph 1 of article 14 in accordance with article 2 of the Algerian Constitution, which provides that Islam is the State religion, and article 35 of that text, which states that freedom of conscience and opinion are inviolable.

Regarding article 20, on the protection of a child temporarily or permanently deprived of his or her environment, my delegation interprets this provision in conformity with our national legislation, in particular article 62 of the family code, which states:

> "Custody" - *hadana* - "consists in the care, schooling and education of the child in the religion of the father and the safeguarding of his or her physical and moral well-being, and the guardian must fulfil this responsibility."

As regards article 21, which deals with adoption, we have to state that Algeria is not bound by this provision, since article 46 of the Algerian family code states:

> "Adoption" - *tabanni* - "is forbidden by the sharia and the law."

The protection and care of the child until majority is guaranteed within the framework of the application of the *kafalah* in Islamic law.

Mr. URIARTE (Chile) (interpretation from Spanish): Last week in the Third Committee we adopted by consensus the Convention on the Rights of the Child, at which time the alternate Permanent Representative of my country made a long statement in explanation of vote and said that we would, of course, sign the Convention. We requested that the explanation of vote be made part of the record.

The PRESIDENT [Mr. GARBA (Nigeria)]: I call on the Secretary-General.

The SECRETARY-GENERAL [Mr. PEREZ DE CUELLAR]: Today our Organization has taken a most important step towards the realization of our common purpose of promoting and encouraging respect for human rights and fundamental freedoms for all, without distinction as to race, sex, language or religion. Thirty years after the adoption of the Declaration of the Rights of the Child the United Nations has given the global community an international instrument of high quality that protects the dignity, equality and basic human rights of the world's children.

This achievement, of which we can be justly proud, rests on more than 10 years of hard effort by the Working Group of the Commission on Human Rights, by Governments and non-governmental organizations, and by specialized agencies and the United Nations Children's Fund (UNICEF). The drafting of the Convention was no easy task. In the years since the Declaration of the Rights of the Child was adopted many perceptions have changed and many concepts have evolved, and the Convention had to be shaped accordingly. The process of its drafting was a model of how our Organization can and should strive to achieve common goals. Unproductive political confrontations were set aside while delegates from countries with different social and economic systems representing the various cultural, ethical and religious approaches to life worked together with non-governmental organizations in a spirit of harmony and mutual respect and with the best interests of the child as their paramount objective. I should like to pay a special tribute to the Government of Poland, which first proposed the drafting of the Convention, and to the Chairman of the Working Group, Professor Adam Lopatka.

The Convention the Assembly has just adopted constitutes an instrument of far-reaching significance, as visionary as it is timely. First, it addresses the needs of those who are humanity's more vulnerable, as well as its most cherished resource. It is axiomatic that they should be afforded special attention. Secondly, it calls for the development of children through access to information, education, play, leisure and cultural activities, and the right to freedom of thought, conscience and religion. And, thirdly, it seeks to ensure the entire spectrum of the rights of the child and the direct involvement of children in the exercise of their rights, while recognizing the equal worth of the diverse cultural values of the human community.

One of the cardinal lessons of the Convention is that the child is not alone. The Convention recognizes the primary role of the family and parents in the care and protection of children, as well as the need for special protection of those who are without families or separated from them. But it also recognizes the role, when necessary, of the community and the State and the crucial contribution that international cooperation and international organizations can make in bringing about conditions in which each child can fully and harmoniously develop his or her personality. Above all, the Convention attempts to provide a framework within which the child, in the light of his or her evolving capacities, can make the difficult transition from infancy to adulthood. It also acknowledges that children are particularly vulnerable to certain kinds of exploitation. In a series of important articles it seeks to protect the child from attacks so prejudicial to his or her welfare as child labour, drug abuse, sexual exploitation and sale, trafficking, and abduction.

The need to furnish the world's children with a means of assuring their fundamental rights is felt with increasing urgency every day. At this meeting the Assembly has taken the first, seminal step. The adoption of the Convention places on the international community, and especially the United Nations, the heavy burden of helping States to implement the promise of the Convention. I wish today to call for States from all regions to ratify the Convention, so that support for the Convention itself and for the committee to be elected by States parties will reflect the wide economic, social and cultural diversity of our membership.

I wish to assure the Assembly of the Secretariat's full commitment to assisting in the implementation of the Convention to the maximum extent allowed by the resources available. I also wish to inform members that during the month of January 1990 there will be a ceremony at which States will be able to sign the text of the Convention.

I congratulate members and urge that we move on to make of the Convention's principles a living reality for each and every child on Earth. In so doing, we shall not only secure the rights of coming generations; we shall also strengthen the foundations of justice, peace and freedom in the world of the future.

The PRESIDENT [Mr. GARBA (Nigeria)]: Thirty years ago today the General Assembly adopted the Declaration of the Rights of the Child, which in its preamble affirmed that "mankind owes to the child the best it has to give" (resolution 386 (XIV)). The 10 principles laid down in that Declaration have served as guideposts and objectives for the work of our Organization since then in promoting and protecting the rights of children throughout the world.

Today, with the adoption of the Convention on the Rights of the Child, the Assembly has taken a new and decisive step along the road towards ensuring respect for the dignity and rights of the child; for the rights of the child have now gone from a declaratory statement of purpose into what will become a binding piece of international legislation.

The Convention is an important achievement by the United Nations and shows the positive and constructive results which international cooperation can yield. It protects a wide range of basic human rights, deals with situations of special concern to children, such as reunification with parents, adoption and foster care and protects the child from such abuses as exploitation for child labour, sexual purposes and sale, trafficking and abduction and all other forms of exploitation prejudicial to the child's welfare.

The Convention we have adopted here today is the result of 10 years of dedicated effort, and I wish to express my profound thanks to all who have contributed to this success - Government representatives, those of specialized agencies and the United Nations Children's Fund and the non-governmental organizations.

The task before us now is to give reality to the promises of the Convention by bringing it into force and applying it worldwide. In this way we can respond and give effect to the statement of the Declaration that mankind owes the child the best it has to give.

We have now concluded our consideration of agenda item 108.

## 13.　General Assembly resolution 44/25 on the "Convention on the Rights of the Child" adopted on 20 November 1989

*The General Assembly,*

*Recalling* its previous resolutions, especially resolutions 33/166 of 20 December 1978 and 43/112 of 8 December 1988, and those of the Commission on Human Rights and the Economic and Social Council related to the question of a convention on the rights of the child,

*Taking note,* in particular, of Commission on Human Rights resolution 1989/57 of 8 March 1989, by which the Commission decided to transmit the draft convention on the rights of the child, through the Economic and Social Council, to the General Assembly, and Economic and Social Council resolution 1989/79 of 24 May 1989,

*Reaffirming* that children's rights require special protection and call for continuous improvement of the situation of children all over the world, as well as for their development and education in conditions of peace and security,

*Profoundly concerned* that the situation of children in many parts of the world remains critical as a result of inadequate social conditions, natural disasters, armed conflicts, exploitation, illiteracy, hunger and disability, and convinced that urgent and effective national and international action is called for,

*Mindful* of the important role of the United Nations Children's Fund and of that of the United Nations in promoting the well-being of children and their development,

*Convinced* that an international convention on the rights of the child, as a standard-setting accomplishment of the United Nations in the field of human rights, would make a positive contribution to protecting children's rights and ensuring their well-being,

*Bearing in mind* that 1989 marks the thirtieth anniversary of the Declaration of the Rights of the Child and the tenth anniversary of the International Year of the Child,

1.　*Expresses its appreciation* to the Commission on Human Rights for having concluded the elaboration of the draft convention on the rights of the child;

2.　*Adopts* and opens for signature, ratification and accession the Convention on the Rights of the Child contained in the annex to the present resolution;

3.　*Calls* upon all Member States to consider signing and ratifying or acceding to the Convention as a matter of priority and expresses the hope that it will come into force at an early date;

4.　*Requests* the Secretary-General to provide all the facilities and assistance necessary for dissemination of information on the Convention;

5.　*Invites* United Nations agencies and organizations, as well as intergovernmental and non-governmental organizations, to intensify their efforts with a view to disseminating information on the Convention and to promoting its understanding;

6.　*Requests* the Secretary-General to submit to the General Assembly at its forty-fifth session a report on the status of the Convention on the Rights of the Child;

7.　*Decides* to consider the report of the Secretary-General at its forty-fifth session under an item entitled "Implementation of the Convention on the Rights of the Child".

[For the final version of the Convention, see annex I]

*61st plenary meeting*
*20 November 1989*

# The Convention
## Title, Preamble and Articles

# Title and Preamble

## A.  Final text adopted by the General Assembly (1989)

*The following text is that approved by the General Assembly in its resolution 44/25 of 20 November 1989.*

Convention on the Rights of the Child

PREAMBLE

*The States Parties to the present Convention,*

*Considering* that, in accordance with the principles proclaimed in the Charter of the United Nations, recognition of the inherent dignity and of the equal and inalienable rights of all members of the human family is the foundation of freedom, justice and peace in the world,

*Bearing in mind* that the peoples of the United Nations have, in the Charter, reaffirmed their faith in fundamental human rights and in the dignity and worth of the human person, and have determined to promote social progress and better standards of life in larger freedom,

*Recognizing* that the United Nations has, in the Universal Declaration of Human Rights and in the International Covenants on Human Rights, proclaimed and agreed that everyone is entitled to all the rights and freedoms set forth therein, without distinction of any kind, such as race, colour, sex, language, religion, political or other opinion, national or social origin, property, birth or other status,

*Recalling* that, in the Universal Declaration of Human Rights, the United Nations has proclaimed that childhood is entitled to special care and assistance,

*Convinced* that the family, as the fundamental group of society and the natural environment for the growth and well-being of all its members and particularly children, should be afforded the necessary protection and assistance so that it can fully assume its responsibilities within the community,

*Recognizing* that the child, for the full and harmonious development of his or her personality, should grow up in a family environment, in an atmosphere of happiness, love and understanding,

*Considering* that the child should be fully prepared to live an individual life in society, and brought up in the spirit of the ideals proclaimed in the Charter of the United Nations, and in particular in the spirit of peace, dignity, tolerance, freedom, equality and solidarity,

*Bearing in mind* that the need to extend particular care to the child has been stated in the Geneva Declaration of the Rights of the Child of 1924 and in the Declaration of the Rights of the Child adopted by the General Assembly on 20 November 1959 and recognized in the Universal Declaration of Human Rights, in the International Covenant on Civil and Political Rights (in particular in articles 23 and 24), in the International Covenant on Economic, Social and Cultural Rights (in particular in article 10) and in the statutes and relevant instruments of specialized agencies and international organizations concerned with the welfare of children,

*Bearing in mind* that, as indicated in the Declaration of the Rights of the Child, "the child, by reason of his physical and mental immaturity, needs special safeguards and care, including appropriate legal protection, before as well as after birth",

*Recalling* the provisions of the Declaration on Social and Legal Principles relating to the Protection and Welfare of Children, with Special Reference to Foster Placement and Adoption Nationally and Internationally; the United Nations Standard Minimum Rules for the Administration of Juvenile Justice (The Beijing Rules); and the Declaration on the Protection of Women and Children in Emergency and Armed Conflict,

*Recognizing* that, in all countries in the world, there are children living in exceptionally difficult conditions, and that such children need special consideration,

*Taking due account* of the importance of the traditions and cultural values of each people for the protection and harmonious development of the child,

*Recognizing* the importance of international cooperation for improving the living conditions of children in every country, in particular in the developing countries,

*Have agreed* as follows:

## B.    First Polish draft convention and comments (1978)

*In a letter dated 17 January 1978 addressed to the Director of the Division of Human Rights (see E/CN.4/1284), the Permanent Representative of Poland to the United Nations Office at Geneva proposed that "The question of the convention on the rights of the child" be included in the agenda of the thirty-fourth session of the Commission on Human Rights. At that session, the Polish delegation submitted a draft resolution (E/CN.4/L.1366) which contained a draft convention based on the provisions of the 1959 Declaration of the Rights of the Child. The resolution was subsequently revised (E/CN.4/L.1366/Rev.1) and two additional articles (XI and XII) were added to the draft convention annexed to the final version of the draft resolution (E/CN.4/L.1366/Rev.2) which was then adopted by the Commission on Human Rights (see E/CN.4/1292, pp. 122 to 127) as resolution 20 (XXXIV) of 8 March 1978.*

### 1.    The first Polish draft

*The following text is taken from the 1978 report of the Commission on Human Rights (E/CN.4/1292, p. 123).*

DRAFT CONVENTION ON THE RIGHTS OF THE CHILD

*The States Parties to the present Convention,*

*Bearing in mind* that the peoples of the United Nations have, in the Charter, reaffirmed their faith in fundamental human rights and in the dignity and worth of the human person, and have determined to promote social progress and better standards of life in larger freedom,

*Recognizing* that the United Nations have, in the Universal Declaration of Human Rights and in the International Covenants on Human Rights, proclaimed and agreed that everyone is entitled to all the rights and freedoms set forth therein, without distinction of any kind, such as race, colour, sex, language, religion, political or other opinion, national or social origin, property, birth of other status,

*Recognizing also* that the child, by reason of his physical and mental immaturity, needs special safeguards and care, including appropriate legal protection, before as well as after birth,

*Having in mind* that the need for such special safeguards has been stated in the Geneva Declaration of the Rights of the Child of 1924 and in the United Nations Declaration of the Rights of the Child of 1959 and recognized in the Universal Declaration of Human Rights, in the International Covenant on Civil and Political Rights (in particular in its articles 23 and 24), in the International Covenant on Economic, Social and Cultural Rights (in particular in its article 10) and in the statutes of specialized agencies and international organizations concerned with the welfare of children,

*Proclaiming* that mankind owes to the child the best it has to give,

*Have agreed as follows:*

### 2.    Comments on the first Polish draft

*The Secretary-General was requested in Commission on Human Rights resolution 20 (XXXIV) of 8 March 1978 to invite Member States, competent specialized agencies, regional intergovernmental organizations and non-governmental*

*organizations to communicate to him their views, observations and suggestions concerning the draft convention submitted by Poland. The views received are contained in documents E/CN.4/1324 and Corr.1 and Add.1-5. The following comments relate to the preamble.*

## (a)      Bulgaria

*The following is taken from document E/CN.4/1324/Add.1.*

> The preamble should point out that it is necessary to adopt a convention on the rights of the child because in many countries the principles embodied in the Declaration of the Rights of the Child are still not being implemented (child labour practices, which are injurious to the health of children and prevent their proper development, still persist; infant mortality is high; normal conditions in which all children can be cared for and given education, medical services and so forth, have not yet been created).

## (b)      Federal Republic of Germany

*The following is taken from document E/CN.4/1324.*

> See paragraph 7, Federal Republic of Germany, under General Comments.

*The paragraph cited, which appears elsewhere in document E/CN.4/1324, is as follows:*

> 7.        Conversely, the provisions of the draft relating to the objectives, content and methods of education cannot be considered as either rights of the individual or undertakings on the part of States. The provisions in question are contained in the first sentence of article VI, the first part of article VII, paragraph 2, and the second sentence of article 10 of the draft. It is the responsibility and duty of the parents whose rights are also recognized in the draft to take binding decisions in this regard. The provisions referred to can more appropriately be made the subject of a recommendation to be incorporated in the preamble to the convention.

## (c)      Norway

*The following general comments on the draft convention, including its title, are taken from document E/CN.4/1324.*

> [...]

> 2.        In the opinion of the Norwegian authorities, the interests of children would best be served if seen in conjunction with the interests of adults. Today the interests of children are very often overlooked in the decision-making process. Therefore, a convention on the subject of the rights of children should deal with children as a group. This aspect ought to be emphasized by using the noun "child" in its plural form throughout the convention. By the use of "children" and, consequently, "they", "them" and "their", the terms "he", "whom" and "his" could be avoided, and the equal status of the two sexes would appear more clearly.

> 3.        On this basis, the following amendments to the draft convention are suggested:

> Throughout the draft convention, substitute "children" for "the child", "they" for "he", "them" for "him", and "their" for "his".

> [...]

*The following specific comments are also taken from document E/CN.4/1324.*

> Add as *3rd and 4th preambular paragraphs*:

>> "Recognizing also that the best interest of children shall be the guiding principle for those responsible for the upbringing, education and development of children.

>> Recognizing also that family and society share the responsibility for children."

**(d)      Sweden**

*The following is taken from document E/CN.4/1324.*

See paragraph 7, Sweden, under General Comments.

*The paragraph cited, which appears elsewhere in document E/CN.4/1324, is as follows:*

7.          Finally, it is essential that a new convention on the rights of the child should be brought into line with other existing international agreements, in particular the two International Covenants on Human Rights, and with certain new instruments now being prepared, for instance the Convention on the Elimination of Discrimination against Women. It may prove useful also to record in the preamble to the convention or in a separate resolution certain new objectives or guidelines which are difficult to express as obligations in the operative part of the convention but which should be pursued by States in their long-term policies for the protection of children and the safeguarding of their rights.

**(e)      United Nations Educational, Scientific and Cultural Organization (UNESCO)**

*The following is taken from document E/CN.4/1324.*

The draft preamble should, at the very least, contain a reference to the three standard-setting UNESCO instruments mentioned above (see paragraph 1, United Nations Educational, Scientific and Cultural Organization, under General Comments).

*The paragraph cited, which appears elsewhere in document E/CN.4/1324, is as follows:*

1.          The draft text as proposed by the United Nations does not appear to accord sufficient importance to the right of the child to cultural development by acknowledging, inter alia, broader rights to education and cultural identity. In our view, this draft should:

(i)    Mention, in particular, the right to be different as defined in article 1, paragraph 2, of the draft declaration on race and racial prejudice to be submitted to the General Conference at its twentieth session;

(ii)   Be based more closely on the following three standard-setting instruments adopted under the auspices of UNESCO:

The Convention against Discrimination in Education,

The Recommendation concerning Education for International Understanding, Cooperation and Peace and Education relating to Human Rights and Fundamental Freedoms,

The Recommendation on Participation by the People at Large in Cultural Life and Their Contribution to It;

(iii)  Mention, in this year of the thirtieth anniversary of the Universal Declaration on Human Rights, the right of the child to be educated in respect of human rights;

(iv)   Provide for the teaching of the rights of the child to adults (a similar idea has already been considered at the International Congress on the Teaching of Human Rights held in Vienna from 12 to 16 September 1978, since the recommendations made by the rapporteurs of the Congress contain a paragraph 11 which acknowledges the right of the child to receive an education in human rights and suggests the preparation of a specific programme of instruction on the rights of the child).

**(f)      World Health Organization (WHO)**

*The following is taken from document E/CN.4/1324.*

Although the draft convention refers to "the statutes of specialized agencies and international organizations concerned with the welfare of children", it would seem most appropriate that some express reference be made to WHO in the preamble to the draft convention along the following lines:

> "Reaffirming the principles laid down in the Constitution of the World Health Organization concerning the health of the child and the mother;
>
> Bearing in mind that health development of the child is of basic importance and that the promotion of maternal and child health and welfare and the fostering of the ability of the child to live harmoniously in a changing total environment are necessary for the achievement of the purposes of this Convention."

### (g)  Women's International Democratic Federation

*The following is taken from document E/CN.4/1324.*

> After the fifth preambular paragraph of the draft convention, which begins *"Having in mind"*, add the idea expressed at the tenth special session of the United Nations devoted to disarmament stressing the hope that Governments will take steps to ensure that a portion of the resources that could be saved by reducing world arms expenditures is utilized, through national or multinational programmes, to meet the basic needs of children throughout the world, particularly in the developing countries.

## C.  First reading (1979-1988)

*In 1979, the Commission on Human Rights decided to establish an informal open-ended Working Group to meet for one week to consider the question of a draft convention on the rights of the child during the session of the Commission. The Working Group met again in 1980 and was authorized in 1981 and each year thereafter to meet prior to the Commission session. In 1988, the working group met for two weeks in order to complete the first reading. The title and preamble were adopted by the Working Group in 1979 and 1980. An additional preambular paragraph was adopted in 1988. It should be noted that the order of the preambular paragraphs was changed on second reading.*

### 1.  Proposals submitted to the Working Group (1979)

*The following proposals are taken from paragraph 23 of the 1979 report of the Working Group to the Commission on Human Rights (E/CN.4/L.1468), which is reproduced in paragraph 244 of the 1979 report of the Commission on Human Rights (E/CN.4/1347). The proposals were not discussed by the Working Group owing to lack of time.*

### (a)  France and Federal Republic of Germany

The following provisions of the draft convention should not be included in the convention itself but set out in the preamble or in an annexed recommendation of a pedagogical nature:

> Article II,
> Article VI (first sentence),
> Article VII (paragraph 2, from "The best interests" to "guidance"),
> Article VIII,
> Article X (second sentence).

### (b)  Sweden

New preambular paragraphs for insertion before the last preambular paragraph of the draft convention:

> "*Aware* that children have inherent rights and needs of their own,
>
> *Also aware* of the changing role and structure of the family in many parts of the world,

*Recognizing* that the conditions for children have changed considerably in many countries since the time of the adoption of the United Nations Declaration of the Rights of the Child, entailing some improvements but also creating new problems for children, partly due to the environmental situation and to increased migration,

*Acknowledging* that these developments necessitate the elaboration of new special safeguards and of concrete obligations for States,"

### (c)  United Kingdom of Great Britain and Northern Ireland

New preambular paragraph for insertion after the second preambular paragraph of the draft convention:

"*Recalling* that in the Universal Declaration of Human Rights, the United Nations has proclaimed that childhood is entitled to special care and assistance,"

### (d)  United States of America

New preambular paragraph 3:

"*Recognizing* that these rights derive from the inherent dignity of the human person,"

## 2.  Discussion and adoption by the Working Group (1979)

*The following is taken from paragraphs 9 to 22 of the 1979 report of the Working Group to the Commission on Human Rights (E/CN.4/L.1468), which is reproduced in paragraph 244 of the 1979 report of the Commission on Human Rights (E/CN.4/1347).*

9.      A number of representatives expressed a preference for the title as contained in the draft convention while others felt that the convention should deal with children as a group and that this aspect ought to be emphasized by using the term "children" throughout the convention, so there would be no discrimination between sexes. The working group decided to adopt the present title of the draft convention on the understanding that it might later decide to change it.

*First preambular paragraph*

10.      At the 4th meeting, the working group considered the first preambular paragraph of the draft convention. One representative said that the first preambular paragraph should incorporate some of the provisions of the United Nations Charter.

11.      The representative of the United States of America proposed that the phrase "in the equal rights of men and women", taken from the second preambular paragraph of the Charter, should be inserted in this paragraph between the words "person" and "and have determined". Other representatives considered the proposal unnecessary, the reference to the dignity and worth of the human person in the original text being sufficient; they preferred the text as it stood.

12.      The representative of Australia proposed that the words "to promote economic and social progress and development as well as universal respect for, and observance of, human rights and fundamental freedoms for all without distinction as to race, sex, language, or religion", which reflected a similar provision of article 55 of the Charter, should be added after the words "have determined" in the first preambular paragraph.

13.      Several delegations, expressing their support for the paragraph as it stood, considered the wording to be sufficiently precise and that any additions to it might overburden the text. The amendment put forward by Australia was withdrawn in the light of those comments.

14.      The discussion concerning the first preambular paragraph continued at the 5th meeting of the working group. Some representatives were of the opinion that the text of the first preambular paragraph should be

retained as it appeared in the draft convention. The first preambular paragraph of the draft convention was finally adopted without change, as follows:

> "*Bearing in mind* that the peoples of the United Nations have, in the Charter, reaffirmed their faith in fundamental human rights and in the dignity and worth of the human person, and have determined to promote social progress and better standards of life in larger freedom,".

15.     The representative of Canada proposed at the 6th meeting that the first preambular paragraph of the International Covenant on Civil and Political Rights and of the International Covenant on Economic, Social and Cultural Rights should also be the first preambular paragraph of the convention on the rights of the child. The paragraph read as follows:

> "*Considering* that, in accordance with the principles proclaimed in the Charter of the United Nations, recognition of the inherent dignity and of the equal and inalienable rights of all members of the human family is the foundation of freedom, justice and peace in the world,".

16.     The working group accepted the proposal submitted by Canada.

*Second preambular paragraph*

17.     The working group proceeded to consider the second preambular paragraph of the draft convention. During the discussion, the reference in the preamble to international instruments was questioned by some representatives and it was suggested that references should be limited to the United Nations Charter. One representative stated that it would be appropriate to make special mention of certain articles of the Universal Declaration of Human Rights, where specific reference was made to children, namely articles 25 and 26.

18.     It was understood that the phrase "religion, political or other opinion, national or social origin, property, ...", in the second preambular paragraph, was also intended to prevent discrimination against children on account of the political opinions, religious beliefs or property of their parents or relatives.

19.     A number of representatives were in favour of adopting the second preambular paragraph as it stood, considering that it was appropriate to refer to previous international instruments which were all relevant. It was therefore agreed to adopt the paragraph under discussion in its original form.

20.     The second preambular paragraph, as adopted by the working group, read as follows:

> "*Recognizing* that the United Nations has, in the Universal Declaration of Human Rights and in the International Covenants on Human Rights, proclaimed and agreed that everyone is entitled to all the rights and freedoms set forth therein, without distinction of any kind, such as race, colour, sex, language, religion, political or other opinion, national or social origin, property, birth or other status,".

*Other provisions of the draft convention*

21.     At the 6th meeting, the representatives of France and the Federal Republic of Germany reminded the working group of the recommendations of their Governments contained in the report of the Secretary-General concerning the desirability of convening a group of experts to draw up the convention.

22.     The representative of Poland proposed a text for insertion after the second preambular paragraph of the draft convention which would stress the importance of the family as the basic unit of society and the natural environment for the growth and well-being of children. Taking into account comments made by various delegations, he submitted a new text which was adopted by the working group at its 7th meeting. The text, as adopted, read as follows:

> "*Convinced* that the family, as the basic unit of society and the natural environment for the growth and well-being of all its members and particularly children, should be afforded the necessary protection and assistance so that it can fully assume its responsibilities within the community,".

One representative stated that he did not oppose the substance of the provision but questioned whether the convention would in fact address the issue of family protection and said that the preambular phrase might have to be re-examined in the light of the operative portion of the convention.

## 3. Revised Polish draft (1979)

*A revised version of the draft convention was included in a note verbale dated 5 October 1979 addressed to the Division of Human Rights from the Permanent Representation of the Polish People's Republic to the United Nations Office at Geneva. This draft formed the basis for discussion at the 1980 session of the Working Group. The following text is taken from Commission on Human Rights document E/CN.4/1349, which was reissued for technical reasons. Preambular paragraphs marked with an asterisk (\*/) had already been adopted by the Working Group at its 1979 session.*

*The States Parties to the Convention,*

*Considering* that in accordance with the principles proclaimed in the Charter of the United Nations, recognition of the inherent dignity and of the equal and inalienable rights of all members of the human family is the foundation of freedom, justice and peace in the world, \*/

*Bearing in mind* that the peoples of the United Nations have, in the Charter, reaffirmed their faith in fundamental human rights and in the dignity and worth of the human person, and have determined to promote social progress and better standards of life in larger freedom, \*/

*Recognizing* that the United Nations have, in the Universal Declaration of Human Rights and in the International Covenants on Human Rights, proclaimed and agreed that everyone is entitled to all the rights and freedoms set forth therein, without distinction of any kind, such as race, colour, sex, language, religion, political or other opinion, national or social origin, property, birth or other status, \*/

*Convinced* that the family, as the basic unit of society and the natural environment for the growth and well-being of all its members and particularly children, should be afforded the necessary protection and assistance so that it can fully assume its responsibilities within the community, \*/

*Recognizing* that the child due to the needs of his physical and mental development requires particular care and assistance with regard to health, physical, mental, moral and social development as well as legal protection in conditions of freedom, dignity and security,

*Recognizing* that the child, for the full and harmonious development of his personality, should grow up in family environment, in an atmosphere of love and understanding,

*Bearing in mind* that the need for extending particular care to the child has been stated in the Geneva Declaration of the Rights of the Child of 1924 and in the Declaration of the Rights of the Child adopted by the United Nations in 1959 and recognized in the Universal Declaration of Human Rights, in the International Covenant on Civil and Political Rights (in particular in the articles 23 and 24), in the International Covenant on Economic, Social and Cultural Rights (in particular in its article 10) and in the statutes of specialized agencies and international organizations concerned with the welfare of children,

*Considering* that the child should be fully prepared to live an individual life in society, and brought up in the spirit of the ideals proclaimed in the Charter of the United Nations, and in particular in the spirit of peace, dignity, tolerance, freedom and brotherhood,

*Have agreed as follows:*

## 4. Discussion and adoption by the Working Group (1980)

*The following is taken from paragraphs 4 to 27 of the 1980 report of the Working Group to the Commission on Human Rights (E/CN.4/L.1542), which is reproduced in paragraph 277 of the 1980 report of the Commission on Human Rights (E/CN.4/1408).*

4.      In the course of the general discussion at that meeting, some representatives suggested that the term "child" should be clearly defined, and perhaps replaced by a more precise term with greater juridical significance, such as "minor", before proceeding with the adoption of further paragraphs. It was also pointed out that, at the previous session, the Working Group had adopted the title of the convention on the understanding that it might later decide to change it. However, other representatives expressed support for the idea of proceeding with the discussion and formulation of the rest of the preamble immediately. It was therefore decided to postpone the discussion of the definition until the Working Group considered article 1 of the draft convention.

*Fifth preambular paragraph*

5.      At its second meeting, the Working Group began its consideration of the rest of the preamble.

6.      The representative of the Holy See, in agreement with other delegations, suggested that the text of the fifth preambular paragraph should be amended by inserting the words, taken from the Declaration of the Rights of the Child, "before as well as after birth" after the words "particular care and assistance". A number of delegations argued in support of the amendment on the grounds that their national legislation contained provisions protecting the rights of the unborn child from the time of conception. They stated that the purpose of the amendment was not to preclude the possibility of abortion, since many countries had adopted legislation providing for abortion in certain cases, such as a threat to the health of the mother. Some delegations referred to the fact that the Declaration of the Rights of the Child of 1959 contained the sentence proposed.

7.      Other delegations, however, opposed the amendment. In their view, this preambular paragraph should be indisputably neutral on issues such as abortion. They stated that the definition of "child" should be contained in article 1 and that nothing in the preamble should prejudge or slant the definition formulated in article 1.

8.      Some representatives appealed to the proponents of the amendment not to insist on it at that stage, and to accept the text contained in the draft on the understanding that the Working Group could revert to it at a later stage. The representative of Ireland suggested that the amendment could be inserted in the text in square brackets and the Working Group could make a final decision after having discussed article 1. The representative of the Holy See expressed agreement with the proposed solution, which was supported by a number of other delegations. The fifth preambular paragraph was therefore adopted with the proposed amendment in square brackets, on the understanding that the final language would be agreed upon after the adoption of article 1.

9.      Subsequently, at the third meeting, the representative of Greece suggested that the words "physical and mental" before the word "development" at the beginning of the paragraph should be deleted since they were already contained later on in the paragraph. It was decided that the Working Group should consider this proposal when it came back to this paragraph to decide on its final formulation.

10.     Debate on the amendment proposed by the Holy See was resumed at the fourth meeting, after adoption of article 1. Several delegations argued that the text inserted in square brackets should be deleted in order to ensure the neutrality of the preamble. One representative expressed the view that, since article 1 had been adopted with a neutral wording, the convention should not appear to give a different interpretation in the preamble. It was also stated that since national legislation differed greatly on the question of abortion, the convention could be widely ratified only if it did not take sides on the issue.

11.     Other delegations, speaking in support of the amendment, stated that, in their view, the wording was sufficiently neutral since it did not specify the length of the period before birth which was covered. They again argued that all national legislations included provisions for the protection of the child before birth. One delegation considered that the proposal could be extended to cover legal protection in view of the fact that most legislations protected, for example, the inheritance rights of children who had not even yet been born.

12.        A number of representatives expressed the view that, if agreement could not be reached at the current session, discussion should proceed on the rest of the convention in the hope that the group might achieve a consensus after further consultations. One delegate pointed out that a compromise might be possible on the basis of the fact that all delegations agreed that some kind of protection and assistance before birth was necessary: in his view, the disagreement lay in the precise definition of what kind of protection and assistance should be specified in the convention.

13.        The observer of the International Union for Child Welfare, supported by some delegations, suggested that, since the seventh preambular paragraph of document E/CN.4/1349 made reference to the Declaration of the Rights of the Child of 1959, the Holy See amendment could be deleted on the understanding that the Declaration (including its third preambular paragraph containing a wording similar to the proposed amendment) remained in force under the proposed convention. Other delegations, however, opposed returning to the original text.

14.        At the same meeting, the Working Group decided on a further postponement of the issue until an acceptable compromise could be found.

15.        At the fifth meeting of the Working Group, the Chairman announced that a compromise text had been elaborated following consultation. The new text would amend the beginning of the paragraph to read:

> "*Recognizing* that, as stated in the Declaration of the Rights of the Child, the child due to the needs of his physical and mental development ...".

The rest of the original preambular paragraph would remain, without the insertion in square brackets proposed by the Holy See.

16.        Further discussion ensued, in the course of which the delegate of Australia proposed that the reference to the Declaration of the Rights of the Child be made more specific by adding the words "adopted in 1959".

17.        The delegate of the United States proposed that the words "as stated in" be changed to "as indicated in"; that a semicolon be inserted after the words "moral and social development" and that the words "as well as legal protection" be changed to read "and also requires legal protection".

18.        Some delegations objected to the amendment proposed by the United States, indicating that they needed time to reflect on its legal significance. Others were not satisfied by that delegation's explanation that the amendment was necessary in order to ensure the complete neutrality of the text, and expressed concern that the draft convention would be slanted in favour of legalizing abortion. They re-emphasized their contention that the draft convention should ensure protection for children both before and after birth. In reply, the delegate of the United States argued that any attempt to institutionalize a particular point of view on abortion in the draft convention would make the convention unacceptable from the outset to countries espousing a different point of view. Accordingly, he insisted that the draft convention must be worded in such a manner that neither proponents nor opponents of abortion can find legal support for their respective positions in the draft convention.

19.        After further discussion, a compromise text was adopted which read as follows:

> "*Recognizing* that, as indicated in the Declaration of the Rights of the Child adopted in 1959, the child due to the needs of his physical and mental development requires particular care and assistance with regard to health, physical, mental, moral and social development, and requires legal protection in conditions of freedom, dignity and security."

*Sixth preambular paragraph*

20.        At the second meeting of the Working Group, the representative of the Netherlands proposed that the word "happiness" be inserted immediately before the words "love and understanding" at the end of the paragraph.

21.	The Working Group then adopted the sixth preambular paragraph with the proposed amendment.

*Seventh preambular paragraph*

22.	The Working Group adopted the seventh preambular paragraph without changes at its second meeting.

*Eighth preambular paragraph*

23.	At the second meeting of the Working Group, the representative of the Netherlands proposed to insert the word "individual" before the word "freedom" in the last part of the paragraph.

24.	Some delegations, however, opposed the amendment on the grounds that it detracted from the notion of freedom contained in the text. One representative stated that the text could be approved as it stood, on the understanding that the Working Group could return to it at a later stage if it was felt that the concept of individual freedom was not sufficiently covered by other articles of the draft convention.

25.	The eighth preambular paragraph was then adopted without changes on the above-mentioned understanding.

*New preambular paragraph*

26.	At the third meeting, the representative of the United Kingdom reproposed a new preambular paragraph which had been submitted by his delegation the year before but had not been considered owing to lack of time. The new paragraph, which he suggested should be inserted between the third and fourth preambular paragraphs of the new draft, read as follows:

> "*Recalling* that in the Universal Declaration of Human Rights, the United Nations had proclaimed that childhood is entitled to special care and assistance,".

27.	Several delegations expressed support for this proposal. Some delegations pointed out that they did not oppose the insertion of the new paragraph although, in their view, it was somewhat repetitious of preambular paragraph five. The new paragraph was therefore adopted for insertion into the preamble as proposed. Subsequently, one delegation observed that the order of the paragraphs in the preamble could be rearranged at a later stage for the sake of logical consistency.

## 5.	Comment submitted to the Working Group (1986)

### (a)	Bangladesh

*The following comment regarding the preamble is contained in a paper submitted by the Permanent Representative of Bangladesh to the United Nations Office at Geneva with the request that the paper be annexed to the report of the Working Group. For the complete text, including general comments on the draft convention, see document E/ CN.4/1986/39, annex IV.*

> *Preamble,*
>
> In the preamble Bangladesh is not in favour of specific references to international instruments such as Universal Declaration of Human Rights, etc., since the convention itself will be the operative instrument in this area. References to such declarations may give rise to conflicting legal interpretations since some countries that may become parties to the draft convention may not be parties to, e.g., the international covenants.

## 6.	Proposals submitted to the Working Group (1988)

### (a)	Italy

*For the text of this proposal see paragraph 9 in section 7 below.*

**(b)    International Planned Parenthood Federation**

*The following is taken from document E/CN.4/1988/WG.1/WP.2, pages 4 and 6.*

> *Additions to the preamble*

> 1.    *Additional paragraph* (Protection of the educational rights of adolescent girls)

> "Adhering to the principle that the right to education should be fully realized on the basis of equal opportunity and correspondingly that girls should not suffer discrimination as a result of marriage, pregnancy and/or exigencies of childcare,"

> 2.    *Additional paragraph* (Compensation for the historical priority given to the rights of boys)

> "Recognizing that the health risks confronting girls demand that emphasis be placed on protecting their rights comparable to the priority historically and universally awarded the rights of young males,"

## 7.    Discussion and adoption by the Working Group (1988)

*The following is taken from the 1988 report of the Working Group to the Commission on Human Rights (E/CN.4/1988/28, paras. 9 to 13).*

> *Preamble, additional paragraph (Special consideration for children living in exceptionally difficult conditions)*

9.    Italy, upon the suggestion of some non-governmental organizations, proposed the addition of an eighth paragraph to the preamble (E/CN.4/1988/WG.1/WP.24) which read as follows:

> "*Recognizing* that there are in the world children living in exceptionally difficult conditions which do not correspond to those generally obtaining in their country, and that such children need special consideration."

10.    The view was expressed that this proposal would entail undesirable discrimination as it singled out one specific category of children that required special consideration. The following alternative wordings were proposed:

> "*Recognizing* that children who live in exceptionally difficult situations need special consideration,

> *Recognizing* that there are in the world children who live in exceptionally difficult conditions, and that such children need special consideration,

> *Recognizing* the special needs of children living in exceptionally difficult conditions which do not correspond to those generally obtaining in their own country,"

11.    The view was also expressed that the situation of children living in permanently exceptionally difficult conditions was a reality which should be mentioned; attention should be given to the difficult situation of children living in a particular society where all children were supposedly living well. It was recalled that the proposal made in working paper 24 had been discussed in the context of the question of national reports and concerned children living in conditions which did not correspond to those generally prevailing in their country. On the other hand, it was said that positive discrimination regarding children in difficult conditions would be acceptable in general terms but should not be included in the preamble to the convention so as not to restrict it.

12.    A small drafting group was established (Holy See, United Kingdom, Venezuela) and, with the collaboration of Argentina and Spain, submitted the following text:

> "*Recognizing* that, in rich as well as in poor countries, there are children living in exceptionally difficult conditions, and that such children need special consideration,"

13.      Most of the participants strongly supported the proposal to replace the words "in rich as well as in poor countries" by "in all countries in the world" in order not to restrict the idea that marginalized children needed special consideration wherever they might be. The eighth preambular paragraph, as adopted, read as follows:

> "*Recognizing* that in all countries in the world there are children living in exceptionally difficult conditions, and that such children need special consideration,"

## 8.      Text as adopted at first reading

*The following is taken from document E/CN.4/1988/WG.1/WP.1/Rev.1.*

Draft convention on the rights of the child

*The States Parties to the Convention,*

*Considering* that in accordance with the principles proclaimed in the Charter of the United Nations, recognition of the inherent dignity and of the equal and inalienable rights of all members of the human family is the foundation of freedom, justice and peace in the world,

*Bearing in mind* that the peoples of the United Nations have, in the Charter, reaffirmed their faith in fundamental human rights and in the dignity and worth of the human person, and have determined to promote social progress and better standards of life in larger freedom,

*Recognizing* that the United Nations has, in the Universal Declaration of Human Rights and in the International Covenants on Human Rights, proclaimed and agreed that everyone is entitled to all the rights and freedoms set forth therein, without distinction of any kind, such as race, colour, sex, language, religion, political or other opinion, national or social origin, property, birth or other status,

*Recalling* that, in the Universal Declaration of Human Rights, the United Nations has proclaimed that childhood is entitled to special care and assistance,

*Convinced* that the family, as the basic unit of society and the natural environment for the growth and well-being of all its members and particularly children, should be afforded the necessary protection and assistance so that it can fully assume its responsibilities within the community,

*Recognizing* that, as indicated in the Declaration of the Rights of the Child adopted in 1959, the child due to the needs of his physical and mental development requires particular care and assistance with regard to health, physical, mental, moral and social development, and requires legal protection in conditions of freedom, dignity and security,

*Recognizing* that the child, for the full and harmonious development of his personality, should grow up in a family environment, in an atmosphere of happiness, love and understanding,

*Recognizing* that in all countries in the world there are children living in exceptionally difficult conditions, and that such children need special consideration,

*Bearing in mind* that the need for extending particular care to the child has been stated in the Geneva Declaration of the Rights of the Child of 1924 and in the Declaration of the Rights of the Child adopted by the United Nations in 1959 and recognized in the Universal Declaration of Human Rights, in the International Covenant on Civil and Political Rights (in particular in articles 23 and 24), in the International Covenant on Economic, Social and Cultural Rights (in particular in its article 10) and in the statutes of specialized agencies and international organizations concerned with the welfare of children,

*Considering* that the child should be fully prepared to live an individual life in society, and brought up in the spirit of the ideals proclaimed in the Charter of the United Nations, and in particular in the spirit of peace, dignity, tolerance, freedom and brotherhood,

*Have agreed as follows:*

# D.    Technical review (1988)

*In a letter addressed to the Secretary-General (see document E/CN.4/1988/28, para. 248), the Working Group requested that a technical review of the draft convention be undertaken by the United Nations Secretariat in advance of the second reading. Among the aims of the technical review were to identify overlap and repetition between and within draft articles; to check for linguistic consistency and accuracy in the text; to compare the standards established with those in other widely accepted human rights instruments; and to make recommendations as to how any overlaps or inconsistencies might be corrected in the second reading.*

*The Secretary-General subsequently requested comments on matters within their respective mandates from a number of the specialized agencies and other United Nations bodies, and from the International Committee of the Red Cross. The comments were compiled in the technical review of the text of the draft convention on the rights of the child (E/CN.4/1989/WG.1/CRP.1 and Add.1), which was taken into account by the Working Group during the second reading of the draft convention.*

## 1.    Comment by the Legal Counsel

*The following is taken from document E/CN.4/1989/WG.1/CRP.1, page 10.*

> The expression "Statutes of specialized agencies" used in the ninth preambular paragraph is too narrow a term to adequately cover all constitutional instruments and other legal documents adopted by the specialized agencies.

## 2.    Comment by the Social Development Division, Centre for Social Development and Humanitarian Affairs

*The following is taken from document E/CN.4/1989/WG.1/CRP.1, page 10.*

> The "Beijing Rules" (General Assembly resolution 40/33) should be mentioned in the preamble of the draft convention, since they are the major international instrument on juvenile justice, and the same mention could be made of the "Standard Minimum Rules for the Treatment of Prisoners".

## 3.    Comment by the United Nations Educational, Scientific and Cultural Organization (UNESCO)

*The following is taken from document E/CN.4/1989/WG.1/CRP.1, pages 10-12.*

> In the English version the first phrase should read: "The States Parties to the present Convention";

> The 10 *considerata* in the preamble do not once mention the primary societal function involving children namely education - although mention is made of the needs of the child's physical and mental development, which require particular care and assistance. Nor is there any mention of the two principal normative instruments assuring the child's right to education, the Convention and the Recommendation against Discrimination in Education (UNESCO 1960); they could be referred to, for instance, in the final paragraph of the Preamble which deals with the content and spirit of the child's upbringing (education) in terms very close to those in article 5 of the Convention/Recommendation.

> The text contains a few scattered mentions of educational measures (e.g. articles 8 bis, 12.3 and 4, 18 bis and 19.3), but the right to education is dealt with in article 15 (not high on the list of rights) and the aims of education in article 16, both of which cover ground already covered in UNESCO's Convention/Recommendation (hereafter called C/R).

It seems to us that among the many positive principles and values conducive to the child's development, as included in the text, the principle of equality is largely ignored. It is particularly essential when it comes to equal treatment of boys and girls within and outside of the family. Since much of the later discrimination of girls can be traced back to their unequal treatment in early years, it is suggested that the element of equality be inserted into the Preamble as their basic right.

Possibly a corresponding addition could be made *on page 5 to the second paragraph* to read:

"in an atmosphere of happiness, love, equality and understanding"

*and to the fifth paragraph*

"and in particular in the spirit of peace, dignity, tolerance, freedom, equality and solidarity" (omitting "brotherhood").

In conformity with article 10 of the International Covenant on Economic, Social and Cultural Rights and with article 23 of the International Covenant on Civil and Political Rights, paragraph 5 should read:

English version:

"*Convinced* that the family, as the fundamental group unit of society ..."

French version:

"*Convaincu* que la famille, élement fondamental ..."

Paragraph 6, in accordance with paragraph 3 of the Preamble and principle 2 of the Declaration of the Rights of the Child, should read:

"*Recognizing* that, as the Declaration of the Rights of the Child adopted by the General Assembly of the United Nations on 20 November 1959 states, the child, by reason of his physical and mental immaturity, needs special assistance, particular care and appropriate legal protection, before as well as after birth, to enable him to develop physically, mentally, intellectually, morally, spiritually and socially in a healthy and normal manner and in conditions of freedom, dignity and security,".

Pages 4 and 5, paragraphs 5 and 7, the *family* is emphasized. It should be noted that there are different types and forms of families and that all children (such as refugees or victims of war) do not have a family environment, and they should also have the right to a full and harmonious development of their personality in an atmosphere of happiness, love and understanding. Consequently, "convinced that the different forms of the family ..." should be added to paragraph 5 and in paragraph 7 the word "family" should be abolished.

French version: paragraph 9 should read:

"*Ayant présent à l'esprit* que la nécessité d'accorder une protection spéciale à l'enfant a été enoncée dans la Déclaration de Genève de 1924 sur les droits de l'enfant et dans la Déclaration des droits de l'enfant adoptée par l'Assemblée générale des Nations Unies en 1959, et qu'elle a été reconnue dans la Déclaration universelle des droits de l'homme, et le Pacte international relatif aux droits civils et politiques (en particulier aux articles 23 et 24), dans le Pacte international relatif aux droits économiques, sociaux et culturels (en particulier à l'article 10) et dans les constitutions des institutions spécialisées et des organisations internationales qui se consacrent au bien-être de l'enfant."

## 4.     Additional comments and clarifications by the Secretariat

*The following is taken from document E/CN.4/1989/WG.1/CRP.1/Add.1, paragraphs 7 and 8.*

7.      In connection with the comment by the Legal Counsel (document E/CN.4/1989/WG.1/CRP.1) that the expression "statutes of specialized agencies" is too narrow, the Working Group may wish to add the words *"and relevant instruments"*.

8.        Given their direct relevance to the understanding and interpretation of certain articles in the draft convention, the Working Group may wish to refer in the Preamble to three resolutions recently adopted by the General Assembly, namely, the Declaration on Social and Legal Principles relating to the Protection and Welfare of Children, with Special Reference to Foster Placement and Adoption Nationally and Internationally, adopted by General Assembly resolution 41/85 of 3 December 1986; the United Nations Standard Minimum Rules for the Administration of Juvenile Justice ("The Beijing Rules"), adopted by General Assembly resolution 40/33 of 29 November 1985; and the Declaration on the Protection of Women and Children in Emergency and Armed Conflict, adopted by resolution 3318 (XXIX) of 14 December 1974. This could be accomplished, for example, by a new ninth preambular paragraph beginning with the words *"Recalling the provisions of ..."*.

## E.    Second reading (1988-1989)

*In a letter addressed to the Secretary-General (see document E/CN.4/1988/28, para. 248), the Working Group requested that the draft convention as adopted at first reading be circulated to all Member States so that their comments could be taken into account during the second reading of the draft. The Working Group conducted the second reading from 28 November to 9 December 1988 and adopted its report from 21 to 23 February 1989.*

## 1.        Proposals submitted to the Working Group at second reading

*The following States submitted written proposals for consideration by the Working Group on second reading.*

### (a)      Argentina

*The following is taken from document E/CN.4/1989/WG.1/WP.24.*

*Order of the Preamble*

| *WP.2 text including suggested revisions* | *New order suggested* |
|---|---|
| Paras. 1, 2, 3, 4, 5 .......................................... remain the same |
| Para. 6 ......................................... becomes  9 |
| Para. 7 ......................................... becomes  6 |
| Para. 8 ......................................... becomes  11 |
| Para. 9 (New para. about traditions and values Re. WP.17, para. 2).............. becomes  12 |
| Para. 10 ("*Recalling* the provisions ...") ........................................ remains  10 |
| Para. 11 ......................................... becomes  8 |
| Para. 12 ......................................... becomes  7 |
| Para. 13 (New para. about international cooperation, |
|         Re. Senegal (WP.17, para. 1) and drafting group's |
|         United States of America, Senegal, Morocco, |
|         Philippines, Canada, Norway proposals)................................ becomes 13 |

### (b)      Federal Republic of Germany

*The following is taken from document E/CN.4/1989/WG.1/WP.6.*

Reformulate preambular paragraph 6 as follows:

> "*Recognizing* that, as indicated in the Declaration of the Rights of the Child adopted in 1959, 'the child, by reason of his physical and mental immaturity, needs special safeguards and care, including appropriate legal protection, before as well as after birth', ..."

**(c)    Holy See, Ireland, Malta and the Philippines**

*The following is taken from document E/CN.4/1989/WG.1/WP.8.*

> Add the words "before as well as after birth" at the end of preambular paragraph 6 (document E/CN.4/1988/WG.1/WP.1/Rev.2).

**(d)    Malta**

*The following is taken from document E/CN.4/1989/WG.1/WP.9.*

> It is the submission of the Government of Malta that the text of the proposed convention as contained in document E/CN.4/1988/WG.1/WP.1/Rev.2 of 6 April, 1988 represents, in one important respect, a retreat from the principles enunciated in the 1959 United Nations Declaration of the Rights of the Child. Unlike the Declaration, the draft convention in its present form makes no mention of the rights of the child *before birth*, and as such falls short of the comprehensive protection enunciated by the Declaration.

> It is accordingly the view of the Government of Malta that the text of the draft convention should be amended as follows:

> > 1)    At the end of the sixth preambular paragraph, after the words "conditions of freedom, dignity and security" add the words "before as well as after birth";

> > 2)    In Article 1, after the words "human being", add the words "from conception".

**(e)    Senegal**

*The following is taken from document E/CN.4/1989/WG.1/WP.17.*

> 1.    Insert after the eighth preambular paragraph:

> > "*Recognizing* the importance of international cooperation and assistance for the developing countries in order to improve the living conditions of children in those countries confronted with serious economic and social difficulties."

> 2.    Insert after preambular paragraph 9:

> > "*Taking due account* of the importance of the traditions and cultural values of each people for the protection and harmonious development of the child."

> 3.    In paragraph 10 insert the words in italics:

> > "*Considering* that the child should be fully prepared to live an individual *and collective/community* life in society, and brought up in the spirit of the ideals proclaimed in the Charter of the United Nations, and in particular in the spirit of peace, dignity, tolerance, freedom and brotherhood."

> [...]

## 2.    Discussion and adoption at second reading

*The following is taken from the 1989 report of the Working Group to the Commission on Human Rights (E/CN.4/1989/48, paras. 25 to 74).*

> *Title of the convention*

> 25.    The representative of Senegal expressed doubt whether the present title which read "A draft convention on the rights of the child" faithfully reflected all those concerns which the delegations had when elaborating this draft. He consequently proposed the following new title: "A draft convention on the protection of the child".

26.     Several representatives (Netherlands, Norway and Argentina) indicated their preference for retaining the title as it stood since the proposed new wording for the title was, in their view, too restrictive.

27.     The representative of Senegal did not insist on his proposal, and the Working Group, after having deleted the word "draft", agreed to adopt the title reading: "convention on the rights of the child".

*Preamble*

28.     The first line of the preamble as adopted at first reading and which read "The States Parties to the Convention" was adopted with the addition of the word "present" before the word "Convention", as proposed by the Legal Counsel and UNESCO.

*Preambular paragraphs 1, 2, 3 and 4* (paragraphs 1, 2, 3 and 4)

29.     Paragraphs 1, 2, 3 and 4 of the preamble as adopted at first reading were approved by the Working Group without any changes. Paragraphs 1, 2, 3 and 4 of the preamble, therefore, read as follows:

> "*Considering* that in accordance with the principles proclaimed in the Charter of the United Nations, recognition of the inherent dignity and of the equal and inalienable rights of all members of the human family is the foundation of freedom, justice and peace in the world,
>
> *Bearing in mind* that the peoples of the United Nations have, in the Charter, reaffirmed their faith in fundamental human rights and in the dignity and worth of the human person, and have determined to promote social progress and better standards of life in larger freedom,
>
> *Recognizing* that the United Nations has, in the Universal Declaration of Human Rights and in the International Covenants on Human Rights, proclaimed and agreed that everyone is entitled to all the rights and freedoms set forth therein, without distinction of any kind, such as race, colour, sex, language, religion, political or other opinion, national or social origin, property, birth or other status,
>
> *Recalling* that, in the Universal Declaration of Human Rights, the United Nations has proclaimed that childhood is entitled to special care and assistance,"

*Preambular paragraph 5* (paragraph 5)

30.     After a brief discussion, the Working Group agreed to adopt paragraph 5 of the preamble with a small change proposed by the Chairman. The words "as the basic unit of society" were thus replaced by the words "as the fundamental group of society".

31.     The fifth preambular paragraph, as adopted, reads as follows:

> "*Convinced* that the family, as the fundamental group of society and the natural environment for the growth and well-being of all its members and particularly children, should be afforded the necessary protection and assistance so that it can fully assume its responsibilities within the community,"

*Preambular paragraph 6* (paragraph 9)

32.     With regard to paragraph 6 of the preamble, two proposed amendments to the text already adopted at first reading were submitted by the Federal Republic of Germany (E/CN.4/1989/WG.1/WP.6) and by the Holy See, Ireland, Malta and the Philippines (E/CN.4/1989/WG.1/WP.8).

33.     In introducing his proposal (E/CN.4/1989/WG.1/WP.6), the representative of the Federal Republic of Germany explained that his amendment sought to replace a part of preambular paragraph 6 by a literal quotation of the Declaration of the Rights of the Child of 1959. It was suggested to reformulate paragraph 6 as follows:

> "*Recognizing* that, as indicated in the Declaration of the Rights of the Child adopted in 1959, 'the child, by reason of his physical and mental immaturity, needs special safeguards and care, including appropriate legal protection, before as well as after birth', ...".

34.     The other proposal (E/CN.4/1989/WG.1/WP.8) was introduced by the representative of the Philippines and sought to add the words "before as well as after the birth" at the end of preambular paragraph 6. At a later stage, the representative of the Philippines stated that the co-sponsors of this amendment would have no difficulty if the Working Group preferred the text submitted by the Federal Republic of Germany.

35.     In a prolonged discussion that followed, a number of delegations, including Italy, Venezuela, Senegal, Kuwait, Argentina, Austria, Colombia, Egypt and one non-governmental organization, supported the idea of retaining the concept of the 1959 Declaration of the Rights of the Child in the text of the draft convention, as proposed in both amendments. The importance of protection of the child even before it is born was repeatedly stressed in this connection. It was further stated that in all national legal systems protection was provided to the unborn child and the draft convention should not ignore this fact.

36.     Other delegations, including Norway, the Netherlands, India, China, the Union of Soviet Socialist Republics, Denmark, Australia, Sweden, the German Democratic Republic and Canada, however, opposed what in their view amounted to reopening the debate on this controversial matter which, as they indicated, had been extensively discussed at earlier sessions of the Working Group with no consensus achieved. It was also pointed out by some delegations that an unborn child is not literally a person whose rights could already be protected, and that the main thrust of the convention was deemed to promulgate the rights and freedoms of every human being after his birth and to the age of 18 years. The view was also expressed that the Declaration of 1959, being a document of almost 30 years, is to be superseded by the present new draft and, therefore, there was no need to stick to all of its provisions.

37.     The representative of Poland stated that the present formulation of preambular paragraph 6 was a delicate balance which the Working Group had reached in the course of continued discussions. In his view, the present compromise wording of this paragraph did not exclude the protection of the child before birth, nor did it contradict a wider interpretation of the text or the application of other more comprehensive provisions, as laid down in article 21 of the draft convention. In the course of the debate, a reference was also made to article 1 bis of the draft which provided for measures to ensure the survival and development of the child.

38.     On the other hand, the authors of the amendments as well as some other delegations insisted on their view that the future convention could not ignore an important issue of the rights of the unborn child. In the circumstances, proposals were made to put the amendments of the Federal Republic of Germany in square brackets or even to include them in a new section in the text entitled "Proposals on which no consensus was reached". Another opinion was that it would be preferable not to use the square brackets at this stage of work on the draft convention.

39.     In the course of a procedural debate that followed, the representative of the Federal Republic of Germany indicated that he would formally request a vote in the Working Group if his proposal was not duly reflected in the text of preambular paragraph 6.

40.     The representative of Italy observed that no State was manifestly opposed to the principles contained in the Declaration of the Rights of the Child and, therefore, according to the Vienna Convention on the Law of Treaties, the rule regarding the protection of life before birth could be considered as "jus cogens" since it formed part of the common conscience of members of the international community. She further indicated that the concept of "responsible motherhood", affirmed in many modern judicial systems, was not against the protection of children before birth.

41.     It was stated by some delegations that the Working Group should avoid taking a vote and that the holding of informal consultations could help to find a way out of this situation. At the suggestion of the Chairman, an informal drafting group was set up to undertake such consultations.

42.     Another amendment to preambular paragraph 6 was put forward by the representative of Egypt. He proposed orally that the word "psychological" be added after the word "moral".

43.　　On behalf of the drafting group on preambular paragraph 6, the representative of Italy submitted a compromise text (E/CN.4/1989/WG.1/WP.19) which read as follows:

> "The drafting group composed of the Federal Republic of Germany, Ireland, Italy, Netherlands, Poland, Sweden and the United States of America in a spirit of collaboration has adopted unanimously the following proposal:
>
> *Bearing in mind* that, as indicated in the Declaration of the Rights of the Child adopted by the General Assembly of the United Nations on 20 November 1959, 'the child, by reason of his physical and mental immaturity, needs special safeguards and care, including appropriate legal protection, before as well as after birth,'"

The same drafting group, in agreeing to this text, urges that the following statement be placed in the *travaux préparatoires* by the Chairman on behalf of the entire Working Group.

> "In adopting this preambular paragraph, the Working Group does not intend to prejudice the interpretation of article 1 or any other provision of the Convention by States Parties."

44.　　The representative of the United Kingdom of Great Britain and Northern Ireland stated that she understood that reference to article 1 in the above statement included reference to article 1 bis.

45.　　The representative of Senegal said that, in the view of certain delegations, the reference to the statement by the Chairman of the Working Group in no way prejudged the interpretation of the future convention.

46.　　The text of preambular paragraph 6 as proposed by the drafting group was adopted and the Chairman read into the record the requested statement as set out above.

47.　　In connection with that statement, the representative of the United Kingdom requested confirmation from the Legal Counsel that the statement would be taken into account if, in the future, doubts were raised as to the method of interpreting article 1. The response by the Legal Counsel to that request is annexed to the present report.

*Preambular paragraph 7* (paragraph 6)

48.　　With regard to paragraph 7 of the preamble, the representative of the United States of America stated that he would prefer the original language of this paragraph without adding the word "equality" before the words "and understanding", as proposed by UNESCO. The Working Group then approved the text of paragraph 7 of the preamble as adopted at first reading, with a small change orally proposed by Australia to insert the words "or her" before the word "personality".

49.　　The text thus approved reads as follows:

> "*Recognizing* that the child, for the full and harmonious development of his or her personality, should grow up in a family environment, in an atmosphere of happiness, love and understanding,"

*Paragraph 8* (paragraph 11)

50.　　Paragraph 8 of the preamble as adopted at first reading was approved by the Working Group without any changes. It reads as follows:

> "*Recognizing* that in all countries in the world there are children living in exceptionally difficult conditions, and that such children need special consideration."

*Additional paragraph 9* (paragraph 10)

51.　　A new paragraph 9 of the preamble proposed by the Social Development Division (E/CN.4/1989/WG.1/CRP.1 and E/CN.4/1989/WG.1/CRP.1/Add.1) was adopted by the Working Group without changes.

52.    Paragraph 9, as adopted, reads as follows:

> "*Recalling* the provisions of the Declaration on Social and Legal Principles relating to the Protection and Welfare of Children, with Special Reference to Foster Placement and Adoption Nationally and Internationally (General Assembly resolution 41/85 of 3 December 1986); the United Nations Standard Minimum Rules for the Administration of Juvenile Justice ('The Beijing Rules') (General Assembly resolution 40/33 of 29 November 1985); and the Declaration on the Protection of Women and Children in Emergency and Armed Conflict (General Assembly resolution 3318 (XXIX) of 14 December 1974),"

53.    The representative of Argentina expressed the view that a better location in the preamble could be found for this new paragraph.

*Second additional paragraph 9* (paragraph 12)

54.    Senegal submitted a proposal (E/CN.4/1989/WG.1/WP.17), paragraphs 1, 2 and 3 of which contained amendments relating to the preamble of the draft convention.

55.    The second amendment of Senegal, which was considered first by the Working Group, sought to insert after preambular paragraph 8 a new paragraph reading as follows:

> "*Taking due account* of the importance of the traditions and cultural values of each people for the protection and harmonious development of the child."

56.    The Working Group adopted this proposal.

*Paragraph 10* (paragraph 8)

57.    Paragraph 10 of the preamble as adopted at first reading was approved by the Working Group with the addition of the words "and relevant instruments" before the words "of specialized agencies", as proposed by the Legal Counsel.

58.    The tenth preambular paragraph, as adopted, reads as follows:

> "*Bearing in mind* that the need for extending particular care to the child has been stated in the Geneva Declaration of the Rights of the Child of 1924 and in the Declaration of the Rights of the Child adopted by the United Nations in 1959 and recognized in the Universal Declaration of Human Rights, in the International Covenant on Civil and Political Rights (in particular in articles 23 and 24), in the International Covenant on Economic, Social and Cultural Rights (in particular in its article 10) and in the statutes and relevant instruments of specialized agencies and international organizations concerned with the welfare of children,"

59.    With regard to preambular paragraph 10 and at the meeting subsequent to its adoption, the representative of Senegal called attention to his delegation's proposed amendment (E/CN.4/1989/WG.1/WP.17) which sought to add the words "and collective/community" in preambular paragraph 10 as adopted at first reading. The Chairman ruled that, since paragraph 10 had already been adopted without objection by the Working Group at its previous meeting, the proposal could not be considered.

60.    The representative of Senegal made a declaration in this connection, stating that with deep regret the delegation of Senegal felt compelled to enter a reservation to that paragraph of the preamble.

*Paragraph 11* (paragraph 7)

61.    In connection with preambular paragraph 11, the representative of the United States of America stated that he would prefer the text of this paragraph without the words "equality and solidarity", the addition of which at the end of the paragraph was proposed by UNESCO. He could still go along with the word "equality"; the word "solidarity" should be better replaced by the word "friendship".

62.     After a brief discussion in which the words "fraternity" and "brotherhood" were proposed as possible alternatives to the word "solidarity", the Working Group decided to approve the text of paragraph 11 as adopted at first reading with the addition of the words "equality and solidarity" after the word "freedom".

63.     Paragraph 11 thus adopted reads as follows:

> "*Considering* that the child should be fully prepared to live an individual life in society, and brought up in the spirit of the ideals proclaimed in the Charter of the United Nations, and in particular in the spirit of peace, dignity, tolerance, freedom, equality and solidarity,"

*New preambular paragraph 11 (paragraph 13)*

64.     The Working Group then considered amendment 1 of E/CN.4/1989/WG.1/WP.17 submitted by Senegal. The representatives of Brazil and Italy supported the proposal submitted by the representative of Senegal. The proposal was to insert, after preambular paragraph 9, a new paragraph reading as follows:

> "*Recognizing* the importance of international cooperation and assistance for the developing countries in order to improve the living conditions of children in those countries confronted with serious economic and social difficulties."

65.     The representative of Venezuela orally proposed a sub-amendment to this amendment of Senegal, by which the word "particularly" was to be added before the words "serious economic and social difficulties". The sub-amendment was accepted by the representative of Senegal.

66.     Several participants expressed their support for the proposal of Senegal as sub-amended. It was pointed out that the draft convention should take due account of the special needs of the developing countries.

67.     Some other delegations, while not opposing in principle the inclusion of this new paragraph, indicated that the purposes of this amendment had already been covered in the body of the draft convention, namely in article 12 bis, paragraph 4, and article 24 which relate to questions of international cooperation. Besides, international cooperation was also needed to improve the living conditions of children in developed countries, namely, those belonging to certain minority groups.

68.     The representative of the United States of America indicated that the convention will primarily create obligations for ratifying Governments to respect the rights of, and to render assistance to, their own citizens. He further stated that, while Governments should cooperate with each other in this regard, the Working Group should let other legal instruments and other fora deal with the subject of international assistance.

69.     After a brief discussion, it was decided to set up a small drafting group composed of Senegal, the United States of America, Morocco, Canada, Norway and the Philippines to formulate a compromise wording of this paragraph.

70.     After some consultations, the representative of the United States of America read out a compromise text of amendment 1 of the proposal of Senegal.

71.     This compromise text was then adopted by the Working Group as a new preambular paragraph 11, which reads as follows:

> "*Recognizing* the importance of international cooperation for improving the living conditions of children in every country, in particular in the developing countries,"

*Reordering of the preambular paragraphs*

72.     The representative of Argentina introduced his delegation's proposals to rearrange the order of the 13 preambular paragraphs (contained in document E/CN.4/1989/WG.1/WP.24) in order to take into account chronological sequence and groups of subject matter. It was emphasized by him that this in no way affected the substance of the paragraphs but merely sought to introduce some logic in their order.

73. The representative of the United States of America supported the proposal by the representative of Argentina.

74. The Working Group adopted the order of the preambular paragraphs as proposed by the representative of Argentina (E/CN.4/1989/WG.1/WP.24).

## 3. Statements made after the adoption of the draft convention

*The following is taken from the 1989 report of the Working Group to the Commission on Human Rights (E/CN.4/1989/48, paras. 21, 23 and 24).*

21. [...] In the absence of the advice from Legal Counsel on the Chairman's statement regarding paragraph 6 (new paragraph 9) of the preamble, the United Kingdom also stated that their Government might have to lodge a reservation with regard to article 1 and 1 bis at the time of ratification.

23. The observer for New Zealand stated that the text of the draft convention, with particular reference to its preamble, is *ad referendum* to his Government which may have further views to express and positions to adopt on the text at a later stage.

24. Statements to this effect were also made by the representatives of India, the United Kingdom of Great Britain and Northern Ireland and Venezuela.

## 4. Statements made during the adoption of the report

*The following is taken from the 1989 report of the Working Group to the Commission on Human Rights (E/CN.4/1989/48, para. 731).*

731. The representative of the United Kingdom in connection with the adoption of paragraph 43 of the report, said that the United Kingdom understood that the reference to article 1 in the Chairman's statement in that paragraph included a reference to article 1 bis. The representative of Ireland stated that he had no recollection of such a statement having been made at the time that the text of preambular paragraph 6 was adopted. He therefore questioned the appropriateness of its inclusion in the official report of the Working Group.

## 5. Response of the Legal Counsel

*The following response of the Legal Counsel to the request for confirmation by the representative of the United Kingdom regarding preambular paragraph 6 (paragraph 9) is taken from the annex to the 1989 report of the Working Group to the Commission on Human Rights (E/CN.4/1989/48).*

Regarding your request of 30 November 1988 on whether the Chairman of the Working Group preparing the draft convention on rights of the child may on behalf of the entire Working Group include a statement in the *travaux préparatoires* which would read "in adopting this preambular paragraph, the Working Group does not intend to prejudice the interpretation of article 1 or any other provision of the Convention by States Parties", we have not, of course, seen the text of the preambular paragraph in question or the text of any of the provisions of the draft convention and, thus, our views set out below are somewhat abstract in nature.

1. The preamble to a treaty serves to set out the general considerations which motivate the adoption of the treaty. Therefore, it is at first sight strange that a text is sought to be included in the *travaux préparatoires* for the purpose of depriving a particular preambular paragraph of its usual purpose, i.e. to form part of the basis for the interpretation of the treaty. Also, it is not easy to assess what conclusions States may later draw, when interpreting the treaty, from the inclusion of such a text in the *travaux préparatoires*. Furthermore, seeking to establish the meaning of a particular provision of a treaty, through an inclusion in the *travaux préparatoires* may not optimally fulfil the intended purpose, because, as you know, under article 32 of the

Vienna Convention on the Law of Treaties, *travaux préparatoires* constitute a "supplementary means of interpretation" and hence recourse to *travaux préparatoires* may only be had if the relevant treaty provisions are in fact found by those interpreting the treaty to be unclear.

2.      Nevertheless, there is no prohibition in law or practice against inclusion of an interpretative statement in *travaux préparatoires*. Though this is better done through the inclusion of such interpretative statement in the final act or in an accompanying resolution or other instrument. (Inclusion in the final act, etc. would be possible under article 31 of the Vienna Convention on the Law of Treaties.) Nor is there a prohibition in law or practice from making an interpretative statement; in the negative sense, intended here as part of the *travaux préparatoires*.

Carl August Fleischhauer
THE LEGAL COUNSEL
*9 December 1988*

# Article 1 (Definition of a child)

## A.    Final text adopted by the General Assembly (1989)

*The following text is that approved by the General Assembly in its resolution 44/25 of 20 November 1989.*

> For the purposes of the present Convention, a child means every human being below the age of eighteen years unless, under the law applicable to the child, majority is attained earlier.

## B.    First Polish draft convention and comments (1978)

### 1.    The first Polish draft

*Article I of the Polish draft is most closely related to the substantive concerns covered under present article 1. The following text is taken from the 1978 report of the Commission on Human Rights (thirty-fourth session, document E/CN.4/1292, p. 124).*

*Article I*

> Every child, without any exception whatsoever, shall be entitled to the rights set forth in this Convention, without distinction or discrimination on account of race, colour, sex, language, religion, political or other opinion, national or social origin, property, birth or other status, whether of himself or of his family.

### 2.    Comments on the first Polish draft

*Draft article I gave rise to the following comments.*

### (a)    Austria

*The following is taken from document E/CN.4/1324.*

> The draft does not define the term "child". More especially, it does not say up to what age an individual may be described as a child.

### (b)    Barbados

*The following is taken from document E/CN.4/1324.*

> [...]
>
> 3.        The child's right to life has not been articled. How far should this right go? Does the child include the unborn child, or the foetus? Under specified circumstances, should a foetus be aborted without an offence being committed or at the relevant time was the foetus a human life? All these are questions which should be considered before the child's right to life is articled.

### (c)    Dominican Republic

*The following is taken from document E/CN.4/1324.*

> The Dominican Republic, aware not only that, for the reasons stated in the introduction, the child is physically and mentally immature, but also that, for the same biological and mental reasons, legislators in almost every country have created levels of dependency and responsibility such as parental authority and guardianship of children and adolescents, wishes to suggest that in article 1, the words "political or other opinion" should be deleted, since although the child's incapacity is recognized in the preamble, they could be interpreted as meaning that his opinions would still have some relevance. We would suggest that the article in question should be amended to read as follows:

"Every child, without any exception whatsoever, shall be entitled to the rights set forth in this Convention, without distinction or discrimination on account of race, colour, sex, language, religion, national or social origin, property, birth or other status, whether of himself or of his family or guardians. Moreover, the political opinions or allegiances of the family or guardians of the child shall not be a consideration preventing or impending the full enjoyment of these rights."

## (d)    France

*The following is taken from document E/CN.4/1324/Add.1.*

1.      The first article of the convention should give a restrictive definition of the term "child", since it is important to have a clear understanding of what is meant by that term. In some national legislative bodies, including that of France, a "child" is a "minor". But the age at which a child attains his majority varies from one country to another. The first thing to be done is therefore to specify the scope of the convention.

2.      Once the term "child" has been defined, the draft text should state clearly that it is in the best interests of the child, who is unable to express his own wishes, to be represented by his father and his mother.

## (e)    Federal Republic of Germany

*The following is taken from document E/CN.4/1324.*

See paragraphs 3, 8 and 10, General Comments, and paragraph 2, Specific Comments, Federal Republic of Germany.

*Paragraphs 3, 8 and 10, which appear elsewhere in document E/CN.4/1324, are reproduced below. There is no paragraph 2 under the specific comments of the Federal Republic of Germany in the document.*

3.      Without prejudice to a final assessment, we consider that articles I, III, IV (understood as the right of the child to have his needs provided for in the broadest sense), the first and second sentences of article VI, the first sentence of article VII, paragraph 1 (right to education), and the second part of article VII, paragraph 2 (primary right of parents) should be grouped together in a separate section as rights of the individual.

[...]

8.      The Federal Government also expresses reservations as to the comprehensiveness of the safeguards provided regarding efforts to ensure the protection of the child which have been undertaken elsewhere in the United Nations. This applies particularly to natural children whose status has long been the subject of consultations within the Sub-Commission on Prevention of Discrimination and Protection of Minorities of the United Nations Commission on Human Rights. This question should receive special attention. Another matter that should receive special attention in this context is whether the application of the convention to natural children is also provided for in the present draft. Admittedly, article I provides that every child shall be entitled to the rights set forth in the convention, without distinction or discrimination on account of birth or status, among other factors. Furthermore, the wording of principle 1 of the Declaration of the Rights of the Child of 20 November 1959, on which article I of the draft convention is based, seems to have been designed to assure natural children of the same rights as those enjoyed by legitimate children. However, the other provisions of the Declaration of 20 November 1959, and consequently of the draft convention based on it, do not take account of the situation of natural children. For instance, the second part of article VII, paragraph 2, provides that responsibility for the education and guidance of the child lies in the first place with "his parents". This provision needs to be modified to cover the situation of natural children, most of whom are brought up in the family of the mother.

[...]

10.     In the view of the Federal Government, another question that should be considered is whether the draft convention should also make specific provision for the protection of adopted children and children

who are brought up by foster-parents. Efforts have been in progress for a number of years within the United Nations to draft a convention or, at the very least, a declaration on adoption. In this connection, particular reference should be made to Economic and Social Council resolution 1925 (LVIII) of 6 May 1975. The present draft convention also deals with adopted children in so far as its article I prohibits any distinction in the treatment of children on account of their "status". However, as in the case of natural children, the draft contains no other provision relating specifically to adoption or to the situation of the foster-child. Consequently, it should also be made clear whether the protection of adopted children and foster-children should be dealt with separately, or whether it is preferable to treat these questions in greater detail on the basis and in the framework of the proposed convention, after they have been raised in article I of the draft. One reason why this is essential is to avoid any conflict between the different United Nations instruments on the protection of the child.

## (f) Madagascar

*The following is taken from document E/CN.4/1324.*

If it proves impossible to reach a consensus on the term "child" (which would be the ideal solution), it will be necessary to seek a broad interpretation of this term or to harmonize the various criteria adopted by States regarding the age of the child.

## (g) Malawi

*The following is taken from document E/CN.4/1324/Add.4.*

We feel that clarifications on the following points are necessary:

    (1)      the meaning the convention attributes to the term, "child";

    (2)      any extensions attributed to the term "child" like, for example, in our Wills and Inheritance Act (Cap. 10.02) Section 2(1), whereby the word "child", includes an illegitimate adopted child and a grandchild; and

    (3)      the question of whether or not the convention intends to leave interpretation matters to Municipal Law.

## (h) New Zealand

*The following is taken from document E/CN.4/1324/Add.5.*

Acceptable.

*The following comments submitted by New Zealand on article IV of the first Polish draft concern article 1 and are therefore also reproduced here.*

*Article IV*

A point of some importance which this article, and indeed all the articles raise to some degree, is the definition of a child. Does the definition begin at conception, at birth, or at some point in between? Perhaps of equal importance, in view of the special protection clause (article II), is a definition of the end of childhood. It seems that it would be very difficult to declare an across-the-board age and that the end of childhood would be related to specific issues (right to leave home, vote, drive a motor vehicle, have sexual intercourse, etc.) which would be covered by specific legislation in each country.

## (i) Portugal

*The following is taken from document E/CN.4/1324.*

[...]

2.        However, the competent Portuguese authorities are of the view that the wording of the draft could be improved. The rights of the child prior to birth could be more clearly defined.

## (j)      International Committee of the Red Cross

*The following is taken from document E/CN.4/1324.*

1.        In analysing the draft convention on the rights of the child, ICRC must consider the relationship between the draft and the provisions of the Geneva instruments concerning protection of the child.

2.        An examination of article I of the draft shows that its material scope has not been defined. The article provides that the convention shall apply to every child "without any exception whatsoever". In the absence of any clarification, it could be inferred from this that the material scope is very broad and that the draft is to be applied in times of peace as well as in times of armed conflict.

3.        Only article VIII stipulates that "the child shall *in all circumstances* be among the first to receive protection and relief". It seems to us that the words "in all circumstances" apply to all the provisions and have been inserted in this article only to emphasize the fact that the child must *always* be among the first to receive protection and relief. Moreover, consideration of the provisions themselves shows that they are very general in nature and capable of being observed at all times. The provisions attempt not so much to grant the child specific rights connected with a particular situation, but to deal with general questions so as to guarantee the child a harmonious background for his physical and mental development.

4.        The personal scope of the draft has been defined, for the convention is to apply to children (article I). The notion of "child" has not, however, been made clear. The concept varies from one culture to another. This silence seems wise and will facilitate universal application of the convention irrespective of local peculiarities.

5.        The context of the Geneva Conventions and the Additional Protocols is much more precise. Their scope has been strictly defined - they apply in situations of armed conflict. The notion of "child" has not been defined for the purpose of the Conventions and the Protocols as a whole. An age-limit of either 15 or 18 years has, however, often been added. The provisions relating to the protection of children therefore have a specific character. They define the rights of the child in precise and practical terms.

6.        We are confronted, on the one hand, by a draft convention characterized by the general and global nature of both its scope and its provisions and, on the other, by the provisions of the Geneva instruments, which are more precise and which apply only in times of armed conflict. The two texts are not incompatible. It is necessary to point out, however, that the protection accorded by existing law must not be reduced by the draft convention. We considered whether it was necessary to express this idea by means of a reservation upholding existing law. This does not seem to be the case, since the provisions of positive law, which go further than the proposed law, must be regarded as *leges speciales*. This is particularly true of the 1949 Geneva Conventions and the Protocols additional thereto which, as *leges speciales* for situations of armed conflict, will remain fully in force. If, however, there was any doubt on this point, a clause should be formulated and inserted in the draft.

7.        In order to avoid any ambiguity, we propose that the material scope of the draft should be clarified by the addition of the words "in all circumstances" after the words "shall be entitled" in article I.

## (k)      Society for Comparative Legislation

*The following is taken from document E/CN.4/1324.*

Every child up to the age of 16 years, and possibly beyond in certain particular cases, shall, without any exception whatsoever, be entitled to the rights set forth in this Convention, without distinction or discrimination on account of race, colour, sex, language, religion, political or other opinion, national or social origin, property, birth or other status, whether of himself or of his family.

## C.   First reading (1979-1988)

*The text of article 1, which was based on article 1 of the revised Polish draft, was discussed and adopted by the Working Group in 1980. Additional proposals were submitted to the Working Group in 1987 and 1988 but further consideration was deferred until the second reading. This article was referred to as article 1 throughout the first and second readings.*

### 1.   Revised Polish draft (1979)

*This draft formed the basis for discussion at the 1980 session of the Working Group. The following text is taken from Commission on Human Rights document E/CN.4/1349, which was reissued for technical reasons.*

*Article 1*

According to the present Convention a child is every human being from the moment of his birth to the age of 18 years unless, under the law of his State, he has attained his age of majority earlier.

### 2.   Discussion and adoption by the Working Group (1980)

*The following is taken from the 1980 report of the Working Group to the Commission on Human Rights (E/CN.4/ L.1542, paras. 28-36), which is reproduced in the 1980 report of the Commission on Human Rights (thirty-sixth session, document E/CN.4/1408, para. 277).*

28.      At its third meeting, the Working Group considered article 1 of the draft convention. There was considerable debate concerning the initial and terminal points which define the concept of child, as contained in the article.

29.      Some delegates opposed the idea that childhood begins at the moment of birth, as stated in the draft article, and indicated that this is contrary to the legislation of many countries. They argued that the concept should be extended to include the entire period from the moment of conception. Other delegates asserted that the attempt to establish a beginning point should be abandoned and that wording should be adopted which was compatible with the wide variety of domestic legislation on this subject.

30.      The representative of Morocco proposed that the words "from the moment of his birth" should be deleted from the article in order to solve the difficulty. Several delegations supported the proposed amendment.

31.      The first part of the article was therefore adopted with the amendment proposed by Morocco.

32.      Concerning the terminal point of the concept of child as defined in the article, some delegates pointed out that the age of 18 appeared to be quite late in light of some national legislations and that a lower age-limit should be recommended. It was suggested that, since the General Assembly had set the age-limit at 15 in connection with the International Year of the Child, the same position should be adopted in the draft convention. It was also pointed out that 14 was the age of the end of compulsory education in many countries, and the legal marriage age for girls in many parts of the world. In this view, setting the age-limit at 14 would also establish a clear distinction between the concept of minor and that of child, since the former was protected under many national legislations while the latter was not.

33.      Other delegates, however, opposed the lowering of the age-limit to 15 because their domestic legislation embodied protective measures for children beyond that age, and they believed that the draft convention should apply to as large an age group as possible. They argued in favour of retaining the wording of the draft article which, in any event, is qualified by the reference to national legislation.

34.    The observer for the International Union for Child Welfare, a non-governmental organization in consultative status, suggested that reference to an upper age-limit could be eliminated by amending the text of the article to read:

> "According to the present Convention a child is every human being who has not attained the age of majority in conformity with the law of his State."

35.    A number of delegations, however, opposed the idea of making the definition depend on the concept of majority age, since this varied widely between countries and also within national legislations, according to whether the civil, penal, political or other aspects of majority were at issue. Others, while not opposing this formulation, pointed out that the original text took care of the objections raised by making reference to national legislation.

36.    At the fourth meeting of the Working Group, the second part of article 1 was adopted in its original version. One representative recalled that he had expressed reservations concerning the specifying of the age of 18 in article 1 and said that his delegation might consider it necessary to refer again to this matter, including in the plenary of the Commission. Another delegation reserved its position on the number "18", stating that a person at that age is not a child.

## 3.    Proposal submitted to the Working Group (1984)

### (a)    International Federation of Women in Legal Careers and the International Abolitionist Federation

*The following is taken from document E/CN.4/1983/NGO/33, which appeared after the 1983 session of the Working Group.*

> *Article 1* (Age)
>
> In view of increasingly early development of children and the present tendency to include young people in discussions relating to family decisions or outside problems, we consider that a second paragraph should be added, reading: "Account shall, however, be taken of the passage from childhood to adolescence, which will lead to a different approach to the rights and duties of the child."

## 4.    Question raised before the Working Group (1984)

*The following is taken from the 1984 report of the Working Group (E/CN.4/1984/71, paragraph 12).*

> 12.    The Japanese delegation asked whether, for the purposes of article 1 of the draft convention, an 18-year-old human being was to be considered a child.

## 5.    Proposal submitted to the Working Group (1987)

### (a)    Netherlands and Austria

*The following proposal concerning "article 1 bis" was submitted jointly by the Netherlands and Austria to the Working Group at its 1987 session. However, the proposal was not discussed at that time and therefore appears in the annex to the 1987 report of the Working Group to the Commission on Human Rights (E/CN.4/1987/25). It was subsequently reproduced in document E/CN.4/1988/WG.1/WP.2 and is referred to in paragraph 221 of document E/CN.4/1988/28 reproduced in section 7 below.*

> *Article 1 bis*
>
> "The States Parties to the present Convention shall not provide any discrimination, in particular on the grounds of sex, in establishing the age of majority."

## 6. Proposal submitted to the Working Group (1988)

### (a) Finland

*For the text of this proposal, and the remarks of the observer from Finland in withdrawing it, see paragraphs 224 and 225 in section 7 below.*

## 7. Discussion in the Working Group (1988)

*The following is taken from the 1988 report of the Working Group to the Commission on Human Rights (E/CN.4/1988/28, paras. 221, 224, 225 and 235).*

1. *Article 1 bis (Prevention of discrimination, particularly on the grounds of sex)*

221. The proposal submitted by the Netherlands (E/CN.4/1988/WG.1/WP.2, chapt. II) concerned the obligation of the States Parties not to discriminate, in particular on grounds of sex, in establishing the age of majority. Some participants requested clarification of the reasons why the proposal had been submitted, since articles 1 and 4 of the draft convention established the age of majority and the principle of non-discrimination. The observer for the Netherlands explained that he would accept that article 4 covered that point if the age of adulthood were established in the convention but, given the terms in which article 1 had been drafted, he thought that article 4 did not suffice. However, he understood that some of the questions put to him needed clarification. The discussion of the proposal was deferred to the second reading.

[...]

1. *Article 1 (Child-age)*

224. The Working Group had before it a proposal submitted by Finland (E/CN.4/1988/WG.1/WP.10) which read as follows:

"Article 1

1. For the purposes of the present Convention, *a child* means every human being who has not attained the age of 18 years.

2. No provision of the present Convention shall be applied to a child who has attained the age of [15] years and who no longer is a minor, where the application would be manifestly incompatible with the legal status of that child.

[3. In terms of paragraph 2 of this article, *a child who no longer is a minor* means a child who:

    (a) has full legal capacity; or

    (b) has become emancipated in all matters relating to his or her person; or

    (c) has the right to determine his or her own residence; or

    (d) has the capacity to enter into certain contractual relationships; or

    (e) has the capacity to dispose of certain parts of his or her property.]"

225. The observer for Finland stated that article 1 needed fundamental revision in various respects. The use of the age of majority as one of the central devices to delimit the scope of application of the convention could weaken the whole convention considerably. It was to be hoped that the proposal which Finland was withdrawing would give some indication for future revision of article 1, in particular with respect to the emphasis to be given to the crucial links between article 1 and other articles, such as article 20 on children in armed conflicts.

[...]

C.        *Other proposals*

235.        During its session, statements were made to the effect that the proposals relating to the following articles should be considered by the working group during the second reading of the draft convention.

[...]

1.        *Article 1, revision (Child-age), proposal from Finland, E/CN.4/1988/WG.1/WP.10 (see paras. 224 and 225 above)*

[...]

## 8.        Text as adopted at first reading

*The following is taken from E/CN.4/1988/WG.1/WP.1/Rev.1.*

*Article 1*

According to the present Convention a child is every human being to the age of 18 years unless, under the law of his State, he has attained his age of majority earlier.

# D.    Technical review (1988)

## 1.        Comment by the Legal Counsel

*The following is taken from document E/CN.4/1989/WG.1/CRP.1, page 12.*

Would be clearer if it were to read:

"For the purpose of the present Convention, a child means every human being who has not as yet attained the age of 18 years unless, according to the law of his State of nationality, he has attained the age of majority earlier."

## 2.        Comment by the United Nations Educational, Scientific and Cultural Organization (UNESCO)

*The following is taken from document E/CN.4/1989/WG.1/CRP.1, page 12.*

Article 1 should begin as follows:

*English version*: "For the purpose of ..."

*French version*:  "Aux fins de la présente Convention ..."

## 3.        Comment by the United Nations Children's Fund (UNICEF)

*The following is taken from document E/CN.4/1989/WG.1/CRP.1, page 12.*

*Gender neutrality*:

A possible reformulation of the article is:

"According to the present Convention a child is every human being to the age of 18 years unless, under the law of *the child's* State, [ ] the age of majority is attained earlier."

# E.    Second reading (1988-1989)

## 1.    Proposals submitted to the Working Group at second reading

### (a)    Finland

*For the text of this proposal, see paragraph 76 in section 2 below.*

### (b)    India

*For the text of this proposal, see paragraph 76 in section 2 below.*

### (c)    Kuwait

*The following is taken from document E/CN.4/1989/WG.1/WP.18.*

Article 1, concerning the definition of a child, should read as follows:

"A child is every human being who has not attained the age of majority as defined by the law of his country."

### (d)    Libyan Arab Jamahiriya

*The following is taken from document E/CN.4/1989/WG.1/WP.18.*

[...]

*Article 1: Proposed alternative wording*

"Under the present Convention, a child is every human being under the age of 18 years unless, under the law of his country, he has attained the age of majority earlier."

[...]

### (e)    Malta

*The following is taken from document E/CN.4/1989/WG.1/WP.9.*

It is the submission of the Government of Malta that the text of the proposed convention as contained in document E/CN.4/1988/WG.1/WP.1/Rev.2 of 6 April, 1988 represents, in one important respect, a retreat from the principles enunciated in the 1959 United Nations Declaration of the Rights of the Child. Unlike the Declaration, the draft convention in its present form makes no mention of the rights of the child *before birth*, and as such falls short of the comprehensive protection enunciated by the Declaration.

It is accordingly the view of the Government of Malta that the text of the draft convention should be amended as follows:

1)    At the end of the sixth preambular paragraph [new paragraph 9], after the words "conditions of freedom, dignity and security" add the words "before as well as after birth";

2)    In Article 1, after the words "human being", add the words "from conception".

### (f)    Senegal

*For the text of this proposal, see paragraph 76 in section 2 below.*

### (g)    Venezuela

*For the text of this proposal, see paragraph 87 in section 2 below.*

**(h)    World Association of Children's Friends**

*The following is taken from document E/CN.4/1988/WG.1/NGO/1.*

*Article 1*

According to the present Convention, a child is every human being to the age of 18 years unless, under the law of his State, he has attained his age of majority earlier.

*Addition*:

The present Convention also extends, in accordance with article 21 quater, to the protection of the conceived, unborn child from genetic experiments and manipulations injurious to his physical, moral or mental integrity or to his health.

Article 21 quater

The States Parties to the present Convention shall take all steps to prohibit, at the least:

> Any creation of identical human beings by cloning or other methods, whether or not for purposes of racial selection;
>
> Implantation of a human embryo in the uterus of another species or vice versa;
>
> The fusion of human gametes with those of another species; 1/
>
> The creation of embryos using sperm from other individuals;
>
> The fusion of embryos or any other operation likely to result in terata;
>
> Ectogenesis;
>
> The possible creation of children from persons of the same sex;
>
> The selection of sex by genetic manipulation for non-therapeutic purposes;
>
> The creation of identical twins;
>
> Research and experimentation on human embryos, whether viable or not;
>
> Experimentation on living embryos, whether viable or not.

*Note*

1/    The hamster test for studying male fertility might be an exception, if subject to strict regulation.

## 2.    Discussion and adoption at second reading

*The following is taken from the 1989 report of the Working Group to the Commission on Human Rights (E/CN.4/1989/48, paras. 75-90).*

75.    The Working Group had before it a text of the article as adopted at first reading into which was incorporated suggested revisions by the Legal Counsel, UNESCO and UNICEF contained in document E/CN.4/1989/WG.1/WP.9 which read as follows:

> *"For the purpose of* the present Convention, a child *means* every human being to the age of 18 years unless, under the law of (his) *the child's* State, *the* age of majority is attained earlier."

76.      The Working Group also had before it a proposal by Malta contained in document E/CN.4/1989/ WG.1/WP.9 which read as follows:

"In article 1, after the words 'human being', add the words 'from conception'."

a proposal by Finland contained in document E/CN.4/1989/WG.1/WP.12 which read as follows:

"For the purpose of the present Convention a child means every human being who is a minor and has not attained the age of 18 years."

a proposal by Senegal (contained in document E/CN.4/1989/WG.1/WP.17) which read as follows:

"According to the present Convention a child is every human being, *from his conception until at least*, the age of 18 years unless, under the law of his State, he has attained the age of majority earlier."

and a proposal by India (contained in document E/CN.4/1989/WG.1/WP.14) which read as follows:

"According to the present Convention a child is every human being up to the age of 18 years unless, under the law of his State, he has ceased to be a child earlier or different age-limits for different purposes are recognized."

77.      The representatives of Malta and Senegal stated that, in light of the text of preambular paragraph 6 as adopted, they would not insist on the adoption of the ideas contained in their respective proposals and therefore withdrew them. They both however indicated that they wished the report of the Working Group to show that their respective Governments took the view that the protection of the child should begin with conception and not just from birth. The observer for the Holy See made a statement indicating that had these proposals not been withdrawn his delegation would have supported them.

78.      The representatives of Finland and the United States of America stated, with reference to the revised text contained in document E/CN.4/1989/WG.1/WP.2, that the phrase "under the law of (his) *the child's* State" did not clarify exactly which law would be applicable and therefore wished to see the words omitted from the final text. It was suggested that the words "under the law applicable to the child" be used.

79.      The representatives of Finland and India, supported by the representative of the United States of America, took the view that as the concept of majority differed from context to context, and from one legislation to another, it should not be included in a final text of the article.

80.      The representative of the Netherlands expressed general support for the proposal by the representative of Finland. He further indicated with reference to the revised text contained in document E/ CN.4/1989/WG.1/WP.2 that the words "the age of" be deleted since majority may be attained by satisfying criteria other than age. It was suggested that the words "majority is attained earlier" be used.

81.      The representative of Kuwait did not wish the specific age-limit of 18 to be included in a final text.

82.      The representative of Nepal took the view that an upper age-limit of 16 years be set for the definition of a child so as to take into account the concerns of poorer States who may not be able to shoulder the burdens imposed by this convention for children up to 18 years of age. He took the view that this would leave more wealthy States with the option to expand their definition as they deem fit. The representative of Portugal expressed general support for the revised text contained in document E/CN.4/1989/WG.1/WP.2. She stated that mentioning the age of 18 years would underline the recognition of the need to ensure special protection to human beings under that age. A definition based on the simple notion of majority would not therefore seem to be desirable, taking into account the different solutions existing in various legal systems.

83.      The representatives of Argentina, Ireland and Morocco expressed support for the revised text contained in document E/CN.4/1989/WG.1/WP.2 and expressed hesitation about the Finnish proposal as it sought to introduce the concept of a "minor" into a text of the article.

84.     The representative of Japan indicated that an upper age-limit be expressed as "below the age of 18" rather than "to the age of 18".

85.     The text of article 1, as adopted on second reading, reads as follows:

"For the purposes of the present Convention a child means every human being below the age of 18 years unless, under the law applicable to the child, majority is attained earlier."

[...]

87.     The representative of Venezuela submitted document E/CN.4/1989/WG.1/WP.10 which reads as follows:

*Article 1 and 1 bis*

*Merge* the present article 1 with article 1 bis to form a single article 1 reading:

"1.     For the purpose of the present Convention, "child" means every human being up to the age of 18 years unless, under the law of his State, he has attained the age of majority earlier.

2.     The States Parties to the present Convention recognize that every child has the inherent right to life.

3.     States Parties shall ensure to the maximum extent possible the healthy growth and development of the child."

[...]

90.     The representative of Venezuela withdrew the amendment and stated that the problem would be one of interpretation by local authorities.

## 3.     Statement made after the adoption of the draft convention

### (a)     United Kingdom of Great Britain and Northern Ireland

*The following is taken from the 1989 report of the Working Group to the Commission on Human Rights (E/CN.4/1989/48, para. 21).*

21.     [...] In the absence of the advice from Legal Counsel on the Chairman's statement regarding paragraph 6 [new paragraph 9] of the preamble, the United Kingdom also stated that their Government might have to lodge a reservation with regard to article 1 and 1 bis at the time of ratification.

## 4.     Statements made during the adoption of the report

*The following is taken from the 1989 report of the Working Group to the Commission on Human Rights (E/CN.4/1989/48, para. 731).*

731.     The representative of the United Kingdom in connection with the adoption of paragraph 43 of the report, said that the United Kingdom understood that the reference to article 1 in the Chairman's statement in that paragraph included a reference to article 1 bis. The representative of Ireland stated that he had no recollection of such a statement having been made at the time that the text of preambular paragraph 6 [new paragraph 9] was adopted. He therefore questioned the appropriateness of its inclusion in the official report of the Working Group.

## 5.     Response of the Legal Counsel

*The following response of the Legal Counsel to the request for confirmation by the representative of the United Kingdom regarding preambular paragraph 6 (new paragraph 9) is taken from the annex to the 1989 report of the Working Group to the Commission on Human Rights (E/CN.4/1989/48).*

Regarding your request of 30 November 1988 on whether the Chairman of the Working Group preparing the draft convention on rights of the child may on behalf of the entire Working Group include a statement in the *travaux préparatoires* which would read "in adopting this preambular paragraph, the Working Group does not intend to prejudice the interpretation of article 1 or any other provision of the Convention by States Parties", we have not, of course, seen the text of the preambular paragraph in question or the text of any of the provisions of the draft convention and, thus, our views set out below are somewhat abstract in nature.

1.      The preamble to a treaty serves to set out the general considerations which motivate the adoption of the treaty. Therefore, it is at first sight strange that a text is sought to be included in the *travaux préparatoires* for the purpose of depriving a particular preambular paragraph of its usual purpose, i.e. to form part of the basis for the interpretation of the treaty. Also, it is not easy to assess what conclusions States may later draw, when interpreting the treaty, from the inclusion of such a text in the *travaux préparatoires*. Furthermore, seeking to establish the meaning of a particular provision of a treaty, through an inclusion in the *travaux préparatoires* may not optimally fulfil the intended purpose, because, as you know, under article 32 of the Vienna Convention on the Law of Treaties, *travaux préparatoires* constitute a "supplementary means of interpretation" and hence recourse to *travaux préparatoires* may only be had if the relevant treaty provisions are in fact found by those interpreting the treaty to be unclear.

2.      Nevertheless, there is no prohibition in law or practice against inclusion of an interpretative statement in *travaux préparatoires*. Though this is better done through the inclusion of such interpretative statement in the final act or in an accompanying resolution or other instrument. (Inclusion in the final act, etc. would be possible under article 31 of the Vienna Convention on the Law of Treaties.) Nor is there a prohibition in law or practice from making an interpretative statement; in the negative sense, intended here as part of the *travaux préparatoires*.

Carl August Fleischhauer
THE LEGAL COUNSEL
*9 December 1988*

# Article 2 (Non-discrimination)

## A.  Final text adopted by the General Assembly (1989)

*The following text is that approved by the General Assembly in its resolution 44/25 of 20 November 1989.*

1.    States Parties shall respect and ensure the rights set forth in the present Convention to each child within their jurisdiction without discrimination of any kind, irrespective of the child's or his or her parent's or legal guardian's race, colour, sex, language, religion, political or other opinion, national, ethnic or social origin, property, disability, birth or other status.

2.    States Parties shall take all appropriate measures to ensure that the child is protected against all forms of discrimination or punishment on the basis of the status, activities, expressed opinions, or beliefs of the child's parents, legal guardians, or family members.

## B.  First Polish draft convention and comments (1978)

### 1.  The first Polish draft

*Articles I and X of the Polish draft are most closely related to the substantive concerns covered under present article 2. The following text of those two articles is taken from the 1978 report of the Commission on Human Rights (thirty-fourth session, document E/CN.4/1292, pp. 124-125).*

*Article I*

Every child, without any exception whatsoever, shall be entitled to the rights set forth in this Convention, without distinction or discrimination on account of race, colour, sex, language, religion, political or other opinion, national or social origin, property, birth or other status, whether of himself or of his family.

*Article X*

The child shall be protected from practices which may foster racial, religious or any other form of discrimination. He shall be brought up in a spirit of understanding, tolerance, friendship among peoples, peace and universal brotherhood, and in full consciousness that his energy and talents should be devoted to the service of his fellow men.

### 2.  Comments on article I of the first Polish draft which pertain to non-discrimination

#### (a)  Dominican Republic

*The following is taken from document E/CN.4/1324.*

The Dominican Republic, aware not only that, for the reasons stated in the introduction, the child is physically and mentally immature, but also that, for the same biological and mental reasons, legislators in almost every country have created levels of dependency and responsibility such as parental authority and guardianship of children and adolescents, wishes to suggest that in article 1, the words "political or other opinion" should be deleted, since although the child's incapacity is recognized in the preamble, they could be interpreted as meaning that his opinions would still have some relevance. We would suggest that the article in question should be amended to read as follows:

"Every child, without any exception whatsoever, shall be entitled to the rights set forth in this Convention, without distinction or discrimination on account of race, colour, sex, language, religion, national or social origin, property, birth or other status, whether of himself or of his family or guardians. Moreover, the political opinions or allegiances of the family or guardians of the child shall not be a consideration preventing or impending the full enjoyment of these rights."

## (b)    German Democratic Republic

*The following is taken from document E/CN.4/1324.*

[...]

2.      Drawing on its previous experience in this field, the German Democratic Republic should like to make the following suggestion to make the language more precise:

> "An explicit provision should be included in the Convention to preclude discrimination against children of unmarried parents. On this subject, the German Democratic Republic earlier submitted to the Secretary-General of the United Nations detailed observations on the 'Draft general principles on equality and non-discrimination in respect of children born out of wedlock'."

3.      The German Democratic Republic believes that the principles set forth in the draft convention on the rights of the child, and in particular the provisions of article I on non-discrimination and the attendant right of all children to physical and spiritual development without distinction, are in accordance with one of the principal tasks facing the United Nations, i.e. to support the peoples in their struggle against colonialism, neocolonialism, racial discrimination and apartheid. It is the German Democratic Republic's understanding that in implementing the convention one should be aware of the inseparable unity of the striving for peace and détente, and the happiness, advancement and protection of children all over the world.

## (c)    Federal Republic of Germany

*The following is taken from document E/CN.4/1324.*

See paragraphs 3, 8 and 10, General Comments, and paragraph 2, Specific Comments, Federal Republic of Germany.

*Paragraphs 3, 8 and 10, which appear elsewhere in document E/CN.4/1324, are reproduced below. There is no paragraph 2 under the specific comments of the Federal Republic of Germany in the document.*

3.      Without prejudice to a final assessment, we consider that articles I, III, IV (understood as the right of the child to have his needs provided for in the broadest sense), the first and second sentences of article VI, the first sentence of article VII, paragraph 1 (right to education), and the second part of article VII, paragraph 2 (primary right of parents) should be grouped together in a separate section as rights of the individual.

[...]

8.      The Federal Government also expresses reservations as to the comprehensiveness of the safeguards provided regarding efforts to ensure the protection of the child which have been undertaken elsewhere in the United Nations. This applies particularly to natural children whose status has long been the subject of consultations within the Sub-Commission on Prevention of Discrimination and Protection of Minorities of the United Nations Commission on Human Rights. This question should receive special attention. Another matter that should receive special attention in this context is whether the application of the convention to natural children is also provided for in the present draft. Admittedly, article I provides that every child shall be entitled to the rights set forth in the convention, without distinction or discrimination on account of birth or status, among other factors. Furthermore, the wording of principle 1 of the Declaration of the Rights of the Child of 20 November 1959, on which article I of the draft convention is based, seems to have been designed to assure natural children of the same rights as those enjoyed by legitimate children. However, the other provisions of the Declaration of 20 November 1959, and consequently of the draft convention based on it, do not take account of the situation of natural children. For instance, the second part of article VII, paragraph 2, provides that responsibility for the education and guidance of the child lies in the first place with "his parents". This provision needs to be modified to cover the situation of natural children, most of whom are brought up in the family of the mother.

[...]

10.    In the view of the Federal Government, another question that should be considered is whether the draft convention should also make specific provision for the protection of adopted children and children who are brought up by foster-parents. Efforts have been in progress for a number of years within the United Nations to draft a convention or, at the very least, a declaration on adoption. In this connection, particular reference should be made to Economic and Social Council resolution 1925 (LVIII) of 6 May 1975. The present draft convention also deals with adopted children in so far as its article I prohibits any distinction in the treatment of children on account of their "status". However, as in the case of natural children, the draft contains no other provision relating specifically to adoption or to the situation of the foster-child. Consequently, it should also be made clear whether the protection of adopted children and foster-children should be dealt with separately, or whether it is preferable to treat these questions in greater detail on the basis and in the framework of the proposed convention, after they have been raised in article I of the draft. One reason why this is essential is to avoid any conflict between the different United Nations instruments on the protection of the child.

## (d)    Malawi

*The following is taken from document E/CN.4/1324/Add.4.*

We feel that clarifications on the following points are necessary:

(1)    the meaning the convention attributes to the term, "child";

(2)    any extensions attributed to the term "child" like, for example, in our Wills and Inheritance Act (Cap. 10.02) Section 2(1), whereby the word "child" includes an illegitimate adopted child and a grandchild; and

(3)    the question of whether or not the convention intends to leave interpretation matters to Municipal Law.

## (e)    Spain

*The following is taken from document E/CN.4/1324.*

Insert the words "in or out of wedlock" between the word "birth" and the words "or other status".

## (f)    International Committee of the Red Cross

*The following is taken from document E/CN.4/1324.*

1.    In analysing the draft convention on the rights of the child, ICRC must consider the relationship between the draft and the provisions of the Geneva instruments concerning protection of the child.

2.    An examination of article I of the draft shows that its material scope has not been defined. The article provides that the convention shall apply to every child "without any exception whatsoever". In the absence of any clarification, it could be inferred from this that the material scope is very broad and that the draft is to be applied in times of peace as well as in times of armed conflict.

3.    Only article VIII stipulates that "the child shall *in all circumstances* be among the first to receive protection and relief". It seems to us that the words "in all circumstances" apply to all the provisions and have been inserted in this article only to emphasize the fact that the child must *always* be among the first to receive protection and relief. Moreover, consideration of the provisions themselves shows that they are very general in nature and capable of being observed at all times. The provisions attempt not so much to grant the child specific rights connected with a particular situation, but to deal with general questions so as to guarantee the child a harmonious background for his physical and mental development.

4.      The personal scope of the draft has been defined, for the convention is to apply to children (article I). The notion of "child" has not, however, been made clear. The concept varies from one culture to another. This silence seems wise and will facilitate universal application of the convention irrespective of local peculiarities.

5.      The context of the Geneva Conventions and the Additional Protocols is much more precise. Their scope has been strictly defined - they apply in situations of armed conflict. The notion of "child" has not been defined for the purpose of the Conventions and the Protocols as a whole. An age-limit of either 15 or 18 years has, however, often been added. The provisions relating to the protection of children therefore have a specific character. They define the rights of the child in precise and practical terms.

6.      We are confronted, on the one hand, by a draft convention characterized by the general and global nature of both its scope and its provisions and, on the other, by the provisions of the Geneva instruments, which are more precise and which apply only in times of armed conflict. The two texts are not incompatible. It is necessary to point out, however, that the protection accorded by existing law must not be reduced by the draft convention. We considered whether it was necessary to express this idea by means of a reservation upholding existing law. This does not seem to be the case, since the provisions of positive law, which go further than the proposed law, must be regarded as *leges speciales*. This is particularly true of the 1949 Geneva Conventions and the Protocols additional thereto which, as *leges speciales* for situations of armed conflict, will remain fully in force. If, however, there was any doubt on this point, a clause should be formulated and inserted in the draft.

7.      In order to avoid any ambiguity, we propose that the material scope of the draft should be clarified by the addition of the words "in all circumstances" after the words "shall be entitled" in article I.

## (g)      Society for Comparative Legislation

*The following is taken from document E/CN.4/1324.*

Every child up to the age of 16 years, and possibly beyond in certain particular cases, shall, without any exception whatsoever, be entitled to the rights set forth in this Convention, without distinction or discrimination on account of race, colour, sex, language, religion, political or other opinion, national or social origin, property, birth or other status, whether of himself or of his family.

## 3.      Comments on article X of the first Polish draft which pertain to non-discrimination

### (a)      Dominican Republic

*The following is taken from document E/CN.4/1324.*

See Dominican Republic, under Specific Comments, article IX.

*The specific comments referred to, which also appear in document E/CN.4/1324, are reproduced below.*

By way of comment only, we would draw attention to the fact that the provisions of articles IX and X of the draft have been given detailed treatment in various ILO international agreements on other questions; it might be advisable to revise those agreements in case their contents should be expanded.

### (b)      France

*The following is taken from document E/CN.4/1324/Add.1.*

1.      In our view, this article should not form part of the convention itself but should be incorporated into the preliminary declaration which we would like to see included in a text preceding the articles of the convention.

2.      For earlier comments, see paragraph 4 (a), France, under General Comments.

*Subparagraph 4 (a), which also appears in document E/CN.4/1324/Add.1, is reproduced below.*

The provisions that would constitute a recommendation, such as article II, the first sentence of article VI and article X, might be included in a preliminary declaration or a recommendation annexed to the convention[.]

## (c)    **Federal Republic of Germany**

*The following is taken from document E/CN.4/1324.*

See paragraphs 6 and 7, Federal Republic of Germany, under General Comments.

*Paragraphs 6 and 7, which also appear in document E/CN.4/1324, are reproduced below.*

6.      Unlike the series of measures on the rights of the individual, article II, article IV (first and second sentences), article V, article VI (fourth sentence), article VII, paragraph 1 (second sentence), article VII, paragraph 3, article IX and article X (first sentence) can be considered only as undertakings on the part of States.

7.      Conversely, the provisions of the draft relating to objectives, content and methods of education cannot be considered as either rights of the individual or undertakings on the part of States. The provisions in question are contained in the first sentence of article VI, the first part of article VII, paragraph 2, and the second sentence of article X of the draft. It is the responsibility and duty of the parents whose rights are also recognized in the draft to take binding decisions in this regard. The provisions referred to can more appropriately be made the subject of a recommendation to be incorporated in the preamble to the convention.

## (d)    **New Zealand**

*The following is taken from document E/CN.4/1324/Add.5.*

The New Zealand Human Rights Commission has recommended that discrimination on the grounds of sex be specifically stated in the first sentence of article X. Practices fostering discrimination on the basis of sex are often unrecognized and it is necessary to emphasize that sex is as much a ground for discrimination as race and religion so that sex discrimination can be recognized and steps taken towards its elimination.

The present first sentence is also impracticable because of the use of the word "may" and we believe that this word should be omitted. The question also arises that if the practices referred to in the first sentence were to occur in the home of the parents of the child who would decide that the child should be protected, and how the protection would be given? In New Zealand if a child is physically ill-treated the Department of Social Welfare can remove the child from the detrimental environment. We wonder if this is the sort of protection envisaged by the authors of the article.

Clearly, this article has implications for school and classroom practices. For example, in the light of the terms of the article the withdrawal of children from religious instruction could be construed as fostering discrimination. The article's practicability depends on what are seen to be desirable and practised values in the society. Some of the New Zealand curriculum is orientated towards the stated terms, and many schools would say they are meeting them. However, it is important to recognize the school is only one educational force in society and that the influence of the home, mass media, the peer group and other models can overwhelm the force of the school.

Finally while we recognize the claims of customary international legal usage, we would prefer that the use of "his" throughout the text of the draft convention be replaced by "the child", or by the plural "children". It would be unwise for a convention of this type to be open to criticisms of perpetuating sex-role stereotyping.

**(e)      International Council of Women**

*The following is taken from document E/CN.4/1324.*

We would like this article to follow immediately after article I, of which it is the continuation.

**(f)      Society for Comparative Legislation**

*The following is taken from document E/CN.4/1324.*

The child shall be protected from practices which may foster racial, religious or any other form of discrimination. He shall be brought up in a spirit of understanding, tolerance, friendship among peoples, peace and universal brotherhood, and in full consciousness that his energy and talents should be devoted to the service of his fellow men. The child of a divided international family shall preserve his ties with both his parents even if they are of different religions, and in no case shall religion be taken into consideration for the purposes of the devolution of the right of custody.

## C.     First reading (1979-1988)

*The text of article 2, which was based on article 4 of the revised Polish draft, was discussed and adopted by the Working Group in 1981. This article was referred to as article 4 throughout the first and second readings. A related proposal, included below, concerning discrimination based on gender was submitted to the Working Group in 1987 and discussed in 1988 but further consideration was deferred until the second reading. Additionally, a number of proposals concerning a new article on children born out wedlock were made and discussed by the Working Group during the first reading. The final decision not to adopt a separate article on this subject was made, in part, on the basis that that concern was already sufficiently addressed in the present article on non-discrimination.*

### 1.      Proposal submitted to the Working Group (1979)

**(a)      Norway and Sweden**

*The following is taken from paragraph 23 (d) of the 1979 report of the Working Group to the Commission on Human Rights (E/CN.4/L.1468), which is reproduced in the 1979 report of the Commission on Human Rights (E/CN.4/1347, para. 244).*

Article IX

Add the following:

[...]

"The child shall, under no circumstances be subject to imprisonment, humiliation or discrimination because of any act committed or any opinion expressed by the child's parents, relatives or any other person."

### 2.      Revised Polish draft (1979)

*Articles 4 and 5 of the revised draft pertained to the principle of non-discrimination. The following text of those two articles is taken from Commission on Human Rights document E/CN.4/1349, which was reissued for technical reasons.*

*Article 4*

1.      The States parties to the present Convention shall respect and extend all the rights set forth in this Convention to all children in their territories, irrespective of these children's race, colour, sex, religion, political and other opinion, social origin, property, birth in lawful wedlock or out of wedlock or any other distinction whatever.

2.      The States Parties to the present Convention shall undertake appropriate measures individually and within the framework of international cooperation, particularly in the areas of economy, health and education for the implementation of the rights recognized in this Convention.

*Article 5*

The States Parties to the present Convention recognize the right of alien children staying in their territories to enjoy the rights provided for in this Convention.

## 3.      Proposal submitted to the Working Group (1980)

### (a)      Australia

*The following is taken from paragraph 44 (c) of the 1980 report of the Working Group to the Commission on Human Rights (E/CN.4/L.1542), which is reproduced in the 1980 report of the Commission on Human Rights (E/CN.4/1408, para. 277).*

Delete article 4 (2). Insert new article 4 bis:

"The States Parties to the present Convention shall take all appropriate measures, individually or jointly within the framework of international cooperation, for the full and effective implementation of the rights recognized in the Convention."

## 4.      Proposals submitted to the Working Group (1981)

### (a)      Australia

*The following is taken from document HR/(XXXVII)/WG.1/WP.6.*

Replace existing text of Article 5 with:

"A child resident in the territory of a State Party and who is not a national of that State Party shall enjoy in that territory all the rights provided for in this Convention."

### (b)      Brazil

*For the text of this proposal, see paragraph 42 in section 5 below.*

### (c)      Norway

*For the text of this proposal concerning article 4, see paragraph 54 in section 5 below. The following additional proposal is taken from document HR/(XXXVII)/WG.1/WP.10.*

Addition to Article 5 of the "Revised draft convention on the rights of the child" (E/CN.4/1349).

"..., irrespective of the legality of their parents' stay."

### (d)      United States of America

*For the text of the proposed reformulation of article 4, see paragraph 44 in section 5 below. The following additional proposal is taken from document HR/(XXXVII)/WG.1/WP.7.*

Article 4 (Defer consideration until after adoption of all articles granting rights to children)

Paragraph 1 (as separate article):

"Each State Party to the present Convention shall respect and extend all the rights set forth in this Convention to all children lawfully in its territory irrespective of any distinction whatever."

## 5. Discussion and adoption by the Working Group (1981)

*The following is taken from the 1981 report of the Working Group to the Commission on Human Rights (E/CN.4/L.1575, paras. 39-56), which is reproduced in the 1981 report of the Commission on Human Rights (E/CN.4/1475, para. 289).*

39.     Article 4 of the revised Polish draft was as follows:

"1.     The States Parties to the present Convention shall respect and extend all the rights set forth in this Convention to all children in their territories, irrespective of these children's race, colour, sex, religion, political and other opinion, social origin, property, birth in lawful wedlock or out of wedlock or any other distinction whatever.

2.     The States Parties to the present Convention shall undertake appropriate measures individually and within the framework of international cooperation, particularly in the areas of economy, health and education for the implementation of the rights recognized in this Convention."

*Paragraph 1*

40.     A proposal was introduced by the representative of the United States which read as follows:

"Each State Party to the present Convention shall respect and extend all the rights set forth in this Convention to all children lawfully in its territory."

That proposal was regarded by some delegations as containing a principle with which they could not agree, namely, the limitation of the rights set forth in the draft convention to children who were lawfully in the territory of a State Party. Other delegations agreed that the parents' illegal entry into the territory of a State Party could not be invoked in order to limit the rights of their children.

41.     The representatives of Argentina further suggested the insertion of the phrase "or arising under their legal systems" after the word "Convention" in the second line of the text of the revised Polish draft.

42.     Another proposal was submitted by the representative of Brazil after consultations to the effect that the last three lines of paragraph 1 of the revised Polish draft should be replaced by the following text:

".... irrespective of these children's or their family's or legal guardian's race, colour, sex, religion, political and other opinion, social origin, property, family status, language, national origin, educational background, or any other distinction whatever."

43.     Proposals were also made to bring the formulation of the paragraph more closely into line with relevant passages of existing United Nations international instruments particularly the International Convention on the Elimination of All Forms of Racial Discrimination, the International Covenant on Economic, Social and Cultural Rights, the International Covenant on Civil and Political Rights and the UNESCO Convention against Discrimination in Education.

44.     Following consultations, the representative of the United States submitted the following text as a possible compromise:

"1.     The States Parties to the present Convention shall respect and extend all the rights set forth in this Convention to all children (lawfully) in their territories without distinction of any kind, such as race, colour, sex, language, religion, political or other opinion, national or social origin, family status, ethnic origin, economic condition, cultural beliefs or practices, property, educational attainment, and birth or other status.

2.     States Parties to the present Convention shall take appropriate measures to ensure that the child is protected against all forms of discrimination on any basis whatsoever, particularly against any form of discrimination or punishment based on the activities or beliefs of the child's parents, legal guardians, or other family members.

3.      Each State Party to this Convention shall take steps, in accordance with its constitutional processes and its available resources, with a view to achieving the full realization of the rights recognized in the present Convention by all appropriate means, including particularly the adoption of legislative or administrative measures."

45.     The representative of the United States indicated that if paragraph 1 of this new text was adopted without mentioning the term "lawfully" there need not be a provision concerning aliens such as the one embodied in article 5 of the revised Polish draft.

46.     Several delegations supported a proposal to revert to the maximum extent possible to the Polish version of the text under consideration, in particular by retaining article 5 on the rights of alien children.

47.     After further discussion, the representative of the United States proposed to merge paragraphs 1 and 2 of the text presented by him and agreed to withdraw paragraph 3. He also agreed to withdraw the words "lawfully" and "economic condition" on the understanding that article 5 would be deleted. The revised text read as follows:

"The States Parties to the present Convention shall respect and extend all the rights set forth in this Convention to each child in their territories without discrimination or distinction of any kind, irrespective of the child's or his parents' or legal guardians' race, colour, sex, language, religion, political or other opinion, national or social origin, family status, ethnic origin, cultural beliefs or practices, property, educational attainment, and birth or other status, or any other basis, including any form of discrimination or punishment based on the activities or beliefs of the child's parents, legal guardians, or other family members."

48.     The representative of the Byelorussian Soviet Socialist Republic proposed the deletion from the [second] line of that text of the words "discrimination or". The representative of Brazil suggested the addition, in the antepenultimate line, after the words "and birth or", of the phrase "any other distinction whatever". The representative of the United States indicated his preference for the word "basis" rather than the word "distinction".

49.     The Chairman proposed that the text as amended, with the deletion of the phrase "including any form of discrimination or punishment based on the activities or beliefs of the child's parents, legal guardians, or other family members" should be adopted and suggested that a new paragraph be formulated for inclusion in article 4.

50.     The Working Group adopted by consensus paragraph 1 of article 4, in its revised version, which read as follows:

"The States Parties to the present Convention shall respect and extend all the rights set forth in this Convention to each child in their territories without distinction of any kind, irrespective of the child's or his parents' or legal guardians' race, colour, sex, language, religion, political or other opinion, national or social origin, family status, ethnic origin, cultural beliefs or practices, property, educational attainment, birth, or any other basis whatever."

51.     One representative felt that, notwithstanding the fact that the language adopted in paragraph 1 would apply to all children, if article 5 of the revised Polish draft contained a reference to a certain category of children (alien children), that would undermine the universality of paragraph 1. Other delegates agreed that article 5 would no longer be necessary if paragraph 1 of article 4 were adopted, and proposed its deletion. The representative of Italy expressed her reservation on this course of action.

52.     The Working Group decided to delete article 5 of the revised Polish draft.

*Paragraph 2*

53.     The delegation of the United States put forward for consideration by the Working Group the following proposal:

"States Parties to the present Convention shall take appropriate measures to ensure that the child is protected against all forms of discrimination on any basis whatsoever, particularly against any form of discrimination or punishment based on the activities or beliefs of the child's parents, legal guardians, or other family members."

54.     After a lengthy debate that proposal was withdrawn in favour of a revised version of paragraph 2 which had been elaborated by the delegation of Norway and that read as follows:

"States Parties to the present Convention shall take all appropriate measures to ensure that the child is protected against all forms of discrimination or punishment based on the activities, expressed opinions, or beliefs of the child's parents, legal guardians, or other family members."

55.     The representative of the Byelorussian Soviet Socialist Republic proposed that the words "based on" be replaced by the words "on the basis of". The representative of Brazil further suggested the insertion of the word "status" before the word "activities". Several delegations expressed support for those amendments.

56.     Further to a joint proposal by the delegations of Australia and the United States to the effect that the above-mentioned text, with the proposed amendments, become paragraph 2 of article 4, the Working Group adopted by consensus the revised version of paragraph 2 which read as follows:

"States Parties to the present Convention shall take all appropriate measures to ensure that the child is protected against all forms of discrimination or punishment on the basis of the status, activities, expressed opinions, or beliefs of the child's parents, legal guardians, or other family members."

## 6.     Proposal submitted to the Working Group (1984)

### (a)     China

*The following proposal for a new article, not considered by the Working Group until its 1986 session, is taken from the 1984 report of the Working Group to the Commission on Human Rights (E/CN.4/1984/71, annex II).*

The States Parties to the present Convention should protect the interests of the children born out of wedlock and ensure to them the rights as enjoyed by those born in lawful wedlock.

## 7.     Statements made to the Working Group (1984)

### (a)     United Kingdom of Great Britain and Northern Ireland

*The following is taken from the 1984 report of the Working Group to the Commission on Human Rights (E/CN.4/1984/71, para. 9).*

9.     The representative of the United Kingdom stated that, even as a State participating in the work of the open-ended Working Group, his delegation continued to have difficulties with some of the articles already adopted (e.g. articles 2, paragraph 1, 3, paragraph 1, 4, paragraph 1, 6 and 8, paragraphs 1 and 2). Article 2, paragraphs 1 and 2, caused difficulties in relation to United Kingdom nationality law. Article 6, paragraph 1, as currently drafted was not compatible with United Kingdom immigration legislation because the parents of a child who did not have rights of residence in the United Kingdom could not determine that he should live there unless he qualified for residence under United Kingdom immigration rules. In addition, draft articles 3, paragraph 1, 4, paragraph 1, 6, paragraphs 2 and 3, 6 bis, paragraphs 2 and 3, and 8, paragraphs 1 and 2, all posed problems in relation to United Kingdom immigration law. Certain of those draft provisions were difficult or even impossible to reconcile with his country's law and practice. Nevertheless, his delegation had joined the consensus at the Working Group in recognition of the efforts made by other delegations to get an acceptable draft completed and available for comment by Member States with as little delay as possible. However, the United Kingdom thought it important that all States, including those which had not participated in the

Working Group, should have an opportunity to consider and comment on those articles after the current drafting exercise was concluded. If, after the drafting was completed and notwithstanding that certain parts of the text remained substantially as they were now, the United Kingdom authorities were nevertheless to consider that they could proceed to signature and ratification, his delegation foresaw that there would be a need to enter reservations and declarations, in particular to deal with the aforementioned difficulties over immigration and nationality.

**(b)      Netherlands**

*The following is taken from the 1984 report of the Working Group to the Commission on Human Rights (E/CN.4/1984/71, para. 10).*

> 10.      The Netherlands delegation believed that a convention on the rights of the child would only be effective if it were broadly acceptable to a large number of States. It was therefore considered important that all States should have an opportunity to comment on the Working Group's draft before it was submitted to the Commission on Human Rights for finalization. Accordingly, the Netherlands delegation supported the United Kingdom's proposal to that end.

**(c)      Federal Republic of Germany**

*The following is taken from the 1984 report of the Working Group to the Commission on Human Rights (E/CN.4/1984/71, para. 11).*

> 11.      The representative of the Federal Republic of Germany stated that his delegation shared the concerns of the United Kingdom delegation particularly with regard to article 2, paragraph 2, and article 6, paragraphs 1 and 2. Article 2, paragraph 2, posed problems with regard to his country's nationality law. As in the case of the United Kingdom, the provisions of draft article 6, paragraphs 1 and 2, were not compatible with the Federal Republic's immigration legislation. Should article 2, paragraph 2, and article 6, paragraphs 1 and 2, be retained in their present form during the forthcoming deliberations in spite of the concerns of some delegations, and should the draft convention be opened for signature and ratification in that form, his Government might feel obliged to enter reservations to both articles. The representative of the Federal Republic of Germany also expressed his support for the United Kingdom proposal that all States be given an opportunity to comment on the Working Group's completed draft before its submission to the Commission on Human Rights.

## 8.      Proposal submitted to the Working Group (1985)

**(a)      NGO Ad Hoc Group** *(see annex III (B) for participating organizations)*

*The following proposal, made available to the Working Group at its 1985 session, is taken from "Informal consultations among international non-governmental organizations: Report on conclusions" (December 1984). The proposal was later revised and reproduced in document E/CN.4/1986/WG.1/WP.1, page 8.*

> 1.      The States Parties shall protect the interests of children born out of wedlock, in particular by ensuring that they shall enjoy the same legal rights as all other children.

> 2.      The States Parties to the present Convention shall ensure that all children have the right to legal recognition of both maternity and paternity, and that no child shall suffer from discrimination in inheritance rights because of the legal status of his or her parents.

## 9.      Proposals submitted to the Working Group (1986)

**(a)      Austria**

*For the text of this proposal, see paragraph 13 in section 10 below.*

**(b)    China**

*For the text of this proposal, see paragraph 13 in section 10 below.*

**(c)    NGO Ad Hoc Group** *(see annex III (B) for participating organizations)*

*The following proposal for a new article is taken from E/CN.4/1986/WG.1/WP.1, page 8.*

> 1.    The States Parties shall protect the interests of children born out of wedlock, in particular by ensuring that they shall enjoy the same legal rights as all other children.

> 2.    The States Parties to the present Convention shall ensure that all children have the right to legal recognition of both maternity and paternity, and undertake to facilitate the processes for the determination and acknowledgement thereof.

**(d)    International Council of Jewish Women**

*The following proposal, submitted on behalf of the NGO Ad Hoc Group, is taken from document E/CN.4/1986/WG.1/CRP.4.*

> Add [to the proposal of the NGO Ad Hoc Group] a paragraph 3 (...) as follows:

> > 3.    No birth registration record or any record bearing recognition of the child's identity shall be so worded as to cast the stigma of illegitimacy on an individual. All records shall be kept confidential, accessible only to those having legal recourse to them.

## 10.    Discussion in the Working Group (1986)

*The following is taken from the 1986 report of the Working Group to the Commission on Human Rights (E/CN.4/1986/39, paras. 13-21).*

> 13.    For the consideration of this article the Working Group had before it a proposal submitted by the delegation of China contained in document E/CN.4/1986/WG.1/CRP.5 which read:

> > "The States Parties to the present Convention shall take all effective measures to ensure that a child born out of wedlock shall enjoy the same legal rights as those enjoyed by a child born in wedlock, in particular the rights enumerated in the present Convention."

> The Working Group also had before it a proposal by the representative of Austria as follows:

> > "1.    The States Parties to the present Convention recognize that children born out of wedlock shall enjoy equal rights with children born in wedlock.

> > 2.    The States Parties to the present Convention shall take all appropriate measures including legislative and administrative measures to implement this article having regard to the relevant provisions of other international instruments. In particular, the States Parties shall ensure that the child has the right to establish maternal and paternal affiliation."

> A proposal was also submitted by the Informal NGO Ad Hoc Group on the Drafting of the Convention, as contained in document E/CN.4/1986/WG.1/WP.1.

> 14.    During consideration of these proposals, some delegations expressed the view that there was no need to include a specific article relating to children born out of wedlock in the convention as the subject was already covered under article 4 adopted by the Working Group. The delegations of the Netherlands and Norway were in favour of such a provision and suggested the deletion in the proposal by China of the following words: ", in particular the rights enumerated in the present Convention".

> 15.    The representative of Finland was in favour of the proposal submitted by the representative of Austria, but suggested the second sentence of the second paragraph of the Austrian proposal be replaced

by the following: "In particular, the States Parties shall take all appropriate measures to ensure the effective implementation of the child's right to have maternal and paternal affiliation evidenced or established". The representative of Austria supported the revised proposal put forward by the observer for Finland.

16.	The representatives of Australia, Japan, United Kingdom and United States pointed out that the proposal submitted by the delegation of China was in conflict with their domestic laws of succession. The delegations of Algeria, Iraq and Morocco specifically objected to the inclusion in the draft convention of a provision dealing with children born out of wedlock, while the representative of the German Democratic Republic stressed that such a provision should be included in the draft convention.

17.	The representative of China felt that there should definitely be an article stating in clear terms the rights of a child born out of wedlock and suggested inserting the words "according to national laws" after the words "present Convention".

18.	The observer for the Netherlands suggested that in paragraph 1 of the Austrian proposal the words "equal rights with" be replaced by "the same legal rights as". After some further debate on the question, the representative of Austria decided to withdraw his proposal while the representative of France indicated that she was in favour of a separate article on the subject being discussed by the Working Group.

19.	The representative of the United Kingdom put forward the following reformulation of the article under discussion:

> "The States Parties to the present Convention shall through national legislation take all effective measures to ensure that a child born out of wedlock shall enjoy the rights set out in this Convention to the same extent as a child born in wedlock".

20.	The representative of Japan supported the proposal by the representative of the United Kingdom with the exception of the words "through national legislation". The representative of the United Kingdom agreed to their deletion and stated that although he had put forward the above-mentioned proposal, his preference was not to have a separate article on the question under consideration by the Working Group.

21.	The Chairman decided that the Working Group had not reached a consensus on the proposal by the delegation of China.

## 11.	Comment submitted to the Working Group (1986)

### (a)	Bangladesh

*The following comment regarding article 4 (present article 2) is contained in a paper submitted by the Permanent Representative of Bangladesh to the United Nations Office at Geneva in connection with the draft convention on the rights of the child with the request that the paper be annexed to the 1986 report of the Working Group. For the complete text, including general comments on the draft convention, see document E/CN.4/1986/39, annex IV.*

*Article 4 (1)*

*Article 4 (1) is very broadly framed and may not be entirely necessary. The principle of non-discrimination is already enshrined in article 4 (2). We feel that a single provision embodying the principle of non-discrimination would meet the case.*

## 12.	Proposal submitted to the Working Group (1987)

### (a)	Netherlands and Austria

*The following proposal related to article 2 but concerning a proposed new article 1 bis was submitted jointly by the Netherlands and Austria to the Working Group at its 1987 session. However, the proposal was not discussed at that time and it therefore appears in the annex to the 1987 report of the Working Group to the Commission on Human*

*Rights (E/CN.4/1987/25). This proposal was subsequently reproduced in document E/CN.4/1988/WG.1/WP.2 and is referred to in paragraph 221 in section 14 below.*

*Article 1 bis*

"The States Parties to the present Convention shall not provide any discrimination, in particular on the grounds of sex, in establishing the age of majority."

## 13. Proposal submitted to the Working Group (1988)

### (a) Federal Republic of Germany

*The following proposal for a new article is taken from document E/CN.4/1988/WG.1/WP.3.*

The States parties to the present Convention undertake to ensure the conformity of their law with the following provisions:

1.      Maternal affiliation of every child born out of wedlock shall be based solely on the fact of the birth of the child.

2.      Paternal affiliation of every child born out of wedlock may be evidenced or established by voluntary recognition or by judicial decision.

3.      The voluntary recognition of paternity may not be opposed or contested in so far as the internal law provides for these procedures unless the person seeking to recognize or having recognized the child is not the biological father.

4.      In actions relating to paternal affiliation, scientific evidence which may help to establish or disprove paternity shall be admissible.

5.      (a)      The father and mother of a child born out of wedlock shall have the same obligation to maintain the child as if it were born in wedlock.

        (b)      Where a legal obligation to maintain a child born in wedlock falls on certain members of the family of the father or mother, this obligation shall also apply for the benefit of a child born out of wedlock.

6.      (a)      Where the affiliation of a child born out of wedlock has been established as regards both parents, parental authority may not be attributed automatically to the father alone.

        (b)      There shall be power to transfer parental authority; cases of transfer shall be governed by the internal law.

7.      Where the father or mother of a child born out of wedlock does not have parental authority over or the custody of the child, that parent may obtain a right of access to the child in appropriate cases.

8.      A child born out of wedlock shall have the same right of succession in the estate of its father and its mother, and of a member of its father's or mother's family, as if it had been born in wedlock.

9.      The marriage between the father and mother of a child born out of wedlock shall confer on the child the legal status of a child born in wedlock.

## 14. Discussion in the Working Group (1988)

*The following is taken from the 1988 report of the Working Group to the Commission on Human Rights (E/CN.4/1988/28, paras. 221 and 226-230).*

*Article 1 bis (Prevention of discrimination, particularly on the grounds of sex)*

221.     The proposal submitted by the Netherlands (E/CN.4/1988/WG.1/WP.2, chapt. II) concerned the obligation of the States Parties not to discriminate, in particular on grounds of sex, in establishing the age of majority. Some participants requested clarification of the reasons why the proposal had been submitted, since articles 1 and 4 of the draft convention established the age of majority and the principle of non-discrimination. The observer for the Netherlands explained that he would accept that article 4 covered that point if the age of adulthood were established in the convention but, given the terms in which article 1 had been drafted, he thought that article 4 did not suffice. However, he understood that some of the questions put to him needed clarification. The discussion of the proposal was deferred to the second reading.

[...]

*Article 4 bis (Children born out of wedlock)*

226.     The working group had before it a proposal submitted by the Federal Republic of Germany (E/CN.4/1988/WG.1/WP.3). In introducing the proposal, the representative of the Federal Republic of Germany stated that the convention would not serve its purposes if it did not cover the situation of children born out of wedlock, who suffered a kind of discrimination. His delegation's proposal reproduced the terms of the European Convention on the matter. He recognized that the proposal could be objected to because national legislation in many countries was not in agreement with it, but he thought that the points proposed were minimal.

227.     One speaker stated that an article reading, "Children born out of wedlock shall have the same rights as children born in wedlock" should be included.

228.     Several speakers stated that the question of children born out of wedlock had been discussed at previous sessions of the working group, in which it had been evident that it was impossible to reach a consensus. A much shorter draft than the one proposed by the Federal Republic of Germany had been suggested but consensus thereon had not been reached. It was therefore impossible to insert such a detailed proposal at the current stage. Furthermore, in the discussion on that question in 1986, it had been made very clear that the problem was indeed covered by article 4 which established the principle of non-discrimination on the basis of birth.

229.     The question, according to some speakers, caused many problems. Although the principle of recognizing children born out of wedlock was a good one, there were many countries in which it had not been incorporated in the legislation and customs and culture were in contradiction with it.

230.     The representative of the Federal Republic of Germany stated that his proposal was aimed at extending the benefits of a convention, which was supposed to protect one of the weakest parts of society, to a portion of it which was even weaker, but having heard the various speakers he would withdraw his proposal.

## 15.     Text as adopted at first reading

*The following is taken from document E/CN.4/1988/WG.1/WP.1/Rev.1.*

### Article 4

1.     The States Parties to the present Convention shall respect and extend all the rights set forth in this Convention to each child in their territories without distinction of any kind, irrespective of the child's or his parents' or legal guardians' race, colour, sex, language, religion, political or other opinion, national or social origin, family status, ethnic origin, cultural beliefs or practices, property, educational attainment, birth, or any other basis whatever.

2.       States Parties to the present Convention shall take all appropriate measures to ensure that the child is protected against all forms of discrimination or punishment on the basis of the status, activities, expressed opinions, or beliefs of the child's parents, legal guardians, or other family members.

# D.   Technical review (1988)

## 1.       Comments regarding draft article 4 (non-discrimination)

### (a)       Comment by the United Nations Educational, Scientific and Cultural Organization (UNESCO)

*The following is taken from document E/CN.4/1989/WG.1/CRP.1, page 15.*

In this article, paragraph 1, the word "disability" should be added to the list.

*French version*

Article 4 should come immediately after article 1. The Declaration of the Rights of the Child devotes its first principle to confirm that the rights should be recognized for all children without exception. In paragraph 1 in fine, it is suggested to replace the expression "ou de toute autre considération" by "de toute autre situation" used in the preamble of the convention and in the International Covenants on Human Rights.

### (b)       Comment by the United Nations Children's Fund (UNICEF)

*The following is taken from document E/CN.4/1989/WG.1/CRP.1, pages 15-17.*

In any human rights treaty the obligations clauses constitute the foundation stones on which the treaty is constructed. They lay down the nature of the basic obligations which a State will undertake if it chooses to ratify, or accede to, the treaty and thus determine, in many respects, the precise scope and content of a State Party's obligations with respect to each of the individual rights formulated in the remainder of the treaty. In the case of the draft convention, the basic obligations clauses are to be found in articles 4, 5 and 5 *bis.*

The first part of paragraph 1 of article 4 provides that:

> "The States Parties to the present Convention shall respect and extend all the rights set forth in this Convention to each child in their territories, without distinction of any kind ..."

*"Respect and extend"*: In comparing this standard with those in other widely accepted human rights instruments and, particularly the two International Covenants, it can be seen that there is a significant difference. Under the International Covenant on Civil and Political Rights (article 2, paragraph 1) each State Party "undertakes to respect and to ensure". Under the comparable provision of the International Covenant on Economic, Social and Cultural Rights (article 2, paragraph 2) States Parties "undertake to guarantee". The obligation to "ensure" is also contained in both of the International Covenants (in article 3 of each) with respect to the equal rights of men and women to the enjoyment of the rights in question.

The two most comprehensive, United Nations non-discrimination conventions contain basic obligations clauses which are considerably more complex than, and at least equally demanding as, the relevant provisions of the Covenant. Thus, the Convention on the Elimination of All Forms of Racial Discrimination uses phrases such as:

> "Each State Party undertakes to engage in no act ... and to ensure that ..." (article 2 (1) (a)).

> "Each State Party undertakes not to ..." (article 2 (1) (b)).

> "Each State Party shall take effective measures ..." (article 2 (1) (c)).

> "Each State Party shall prohibit and bring to an end by all appropriate means ..." (article 2 (1) (d)).

The Convention on the Elimination of All Forms of Discrimination against Women uses comparable language including, in particular an undertaking by States Parties "... to ensure, through law and other appropriate means, the practical realization of" the principle of equality of men and women (article 2 (a)).

Two conclusions emerge from this survey. The first is that the verb "to extend" is not used in any of the principal human rights instruments and has not acquired, in any international legal context, any precise technical or general meeting. Nor do the *travaux préparatoires* to the draft convention shed any light on the intended meaning of the term.

It is thus unclear what is meant by the undertaking to "...extend all the rights set forth in this Convention to each child...". It seems reasonable to assume, however, that it does not actually detract in any way from the level of obligation reflected in the undertaking "to respect" "all the rights set forth" in the convention. There is thus no need to recommend its deletion, except that it might appear somewhat superfluous.

The second conclusion is that the undertaking to "respect and extend" constitutes a very considerably lower level of obligation than the undertaking to "respect and ensure" which is contained in the great majority of existing international human rights treaties. It has been widely and consistently acknowledged both by the States Parties to the treaties and by the relevant supervisory bodies (such as the Human Rights Committee) that the obligation to "respect" requires a State not to violate the rights in question, whereas the obligation to "ensure" implies an affirmative obligation on the part of the State to take whatever measures are necessary to enable individuals to enjoy and exercise the relevant rights.

Since the obligation to "respect and ensure" human rights is already incumbent upon States pursuant to the wide range of existing treaties, the inclusion of a substantially lower obligation to "respect and extend", as proposed in the draft convention, would therefore represent a major diminution in the level of protection already provided to children under existing standards. In order to avoid such a result, consideration might be given to deletion of the verb "extend" and its replacement by "ensure" in the first part of article 4, *paragraph 1.*

*"In their territories"*: This provision effectively defines and limits the range of children whose rights each State Party will be required to respect. It may be compared with the International Covenant on Civil and Political Rights which provides that the obligations of a State Party to that treaty apply "to all individuals within its territory and subject to its jurisdiction" (article 2 (1)). The latter phrase has been omitted from the draft convention, thus giving its provisions a more limited range of application than is the case with the Covenant. By way of example, the implications of the draft convention's non-applicability to individuals who are not within the State Party's territory, but are subject to its jurisdiction, may be illustrated by reference to article 6 *bis, paragraph 2.* Under that provision "a child whose parents reside in different States shall have the right to maintain on a regular basis save in exceptional circumstances personal relations and direct contacts with both parents...". If a child, having left his or her own country in order to maintain contact with his or her parents who reside elsewhere, was then refused permission to re-enter his or her home State, the rights granted by the convention would not be able to be invoked vis-à-vis the relevant State Party because the child would not, at the time of the request, be within the territory of the State.

The *travaux préparatoires* do not indicate that any deliberate decision was taken to exclude persons subject to the jurisdiction of States Parties, but outside their territories. Consideration might thus be given to adding the phrase "or subject to their jurisdiction" after the word "territories" in article 4, *paragraph 1.*

*Gender neutrality*

Paragraph 1. The middle part of the article could read:

> "...irrespective of the child's or a parent's or legal guardian's race,..."

### (c)       Additional comments and clarifications by the Secretariat

*The following is taken from document E/CN.4/1989/WG.1/CRP.1/Add.1, paragraph 11.*

11.     In paragraphs 1 and 2, the Working Group may wish to delete the word "legal" before the word "guardian" so that the listing corresponds with the responsible persons listed in article 5 bis.

## 2.     Comments regarding discrimination against female children

### (a)     Comment by the Food and Agriculture Organization of the United Nations (FAO)

*The following is taken from document E/CN.4/1989/WG.1/CRP.1, page 8.*

> The convention should include provisions to prevent discrimination against female children as far as food and education are concerned.

### (b)     Comment by the United Nations Educational, Scientific and Cultural Organization (UNESCO)

*The following is taken from document E/CN.4/1989/WG.1/CRP.1, page 8.*

> See also comment of UNESCO relating to the preamble.

*The following text concerning discrimination against girls is taken from the comment of UNESCO relating to the preamble, which also appears in document E/CN.4/1989/WG.1/CRP.1.*

> [...]

> It seems to us that among the many positive principles and values conducive to the child's development, as included in the text, the principle of equality is largely ignored. It is particularly essential when it comes to equal treatment of boys and girls within and outside of the family. Since much of the later discrimination of girls can be traced back to their unequal treatment in early years, it is suggested that the element of equality be inserted into the Preamble as their basic right.

> [...]

# E.     Second reading (1988-1989)

## 1.     Proposal submitted to the Working Group at second reading

### (a)     Mexico

*For the text of this proposal, see paragraph 151 in section 2 below.*

## 2.     Discussion and adoption at second reading

*The following is taken from the 1989 report of the Working Group to the Commission on Human Rights (E/CN.4/1989/48, paras. 146-169).*

> 146.     The Working Group had before it a text (contained in document E/CN.4/1989/WG.1/WP.2) of paragraph 1 as adopted during the first reading incorporating suggested revisions by UNICEF, UNESCO and the technical review conducted by the Secretariat. The text read as follows:

>> "1.     (The) States Parties (to the present Convention) shall respect and (extend) *ensure* all the rights set forth in this Convention to each child in their territories or *subject to their jurisdiction* without distinction of any kind, irrespective of the child's or his *or her* parents' or (legal) guardian's race, colour, sex, language, religion, political or other opinion, national or social origin, family status, ethnic origin, cultural beliefs or practices, property, educational attainment, birth, *disability*, or any other basis whatever."

147.     With regard to the revised text, the representatives of the United Kingdom of Great Britain and Northern Ireland, United States of America, Union of Soviet Socialist Republics, and Argentina questioned why the revised text was inconsistent with the language of earlier instruments in talking of children in their territories "or" subject to their jurisdiction. The representative of the Union of Soviet Socialist Republics indicated that although he had no strong feelings as regards the suggested revision, he however felt that the introduction of this new idea may lead to some misunderstanding. The observer for Australia indicated that it was the intention of the suggested revision to take the text further than existing instruments.

148.     The representative of Portugal indicated general support for the revised text in document E/CN.4/1989/WG.1/WP.2 and proposed that the words "basis whatever" be substituted by the word "status" in order to make the text consistent with previous international human rights instruments, including the International Covenant on Civil and Political Rights. The representatives of Italy, Sweden, Australia, the Netherlands and the Federal Republic of Germany expressed similar positions.

149.     In view of the Working Group's inability to arrive at a consensus, the Chairman suspended the discussion and appointed a small drafting group to discuss suitable wording for the paragraph.

150.     The Working Group had before it a text (contained in document E/CN.4/1989/WG.1/WP.2) of paragraph 2 as adopted during first reading including a suggested revision as to the reference to States Parties. The text read as follows:

> "2.     States Parties (to the present Convention) shall take all [appropriate] measures to ensure that the child is protected against all forms of discrimination or punishment on the basis of the status, activities, expressed opinions, or beliefs of the child's parents, legal guardians, or other family members."

151.     The Working Group also had before it a proposal by the representative of Mexico (E/CN.4/1989/WG.1/WP.27). The proposal read as follows:

> "Delete the words 'expressed opinions, or beliefs'".

152.     The representative of Mexico indicated that the intention of the proposal was to allow countries to use the education of children as a tool in their drive against ignorance, prejudice and superstition.

153.     A number of States indicated their difficulty in accepting the proposal because it would imply the acceptance of discrimination against, and punishment of, children on the basis of the opinions and beliefs of their parents. The representative of Mexico therefore withdrew his proposal and indicated that the Mexican Government would interpret the existing text in accordance with its domestic legislation.

154.     The representative of Canada raised the question of whether the words "the child" should be added to paragraph 2 to ensure that the child was protected against all forms of discrimination or punishment on the basis of his or her status, activities, etc., as well as those of the child's parents, legal guardians, or other family members.

155.     Concerns were raised by the representatives of Venezuela and Colombia about the translation of "legal guardian" into Spanish. The representative of Portugal raised similar concerns about the French text, the representative of the Union of Soviet Socialist Republics about the Russian text and the representative of China about the Chinese text.

156.     In view of the Working Group's inability to arrive at a consensus, the Chairman suspended the discussion of the paragraph and requested the drafting group appointed to consider paragraph 1 to also consider paragraph 2.

157.     The delegation of Australia gave a reading of the compromise text prepared by the drafting group composed of China, Italy, Kuwait, Portugal, Senegal and the Union of Soviet Socialist Republics under the supervision of Australia. The text contained in document E/CN.4/1989/WG.1/WP.34 read as follows:

"1.     States Parties shall respect and ensure the rights set forth in this Convention to each child in their territories and subject to their jurisdiction without discrimination of any kind, irrespective of the child's or his or her parents' or legal guardian's race, colour, sex, language, religion, political or other opinion, national, ethnic or social origin, property, disability, birth or other status.

2.     States Parties shall take all appropriate measures to ensure that the child is protected against all forms of discrimination or punishment on the basis of the status, activities, expressed opinions, or beliefs of the child, the child's parents, legal guardians, or family members."

158.    The delegate then gave some explanations on the deliberations of the drafting group.

159.    Several delegations drew attention to the need to ensure that the translation into Arabic, Chinese, French and Spanish of the English term "legal guardians" reflected the meaning of the English text exactly; it was suggested to use "représentant légal" in French and "representantes legales" in Spanish.

160.    Poland drew attention to the second line of the first paragraph and asked what would be the status of children "within a territory but not subject to the jurisdiction of the country" (such as diplomats' children). The delegate proposed that "or subject to their jurisdiction" be preferred to "and subject to their jurisdiction".

161.    The observer for Australia recognized the problem but said that they had used the Covenants as models and that in the case of the diplomat's children, these latter would be governed by their own laws.

162.    The observer for Finland, while supporting the proposal, recognized that an important issue had been raised and proposed, in order to cover every possible situation, the deletion of the reference to territories and keeping only the reference to jurisdiction, such as in the European Convention.

163.    Australia agreed with this proposal made by Finland.

164.    The delegates of the United States of America and the Netherlands referred to the deletion of the words "cultural beliefs and practices" from paragraph 1 and expressed their preference for their retention. With respect to the second paragraph of article 4, the delegate of the United States of America questioned the inclusion of the words "the child" before the words "the child's parents". He noted that children may legitimately be punished by their parents or guardians for their own activities and expressed opinions.

165.    The observer for Australia said that he would have trouble accepting the reinsertion of these words since some delegations had problems with them.

166.    With regard to the deletion of the words "family status", the delegate of Sweden stated his understanding that the problems referred to under that term, including that of children born out of wedlock, were covered by the words "other status".

167.    The delegate of Senegal said that the use of the words "or other status" would cover every possible status.

168.    The delegate of India declared that the compromise text was good but that he reserved his position on the use of "ensure" instead of "extend".

169.    The text as amended was adopted to read:

"1.     States Parties shall respect and ensure the rights set forth in this Convention to each child within their jurisdiction without discrimination of any kind, irrespective of the child's or his or her parents' or legal guardian's race, colour, sex, language, religion, political or other opinion, national, ethnic or social origin, property, disability, birth or other status.

2.     States Parties shall take all appropriate measures to ensure that the child is protected against all forms of discrimination or punishment on the basis of the status, activities, expressed opinions, or beliefs of the child's parents, legal guardians, or family members."

## 3.    Statement made during the adoption of the report

### (a)    Federal Republic of Germany

*The following is taken from the 1989 report of the Working Group to the Commission on Human Rights (E/CN.4/1989/48, para. 721).*

> 721.    The delegation of the Federal Republic of Germany stated its desire that the discussion on substantive articles of the draft convention not be reopened. However, it expressed its disappointment that nothing more could be done for the protection of an extremely weak group of children, the children born out of wedlock. In January 1988 it had tabled a detailed proposal on this issue which unfortunately had to be withdrawn but which it would have to present once again if the discussion of the substance of the draft is reopened again. The representative of the Federal Republic of Germany further asked that the following declarations be entered in the report:
>
> > (a)    Nothing in the convention on the rights of the child shall be interpreted as legitimizing the illegal entry and presence on the territory of the Federal Republic of Germany of any alien, nor shall any provision be interpreted as restricting the right of the Federal Republic of Germany to promulgate laws and regulations concerning the entry of aliens and the conditions of their stay or to establish differences between nationals and aliens.
> >
> > [...]

## F.    Related references

*For further research, see under the chapter on "Articles proposed but not adopted by the Working Group" the consideration by the Working Group of a proposed article on illegal alien entry.*

# Article 3 (Best interests of the child)

## A. Final text adopted by the General Assembly (1989)

*The following text is that approved by the General Assembly in its resolution 44/25 of 20 November 1989.*

1. In all actions concerning children, whether undertaken by public or private social welfare institutions, courts of law, administrative authorities or legislative bodies, the best interests of the child shall be a primary consideration.

2. States Parties undertake to ensure the child such protection and care as is necessary for his or her well-being, taking into account the rights and duties of his or her parents, legal guardians, or other individuals legally responsible for him or her, and, to this end, shall take all appropriate legislative and administrative measures.

3. States Parties shall ensure that the institutions, services and facilities responsible for the care or protection of children shall conform with the standards established by competent authorities, particularly in the areas of safety, health, in the number and suitability of their staff, as well as competent supervision.

## B. First Polish draft convention and comments (1978)

### 1. The first Polish draft

*Article II of the Polish draft is most closely related to the substantive concerns covered under present article 3. The following text is taken from the 1978 report of the Commission on Human Rights (thirty-fourth session, document E/CN.4/1292, p. 124).*

*Article II*

The child shall enjoy special protection and shall be given opportunities and facilities, by law and by other means, to enable him to develop physically, mentally, morally, spiritually and socially in a healthy and normal manner and in conditions of freedom and dignity. In the enactment of laws for this purpose, the best interests of the child shall be the paramount consideration.

### 2. Comments on the first Polish draft

*Article II of the draft gave rise to the following comments.*

### (a) Dominican Republic

*The following is taken from document E/CN.4/1324.*

1. We consider it appropriate to add, after the word "dignity" at the end of the first sentence of article II, the words "Children of working mothers shall enjoy, from the time of their birth until they reach school age, the assistance of centres or day nurseries which guarantee the care and assistance necessary for their full development during these early years of their life."

2. The last part of this article could constitute a final clause for the operative part of the convention, contained in a separate article reading as follows:

"In order to achieve the purposes of the present Convention, the States Parties thereto shall, when enacting laws governing this subject in their respective countries, give paramount consideration to the best interests of the child".

**(b)    France**

*The following is taken from document E/CN.4/1324/Add.1.*

See paragraph 4 (a), France, under General Comments.

*Subparagraph 4 (a), which also appears in document E/CN.4/1324/Add.1 reads as follows.*

The provisions that would constitute a recommendation, such as article II, the first sentence of article VI and article X, might be included in a preliminary declaration or a recommendation annexed to the convention[.]

**(c)    Federal Republic of Germany**

*The following is taken from document E/CN.4/1324.*

See paragraph 6, Federal Republic of Germany, under General Comments.

*Paragraph 6, which also appears in document E/CN.4/1324, is reproduced below.*

6.    Unlike the series of measures on the rights of the individual, article II, article IV (first and second sentences), article V, article VI (fourth sentence), article VII, paragraph 1 (second sentence), article VII, paragraph 3, article IX and article X (first sentence) can be considered only as undertakings on the part of States.

**(d)    New Zealand**

*The following is taken from document E/CN.4/1324/Add.5.*

We accept the general intent of article II. However, we presume that key phrases such as "special protection", "healthy and normal manner" and "the best interests of the child" will be open, through the general terms in which they are couched, to varied interpretations and will in fact be defined nationally in terms of the laws and the child-rearing practices which are adopted and acceptable in that nation.

**(e)    Spain**

*The following is taken from document E/CN.4/1324.*

Between the words "normal manner" and the words "and in the conditions of freedom and dignity" insert the words "avoiding anything that damages or may impair his physical or mental health, especially drugs in any of their forms".

**(f)    Food and Agriculture Organization of the United Nations (FAO)**

*The following is taken from document E/CN.4/1324.*

There is no mention in the article of the emotional development of the child. Statements referring to his/her overall growth and development refer instead to moral and spiritual development, supposedly to cover this important area of development.

**(g)    United Nations Educational, Scientific and Cultural Organization (UNESCO)**

*The following is taken from document E/CN.4/1324.*

Alongside physical, mental, moral, spiritual and social development, an explicit reference should be made to *"cultural development with due regard for national or regional realities".*

**(h)    World Health Organization (WHO)**

*The following is taken from document E/CN.4/1324.*

Article II, first line:

> It is not clear against what the "special protection" is to be provided. Would it be against harmful social environment, against disease, against abuse, etc.? Perhaps this point should be clarified.

Article II, second line:

> It is not clear what the term "other means" is meant to cover. Is it intended to refer to measures which are not law in the strict sense, such as administrative acts or practical measures? This needs to be clarified.

### (i)      Society for Comparative Legislation

*The following is taken from document E/CN.4/1324. Paragraph 2 below appears elsewhere in the first Polish draft as paragraph 2 of article VII, which concerns the rights of the child to education and recreation.*

> 1.      The child shall enjoy special protection and shall be given opportunities and facilities, by law and by other means, to enable him to develop physically, mentally, morally, spiritually and socially in a healthy and normal manner and in conditions of freedom and dignity. In the enactment of laws for this purpose, the best interests of the child shall be the paramount consideration.

> 2.      The best interests of the child shall be the guiding principle of those responsible for his education and guidance; that responsibility lies in the first place with his parents.

## C.    First reading (1979-1988)

*The text of article 3, which was based on article 3 of the revised Polish draft, was discussed and adopted by the Working Group in 1981. This article was referred to as article 3 throughout the first and second readings.*

### 1.      Proposal submitted to the Working Group (1979)

### (a)      France and Federal Republic of Germany

*The following is taken from paragraph 23 (e) of the 1979 report of the Working Group to the Commission on Human Rights (E/CN.4/L.1468), which is reproduced in paragraph 244 of the 1979 report of the Commission on Human Rights (E/CN.4/1347).*

> The following provisions of the draft convention should not be included in the convention itself but set out in the preamble or in an annexed recommendation of a pedagogical nature:
>
> Article II;
> Article VI (first sentence);
> Article VII (paragraph 2, from "The best interests" to "guidance");
> Article VIII;
> Article X (second sentence).

### 2.      Revised Polish draft (1979)

*The following text is taken from Commission on Human Rights document E/CN.4/1349, which was reissued for technical reasons.*

*Article 3*

> 1.      In all actions concerning children, whether undertaken by their parents, guardians, social or State institutions, and in particular by courts of law and administrative authorities, the best interest of the child shall be the paramount consideration.

2.      The States Parties to the present Convention undertake to ensure the child such protection and care as his status requires, taking due account of the various stages of his development in family environment and in social relations, and, to this end, shall take necessary legislative measures.

3.      The States Parties to the present Convention shall create special organs called upon to supervise persons and institutions directly responsible for the care of children.

## 3.      Proposals submitted to the Working Group (1980)

### (a)      Australia

*For the text of this proposal, see paragraph 21 in section 4 below.*

### (b)      United States of America

*For the text of this proposal, see paragraph 20 in section 4 below.*

## 4.      Discussion and adoption by the Working Group (1981)

*The following is taken from the 1981 report of the Working Group to the Commission on Human Rights (E/CN.4/L.1575, paras. 19-38), which is reproduced in paragraph 289 of the 1981 report of the Commission on Human Rights (E/CN.4/1475).*

19.      Article 3 of the revised Polish draft was as follows:

"1.      In all actions concerning children, whether undertaken by their parents, guardians, social or State institutions, and in particular by courts of law and administrative authorities, the best interest of the child shall be the paramount consideration.

2.      The States parties to the present Convention undertake to ensure the child such protection and care as his status requires, taking due account of the various stages of his development in family environment and in social relations, and, to this end, shall take necessary legislative measures.

3.      The States parties to the present Convention shall create special organs called upon to supervise persons and institutions directly responsible for the care of children."

20.      The representative of the United States of America reintroduced a new article 3 which had been submitted by his delegation the year before but had not been considered owing to lack of time. The new article read as follows:

"1.      In all official actions concerning children, whether undertaken by public or private social welfare institutions, courts of law, or administrative authorities, the best interests of the child shall be a primary consideration.

2.      In all judicial or administrative proceedings affecting a child that has reached the age of reason, an opportunity for the views of the child to be heard as an independent party to the proceedings shall be provided, and those views shall be taken into consideration by the competent authorities.

3.      Each State party to this Convention shall support special organs which shall observe and make appropriate recommendations to persons and institutions directly responsible for the care of children.

4.      The States parties to this Convention undertake, through passage of appropriate legislation, to ensure such protection and care for the child as his status requires."

21.      The delegation of Australia also had submitted in 1980 the following text to replace paragraphs 2 and 3 of article 3:

> "2.      The States parties to the present Convention undertake to ensure the child such protection and care as is necessary for his well-being, taking into account the rights and responsibilities of his parents and the stage of the child's development towards full responsibility and, to this end, shall take all necessary legislative and administrative measures.
>
> 3.      The States parties to the present Convention shall ensure competent supervision of persons and institutions directly responsible for the care of children."

This proposal was reintroduced at the 1981 session of the Working Group.

*Paragraph 1*

22.      A number of speakers agreed that the Polish version of this paragraph was wider and better protected the child, but in search for compromise it was agreed to take as a basis for discussion the proposal of the United States delegation.

23.      A discussion ensued as to whether, on general humanitarian grounds, the best interests of the child should be the pre-eminent consideration in actions undertaken by his parents, guardians, social or State institutions. The imposition of obligations on parents and guardians by an international convention was questioned, but the inclusion of obligations in this provision was felt by some delegations to provide greater protection for the child. Moreover, the word "paramount" used in the revised Polish draft to qualify the consideration to be given to the interests of the child was considered too broad by some delegations which felt that the best interests of the child should be "a primary consideration".

24.      In the course of the discussion a speaker stated that the interests of the child should be a primary consideration in actions concerning children but were not the overriding, paramount consideration in every case, since other parties might have equal or even superior legal interests in some cases (e.g. medical emergencies during childbirth). He also pointed out that his delegation did not attempt to regulate private family decisions but only official actions. The view was also expressed by some representatives that paragraph 1 did not need to have a reference to specific obligations of States parties in respect of the best interests of the child; paragraph 1 enunciated general principles while the specific obligations of States parties would be listed in the following provisions which would also take into consideration actions concerning children and undertaken by their parents or guardians.

25.      After further discussion, agreement was reached to delete the word "official" from the first line of the proposal made by the representative of the United States of America.

26.      The Working Group adopted by consensus paragraph 1 as proposed by the delegation of the United States of America, with the deletion of the word "official".

*Paragraph 2*

27.      One representative suggested that the Working Group consider paragraph 2 as proposed by the delegation of the United States of America, since it made reference to judicial and administrative proceedings. The representative of the United States explained that paragraph 2, as submitted by his delegation, contained concepts that were missing in the draft convention.

28.      Some speakers indicated that the opportunity for the views of the child to be heard, mentioned in the amendment proposed by the delegation of the United States, was also mentioned in article 7 of the revised Polish draft, but others pointed out that the amendment by the United States delegation to paragraph 2 of article 3 made specific reference to all judicial or administrative proceedings affecting a child in this respect and followed logically from paragraph 1 of article 3 as a means by which judicial or administrative authorities could ascertain a child's best interests in a given case.

29.     One delegate stated that although the idea contained in the paragraph under consideration was correct, the characterization of "the age of reason" was very difficult. He also believed that views of children could be expressed in court through their legal guardians. The observer of the International Association of Penal Law suggested that language should be borrowed from article 7 to replace the phrase "has reached the age of reason". The Working Group agreed to replace the words "the age of reason" by the following words of article 7: "is capable of forming his own views".

30.     The representative of Brazil said that it would be preferable to insert the words "shall be provided" after the words "an opportunity". A further suggestion, made by the representative of the Netherlands, was that in the [second] line of the paragraph, the phrase "either directly or indirectly through a representative" should be inserted after the word "heard". In addition, proposals were made to delete the word "independent" from the [second] line of the paragraph and to add the following phrase at the end of that paragraph: "in a manner consistent with the procedures followed in the State Party for the application of its legislation".

31.     One representative stated that, because no provision had yet been made for determining the best interests of a child not capable of forming his own views, the Working Group might need to revert to that point at a later stage.

32.     The paragraph as revised and adopted by the Working Group read as follows:

"In all judicial or administrative proceedings affecting a child that is capable of forming his own views, an opportunity shall be provided for the views of the child to be heard, either directly or indirectly through a representative, as a party to the proceedings, and those views shall be taken into consideration by the competent authorities, in a manner consistent with the procedures followed in the State Party for the application of its legislation."

*Paragraph 3*

33.     The Working Group considered the proposal submitted by the delegation of Australia to replace paragraph 2 of article 3 of the revised Polish draft. The representative of Australia pointed out that his proposal took into account a basic aim of the Conference on the Legal Protection of the Rights of the Child held in Warsaw on 16-19 January 1979, namely the need to secure the rights of the child through support to the family in need.

34.     After an exchange of views, it was agreed to insert, in the third line of the text, the phrase "legal guardians" after the word "parents". Further to the Chairman's request that a compromise text be elaborated following consultations, the delegation of the United States submitted a text that read as follows:

"The States Parties to the present Convention undertake to ensure the child such protection and care as is necessary for his well-being, taking into account the rights and duties of his parents, legal guardians, or other individuals legally responsible for him and, to this end, shall take all appropriate legislative and administrative measures."

35.     That text of paragraph 3 was adopted by consensus by the Working Group.

*Paragraph 4*

36.     The amendment put forward by the Australian delegation to replace paragraph 3 of article 3 was considered by the Working Group.

37.     There was a discussion on the word "persons". The representative of Norway suggested that the word "persons" be replaced by the word "personnel". The representative of the United States proposed that the word "persons" be replaced by the word "officials" or by the phrase "officials and personnel of institutions" and explained that the term "officials" would cover, for example, the board of directors of a hospital or an orphanage; he indicated that if those amendments were accepted by the Working Group, paragraph 3 of article 3 submitted by his delegation would be withdrawn in favour of the Australian amendment.

38.     After discussion, the Working Group adopted the proposed amendments. The paragraph, as adopted, reads as follows:

> "The States Parties to the present Convention shall ensure competent supervision of officials and personnel of institutions directly responsible for the care of children."

The Working Group later decided that text should become paragraph 4 of article 3.

## 5.     Proposal submitted to the Working Group (1983)

### (a)     Belgium

*The following is taken from document E/CN.4/1983/WG.1/WP.21.*

> *Article 3*
>
> [...]
>
> 3.     The States parties to the present Convention undertake to ensure the child *the right to physical and moral integrity*, as well as such protection and care as is necessary for his well-being, taking into account the rights and duties of his parents, legal guardians, or other individuals legally responsible for him, and, to this end, shall take all appropriate legislative and administrative measures.

## 6.     Proposals submitted to the Working Group (1984)

### (a)     International Federation of Women in Legal Careers and the International Abolitionist Federation

*The following is taken from document E/CN.4/1983/NGO/33, which appeared after the 1983 session of the Working Group.*

> *Article 3* (Rights of children)
>
> We support the amendment proposed by the Belgian delegation [concerning paragraph 3.]
>
> [...]
>
> We would also suggest that paragraph 4 of the article read:
>
> > "The States Parties to the present Convention shall ensure that children are placed in institutions only in exceptional cases and that the officials and personnel of such institutions are properly qualified and subject to regular supervision."

### (b)     International Federation of Human Rights, International Federation of Women in Legal Careers, Pax Romana

*The following is taken from document E/CN.4/1984/WG.1/WP.6.*

> [...]
>
> B.     CONCEPT OF THE BEST INTERESTS OF THE CHILD (art. 3 of the draft convention)
>
> It would appear essential to stipulate in the draft convention that the authorities which will be called upon to rule on the best interests of the child should take their decisions in the light of "all national and international elements of the personal and family situation of the child".
>
> Because of its general nature, there is a danger that the concept of the best interests of the child as recognized in article 3 of the draft convention may induce States, when children are of dual origin, to give this concept a purely nationalist content and interpretation.

Whereas this concept of the best interests of the child should in principle bring the legislations of the various States closer together, in this instance there is a possibility that it may drive them further apart. The convention would thus be in danger of losing its universal character and its role as a reference instrument.

## 7.     Statements made to the Working Group (1984)

### (a)     United Kingdom of Great Britain and Northern Ireland

*The following is taken from the 1984 report of the Working Group to the Commission on Human Rights (E/CN.4/1984/71, para. 9).*

> 9.     The representative of the United Kingdom stated that, even as a State participating in the work of the open-ended Working Group, his delegation continued to have difficulties with some of the articles already adopted (e.g. articles 2, paragraph 1, 3, paragraph 1, 4, paragraph 1, 6 and 8, paragraphs 1 and 2). Article 2, paragraphs 1 and 2, caused difficulties in relation to United Kingdom nationality law. Article 6, paragraph 1, as currently drafted was not compatible with United Kingdom immigration legislation because the parents of a child who did not have rights of residence in the United Kingdom could not determine that he should live there unless he qualified for residence under United Kingdom immigration rules. In addition, draft articles 3, paragraph 1, 4, paragraph 1, 6, paragraphs 2 and 3, 6 bis, paragraphs 2 and 3, and 8, paragraphs 1 and 2, all posed problems in relation to United Kingdom immigration law. Certain of those draft provisions were difficult or even impossible to reconcile with his country's law and practice. Nevertheless, his delegation had joined the consensus at the Working Group in recognition of the efforts made by other delegations to get an acceptable draft completed and available for comment by Member States with as little delay as possible. However, the United Kingdom thought it important that all States, including those which had not participated in the Working Group, should have an opportunity to consider and comment on those articles after the current drafting exercise was concluded. If, after the drafting was completed and notwithstanding that certain parts of the text remained substantially as they were now, the United Kingdom authorities were nevertheless to consider that they could proceed to signature and ratification, his delegation foresaw that there would be a need to enter reservations and declarations, in particular to deal with the aforementioned difficulties over immigration and nationality.

### (b)     Federal Republic of Germany

*The following is taken from the 1984 report of the Working Group to the Commission on Human Rights (E/CN.4/1984/71, para. 11)*

> 11.     The representative of the Federal Republic of Germany stated that his delegation shared the concerns of the United Kingdom delegation particularly with regard to article 2, paragraph 2, and article 6, paragraphs 1 and 2. Article 2, paragraph 2, posed problems with regard to his country's nationality law. As in the case of the United Kingdom, the provisions of draft article 6, paragraphs 1 and 2, were not compatible with the Federal Republic's immigration legislation. Should article 2, paragraph 2, and article 6, paragraphs 1 and 2, be retained in their present form during the forthcoming deliberations in spite of the concerns of some delegations, and should the draft convention be opened for signature and ratification in that form, his Government might feel obliged to enter reservations to both articles. The representative of the Federal Republic of Germany also expressed his support for the United Kingdom proposal that all States be given an opportunity to comment on the Working Group's completed draft before its submission to the Commission on Human Rights.

## 8.     Comment submitted to the Working Group (1986)

### (a)     Bangladesh

*The following comment regarding article 3 is contained in a paper submitted by the Permanent Representative of Bangladesh to the United Nations Office in Geneva in connection with the draft convention on the rights of the child with the request that the paper be annexed to the 1986 report of the Working Group. For the complete text, including general comments on the draft convention, see document E/CN.4/1986/39, annex IV.*

The mandatory nature of article 3 (2) requires to be modified by substituting the word "shall" after the words "an opportunity" in line 2 by "should".

## 9.     Text as adopted at first reading

*The following is taken from document E/CN.4/1988/WG.1/WP.1/Rev.1.*

*Article 3*

1.        In all actions concerning children, whether undertaken by public or private social welfare institutions, courts of law, or administrative authorities, the best interests of the child shall be a primary consideration.

2.        In all judicial or administrative proceedings affecting a child that is capable of forming his own views, an opportunity shall be provided for the views of the child to be heard, either directly or indirectly through a representative, as a party to the proceedings, and those views shall be taken into consideration by the competent authorities, in a manner consistent with the procedures followed in the State Party for the application of its legislation.

3.        The States Parties to the present Convention undertake to ensure the child such protection and care as is necessary for his well-being, taking into account the rights and duties of his parents, legal guardians, or other individuals legally responsible for him and, to this end, shall take all appropriate legislative and administrative measures.

4.        The States Parties to the present Convention shall ensure competent supervision of officials and personnel institutions directly responsible for the care of children.

## D.     Technical review (1988)

## 1.     Comment by the International Labour Organization (ILO)

*The following is taken from document E/CN.4/1989/WG.1/CRP.1, page 13.*

In paragraph 4, the following words (*italics*) might be added:

"... shall ensure *appropriate training, qualifications* and competent supervision of ..." the staff of childcare institutions. A parallel may be drawn with article 8, paragraph 4 of which refers to "standards established ... in the number and suitability" of the staff of childcare institutions and services.

## 2.     Comment by the World Health Organization (WHO)

*The following is taken from document E/CN.4/1989/WG.1/CRP.1, page 13.*

Paragraph 3 of this article refers to the undertaking of the States Parties to the draft convention "to ensure the child such protection and care as is necessary for his well-being". This provision echoes article 2, paragraph 1 of the World Health Organization Constitution, whereby it is stated that one of the functions of the Organization shall be "to promote maternal and child health and welfare". The same applies to a certain extent to article *8 bis, paragraph 1*, article *14, paragraph 1* and article *18, paragraph 1*.

## 3.     Comment by the United Nations Children's Fund (UNICEF)

*The following is taken from document E/CN.4/1989/WG.1/CRP.1, pages 13-14.*

*Paragraph 1*

This provision reads:

> "In all actions concerning children, whether undertaken by public or private social welfare institutions, courts of law, or administrative authorities, the best interests of the child shall be a primary consideration."

By stating that the child's best interest shall be "a primary consideration" this provision uses what amounts to a twofold qualification. The word "primary" implies that other considerations, although not deemed primary, may nevertheless be taken into account. The article "a" indicates that there may be several considerations, each of which is primary. The issue which arises by virtue of standards incorporated in other widely accepted human rights instruments is whether a single qualification is not sufficient. If this were considered to be the case, the wording could be changed to indicate that the child's best interests would be "the primary consideration".

In this regard, note might be taken of article 5 of the Convention on the Elimination of All Forms of Discrimination Against Women which obligates States Parties to take all appropriate measures:

> "(b)    To ensure that family education includes a proper understanding of maternity as a social function and the recognition of the common responsibility of men and women in the upbringing and development of their children, it being understood that the interest of the children is the primordial consideration in all cases."

Similarly article 5 of the Declaration on Social and Legal Principles relating to the Protection and Welfare of Children, with Special Reference to Foster Placement and Adoption Nationally and Internationally, provides that:

> "In all matters relating to the placement of a child outside the care of the child's own parents, the best interests of the child, particularly his or her need for affection and right to security and continuing care, should be the paramount consideration."

*Paragraph 2*

The reference to a child "capable of forming his own views" is presumably intended to refer to a child capable of "expressing" those views since even very young children, who are not able to talk, can still "form" views and communicate them in one way or another.

*Gender Neutrality*

Paragraph 2. The first part of the paragraph might be reformulated as follows:

> "In all judicial or administrative proceedings affecting a child who is capable of forming his *or her* own views..."

Paragraph 3. A possible reformulation of the article is:

> "The States Parties to the present Convention undertake to ensure such protection and care as are necessary for *the child's* well-being, taking into account the rights and duties of his *or her* parents, legal guardians, or other individuals legally responsible *for the child*...".

## 4.    Additional comments and clarifications by the Secretariat

*The following is taken from document E/CN.4/1989/WG.1/CRP.1/Add.1, paragraph 10.*

> 10.    The draft convention contains numerous clauses requiring or calling for legislative measures for ensuring various rights of the child. The Working Group may therefore wish to insert in paragraph 1, together with the other institutions listed, a reference to *"legislative bodies"*.

# E.    Second reading (1988-1989)

## 1.    Proposal submitted to the Working Group at second reading

### (a)    Latin American meeting

*By note verbale to the Centre for Human Rights, the Permanent Mission of Argentina requested that the report and recommendations of the Latin American meeting [of NGOs] in support of the United Nations draft convention on the rights of the child be circulated as an official information document at the Working Group. The meeting took place in Buenos Aires from 29 September to 2 October 1988. The following is taken from document E/CN.4/1989/WG.1/WP.1.*

> In article 3, paragraph 4:
>
> > "... shall ensure *training* and supervision ...".

## 2.    Discussion and adoption at second reading

*The following discussion is taken from the 1989 report of the Working Group to the Commission on Human Rights (E/CN.4/1989/48, paras. 117-145).*

> *Paragraph 1*

117.    The Working Group had before it a text (contained in document E/CN.4/1989/WG.1/WP.2) of the paragraph as adopted during the first reading incorporating suggested revisions by UNICEF and the technical review carried out by the Secretariat. The text read as follows:

> "1.    In all actions concerning children, whether undertaken by public or private social welfare institutions, courts of law, administrative authorities or *legislative bodies*, the best interests of the child shall be *the* (a) primary consideration."

118.    The observers for Kuwait, Portugal and Australia expressed support for the revised text as contained in document E/CN.4/1989/WG.1/WP.2. The latter did so because the revised text reflected existing international standards, for instance as contained in article 5 of the Convention on the Elimination of All Forms of Discrimination against Women.

119.    The observer for the Netherlands expressed general satisfaction with the revised text but suggested that the word "primary" be replaced by the word "paramount".

120.    The representative of Venezuela suggested that, although her delegation was not opposed to the phrase "best interests of the child" being included in the final text, she however wished to draw attention to the subjectivity of the term, especially if the convention contained no prior stipulation that the "best interests of the child" were his all-round - in other words, physical, mental, spiritual, moral and social - development. That would mean leaving the interpretation of the "best interests of the child" to the judgement of the person, institution or organization applying the rule. In the ensuing debate a number of delegations expressed satisfaction with the phrase and the representative of Venezuela therefore withdrew her suggestion.

121.    With regard to the revised text as contained in document E/CN.4/1989/WG.1/WP.2, a number of delegations questioned whether the best interests of the child should be the primary consideration in all actions. It was generally noted that there were situations in which the competing interests, inter alia, of justice and of the society at large should be of at least equal, if not greater, importance than the interests of the child.

122.    In an effort to allay such concerns the observer for Canada suggested that, as adopted during the first reading, the paragraph should make the interests of the child "a" primary consideration, noting that other instruments making the interests of the child *the* primary consideration were directed to more limited circumstances than those provided for in this paragraph. The observer for Canada otherwise expressed

support for the revised text. A similar position was taken by the representatives of the United States of America, Japan and Argentina.

123.     The observer for Finland suggested that the interests of the child should be "the" primary consideration only in actions involving his or her "welfare". Although the proposal was supported by the observer for the Netherlands, it was opposed by the delegations of Portugal, Australia, Canada and Senegal because it sought to narrow the scope of protection the paragraph afforded to children.

124.     The representative of the United Kingdom suggested that either the word "all" should be deleted or the interests of the child should only be "of" primary consideration. The latter proposal was also made by the representative of Norway. The observer for Australia questioned whether the meaning of the latter proposal differed from "a" primary consideration, as adopted during the first reading.

125.     In view of the strength of reservations voiced about making the interests of the child "the" primary consideration in all situations and taking into account the fact that the delegations which felt that it should be did not insist on this revision, consensus was reached to make the interests of the child only "a" primary consideration in all actions, as it had been in the text adopted during the first reading.

126.     The Working Group then proceeded to adopt the text of paragraph 1 of article 3 as follows:

> "1.     In all actions concerning children, whether undertaken by public or private social welfare institutions, courts of law, administrative authorities or legislative bodies, the best interests of the child shall be a primary consideration."

*Paragraph 2* [later deleted; see paragraph 140 below]

127.     The Working Group had before it a text (contained in document E/CN.4/1989/WG.1/WP.2) of the paragraph as adopted during the first reading incorporating a suggested revision as to gender-neutral language. The text read as follows:

> "2.     In all judicial or administrative proceedings affecting a child that is capable of forming his *or her* own views, an opportunity shall be provided for the views of the child to be heard, either directly or indirectly through a representative, as a party to the proceedings, and those views shall be taken into consideration by the competent authorities, in a manner consistent with the procedures followed in the State Party for the application of its legislation."

128.     The observer for Finland suggested that the scope of this paragraph overlapped with the scope of article 7 and therefore proposed that discussion be postponed until the consideration of that article.

129.     Consideration of the paragraph was suspended pending the outcome of the deliberations of a drafting group set up to resolve the issue. As indicated below, upon the proposal of the drafting group, paragraph 2 was deleted from draft article 3 in order to discuss it under article 7. The delegate of Portugal reserved her position on paragraph 2 for discussion in connection with article 7.

*Paragraph 3* [new paragraph 2 after the deletion of former paragraph 2]

130.     The Working Group had before it a text (contained in document E/CN.4/1989/WG.1/WP.2) of the paragraph as adopted during the first reading incorporating suggested revisions on gender-neutral language and a reference to States Parties. The text read as follows:

> "3.     (The) States Parties (to the present Convention) undertake to ensure the child such protection and care as is necessary for his *or her* well-being, taking into account the rights and duties of his *or her* parents, legal guardians, or other individuals legally responsible for him *or her*, and, to this end, shall take all (appropriate) legislative and administrative measures."

131.     Paragraph 3 was adopted taking into account the suggested revisions and removing the brackets around the word "appropriate". The text as adopted reads as follows:

"3.    States Parties undertake to ensure the child such protection and care as is necessary for his or her well-being, taking into account the rights and duties of his or her parents, legal guardians, or other individuals legally responsible for him or her, and, to this end, shall take all appropriate legislative and administrative measures."

*Paragraph 4* [new paragraph 3 after the deletion of former paragraph 2]

132.    The Working Group had before it a text (contained in document E/CN.4/1989/WG.1/WP.2) of the paragraph as adopted during the first reading including suggested revisions by the International Labour Organization and regarding a reference to States Parties. The text read as follows:

"4.    (The) States Parties (to the present Convention) shall ensure *(appropriate) training, qualifications and* competent supervision of officials and personnel of institutions directly responsible for the care of children."

133.    The observer for Canada, supported by the observer for New Zealand, suggested there was a growing tendency in many countries to move away from institutionalized care of children and therefore proposed the inclusion of such words as "programmes" or "organizations" in addition to, or with the deletion of, "institutions".

134.    The representative of Venezuela proposed that the idea of technical supervision for children in institutions until they rejoin their families should be included in the paragraph. After a discussion, the representative of Venezuela withdrew the proposal.

135.    The representative of India expressed a preference for the text of the paragraph as adopted during the first reading, without revisions. He did so because he felt that it was enough to supervise institutions run by volunteer organizations without imposing unnecessary bureaucratic requirements. The observer for Kuwait agreed with the representative of India as to his concerns and suggested that the new idea from the ILO in the revised text was already covered in article 8, paragraph 4.

136.    In the ensuing debate the representatives of Canada, Norway and Australia proposed that since the idea contained in article 3 (4) was covered in article 8 (4) it should be deleted from article 3 and left only in article 8. The observer for New Zealand indicated that he had no strong views on the placement of the substance contained in the paragraph as long as it was left in either article. The representative of India noted that the paragraphs in articles 3 and 8 were different in scope because the latter covered only children with parents or guardians whereas the former concerned children generally, and would therefore include such children as destitutes who would otherwise be excluded from the protection afforded by article 8. The observer for the ILO indicated that in submitting its suggested revisions the ILO took the view that the paragraphs in articles 3 and 8 were different in scope. The observer for the ILO did not however insist on the adoption of its suggested revisions and withdrew its proposal.

137.    The representative of Senegal suggested that the idea of supervising childcare institutes and monitoring the children in them be separated from article 3 and be incorporated in an article 3 bis.

138.    It was then suggested by the Chairman that discussion of paragraph 4 should be suspended and that the same drafting group considering paragraph 2 should also discuss and try to resolve any possible overlap between article 3 (4) and article 8 (4).

139.    On behalf of the special drafting group composed of Canada, Finland, Morocco and the Union of Soviet Socialist Republics, the delegate of Finland stated that their proposal was to delete paragraphs 2 and 4 from article 3 and incorporate them in, respectively, articles 7 and 8.

140.    The Working Group decided to delete paragraph 2 from article 3 in order to discuss it under article 7. Former paragraph 3 thus became new paragraph 2.

141.    With regard to the proposed deletion of paragraph 4, the delegate of India expressed his concern since that paragraph was the logical continuation of the preceding paragraph (new 2, former 3). He consequently

objected to its removal to article 8 and proposed it be maintained under article 3, since the two articles did not deal with the same type of institution. Canada drew the Working Group's attention to another article dealing with institutions, namely article 10. The representative of the ILO stated her understanding that different institutions were dealt with under articles 3 and 8.

142.    The delegation of Finland proposed to postpone the discussion on paragraph 4, so that the drafting group could decide on its placement; article 8, article 10, or a new article were mentioned as possibilities for placing this paragraph. Upon the request made by Finland and then by the Federal Republic of Germany, the Chairman adjourned the discussion on paragraph 4 and decided that India should join the drafting group.

143.    The observer for Finland introduced a proposal submitted by the drafting group with regard to a new paragraph 3 of article 3. The proposal read as follows:

> "3.     States Parties shall ensure that the institutions, services and facilities responsible for the care or protection of children shall conform with the standards established by competent authorities, particularly in the areas of safety, health, in the number and suitability of their staff as well as competent supervision."

144.    In introducing this proposal, the observer for Finland pointed out that this text repeated to some extent the provisions of article 8, paragraph 4 of the draft convention as adopted at first reading. He suggested that the working group should decide what to do with this paragraph later on when it came to article 8. He also mentioned that the amendments proposed by the ILO (E/CN.4/1989/WG.1/WP.2, p. 15) were not included in the text. In the view of the drafting group the purpose of these amendments which related to appropriate training and qualification of officials and personnel of childcare institutions was adequately covered by the inclusion of the words "suitability of their staff".

145.    The Working Group then adopted paragraph 3 of article 3 as proposed by the drafting group which reads as follows:

> "3.     States Parties shall ensure that the institutions, services and facilities responsible for the care or protection of children shall conform with the standards established by competent authorities, particularly in the areas of safety, health, in the number and suitability of their staff as well as competent supervision."

# Article 4 (Implementation of rights)

## A. Final text adopted by the General Assembly (1989)

*The following text is that approved by the General Assembly in its resolution 44/25 of 20 November 1989.*

> States Parties shall undertake all appropriate legislative, administrative, and other measures for the implementation of the rights recognized in the present Convention. With regard to economic, social and cultural rights, States Parties shall undertake such measures to the maximum extent of their available resources and, where needed, within the framework of international cooperation.

## B. First Polish draft convention and comments (1978)

*Although there was no article in the Polish draft equivalent to present article 4 of the Convention, the following comments address similar concerns.*

### (a)    Colombia

*The following is taken from document E/CN.4/1324/Add.2.*

> [...]

> 3.        Any plan or programme which a nation may adopt in relation to children should consider the child as an active and participating member of a society in general and of a family in particular, so that his actions are not dissociated from the social environment in which he lives, and so that he is not regarded as an abstract subject alien to any objective reality.

> [...]

> 5.        Steps should be taken in the States Members of the United Nations to promote solidarity with the children of developing countries.

### (b)    Cyprus

*The following is taken from document E/CN.4/1324.*

> 1.        A provision could be included in the draft convention which would take into account the economic capabilities of the Contracting Parties as regards the implementation of the convention. Article 2, paragraph 1, of the International Covenant on Economic, Social and Cultural Rights could serve as a model for drafting this article;

> [...]

### (c)    Norway

*The following is taken from document E/CN.4/1324.*

> [...]

> 4.        It should also be considered to impose on the States Parties an obligation to establish or designate national administrative organs to be responsible for the protection and promotion of the rights of children.

## C. First reading (1979-1988)

*The text of article 4, which was based on article 4, paragraph 2, of the revised Polish draft, was discussed and adopted by the Working Group in 1981. This article was referred to as article 5 throughout the first and second readings.*

# 1. Revised Polish draft (1979)

*The following text of draft article 4, in which paragraph 2 addresses the concerns under the present article, is taken from Commission on Human Rights document E/CN.4/1349, which was reissued for technical reasons.*

*Article 4*

1.     The States Parties to the present Convention shall respect and extend all the rights set forth in this Convention to all children in their territories, irrespective of these children's race, colour, sex, religion, political and other opinion, social origin, property, birth in lawful wedlock or out of wedlock or any other distinction whatever.

2.     The States Parties to the present Convention shall undertake appropriate measures individually and within the framework of international cooperation, particularly in the areas of economy, health and education for the implementation of the rights recognized in this Convention.

# 2. Proposal submitted to the Working Group (1980)

## (a)     Australia

*The following is taken from the 1980 report of the Working Group to the Commission on Human Rights (E/CN.4/L.1542, paragraph 44 (c)).*

Delete Article 4 (2).

Insert new article 4 bis:

"The States Parties to the present Convention shall take all appropriate measures, individually or jointly within the framework of international cooperation, for the full and effective implementation of the rights contained in the Convention."

# 3. Proposals submitted to the Working Group (1981)

## (a)     Brazil

*For the text of this proposal, see section 4, paragraph 60, below.*

## (b)     Norway

*The following is taken from document HR/(XXXVII)/WG.1/WP.4.*

Replace Article 4 paragraph 2 of the "Revised draft convention on the rights of the child" (E/CN.4/1349) by:

The States Parties to the present Convention shall undertake appropriate measures individually and within the framework of international cooperation, through legislation in local and national planning, in the economy and in the areas of health, social welfare and education, for the implementation of the rights recognized in this Convention.

## (c)     United States of America

*The following text, taken from document HR/(XXXVII)/WG.1/WP.14, was included in a proposed article 4 dealing, in particular, with the question of non-discrimination.*

[...]

3.     Each State party to this Convention shall take steps, in accordance with its constitutional processes and its available resources, with a view to achieving the full realization of the rights recognized in the present Convention by all appropriate means, including particularly the adoption of legislative or administrative measures.

## 4.     Discussion and adoption by the Working Group (1981)

*The following is taken from paragraphs 57-61 of the 1981 report of the Working Group to the Commission on Human Rights (E/CN.4/L.1542), which is reproduced in paragraph 289 of the 1981 report of the Commission on Human Rights (E/CN.4/1475).*

57.     The Working Group discussed the question of how concretely the obligation of States Parties under the future convention on the rights of the child should be laid down in order to ensure the implementation of the rights recognized in the convention. Norway favoured the following formulation:

> "The States Parties to the present Convention shall undertake appropriate measures individually and within the framework of international cooperation, through legislation, in local and national planning, in the economy and in the areas of health, social welfare and education, for the implementation of the rights recognized in this Convention."

58.     In this connection, a proposal submitted in 1980 by the representative of Australia which had not been considered owing to lack of time, was reintroduced. It read as follows:

> "The States Parties to the present Convention shall take all appropriate measures, individually or jointly within the framework of international cooperation, for the full and effective implementation of the rights contained in the Convention."

59.     Some delegations felt that the amendment proposed by Norway was more in line with the original text of the revised Polish draft which read: "The States Parties to the present Convention shall undertake appropriate measures individually and within the framework of international cooperation, particularly in the areas of economy, health and education for the implementation of the rights recognized in this Convention." In addition, paragraph 3 of article 4 of the text submitted by the representative of the United States (see paragraph 44) was again brought to the attention of the Working Group in view of its more generalized formulation.

60.     The Working Group moved to a text elaborated after consultations and proposed by the representative of Brazil, which read as follows:

> "The States Parties to the present Convention shall undertake all appropriate administrative and legislative measures, in accordance with their available resources and, where needed, within the framework of international cooperation, for the implementation of the rights recognized in this Convention."

61.     Several delegations expressed support for that proposal, and the Working Group adopted it by consensus as a separate article. The Group decided at a later stage of the proceedings that it should become article 5.

## 5.     Proposal submitted to the Working Group (1988)

### (a)     United States of America

*The following is taken from document E/CN.4/1988/WG.1/WP.17.*

*Article 23 bis*

1.     Where a State Party is constituted as a federal State, the national Government of such State Party shall undertake appropriate measures to implement the provisions of this Convention in so far as it exercises legislative and judicial jurisdiction over the subject matter thereof.

2.     In so far as the subject matter of the provisions of this Convention falls within the jurisdiction of the constituent units of the federal State, the national Government shall take suitable measures, in accordance

with its constitution and its laws, to the end that the competent authorities of the constituent units may take appropriate measures for the fulfilment of this Convention.

## 6. Discussion in the Working Group (1988)

*The following is taken from the 1988 report of the Working Group to the Commission on Human Rights (E/CN.4/1988/28, paras. 231-234).*

231. The representative of the United States of America, in introducing a proposal (E/CN.4/1988/WG.1/WP.17) for a provision concerning the obligation of federal or non-unitary States, emphasized that the proposal was made in order to assist implementation of the convention in a federal structure and would not affect implementation in unitary States.

232. On the basis that the proposal could enable some federal States to become parties to the convention, which was one of the main purposes of such an instrument, a number of speakers said that they did not oppose its inclusion, but indicated that the central Government had a primary responsibility for implementation.

233. Other speakers stated that federal clauses might establish a difference between federal States and the others, which was not considered appropriate, especially for human rights instruments. They objected in particular to the wording used in the proposal which did not reflect the consensus developed in the world on the language to be used in federal clauses. Some words of the proposal concerning the obligation of the central or national Governments to implement the convention were considered vague (e.g. "suitable measures" or "appropriate measures") and unacceptable, in particular in the context of a human rights instrument. The wording of the proposal, if adopted, would considerably narrow the application of the convention in federal States. It was suggested that, as the federal States had organized their internal relations in different ways, they might study the possibility of making reservations.

234. The representative of the United States of America said that in view of the complexity of the question, he would withdraw the proposal. This might be a matter for a reservation upon consideration of ratification.

## 7. Text as adopted at first reading

*The following is taken from document E/CN.4/1988/WG.1/WP.1/Rev.1.*

*Article 5*

The States Parties to the present Convention shall undertake all appropriate administrative and legislative measures, in accordance with their available resources and, where needed, within the framework of international cooperation, for the implementation of the rights recognized in this Convention.

## D. Technical review (1988)

## 1. Comment by the United Nations Children's Fund (UNICEF)

*The following is taken from document E/CN.4/1989/WG.1/CRP.1, pages 17-20.*

In order to review and compare the standards established in article 5 with those contained in other widely accepted human rights instruments, it is convenient, for analytical purposes, to examine separately each of the three main elements contained in the present formulation.

*Obligation to implement*

> "The States Parties to the present Convention shall undertake all appropriate administrative and legislative measures for the implementation of the rights recognized in this Convention."

The use of the word "appropriate" in this context is consistent with the terminology used in some of the other comparable instruments. Thus, for example, article 2, paragraph 1, of the International Covenant on Economic, Social and Cultural Rights uses the phrase "by all appropriate means". The other International Covenant uses the phrase "necessary steps" (article 2, paragraph 2). There would not appear to be any significant differences in either the type or level of obligation implied by the use of "appropriate" as against the use of "necessary". In practice, it may be assumed that if a measure is necessary, it is also appropriate that it be taken.

The measures which States Parties are required to undertake pursuant to this provision are limited to those which are "administrative and legislative" in nature. It may be noted that other articles of the draft convention, dealing with specific issues go further and specify that other measures are also to be taken. Thus, for example, article 8 bis requires States Parties to "take all appropriate legislative, administrative, social and educational measures" to protect the child from various forms of abuse. A significant number of other articles do not, however, contain such provisions. The question which thus arises is whether the two categories specified (administrative and legislative) can be considered to be exhaustive of the measures which would be "appropriate" to deal with each of the substantive issues raised in the convention. In theory, the answer will depend on what is considered to constitute a legislative or, more problematically, an administrative measure.

In practice, precise categorization of a particular measure may give rise to difficulties. For that reason, virtually all of the existing, widely accepted human rights instruments use terms such as "legislative or other measures" (article 2, paragraph 2, of the International Covenant on Civil and Political Rights), "all appropriate means, including particularly the adoption of legislative measures" (article 2, paragraph 1, of the International Covenant on Economic, Social and Cultural Rights) or "all appropriate measures, including legislation" (article 3 of the Convention on the Elimination of All Forms of Discrimination against Women). All of these formulas are open-ended in contrast to the more restrictive approach reflected in the draft convention.

It could be argued that, on the basis of the existing formulation, a State Party would not be obligated to undertake a measure which, although widely considered to be "appropriate" in order to deal with a particular problem, is neither administrative nor legislative in nature. The response might be that anything which a Government might do, will, almost by definition, be covered by one or other of those two categories. (Are educational measures to be considered administrative?) In any event there is nothing in the *travaux préparatoires* to indicate an intent on the part of the Working Group to achieve a restrictive listing of the appropriate measures. Therefore, in order to avoid any challenge which might arise, and to ensure that the type of obligations provided for in existing treaties are not diminished, consideration might be given to amending the relevant phrase so as to read:

"all appropriate administrative, [ ] legislative *and other* measures...".

Such an amendment would also be desirable in order to ensure consistency with subsequent articles, many of which refer to measures going beyond those of a legislative or administrative nature. Thus, for example, article 18 sixt requires that "all appropriate measures" be taken, while article 18 bis refers to "all appropriate measures, including legislative, social and educational measures".

### "In accordance with their available resources"

Article 5 of the draft convention provides that the appropriate measures required for the implementation of the rights recognized are to be undertaken "in accordance with the available resources" of the States Parties. With respect to those rights which can be classified as being economic, social or cultural in nature, the inclusion of a resource availability clause reflects, in a general sense, the approach taken in article 2, paragraph 1, of the International Covenant on Economic, Social and Cultural Rights. However, the obligation of each State Party to that Covenant is to "take steps to the maximum of its available resources". This is a stronger and more demanding obligation than that which is embodied in the draft convention. Thus, in order to ensure that the level of obligation provided for in the case of economic, social and cultural rights is not lower than that already accepted by a large number of States, consideration might be given to amending the relevant part of article 5 to read:

> "The States Parties to the present Convention shall undertake all appropriate administrative and legislative measures, *to the maximum of their available resources*, and ...".

But that amendment would not resolve all of the problems that arise in connection with the phrase in question. A more fundamental issue, and one with far-reaching consequences, is whether the fact that the obligation to implement all of the rights recognized in the draft convention (and not only those dealing with economic, social and cultural rights) is subject to the availability of resources, is in conformity with the standards already established in widely accepted human rights instruments. The issue is perhaps best illustrated by taking an example. Under the terms of article 5, as presently drafted, the obligations of a State Party to "respect the right of the child to freedom of thought, conscience and religion" (article 7 bis) and to respect "the right of the child not to be subjected to arbitrary or unlawful interference with his or her privacy, family, home or correspondence ..." (article *7 quater*) are made subject to the availability of resources. Thus, if a State Party is able to demonstrate that it does not have available resources, its refusal to take appropriate steps to "respect and extend" the rights mentioned would not amount to a violation of the draft convention. By contrast, however, such a situation would clearly amount to a violation of existing, widely accepted international standards. For example, none of the obligations undertaken by States Parties to the International Covenant on Civil and Political Rights, the Convention on the Elimination of All Forms of Discrimination against Women or the International Convention on the Elimination of All Forms of Racial Discrimination are made subject to the availability of resources. In this respect, article 5 of the draft convention would achieve a radical diminution of the standards contained in existing instruments and would run counter to all of the assumptions that have hitherto governed the recognition of civil and political rights in international law.

It might at first glance be assumed that this problem stems from the inclusion of both sets of rights (economic, social and cultural on the one hand, and civil and political on the other) in the same instrument, rather than following the precedent set by the two International Covenants. But this assumption does not withstand scrutiny. In the first place, many other international instruments deal with both types of rights without applying different standards from one type to another. Thus, article 3 of the Convention on the Elimination of All Forms of Discrimination against Women provides that "States Parties shall take in all fields, in particular in the political, social, economic and cultural fields, all appropriate measures, including legislation, to ensure the full development and advancement of women...". The Convention on the Elimination of All Forms of Racial Discrimination also contains provisions relating to both sets of rights.

In the second place, it is unnecessary to include a resource availability clause in the article defining the nature of States Parties' overall obligations since each of the subsequent provisions of the draft convention dealing with economic or social rights contains a specific phrase effectively limiting the States Parties' obligations in the light of resource availability. For example, assistance in the provision of special care to disabled children is made "subject to available resources" (article *12, paragraph 2*). Other resource availability qualifications are contained, inter alia, in articles *12 bis*, *13*, *14* and *15*.

It is recommended, therefore, that consideration be given to deletion from article 5 of the phrase "in accordance with their available resources".

### "Where needed, within the framework of international cooperation"

This provision recalls the pledge of Member States under articles 55 and 56 of the United Nations Charter "to take joint and separate action in cooperation with the Organization for the achievement of "inter alia" universal respect for, and observance of, human rights and fundamental freedoms". It differs slightly from the formulation used in article 2, paragraph 1, of the International Covenant on Economic, Social and Cultural Rights by which States Parties undertake "to take steps, individually and through international assistance and cooperation, especially economic and technical...". It can be assumed, however, in the light of current international usage, that the phrase "international cooperation" encompasses the notion of assistance. There would thus appear to be no inconsistency between this part of the draft convention and existing standards.

## 2.   Additional comments and clarifications by the Secretariat

*The following is taken from document E/CN.4/1989/WG.1/CRP.1/Add.1, paragraph 12.*

12.     With regard to the words "administrative and legislative", along the lines suggested by UNICEF (document E/CN.4/1989/WG.1/CRP.1), the Working Group may wish to rearrange the phrase to read "*legislative, administrative and other ...*".

# E.   Second reading (1988-1989)

## 1.   Discussion and adoption at second reading

*The following is taken from the 1989 report of the Working Group to the Commission on Human Rights (E/CN.4/1989/48, paras. 170 to 177).*

170.     The Working Group had before it article 5 as adopted at first reading, together with suggested revisions contained in E/CN.4/1989/WG.1/WP.2:

> "(The) States Parties (to the present Convention) shall undertake all (appropriate) legislative, administrative, and other measures (in accordance with their available resources), and, where needed, within the framework of international cooperation, for the implementation of the rights recognized in this Convention."

171.     The delegate of the United States of America suggested that the words "appropriate" as well as "and other" be retained. The delegate of Kuwait agreed upon the inclusion of the words "and other" while stating her delegation's wish that article 5 be drafted to cover all rights.

172.     The delegate of the United States of America then proposed the deletion of the words "in accordance with their available resources", along with the delegations of Canada, Sweden, New Zealand, Argentina, Portugal and the United Kingdom. They stated that the civil and political rights guaranteed in the International Covenant on Civil and Political Rights were not subjected to the availability of resources and that the Covenant's standards should not be weakened in the child's convention. With regard to economic, social and cultural rights, they recognized that certain of these rights could be implemented only if sufficient resources were available or were provided for in the International Covenant on Economic, Social and Cultural Rights.

173.     But the delegations of Brazil, India, Venezuela, Libya and Algeria pronounced themselves against the deletion of the words "in accordance with their available resources", given their preoccupation with the economic difficulties faced by the developing countries. The delegate of Venezuela proposed the inclusion of the word "maximum" before the word "available".

174.     Several proposals were made for compromise wording, such as the one submitted by the United Kingdom in order to save civil and political rights without endangering economic, social and cultural rights:

> "... in accordance with their available resources with respect to economic, social and cultural rights....".

175.     Poland proposed that, along with the deletion of the phrase, the word "appropriate" be included in the report and that it be understood in the light of economic, social and cultural rights. The delegation of Senegal declared itself in favour of the Polish proposal.

176.     The Chairman established a drafting group composed of the United States of America, Senegal, India and Sweden in order to come up with a unified proposal.

177.     The representative of the United States of America on behalf of the drafting group on article 5 introduced the text of this article as agreed in the drafting group, which was subsequently adopted by the Working Group. The text reads as follows:

> "States Parties shall undertake all appropriate legislative, administrative, and other measures for the implementation of the rights recognized in this Convention. In regard to economic, social and cultural rights, States Parties shall undertake such measures to the maximum extent of their available resources and, where needed, within the framework of international cooperation."

# Article 5 (Parental guidance and the child's evolving capacities)

## A. Final text adopted by the General Assembly (1989)

*The following text is that approved by the General Assembly in its resolution 44/25 of 20 November 1989.*

> States Parties shall respect the responsibilities, rights and duties of parents or, where applicable, the members of the extended family or community as provided for by local custom, legal guardians or other persons legally responsible for the child, to provide, in a manner consistent with the evolving capacities of the child, appropriate direction and guidance in the exercise by the child of the rights recognized in the present Convention.

## B. First Polish draft convention and comments (1978)

*Neither the draft convention submitted by Poland nor the views received on it (see E/CN.4/1324 and Corr.1 and Add.1-5) addressed the issues raised under article 5 of the Convention.*

## C. First reading (1979-1988)

*This article was referred to as article 5 bis throughout the first and second readings.*

### 1. Proposal submitted to the Working Group (1981)

**(a) Denmark**

*The following is taken from document HR/(XXXVII)/WG.1/WP.21.*

> [...]
>
> Delete article 6 of the "Revised draft convention on the rights of the child" (E/CN.4/1349), and replace by the following:
>
> > "Parents or other guardians have the main responsibility for the child. Every State Party has, however, the responsibility to satisfy the needs of the child and ensure the child the rights set forth in this Convention."

### 2. Proposal submitted to the Working Group (1984)

**(a) NGO Ad Hoc Group** *(see annex III (B) for participating organizations)*

*The following proposal, which was made available to the Working Group at its 1984 session in the Report on informal consultations among international non-governmental organizations (December 1983), is taken from document E/CN.4/1985/WG.1/WP.1, page 17.*

> 1.     The protection of the child's interests cannot be dissociated from the protection of the child's natural family.
>
> 2.     The responsibility of parents is to do everything in their power to ensure their children's well-being and harmonious development. Parents shall participate in all decision-making and orientation with regard to their children's education and future.
>
> 3.     The States Parties to the present Convention undertake to recognize, support and protect the family unit in every way to enable it to carry out its function as provider of the most suitable environment for the child's emotional, physical, moral and social development.

### 3.    Proposals submitted to the Working Group (1987)

*The following States submitted written proposals to the Working Group.*

**(a)    Australia and the United States of America**

*For the text of this proposal, see paragraph 100 in section 4 below.*

**(b)    Netherlands**

*For the text of this proposal, see paragraph 105 in section 4 below.*

### 4.    Discussion in the Working Group (1987)

*The following is taken from the 1987 report of the Working Group to the Commission on Human Rights (E/CN.4/1987/25, paras. 100 to 110).*

100.    The Working Group had before it the following proposal by the delegations of Australia and the United States for an article 5 bis:

> "To help the child enjoy the rights enumerated in this Convention, States Parties undertake to protect the family as the natural and fundamental unit of society. Parents or legal guardians shall enjoy the primary rights and responsibilities for the care, upbringing and development of the child, having due regard for the importance of allowing the child to develop the skills and knowledge required for an independent adulthood."

101.    The representative of the United States explained that his country attached great importance to the family as the natural and fundamental group unit of society. He explained that the family should be explicitly protected, with language similar to that contained in paragraph 1 of articles 10 and 23, respectively, of the International Covenants on Economic, Social and Cultural Rights, and Civil and Political Rights, and that such protection should be included in the draft convention. The United States representative requested that the article under consideration by the Group be included early in the draft convention as article 5 bis, in order to emphasize its importance and relationship to all the other rights contained in the draft convention.

102.    During the debate, the attention of the Working Group was drawn to the possible overlap of the proposal with the already existing articles in the draft convention and in the International Covenants on Civil and Political Rights and on Economic, Social and Cultural Rights.

103.    Some delegations specifically drew the attention of the Working Group to the fact that the proposal did not introduce any new element, as compared to paragraph 3 of article 7 bis [article 14 of the final text] of the draft convention.

104.    The delegation of Canada indicated that it would support such a provision - already included in articles 7 bis and 15 [article 28 of the final text] - to the extent that the proposed article 5 bis would deal with the parental responsibility in the exercise of its rights over the child, with due regard for the evolving capacities of the child and for the child's need to mature into an independent adulthood. However, the observer for Canada concluded that as the concept was already included in the aforementioned articles 7 bis and 15, it would be possible that on the second reading of the draft convention, a generally applicable article could be developed from the - by that time - adopted limited provisions. The delegation of Finland agreed with the suggestions made by the observer for Canada.

105.    The observer for the Netherlands suggested that the latter part of the proposal by the American and Australian delegations be combined with paragraph 3 of article 7 bis in the following manner:

> "The States Parties to the present Convention shall respect the rights and duties of the parents and, where applicable, legal guardians, to provide direction to the child in the exercise of his rights

enumerated in this Convention in a manner consistent with the evolving capacities of the child, having due regard for the importance of allowing the child to develop the skills and knowledge required for an independent adulthood."

106.     The observer for Canada supported the revised proposal put forward by the delegation of the Netherlands. However, with respect to that part of the original proposal, which was based on the protection given to the family under article 23 of the International Covenant on Civil and Political Rights, the Canadian delegation had expressed concern that because article 23 was intended to protect the family from the State, incorporation of such a provision in a convention on the rights of the child must also ensure that the rights of the child would not be left solely to the wishes of the family, without any protection whatsoever from the State; in other words, in protecting the family from the State, the family must not be given arbitrary control over the child. Any protection from the State given to the family must be equally balanced with the protection of the child within the family.

107.     The representative of Austria, while agreeing with the insertion of a separate article along those lines strongly supported the first sentence of the original proposal feeling that, although it appeared in the Covenants, it would be regrettable if it did not also appear in the draft convention.

108.     The Chairman then suggested keeping the first sentence, as it appeared in the original proposal, with the following modifications: to add the words "to the present Convention" between "States Parties" and "undertake" and the words "and assist" between "protect" and "the family". The delegations of Austria and the United States were amenable to the insertion of the above-mentioned words as proposed by the Chairman.

109.     The representative of Australia said that the revised proposal by the delegation of the Netherlands was a good one and therefore should be included in the draft convention, and that during the second reading, references that would appear to be a duplication of already existing texts of the draft convention would be struck out. In addition, he proposed to introduce the words "within the family" between "to provide" and "direction to the child".

110.     After some further exchange of views and after listening to the opinion put forward by the delegation of Finland to the effect that the discussions on this question should be postponed until the second reading of the draft convention, the Chairman proceeded to adjourn the debate with the request that a new proposal for an article 5 bis be prepared.

## 5.     Proposals submitted to the Working Group (1988)

*The following States and organizations submitted written proposals to the Working Group.*

### (a)     Australia, Austria, Netherlands and the United States of America

*For the text of this proposal, see paragraph 27 in section 6 below.*

### (b)     Federal Republic of Germany

*For the text of this proposal, see paragraph 29 in section 6 below.*

### (c)     NGO Ad Hoc Group *(see annex III (B) for participating organizations)*

*The following is taken from document E/CN.4/1988/WG.1/WP.2, page 13.*

In this Convention, the term "parents" shall be interpreted to include, where appropriate, other family members or guardians who have de facto responsibility for the care and upbringing of the child.

## 6.     Discussion and adoption by the Working Group (1988)

*The following is taken from the 1988 report of the Working Group to the Commission on Human Rights (E/CN.4/1988/28, paras. 27 to 34, 237 and 242).*

27.     Australia, Austria, the Netherlands, and the United States of America submitted the following proposal (E/CN.4/1988/WG.1/WP.22):

"*Article 5 ter*

"The States Parties to the present Convention shall respect the rights and duties of the parents and, where applicable, legal guardians, to provide direction to the child in the exercise of his or her rights enumerated in the present Convention in a manner consistent with the evolving capacities of the child, having due regard to the importance of promoting the development of the skills and knowledge required for an independent adulthood."

28.     In introducing this proposal, the observer for Australia stated that the proposed article would incorporate into the convention two important general concepts: (a) the evolving capacities of the child, and his or her rights as enumerated in the draft convention, and (b) the rights and duties of the parents who raised the child, who provided guidance to and took primary responsibility for the child.

29.     The representative of the Federal Republic of Germany was of the view that the draft convention dealt with the rights of the child and not those of the parents and therefore proposed the insertion of the following paragraph 2 in article 21 [article 41 of the final text], as adopted:

"Nothing in this Convention shall affect the right and the duty of parents and, where applicable, legal guardians to take measures as are required for the upbringing and well-being of the child".

30.     In the course of the debate, most of the participants expressed the view that article 5 ter in working paper 22 reflected the concerns of the working group. It was recalled that this matter had been discussed at length at past sessions of the Working Group, resulting in a compromise in article 7 bis, paragraph 3; article 5 ter in working paper 22, based on that compromise, reflected the delicate balance between the rights of children and the correlative rights of parents. If the emphasis was placed on the evolving capacities of the child in accordance with his age, the parents also had a role to play. Attention should be given to the growing child, and to his evolving capacities in a positive environment. The parents' rights in respect of bringing up the child were already well protected in article 8 [article 18 of the final text].

31.     The representative of the United Kingdom was of the view that the proposed amendment by the Federal Republic of Germany was not as detailed as the proposal made in working paper 22 as to the definition of the duties of parents and proposed the following wording for article 5 ter:

"Nothing in this Convention shall affect the right and duty of parents or, where applicable, legal guardians to provide in a manner consistent with the child's evolving capacities, appropriate direction and guidance to him or her in the exercise of the rights of the child recognized in the present Convention."

32.     The representative of Norway expressed the view that article 5 ter in working paper 22 was more consistent with the compromise and delicate balance which were found in article 15 relating to education. He proposed the following rewording of the text proposed by the United Kingdom:

"The States Parties to the present Convention shall respect the responsibilities of parents or, where applicable, legal guardians, to provide in a manner consistent with his or her evolving capacities, appropriate direction and guidance to the child in the exercise of the rights of the child recognized in the present Convention."

33.     Several participants expressed their support for the new text. The attention of the Working Group was drawn to the broader context of article 3 which listed parents, legal guardians, and other individuals legally responsible for the child. Finally, after some amendments proposed by the United Kingdom, the Working Group reached a consensus and adopted the following article 5 bis:

"The States Parties to the present Convention shall respect the responsibilities, rights, and duties of parents or, where applicable, legal guardians or other individuals legally responsible for the child, to provide, in a manner consistent with the evolving capacities of the child, appropriate direction and guidance in the exercise by the child of the rights recognized in the present Convention."

34.     The representative of the Federal Republic of Germany stated that he had joined the consensus on article 5 bis, although the text was not entirely satisfactory to his delegation, largely because article 5 bis addressed the rights of parents only in connection with a responsibility that States would have under the convention, namely to respect the parents' rights. His delegation would favour an interpretational clause which would state clearly that the draft convention was under no circumstances to be interpreted in a way that would affect the rights of parents or legal guardians. Should article 5 bis be retained in its present form or should an interpretational clause not be included so as to meet its concerns, his Government might enter reservations or declarations in case of ratification.

[...]

*Technical review of the draft convention*

237.     The question of a technical review of the draft convention was discussed on the basis of a proposal submitted by Australia (E/CN.4/1988/WG.1/WP.20). In the course of the discussion the members of the working group expressed their views on the main aspects to be considered when undertaking a technical review of the text.

[...]

242.     In connection with internal consistency, some speakers wished to have a list of definitions of terms used in the convention, which would be of great help for a correct understanding of the legal and practical effects of its provisions. For example, there was no definition of the concept of "parents" or "legal guardians". Were only biological parents concerned, or were other persons also entitled to be considered parents for some purposes, with equal responsibilities in relation to the child or children concerned? There was an analysis of definitions prepared by a non-governmental organization which could be of some help when preparing such a list for the convention. This should be considered during the quality control exercise so that the issue could be resolved at [the] second reading.

## 7.     Text as adopted at first reading

*The following is taken from document E/CN.4/1988/WG.1/WP.1/Rev.1.*

*Article 5 bis*

The States Parties to the present Convention shall respect the responsibilities, rights, and duties of parents or, where applicable, legal guardians or other individuals legally responsible for the child, to provide, in a manner consistent with the evolving capacities of the child, appropriate direction and guidance in the exercise by the child of the rights recognized in the present Convention.

# D.     Technical review (1988)

## 1.     Additional comments and clarifications by the Secretariat

*The following is taken from document E/CN.4/1989/WG.1/CRP.1/Add.1, paragraph 13.*

13.     The draft convention as a whole may not adequately recognize the role of the extended family and community when parental care is not available. Because cultures, traditions and customs in many countries and areas provide for such a role, the Working Group may wish to broaden article 5 *bis* accordingly. Taking also into account the wording of article 10 [article 20 of the final text], both paragraphs 1 and 2, which

mention the "family environment" in a similar context, it would seem desirable to include in article *5 bis*, as the relevant umbrella article, a reference to these circumstances. This might be accomplished by adding the words *"the extended family or community as provided for by local custom"* after the word "applicable".

# E. Second reading (1988-1989)

## 1. Proposal submitted to the Working Group at second reading

### (a) Senegal

*For the text of this proposal, see paragraph 704 in section 3 below.*

## 2. Discussion and adoption at second reading

*The following is taken from the 1989 report of the Working Group to the Commission on Human Rights (E/CN.4/1989/48, paras. 178 to 185).*

178.     The Working Group had before it the following text of article 5 bis as adopted at first reading:

"The States Parties to the present Convention shall respect the responsibilities, rights, and duties of parents or, where applicable, legal guardians or other individuals legally responsible for the child, to provide, in a manner consistent with the evolving capacities of the child, appropriate direction and guidance in the exercise by the child of the rights recognized in the present Convention."

179.     The revisions suggested to this article in the course of the technical review (E/CN.4/1989/WG.1/WP.2, p.21) included the deletion of "The" before, and of the words "to the present Convention" after, the words "States Parties", and the insertion of the words "the extended family or community as provided for by local custom" after the words "where applicable". It was also proposed to consider whether the word "appropriate" before the words "direction and guidance" should be maintained in the text of the article.

180.     Several delegations voiced their support for the idea of giving recognition in the convention to the notion of extended family or community responsibility for the child. While there was no strong opposition to its inclusion in article 5 bis, it was nevertheless argued that the introduction of this concept would change essentially the traditional triangular responsibility for the child. One participant expressed his preference for the text of this article as adopted at first reading.

181.     The representative of the United States of America proposed to insert the words "members of" before the words "extended family or community".

182.     The representative of the United Kingdom of Great Britain and Northern Ireland suggested that the word "individuals" be deleted from the text and the word "other" which preceded be made plural.

183.     The representative of the Union of Soviet Socialist Republics proposed to replace the word "individuals" by the word "persons" which, in his view, could be interpreted as including also the personnel of State children's institutions.

184.     The observer for Sweden said he would prefer that the word "appropriate" be maintained in the text of the article.

185.     The Working Group then adopted article 5 bis reading as follows:

"States Parties shall respect the responsibilities, rights, and duties of parents, or, where applicable, the members of the extended family or community as provided for by local custom, legal guardians or other persons legally responsible for the child, to provide, in a manner consistent with the evolving capacities of the child, appropriate direction and guidance in the exercise by the child of the rights recognized in the present Convention."

## 3. Proposals discussed but not adopted

*The following is taken from the 1989 report of the Working Group to the Commission on Human Rights (E/CN.4/1989/48, paras. 704 to 711).*

*Proposals relating to article 5*

704. In connection with its discussion of article 5, the representative of Senegal submitted a proposal (E/CN.4/1989/WG.1/WP.17, paragraphs 5 and 6) which sought to insert two new articles reading as follows:

*"Article 5 ter* (article 8 ter)

The States Parties shall grant the protection necessary to the family, the natural environment of the child and shall attend to his physical and moral health.

Accordingly, the States Parties shall provide, in case of need, appropriate assistance to the family with a view to helping it to assume its responsibilities for the harmonious development of the child.

*Article 5 quater* (article 8 quater)

The child has the duty to respect his parents and to give them assistance, in case of need."

705. In introducing his proposals the representative of Senegal indicated that he did not insist on consideration by the Working Group of article 5 ter which was thus withdrawn, but he would maintain his proposal with regard to a new article 5 quater which would thus become article 5 ter.

706. Some participants said that, although they shared the concern of the author of the proposal, they still were hesitant to support it because the duty to respect parents was, in their view, more a moral obligation than a legal one. It was also pointed out that in practical terms it would be hardly possible for the States Parties to report on their compliance with such a provision of the convention.

707. Some other delegations, however, voiced their support for the inclusion of this article or at least of this idea into the future convention. It was argued that in quite a number of international instruments the rights were accompanied by corresponding duties, and in this convention certain duties might also be laid down.

708. The representative of Ireland orally proposed to change the second part of the article to read: "...and to accord them appropriate assistance". The observer for Egypt suggested that after the word "assistance" the words "if they are capable of doing so" be added.

709. The observer for Canada expressed the view that consideration of the proposal of Senegal would be more appropriate within the framework of issues under article 16 [article 29 of the final text] which related to the objectives of education of the child.

710. The representative of Senegal agreed with this idea and indicated that he would be prepared to discuss his proposal under article 16.

711. The Chairman announced that Senegal was thus included as a member in the Working Group on education issues.

# Article 6 (Right to life, survival and development)

## A. Final text adopted by the General Assembly (1989)

*The following text is that approved by the General Assembly in its resolution 44/25 of 20 November 1989.*

> 1. States Parties recognize that every child has the inherent right to life.
>
> 2. States Parties shall ensure to the maximum extent possible the survival and development of the child.

## B. First Polish draft convention and comments (1978)

### 1. Comment on the first Polish draft

*Although the draft convention did not address the issues raised under present article 6, the comment of Barbados did.*

#### (a) Barbados

*The following is taken from document E/CN.4/1324.*

> [...]
>
> 3. The child's right to life had not been articled. How far should this right go? Does the child include the unborn child, or the foetus? Under specified circumstances, should a foetus be aborted without an offence being committed or at the relevant time was the foetus a human life? All these are questions which should be considered before the child's right to life is articled.

## C. First reading (1979-1988)

*This article was referred to as article 1 bis throughout the first and second readings.*

### 1. Proposal submitted to the Working Group (1988)

#### (a) India

*For the text of this proposal, see paragraph 14 in section 2 below.*

### 2. Discussion and adoption by the Working Group (1988)

*The following is taken from the 1988 report of the Working Group to the Commission on Human Rights (E/CN.4/1988/28, paras. 14 to 26).*

> 14. The Working Group had before it a proposal submitted by India (E/CN.4/1988/WG.1/WP.13) which read as follows:
>
> > "Article 1 bis or 2 bis
> >
> > "The States Parties to the present Convention undertake to create an environment, within their capacities and constitutional processes, which ensures, to the maximum extent possible, the survival and healthy development of the child."
>
> 15. During the course of the debate, several governmental representatives commented that the concept of survival was not legally defined and one representative expressed the belief that it could even prove harmful to the concept of the right to development, as her delegation understood it. A number of specific amendments were proposed and the following alternative wordings were suggested:

"The States Parties to the present Convention shall respect the right of the child to survival. The States Parties shall, within their capacities and constitutional processes, take all necessary measures to ensure, to the maximum extent possible, the survival and healthy development of the child."

"The States Parties to the present Convention undertake to promote conditions which ensure, to the maximum extent possible, the survival of the child."

"The States Parties to the present Convention undertake to create within the available resources the psychosocial conditions which will guarantee, to the maximum extent possible, the life and the full development of the child."

"The States Parties to the present Convention undertake to promote conditions which guarantee the life and healthy development of the child."

16.        At the request of the Chairman, the observer for the United Nations Children's Fund explained what the Fund understood by survival.

17.        The representative of India was of the view that the right to survival should be stressed, bearing in mind, as indicated by UNICEF, that many children died from preventable causes and that children could also survive in very poor conditions, the right to survival should be supplemented by the notion of healthy development.

18.        The discussions focused mainly on the definition of the concepts of survival, right to survival, right to development and the child's development. The view was expressed that life and survival were complementary and were not mutually exclusive, and that survival could even mean the diminution of infant mortality. In this regard, the Italian representative remarked that the international norm concerning the right to life, contained in the Universal Declaration of Human Rights (article 3) and expressed, through a different formulation, in article 6 of the International Covenant on Civil and Political Rights, has the nature of an intransgressible norm (*jus cogens*). The Italian representative insisted therefore that a specific provision on the right to life be inserted. Others observed that, in discussing the inclusion of a child's right to life, the Working Group had agreed not to reopen the discussion concerning the moment at which life begins.

19.        It was stated that the right to survival carried with it a more positive connotation than the right to life, it meant the right to have positive steps taken to prolong the life of the child. The view was further expressed that conditions should be defined in order to permit the exercise of the right to life, and not the right to mere survival. Two speakers stated that, despite the explanations that had been given on the word "survival", they continued to have serious doubts about the inclusion of this concept in the convention. The following text was proposed:

"The States Parties to the present Convention undertake to promote conditions which protect, to the maximum extent possible, the life of the child."

20.        The following texts were also proposed:

"The States Parties to the present Convention undertake to promote conditions which ensure, to the maximum extent possible, the survival and healthy development of the child." (The word "survival" in English to be put in brackets in the French and Spanish texts.)

"States Parties shall protect the right to life of children and ensure the survival and healthy development of children."

21.        In summing up the debate, the Chairman-Rapporteur stated that the right to life had been omitted from the draft convention, and that the proposal made in working paper 13 was intended to remedy that shortcoming. The right to life, already enshrined in the International Covenants on Human Rights, should be included in the draft convention and listed as a priority before other rights of the child. The approach to the right to life in the Covenants was rather negative, while that of the convention should be positive and

should take into account economic, social and cultural conditions. He proposed that a small drafting group (Argentina, Bulgaria, India, Italy, Norway, UNICEF and the United Kingdom) should work out a compromise text.

22.     The small drafting group submitted the following compromise text:

"1.     The States Parties to the present Convention recognize that every child has the inherent right to life.

2.     States Parties shall ensure, to the maximum extent possible, the survival and development of the child."

23.     The representative of India stated that the text had been drafted in order to cover the following main concerns: (a) the inherent right to life of the child, and (b) the focus on obligations for States Parties to promote measures and conditions for the survival and development of the child.

24.     After an extensive discussion, the representative of Venezuela said she would yield to the Working Group, simply and solely to enable work to go forward on the text of the convention, but that she regretted the inclusion of paragraph 2 of the proposed compromise text since, in her view, it will diminish the concept of the right to life conferred on all human beings in existing international instruments; she requested that some thought should be given to that, and that her position should be reflected in the report to be submitted to the Commission on Human Rights.

25.     The observer for the Holy See stated that it recognized the rights of the child began before birth. The Holy See affirmed that a child and its life existed from the moment of conception which was the transmission of life in marriage to which the mission of transmitting life was exclusively entrusted. Consequently, a conceived child was entitled to rights. Human life shall absolutely be respected and protected from the moment of conception.

26.     The Working Group finally adopted the text submitted by the small drafting group.

## 3.     Text as adopted at first reading

*The following is taken from document E/CN.4/1988/WG.1/WP.1/Rev.1.*

*Article 1 bis*

1.     The States Parties to the present Convention recognize that every child has the inherent right to life.

2.     States Parties shall ensure to the maximum extent possible the survival and development of the child.

## D.     Technical review (1988)

*There were no comments concerning either article 1 bis or the issues raised thereunder.*

## E.     Second reading (1988-1989)

## 1.     Proposals submitted to the Working Group at second reading

*The following States submitted written proposals for consideration by the Working Group at second reading.*

### (a)     Kuwait

*The following is taken from document E/CN.4/1989/WG.1/WP.18.*

[...]

Article 1 bis should read as follows:

> "The States Parties to the present Convention shall respect the child's right to life and, to this end, shall take all constitutional and legal measures needed to guarantee that right."

## (b)    Venezuela

*For the text of this proposal, see paragraph 87 in section 2 below.*

## 2.    Discussion and adoption at second reading

*The following is taken from the 1989 report of the Working Group to the Commission on Human Rights (E/CN.4/1989/48, paras. 86 to 91).*

86.    The Working Group had before it article 1 bis as adopted in the first reading which reads as follows (E/CN.4/1989/WG.1/WP.2):

> "1.    The States Parties to the present Convention recognize that every child has the inherent right to life.
>
> 2.    States Parties shall ensure to the maximum extent possible the survival and development of the child."

87.    The representative of Venezuela submitted document E/CN.4/1989/WG.1/WP.10 which reads as follows:

> *Article 1 and 1 bis*
>
> Merge the present article 1 with article 1 bis to form a single article 1 reading:
>
> > "1.    For the purposes of the present Convention, 'child' means every human being up to the age of 18 years unless, under the law of his State, he has attained the age of majority earlier.
> >
> > 2.    The States Parties to the present Convention recognize that every child has the inherent right to life.
> >
> > 3.    States Parties shall ensure to the maximum extent possible the healthy growth and development of the child."

88.    The observer for the World Health Organization expressed reservations with regard to the replacement of the word "survival" and explained that the term "survival" had a special meaning within the United Nations context, especially for his organization and UNICEF. "Survival" included growth monitoring, oral rehydration and disease control, breastfeeding, immunization, child spacing, food and female literacy; the term "growth" represented only a part of the concept of "survival" and the change would be a step backwards from standards already accepted.

89.    Delegates from Australia, Norway, Italy, Sweden and India stated their preference for the retention of the word "survival", reminding the Working Group of the spirit of collaboration under which this particular article was drafted 10 months ago. The representative of Italy indicated that in the language of international organizations the two words "survival" and "development" had come to acquire the special meaning of ensuring the child's survival in order to realize the full development of his or her personality, both from the material and spiritual points of view.

90.    The representative of Venezuela withdrew the amendment and stated that the problem would be one for interpretation by local authorities.

91.     The article was adopted and reads as follows:

"1.     States Parties recognize that every child has the inherent right to life.

2.     States Parties shall ensure to the maximum extent possible the survival and development of the child."

## 3.     Statement made after the adoption of the draft convention

*The following is taken from the 1989 report of the Working Group to the Commission on Human Rights (E/CN.4/1989/48, paragraph 21).*

### (a)     United Kingdom of Great Britain and Northern Ireland

21.     The representative of the United Kingdom of Great Britain and Northern Ireland stated that nothing in this convention may be interpreted as affecting in any way the operation of the United Kingdom immigration or nationality legislation in so far as it relates to the entry of aliens and the terms and conditions of their stay in the United Kingdom, and to the acquisition and possession of citizenship. In the absence of the advice from Legal Counsel on the Chairman's statement */ regarding paragraph 6 (new paragraph 9) of the Preamble, the United Kingdom also stated that their Government might have to lodge a reservation with regard to article 1 and 1 bis at the time of ratification.

*/      *In adopting preambular paragraph 9, which reads:*

> *Bearing in mind, as indicated in the Declaration of the Rights of the Child, "the child, by reason of his physical and mental immaturity, needs special safeguards and care, including appropriate legal protection, before as well as after birth",*

*the following statement was to be included in the travaux préparatoires: "In adopting this preambular paragraph, the Working Group does not intend to prejudice the interpretation of article 1 or any other provision of the Convention by States Parties."*

## 4.     Response of the Legal Counsel

*The following is taken from the annex to the 1989 report of the Working Group to the Commission on Human Rights (E/CN.4/1989/48).*

Regarding your request of 30 November 1988 on whether the Chairman of the Working Group preparing the draft convention on the rights of the child may on behalf of the entire Working Group include a statement in the *travaux préparatoires* which would read "in adopting this preambular paragraph, the Working Group does not intend to prejudice the interpretation of article 1 or any other provision of the Convention by States Parties", we have not, of course, seen the text of the preambular paragraph in question or the text of any of the provisions of the draft convention and, thus, our views set out below are somewhat abstract in nature.

1.     The preamble to a treaty serves to set out the general considerations which motivate the adoption of the treaty. Therefore, it is at first sight strange that a text is sought to be included in the *travaux préparatoires* for the purpose of depriving a particular preambular paragraph of its usual purpose, i.e. to form part of the basis for the interpretation of the treaty. Also, it is not easy to assess what conclusions States may later draw, when interpreting the treaty, from the inclusion of such a text in the *travaux préparatoires*. Furthermore, seeking to establish the meaning of a particular provision of a treaty, through the inclusion in the *travaux préparatoires* may not optimally fulfil the intended purpose, because, as you know, under article 32 of the Vienna Convention on the Law of Treaties, *travaux préparatoires* constitute a "supplementary means of interpretation" and hence recourse to *travaux préparatoires* may only be had if the relevant treaty provisions are in fact found by those interpreting the treaty to be unclear.

2.      Nevertheless, there is no prohibition in law or practice against inclusion of an interpretive statement in *travaux préparatoires*. Though this is better done through the inclusion of such interpretive statement in the final act or in an accompanying resolution or other instrument. (Inclusion in the final act, etc. would be possible under article 31 of the Vienna Convention on the Law of Treaties.) Nor is there a prohibition in law or practice from making an interpretative statement; in the negative sense, intended here as part of the *travaux préparatoires*.

Carl August Fleischhauer
THE LEGAL COUNSEL
*9 December 1988*

## 5.      Statements made during the adoption of the report

*The following is taken from the 1989 report of the Working Group to the Commission on Human Rights (E/CN.4/1989/48, paragraph 731).*

731.      The representative of the United Kingdom in connection with the adoption of paragraph 43 of the report, said that the United Kingdom understood that the reference to article 1 in the Chairman's statement in that paragraph included a reference to article 1 bis. The representative of Ireland stated that he had no recollection of such a statement having been made at the time that the text of preambular paragraph 6 was adopted. He therefore questioned the appropriateness of its inclusion in the official report of the Working Group.

# Article 7 (Name and nationality)

## A.    Final text adopted by the General Assembly (1989)

*The following text is that approved by the General Assembly in its resolution 44/25 of 20 November 1989.*

1.    The child shall be registered immediately after birth and shall have the right from birth to a name, the right to acquire a nationality and, as far as possible, the right to know and be cared for by his or her parents.

2.    States Parties shall ensure the implementation of these rights in accordance with their national law and their obligations under the relevant international instruments in this field, in particular where the child would otherwise be stateless.

## B.    First Polish draft convention and comments (1978)

### 1.    The first Polish draft

*The following text is taken from the 1978 report of the Commission on Human Rights (E/CN.4/1292, p. 124).*

*Article III*

The child shall be entitled from his birth to a name and a nationality.

### 2.    Comments on the first Polish draft

*Article III of the draft gave rise to the following comments.*

#### (a)    Federal Republic of Germany

*The following is taken from document E/CN.4/1324, page 30.*

1.    See paragraph 3, Federal Republic of Germany, under General Comments.

[...]

In the opinion of the Federal Government, article III of the draft gives rise to serious reservations. Although this provision provides that every child shall be entitled from his birth to a nationality, it does not indicate how this right is to be implemented. Unlike the texts of other provisions concerning nationality (article 15 of the Universal Declaration of Human Rights of 10 December 1948 and article 24, paragraph 3, of the International Covenant on Civil and Political Rights of 19 December 1966), article III of the draft implies that the convention wishes to establish the child's nationality.

2.    The same inference could also be drawn from article I of the draft convention, according to which every child shall immediately be entitled to the rights provided for in the convention. If draft article III was merely in the nature of a programme, this provision would be superfluous.

3.    Immediate application of article III must not, moreover, cause us to forget that the absence of the other essential requirements for the acquisition of a nationality means that, in its present wording, this article is doomed to failure, because it cannot be supposed that the convention wishes to compel every Contracting Party to introduce the principle of *"jus soli".*

4.    Nowhere does the acquisition of nationality by birth depend solely on the natural fact of birth; quite the contrary, apart from birth, all nationality laws require additional elements which must be related to the birth and which are the really essential factors conferring nationality. These correlative factors sanctified as principles by international law, which in general govern acquisition of a nationality through birth in the

State granting it, are:

- descent from parents having the nationality of the State in question;

- birth in the territory of that State.

5.      The reluctance of States Members of the United Nations to meet the minimal requirements imposed by the rules of the Convention on the Reduction of Statelessness of 30 August 1961 is shown by the small number of States that has accepted that instrument. In the circumstances, it would seem ill-advised to expect article III of the draft convention to provide a solution to the fundamental problem, which in practice is still unresolved, of the acquisition of nationality by birth. The draft would in no way be impaired if this provision were omitted. In its place, it would be better to urge Members of the United Nations to accept the Convention of 30 August 1961 or to take account of that Convention's principles in their internal law.

*Paragraph 3 of the general comments of the Federal Republic of Germany, also contained in document E/CN.4/1324, reads as follows.*

3.      Without prejudice to a final assessment, we consider that articles I, III, IV (understood as the right of the child to have his needs provided for in the broadest sense), the first and second sentences of article VI, the first sentence of article VII, paragraph 1 (right to education), and the second part of article VII, paragraph 2 (primary right of parents) should be grouped together in a separate section as rights of the individual.

## (b)    Malawi

*The following is taken from document E/CN.4/1324/Add.4.*

We are concerned with the nationality requirement since nationality is a matter of Municipal Law. It is a fact that each State decides who are to be its nationals and who are not going to be its nationals. This serves, above all, to determine that the person upon whom nationality is conferred enjoys the rights and is bound by the obligations which the law of the State in question grants and imposes on its nationals.

Because of the foregoing, there are some people who are considered as stateless persons and others who are considered as persons with dual nationality.

We, therefore, feel that clarifications on the following points are also necessary:

(1)    the nationality that would be conferred upon children born from stateless persons or persons with dual nationality;

(2)    the question of whether or not nationality is going to be conferred purely on the basis of a child's birth place;

(3)    the question of whether or not the article is imposing on States Parties something which is supposed to be taken care of by Municipal Law; and

(4)    the guarantee that the State Party will have its nationality on the child; the child will honour the obligations that the State in question expects of the child, for example, like accepting to go to war when called upon to defend the State.

## (c)    New Zealand

*The following is taken from document E/CN.4/1324/Add.5.*

Acceptable.

## (d)    Sweden

*The following is taken from document E/CN.4/1324, page 31.*

The child's right to a nationality, which is dealt with in principle 3 of the 1959 Declaration, is an important point which requires further examination. A child should not be stateless if at least one of its parents has a nationality. In cases where both parents are stateless, the child should be able to acquire the nationality of the State in which it was born or in which it resides.

# C.  First reading (1979-1988)

*This article was referred to as article 2 throughout the first and second readings.*

## 1.  Revised Polish draft (1979)

*The following text is taken from Commission on Human Rights document E/CN.4/1349, which was reissued for technical reasons.*

*Article 2*

1.  The child shall have the right from his birth to a name and a nationality.

2.  The States Parties to the present Convention undertake to introduce into their legislation the principle according to which a child shall acquire the nationality of the State in the territory of which he has been born if, at the time of the child's birth, the application of the proper national law would not grant him any nationality whatever.

## 2.  Proposals submitted to the Working Group (1980)

### (a)  Australia

*For the text of this proposal, see paragraph 40 in section 3 below.*

### (b)  United States of America

*For the text of this proposal, see paragraph 37 in section 3 below.*

## 3.  Discussion and adoption by the Working Group (1980)

*The following is taken from paragraphs 37 to 43 of the 1980 report of the Working Group to the Commission on Human Rights (E/CN.4/L.1542), which is reproduced in paragraph 277 of the 1980 report of the Commission on Human Rights (E/CN.4/1408).*

37.  At the fourth meeting, the Working Group considered article 2 (1) of the draft convention. The representative of the United States of America proposed that the wording of the article should be amended to read:

"1.  In accordance with the laws or practices of each Contracting State, the child shall have the right from his birth to acquire a name and a nationality."

He pointed out that the proposed amendment would bring the draft convention in line with article 24 of the International Covenant on Civil and Political Rights and would help to prevent difficulties under the immigration and nationality laws of various States. In particular, he maintained that the amendment would avoid any implication that the draft convention would automatically entitle stateless children entering the territory of a State party to the nationality of that State.

38.  Some delegations opposed the amendment on humanitarian grounds, in order to provide protection for stateless children. It was also argued that the wording of article 2 (1) was of a general nature, while the second paragraph would include more specific provisions.

39.     On the suggestion of the Chairman, the Working Group adopted the following compromise text:

"1.      The child shall have the right from his birth to a name and to acquire a nationality."

40.     At the fifth meeting, the delegation of Australia submitted the following amendment to article 2 (2):

"2.      The States parties to the present Convention shall ensure that their legislation recognizes the principle according to which a child shall acquire the nationality of the State in the territory of which he has been born if, at the time of the child's birth, he is not granted nationality by any other State in accordance with its laws."

41.     The representative of Australia explained that the first part of his amendment was meant to remove the implication in the original draft that the principle in question was not already contained in most national legislations; the second, and most important, part was aimed at bringing the draft convention as close as possible to the general principles of the Convention on the Reduction of Statelessness of 1961.

42.     Discussion on the proposed amendment began at the fifth meeting of the Working Group. Some delegations expressed their opposition on the grounds that the law of their countries did not provide for automatic granting of nationality to children of foreign parents born there.

43.     The Working Group, however, was unable to continue consideration of article 2 (2) because of lack of time.

## 4.      Discussion and adoption by the Working Group (1981)

*The following is taken from paragraphs 12 to 18 of the 1981 report of the Working Group to the Commission on Human Rights (E/CN.4/L.1575), which is reproduced in paragraph 289 of the 1981 report of the Commission on Human Rights (E/CN.4/1475).*

12.     Paragraph 2 of article 2 of the revised Polish draft was as follows:

"The States parties to the present Convention undertake to introduce into their legislation the principle according to which a child shall acquire the nationality of the State in the territory of which he has been born if, at the time of the child's birth, the application of the proper national law would not grant him any nationality whatever."

13.     At the Working Group's session of 1980, the representative of Australia submitted the following amendment to paragraph 2 of article 2:

"The States parties to the present Convention shall ensure that their legislation recognizes the principle according to which a child shall acquire the nationality of the State in the territory of which he has been born if, at the time of the child's birth, he is not granted nationality by any other State in accordance with its laws."

This proposal was reintroduced at the 1981 session of the Group.

14.     Some speakers felt that there were no substantial differences between the text of the revised Polish draft convention and the proposal submitted by Australia. They also felt that both the Australian and Polish delegations were inspired by humanitarian principles in proposing their formulations for the paragraph, recalling that this paragraph was aimed at providing every child with a nationality so as to prevent cases of statelessness among children.

15.     The representative of Poland withdrew paragraph 2 of article 2 of the revised Polish draft in favour of the Australian amendment.

16.     It had been noted by some speakers that the Australian proposal was largely aimed at bringing the draft convention as close as possible to the general principles of the Convention on the Reduction of Statelessness of 1961.

17.      During the ensuing discussion, some speakers drew the attention of the Working Group to the problems that might arise from the fact that many Member States of the United Nations had based their legislation on nationality on principles other than those laid down in the Convention on the Reduction of Statelessness and the proposed paragraph 2. For, in the view of these speakers, there were countries where the *jus sanguinis* basis of nationality prevailed, as opposed to the *jus soli* approach in the Polish and Australian texts, and therefore the Working Group should consider the need for a compromise formula in order to prevent possible reservations by States to this provision of the convention on the rights of the child at the time of ratification.

18.      The Working Group adopted by consensus paragraph 2 of article 2, as proposed by Australia, on the understanding that at a later stage, if necessary, the Working Group would resume the consideration of those problems pointed out by some members of the Group.

## 5.      Proposal submitted to the Working Group (1984)

### (a)      International Federation of Women in Legal Careers and the International Abolitionist Federation

*The following is taken from document E/CN.4/1983/NGO/33, which appeared after the 1983 session of the Working Group.*

> *Article 2* (Nationality)
>
> Noting that in some cases the minor children of political refugees who have given up their nationality have to wait for a fairly long time to acquire the nationality of the country in which they are living, although in principle it should be theirs by right, we would suggest that the words "without delay or prior conditions" be added after the words "the principle according to which a child shall acquire" and before the words "the nationality of the State...".
>
> We would like to add the following paragraph 3:
>
>> "The acquisition of a name or nationality may not constitute grounds for discrimination against either of the parents or between children born in wedlock and children born out of wedlock."

## 6.      Statements made before the Working Group (1984)

*The following is taken from the 1984 report of the Working Group to the Commission on Human Rights (E/CN.4/1984/71, paras. 9 and 11).*

### (a)      United Kingdom of Great Britain and Northern Ireland

9.      The representative of the United Kingdom stated that, even as a State participating in the work of the open-ended Working Group, his delegation continued to have difficulties with some of the articles already adopted (e.g. articles 2, paragraph 1 [new article 7 (1)], 3, paragraph 1 [new article 3 (1)], 4, paragraph 1 [new article 4 (1)], 6 and 8 [new articles 9 and 18], paragraphs 1 and 2). Article 2, paragraphs 1 and 2, caused difficulties in relation to United Kingdom nationality law. Article 6, paragraph 1 [new article 9 (1)], as currently drafted was not compatible with United Kingdom immigration legislation because the parents of a child who did not have rights of residence in the United Kingdom could not determine that he should live there unless he qualified for residence under United Kingdom immigration rules. In addition, draft articles 3, paragraph 1 [new article 3 (1)], 4, paragraph 1 [new article 4 (1)], 6, paragraphs 2 and 3 [new article 9 (2) (3)], 6 bis, paragraphs 2 and 3 [new article 10 (2) (3)], and 8, paragraphs 1 and 2 [new article 18 (1) (2)], all posed problems in relation to United Kingdom immigration law. Certain of those draft provisions were difficult or even impossible to reconcile with his country's law and practice. Nevertheless, his delegation had joined the consensus at the Working Group in recognition of the efforts made by other delegations to get an acceptable draft completed and available for comment by Member States with as little delay as possible. However, the United Kingdom thought it important that all States, including those which had not participated in the Working Group, should have an

opportunity to consider and comment on those articles after the current drafting exercise was concluded. If, after the drafting was completed and notwithstanding that certain parts of the text remained substantially as they were now, the United Kingdom authorities were nevertheless to consider that they could proceed to signature and ratification, his delegation foresaw that there would be a need to enter reservations and declarations, in particular to deal with the aforementioned difficulties over immigration and nationality.

## (b)    Federal Republic of Germany

11.    The representative of the Federal Republic of Germany stated that his delegation shared the concerns of the United Kingdom delegation particularly with regard to article 2, paragraph 2 [new article 7 (2)], and article 6, paragraph 1 and 2 [new article 9 (1) (2)]. Article 2, paragraph 2 [new article 7 (2)], posed problems with regard to his country's nationality law. As in the case of the United Kingdom, the provisions of draft article 6, paragraphs 1 and 2 [new article 9 (1) (2)], were not compatible with the Federal Republic's immigration legislation. Should article 2, paragraph 2, and article 6, paragraphs 1 and 2, be retained in their present form during the forthcoming deliberations in spite of the concerns of some delegations, and should the draft convention be opened for signature and ratification in that form, his Government might feel obliged to enter reservations to both articles. The representative of the Federal Republic of Germany also expressed his support for the United Kingdom proposal that all States be given an opportunity to comment on the Working Group's completed draft before its submission to the Commission on Human Rights.

## 7.    Comment submitted to the Working Group (1986)

### (a)    Bangladesh

*The following comment is contained in a paper submitted by the Permanent Representative of Bangladesh to the United Nations Office at Geneva in connection with the draft convention on the rights of the child with the request that the paper be annexed to the report of the Working Group. For the complete text, including general comments on the draft convention, see document E/CN.4/1986/39, annex IV.*

Paragraph 2 of article 2 as it stands will create serious and complex problems with regard to nationality and the status of children. If the article 2 (2) in its present form is adopted in the final text, it is the view of Bangladesh that this will lead to far-reaching legal reservations by a large number of States including Bangladesh.

## 8.    Comment submitted to the Working Group (1987)

### (a)    Morocco

*On 30 January 1987, the Permanent Representative of Morocco submitted to the United Nations Office at Geneva a paper containing its comments on certain articles of the draft convention and requested that those comments be brought to the attention of the Working Group. The following is taken from document E/CN.4/1987/WG.1/WP.35.*

Morocco fully supports the resolutions of the General Assembly aiming to ensure the rapid adoption of the draft convention on the rights of the child, but it considers that the implementation of the convention should not shake the foundations of the family or respect for its traditional rules.

The rights of the child are conceived in different ways throughout the world because of differences in legal systems, moral values, religious beliefs and family rules. Nevertheless, the family remains linked with the culture, the evolution and the beliefs of each society.

The Muslim societies, including Morocco, have not neglected the rights of the child. However, the Muslim conception has made the child an essential element within the family.

A reading of the draft convention on the rights of the child in its present form calls for comments on the following points:

- Nationality of the child born of stateless parents
- Situation of children born outside marriage
- Recognition of children
- Adoption
- Succession

*Article 2* (Nationality)

In accordance with the Moroccan code governing nationality, the acquisition of Moroccan nationality is subject to certain conditions. According to article 6 of this code, the nationality of the child follows that of his father (*jus sanguinis*). Similarly, the child is entitled to Moroccan nationality if born of a Moroccan mother and an unidentified father.

However, Moroccan nationality cannot be granted to a child born of stateless parents.

[...]

## 9. Text as adopted at first reading

*The following is taken from document E/CN.4/1988/WG.1/WP.1/Rev.1.*

*Article 2*

1. The child shall have the right from his birth to a name and to acquire a nationality.

2. The States Parties to the present Convention shall ensure that their legislation recognizes the principle according to which a child shall acquire the nationality of the State in the territory of which he has been born if, at the time of the child's birth, he is not granted nationality by any other State in accordance with its laws.

## D. Technical review (1988)

## 1. Comment by the United Nations Educational, Scientific and Cultural Organization (UNESCO)

*The following is taken from document E/CN.4/1989/WG.1/CRP.1, page 12.*

A new paragraph should be added between its present paragraphs 1 and 2, the present paragraph 2 becoming paragraph 3.

This new paragraph should read:

"2. The child shall have the right from birth to respect for his/her human, racial, national and cultural identity and dignity, as well as have the duty to respect the human, racial, national and cultural identity and dignity of others."

## 2. Comment by the United Nations Children's Fund (UNICEF)

*The following is taken from document E/CN.4/1989/WG.1/CRP.1, page 13.*

*Gender neutrality*

Paragraph 1. Omission of the pronoun "his" is proposed.

Paragraph 2. The latter part of the paragraph might be reformulated as follows:

"...a child shall acquire the nationality of the State in the territory of which he *or she* has been born if, at the time of birth, *the child* is not granted nationality by any other State in accordance with its laws".

### 3.    Additional comments and clarifications by the Secretariat

*The following is taken from document E/CN.4/1989/WG.1/CRP.1/Add.1, paragraph 9.*

9.        In line with article 24, paragraph 2, of the International Covenant on Civil and Political Rights, the words *"and registration"* may be added after the word "name" in paragraph 1.

## E.    Second reading (1988-1989)

### 1.    Proposals submitted to the Working Group at second reading

#### (a)    Algeria, Egypt, Iraq, Jordan, Kuwait, Libyan Arab Jamahiriya, Morocco, Oman, Pakistan and Tunisia

*For the text of this proposal, see paragraph 93 in section 2 below.*

#### (b)    Federal Republic of Germany

*For the text of the two proposals submitted by the Federal Republic of Germany, see section 2, paragraph 98, and section 3, paragraph 695, below.*

#### (c)    Netherlands

*For the text of this proposal, see paragraph 99 in section 2 below.*

#### (d)    Latin American meeting

*The following is taken from document E/CN.4/1989/WG.1/WP.1.*

In article 2: "... from his birth to assume an *identity*, a *family*, a name ...".

### 2.    Discussion and adoption at second reading

*The following is taken from the 1989 report of the Working Group to the Commission on Human Rights (E/CN.4/1989/48, paras. 92 to 116).*

92.        In connection with this article, the Working Group had before it the text of article 2 as adopted at first reading together with suggestions for revision, contained in E/CN.4/1989/WG.1/WP.2:

"1.        The child shall have the right from his *or her* birth to a name *and registration* and to acquire a nationality.

2.        *The child shall have the right from birth to respect for his or her human, racial, national and cultural identity and dignity, as well as have the duty to respect the human, racial, national and cultural identity and dignity of others.*

3.        (The) States Parties (to the present Convention) shall ensure that their legislation recognizes the principle according to which a child shall acquire the nationality of the State in the territory of which he or she has been born if, at the time of the child's birth, he *or she* is not granted nationality by any other State in accordance with its laws."

93.        On behalf of Algeria, Egypt, Iraq, Jordan, Kuwait, Libyan Arab Jamahiriya, Morocco, Oman, Pakistan and Tunisia, the delegation of Egypt proposed the following amendments contained in E/CN.4/1989/WG.1/WP.4:

1.      Paragraph 1 should be amended to read as follows:

> "The child shall have the right from his birth to know and belong to his parents, as well as the right to a name and to acquire a nationality."

2.      Paragraph 2 should be amended to read as follows:

> "The States Parties to the present Convention shall diligently endeavour to grant their nationality, in accordance with their laws, to a child born in their territory if, at the time of the child's birth, he is not granted nationality by any other State."

94.     According to the delegate of Egypt, the purpose of the first amendment was that of ensuring the psychological stability of the child, which was of equal importance to his physical and mental growth and helped to form his personality. In most cases the right to know his parents was quite essential to the child and equal to his right to a name or a nationality, which were only important for him at a certain age. The purpose of the second was to allow a country to apply freely either one of the two legal systems prevailing, that is, *jus sanguinis* or *jus soli*, regarding nationality.

95.     Iraq urged the Working Group to consider this proposal contained in E/CN.4/1989/WG.1/WP.4 since the preference for *jus soli* was not in conformity with many legal systems.

96.     With regard to paragraph 1 of the proposal, the German Democratic Republic, the Union of Soviet Socialist Republics and the United States of America referred to the exceptions in their legislation concerning the right of "secret adoption", that is, when the adopted child did not have the right to know his natural parents, and pointed out that "the right to know one's parents" could not be applied everywhere. They also drew the Working Group's attention on the use of the word "belonging" as an implication of the idea of property. They also underlined that the concepts of *jus sanguinis* and *jus soli* were of equal importance. The delegation of Portugal expressed the view that the idea of "belonging" is not applicable to children and that there were situations where the right to know one's parents could not be applied.

97.     The delegate of Egypt reiterated the objective of the first amendment and stated he would seek new compromise language.

98.     The representative of the Federal Republic of Germany submitted a proposal for amendment (E/CN.4/1989/WG.1/WP.7) which read as follows:

> "Reformulate paragraph 2 of article 2 as follows (amendments in italics):
>
> 2.      The States Parties to the present Convention shall ensure that their legislation recognizes the principle according to which a child *upon application or without any further action* shall acquire the nationality of the State in the territory of which he has been born if, at the time of the child's birth, he is not granted nationality by any other State in accordance with its laws."

99.     The delegate of the Netherlands drew attention to the concept of permanent residency contained in his own proposal (E/CN.4/1989/WG.1/WP.23 (revised)) which read as follows:

> "2.      The States Parties to the present Convention shall ensure that their legislation recognizes the principle according to which a child shall acquire the nationality of the State in the territory of which he or she has been born *and has habitually resided for such period as may be fixed by the States Parties, not exceeding five years immediately preceding the lodging of the application, nor ten years in all*, if he or she *would otherwise be stateless*."

100.    He then explained that the words "time of the child's birth" were to be deleted from the proposal of the Federal Republic of Germany in order to avoid statelessness and added that he judged unnecessary the use of the words "upon application" contained in that same proposal.

101.    The representative of the Federal Republic of Germany explained that with the use of the words "upon application", the draft convention was being brought closer to the general principle of the Convention on the Reduction of Statelessness of 1961.

102.    The delegate of the Union of Soviet Socialist Republics stated that the proposal of the Federal Republic of Germany referred to the above-mentioned Convention word for word, but that many countries that had not ratified this Convention would have problems in adopting this paragraph. He declared that the Dutch proposal in WP.23 overlapped with other views such as the one expressed by UNESCO and proposed the forming of a small drafting group and the use of more flexible wording as in E/CN.4/1989/WG.1/WP.25, which he proposed:

"To replace paragraph 2 of article 2 by the following text:

"2.    The States Parties shall ensure the realization of this right in accordance with their national legislation and their international legal obligations in this field."

103.    The Chairman decided to establish a drafting group composed of Algeria, Australia, the Federal Republic of Germany, the German Democratic Republic, Kuwait, the Netherlands, and the Union of Soviet Socialist Republics, with the United States of America as its Coordinator.

104.    The representative of the United States of America introduced the proposals submitted by the drafting group on article 2, composed of the United States of America, Algeria, Australia, the Federal Republic of Germany, the German Democratic Republic, Kuwait, the Netherlands and the Union of Soviet Socialist Republics (E/CN.4/1989/WG.1/WP.26). The proposed text for article 2 read as follows:

"1.    The child shall have the right from birth to a name and registration and to acquire a nationality, and, as far as possible, to know and be cared for by his or her parents.

2.    States Parties shall ensure the implementation of these rights in accordance with their national law and their obligations under the relevant international instruments in this field, in particular where the child would otherwise be stateless."

105.    The representative of the Union of Soviet Socialist Republics stated that, since the proposal of his delegation relating to paragraph 2 of article 2 (E/CN.4/1989/WG.1/WP.25) was taken into account in the text submitted by the drafting group, he would not insist on consideration of his proposals by the working group.

106.    The participants favoured in general the proposals submitted by the drafting group. The discussion focused mainly on the question of registration of the child. It was pointed out that the proposed text of article 2 differed substantially from the provision of article 24, paragraph 2, of the International Covenant on Civil and Political Rights which stated that "Every child shall be registered immediately after birth...".

107.    Some doubts were also expressed with regard to the words "as far as possible" contained in paragraph 2 of article 2. This expression was viewed by some participants as giving rise to an arbitrary interpretation of this article of the convention.

108.    The observer for New Zealand proposed orally that the words "as far as possible" be replaced by "subject to the provisions of this Convention". Another alternative formulation was put forward by the representative of the United States of America who suggested the wording "in the best interests of the child". The observer for Sweden proposed to make a combination of two proposals reading "as far as possible and subject to the provisions of the Convention".

109.    The observer for the Netherlands indicated that the right of the child to acquire a nationality is not directly linked to the fact of birth. He therefore suggested that certain modifications should be made in this connection in the text proposed by the drafting group.

110.     The observer for Egypt orally proposed that the words "and/or" be added before the words "their obligations" in the second paragraph of article 2.

111.     The representative of Italy proposed to introduce in the text of article 2 a phrase stating that "No child can be arbitrarily deprived of his or her family". Some other delegations pointed out that such provision had been already included in the body of the draft convention and therefore there was no need to repeat it in article 2.

112.     After some more discussion, the representative of the United States of America on behalf of the drafting group proposed a compromise text of the first paragraph of article 2 which read as follows:

> "The child shall be registered immediately after birth and shall have the right from birth to a name, the right to acquire a nationality and, as far as possible, the right to know and be cared for by his or her parents."

113.     It was proposed that the second paragraph of article 2 should stay unchanged as submitted originally by the drafting group.

114.     This proposal was accepted by the working group and it thus adopted article 2 which reads as follows:

> "1.     The child shall be registered immediately after birth and shall have the right from birth to a name, the right to acquire a nationality, and, as far as possible, the right to know and be cared for by his or her parents.
>
> 2.     States Parties shall ensure the implementation of these rights in accordance with their national law and their obligations under the relevant international instruments in this field, in particular where the child would otherwise be stateless."

115.     The representative of Sweden stated that his delegation was able to join in the consensus on article 2 on the understanding that the provisions of this article should be interpreted in the best interests of the child.

116.     The observer for Canada pointed out that certain provisions of article 2 as adopted had been already included in some of the other articles of the draft convention, in particular in article 6 [new article 9]. He urged the Working Group to avoid such duplication in future.

[...]

## 3.     Proposals discussed but not adopted by the Working Group

*The following is taken from the 1989 report of the Working Group to the Commission on Human Rights (E/CN.4/1989/48, paras. 695 to 703).*

*Proposal relating to article 2*

695.     In connection with the discussion of article 2, the delegation of the Federal Republic of Germany submitted the following proposal (E/CN.4/1989/WG.1/WP.5):

*Article 2* (new)

Replace article 2 by the following:

> "*Article 2* (new)[*]
>
> (1)     The States Parties shall ensure
>
> (a)     that all human rights recognized by them also apply to children,

(b)      that general human rights as enshrined in the International Covenant on Civil and Political Rights even apply to children, if a State Party to the present Convention is not a Party to the Covenant.

(2)      In order to take into account the evolving capacities of the child to take decisions under his own responsibility, provision may be made for the child to exercise some of his rights to be specified under the law of his State as if he had attained the age of majority; in this case, State Parties shall ensure that the legal effects of the decision taken by the child are recognized, except the child acted before having attained the minimum age prescribed under the law of his State."

[* In the case of adoption of paragraph 1 of the proposed article 2 (new), numerous repetitious draft articles are to be deleted, especially article 1 bis [new article 6], (identical with parts of article 6 (1) of the Covenant); article 2 (1) [new article 7 (1)] (nearly identical with article 24 (2) and (3) of the Covenant; articles 7a [new article 13], 7 bis [new article 14], 7 ter [new article 15] and 7 quater [new article 16] (more or less identical with articles 19, 18, 21/22 and with article 17 of the Covenant); and article 19 [new article 37] of the draft convention (a selective repetition of article 14 of the Covenant).]

696.      The delegate of the Federal Republic of Germany pointed out that many rights which under the International Covenants already apply to children, were included again specifically for children in the draft convention, but on the other hand, not all the rights guaranteed by the Covenants appeared in the draft convention, for example, the right of self-determination, the equal rights of men and women, the ban on slavery, the right of a person arrested or detained to be brought promptly before a judge, even though they also should apply to children. The delegate said that this selective double-regulation of rights would create problems and even contradictions with the Covenants and that a general clause ensuring the application of general human rights to children, should be substituted for the present article 2.

697.      The observer for Australia stated that the proposal of the Federal Republic of Germany to replace article 2 was totally new, bringing into question the whole approach to the convention to existing rights. It may well have been a better way to proceed had it been introduced eight years before, but that had not happened and now its acceptance would only serve to delay adoption of the convention.

698.      The delegate of India stated that the proposal of the Federal Republic of Germany to replace article 2 with a new article covered entirely new areas, and he expressed his opposition to consider such a proposal at this late stage.

699.      The delegation of Portugal pointed out that the proposal of the Federal Republic of Germany referred solely to the Covenant on Civil and Political Rights, while other important conventions, including the Covenant on Economic, Social and Cultural Rights and the Geneva Conventions and Protocols, had been omitted. Moreover, the representative of Portugal pointed out that it seemed unlikely that a State which is not a party to the Covenant on Civil and Political Rights would be open to the idea of feeling bound by its provisions.

700.      The delegate of Poland said that it was too late to adopt the proposal of the Federal Republic of Germany and pointed out the problem that would be posed by the countries which were not parties to the Covenant on Civil and Political Rights. He added that despite repetitions between the draft convention and the Covenant, the former was an independent instrument and that work on this convention should continue.

701.      Noting the importance of the issue raised by the Federal Republic of Germany, the delegate of Ireland, reminded the Working Group that article 21 of the draft convention allowed the application of the highest human rights standards enshrined in other international instruments and suggested that article 21 might be moved forward to follow article 1 bis.

702.    The observer for Finland drew the Working Group's attention to the issue raised under the present article 21 and stated that this had already been addressed by Finland and the ILO in E/CN.4/1989/WG.1/CRP.1, and proposed the inclusion of these two suggestions in article 21.

703.    The representative of the Federal Republic of Germany withdrew his proposals relating to article 2 (E/CN.4/1989/WG.1/WP.5).

# Article 8 (Preservation of identity)

## A.    Final text adopted by the General Assembly (1989)

*The following text is that approved by the General Assembly in its resolution 44/25 of 20 November 1989.*

> 1.    States Parties undertake to respect the right of the child to preserve his or her identity, including nationality, name and family relations as recognized by law without unlawful interference.

> 2.    Where a child is illegally deprived of some or all of the elements of his or her identity, States Parties shall provide appropriate assistance and protection, with a view to speedily re-establishing his or her identity.

## B.    First Polish draft convention and comments (1978)

*Neither the first Polish draft nor the views received on it (see document E/CN.4/1324 and Corr.1 and Add.1-5) addressed the issues raised in article 8 of the Convention.*

## C.    First reading (1979-1988)

*The text of article 8 was proposed to the Working Group in 1985 and discussed and adopted in 1986. This article was referred to as article 9 bis throughout the first and second readings.*

### 1.    Proposal submitted to the Working Group (1985)

#### (a)    Argentina

*The following is taken from the 1985 report of the Working Group to the Commission on Human Rights (E/CN.4/1985/64, para. 9 and annex II).*

> 9.    The representative of Argentina introduced a new article for consideration by the Working Group at its next session to be held in 1986. He stated that such an article constituted a safeguard to preserve personal, legal and family identity of children throughout the world.

> *New article* (Argentina)

> The child has the inalienable right to retain his true and genuine personal, legal and family identity.

> In the event that a child has been fraudulently deprived of some or all of the elements of his identity, the State must give him special protection and assistance with a view to re-establishing his true and genuine identity as soon as possible. In particular, this obligation of the State includes restoring the child to his blood relations to be brought up.

### 2.    Modified proposal submitted by Poland (1986)

*At its 1986 session, the Working Group had before it an elaboration of the draft convention that had been made available to the General Assembly in 1985 (see document A/C.3/40/3) by the Polish delegation with a view to expediting the drafting process. That document contained the text of the articles that had already been adopted as well as modifications of a number of proposals that had been made to the Working Group. For the text of the Polish proposal, see section 4, paragraph 33, below.*

### 3.    Proposal submitted to the Working Group (1986)

#### (a)    **NGO Ad Hoc Group** *(see annex III (B) for participating organizations)*

*The following is taken from document E/CN.4/1986/WG.1/WP.1, page 26.*

> The States Parties to the present Convention shall take all appropriate measures to enable the child to exercise his/her inalienable right to know and to retain his/her true and genuine personal, legal and family identity.

## 4.    Discussion and adoption by the Working Group (1986)

*The following is taken from the 1986 report of the Working Group to the Commission on Human Rights (E/CN.4/1986/39, paras. 33 to 49).*

33.     In 1985, the delegation of Argentina submitted a proposed new article to be incorporated in the draft convention as article 9 bis to read as follows:

> "The child has the inalienable right to retain his true and genuine personal, legal and family identity.
>
> In the event that a child has been fraudulently deprived of some or all of the elements of his identity, the State must give him special protection and assistance with a view to re-establishing his true and genuine identity as soon as possible. In particular, this obligation of the State includes restoring the child to his blood relations to be brought up."

The proposal was reintroduced at the current session as originally presented. There was also a proposal from the delegation of Poland, contained in document A/C.3/40/3, that read:

> "1.     The States Parties undertake to guarantee to the child the right to preserve his true and genuine personal, legal and family identity.
>
> 2.     If a child has been fraudulently deprived of some or all of the elements of his identity, the States Parties shall provide the child with necessary assistance and protection, with a view to speedily re-establishing his true and genuine identity."

In addition, a proposal was submitted by the Informal NGO Ad Hoc Group on the Drafting of the Convention, contained in document E/CN.4/1986/WG.1/WP.1.

34.     The representative of Norway asked the delegation of Argentina whether it was necessary to have such an article in the convention, pointing out that the true and genuine personal identity of the child was embodied in articles 2, 6 and 8 which had already been adopted by the Working Group.

35.     The representative of Argentina said that, while articles 2, 6 and 8 of the convention referred to the question, they did so in general terms, and that the importance of the article submitted by his delegation stemmed both from the special protection that was to be given by the State to the child as soon as possible, when the right of the child to preserve his or her true identity had been violated, and from the distinction made between the child's true and genuine identity and his or her legal one.

36.     The observer for the Netherlands said he shared the opinion put forward by the Norwegian delegation, reminding the Working Group that it had previously adopted article 11 on adoption procedure. In view of the existence in the convention of articles 2, 6, 8 and 11, he wondered whether there was any need for the article under discussion, especially in view of the many family law problems concealed therein.

37.     The representative of Austria expressed his agreement with the views of the delegations of Norway and the Netherlands. The representative of the United States also shared the concerns of those delegations, while the observer for Canada held the same opinions as previous speakers indicating at the same time that identity per se, so broadly stated, had no place whatsoever in Canadian legislation.

38.     The representative of Argentina insisted on the need for a specific article relating to that question in order to cover the legal void which otherwise would exist in the convention on the rights of the child.

The representative of Brazil, while supporting the Argentine proposal, thought that articles 2, 6, 8 and 11 of the draft convention already dealt with some of the aspects covered by the Argentine proposal and requested the formation of a working party to redraft the article submitted by the Argentine delegation. The representative of Bangladesh supported the idea of forming a working party and considered - echoing an earlier observation by the representative of the United Kingdom - that the word "inalienable" qualifying the term "right" in the first sentence of the Argentine proposal did not have to be retained and furthermore that the word "fraudulently" at the beginning of the second paragraph could be avoided.

39.     The Argentine delegation, replying to the observations made by the delegation of Bangladesh, said that the word "inalienable" was not a major concern but that the word "fraudulently" certainly was. Consequently, before joining the proposed working party, it wished to place on record its desire to retain the word "fraudulently" in the text to be produced by the aforementioned working party.

40.     Further to the Chairman's suggestion that the working party should include the delegations of Argentina, the Netherlands, Norway and Poland with the assistance of the International Commission of Jurists, and that it should take into account the views exchanged during the discussion of the Argentine proposal, the representative of Argentina submitted a text that read as follows:

> "1.     The States Parties undertake to respect the right of the child to preserve his or her family identity without unlawful interference.
>
> 2.     Where a child is illegally separated or removed from his or her lawful custodians or otherwise fraudulently or illegally deprived of some or all of the elements of this identity, the States Parties shall provide special assistance and protection, with a view to speedily re-establishing his or her rightful family identity."

41.     The delegation of the Netherlands observed that the concept of family identity as such was not known in every State and, for that reason, he wished to introduce in the first paragraph after the words "family identity" the phrase "as recognized by law". The delegations of Australia and Finland expressed similar views and their desire that the representative of Argentina should clarify the meaning of the expression "family identity".

42.     The representative of Argentina replied that paragraph 2 of the redrafted proposal supplied a context for the concept of "family identity", and added that he would have no objection to incorporating the proposal of the delegation of the Netherlands in paragraph 1 of the text.

43.     The delegation of Norway suggested that the words "family relations" should replace "family identity", and the observer for Finland indicated that he was able to accept that proposal.

44.     The representative of Austria said that he shared the doubts of previous speakers concerning the article under discussion, because the concept of "family identity" was unknown in Austrian law, and the reply by the representative of Argentina had not removed those doubts. He asked the representative of Argentina to provide the Working Group with a clear definition of the concept of "family identity".

45.     The delegations of France and the United Kingdom shared the concerns voiced by other delegations. The representative of Argentina then stated that for the interpretation of "family identity" reference must be made, within the national context, to the national legislation and, within the international context, to the Protocols additional to the Geneva Conventions of 1949.

46.     The representative of Australia, indicating that the concept of "family identity" was unknown in Australian law, requested that the representative of Argentina provide the Working Group with definitions in national legislations of the term "family identity" for he still did not understand its meaning. The Chairman then suggested that, in the first paragraph, the word "family" be deleted and that between the words "identity" and "without unlawful interference" the words "nationality, name, family relations" should be inserted, the amendment being placed in brackets. The representative of Bulgaria proposed that, after the

wording suggested by the Chairman, the following phrase be added: "in accordance with their legal system and judicial practice".

47.        The observer for the Netherlands reiterated his previous proposal to introduce the phrase "as recognized by law" in paragraph 1 and suggested its addition after the words "family relations". He also objected to the utilization in paragraph 2 of the two words "fraudulently" and "illegally", indicating his preference for the word "fraudulently", in addition, he proposed that, in the same paragraph, the word "special" should be replaced by "appropriate". The latter proposal was supported by the delegation of the United States.

48.        The delegation of Australia proposed the deletion of the word "family" before the word "identity" at the end of paragraph 2. The representative of Austria associated himself with the remarks made by the observer for the Netherlands regarding the deletion of the word "fraudulently" and the replacement of the word "special" by the word "appropriate".

49.        After a further exchange of views, the Working Group approved the following text:

"1.        The States Parties to the present Convention undertake to respect the right of the child to preserve his or her identity (nationality, name, family relations, as recognized by law) without unlawful interference.

2.        Where a child is illegally deprived of some or all of the elements of his or her identity, the States Parties shall provide appropriate assistance and protection, with a view to speedily re-establishing his or her identity."

## 5.        Text as adopted at first reading

*The following is taken from document E/CN.4/1988/WG.1/WP.1/Rev.1.*

*Article 9 bis*

1.        The States Parties to the present Convention undertake to respect the right of the child to preserve his or her identity (nationality, name, family relations as recognized by law) without unlawful interference.

2.        Where a child is illegally deprived of some or all of the elements of his or her identity, the States Parties shall provide appropriate assistance and protection, with a view to speedily re-establishing his or her identity.

# D.        Technical review (1988)

## 1.        Additional comments and clarifications by the Secretariat

*The following is taken from document E/CN.4/1989/WG.1/CRP.1/Add.1, paragraphs 22 and 23.*

22.        In paragraph 1, for linguistic reasons, it may be suggested that the brackets be removed and the word "including" be added so that other elements of identity will not be excluded. The relevant part of the paragraph would then read:

"... to preserve his or her identity, *including* nationality, name and family relations as recognized by law, without ...".

23.        Keeping in mind the provision of article 2 which does not allow for exceptions, as is the case with article 24, paragraphs 2 and 3, of the International Covenant on Civil and Political Rights, the reference in paragraph 2 of article 9 bis to "illegally" raises the question when or whether a child can be legally deprived of some and especially all of the elements of his or her identity. The question of compatibility with article 10, paragraph 2, is also raised by the use of this term. For this reason, the Working Group may wish to consider deleting the word "illegally" in order to avoid implying that a child can be legally deprived of, for example, his or her cultural background.

# E.  Second reading (1988-1989)

## 1.  Discussion and adoption at second reading

*The following is taken from the 1989 report of the Working Group to the Commission on Human Rights (E/CN.4/1989/48, paras. 333 to 338).*

333.  The Working Group had before it article 9 bis as adopted at first reading (E/CN.4/1989/WG.1/WP.2):

> "1.  The States Parties to the present Convention undertake to respect the right of the child to preserve his or her identity (nationality, name, family relations) as recognized by law without unlawful interference.
>
> 2.  Where a child is illegally deprived of some or all of the elements of his or her identity, the States Parties shall provide appropriate assistance and protection, with a view to speedily re-establishing his or her identity."

334.  The Chairman declared that no major amendment was proposed except for the small changes suggested by the Secretariat in E/CN.4/1989/WG.2/CRP.1/Add.1, namely the suppression of brackets and addition of the word "including" before "nationality" under paragraph 1 and the deletion of the word "illegally" under paragraph 2.

335.  The representatives of Argentina, Norway and the Netherlands accepted the suppression of brackets under paragraph 1 but insisted upon keeping the word "illegally" under paragraph 2. The observer for Australia agreed in view of the situation in some countries but pointed out that the word "illegally" would be meaningless in the Australian context since there it was simply not possible "legally" to deprive someone of their identity.

336.  The representative of Mexico stated that the wording should be more explicit as to the commitments made by the States under paragraph 1 and that the biological elements of the identity should also be included.

337.  The Working Group adopted article 9 bis keeping the changes under paragraph 1 and leaving paragraph 2 unchanged.

338.  The final version of article 9 bis reads as follows:

> "1.  States Parties undertake to respect the right of the child to preserve his or her identity, including nationality, name and family relations as recognized by law without unlawful interference.
>
> 2.  Where a child is illegally deprived of some or all of the elements of his or her identity, States Parties shall provide appropriate assistance and protection, with a view to speedily re-establishing his or her identity."

# Article 9 (Separation from parents)

## A. Final text adopted by the General Assembly (1989)

*The following text is that approved by the General Assembly in its resolution 44/25 of 20 November 1989.*

1. States Parties shall ensure that a child shall not be separated from his or her parents against their will, except when competent authorities subject to judicial review determine, in accordance with applicable law and procedures, that such separation is necessary for the best interests of the child. Such determination may be necessary in a particular case such as one involving abuse or neglect of the child by the parents, or one where the parents are living separately and a decision must be made as to the child's place of residence.

2. In any proceedings pursuant to paragraph 1 of the present article, all interested parties shall be given an opportunity to participate in the proceedings and make their views known.

3. States Parties shall respect the right of the child who is separated from one or both parents to maintain personal relations and direct contact with both parents on a regular basis, except if it is contrary to the child's best interests.

4. Where such separation results from any action initiated by a State Party, such as the detention, imprisonment, exile, deportation or death (including death arising from any cause while the person is in the custody of the State) of one or both parents or of the child, that State Party shall, upon request, provide the parents, the child or, if appropriate, another member of the family with the essential information concerning the whereabouts of the absent member(s) of the family unless the provision of the information would be detrimental to the well-being of the child. States Parties shall further ensure that the submission of such a request shall of itself entail no adverse consequences for the person(s) concerned.

## B. First Polish draft convention and comments (1978)

### 1. The first Polish draft

*The following text is taken from the 1978 report of the Commission on Human Rights (E/CN.4/1292, p. 124).*

*Article VI*

The child, for the full and harmonious development of his personality, needs love and understanding. He shall, wherever possible, grow up in the care and under the responsibility of his parents and, in any case, in an atmosphere of affection and of moral and material security; a child of tender years shall not, save in exceptional circumstances, be separated from his mother. Society and the public authorities shall have the duty to extend particular care to children without a family and to those without adequate means of support. Payment of State and other assistance towards the maintenance of children of large families is desirable.

### 2. Comments on the first Polish draft

*Article VI of the draft convention gave rise to the following comments.*

#### (a) Barbados

*The following is taken from document E/CN.4/1324.*

The payment of State and other assistance towards the maintenance of children of large families is desirable but it is suggested that a family should be encouraged to limit its size especially where it becomes difficult to provide adequately for these children.

## (b) Bulgaria

*The following is taken from document E/CN.4/1324.*

Add the words: "and children from incomplete families (children of unmarried mothers, widows, divorced parents) or children who have been abandoned by their parents" to the penultimate sentence of article VI.

## (c) Finland

*The following is taken from document E/CN.4/1324.*

"Where necessary, Governments should, by economic or other arrangements, ensure the possibilities for parents to take care of their children" (to be inserted after the first sentence);

The wording "be separated from his mother", at the end of the second sentence to be replaced by the wording "be separated from his parents";

The last sentence to be replaced by the following sentence: "Governments shall ensure the livelihood of families with children and provide the necessary family counselling and domestic services".

## (d) France

*The following is taken from document E/CN.4/1324/Add.1.*

1.    In the light of the comments made in paragraph 4 (a) above under "General Comments", the first sentence of this article should be included in a preliminary declaration or a recommendation.

2.    Article VI could be improved in two other respects. While a young child should not be separated from his mother, it is equally important that his ties to his father should not be jeopardized. The article might also be completed by a special reference to the situation of children belonging to an international family that has split up. These two points might be worded as follows:

(a)    Add at the end of the second sentence, after the words "A child of tender years shall not, save in exceptional circumstances, be separated from his mother", the words "but neither shall his ties with his father be jeopardized or severed".

(b)    Add at the end of the third sentence the following words: "Children who belong to an international family that has split up shall, so far as possible, preserve their ties with both parents even if they are of different social origin, nationality or religion."

## (e) Federal Republic of Germany

*The following is taken from document E/CN.4/1324.*

See paragraphs 3, 6 and 7, Federal Republic of Germany, under General Comments.

*Paragraphs 3, 6 and 7, which appear elsewhere in document E/CN.4/1324, read as follows.*

3.    Without prejudice to a final assessment, we consider that articles I, III, IV (understood as the right of the child to have his needs provided for in the broadest sense), the first and second sentences of article VI, the first sentence of article VII, paragraph 1 (right to education), and the second part of article VII, paragraph 2 (primary right of parents), should be grouped together in a separate section as rights of the individual.

6.    Unlike the series of measures on the rights of the individual, article II, article IV (first and second sentences), article V, article VI (fourth sentence), article VII, paragraph 1 (second sentence), article VII, paragraph 3, article IX and article X (first sentence) can be considered only as undertakings on the part of States.

7.        Conversely, the provisions of the draft relating to objectives, content and methods of education cannot be considered as either rights of the individual or undertakings on the part of States. The provisions in question are contained in the first sentence of article VI, the first part of article VII, paragraph 2, [article VIII] and the second sentence of article X of the draft. It is the responsibility and duty of the parents whose rights are also recognized in the draft to take binding decisions in this regard. The provisions referred to can more appropriately be made the subject of a recommendation to be incorporated in the preamble to the convention.

## (f)        Greece

*The following is taken from document E/CN.4/1324.*

1.        The Greek Government considers that the role of the father for the normal development of children has been so far underestimated and should be stressed in the future. It suggests the following alteration starting as from the middle of the paragraph.

> "... a child of tender years shall not, save in exceptional circumstances, be separated from his parents."

2.        Because of the growing problem of child abuse (non-accidental injury) by one or both of his parents or his caretakers, the Greek Government feels that special mention should be made of the problems of these children. It suggests the following rewording:

> "... society and the public authorities shall have the duty to extend particular care to children not only without a family, but also those whose families are evaluated as unable to care for the child in the present and future, regardless of support from public authorities. The child in that case deserves to grow up in an environment which can guarantee his optimal development. Payment of State and other assistance ..."

## (g)        New Zealand

*The following is taken from document E/CN.4/1324/Add.5.*

Sentences 1 and 2 are generally acceptable. However, the phrase "separated from his mother" requires qualification. It appears to preclude the choice available to many parents at present to place "the child of tender years" in the day care or childcare situation where the quality of care is judged to be equivalent to or even better than that provided by the family and the mother. There is now a considerable body of evidence which indicates that such practices are not detrimental to the best interests of the child and may in fact be positively in the child's best interests. Moreover there is no principle in New Zealand law whereby a child of "tender years" shall not, save in exceptional circumstances, be separated from his mother. Both parents are entitled to custody of their child and in the event of a dispute over custody, the court is bound to treat the welfare of the child as the first and paramount consideration (Guardianship Act 1968, S. 23). Thus it would be possible for a small child to be separated from his mother if the court thought this was in the best interests of the child. In addition the Family Proceedings Bill would give equal rights to parents in custody disputes, where the paramount consideration is still the welfare of the child. To that extent our law accords with the principle of article II, rather than article VI.

The last sentence of the article as stated is highly debatable. We would prefer that all children, without discrimination according to size of family, were given the same financial benefits by the State. The equalization of family circumstances would be carried out through the taxation structures of the country. We would therefore suggest an alternative wording along the lines of: "Payment of State and other assistance towards the maintenance of all children should be of such a nature that no child is placed at a disadvantage because of the size of the family".

**(h)  Norway**

*The following is taken from document E/CN.4/1324.*

1.  Delete the following phrase:

"a child of tender years shall not, save in exceptional circumstances, be separated from his mother."

2.  Amend the last sentence to read as follows:

"Economic support for families with children, through appropriate mechanisms, is desirable."

**(i)  Spain**

*The following is taken from document E/CN.4/1324.*

1.  After the words "children without a family" insert the words "arranging for them to be placed, wherever possible, in the most appropriate family environment and, with respect to those without means of support, supplying them with the necessary assistance and preventing them from being uprooted from the family environment". The words "and to those without adequate means of support" would accordingly be deleted.

2.  The purpose of this is to avoid the effects of being placed in institutions and, so far as possible, to encourage acceptance in families and adoption.

**(j)  Suriname**

*The following is taken from document E/CN.4/1324.*

See paragraph 2, Suriname, under General Comments.

*Paragraph 2, which appears elsewhere in document E/CN.4/1324, reads as follows.*

2.  In this connection the Government of the Republic of Suriname wishes to state that it attaches particular importance to the articles VI, VII sub[paragraph] 3 and IX sub[paragraphs] 1 and 2 of the above-mentioned draft convention.

**(k)  Sweden**

*The following is taken from document E/CN.4/1324.*

The child's need of close contacts with both parents - and not only with the mother - is a fact which ought to be adequately reflected in the convention. Generally, the equality of children with respect to education, social and health care is a fundamental element.

**(l)  World Health Organization (WHO)**

*The following is taken from document E/CN.4/1324.*

Article VI, [third] line:

We have some difficulties with the reference to "moral security" and would prefer the deletion of "moral". The provision would thus read: "... in an atmosphere of affection and security; ..."

**(m)  International Council of Women**

*The following is taken from document E/CN.4/1324.*

Article VI seems to us to be ambiguously formulated. It is obviously aimed at providing the child with optimum conditions for the harmonious development of his personality but the juxtaposition, in one and the same article of the convention, of love and family allowances is not felicitous. There seems to be a problem of drafting, if not of substance.

**(n)**      **Society for Comparative Legislation**

*The following is taken from document E/CN.4/1324.*

> The child, for the full and harmonious development of his personality, needs love and understanding. He shall, wherever possible, grow up in the care and under the responsibility of his parents and, in any case, in an atmosphere of affection and of moral and material security; a child of tender years shall not, save in exceptional circumstances, be separated from his mother, although his ties with his father shall not thereby be weakened or broken, and a child belonging to a divided international family shall, so far as possible, maintain his ties with both his parents. Society and the public authorities shall have the duty to extend particular care to children without a family, to those belonging to a divided international family and to those without adequate means of support. Payment of State and other assistance towards the maintenance of children of large families is desirable.

**(o)**      **International Humanist and Ethical Union**

*The following is taken from document E/CN.4/1324.*

> In the light of other world problems, especially the population problem, we doubt whether it is desirable to include in article VI the sentence "payment of State and other assistance towards the maintenance of children of large families is desirable". This, in effect, nullifies efforts to decrease population in the world. We agree that States should be encouraged to achieve an adequate standard of living for their citizens and feel that it might be better to replace the above-mentioned sentence by a sentence to that effect.

## C.    First reading (1979-1988)

*The text of article 9, which was based on article 6 of the revised Polish draft, was discussed in 1981, 1982 and 1983. Paragraphs 1 and 2 were adopted in 1982 and paragraphs 3 and 4 were adopted at the 1983 session. Additional proposals were submitted to the Working Group but further consideration was deferred until the second reading. This article was referred to as article 6 throughout the first and second readings.*

### 1.      Revised Polish draft (1979)

*For the text of revised article 6, which was taken from Commission on Human Rights document E/CN.4/1349, see paragraph 62 in section 3 below. Related article 10 of the revised draft, also taken from document E/CN.4/1349, reads as follows:*

> A child of preschool age shall not be separated from his parents, with the exception for cases when such separation is necessary for the child's benefit.

### 2.      Proposals submitted to the Working Group (1981)

**(a)**      **Australia**

*For the text of this proposal, see paragraph 69 in section 3 below.*

**(b)**      **Denmark**

*For the text of this proposal, see paragraph 70 in section 3 below.*

**(c)**      **Norway**

*For the text of this proposal, see paragraph 66 in section 3 below.*

**(d)    Poland**

*For the text of these proposals, see paragraphs 63 and 71 in section 3 below.*

**(e)    United States of America**

*The following text is taken from document  HR/(XXXVII)/WG.1/WP.12.*

Replace existing text of article 6 (...) with the following:

> "Except as otherwise provided in the present Convention, the child shall have the right to reside with his parents or legal guardians, including when necessary the right to be reunited with them if they lawfully reside in another State party. If only one parent or legal guardian of a child resides in another State party, such child's preferred place of residence shall be a primary consideration in the deliberations of any judicial or administrative proceeding held to determine such child's place of residence. Each State party shall process applications for family reunification in a positive, humane, and expeditious manner. Until family reunification in a particular case is accomplished, all States parties involved shall permit frequent and regular family contacts."

*The foregoing proposal was later extensively modified. For the text of the revised proposal, see paragraph 65 in section 3 below.*

## 3.    Discussion in the Working Group (1981)

*The following is taken from paragraphs 62 to 72 of the 1981 report of the Working Group to the Commission on Human Rights (E/CN.4/L.1575), which is reproduced in paragraph 289 of the 1981 report of the Commission on Human Rights (E/CN.4/1475).*

62.    Article 6 of the revised Polish draft read as follows:

> "The parents shall have the right to specify the place of the child's residence unless, guided by his best interests, a competent State organ is authorized, in accordance with national law, to decide in this matter."

63.    The Polish delegation submitted the following revised text to replace the original wording of article 6 of the revised draft convention:

> "The parents have the right to determine the place of the child's residence. If the place of residence determined by parents endangers the child's well-being and in case of disagreement between the parents as well as if the child does not remain under the care of parents, his residence will be decided by a competent State organ, guided by the child's well-being."

64.    The delegation of Australia suggested that article 6 be deleted because a provision concerning the rights accruing to the parents had no place in such a convention.

65.    The representative of the United States proposed that the original wording of articles 6 and 10 of the revised draft convention, be replaced by a revised text which read as follows:

> "1.    States parties shall ensure that a child shall not be involuntarily separated from his parents, except when competent authorities determine, in accordance with procedures and criteria specified by domestic law, that such separation is necessary for the welfare of the child in a particular case, such as one involving maltreatment or abuse of the child by the parents or one where the parents are living separately and a decision must be made as to the child's place of residence. Such determinations shall not be made until all interested parties have been given an opportunity to participate in the proceedings and to make their views known. Such views shall be taken into account by the competent authorities in making their determination.

2.      In cases where both parents lawfully reside in one State party and their child lawfully resides in another State party, the States parties concerned shall deal with applications for family reunification in a positive, humane and expeditious manner. States parties shall charge only moderate fees in connection with such applications and shall not modify in any way the rights and obligations of the applicant(s) or of other members of the family concerned. States parties shall ensure that applications for the purpose of family reunification of parents with their children which are not granted for any reason may be renewed at the appropriate level and will be considered at reasonably short intervals by the authorities of the country of residence or destination, whichever is concerned, and, in such cases, fees will be charged only when applications are granted. Until family reunification in a particular case is accomplished, all State parties involved shall permit frequent and regular family contacts.

3.      The provisions of paragraph 2 shall also apply in cases where a child's only surviving parent lawfully resides in one State party and the child lawfully resides in another State party.

4.      If the parents of a child lawfully reside in different States parties, States parties shall ensure that the child's preference as to which parent he wishes to reside with shall be an important consideration in any determination made by competent authorities concerning the child's place of residence."

66.      Although the representative of Norway submitted a text to replace article 6 only, he shared the view of the United States delegation that there was a strong relationship between articles 6 and 10 of the revised Polish draft convention. The text put forward by Norway read as follows:

"A child shall not, against the will of the parents be separated from them, unless a competent public organ is authorized, in accordance with national law, to make such a decision in order to protect the child."

67.      The representative of Australia maintained his suggestion that article 6 be deleted and requested the sponsors of the amendments and of the original version to delete the article. The representative of the United States agreed with the representative of Australia that the article as drafted should be deleted, but insisted that the convention should contain a provision on family reunification and that article 6 was the logical place for this provision because it dealt with the child's place of residence.

68.      The representative of the Union of Soviet Socialist Republics supported the wording of article 6 of the revised draft convention, stressing the importance of retaining this provision guaranteeing the child's interest with regard to his place of residence. In addition, he pointed out that the proposal made by the delegation of the United States (see paragraph [65]) was aimed at substituting the provision concerning the child's place of residence for a provision on the reunification of families.

69.      One speaker pointed out that it was not the rights of the parents that were emphasized, but the best interests of the child. In that connection, the representative of Australia proposed the following amendment to article 10:

"A child of preschool age shall not be separated from his parents unless extraordinary circumstances determine that such a separation is necessary for the child's welfare."

70.      The representative of Denmark proposed a new text, stating her preference that it should not be incorporated in article 6 but should stand as a separate article. It read as follows:

"Parents or other guardians have the main responsibility for the child. Every State party has, however, the responsibility to satisfy the needs of the child and ensure the child the rights set forth in this Convention."

71.	The representative of Poland, taking account of the views expressed by other delegations, submitted a new revised text of article 6 which read:

> "The States parties shall recognize the right of the child to have his residence to be determined by his parents. If the place of residence specified by the parents is likely to be detrimental to the child's well-being or in the case of disagreement between the parents, a competent public organ, guided by the child's well-being, shall determine his place of residence."

72.	The Working Group was unable to continue consideration of article 6 for lack of time.

## 4.	Modified proposal submitted by Poland (1982)

*At its 1982 session, the Working Group had before it an elaboration of the draft convention that had been made available to the General Assembly in 1981 (see document A/C.3/36/6) by the Polish delegation with a view to facilitating the drafting process. That document contained the text of the articles that had already been adopted as well as a number of modified proposals that had been made to the Working Group. The following text is taken from document A/C.3/36/6, part II.*

> The States Parties to the present Convention shall recognize the right of the child to have his residence to be determined by his parents. If the place of residence specified by the parents is likely to be detrimental to the child's well-being, or in the case of disagreement between the parents, a competent public organ, guided by the child's well-being, shall determine his place of residence.

## 5.	Proposals submitted to the Working Group (1982)

### (a)	France

*For the text of this proposal, see paragraph 15 in section 6 below.*

### (b)	United States of America

*For the text of this proposal, see paragraph 25 in section 6 below.*

### (c)	Joint NGO proposal

*(Co-sponsors: International Council of Women, Friends World Committee for Consultation, International Association of Penal Law, International Catholic Child Bureau, International Catholic Union of the Press, International Commission of Jurists, International Council of Jewish Women, International Federation of Women in Legal Careers, International Federation of Women Lawyers and the World Jewish Congress)*

*For the text of this proposal, see paragraph 13 in section 6 below.*

### (d)	Minority Rights Group

*For the text of this proposal, see paragraph 14 in section 6 below.*

## 6.	Discussion and adoption by the Working Group (1982)

*The following is taken from the 1982 report of the Working Group to the Commission on Human Rights (E/CN.4/1982/30/ Add.1, paras. 9 to 33).*

9.	Article 6 of the revised Polish draft read as follows:

> "The parents shall have the right to specify the place of the child's residence unless, guided by his best interests, a competent State organ is authorized, in accordance with national law, to decide in this matter."

10.	Article 10 of the revised Polish draft read as follows:

"A child of preschool age shall not be separated from his parents, with the exception for cases when such separation is necessary for the child's benefit."

11.	At the Working Group's session of 1981, the delegation of the United States proposed that the original wording of articles 6 and 10 of the revised draft convention be replaced by an amended text which read as follows:

"1.	States Parties shall ensure that a child shall not be involuntarily separated from his parents, except when competent authorities determine, in accordance with procedures and criteria specified by domestic law, that such separation is necessary for the welfare of the child in a particular case, such as one involving maltreatment or abuse of the child by the parents or one where the parents are living separately and a decision must be made as to the child's place of residence. Such determinations shall not be made until all interested parties have been given an opportunity to participate in the proceedings and to make their views known. Such views shall be taken into account by the competent authorities in making their determination.

2.	In cases where both parents lawfully reside in one State Party and their child lawfully resides in another State Party, the States Parties concerned shall deal with applications for family reunification in a positive, humane and expeditious manner. States Parties shall charge only moderate fees in connection with such applications and shall not modify in any way the rights and obligations of the applicant(s) or of other members of the family concerned. States Parties shall ensure that applications for the purpose of family reunification of parents with their children which are not granted for any reason may be renewed at the appropriate level and will be considered at reasonably short intervals by the authorities of the country of residence or destination, whichever is concerned, and, in such cases, fees will be charged only when applications are granted. Until family reunification in a particular case is accomplished, all States Parties involved shall permit frequent and regular family contacts.

3.	The provisions of paragraph 2 shall also apply in cases where a child's only surviving parent lawfully resides in one State Party and the child lawfully resides in another State Party.

4.	If the parents of a child lawfully reside in different States Parties, States Parties shall ensure that the child's preference as to which parent he wishes to reside with shall be an important consideration in any determination made by competent authorities concerning the child's place of residence."

This proposal, which was reintroduced at the 1982 session of the Group, was the subject of some further amendments by its sponsor.

12.	At the Working Group's session of 1981, the representative of Australia proposed to replace the aforementioned text of article 10 by the following:

"A child of preschool age shall not be separated from his parents unless extraordinary circumstances determine that such separation is necessary for the child's welfare."

This proposal was reintroduced at the 1982 session of the Group by several non-governmental organizations as contained in document E/CN.4/1982/WG.1/WP.1.

13.	Several non-governmental organizations suggested the following paragraph, as contained in document E/CN.4/1982/WG.1/WP.1, to replace paragraph 3 of the amendment to articles 6 and 10 originally submitted by the representative of the United States at the Working Group's session in 1981:

"Where a child is placed in the custody of one parent because of a marital dispute between the parents residing in different countries, resulting in divorce, separation or other interlocutory proceedings, and due to conflicting private international law considerations there has been no final determination of the issue of the child's custody or the child is unlawfully held by one parent because of the non-execution of an order of the court of competent jurisdiction, the States Parties shall endeavour to resolve the issue by bilateral agreements or multilateral arrangements reached where appropriate under the auspices of a regional intergovernmental body, the best interest of the child being the guiding principle."

14.     The Minority Rights Group, a non-governmental organization proposed the following text in substitution for the proposed new paragraph 3 mentioned above:

"The States Parties shall endeavour, by new or updated bilateral agreements or multilateral arrangements, reached where appropriate under the auspices of a regional intergovernmental body, the best interest of the child concerned being the guiding principle, to resolve the issues arising:

(i)     When a child has been placed in the custody of one parent or in joint custody because of a marital dispute between the parents residing in different countries, resulting in divorce, separation or other interlocutory proceedings, and due to conflicting private international law considerations there has been no final determination of the issue of the child's custody;

(ii)    When a child is unlawfully held and hidden by one parent because of the non-execution or later breach of an order of the court of competent jurisdiction; or

(iii)   When, there being no order of a court of competent jurisdiction as to custody, one parent assumes control over the child contrary to the wish of the parent normally exercising it; and exercises that control in a country other than that in which the latter parent resides."

The main intention of this proposal was to extend the endeavours which States would undertake to make to children who are in effect kidnapped across international frontiers by a parent, particularly those kidnapped in circumstances where no court order on custody exists; these cases are numerous and may in fact be more numerous than those to which an order of custody applies.

15.     Some speakers drew attention to the situation of children of parents separated by divorce or for other reasons who are not of the same nationality or who may reside in countries other than the country of residence of the child, and to the need of a child in such a situation to retain his links with both his parents. Accordingly, the representative of France made the following proposal: "The child of a separated international family shall, as far as possible, retain his links with both his parents." The French proposal was supported by several delegations, but it was thought that it dealt more properly with paragraph 2 of the article under discussion and it would be very appropriate if it were the first sentence of paragraph 2. At a later stage in the proceedings, the representative of France submitted a new draft to replace his earlier proposal as mentioned above. The text read as follows:

"The child of parents with different nationalities, who are separated, shall, save in exceptional circumstances, be entitled to maintain personal relations with both parents."

The French representative indicated that:

(a)    the convention on the rights of the child would in the future serve as a benchmark for cooperation agreements between States. In view of its importance, the French representative believed that the convention would benefit if it were completed by including a clause concerning a matter which had not so far been dealt with, namely the situation of children of separated parents of different nationalities;

(b)    experience had shown that private family disputes which gave rise to the abduction of children across frontiers occurred more and more frequently and that no country could consider itself exempt. In France, for example, the Ministry of Justice had estimated that there were 1,000 cases of abduction per year involving no fewer than 41 States. It was a situation which gravely affected society;

(c)    the convention, which constituted a basic text at the international level, must by its very nature be universal. Preventive measures should be taken to impede that its provisions be interpreted from a nationalistic point of view. It was absolutely necessary that the child's interests should be evaluated on the basis of all the elements of his family background, whether such elements were national or international. Experience had shown that the nationalistic approach to the child's interests had in most cases resulted in making a legal orphan of a child with a foreign father or mother;

(d)    the convention should not take second place to the existing conventions which have confirmed at the multilateral level the principle of the maintenance of relations between the child and both his parents of different nationalities. The conventions, which had already been ratified by many countries, were the European Convention of Luxembourg of 20 May 1980 on the recognition and enforcement of decisions relating to children's custody and the restoration of custody rights, and The Hague Convention of 25 October 1980 on the Civil Aspects of International Child Abduction.

16.      In connection with a child's place of residence, it was said that the convention also should address itself to certain subjects, namely, the right of the child to liberty of movement and freedom of residence within any State Party together with the right to leave any State - including his own - and to enter his own State, the right of the child to seek asylum from persecution without fear of retaliation, and the right of the child and his parents to be free from arbitrary or unlawful interference with their privacy, family, home or correspondence.

17.      Some delegations strongly opposed any distinction whatsoever of children by age, stating that the essential point was that separation of a child from his parents should not occur under any circumstances, while other delegations continued to find some value in distinguishing the position regarding preschool children, and considered that the same kind of protection cannot be awarded to very young and much older children.

18.      In keeping with the view expressed by his delegation at the Group's 1981 session that the idea contained in article 10 was reflected in paragraph 1 of the United States text for article 6 (set forth in paragraph 11 above) the representative of the United States proposed the merger of these two texts. This suggestion was favourably received by some delegations.

19.      In addition, it was repeatedly emphasized by some delegations that the separation of a child from his parents should preferably be of a temporary or provisional nature, that the separation period should be made as short as possible under national legislation, and that a child should be returned to his parents as soon as circumstances changed favourably making the separation no longer necessary.

20.      The representative of the United States proposed that after the words "competent authorities" in the first sentence of paragraph 1 of the United States text for article 6, the words "subject to judicial review" should be inserted. He also suggested that the Group should consider using, throughout the convention, the term "best interests of the child" rather than the term "welfare of the child". Also, he proposed that the concept of "neglect" of the child should be introduced into the convention and hence suggested the incorporation of the words "or neglect" after the word "abuse" in the first sentence of paragraph 1 of article 6, and the deletion of the word "maltreatment". Further, he proposed the introduction, at the end of the first sentence of the same paragraph, of a new example concerning the child's place of residence to read "or one where there is a disagreement between parent(s) and child as to the child's place of residence". The use of the term "parent(s)" resulted from a suggestion by the representative of Norway that cases of single parents must be covered.

21.      The representative of Norway suggested the deletion of the word "involuntarily" from the first sentence of paragraph 1 of article 6 and the insertion of the words "against their will" after the word "parents" in the same sentence. Further, she proposed that any reference to the age of children should be removed completely from the texts under discussion. This proposal was supported by several delegations.

22.      The delegation of France suggested that the words "in accordance with applicable law and procedures" should replace the words "in accordance with procedures and criteria specified by domestic law" in the first sentence of paragraph 1 of article 6. This proposal was supported by various delegations.

23.      Some speakers questioned the appropriateness of having the letter "s" in the word "parents" between brackets, as in the proposal of the delegation of the United States in paragraph 20, noting that the convention was intended, as far as possible, to cover regular situations where a child has both his parents.

24.      Delegations having found the first lines of paragraph 1 of article 6 up to the words "welfare of the child", as amended, acceptable, the Working Group adopted them by consensus. They read:

> "States Parties shall ensure that a child shall not be separated from his parents against their will, except when competent authorities subject to judicial review determine, in accordance with applicable law and procedures, that such separation is necessary for the best interests of the child."

25.      The representative of the United States submitted the following revised text to replace the original wording of the amendment to articles 6 and 10 presented by his delegation at the Working Group's session of 1981 and reintroduced by him at the beginning of the Group's 1982 session.

> "1.      States Parties shall ensure that a child shall not be separated from his parents against their will, except when competent authorities subject to judicial review determine, in accordance with applicable law and procedures, that such separation is necessary for the best interests of the child in a particular case, such as one involving abuse or neglect of the child by the parents, one where the parents are living separately and a decision must be made as to the child's place of residence, or one where there is a disagreement between parent(s) and child as to the child's place of residence. Such determinations shall not be made until all interested parties have been given an opportunity to participate in the proceedings and to make their views known. Such views shall be taken into account by the competent authorities in making their determination.

> 2.      In cases where both parents lawfully reside in one State Party and their child lawfully resides in another State Party or where the parents of a child lawfully reside in different States Parties, the States Parties concerned shall deal with applications for family reunification or contacts on the basis of family ties in a positive, humane and expeditious manner. States Parties shall make no distinction as to country of origin or destination in dealing with such applications, shall charge only moderate fees in connection with such applications and shall not modify in any way the rights and obligations of the applicant(s) or of other members of the family concerned. States Parties shall ensure that applications for the purpose of family reunification of parents with their children which are not granted for any reason may be renewed at the appropriate level and will be considered at reasonably short intervals by the authorities of the country of residence or destination, whichever is concerned, and, in such cases, fees will be charged only when applications are granted. Until family reunification in a particular case is accomplished, all States Parties involved shall permit frequent and regular family contacts.

> 3.      The provisions of paragraph 2 shall also apply in cases where a child's only surviving parent lawfully resides in one State Party and the child lawfully resides in another State Party, as well as in cases where parents who are nationals of different States Parties apply to transfer the permanent residence of their children and themselves to a Member State in which either one is normally a resident.

> 4.      If the parents of a child lawfully reside in different States Parties, States Parties shall ensure that the child's preference as to which parent he wishes to reside with shall be an important consideration in any determination made by competent authorities concerning the child's place of residence."

26.	A discussion ensued as to whether the examples listed in the second half of the first sentence of the above-mentioned proposal were called for. One delegation expressed its preference for not having any listing of examples whatsoever while another, in supporting this viewpoint, stated that it was impossible to present an exhaustive list of examples and objected in particular to the addition of any example to those already existing in the text submitted by the representative of the United States at the Group's session of 1981.

27.	The representative of the United States agreed to delete the third example contained in the first sentence of its proposal which read "or one where there is a disagreement between parent(s) and child as to the child's place of residence". Further, he suggested that the sentence containing the examples in his proposal should start with the phrase "Such a determination may be necessary".

28.	The Working Group then adopted by consensus the following text:

"Such a determination may be necessary in a particular case, such as one involving abuse or neglect of the child by the parents, or one where the parents are living separately and a decision must be made as to the child's place of residence."

29.	The representative of Poland proposed that the opening sentence of article 6 contained in document A/C.3/36/6 of 7 October 1981 which read as follows: "The States Parties to the present Convention shall recognize the right of the child to have his residence to be determined by his parents", should also be the opening sentence of the paragraph under consideration by the Group. In this connection, the delegation of the United States suggested that the sentence be amended to read: "The States Parties to the present Convention recognize that the child should enjoy parental care and should have his place of residence determined by his parent(s) except as provided herein".

30.	The text originally proposed by the representative of Poland, as amended by the representative of the United States, was supported by the Working Group and was adopted by consensus. The Chairman decided that that text should become paragraph 1 of article 6.

31.	The Working Group then adopted the last two sentences of paragraph 1 in the United States text for article 6, and placed them at the end of paragraph 2 of article 6. These sentences read as follows:

"Such determinations shall not be made until all interested parties have been given an opportunity to participate in the proceedings and to make their views known. Such views shall be taken into account by the competent authorities in making their determination."

32.	The delegation of France requested that at the end of the French version of paragraph 2 the following clause be added: "sous réserve de cas prévu par le paragraphe 3".

33.	Paragraphs 1 and 2 of article 6, as adopted by the Working Group, read as follows:

"1.	The States Parties to the present Convention recognize that the child should enjoy parental care and should have his place of residence determined by his parent(s), except as provided herein.

2.	States Parties shall ensure that a child shall not be separated from his parents against their will, except when competent authorities subject to judicial review determine, in accordance with applicable law and procedures, that such separation is necessary for the best interests of the child. Such a determination may be necessary in a particular case, such as one involving abuse or neglect of the child by the parents or one where the parents are living separately and a decision must be made as to the child's place of residence. Such determinations shall not be made until all interested parties have been given an opportunity to participate in the proceedings and to make their views known. Such views shall be taken into account by the competent authorities in making their determination."

## 7. Proposal submitted to the Working Group (1983)

### (a) Australia

*The following is taken from document E/CN.4/1983/WG.1/WP.12.*

*New article 6 ter*

1.      A child who is separated from one or both parents has the right to maintain personal relations and direct contacts with both parents on a regular basis, save in exceptional circumstances and regardless of whether the parents and the child live in different States.

2.      Where such separation results from judicial or administrative action by a State party, such as detention, imprisonment, exile or deportation of one or both parents or of the child, the State party shall provide the parents and the child with precise information as to the whereabouts of the absent member(s) of the family.

*For a revision of paragraph 2 of this proposal, see paragraph 23 in section 8 below.*

## 8. Discussion and adoption by the Working Group (1983)

*The following is taken from the 1983 report of the Working Group to the Commission on Human Rights (E/CN.4/1983/62, paras. 8-10 and 20-28).*

8.      It will be recalled that paragraphs 1 and 2 of article 6 relating to the question of the determination of the place of residence of the child were adopted by the Working Group last year. At the present session, the discussions which led to the adoption of paragraphs 3 and 4 of article 6, part of article 6 bis and article 6 ter, focused on the proposals and amendments thereto relating to various problems which arise from family separation, such as the right of the child to maintain relations with his parents, the question of family reunification and the illegal abduction of children by one parent. It was also stressed that the national and international aspects of the question should be dealt with separately. All the proposals relating to these problems were considered simultaneously.

9.      The right of the child, who is separated from one or both parents, to maintain relations with both parents, was generally recognized, but in view of some speakers, reference should be made to exceptional circumstances. The exchange of views on that question led to the adoption of paragraph 3 of article 6.

10.      It was suggested that the draft convention should also contain provisions dealing with cases where family separations result from actions initiated by States. It was further stressed, in this connection, that there was a need to ensure that adequate information be provided to the family concerning the whereabouts of the absent parent or child. Various opinions were voiced as regards the type of State action which could lead to family separations. The question was also raised as to whether it was necessary to draw up a list of those actions. The discussions on these points led to the adoption of paragraph 4 of article 6.

[...]

20.      During the discussions, it was suggested that the text of the first paragraph of the proposal by the representative of Australia relating to the right of the child who is separated from one or both parents to maintain relations with both, could be adopted by the Group as *paragraph 3 of article 6*, with the deletion of the words "and regardless of whether the parents and the child reside in different States." It was said in this connection that the international aspects of the question should be dealt with in a separate article. The Group agreed to the adoption of the paragraph on this basis.

21.      Discussion on the proposals relating to action taken by States which result in family separations, led to the adoption of paragraph 4 of article 6.

22.      During the discussions it was suggested to add to the list of actions by States which could result in family separations the case of "death in custody". With regard to the obligation of the States to provide

information, several representatives stressed that such information should be provided only if: (a) a formal request is made and (b) if the information would not be detrimental to the interest of the child.

23.     The representative of Australia revised paragraph 2 of his proposal (E/CN.4/1983/WG.1/WP.20) as follows:

> "Where such separation results from judicial, administrative or any other action initiated by a State Party, such as the detention, imprisonment, exile, deportation or death (including death in custody) of one or both parents or of the child, that State Party shall provide the parents, the child or, if appropriate another member of the family upon request with essential information concerning the whereabouts of the absent member(s) of the family, unless the provision of the information would be detrimental to the well-being of the child. States Parties shall further ensure that the submission of such a request shall of itself entail no adverse consequences for the person(s) concerned."

24.     During the discussions, it was observed that specific references to judicial or administrative action should be deleted as this text refers to any action taken by States.

25.     Several representatives objected to the reference to cases where family separation results from "death in custody", as formulated. In their view, the formulation used seemed to imply the responsibility of the States concerned.

26.     Some representatives continued to maintain that a listing of actions initiated by States were unnecessary.

27.     Paragraph 2 of the Australian proposal was orally revised by the representative of Australia to delete specific references to judicial and administrative action and to replace the words "death in custody" by the words "including death arising from any cause while the person is in the custody of the State".

28.     The paragraph as orally revised was adopted as paragraph 4 of article 6.


## 9.     Proposal submitted to the Working Group (1984)

### (a)     International Federation of Women in Legal Careers and the International Abolitionist Federation

*The following is taken from document E/CN.4/1983/NGO/33, which appeared after the 1983 session of the Working Group.*

> Article 6 (residence of the child)
>
> Article 6 relates to the determination of the place of residence of children whose parents are separated and states at the end of paragraph 2: "Such determinations shall not be made until all interested parties have been given an opportunity to participate in the proceedings and to make their views known". We would like to add: "It shall be understood that the children will have an opportunity to express their preference".


## 10.     Comment submitted to the Working Group (1987)

### (a)     Morocco

*The following is taken from the 1987 report of the Working Group to the Commission on Human Rights (E/CN.4/1987/25, para. 2).*

> 2. [...]. By a note verbale of 30 January 1987, the Permanent Representative of Morocco asked that their observations on the draft convention be brought to the attention of the Working Group; those observations were contained in E/CN.4/1987/WG.1/WP.35.

*The following is taken from document E/CN.4/1987/WG.1/WP.35.*

*Article 6 - Paragraph 2 - Care of children*

Moroccan legislation stipulates that the parents shall have the care of the children during the marriage, but that if the parents are living separately the mother shall have priority in caring for the child.

## 11.    Text as adopted at first reading

*The following is taken from document E/CN.4/1988/WG.1/WP.1/Rev.1.*

1.    The States Parties to the present Convention recognize that the child should enjoy parental care and should have his place of residence determined by his parent(s), except as provided herein.

2.    States Parties shall ensure that a child shall not be separated from his parents against their will, except when competent authorities subject to judicial review determine, in accordance with applicable law and procedures, that such separation is necessary for the best interests of the child. Such a determination may be necessary in a particular case such as one involving abuse or neglect of the child by the parents, or one where the parents are living separately and a decision must be made as to the child's place of residence. Such determinations shall not be made until all interested parties have been given an opportunity to participate in the proceedings and to make their views known. Such views shall be taken into account by the competent authorities in making their determination.

3.    A child who is separated from one or both parents has the right to maintain personal relations and direct contacts with both parents on a regular basis, save in exceptional circumstances.

4.    Where such separation results from any action initiated by a State Party, such as the detention, imprisonment, exile, deportation or death (including death arising from any cause while the person is in the custody of the State) of one or both parents or of the child, that State Party shall, upon request, provide the parents, the child or, if appropriate, another member of the family with essential information concerning the whereabouts of the absent member(s) of the family unless the provision of the information would be detrimental to the well-being of the child. States Parties shall further ensure that the submission of such a request shall of itself entail no adverse consequences for the person(s) concerned.

# D.   Technical review (1988)

## 1.    Comment by the United Nations Children's Fund (UNICEF)

*The following is taken from document E/CN.4/1989/WG.1/CRP.1, page 20.*

*Gender neutrality*

Paragraph 1. A possible reformulation of the paragraph is:

> "The States Parties to the present Convention recognize that the child should enjoy parental care and should have his *or her* place of residence determined by his *or her* parent(s), except as provided herein."

Paragraph 2. The first part of the paragraph might be reformulated as follows:

> "States Parties shall ensure that a child shall not be separated from his *or her* parents against their will..."

# E.   Second reading (1988-1989)

## 1.    Proposals submitted to the Working Group at second reading

### (a)    Canada

*For the text of this proposal, see paragraph 192 in section 2 below.*

**(b)      German Democratic Republic**

*For the text of this proposal, see paragraph 190 in section 2 below.*

**(c)      Federal Republic of Germany and Japan**

*For the text of this proposal, see paragraph 191 in section 2 below.*

**(d)      Venezuela**

*For the text of these proposals, see paragraphs 188 and 189 in section 2 below.*

**(e)      Latin American meeting**

*The following is taken from document E/CN.4/1989/WG.1/WP.1.*

> In article 6: Include a new paragraph 2: "In case of expectant minors, the States parties shall implement compatible policies for the protection of maternity and for attaining integral assistance, keeping the mother-child bond intact, avoiding trafficking and fraudulent adoptions."

## 2.      Discussion and adoption at second reading

*The following is taken from the 1989 report of the Working Group to the Commission on Human Rights (E/CN.4/1989/48, paras. 186 to 207).*

186.      The Working Group had before it the following text of article 6 as adopted at first reading:

> "1.      The States Parties to the present Convention recognize that the child should enjoy parental care and should have his place of residence determined by his parent(s), except as provided herein.

> 2.      States Parties shall ensure that a child shall not be separated from his parents against their will, except when competent authorities subject to judicial review determine, in accordance with applicable law and procedures, that such separation is necessary for the best interests of the child. Such a determination may be necessary in a particular case such as one involving abuse or neglect of the child by the parents, or one where the parents are living separately and a decision must be made as to the child's place of residence. Such determinations shall not be made until all interested parties have been given an opportunity to participate in the proceedings and to make their views known. Such views shall be taken into account by the competent authorities in making their determination.

> 3.      A child who is separated from one or both parents has the right to maintain personal relations and direct contacts with both parents on a regular basis, save in exceptional circumstances.

> 4.      Where such separation results from any action initiated by a State Party, such as the detention, imprisonment, exile, deportation or death (including death arising from any cause while the person is in custody of the State) of one or both parents or [of] the child, that State Party shall, upon request, provide the parents, the child or, if appropriate, another member of the family with essential information concerning the whereabouts of the absent member(s) of the family unless the provision of the information would be detrimental to the well-being of the child. States Parties shall further ensure that the submission of such a request shall of itself entail no adverse consequences for the person(s) concerned."

187.      Three revisions relating to gender neutrality were suggested in the course of the technical review by UNESCO with regard to paragraphs 1 and 2 of the article (E/CN.4/1989/WG.1/CRP.1, p. 20). It was also proposed to consider changing the beginning of paragraph 1 to read: "States Parties recognize that...".

188.      The representative from Venezuela introduced a proposal (E/CN.4/1989/WG.1/WP.36) which sought to replace paragraph 1 of article 6 by the following text:

"1.      The States Parties to the present Convention recognize that the child has a right to enjoy parental care and protection, and should have his place of residence chosen by either of his parents, except as provided herein."

189.      The representative of Venezuela then orally proposed some more amendments relating to paragraphs 2 and 4 of article 6 which were subsequently issued as document E/CN.4/1989/WG.1/WP.43. The amendments read as follows:

*"Paragraph 2*

States Parties shall ensure that a child shall not be separated from his parents against their will, except when competent authorities subject to judicial review determine, in accordance with applicable law and procedures, that such separation is necessary for the best interests of the child, *as in the case of articles [10, 18 et seq. and 19] or where the parents are living separately and have to make* a decision as to the child's place of residence.

*Paragraph 4*

In the *Spanish* version, replace the words 'cuando se le pida' with 'cuando así sea solicitado'." [does not affect the other language versions.]

190.      The representative of the German Democratic Republic introduced a proposal (E/CN.4/1989/WG.1/WP.13) to reformulate paragraph 3 of article 6 to read as follows:

"The States Parties to the present Convention shall respect and promote the right of the child who is separated from one or both parents on a regular basis, save in exceptional circumstances."

191.      The representative of the Federal Republic of Germany introduced a proposal (E/CN.4/1989/WG.1/WP.20) sponsored also by Japan by which a new paragraph 5 was to be added to article 6 reading as follows:

"5.      Nothing in this Convention shall affect in any way the legal provisions of States Parties concerning the immigration and the residence of foreign nationals."

192.      The observer for Canada introduced a proposal (E/CN.4/1989/WG.1/WP.37) to revise article 6 to read as follows:

"1.      States Parties shall ensure that the separation of a child from his or her parents, or other persons who have undertaken responsibility for the child's care, against their wishes shall be authorized only where the competent authorities determine, in accordance with applicable law and procedure that such persons have failed to fulfil their responsibilities in circumstances which indicate that the child's welfare is harmed or threatened. Any care provided for a child who is separated from his or her parents by public authorities shall be in accordance with the best interests of the child.

2.      States Parties recognize that when the parents of a child are living separate and apart from each other and an application is made to the competent authorities for a determination as to which of them shall have custody of the child, the interests of the child shall be the paramount consideration of such authorities in determining who shall be awarded the custody.

3.      In any proceedings pursuant to paragraphs 2 and 3, all interested parties shall be given an opportunity to participate in the proceedings and make their views known.

4.      A child who is separated from one or both parents has the right to maintain personal relations and direct contacts with both parents on a regular basis, except if it is contrary to the child's best interests.

5.      Where such a separation results from any action initiated by a State Party, such as the detention, imprisonment, exile, deportation or death (including death arising from any cause while the person is in the custody of the State) of one or both parents or of the child, that State Party shall,

upon request, provide the parents, the child or, if appropriate, another member of the family with essential information concerning the whereabouts of the absent member(s) of the family unless the provision of the information would be detrimental to the well-being of the child. States Parties shall further ensure that the submission of such a request shall of itself entail no adverse consequences for the person(s) concerned."

193.     The representative of Iraq orally proposed to delete the word "regular" from paragraph 3 of article 6.

194.     The representative of Portugal stated that she could not support the proposal introduced by the Federal Republic of Germany in E/CN.4/1989/WG.1/WP.20, since it was not consistent with article 12 of the Covenant on Civil and Political Rights, concerning the liberty of movement, several recommendations of the Council of Europe, to which Portugal is a member, and the draft convention on migrant workers. She also pointed out that the proposal could be interpreted as a general reservation, not applying only to this article.

195.     After some discussion, the Working Group decided upon the suggestion of the Chairman, to establish a small drafting group composed of Canada, the Federal Republic of Germany, the German Democratic Republic, Japan, the Netherlands, the Philippines, the United Kingdom of Great Britain and Northern Ireland and Venezuela to elaborate a unified text of article 6.

196.     On behalf of the drafting group, the representative of the Federal Republic of Germany introduced the proposals made by the drafting group (E/CN.4/1989/WG.1/WP.55). In doing so, he stated that the group proposed the deletion of paragraph 1 as adopted during the first reading because its contents were covered elsewhere in the convention. He also indicated that old paragraph 2 was to be split up with the bulk of it forming a new paragraph 1 and for the last two sentences of the old paragraph to be more elegantly restyled into a new paragraph 2. He stated that the new paragraph 3 was more consistent with the tone of article 6 in that it imposed State obligations rather than directly creating rights for individuals. He further stated that paragraph 4 remained unchanged from the first reading and that in agreeing to the text in E/CN.4/1989/WG.1/WP.55 the drafting group urged the Chairman to make a statement for the report as to the meaning and intention of the whole article.

197.     The representative of the United States of America suggested that the proposed text for article 6 contained in E/CN.4/1989/WG.1/WP.55 be adopted without any modifications.

198.     The delegations of Finland, Brazil, India and Venezuela expressed their preference for the text of article 6 as adopted during the first reading. In particular, the observer for Finland did so because he took the view that the proposed text in E/CN.4/1989/WG.1/WP.55 added nothing substantial to the old text. However, all four representatives indicated that they would not insist on the adoption of the old text.

199.     The representative of Venezuela proposed with reference to E/CN.4/1989/WG.1/WP.55 that the words "such as the cases in articles 10, 18 and following and 19 or" be inserted after the word "child" in line 5 of paragraph 1 with the deletion of the second sentence of that paragraph from the words "such determination" until "or one", on line 7, inclusive. However, in view of the lack of support for this proposal, the representative of Venezuela withdrew her proposal.

200.     With reference to paragraph 2 of article 6 as contained in E/CN.4/1989/WG.1/WP.55, the representative of India questioned why, since it embodied the latter part of old paragraph 2, the last sentence of old paragraph 2 had been omitted. He strongly urged its inclusion in the text contained in E/CN.4/1989/WG.1/WP.55, because he felt that, in being more forceful, it strengthened the obligation on States Parties. The representatives of the Federal Republic of Germany and Canada indicated that that sentence was not necessary as its meaning was clearly implied by the paragraph as restyled in E/CN.4/1989/WG.1/WP.55. The observer for Finland indicated that it was unnecessary to include that sentence because the idea contained

therein was covered in article 7. The representative of India agreed to join the consensus to leave the sentence out on the understanding that its intent would be covered by article 7.

201.    In the foregoing debate, general agreement was expressed as to the desirability of a statement by the Chairman for the report, as contained in E/CN.4/1989/WG.1/WP.55, regarding articles 6 and 6 bis.

202.    The Working Group then proceeded to adopt article 6 as contained in E/CN.4/1989/WG.1/WP.55 which reads as follows:

> "1.    States Parties shall ensure that a child shall not be separated from his or her parents against their will, except when competent authorities subject to judicial review determine, in accordance with applicable law and procedures, that such separation is necessary for the best interests of the child. Such determination may be necessary in a particular case such as one involving abuse or neglect of the child by the parents, or one where the parents are living separately and a decision must be made as to the child's place of residence.
>
> 2.    In any proceedings pursuant to paragraph 1, all interested parties shall be given an opportunity to participate in the proceedings and make their views known.
>
> 3.    States Parties shall respect the right of the child who is separated from one or both parents to maintain personal relations and direct contact with both parents on a regular basis, except if it is contrary to the child's best interests.
>
> 4.    Where such separation results from any action initiated by a State Party, such as the detention, imprisonment, exile, deportation or death (including death arising from any cause while the person is in the custody of the State) of one or both parents or of the child, that State Party shall, upon request, provide the parents, the child or, if appropriate, another member of the family with the essential information concerning the whereabouts of the absent member(s) of the family unless the provision of the information would be detrimental to the well-being of the child. States Parties shall further ensure that the submission of such a request shall of itself entail no adverse consequences for the person(s) concerned."

203.    After the adoption of the article, the Chairman made a statement for the report. The declaration reads as follows:

> "It is the understanding of the Working Group that article 6 of this convention is intended to apply to separations that arise in domestic situations, whereas article 6 bis is intended to apply to separations involving different countries and relating to cases of family reunification. Article 6 bis is not intended to affect the general right of States to establish and regulate their respective immigration laws in accordance with their international obligations."

204.    The representative of Portugal then made a statement for the report. It reads as follows:

> "In this connection, the delegation of Portugal would like to emphasize that the term 'international obligations' means not only the treaties concluded or ratified by a State but also the principles recognized by the international community, particularly United Nations legal instruments for the promotion and protection of human rights."

205.    The observer for Sweden stated that his delegation fully agreed with the interpretation of the Chairman's declaration made by the representative of Portugal. He further stated that the notion "international obligations" in the Chairman's declaration should include the provisions of this convention and especially article 6 bis.

206.    The representative of Italy indicated her support for, and wished to join in, the expression of the sentiments contained in the statements made by the representative of Portugal.

207.    The representative of the Federal Republic of Germany reserved the right to declare that silence in the face of the Chairman's declaration did not mean agreement with it.

### 3. Statement made after the adoption of the draft convention

#### (a) Japan

*The following is taken from the 1989 report of the Working Group to the Commission on Human Rights (E/CN.4/1989/48, para. 22).*

> 22. The representative of Japan expressed the reservation of his Government with regard to the legal nature of the declaration that the Chairman of the Working Group should make on article 6 bis to the effect that this article was not intended to affect the immigration laws of States Parties. Doubts were also expressed as to the consequences for the national immigration laws of some other provisions of the convention, namely of article 6, paragraphs 2 and 4, and of article 11 bis. The representative of Japan further stated that a number of other newly adopted proposals and articles of the draft convention would be *ad referendum* to his Government which will express its formal view on them at an appropriate opportunity.

### 4. Statements made during the adoption of the report

#### (a) Federal Republic of Germany

*The following is taken from the 1989 report of the Working Group to the Commission on Human Rights (E/CN.4/1989/48, para. 721).*

> 721. [...] The representative of the Federal Republic of Germany further asked that the following declarations be entered in the report:
>
> > (a) Nothing in the convention on the rights of the child shall be interpreted as legitimizing the illegal entry and presence on the territory of the Federal Republic of Germany of any alien, nor shall any provision be interpreted as restricting the right of the Federal Republic of Germany to promulgate laws and regulations concerning the entry of aliens and the conditions of their stay or to establish differences between nationals and aliens.
> >
> > [...]

#### (b) Japan

*The following is taken from the 1989 report of the Working Group to the Commission on Human Rights (E/CN.4/1989/48, para. 722).*

> 722. The representative of Japan drew the attention of the Working Group to the Chairman's declaration contained in paragraph 203 of the report stating that article 6 of the convention (present article 9) was intended to apply to separations that arise in domestic situations and also that article 6 bis (present article 10) was not intended to affect the general right of States to establish and regulate their respective immigration laws in accordance with their international obligations.
>
> [...]

# Article 10 (Family reunification)

## A.    Final text adopted by the General Assembly (1989)

*The following text is that approved by the General Assembly in its resolution 44/25 of 20 November 1989.*

1.    In accordance with the obligation of States Parties under article 9, paragraph 1, applications by a child or his or her parents to enter or leave a State Party for the purpose of family reunification shall be dealt with by States Parties in a positive, humane and expeditious manner. States Parties shall further ensure that the submission of such a request shall entail no adverse consequences for the applicants and for the members of their family.

2.    A child whose parents reside in different States shall have the right to maintain on a regular basis, save in exceptional circumstances, personal relations and direct contacts with both parents. Towards that end and in accordance with the obligation of States Parties under article 9, paragraph 1, States Parties shall respect the right of the child and his or her parents to leave any country, including their own, and to enter their own country. The right to leave any country shall be subject only to such restrictions as are prescribed by law and which are necessary to protect the national security, public order (*ordre public*), public health or morals or the rights and freedoms of others and are consistent with the other rights recognized in the present Convention.

## B.    First Polish draft convention and comments (1978)

*Neither the first draft nor the views received on it (see document E/CN.4/1324 and Corr.1 and Add.1-5) addressed the issues raised in article 10 of the Convention.*

## C.    First reading (1979-1988)

*The text of article 10 was first discussed by the Working Group in 1983, at which time a preliminary version of the article was adopted. Proposals to amend the adopted text were subsequently submitted to the Working Group and in 1987 additional sentences were adopted in both paragraphs 1 and 2. This article was referred to as article 6 bis throughout the first and second readings.*

### 1.    Proposal submitted to the Working Group (1981)

#### (a)    United States of America

*The following text is taken from document HR/(XXXVII)/WG.1/WP.12.*

Replace existing text of article 6 (...) with the following:

"Except as otherwise provided in the present Convention, the child shall have the right to reside with his parents or legal guardians, including when necessary the right to be reunited with them if they lawfully reside in another State party. If only one parent or legal guardian of a child resides in another State party, such child's preferred place of residence shall be a primary consideration in the deliberations of any judicial or administrative proceeding held to determine such child's place of residence. Each State party shall process applications for family reunification in a positive, humane, and expeditious manner. Until family reunification in a particular case is accomplished, all States parties involved shall permit frequent and regular family contacts."

*The foregoing proposal was later extensively modified. The text of the proposal, which is taken from paragraph 65 of the 1981 report of the Working Group to the Commission on Human Rights (E/CN.4/L.1575), reads as follows.*

*[Replace articles 6 and 10 of the revised draft convention with the following:]*

"1.       States Parties shall ensure that a child shall not be involuntarily separated from his parents, except when competent authorities determine, in accordance with procedures and criteria specified by domestic law, that such separation is necessary for the welfare of the child in a particular case, such as one involving maltreatment or abuse of the child by the parents or one where the parents are living separately and a decision must be made as to the child's place of residence. Such determinations shall not be made until all interested parties have been given an opportunity to participate in the proceedings and to make their views known. Such views shall be taken into account by the competent authorities in making their determination.

2.       In cases where both parents lawfully reside in one State Party and their child lawfully resides in another State Party, the States Parties concerned shall deal with applications for family reunification in a positive, humane and expeditious manner. States Parties shall charge only moderate fees in connection with such applications and shall not modify in any way the rights and obligations of the applicant(s) or of other members of the family concerned. States Parties shall ensure that applications for the purpose of family reunification of parents with their children which are not granted for any reason may be renewed at the appropriate level and will be considered at reasonably short intervals by the authorities of the country of residence or destination, whichever is concerned, and, in such cases, fees will be charged only when applications are granted. Until family reunification in a particular case is accomplished, all State Parties involved shall permit frequent and regular family contacts.

3.       The provisions of paragraph 2 shall also apply in cases where a child's only surviving parent lawfully resides in one State Party and the child lawfully resides in another State Party.

4.       If the parents of a child lawfully reside in different States Parties, States Parties shall ensure that the child's preference as to which parent he wishes to reside with shall be an important consideration in any determination made by competent authorities concerning the child's place of residence."

## 2.       Proposal submitted to the Working Group (1982)

### (a)       United States of America

*For the text of this proposal, see paragraph 19 (a) in section 4 below.*

## 3.       Proposals submitted to the Working Group (1983)

### (a)       Australia

*For the text of this proposal, see paragraph 19 (d) in section 4 below.*

### (b)       France

*For the text of this proposal, see paragraph 19 (c) in section 4 below.*

### (c)       United States of America

*For the text of this proposal, see paragraph 19 (b) in section 4 below.*

## 4.       Discussion and adoption by the Working Group (1983)

*The following is taken from the 1983 report of the Working Group to the Commission on Human Rights (E/ CN.4/1983/62).*

8.    It will be recalled that paragraphs 1 and 2 of article 6 relating to the question of the determination of the place of residence of the child were adopted by the Working Group last year. At the present session, the discussions which led to the adoption of paragraphs 3 and 4 of article 6, part of article 6 bis and article 6 ter, focused on the proposals and amendments thereto relating to various problems which arise from family separation, such as the right of the child to maintain relations with his parents, the question of family reunification and the illegal abduction of children by one parent. It was also stressed that the national and international aspects of the question should be dealt with separately. All the proposals relating to these problems were considered simultaneously.

[...]

11.    With regard to the solutions to be given to the question of family reunification, divergent views were expressed. One representative expressed the opinion that all obstacles to emigration for the purpose of family reunification should be removed everywhere and proposed to include in the draft convention, as examples, a number of rights which in his opinion needed special protection. They include, in particular, unimpeded freedom of movement and a guarantee against punishment for children and parents requesting permission to leave a country. All applications to leave should be dealt with, he said, in a humane and expeditious manner.

12.    One speaker stated that the draft convention submitted by Poland emphasized economic and social rights but neglected civil and political rights. Other speakers stressed that, in their view, economic rights were equal or even of greater importance, in some circumstances, for children. It was also noted that the Covenant provided that the rights contained therein could be subject to restrictions in order to protect inter alia, national security and public order. They therefore questioned the need for the adoption of such provisions, and emphasized that there was no need to duplicate the International Covenant on Civil and Political Rights. Otherwise, references should also be made to the International Covenant on Economic, Social and Cultural Rights. One representative further observed that family reunification was broader in scope than the problems being dealt with in the draft convention. With regard to the proposal relating to immunity from punishment for children and parents who request permission to leave a country, some representatives observed that such immunity, if granted, should concern only the fact of making an application. The discussion on these questions led to *the adoption of part of article 6 bis*, which in paragraph 2 refers to the obligations of States Parties, as regards applications by a child or his parents to enter or leave a State party for the purpose of family reunification.

[...]

17.    Mention should further be made of the proposal made by the USSR (in relation to paragraph 1 of article 6 bis) (E/CN.4/1983/WG.1/WP.7), which reads as follows:

> "The States parties to the present Convention recognize that the child should enjoy all the basic human rights in the spirit of the International Covenant on Economic, Social and Cultural Rights and the International Covenant on Civil and Political Rights".

[...]

19.    Proposals dealing with various aspects of the problems arising from family separations were submitted or reintroduced as follows:

(a)    A proposal made by the United States in 1982 (E/1982/12/Add.1/part C, para. 118) was reintroduced at the present session. It reads as follows:

> "1.    The States Parties to the present Convention shall ensure that the child and his parents enjoy the right to liberty of movement and freedom to choose a residence within the territory of any State Party where they are lawfully present.
>
> 2.    The States Parties to the present Convention shall accord to the child and his parents the right to leave any State, including their own, and the right to enter their own State".

(b)    After an exchange of views, the representative of the United States indicated that paragraph 1 of his proposal could be set aside and paragraph 2 could constitute paragraph 1 of article 6 bis (E/1982/12/Add.1/ part C, para. 118 [and] para. 25). He then orally proposed as article 6 bis the following text:

"1.    The States Parties to the present Convention shall accord to the child and his parents the right to leave any State, including their own, and the right to enter their own State.

2.    In cases where both parents lawfully reside in one State Party and their child lawfully resides in another State Party or where the parents of a child lawfully reside in different States Parties, the States Parties concerned shall deal with applications for family reunification or contacts on the basis of family ties in a positive, humane and expeditious manner. States Parties shall make no distinction as to country of origin or destination in dealing with such applications, shall charge only moderate fees in connection with such applications and shall not modify in any way the rights and obligations of the applicant(s) or of other members of the family concerned. States Parties shall ensure that applications for the purpose of family reunification of parents with their children which are not granted for any reason may be renewed at the appropriate level and will be considered at reasonably short intervals by the authorities of the country of residence or destination, whichever is concerned, and, in such cases, fees will be charged only when applications are granted. Until family reunification in a particular case is accomplished, all States Parties involved shall permit frequent and regular family contacts.

3.    The provisions of paragraph 2 shall also apply in cases where a child's only surviving parent lawfully resides in one State Party and the child lawfully resides in another State Party, as well as in cases where parents who are nationals of different States Parties apply to transfer the permanent residence of their children and themselves to a Member State in which either one is normally a resident.

4.    If the parents of a child lawfully reside in different States Parties, States Parties shall ensure that the child's preference as to which parent he wishes to reside with shall be an important consideration in any determination made by competent authorities concerning the child's place of residence."

(c)    The representative of France reintroduced a proposal he submitted last year. As revised, the proposal (E/CN.4/1983/WG.1/WP.6) deals with two questions: (i) the question of personal relations of the child with his parents when the parents are of different nationalities and are separated, and (ii) the question of illegal removal of the child by one parent. It reads as follows:

"1.    The child of parents with different nationalities, who are separated, shall, save in exceptional circumstances, be entitled to maintain personal relations with both parents.

2.    The States parties to the present Convention shall take the necessary measures to prevent the unlawful removal abroad and non-return of children.

The removal and non-return of a child shall be considered unlawful:

(a)    When it occurs in violation of custody rights awarded to a person or an institution by the laws of the State in which the child had his usual place of residence immediately prior to his removal or non-return;

(b)    When such rights were actually exercised at the time of the removal, or would have been so exercised if such events had not taken place. The measures taken by States may be the conclusion of international agreements or accession to existing agreements."

(d)    The representative of Australia proposed the following text (E/CN.4/1983/WG.1/WP.1) as article 6 ter:

"1.     A child who is separated from one or both parents has the right to maintain personal relations and direct contacts with both parents on a regular basis, save in exceptional circumstances and regardless of whether the parents and the child reside in different States.

2.     Where such separation results from judicial or administrative action by a State Party, such as detention, imprisonment, exile or deportation of one or both parents or of the child, the State Party shall provide the parents and the child with precise information as to the whereabouts of the absent member(s) of the family."

[...]

30.     The discussion on the question of family reunification led to the adoption of part of paragraph 2 and paragraph 3 of article 6 bis. In this connection reference is made to paragraph 1 of the French proposal referred to above and to paragraphs 2, 3 and 4 of the proposal by the United States of America (see paragraph 19 above).

31.     The representative of the Ukrainian SSR proposed the following text (E/CN.4/1983/WG.1/WP.11) to be included as a paragraph in article 6 bis, if specific mention of rights already covered by the International Covenant on Civil and Political Rights were not deleted from the proposal made by the representative of the United States of America:

"The above-mentioned rights shall not be subject to any restrictions except those which are provided by law, are necessary to protect national security, public order, public health or morals or the rights and freedoms of others."

32.     During the discussions, it was noted that the wording of this paragraph was identical to a similar text contained in the International Covenant on Civil and Political Rights. It was also argued that the proposals made by the representative of the United States of America constituted a mere repetition of the provisions of the International Covenant on Civil and Political Rights. It was further said that, compared to other paragraphs of the draft convention, the text proposed by the United States was much too long.

33.     In the light of the discussions, the representative of the United States of America submitted a shortened version of his proposal. He maintained that any convention purporting to deal with the rights of children must explicitly and effectively deal with the question of family reunification and the guarantees to be given to applicants who request to leave a country for that purpose. The revised text (E/CN.4/1983/WG.1/WP.8) reads as follows:

"1.     The States Parties to the present Convention shall accord to the child and his parents the right to leave any State, including their own, and the right to enter their own State.

2.     Applications by a child or his parents to leave a State Party for the purpose of family reunification shall be dealt with by States Parties in a positive, humane and expeditious manner. States Parties shall charge only moderate fees in connection with such applications and shall not discriminate against or punish in any way the applicant(s) or other members of the family concerned. States Parties shall ensure that applications for the purpose of reunification of parents with their children which are not granted for any reason may be renewed at the appropriate level and will be considered at reasonably short intervals by the competent authorities, with fees in such cases to be charged only when applications are granted.

3.     States Parties shall recognize the right of a child whose parents lawfully reside in different States Parties to maintain at all times, save in exceptional circumstances, personal relations and direct contacts on the basis of family ties with both parents through regular meetings. In such cases, States Parties shall ensure that the child's preference as to which parent he wishes to reside with shall be an important consideration in any determination made by competent authorities concerning the child's place of residence."

34.      Indicating that the revised text submitted by the United States of America still contains references to rights already covered in the International Covenant on Civil and Political Rights, the representative of the USSR submitted a proposal (E/CN.4/1983/WG.1/WP.7) which reads as follows:

> "The States parties to the present Convention recognize that the child should enjoy all the basic human rights in the spirit of the International Covenant on Economic, Social and Cultural Rights and the International Covenant on Civil and Political Rights."

35.      *No agreement was reached as regards paragraph 1 of article 6 bis.*

36.      The representative of the United States of America proposed orally a new text to constitute paragraph 2 of article 6 bis. The text, which relates to applications by a child or his parents to enter or leave a State Party, reads as follows:

> "In accordance with the obligation of States Parties to ensure that a child is not separated from his parents [against their will] [except in his best interest] [unless in exceptional circumstances] applications by a child or his parents to enter or leave a State Party for the purpose of family reunification shall be dealt with by States Parties in a positive, humane and expeditious manner. In connection with such applications States Parties shall not punish in any way the applicant(s) or other members of the family concerned [Applications which are not granted for any reason may be renewed and may be considered by the competent authorities]."

*The texts of paragraphs 37 and 43 as adopted by the Working Group at its 12th meeting are as follows:*

37.      Some speakers strongly objected to the above-mentioned proposals. In their view the proposals were too broad and would in fact grant immunity to applicants against any punishment for any acts they might commit. Amendments were suggested along those lines. It was also suggested that the second part of the proposal made by the United States should be deleted (see paragraph 36 above). The contrary view was also expressed.

38.      *The Working Group adopted as paragraph 2 of article 6 bis the following text:*

> "In accordance with the obligation of States Parties under article 6 (2), applications by a child or his parents to enter or leave a State Party for the purpose of family reunification shall be dealt with by States Parties in a positive, humane and expeditious manner."

39.      Discussions on the question of the right of the child when parents live in different States to maintain contacts with both parents, led to the adoption of paragraph 3 of article 6 bis. Reference is made to paragraphs 3 and 4 of the original proposal made by the United States of America (see paragraph 19 (b) above).

40.      Referring to his earlier proposal and to the proposal made by the representative of the United States of America on the question under consideration, the representative of France submitted the following text:

> "A child whose parents reside [lawfully] in different States shall have the right to maintain on a regular basis, save in exceptional circumstances, personal relations and direct contacts with both parents."

*Adoption of paragraph 3 of article 6 bis*

41.      With the deletion of the word "lawfully" as proposed by the representative of the United Kingdom, the Working Group adopted the above-mentioned text as paragraph 3 of article 6 bis.

42.      The representative of the United States reintroduced a proposal he made in 1982 according to which the draft convention should contain a provision ensuring the right of the child not to be subjected to arbitrary or unlawful interference by government authorities, The proposal, which was previously designated article 6 ter reads as follows (E/1982/12/Add.1, part C, para. 118):

"The States parties to the present Convention shall ensure that the child and his parents are not subjected to arbitrary or unlawful interference with their privacy, family, home or correspondence."

43.      For some speakers, the inclusion of such provision was not necessary. In their opinion, the fulfilment of the child's basic needs was a more urgent matter.

## 5.    Proposals submitted to the Working Group (1984)

### (a)    United States of America

*The following is taken from annex II to the 1984 report of the Working Group to the Commission on Human Rights (E/CN.4/1984/71).*

*Amendment to article 6 bis*

*1st paragraph*

The States Parties to the present Convention shall accord to the child and his parents the right to leave any State, including their own, and the right to enter their own State.

*2nd paragraph, second sentence*

In connection with such applications States Parties shall not punish in any way the applicant(s) or other members of the family concerned. Applications which are not granted for any reason may be renewed and will be considered in the manner noted above with regard to initial applications.

### (b)    International Federation of Women in Legal Careers and the International Abolitionist Federation

*The following is taken from document E/CN.4/1983/NGO/33, which appeared after the 1983 session of the Working Group.*

*Article 6 bis* (Family reunion)

As we have said before, we would like to see provision made for appeal against decisions taken by States Parties, even if such decisions have been taken in a "positive, humane and expeditious manner". We would therefore suggest the addition of the following paragraph 3:

"Applications that have not been granted for any reason whatsoever may be renewed and reconsidered by the competent authorities."

### (c)    International Social Service

*The following is taken from document E/CN.4/1984/WG.1/WP.3.*

International Social Service would like to see the present text (as in E/CN.4/1983/L.1/Add.1) supplemented, in order to guarantee the right of the individual to leave any State, including his own, and to enter his own State, rights already guaranteed by the Universal Declaration of Human Rights and by the International Covenant on Civil and Political Rights. ISS also stresses the need to facilitate family reunification with the parent or child who has left a given country.

## 6.    Modified proposal submitted by Poland (1986)

*For the text of the Polish proposal, see paragraph 22 in section 8 below.*

## 7.    Proposals submitted to the Working Group (1986)

### (a)    Netherlands, United Kingdom and United States of America

*For the text of this proposal, see paragraph 133 in section 9 below.*

### (b)    United States of America

*For the text of this proposal, see paragraph 22 in section 8 below.*

## 8.    Discussion in the Working Group (1986)

*The following is taken from the 1986 report of the Working Group to the Commission on Human Rights (E/CN.4/1986/39, paras. 22 to 32).*

22.    Discussions held by the Working Group during its 1983 session led to the adoption of part of article 6 bis, namely paragraphs 2 and 3, which read as follows:

"1.    In accordance with the obligation of States Parties under article 6, paragraph 2, applications by a child or his parents to enter or leave a State Party for the purpose of family reunification shall be dealt with by States Parties in a positive, humane and expeditious manner.

2.    A child whose parents reside in different States shall have the right to maintain on a regular basis save in exceptional circumstances personal relations and direct contacts with both parents."

The Polish delegation submitted article 6 bis as contained in document A/C.3/40/3, which read as follows:

"The State Parties to the present Convention, in accordance with article 12 of the International Covenant on Civil and Political Rights, shall recognize the right of the child to leave any States."

The representative of the United States submitted the following revised proposal:

"1.    States Parties shall respect the right of the child and his parents to leave any country, including their own, and to return to their own country.

2.    The right to leave any country shall be subject only to such restrictions as are prescribed by law and which are necessary to protect the national security, public order (*ordre public*), public health or morals or the rights and freedoms of others." (New paragraph)

Renumber existing paragraph 2 as paragraph 3, and add the following concluding sentence:

"3.    States Parties shall ensure that the submission of such a request shall of itself entail no adverse consequence for the person(s) concerned, whether or not similar or related applications have been previously made and granted or denied."

23.    With regard to paragraph 1, the observer for Poland stated that the question of the right, as such, of parents to leave any country - including their own - and to return to it should not be part of a convention on the rights of the child. That view was shared by a number of other delegations including those of Finland, France, the German Democratic Republic and the USSR.

24.    The delegation of Japan found itself in agreement with the proposal put forward by the representative of the United States, although it indicated its preference for the verb "to enter", already used in article 12 of the International Covenant on Civil and Political Rights, rather than the words "to return" in the United States proposal. The representative of the United States accepted the suggestion of the Japanese delegation for reasons of consistency with the International Covenant. However, the observer for Finland and the representative of the USSR insisted on their objection to a right which concerned parents being incorporated into a convention dealing with the rights of the child. At the same time, the delegation of Australia supported the proposal submitted by the representative of the United States with the suggestion that in paragraph 1, the phrase "the right of the child and his parents" be replaced by "the right of children and their parents".

25.      The Chairman observed that the same difference in approach to article 6 bis had persisted within the Working Group for some years, indicating that one solution to the problem could be the establishment of a working party, consisting of the delegations of the United States, Finland, Poland and the USSR, to produce a new text that would be acceptable to the Group. The text in question read as follows:

"1.      In accordance with the obligation of States Parties under article 6, paragraph 2, applications by a child or his parents to enter or leave a State Party for the purpose of family reunification shall be dealt with by States Parties in a positive, humane and expeditious manner. States Parties shall further ensure that the submission of such a request shall of itself entail no adverse consequences for the person(s) concerned.

2.      A child whose parents reside in different States shall have the right to maintain on a regular basis save in exceptional circumstances personal relations and direct contacts with both parents. Toward that end, States Parties shall respect the right of the child and his parents to leave any country, including their own, and to return to their own country. The right to leave any country shall be subject only to such restrictions as are prescribed by law and which are necessary to protect the national security, public order (*ordre public*), public health or morals or the rights and freedoms of others (and is consistent with the other rights recognized in the present Convention)."

26.      The Chairman decided that paragraphs 2 and 3 of article 6 bis that had already been adopted should become paragraphs 1 and 2 respectively.

27.      The representative of the USSR proposed the deletion of the phrase "States Parties shall further ensure that" at the beginning of the second sentence of the above-mentioned paragraph 1. The observer for Canada was opposed to the deletion of this phrase, while the delegation of the Netherlands stated that the sentence under discussion should remain unchanged on the assumption that it must be an obligation of a State Party to ensure that the submission of a request to enter or leave a State Party for the purpose of family reunification should of itself entail no adverse consequences for the person or persons concerned.

28.      Having pointed out that the wording had been taken from paragraph 4 of article 6 that had already been adopted, the delegation of the United States said that it could agree to the deletion of the phrase under discussion if the representative of the USSR insisted, although it would prefer that no such amendment were made. The representative of the Soviet Union then requested that the Working Group should start its consideration of paragraph 2, since his decision whether or not to insist on his amendment would depend on the final wording of the second sentence of paragraph 2.

29.      Some speakers questioned the need for a reference to "*ordre public*" placed between brackets following the words "public order" in the third sentence of paragraph 2. With reference to the term "*ordre public*", the representative of the United States pointed out that the term appeared in the International Covenant on Civil and Political Rights (notably in paragraph 3 of article 12, whose terminology was closely related to the text under discussion by the Group) and that it was more precise than "public order".

30.      The representative of Japan proposed the replacement of the word "return" in the second sentence of paragraph 2 by the word "enter". The delegation of Cyprus expressed its preference for the word "return", finding its use more logical after the phrase "to leave any country" which preceded it. The representative of the United Kingdom indicated his support for the Japanese proposal as did the representative of Australia, who considered that the interests of children who were born abroad must be kept in mind. The latter representatives' views were shared by the delegation of Mexico. The representative of Bangladesh suggested that the two terms be combined by inserting the words "or enter" between the words "return to" and "their own country." The delegation of the United Kingdom expressed its preference for the wording suggested by the representative of Bangladesh.

31.      The representative of the USSR reiterated his objection concerning the inclusion in the draft convention of the specific right of a child's parents to leave any country and to return to it and said that,

in the light of the discussion which had just taken place, he needed to reflect further on the question and proposed that the discussion be postponed.

32.     Noting that only one delegation was unprepared to accept article 6 bis, the representative of the United States expressed the hope that the delegation in question would be prepared to accept the text at the Working Group's next session.

## 9.     Discussion and adoption by the Working Group (1987)

*The following is taken from the 1987 report of the Working Group to the Commission on Human Rights (E/CN.4/1987/25, paras.  9 to 20 and 133 to 138).*

9.     The Working Group had before it the following text of a joint proposal made by the delegations of Finland, Poland, the USSR and the United States for an addition of a second sentence to paragraph 1 and of a second and third sentence to paragraph 2 of article 6 bis:

*Second sentence of paragraph 1*

"States Parties shall further ensure that the submission of such a request shall of itself entail no adverse consequences for the person(s) concerned."

*Second and third sentences of paragraph 2*

"Toward that end, States Parties shall respect the right of the child and his parents to leave any country, including their own, and to return to their own country. The right to leave any country shall be subject only to such restrictions as are prescribed by law and which are necessary to protect the national security, public order (*ordre public*), public health or morals or the rights and freedoms of others (and is consistent with the other rights recognized in the present Convention)."

*Second sentence of paragraph 1*

10.     When discussing the proposal for a second sentence to paragraph 1 of article 6 bis, the representative of Senegal was of the view that this proposal had no significance in an international convention, since it was obvious that the submission of the request by a child or his parents to enter or leave a State Party for the purpose of family reunification should entail no adverse consequences for the persons concerned. He felt that paragraph 1 of article 6 bis, by imposing an obligation upon States, already covered the concerns expressed in the proposal. The representative of the United States explained that the proposal in its entirety reflected a humanitarian concern, that family unity and reunification were basic rights that should be included in the draft convention, and urged the Working Group to adopt the proposal.

11.     The delegation of the Netherlands, supported by the observer for Finland, proposed the deletion of the words "of itself", while the representative of the United Kingdom was of the view that the reason for inclusion of the words "of itself" was justified in certain circumstances, when adverse consequences could arise after States Parties had dealt with requests for family reunification in a positive, humane and expeditious manner, or after family reunification had taken place. The representative of Austria, supporting this view, agreed to these additional words.

12.     The observer for Finland considered that in the phrase "shall of itself entail no adverse consequences for the person(s) concerned", the words "person(s) concerned" should be clarified. He proposed instead the following wording: "shall entail no adverse consequences for the applicants and for the members of their families". The delegation of the Netherlands favoured the proposal put forward by the observer for Finland, a proposal which also met with the acceptance of the representative of the United States.

13.     The Working Group then proceeded to adopt by consensus the following additional sentence to paragraph 1 of article 6 bis:

"States Parties shall further ensure that the submission of such a request shall entail no adverse consequences for the applicants and for the members of their family."

*Second and third sentences of paragraph 2*

14.     The observer for Finland put forward a revised proposal to the one submitted by the delegations of Finland, Poland, the USSR and the United States of America, which read as follows:

"2.        A child shall have the right to maintain [save in exceptional circumstances] personal relations and direct contacts with both parents also where the child and his or her parents live in different States. Toward that end, States Parties shall respect the right of the child and his or her parents to enter or leave their territory temporarily and, where appropriate, on a regular basis. States Parties shall also take all necessary steps to promote and ensure the effective exercise of this right and to secure the fulfilment of any conditions to which the exercise of this right may be subject.

3.        The implementation of the obligations under this article [by States Parties] shall be subjected only to such restrictions as are prescribed by law and which are necessary to protect the national security, public order (*ordre public*), public health or morals or the rights and freedoms of others [and are consistent with the other rights recognized in the present Convention]."

15.     The observer for Finland was of the view that the wording in the revised proposal that he had submitted was more appropriate, and would allow more flexibility in the interpretation of the article so as to ensure the child's right to maintain personal relations and direct contacts with both parents in those cases in which the child and his parents each lived in different States.

16.     The proposal by the observer for Finland met with some reservations, and the Working Group agreed that the text submitted by the delegations of Finland, Poland, the USSR and the United States be taken as the basis for discussion.

17.     The representative of Japan proposed that the word "return" be replaced by the word "enter", in order to allow the entry of a child born outside his or her own country, and the observer for Finland agreed with the proposal. The representative of France proposed the wording "respect the right that the child and his parents have to leave any country", instead of "respect the right of the child and his parents to leave any country". The representative of the German Democratic Republic proposed the addition of the words "and in accordance with the obligation of States Parties under article 6, paragraph 2" after the words "towards that end"; with regard to the proposal by the Japanese delegation, he was in agreement with it and the representative of Australia shared his view.

18.     The delegations of the Netherlands and the United Kingdom expressed their interest in the revised proposal by the observer for Finland. The observer for the Netherlands also said that he would join a consensus with regard to the adoption of the additional sentences to paragraph 2 of article 6 bis, with the understanding that at the appropriate time the Working Group would discuss some elements of the revised proposal submitted by the observer for Finland. The delegation of Finland stated that it would join the consensus on the basis of the proposal under consideration by the Working Group, and with the suggested amendment by the delegation of Japan; the observer for Finland added that his delegation was reserving the right to come back to the matters raised in his proposal at least during the second reading, and voiced his hope that delegations would then accept some of the wording contained in his revised proposal.

19.     The representative of the USSR questioned the appropriateness of having the text at the end of the proposal which was between parentheses added to the proposal. The Chairman suggested the deletion of the parentheses. The representative of the United States proposed to delete the word "to" before the words "their own country", as well as the parenthesis at the end of the proposal, and to replace the word "is" in the [last] line by the word "are". The delegation of Senegal wished to delete the words "Toward that end," at the beginning of the proposal, but this suggestion did not meet with the approval of other members of the

Working Group. The delegation of Poland supported the proposal as amended by the delegations of Japan and the United States.

20.      The Working Group then adopted the following additional sentences to paragraph 2 of article 6 bis:

> "Towards that end and in accordance with the obligation of States Parties under article 6, paragraph 2, States Parties shall respect the right of the child and his parents to leave any country, including their own, and to enter their own country. The right to leave any country shall be subject only to such restrictions as are prescribed by law and which are necessary to protect the national security, public order (*ordre public*), public health or morals or the rights and freedoms of others and are consistent with the other rights recognized in the present Convention."

[...]

133.      The Working Group had before it a proposal for an article 21 bis which was submitted at its 1986 session by the delegations of the Netherlands, the United Kingdom and the United States, and which read as follows:

> "Nothing in this Convention shall be interpreted as legitimizing any alien's illegal entry into and presence in a State, nor shall any provision be interpreted as restricting the right of any State to promulgate laws and regulations concerning the entry of aliens and the terms and conditions of their stay, or to establish differences between nationals and aliens. However, such laws and regulations shall not be incompatible with the international legal obligations of that State, including those in the field of human rights."

134.      The representative of the United Kingdom stated that his delegation would continue to have difficulties with some of the articles already adopted unless such a provision as the above-mentioned one concerning aliens would now be included in the draft convention. For example, paragraphs 1 and 2 of article 2 caused difficulties in relation to his country's nationality law, paragraph 1 of article 6 was not compatible with United Kingdom immigration legislation, and articles 3, paragraph 1, 4, paragraph 1, 6, paragraphs 2 and 3, 6 bis, paragraphs 2 and 3, and 8, paragraphs 1 and 2, all posed problems as well in relation to United Kingdom immigration law. Certain of those provisions were difficult or even impossible to reconcile with his country's law and practice: in common with other States, British legislation did not allow unrestricted entry into the country.

135.      The representative of Senegal questioned the appropriateness of such a proposal, and his doubts were shared by the delegations of Algeria, Argentina, Mexico and Venezuela. The representative of Venezuela referred in particular to the question of adoption and said that if she had the certainty that in cases of adoption such a provision would not hurt the child, she would accept it, but as it stood she was not in a position to do so. In addition, the observer for Finland voiced his doubts as to the relevance, importance and significance of the whole proposal.

136.      The representative of the United States indicated that, while his preference was for the full text, as originally submitted, in a spirit of compromise he proposed to shorten the proposal in the following way:

> "Nothing in this Convention shall be interpreted as legitimizing any alien's illegal entry into and presence in a State."

This proposal was supported by the representative of the United Kingdom.

137.      This abridged version did not meet with the full approval of the delegations of Canada and the Netherlands, while the observer for Finland objected to the inclusion of the proposed article either in its full or abridged version. However, the delegation of the Netherlands held the opinion that the provision under consideration by the Working Group was very relevant to several articles of the draft convention.

138.    The Chairman proposed to put an end to the discussion for lack of a consensus and indicated that if the co-authors of the proposal would elaborate a more acceptable text, in that case the Working Group would resume its discussion on the subject. At a later meeting and in connection with the adoption by the Group of article 6 bis, the representative of the United Kingdom and on behalf of the United States and the Netherlands, stated that they would be presenting a revised proposal for article 21 bis to the next session of the Working Group. The delegations of the Netherlands, the United Kingdom and the United States considered that an article on the lines of article 21 bis was essential to a balanced convention, and this view was supported by the delegation of the Federal Republic of Germany.

## 10.    Text as adopted at first reading

*The following is taken from document E/CN.4/1988/WG.1/WP.1/Rev.1 (article 6 bis).*

1.      In accordance with the obligation of States Parties under article 6, paragraph 2, applications by a child or his parents to enter or leave a State Party for the purpose of family reunification shall be dealt with by States Parties in a positive, humane and expeditious manner. States Parties shall further ensure that the submission of such a request shall entail no adverse consequences for the applicants and for the members of their family.

2.      A child whose parents reside in different States shall have the right to maintain on a regular basis save in exceptional circumstances personal relations and direct contacts with both parents. Towards that end and in accordance with the obligation of States Parties under article 6, paragraph 2, States Parties shall respect the right of the child and his parents to leave any country, including their own, and to enter their own country. The right to leave any country shall be subject only to such restrictions as are prescribed by law and which are necessary to protect the national security, public order (*ordre public*), public health or morals or the rights and freedoms of others and are consistent with the other rights recognized in the present Convention.

# D.    Technical review (1988)

## 1.    Comment by the World Health Organization (WHO)

*The following is taken from document E/CN.4/1989/WG.1/CRP.1, page 21.*

Paragraph 2 of this article deals with the right of the child to leave any country; but this right is subject to restrictions arising, inter alia, from the need to protect "public health". The same applies to article *7a, paragraph 2 (b)*, in connection with the right of freedom of expression, and article *7 ter, paragraph 2*, in connection with the rights of freedom of association and peaceful assembly. These provisions are of interest to the World Health Organization for two reasons:

(1)     The determination of the need to protect health should be made by a competent medical body.

(2)     No abuse should be made with respect to this requirement.

It may be worthwhile pointing out that article 12, paragraph 3 of the International Covenant on Civil and Political Rights contains a similar restriction in relation to the liberty of movement, freedom to leave any country and the freedom to choose residence.

## 2.    Comment by the United Nations Children's Fund (UNICEF)

*The following is taken from document E/CN.4/1989/WG.1/CRP.1, page 21.*

*Gender neutrality*

Paragraph 1. The first part of the paragraph might be reformulated as follows:

"In accordance with the obligation of States Parties under article 6, paragraph 2, applications by a child or *the* child's parents..."

Paragraph 2. The same reformulation might be used in the middle of this paragraph:

"... States Parties shall respect the right of the child and the child's parents to leave any country...."

## 3. Additional comments and clarifications by the Secretariat

*The following is taken from document E/CN.4/1989/WG.1/CRP.1/Add.1, paragraph 14.*

14.     In order to achieve symmetry between the standards laid down in article 6 bis and those in article 12, paragraphs 2 through 4, of the International Covenant on Civil and Political Rights, the Working Group may wish to consider redrafting which would entail, first and foremost:

(a) stating clearly at the beginning of the article the basic rights under elaboration; (b) moving the last sentence of paragraph 2 in article 6 bis to a new paragraph 1 together with the basic rights; and (c) adding a reference to the new paragraph 1 in what becomes paragraph 2. With these changes, article 6 bis would read as follows:

"1.     *The child and his or her parents shall be free to leave any country, including their own.* The right to leave any country shall be subject only to such restrictions as are prescribed by law and which are necessary to protect national security, public order (*ordre public*), public health or morals or the rights and freedoms of others, and are consistent with the other rights recognized in the present Convention. *The child and his or her parents shall not be arbitrarily deprived of the right to enter their own country.*"

2.     In accordance with *paragraph 1 and with* the obligation

[...]     (previous paragraph 1)

3.     (previous paragraph 2 excluding the last sentence)."

# E.     Second reading (1988-1989)

## 1.     Proposal submitted to the Working Group

### (a)     German Democratic Republic

*For the text of this proposal, see paragraphs 209 and 218 in section 2 below.*

## 2.     Discussion and adoption at second reading

*The following is taken from the 1989 report of the Working Group to the Commission on Human Rights (E/CN.4/1989/48, paras. 208 to 223).*

208.     The Working Group had before it a text (E/CN.4/1989/WG.1/WP.2) for article 6 bis as adopted during the first reading into which was incorporated suggested revisions proposed by the technical review of the Secretariat. The text read as follows:

"1.     *The child and his or her parents shall be free to leave any country, including their own. The right to leave any country shall be subject only to such restrictions as are prescribed by law and which are necessary to protect the national security, public order* (ordre public)*, public health or* *morals or the rights and freedoms of others and are consistent with the other rights recognized in the present Convention. The child and his or her parents shall not be arbitrarily deprived of the right to enter their own country.*

2.          In accordance with *paragraph 1 and with* the obligation of States Parties under article 6, paragraph 2, applications by a child or his *or her* parents to enter or leave a State Party for the purpose of family reunification shall be dealt with by States Parties in a positive, humane and expeditious manner. States Parties shall further ensure that the submission of such a request shall entail no adverse consequences for the applicants and for the members of their family.

3.          A child whose parents reside in different States shall have the right to maintain on a regular basis save in exceptional circumstances personal relations and direct contacts with both parents. Towards that end and in accordance with the obligation of States Parties under article 6, paragraph 2, States Parties shall respect the right of the child and his *or her* parents to leave any country, including their own, and to enter their own country. (The right to leave any country shall be subject only to such restrictions as are prescribed by law and which are necessary to protect the national security, public order (*ordre public*), public health or morals or the rights and freedoms of others and are consistent with the other rights recognized in the present Convention.)"

*Paragraph 1*

209.      The Working Group also had before it proposals contained in E/CN.4/1989/WG.1/WP.13 by the representative of the German Democratic Republic reading as follows:

"Change in paragraph 1 'or' by 'and' so that it reads as follows:

'... applications by a child *and* his parents ...'"

210.      The representatives of Argentina, India, Portugal, the Union of Soviet Socialist Republics and the United States of America expressed support for the inclusion of the new paragraph 1 as contained in E/CN.4/1989/WG.1/WP.2 because it reflected rights already enshrined in article 12 of the International Covenant on Civil and Political Rights. The representatives however indicated that they did not insist on its inclusion in the article. The representative of the United Kingdom reserved the right to make a statement concerning his delegation's interpretation of the reference in this article to the right of children and their parents "to enter their own country".

211.      The observer for Australia proposed that since the only new idea raised in the new paragraph 1 was contained in the last sentence, he suggested that that last sentence could be incorporated in the text of article 6 bis as it was adopted during the first reading. The representative of India supported this and suggested that if the new paragraph was not included in the article then that last sentence should be incorporated into the article.

212.      The representatives of Australia, Finland, the Netherlands and Poland expressed a preference for the text of this article as adopted during the first reading. In particular, the representatives of Australia and Poland did so because they wished to maintain the article's emphasis on the issue of family reunification.

213.      The observer for Finland suggested that the scope of the article should be widened and therefore proposed that the words "and family meetings" be included after the words "family reunification". The representatives of Kuwait and the United States of America indicated that the meaning of the words proposed were not clear and therefore they felt that the words should be left out of the text.

214.      The representatives of Australia, Portugal and the United States of America took the view that article 6 bis was intended to cover situations in which children were separated from their parents or where parents were separated themselves, the child living with one of them, and that they were therefore unable to support the proposal by the representative of the German Democratic Republic to change the word "or" in line 2 of old paragraph 1 to the word "and".

215.	The representative of the United Kingdom raised concerns about the interpretation of the word "positive" in line [3] of old paragraph 1. He suggested that as the word could be misinterpreted he would prefer the word "objective" to be used in its place. The representative of France indicated that the translation of the word "positive" into the French text seemed to contain an element of prejudgement and for that reason he would like to see the word "positive" omitted from the text.

216.	The delegations of Sweden and Finland suggested that the word "positive" be retained in the text for article 6 bis as the word had an established usage, at least within the European context. The observer for Finland suggested as an alternative that the use of the word "favourable" might allay the concerns of the United Kingdom delegation. The representative of the United States of America indicated that the word "positive" should be retained in the text of the article because it only obliged States to act positively and in no way prejudged the outcome of their deliberations on questions of family reunification. He further stated that the word "favourable" should not be used as that word seemed to contain an element of prejudgement. As a result of the foregoing debate, the representative of the United Kingdom indicated that his concerns had been allayed and that "positive" should be retained.

217.	The text of article 6 bis, paragraph 1, as adopted during the second reading reads as follows:

"In accordance with the obligation of States Parties under article 6, paragraph 1, applications by a child or his *or her* parents to enter or leave a State Party for the purpose of family reunification shall be dealt with by States Parties in a positive, humane and expeditious manner. States Parties shall further ensure that the submission of such a request shall entail no adverse consequences for the applicants and for the members of their family."

*Paragraph 2*

218.	The representative of the German Democratic Republic drew attention to her proposal of amendment contained in E/CN.4/1989/WG.1/WP.13 which read as follows:

"Delete in paragraph 2 the first sentence and start the second sentence with: In accordance with the obligation of the States Parties under article 6, paragraphs 2 and 3."

219.	The observer for Finland stated that he would not propose any specific amendments but pointed out some interpretation problems as to the amendment proposed by the German Democratic Republic. According to the Finnish delegate, the first sentence had to be kept because even in cases where both parents lived abroad and in the same country, the child should have contacts with both parents and therefore the first sentence should apply.

220.	The representatives of the Federal Republic of Germany and Morocco joined Finland in opposing the amendment.

221.	Given these objections, the German Democratic Republic delegation declared that, despite some legal problems it had with the wording of this paragraph, it would not insist on the amendment. However, the delegate stressed again the difficulties they were having with it and reserved her right to raise the issue at the Commission on Human Rights.

222.	The Working Group then adopted article 6 bis, paragraph 2, without changes except the addition of "or her".

223.	The final version of article 6 bis, paragraph 2, reads as follows:

"A child whose parents reside in different States shall have the right to maintain on a regular basis save in exceptional circumstances personal relations and direct contacts with both parents. Towards that end and in accordance with the obligation of States Parties under article 6, paragraph 2, States Parties shall respect the right of the child and his or her parents to leave any country, including their own, and to enter their own country. The right to leave any country shall be subject only to such restrictions as are prescribed by law and which are necessary to protect the national security, public order (*ordre public*), public health or morals or the rights and freedoms of others and are consistent with the other rights recognized in the present Convention."

## 3.    Statement made after the adoption of the draft convention

### (a)    Japan

*The following is taken from the 1989 report of the Working Group to the Commission on Human Rights (E/CN.4/1989/48, para. 22).*

> 22.      The representative of Japan expressed the reservation of his Government with regard to the legal nature of the declaration that the Chairman of the Working Group should make on article 6 bis to the effect that this article was not intended to affect the immigration laws of States Parties. Doubts were also expressed as to the consequences for the national immigration laws of some other provisions of the convention, namely of article 6, paragraphs 2 and 4, and of article 11 bis. The representative of Japan further stated that a number of other newly adopted proposals and articles of the draft convention would be *ad referendum* to his Government which will express its formal view on them at an appropriate opportunity.

## 4.    Statements made during the adoption of the report

### (a)    Federal Republic of Germany

*The following is taken from the 1989 report of the Working Group to the Commission on Human Rights (E/CN.4/1989/48, para. 721).*

> 721.     [...] The representative of the Federal Republic of Germany further asked that the following declarations be entered in the report:
>
> > (a)      Nothing in the convention on the rights of the child shall be interpreted as legitimizing the illegal entry and presence on the territory of the Federal Republic of Germany of any alien, nor shall any provision be interpreted as restricting the right of the Federal Republic of Germany to promulgate laws and regulations concerning the entry of aliens and the conditions of their stay or to establish differences between nationals and aliens.
> >
> > [...]

### (b)    Japan

*The following is taken from the 1989 report of the Working Group to the Commission on Human Rights (E/CN.4/1989/48, para. 722).*

> 722.     The representative of Japan drew the attention of the Working Group to the Chairman's declaration contained in paragraph 203 of the report stating that article 6 of the convention (present article 9) was intended to apply to separations that arise in domestic situations and also that article 6 bis (present article 10) was not intended to affect the general right of States to establish and regulate their respective immigration laws in accordance with their international obligations. [...]

# Article 11 (Illicit transfer and non-return)

## A. Final text adopted by the General Assembly (1989)

*The following text is that approved by the General Assembly in its resolution 44/25 of 20 November 1989.*

1. States Parties shall take measures to combat the illicit transfer and non-return of children abroad.

2. To this end, States Parties shall promote the conclusion of bilateral or multilateral agreements or accession to existing agreements.

## B. First Polish draft convention and comments (1978)

*Neither the first Polish draft nor the views received on it (see document E/CN.4/1324 and Corr.1 and Add.1-5) addressed the issues raised in article 11 of the Convention.*

## C. First reading (1979-1988)

*The issues raised under article 11 were first discussed by the Working Group at its 1982 session and the text was adopted in 1983. This article was referred to as article 6 ter throughout the first and second readings.*

### 1. Proposals submitted to the Working Group (1982)

#### (a) France

*For the text of this proposal, see paragraph 15 in section 2 below.*

#### (b) Joint NGO proposal

*(Co-sponsors: International Council of Women, Friends World Committee for Consultation, International Association of Penal Law, International Catholic Child Bureau, International Catholic Union of the Press, International Commission of Jurists, International Council of Jewish Women, International Federation of Women in Legal Careers, International Federation of Women Lawyers and the World Jewish Congress). For the text of this proposal, see paragraph 13 in section 2 below.*

#### (c) Minority Rights Group

*For the text of this proposal, see paragraph 14 in section 2 below.*

### 2. Discussion in the Working Group (1982)

*The following is taken from the 1982 report of the Working Group to the Commission on Human Rights (E/CN.4/1982/30/Add.1, paras. 13 to 15).*

13. Several non-governmental organizations suggested the following paragraph, as contained in document E/CN.4/1982/WG.1/WP.1, to replace paragraph 3 of the amendment to articles 6 and 10 originally submitted by the representative of the United States at the Working Group's session in 1981:

"Where a child is placed in the custody of one parent because of a marital dispute between the parents residing in different countries, resulting in divorce, separation or other interlocutory proceedings, and due to conflicting private international law considerations there has been no final determination of the issue of the child's custody or the child is unlawfully held by one parent because of the non-execution of an order of the court of competent jurisdiction, the States Parties shall endeavour to resolve the issue by bilateral agreements or multilateral arrangements reached where appropriate under the auspices of a regional intergovernmental body, the best interest of the child being the guiding principle."

14.     The Minority Rights Group, a non-governmental organization proposed the following text in substitution for the proposed new paragraph 3 mentioned above:

"The States Parties shall endeavour, by new or updated bilateral agreements or multilateral arrangements, reached where appropriate under the auspices of a regional intergovernmental body, the best interest of the child concerned being the guiding principle, to resolve the issues arising:

(i)     When a child has been placed in the custody of one parent or in joint custody because of a marital dispute between the parents residing in different countries, resulting in divorce, separation or other interlocutory proceedings, and due to conflicting private international law considerations there has been no final determination of the issue of the child's custody;

(ii)    When a child is unlawfully held and hidden by one parent because of the non-execution or later breach of an order of the court of competent jurisdiction; or

(iii)   When, there being no order of a court of competent jurisdiction as to custody, one parent assumes control over the child contrary to the wish of the parent normally exercising it; and exercises that control in a country other than that in which the latter parent resides."

The main intention of this proposal was to extend the endeavours which States would undertake to make to children who are in effect kidnapped across international frontiers by a parent, particularly those kidnapped in circumstances where no court order on custody exists; these cases are numerous and may in fact be more numerous than those to which an order of custody applies.

15.     Some speakers drew attention to the situation of children of parents separated by divorce or for other reasons who are not of the same nationality or who may reside in countries other than the country of residence of the child, and to the need of a child in such a situation to retain his links with both his parents. Accordingly, the representative of France made the following proposal: "The child of a separated international family shall, as far as possible, retain his links with both his parents." The French proposal was supported by several delegations, but it was thought that it dealt more properly with paragraph 2 of the article under discussion and it would be very appropriate if it were the first sentence of paragraph 2. At a later stage in the proceedings, the representative of France submitted a new draft to replace his earlier proposal as mentioned above. The text read as follows:

"The child of parents with different nationalities, who are separated, shall, save in exceptional circumstances, be entitled to maintain personal relations with both parents."

The French representative indicated that:

(a)     the convention on the rights of the child would in the future serve as a benchmark for cooperation agreements between States. In view of its importance, the French representative believed that the convention would benefit if it were completed by including a clause concerning a matter which had not so far been dealt with, namely the situation of children of separated parents of different nationalities;

(b)     experience had shown that private family disputes which gave rise to the abduction of children across frontiers occurred more and more frequently and that no country could consider itself exempt. In France, for example, the Ministry of Justice had estimated that there were 1,000 cases of abduction per year involving no fewer than 41 States. It was a situation which gravely affected society;

(c)     the convention, which constituted a basic text at the international level, must by its very nature be universal. Preventive measures should be taken to impede that its provisions be interpreted from a nationalistic point of view. It was absolutely necessary that the child's interests should be evaluated on the basis of all the elements of his family background, whether such elements were national or international. Experience had shown that the nationalistic approach to the child's interests had in most cases resulted in making a legal orphan of a child with a foreign father or mother;

(d)      the convention should not take second place to the existing conventions which have confirmed at the multilateral level the principle of the maintenance of relations between the child and both his parents of different nationalities. The conventions, which had already been ratified by many countries, were the European Convention of Luxembourg of 20 May 1980 on the recognition and enforcement of decisions relating to children's custody and the restoration of custody rights, and The Hague Convention of 25 October 1980 on the Civil Aspects of International Child Abduction.

## 3.      Views of Governments on child removal or detention (1983)

*In its resolution 1982/39, the Economic and Social Council* inter alia *called the attention of States to the proliferation of cases of removal and retention of children and invited them to cooperate actively with a view to preventing the occurrence of such cases and to solving them speedily, out of concern for the interest of the child. In this connection, it invited the Commission on Human Rights, when drafting the convention on the rights of the child, to take into consideration the protection of the rights of the child in cases of unauthorized international removal. It further requested the Secretary-General to consult with Governments on this problem and to report to the Commission on Human Rights at its thirty-ninth (1983) session.*

*In accordance with that resolution, notes verbales relating to this question were sent to all Member States of the United Nations. The following summaries of the replies received were compiled in documents E/CN.4/1983/32 and Adds.1-5, which, with the exception of E/CN.4/1983/32/Add.5 (containing the replies of Barbados and Sudan), were before the Working Group at its 1983 session.*

### (a)      Austria

*The following is taken from document E/CN.4/1983/32.*

The Government refers to the Hague Convention on Civil Aspects of International Child Abduction of 25 October 1980 and makes observations on a number of points including, in particular, the enforcement of decisions concerning custody of children, measures guaranteeing the expeditious return of children in cases of removal, grounds for refusing the return of a child, and the question of the costs incurred through recourse to the assistance of a lawyer.

### (b)      Barbados

*The following is taken from document E/CN.4/1983/32/Add.5.*

The Government of Barbados states that the retention of children, removal or abduction of children by a parent in defiance of a custody order is becoming an increasing problem in Barbados.

This issue has been discussed at several Commonwealth Law Ministers Meetings since 1977 and an attempt is being made by members of the Commonwealth to draft a convention along similar lines as the Hague Convention.

The broad aim of this convention would be to recognize and enforce custody orders made within Commonwealth countries and to ensure that an application to vary or modify a custody order would only be done in the child's country of residence. There is, however, general consensus that in order to alleviate this problem, there must be (a) an intergovernmental agreement and (b) subsequent legislative changes.

The Government has already implemented some initial legislative changes. In the Family Law Bill of 1981, foreign custody orders can be registered and are recognized. A limit is placed on the right of the court in

Barbados to exercise jurisdiction on the matter unless (a) each person having rights in the original order consents to the proceedings or (b) the welfare of the child will be adversely affected by non-action. There is also provision for the transmission of Barbadian custody orders to overseas countries.

The inclusion of the rights of the child in cases of unauthorized removal in the draft convention on the rights of the child would ensure that countries become more aware of the size and scope of the problem and safeguard the right of a child to a stable and secure environment.

### (c)     Colombia

*The following is taken from document E/CN.4/1983/32/Add.2.*

The Government of Colombia reports that chapter 8 of Administrative Decision No. 0773 of 1981 refers expressly to permits to leave Colombia and prescribes the requirements concerning minors.

1.        When both parents agree to the minor's departure: In this case, a statement of intent that has been signed by both parents and authenticated shall be submitted in writing to the Ministry of External Relations so that a passport may be issued to the minor or minors concerned.

2.        When the domicile of one of the parents or legal representatives is unknown, the Minors' Counsel shall, in administrative proceedings, allow or refuse to allow the minor or minors concerned to leave Colombia, as appropriate.

All these decisions must be complied with by the immigration authorities.

In addition to such cases, somewhat irregular de facto situations occur when one of the parents manages, by resorting to bribes, forging signatures or travelling by land to the borders with Ecuador, Brazil, Venezuela, Panama, etc., unlawfully to obtain a visa for other countries from the competent officials.

In view of the foregoing, we consider it advisable, important and urgent that international agreements should be concluded on such matters and that the Commission on Human Right should draft agreements on the rights of children which take account of the protection of their rights in cases of unauthorized and unlawful international travel.

It is extremely important that such agreements should deal not only with the protection of minors, but also provide for machinery to pave the way for, facilitate and make possible the repatriation of a minor or minors unlawfully removed from Colombia.

### (d)     Cyprus

*The following is taken from document E/CN.4/1983/32.*

The Government states that it supports Economic and Social Council resolution 1982/39 and that it is also considering the ratification of the European Convention on Recognition and Enforcement of Decisions concerning Custody of Children and on Restoration of Custody of Children, of 20 May 1980.

### (e)     Denmark

*The following is taken from document E/CN.4/1983/32.*

The Government states that it is considering whether to accede to the European Convention on Recognition and Enforcement of Decisions concerning Custody of Children and on Restoration of Custody of Children, drafted within the framework of the Council of Europe, or to the Hague Convention on Civil Aspects of International Child Abduction of 25 October 1980.

### (f)     Ethiopia

*The following is taken from document E/CN.4/1983/32.*

The Government expresses its full support for Economic and Social Council resolution 1982/39 and declares that States should organize some form of cooperation for preventing the occurrence of cases such as those referred to in the resolution. The Government further notes that it is in favour of the elaboration of an international convention on the question.

## (g)    Federal Republic of Germany

*The following is taken from document E/CN.4/1983/32.*

The Government states that it welcomes Economic and Social Council resolution 1982/39. It further states that is willing to cooperate with other States on the basis of the Hague Convention on Civil Aspects of International Child Abduction of 25 October 1980, and that it therefore intends to ratify the Hague Convention.

## (h)    Greece

*The following is taken from document E/CN.4/1983/32.*

The Government states that it attaches great importance to the inclusion, in drafting the convention on the rights of the child, of sufficient and effective safeguards for the prevention of unauthorized removals from State to State.

The efforts being made to construct a complete and up-to-date system for the protection of the child against unauthorized removal across frontiers, may find inspiration in the European Convention on Recognition and Enforcement of Decisions concerning Custody of Children and on Restoration of Custody of Children, of 20 May 1980, which Greece has already signed and intends to ratify shortly.

## (i)    Kuwait

*The following is taken from document E/CN.4/1983/32/Add.1.*

The Government states that its legislation fully safeguards the right of the child to live undisturbed under the protection of the person legally responsible for his welfare, irrespective of whether that person is the child's guardian, trustee or any other individual in whose custody the child had been placed. According to articles 178 to 184 of the Penal Code, it is absolutely forbidden to remove a child under 21 years of age from his environment or from the place in which he normally lives if such removal would entail the severance of the child's links with his family, who are responsible for his welfare.

The State of Kuwait intends to cooperate with other State Members of the United Nations with a view to the adoption of measures and rules to prevent the removal or retention of children.

*The following additional text is taken from document E/CN.4/1983/32/Add.4.*

The Government states that Kuwaiti legislation contains numerous provisions under the Personal Status Act to protect the child's individuality, development and maintenance. Chapter II of the Constitution stipulates that the family is the foundation of society and is based on religion, morality and patriotism. The law shall safeguard the family and strengthen its bonds, thereby ensuring the protection of mothers and children.

Article 10 of the Constitution stipulates that: "The State shall provide for the welfare of the younger generation, protect it from exploitation, and preserve it from moral, physical and spiritual neglect."

In the event of a conflict between spouses, the customary practice followed by the courts in the State of Kuwait is to grant child custody to the mother, since she is regarded as the person most likely to show concern for the welfare of the child during the early stages of his life. The child remains in the custody of his mother, or whoever replaces her, until he comes of age as prescribed in the Islamic sharia.

The nationality Act No. 15 of 1959 ensures extensive protection for mothers and children.

## (j)     Netherlands

*The following is taken from document E/CN.4/1983/32.*

The Government notes that it intends to ratify the two recently concluded international instruments which deal with the problem of preventing the occurrence of cases of removal of children, namely: the Hague Convention on Civil Aspects of International Child Abduction, and the European Convention on Recognition and Enforcement of Decisions concerning Custody of Children and on Restoration of Custody of Children. Interested States should organize cooperation in this field by acceding to one or both Conventions. Furthermore, if the Commission on Human Rights intends to include in the draft convention on the rights of the child provisions concerning the removal of children, it should pay due attention to existing instruments in order to ensure the effective prevention of unauthorized removal of children.

## (k)     Norway

*The following is taken from document E/CN.4/1983/32.*

It is the Government's view that the question of the unauthorized removal of children should be taken into consideration when drafting a convention on the rights of the child. At the same time, the need for coordination with the work already done by other international organizations should also be taken into account. The Government is, in principle, in favour of adhering to one or both conventions on the subject, namely, the Hague Convention on Civil Aspects of International Child Abduction and the convention elaborated by the Council of Europe.

## (l)     Pakistan

*The following is taken from document E/CN.4/1983/32.*

The Government states that it does not permit the removal or retention of children from their parents' family by other persons. The family courts decide on custody in cases arising out of divorce. The Government supports the proposal that all countries should cooperate closely through accession to the Hague Convention on Civil Aspects of International Child Abduction of 25 October 1980, which is open to all States.

## (m)     Qatar

*The following is taken from document E/CN.4/1983/32.*

The Government states that it endorses Economic and Social Council resolution 1982/39. Islamic law recognizes the need to protect children. The Government proposes that one of the aspects of the question which should be considered is the importance of ensuring adequate services for the fundamental needs of children suffering from the problem of removal.

## (n)     Singapore

*The following is taken from document E/CN.4/1983/32.*

The Government states that there are adequate laws in Singapore to cover the protection of the rights of children and young persons, namely, the Laws of Children and Young Persons Act, the Women's Charter and the Penal Code. In addition to these laws, the Ministry of Social Affairs of Singapore contains two divisions - the Counselling and Advice Division and the Protection and Welfare of Children and Young Persons Division - which deal with all problems connected with children and young persons. Any parent who is aggrieved by the unauthorized removal of a child by one spouse can have recourse to the Courts, provided he or she is a Singapore citizen or has resided in Singapore continuously for a period of not less than six months. There is provision for an expedited order where the Court is satisfied that there is an imminent danger of the child being taken out of the country. The Court is also empowered to order a child to be kept at a place of safety to await a decision. The Penal Code also has a provision which safeguards a child against kidnapping from lawful guardianship.

## (o)  Spain

*The following is taken from document E/CN.4/1983/32/Add.1.*

The Government states that it shares the concern underlying the text of Economic and Social Council resolution 1982/39 in view of the increasing number of cases of Spanish nationals becoming involved in situations of this type, usually as a result of marriages with aliens. Noting that it had played an active part in the preparation of the Hague Convention on Civil Aspects of International Child Abduction to which it intends to accede, the Government adds that it would be very opportune if, at its thirty-ninth session, the Commission on Human Rights completes its work on the elaboration of that convention on the rights of the child with a view to achieving the speedy solution of the cases referred to in the Council's resolution 1982/39.

## (p)  Sudan

*The following is taken from document E/CN.4/1983/32/Add.5.*

The Government states that it fully supports Economic and Social Council resolution 1982/39. Although cases of retention and international removal of children rarely occur because of the existence of strong social and family ties, Sudan welcomes international cooperation and the exchange of experience in the field of the rights of the child.

The Constitution and other legislative acts clearly indicate the importance of moral, spiritual, mental, physical and social values for the development of the child.

## (q)  Switzerland

*The following is taken from document E/CN.4/1983/32.*

The Government states that it has taken the necessary steps for the ratification, in the near future, of the Hague Convention on Civil Aspects of International Child Abduction of 25 October 1980, as well as of the European Convention on Recognition and Enforcement of Decisions concerning Custody of Children and on Restoration of Custody of Children, of 20 May 1980. The Swiss Government also proposes to begin negotiations with certain States not intending to become parties to either of the above-mentioned Conventions, with a view to examining the possibility of concluding bilateral agreements with those States for mutual aid in the event of international child abduction by a parent or close relative.

Within the framework of the draft convention on the rights of the child, Switzerland supports the proposal to grant to a child having parents of different nationalities who are separated the right to maintain personal relations with both parents.

## (r)  Thailand

*The following is taken from document E/CN.4/1983/32.*

The Government states that the protection of children and of youth is the responsibility of various governmental organizations. The services provided to disadvantaged children include family assistance, protection measures, adoption arrangements and the promotion of voluntary child welfare institutions.

*The following additional text is taken from document E/CN.4/1983/32/Add.3.*

The Government states that cases of unauthorized removal and retention of children in Thailand are not only the result of conflicts arising between couples of different nationalities, but also of an increasing demand for children for adoption abroad.

It is the Government's view that national legislative measures are not sufficient to control infringements of the rights and benefits of such children. It therefore suggests that the Commission on Human Rights should take up this problem when drafting the convention on the rights of the child. At the same time, the public should be made aware that a child given for adoption should be provided with the facilities to develop in conditions of freedom and dignity.

**(s)    Yugoslavia**

*The following is taken from document E/CN.4/1983/32/Add.2.*

According to Yugoslav law, parents shall exercise the parental right together and by mutual consent, and in case of disagreement the guardianship authority shall decide. If parents are separated, the parental right shall be exercised by the parent with whom the child lives; in the case of parental disagreement, a decision shall be reached by the guardianship authority or, in specified cases, by the court. Furthermore, if, in case of the separation of parents, dissolution or annulment of their marriage, the child has been entrusted by a court decision or by the decision of any other competent authority to the care and upbringing of one of the parents, that parent shall exercise the parental right.

In exceptional cases, Yugoslav laws provide that a child may be removed from a parent by a decision of the guardianship authority, if the child's proper upbringing is seriously threatened. The act of removal of the child in such cases does not imply that any other rights and duties of parents have ceased. Anyone who removes or retains a child not entrusted to him/her would be subject to civil and criminal liability. The penal laws of the Republics and autonomous provinces provide for a specific type of offence (removal of a minor) for which, in cases of unauthorized removal of a minor by a natural parent, adoptive parent, guardian or any other person, the offender may be punished with imprisonment.

## 4.    Proposals submitted to the Working Group (1983)

**(a)    France**

*For the text of these proposals, see paragraphs 19 and 47 in section 5 below.*

**(b)    Minority Rights Group**

*For the text of this proposal, see paragraph 50 in section 5 below.*

## 5.    Discussion and adoption by the Working Group (1983)

*The following is taken from the 1983 report of the Working Group to the Commission on Human Rights (E/CN.4/1983/62, paras. 8, 13, 19 and 45 to 51).*

8.        It will be recalled that paragraphs 1 and 2 of article 6 relating to the question of the determination of the place of residence of the child were adopted by the Working Group last year. At the present session, the discussions which led to the adoption of paragraphs 3 and 4 of article 6, part of article 6 bis and article 6 ter, focused on the proposals and amendments thereto relating to various problems which arise from family separation, such as the right of the child to maintain relations with his parents, the question of family reunification and the illegal abduction of children by one parent. It was also stressed that the national and international aspects of the question should be dealt with separately. All the proposals relating to these problems were considered simultaneously.

[...]

13.       The illegal abduction of children was considered by many speakers as a very important question. It was observed that when parents of different nationalities are separated and reside in different States, such

situations often give rise to the abduction of children across frontiers. The need for effective remedy was stressed. In the view of some speakers, however, what constituted "illegal abduction by one parent" could not be easily defined, as international private law varied from country to country. Nevertheless, in order to find solutions to this problem, most speakers agreed on the need for the conclusion of bilateral agreements or appropriate additions to existing multilateral agreements. The discussion on this question led to the adoption of article 6 ter.

[...]

19.        [...]

(c)        The representative of France reintroduced a proposal he submitted last year. As revised, the proposal (E/CN.4/1983/WG.1/WP.6) deals with two questions: (i) the question of personal relations of the child with his parents when the parents are of different nationalities and are separated, and (ii) the question of illegal removal of the child by one parent. It reads as follows:

> "1.        The child of parents with different nationalities, who are separated, shall, save in exceptional circumstances, be entitled to maintain personal relations with both parents.

> 2.        The States Parties to the present Convention shall take the necessary measures to prevent the unlawful removal abroad and non-return of children.

> The removal and non-return of a child shall be considered unlawful:

> (a)        When it occurs in violation of custody rights awarded to a person or an institution by the laws of the State in which the child had his usual place of residence immediately prior to his removal or non-return;

> (b)        When such rights were actually exercised at the time of the removal, or would have been so exercised if such events had not taken place. The measures taken by States may be the conclusion of international agreements or accession to existing agreements."

[...]

45.        Discussions on the question of unlawful removal of children across frontiers led to the adoption of article 6 ter. The representative of France referred to paragraph 2 of his earlier proposal (see paragraph 19 above) and said that it could constitute a new article 6 ter, with the provisions of article 6 bis, paragraph 2 in relation with the provisions of article 3, paragraph 1.

46.        During the discussion on the proposal doubts were expressed concerning the two criteria proposed for considering the removal of children unlawfully. Such criteria, it was stated, varied according to different legal systems. Speakers also emphasized the need for more international cooperation, through bilateral or multilateral agreements and consultations between national authorities as regards the measures to be taken by States against abduction of children.

47.        In the light of the discussions the representative of France revised paragraph 2 of his proposal (E/CN.4/1983/WG.1/WP.17) as follows:

> "1.        The States Parties to the present Convention shall take appropriate measures to combat the unlawful abduction of children abroad and their non-return.

> 2.        To that end, States shall promote the conclusion of bilateral or multilateral agreements or accession to existing agreements, and the institution of periodic consultations between the national authorities concerned."

*Adoption of paragraphs 1 and 2 of article 6 ter*

48.    *Paragraph 1 of the revised proposal submitted by France was adopted by the Group as paragraph 1 of article 6 ter.*

49.    With the insertion of the word "Parties" after the word "States" in the first line of paragraph 2 of the revised proposal, *that paragraph was provisionally adopted by the Group as paragraph 2 of article 6 ter.*

50.    The Minority Rights Group, a non-governmental organization, introduced a proposal under which a third paragraph would be added to article 6 ter (E/CN.4/1983/WG.1/WP.18). The text of the proposal reads as follows:

> "Children cannot be divorced from their parents. Any arbitrary removal must be seen as contrary to the interest of the child, in accordance with the principles of human rights.
>
> This Convention must comprise a measure expressing condemnation of such acts and the States Parties' duty to dissuade their perpetration.
>
> The act of abduction shall not be treated differently for reasons of parents' nationality, sex, race or religion, or the status of the parents' separation proceedings."

51.    The Chairman noted that that proposal did not command unanimous support. The Group concerned should review its proposal in the light of delegates' remarks.

## 6.    Text as adopted at first reading

*The following is taken from document E/CN.4/1988/WG.1/WP.1/Rev.1.*

*Article 6 ter*

1.    The States Parties to the present Convention shall take appropriate measures to combat the illicit transfer and non-return of children abroad.

2.    To this end, the States Parties shall promote the conclusion of bilateral or multilateral agreements or accession to existing agreements, as well as the introduction of periodic consultations between the competent national authorities.

# D.    Technical review (1988)

*There were no comments specifically referring to the text of article 6 ter.*

# E.    Second reading (1988-1989)

## 1.    Discussion and adoption at second reading

*The following is taken from the 1989 report of the Working Group to the Commission on Human Rights (E/CN.4/1989/48, paras. 224 to 233).*

224.    The Working Group had before it article 6 ter as adopted at first reading:

> "1.    The States Parties to the present Convention shall take appropriate measures to combat the illicit transfer and non-return of children abroad.
>
> 2.    To this end, the States Parties shall promote the conclusion of bilateral or multilateral agreements or accession to existing agreements, as well as the introduction of periodic consultations between the competent national authorities."

225.     The observer for Finland suggested the deletion of the end of paragraph 2: "... the introduction of periodic consultations between the competent national authorities", since those mechanisms were already provided by international conventions and that here it appeared superfluous, given that within this convention, there would be a committee supervising the matter. The delegate then appealed to the French delegation, which had sponsored this clause, to reconsider it.

226.     The delegation of the Netherlands joined Finland in this suggestion and also proposed the deletion of the word "appropriate" under paragraph 1.

227.     The representative of France agreed to the deletion as suggested by Finland.

228.     The representative of Mexico while expressing his regrets over the deletion, declared he had neither objections nor amendments to suggest. The delegate asked, however, for more specific measures against the sale of children and said that the measures proposed in article 6 ter were too general.

229.     The observer for Canada stated that article 18 already dealt with the sale of children so there was no necessity to broaden article 6 ter further, and that he had no objection to the deletion of the end of paragraph 2 as proposed by Finland. Finally, he said that paragraph 1 of the original text had been proposed in French, using language from the French version of the Hague Convention on International Child Abduction and therefore the English translation of the original paragraph 1 should also use the language from the English version of the Hague Convention. Accordingly, the phrase "illicit transfer and non-return" should be changed to "wrongful removal and retention".

230.     The observer for Finland pointed out that in the Hague Convention the French text used the expression "déplacement illicite" whereas the corresponding expression in the English text was "wrongful removal" and that the 1980 European Convention used the expressions "sans droit" and "illicite" in the French text and the word "improper" in the English text. He suggested that it might be better to avoid the use of "wrongful" in the English text since that word had a specific meaning within the Hague Convention, slightly different from "improper" in the European Convention, and proposed, in order to cover all those nuances and possibilities that the word "illicit" be kept in the English text.

231.     The delegation of Italy proposed the use of "abduction" instead of "illicit transfer and non-return".

232.     As far as article 18 quater was concerned, the representative of the Federal Republic of Germany suggested the deletion of article 6 ter in order to keep only article 18 quater whereas Senegal proposed the addition of article 18 quater under article 6 ter as the third paragraph.

233.     After a short discussion, the Working Group adopted article 6 ter which reads as follows:

"1.     States Parties shall take measures to combat the illicit transfer and non-return of children abroad.

2.     To this end, States Parties shall promote the conclusion of bilateral or multilateral agreements or accession to existing agreements."

# Article 12 (Respect for the views of the child)

## A.  Final text adopted by the General Assembly (1989)

*The following text is that approved by the General Assembly in its resolution 44/25 of 20 November 1989.*

> 1.     States Parties shall assure to the child who is capable of forming his or her own views the right to express those views freely in all matters affecting the child, the views of the child being given due weight in accordance with the age and maturity of the child.

> 2.     For this purpose, the child shall in particular be provided the opportunity to be heard in any judicial and administrative proceedings affecting the child, either directly, or through a representative or an appropriate body, in a manner consistent with the procedural rules of national law.

## B.  First Polish draft convention and comments (1978)

*Neither the first Polish draft nor the views received on it (see document E/CN.4/1324 and Corr.1 and Add.1-5) addressed the issues raised in article 12 of the Convention.*

## C.  First reading (1979-1988)

*The issues raised under article 12 were first discussed by the Working Group at its 1981 session, at which time the text was adopted. This article was referred to as article 7 throughout the first and second readings. The unofficial heading for this article, "the child's right to express opinions", was reformulated by the Committee on the Rights of the Child at its first session (1991). The reporting guidelines of the Committee refer to the article as "respect for the views of the child".*

### 1.  Revised Polish draft (1979)

*The following text is taken from Commission on Human Rights document E/CN.4/1349, which was reissued for technical reasons.*

*Article 7*

> The States parties to the present Convention shall enable the child who is capable of forming his own views the right to express his opinion in matters concerning his own person, and, in particular, marriage, choice of occupation, medical treatment, education and recreation.

### 2.  Proposal submitted to the Working Group (1980)

#### (a)    United States of America

*For the text of this proposal, see paragraph 20 in section 4.  The text was first proposed by the United States as paragraph 2 of article 3 pertaining to the best interests of the child. In 1981, the same text was also proposed as article 7 pertaining to the views of the child.*

### 3.  Proposals submitted to the Working Group (1981)

#### (a)    Australia

*For the text of this proposal, see paragraph 74 in section 4 below.*

**(b)**     **Denmark**

*For the text of this proposal, see paragraph 75 in section 4 below.*

**(c)**     **United States of America**

*The following text is taken from document HR/(XXXVII)/WG.1/WP.3.*

> In all judicial or administrative proceedings affecting a child that is capable of forming his own views, an opportunity shall be provided for the views of the child to be heard, either directly or indirectly through a representative, as an independent party to the proceedings, and those views shall be taken into consideration by the competent authorities.

*For a revised version of this proposal, see paragraph 76 in section 4 below.*

## 4.     Discussion and adoption by the Working Group (1981)

*The following is taken from paragraphs 19-21, 27-32 and 73-81 of the 1981 report of the Working Group to the Commission on Human Rights (E/CN.4/L.1575), which is reproduced in paragraph 289 of the 1981 report of the Commission on Human Rights (E/CN.4/1475).*

19.     Article 3 of the revised Polish draft was as follows:

> "1.     In all actions concerning children, whether undertaken by their parents, guardians, social or State institutions, and in particular by courts of law and administrative authorities, the best interest of the child shall be the paramount consideration.

> 2.     The States parties to the present Convention undertake to ensure the child such protection and care as his status requires, taking due account of the various stages of his development in family environment and in social relations, and, to this end, shall take necessary legislative measures.

> 3.     The States parties to the present Convention shall create special organs called upon to supervise persons and institutions directly responsible for the care of children."

20.     The representative of the United States of America reintroduced a new article 3 which had been submitted by his delegation the year before but had not been considered owing to lack of time. The new article read as follows:

> "1.     In all official actions concerning children, whether undertaken by public or private social welfare institutions, courts of law, or administrative authorities, the best interests of the child shall be a primary consideration.

> 2.     In all judicial or administrative proceedings affecting a child that has reached the age of reason, an opportunity for the views of the child to be heard as an independent party to the proceedings shall be provided, and those views shall be taken into consideration by the competent authorities.

> 3.     Each State party to this Convention shall support special organs which shall observe and make appropriate recommendations to persons and institutions directly responsible for the care of children.

> 4.     The States parties to this Convention undertake, through passage of appropriate legislation, to ensure such protection and care for the child as his status requires."

21.     The delegation of Australia also had submitted in 1980 the following text to replace paragraphs 2 and 3 of article 3:

"2.       The States parties to the present Convention undertake to ensure the child such protection and care as is necessary for his well-being, taking into account the rights and responsibilities of his parents and the stage of the child's development towards full responsibility and, to this end, shall take all necessary legislative and administrative measures.

3.       The States parties to the present Convention shall ensure competent supervision of persons and institutions directly responsible for the care of children."

This proposal was reintroduced at the 1981 session of the Working Group.

[...]

*Paragraph 2*

27.       One representative suggested that the Working Group consider paragraph 2 as proposed by the delegation of the United States of America, since it made reference to judicial and administrative proceedings. The representative of the United States explained that paragraph 2, as submitted by his delegation, contained concepts that were missing in the draft convention.

28.       Some speakers indicated that the opportunity for the views of the child to be heard, mentioned in the amendment proposed by the delegation of the United States, was also mentioned in article 7 of the revised Polish draft, but others pointed out that the amendment by the United States delegation to paragraph 2 of article 3 made specific reference to all judicial or administrative proceedings affecting a child in this respect and followed logically from paragraph 1 of article 3 as a means by which judicial or administrative authorities could ascertain a child's best interests in a given case.

29.       One delegate stated that although the idea contained in the paragraph under consideration was correct, the characterization of "the age of reason" was very difficult. He also believed that views of children could be expressed in court through their legal guardians. The observer of the International Association of Penal Law suggested that language should be borrowed from article 7 to replace the phrase "has reached the age of reason". The Working Group agreed to replace the words "the age of reason" by the following words of article 7: "is capable of forming his own views".

30.       The representative of Brazil said that it would be preferable to insert the words "shall be provided" after the words "an opportunity". A further suggestion, made by the representative of the Netherlands, was that in the [second] line of the paragraph, the phrase "either directly or indirectly through a representative" should be inserted after the word "heard". In addition, proposals were made to delete the word "independent" from the [second] line of the paragraph and to add the following phrase at the end of that paragraph: "in a manner consistent with the procedures followed in the State Party for the application of its legislation".

31.       One representative stated that, because no provision had yet been made for determining the best interests of a child not capable of forming his own views, the Working Group might need to revert to that point at a later stage.

32.       The paragraph as revised and adopted by the Working Group read as follows:

"In all judicial or administrative proceedings affecting a child that is capable of forming his own views, an opportunity shall be provided for the views of the child to be heard, either directly or indirectly through a representative, as a party to the proceedings, and those views shall be taken into consideration by the competent authorities, in a manner consistent with the procedures followed in the State Party for the application of its legislation."

[...]

73.       Article 7 of the revised Polish draft read as follows:

"The States parties to the present Convention shall enable the child who is capable of forming his own views the right to express his opinion in matters concerning his own person, and in particular, marriage, choice of occupation, medical treatment, education and recreation."

74.     The representative of Australia proposed that the article should read:

"The States parties to the present Convention shall assure to the child the right to express his opinion in matters concerning his own person, and in particular marriage, choice of occupation, medical treatment, education and recreation. In all such matters the wishes of the child shall be given due weight in accordance with his age and maturity."

75.     The delegation of Denmark felt that it was not sufficient to state that the child has the right to express his opinion in matters concerning his own person; therefore, the concept that the child should as soon as possible have an influence in matters concerning his person should be expanded. Accordingly, the representative of Denmark proposed the following amendment:

"Parents or other guardians have the right and duty to decide in matters concerning the person of the child. But the child shall, as soon as possible, have an influence in such matters. As the child gets older, the parents or the guardian should give him more and more responsibility for personal matters with the aim of preparing the child for the life of a grown-up."

76.     The representative of the United States put forward for consideration a revised version of article 7 which read:

"The States parties to the present Convention shall enable the child who is capable of forming his own views the right to express his opinion effectively and non-violently in matters concerning his own person, and in particular, religion, political and social beliefs, matters of conscience, cultural and artistic matters, marriage, choice of occupation, medical treatment, education, travel, place of residence, and recreation."

77.     A discussion was held on the phrases "The States parties to the present Convention shall enable the child" (first line of the revised Polish draft and of the proposal of the delegation of the United States) and "The States parties to the present Convention shall assure to the child" (first line of the Australian proposal) as well as the term "effectively" qualifying the phrase "to express his opinion". One speaker pointed out that the State is under no obligation, as a matter of law, towards children: the child should have a degree of freedom comparable to that enjoyed by an individual under the Covenants and comparable instruments of law.

78.     Most delegations felt that the matters concerning the child in which the States parties to the convention would enable him to express his opinion should not be subject to the limits of a list, and therefore the list ought to be deleted.

79.     The representative of the United States suggested the insertion of the word "all" before the word "matters" if the Working Group decided to eliminate the aforementioned list. The representative of Canada proposed the insertion of the word "freely" after the word "opinion".

80.     After further discussion, a compromise text was adopted which read as follows:

"The States parties to the present Convention shall assure to the child who is capable of forming his own views the right to express his opinion freely in all matters, the wishes of the child being given due weight in accordance with his age and maturity."

81.     One delegation stated that the text as adopted would need to be examined carefully from a legal point of view to determine whether it might comply with general rules relating to standing in legal and administrative proceedings. The representative also noted that it might be necessary at a later stage for the Working Group to consider the desirability of including provisions concerning the need to discover the best interests of children not yet capable of forming their own views.

## 5. Comment submitted to the Working Group (1986)

### (a) Bangladesh

*The following comment regarding article 7 (present article 12) is contained in a paper submitted by the Permanent Representative of Bangladesh to the United Nations Office at Geneva with the request that the paper be annexed to the report of the Working Group. For the complete text, including general comments on the draft convention, see document E/CN.4/1986/39, annex IV.*

Article 7 is an article which it will be difficult to implement since it has not been sufficiently crystallized into recognizable legal categories.

## 6. Proposal submitted to the Working Group (1988)

### (a) NGO Ad Hoc Group *(see annex III (B) for participating organizations)*

*In a paper submitted to the Working Group, the NGO Ad Hoc Group proposed an alternative article 7 to take "into account the need to distinguish between freedom of expression, freedom of association, freedom of peaceful assembly and protection of privacy." The following proposal is taken from document E/CN.4/1988/WG.1/WP.2, page 10.*

1.    The States parties to the present Convention shall assure to the child who is capable of forming his or her own views the right to express an opinion freely in all matters. The wishes of the child shall be given due weight in accordance with his of her age and maturity.

2.    Every child shall have the right to seek, receive and impart information and ideas, either orally, in writing, in art form or in any other media of the child's choice.

## 7. Text as adopted at first reading

*The following is taken from document E/CN.4/1988/WG.1/WP.1/Rev.1.*

*Article 7*

The States Parties to the present Convention shall assure to the child who is capable of forming his own views the right to express his opinion freely in all matters, the wishes of the child being given due weight in accordance with his age and maturity.

# D.   Technical review (1988)

## 1.   Comment by the United Nations Children's Fund (UNICEF)

*The following is taken from document E/CN.4/1989/WG.1/CRP.1, pages 21-22.*

As noted above in respect of *article 3, paragraph 2,* consideration might be given to using the phrase "expressing his own views" rather than "forming his own views". Similarly, the word "wishes" might be replaced by the word "views", since the intention appears to be to take account of all views and not only those which constitute wishes.

*Gender neutrality*

The article could be reformulated as follows:

"The States Parties to the present Convention shall assure to the child who is capable of forming his *or her* own views the right to express [ ] opinions freely in all matters, the wishes of the child being given due weight in accordance with *the child's* age and maturity."

## 2. Additional comments and clarifications by the Secretariat

*The following is taken from document E/CN.4/1989/WG.1/CRP.1/Add.1, paragraph 15.*

15.     Because article 7 introduces a new restriction on the freedom of expression, namely, that the child be capable of forming his/her own views, there arises a possible conflict with article 7a which itself follows article 19, paragraphs 2 and 3, of the International Covenant on Civil and Political Rights. Taking into account, in addition, the comments by UNICEF in document E/CN.4/1989/WG.1/CRP.1 concerning the word "wishes", the Working Group may wish to delete article 7 and add a new paragraph 3 to article 7a reading:

> *"(c)     The views of the child shall be given due weight in accordance with his or her age and maturity."*

# E.     Second reading (1988-1989)

## 1.     Discussion and adoption at second reading

*The following is taken from the 1989 report of the Working Group to the Commission on Human Rights (E/CN.4/1989/48, paras. 234 to 267).*

234.     The Working Group had before it article 7 as adopted at first reading (E/CN.4/1989/WG.1/WP.2):

> "The States Parties to the present Convention shall assure to the child who is capable of forming his own views the right to express his opinion freely in all matters, the wishes of the child being given due weight in accordance with his age and maturity."

235.     The Working Group also had before it a proposal submitted by Finland on behalf of a drafting group (E/CN.4/1989/WG.1/WP.35) which read as follows:

> "1.     The States Parties to the present Convention shall assure to the child who is capable of forming his *or her* own views the right to express those views freely in all matters *affecting the child*, the *views* of the child being given due weight in accordance with (his) *the* age and maturity of *the child*.
>
> 2.     *For this purpose, the child shall in particular be provided the opportunity to be heard in any judicial and administrative proceedings affecting the child, either directly, through a representative or an appropriate body, in accordance with the procedural rules of national law."*

236.     The observer for Finland stated that the basic idea contained in this proposal had already been introduced in relation to article 3, paragraph 2, and that the purpose was the addition of article 3, paragraph 2 (which had been deleted) under article 7 as paragraph 2, with some changes (underlined in E/CN.4/1989/WG.1/WP.35).

237.     The observer for the Netherlands declared that it could warmly support the proposal if only the meaning of "in accordance with the procedural rules of national law" was clearer. It then suggested the use of "in a manner consistent with the procedural ...".

238.     The Finnish delegate answered that the purpose was not to change the text in a substantive manner and that in case the hearing of the child's opinion required some international legal assistance, the requesting State's procedure should also be taken into account. He otherwise agreed with the use of "in a manner consistent with".

239.     The delegation of Venezuela pronounced itself in favour of the proposal of the Netherlands or suggested the use of "applicable rules of national law".

240.     The delegate of Norway expressed its satisfaction with the proposal.

241. The representative of the Union of Soviet Socialist Republics asked for clarification of the meaning of "… in all matters affecting the child" under paragraph 1.

242. The representative of Japan stated that he supported the proposal with the understanding that "affecting the child" meant "affecting the rights of the child".

243. The observer for Finland repeated its earlier wish of not undertaking substantive changes and since it was based on article 3, paragraph 2, the text should remain this way and could also be interpreted the way Japan suggested.

244. The delegate of Italy, while in agreement with Finland, proposed to introduce the expression "regarding the rights of the child" as a technical suggestion.

245. The observer for Kuwait expressed her support for the proposal as in E/CN.4/1989/WG.1/WP.35.

246. The delegation of the Union of Soviet Socialist Republics, while declaring that the article did not pose any problem as a whole, drew attention to the difficulty of interpretation especially in relation with article 7a, paragraph 1, since both referred to the same rights, but through a different wording. The delegate asked for more specificity under paragraph 1 and pronounced himself in favour of the Japanese proposal, namely the use of "… affecting the rights of the child …".

247. The representative of Portugal expressed her concern over the neglect of the word "directly" under paragraph 2 of the proposal and drew attention to the danger it represented as a restriction of the child's own freedom of expression.

248. The observer for Canada stated that the concern expressed by Portugal was not founded since the actual wording in English already provided for the alternatives but that the word "or" could be added for more clarity. He observed, however, that if the Japanese proposal was accepted, the matters dealt with in the convention not covering the rights (and still affecting the children) could be endangered.

249. The observer for Finland proposed that paragraph 1 remain as in E/CN.4/1989/WG.1/WP.35 with the deletion of the word "his" already in brackets, and that under paragraph 2, "in accordance with" be replaced by "in a manner consistent with".

250. The Chairman proposed the addition of the word "or" after the word "directly" under paragraph 2, in order to satisfy Portugal's concern.

251. The representative of Japan agreed with the last Finnish proposal.

252. Reservations were expressed by the delegations of China, Japan and the Union of Soviet Socialist Republics.

253. The Working Group then adopted paragraph 1 to read as follows:

"1. States Parties shall assure to the child who is capable of forming his or her own views the right to express those views freely in all matters affecting the child, the views of the child being given due weight in accordance with the age and maturity of the child."

254. Following the adoption of paragraph 1, the observer for Finland gave a reading of paragraph 2 as it appears in E/CN.4/1989/WG.1/WP.35 with the addition of the word "or" after the word "directly".

255. The delegate of Venezuela repeated her wish for the deletion of "the procedural laws" in favour of the "applicable rules of national law".

256. The observer for Finland objected to this change and judged essential that the "procedural laws" be referred to.

257. The delegation of Japan agreed with the view expressed by the observer for Finland.

258.     The delegate of Venezuela withdrew her proposal.

259.     The representative of Senegal declared that since national law already contained procedural rules, the inclusion of the latter was unnecessary.

260.     The delegate of the Federal Republic of Germany expressed its agreement with the Senegalese position.

261.     The delegate from India proposed the replacement of "procedural rules" by "in accordance with procedure established by law".

262.     The delegation of Italy suggested "in a manner consistent with national law".

263.     The observers for Canada and Finland spoke in favour of the text as originally proposed.

264.     The Working Group adopted paragraph 2 of article 7 reading as follows:

> "2.     For this purpose, the child shall in particular be provided the opportunity to be heard in any judicial and administrative proceedings affecting the child, either directly, or through a representative or an appropriate body, in a manner consistent with the procedural rules of national law."

265.     The delegation of India made a declaration to the effect that in its understanding the expression "procedural rules of national law" in article 7a, paragraph 2, adopted at second reading had the same meaning as the expression "procedures followed in the State Party for the application of its legislation" contained in article 3, paragraph 2, of the draft convention as adopted at first reading.

266.     The delegation of Senegal also made the following declaration in this regard:

> While associating itself with the consensus for the adoption of article 7, Senegal wishes to specify that the English expression "with the procedural rules of national law" should be understood to mean the more generic and precise French term *de législation nationale applicable*.

267.     The observer for Finland voiced his support for the declaration made by the delegation of India.

## F.     Related references

*For further research, see the legislative history of article 3, particularly paragraph 2 of the article as adopted at the first reading, which was subsequently deleted at the second reading in view of its overlap with article 12.*

# Article 13 (Freedom of expression)

## A.   Final text adopted by the General Assembly (1989)

*The following text is that approved by the General Assembly in its resolution 44/25 of 20 November 1989.*

> 1.       The child shall have the right to freedom of expression; this right shall include freedom to seek, receive and impart information and ideas of all kinds, regardless of frontiers, either orally, in writing or in print, in the form of art, or through any other media of the child's choice.
>
> 2.       The exercise of this right may be subject to certain restrictions, but these shall only be such as are provided by law and are necessary:
>
> > (a)       For respect of the rights or reputations of others; or
> >
> > (b)       For the protection of national security or of public order (*ordre public*), or of public health or morals.

## B.   First Polish draft convention and comments (1978)

*Neither the first Polish draft nor the views received on it (see document E/CN.4/1324 and Corr.1 and Add.1-5) addressed the issues raised in article 13 of the Convention.*

## C.   First reading (1979-1988)

*The issues raised under article 13 were first discussed by the Working Group in 1987 and a text concerning freedom of expression was adopted in 1988. This article was referred to as article 7a throughout the first and second readings.*

### 1.       Proposal submitted to the Working Group (1985)

#### (a)       United States of America

*The following is taken from the 1985 report of the Working Group to the Commission on Human Rights (E/CN.4/1985/64, annex II, p. 3).*

> *Article 16 bis*
>
> The States Parties to the present Convention shall ensure that the child shall enjoy civil and political rights and freedoms in public life to the fullest extent commensurate with his age including in particular, freedom from arbitrary governmental interference with privacy, family, home or correspondence; the right to petition for redress of grievances; and, subject only to such reasonable restrictions provided by law as are necessary for respect of the rights and legally protected interests of others or for the protection of national security, public safety and order, or public health and morals, freedom of association and expression; and the right of peaceful assembly.

### 2.       Proposal submitted to the Working Group (1987)

#### (a)       United States of America

*For the text of this proposal, see paragraph 111 in section 3 below.*

### 3.       Discussion in the Working Group (1987)

*The following is taken from the 1987 report of the Working Group to the Commission on Human Rights (E/CN.4/1987/25, paras. 111-118).*

111.    The Working Group had before it the following revised proposal, submitted by the delegation of the United States, of a text that had been put forward by the representative of the United States during the Working Group's 1986 session:

"1.    States Parties to the present Convention recognize the rights of the child to freedom of expression, freedom of association and freedom of peaceful assembly.

2.    States Parties recognize the right of the child not to be subjected to arbitrary or unlawful interference with his or her privacy, family, home or correspondence.

3.    The exercise of the rights to freedom of expression, association and peaceful assembly shall be subject only to those restrictions which are provided by law and which are necessary in a democratic society in the interests of national security, public order ("*ordre public*"), the protection of public health and morals or the protection of the rights and freedoms of others.

4.    In no case shall a child be subjected to incarceration or other confinement for the legitimate exercise of these rights or other rights recognized in this Convention.

5.    This article shall not be interpreted as affecting the lawful rights and duties of parents or legal guardians, which should be exercised in a manner consistent with the evolving capacities of the child."

112.    The representative of the United States said that the protection of children's civil and political rights was of fundamental importance to his country, particularly because the "child", as defined in the draft convention, included adolescents who had often acquired the skills needed to participate fully and effectively in society. He noted that the draft convention already protected certain other fundamental rights, including the right to freedom of religion. He also explained that the rights in the draft article were universally accepted and were contained in the Universal Declaration of Human Rights and in the International Covenant on Civil and Political Rights.

113.    The Chairman suggested that the proposal submitted by the representative of the United States could carry the number 7 ter, and this suggestion met with the agreement of the American delegation.

114.    A lengthy discussion ensued dealing with the merits of such a proposal. During this general discussion, some delegations made observations concerning different aspects of the proposal. For example, the representative of the United Kingdom said, inter alia, that already existent international instruments dealt with certain parts of the proposal, and suggested that the language in which the draft article was worded called for some clarification. The delegation of Australia, although generally supporting the proposal, raised some questions remarking among other things that there appeared to be confusion about the freedoms of association and expression and that of privacy, as well as that the proposal made no provision whatsoever for the evolving sense of responsibility of children.

115.    The delegation of Norway, in supporting the American proposal, shared the concern of the Australian delegation that there was a need for a general provision dealing with the evolving capacities of the child. The observer for Canada indicated her support for the proposal put forward by the United States representative and her wish that the principle set out in paragraph 5 of draft article 7 ter be dealt with in a comprehensive manner in a general article. The representative of Argentina, although in general favourable to the draft article, voiced the same concerns as other delegations regarding its paragraph 5, and found that there was much to be clarified in the proposal being considered by the Working Group.

116.    The representative of the USSR indicated that he was not in a position to support draft article 7 ter as it stood, and considered that the draft convention should deal with new issues and not reproduce provisions already existing in international instruments. He raised the question as to why the proposal focused on certain civil and political rights and bypassed others, suggesting to break down the proposed article and

proceed to separate the civil from the political rights in an approach that would not be selective, yet fully consistent with the provisions of the International Covenant on Civil and Political Rights.

117.      The Chinese delegation was not in a position to accept the United States proposal. It was of the opinion that the freedoms of association, peaceful assembly and privacy could not be enjoyed by children in the same way as they are enjoyed by adults because the intellect of a child was not as developed as that of an adult, and therefore a child could only engage in activities commensurate with its intellect. The observer for Sweden indicated her support for the text tabled by the delegation of the United States, but called for a separate article on the evolving capacities of the child.

118.      The Chairman voiced his hope that the representative of the United States would propose a revised text for article 7 ter and that in doing so would take into account the Working Group's observations. The delegation of the United States accepted the Chairman's suggestion to consider the comments made by other delegations and to resubmit article 7 ter for consideration by the Working Group at its 1988 session. It stated that in doing so, it was its understanding that the proposal would be considered early in the Working Group's deliberations.

## 4.      Proposals submitted to the Working Group (1988)

### (a)      United States of America

*For the text of this proposal, see paragraph 35 in section 5 below.*

### (b)      NGO Ad Hoc Group *(see annex III (B) for participating organizations)*

*In a paper submitted to the Working Group, the NGO Ad Hoc Group proposed an alternative article 7 to take "into account the need to distinguish between freedom of expression, freedom of association, freedom of peaceful assembly and protection of privacy." The following proposal is taken from document E/CN.4/1988/WG.1/WP.2, page 10.*

1.      The States parties to the present Convention shall assure to the child who is capable of forming his or her own views the right to express an opinion freely in all matters. The wishes of the child shall be given due weight in accordance with his of her age and maturity.

2.      Every child shall have the right to seek, receive and impart information and ideas, either orally, in writing, in art form or in any other media of the child's choice.

## 5.      Discussion and adoption by the Working Group (1988)

*The following is taken from the 1988 report of the Working Group to the Commission on Human Rights (E/CN.4/1988/28, paras. 35-46).*

35.      The Working Group had before it a proposal submitted by the United States of America on civil and political rights of the child (E/CN.4/1988/WG.1/WP.18) which read as follows:

[...]

"I. ADDITIONS TO ARTICLE 7 (FREEDOM OF EXPRESSION)

1.      (Already adopted) The States Parties to the present Convention shall assure to the child who is capable of forming his (or her) own views the right to express his (or her) own opinion freely in all matters, the wishes of the child being given due weight in accordance with his (or her) age and maturity.

(Additional sentence) This right shall include freedom to seek, receive and impart information and ideas of all kinds, regardless of frontiers, either orally, in writing or in print, in the form of art, or through any other media of the child's choice.

2.	(Additional paragraph) The exercise of this right may be subject to certain restrictions, but these shall only be such as are provided by law and are necessary:

(a)	For respect of the rights and reputations of others; or

(b)	For the protection of national security or of public order (*ordre public*), or of public health or morals.

3.	(Additional paragraph) States Parties shall respect the rights and duties of parents and, where applicable, legal guardians, to provide direction to the child in the exercise of this right in a manner consistent with the evolving capacities of the child."

[...]

36.	In introducing that proposal, the representative of the United States of America stated that children not only had the right to expect certain benefits from their Governments; they also had civil and political rights to protect them from abusive action of their Governments. These rights are largely the same as those enjoyed by adults, although it is generally recognized that children do not have the right to vote. While children might need direction and guidance from parents or legal guardians in the exercise of these rights, this does not affect the content of the rights themselves. The United States proposal was intended to complete the process already begun by the Working Group of incorporating provisions from the International Covenant on Civil and Political Rights into the draft convention. The proposal reflects the recognition contained in the International Covenant that the ability of all individuals to exercise civil and political rights is not absolute, but is subject to certain limited restrictions that may be imposed by States. The proposal was designed to incorporate into the draft convention the right to freedom of expression, the right to freedom of association and to peaceful assembly, and certain privacy rights as elaborated in the International Covenant. The representative of the United States reminded the Working Group that these rights protect children from action of the State, and would not affect the legitimate rights of parents or legal guardians to provide direction and guidance to children.

37.	The idea of including civil and political rights in the draft convention to reinforce the protection of children was strongly supported by several participants. However, the legitimate rights of parents and tutors should be safeguarded, the balance between rights of children and rights of the family should be preserved and the wording of the article should be in line with the Covenants.

38.	The view was expressed that, if parents should be protected from States, the child should be protected from parents. The following additional paragraph was thus proposed for insertion in article 7 quater:

"States Parties to the present Convention shall respect the right of the child to the protection of law against such interference or attacks."

39.	The representative of the United States of America stated that the proposed additional sentence on the freedom to seek, receive and impart information and ideas of all kinds had been taken verbatim from article 19, paragraph 2, of the International Covenant on Civil and Political Rights.

40.	The observer for Finland was of the view that criticisms could be avoided if the proposal dealt with the child's right to express opinion instead of the child's freedom of opinion. He proposed the inclusion of paragraphs 2 and 3 of article 7 in a separate article 7 ter:

"1.	The child shall have the right to hold opinions.

2.	The child shall have the right of expression: this right shall include freedom to seek, receive and impart information and ideas of all kinds, regardless of frontiers, either orally, in writing or in print, in the form of art, or through any other media of the child's choice."

41.	The representative of China, supporting the view that the child should have the right fully to express its own views on questions concerning it, proposed that article 7 be revised. As to the right of the child to seek, receive and impart information, the second additional sentence could be amalgamated with the first one, to read as follows:

> "The States Parties to the present Convention shall assure to the child who is capable of forming his or her own views the freedom to seek, receive and impart information and ideas of all kinds, the right to express his or her own opinion freely in all matters, the wishes of the child being given due weight in accordance with his or her age and maturity."

42.    The observer for Morocco reiterated the following reservations made with regard to article 7 bis at previous sessions of the Working Group: the combination of the provisions in articles 3 and 7 led to the following results: (a) the best interests of the child prevailed over any other consideration; (b) a child who was capable of forming his own views could be heard in a juridical proceeding; (c) the commitment by States to the convention was compulsory regardless of religious considerations. The above rule not only raised a problem of assessment of the best interests of the child and his capacity of forming his own views, but was in contradiction with certain provisions of the Moroccan Code on Personal Status. Furthermore, article 7 bis, which allowed the child (under the age of 18) freely to choose his religion, ran counter to the principles of Muslim law: the child of a Muslim was bound to be a Muslim, and in order to renounce that fact, he had to conform to the rules of Muslim law on the matter.

43.    There was a general consensus on not reopening the discussion on texts already adopted. It was stated that article 7, as already adopted, reflected globally all points of view and covered all aspects relating to divorce, adoption, custody and career development concerning minors.

44.    A small drafting group (Finland, Poland, Senegal, and the United States of America), referring to article 19 of the International Covenant on Civil and Political Rights, submitted the following text:

> "1.    The child shall have the right to hold opinions without interference.
>
> 2.    The child shall have the right to freedom of expression; this right shall include freedom to seek, receive and impart information and ideas of all kinds, regardless of frontiers, either orally, in writing or in print, in the form of art, or through any other media of the child's choice.
>
> 3.    The exercise of this right provided for in paragraph 2 of this article may be subject to certain restrictions, but these shall only be such as are provided by law and are necessary:
>
> > (a)    For respect of the rights and reputations of others; or
> >
> > (b)    For the protection of national security or of public order (*ordre public*), or of public health or morals.
>
> 4.    States Parties shall respect the rights and duties of parents and, where applicable, legal guardians, to provide direction to the child in the exercise of this right in a manner consistent with the evolving capacities of the child."

45.    It was proposed that the words "without interference" should be deleted, since in Spanish, the word "*interferencia*" meant obstacles, and to incorporate paragraph 1 as amended into paragraph 2 or to delete paragraph 1.

46.    The Working Group reached consensus on deleting paragraph 1, and adopted paragraphs 2 and 3 of article 7a, to be renumbered accordingly, which read as follows:

> "1.    The child shall have the right to freedom of expression; this right shall include freedom to seek, receive and impart information and ideas of all kinds, regardless of frontiers, either orally, in writing or in print, in the form of art, or through any other media of the child's choice.
>
> 2.    The exercise of this right may be subject to certain restrictions, but these shall only be such as are provided by law and are necessary:

(a)     for respect of the rights and reputations of others; or

(b)     for the protection of national security or of public order (*ordre public*), or of public health or morals."

## 6.     Text as adopted at first reading

*The following is taken from document E/CN.4/1988/WG.1/WP.1/Rev.1.*

*Article 7a*

1.     The child shall have the right to freedom of expression; this right shall include freedom to seek, receive and impart information and ideas of all kinds, regardless of frontiers, either orally, in writing or in print, in the form of art, or through any other media of the child's choice.

2.     The exercise of this right may be subject to certain restrictions, but these shall only be such as are provided by law and are necessary:

(a)     for respect of the rights and reputations of others; or

(b)     for the protection of national security or of public order (*ordre public*), or of public health or morals.

# D.     Technical review (1988)

## 1.     Comment by the United Nations Children's Fund (UNICEF)

*The following is taken from document E/CN.4/1989/WG.1/CRP.1, page 22.*

*Paragraph 2 (a)*

In order to ensure consistency with the International Covenant on Civil and Political Rights (article 19, paragraph 3) the subparagraph should refer to the "rights or reputations of others".

## 2.     Additional comments and clarifications by the Secretariat

*The following is taken from document E/CN.4/1989/WG.1/CRP.1/Add.1.*

16.     See above under article 7.

*The comments referred to are the following:*

15.     Because article 7 introduces a new restriction on the freedom of expression, namely, that the child be capable of forming his/her own views, there arises a possible conflict with article 7a which itself follows article 19, paragraphs 2 and 3, of the International Covenant on Civil and Political Rights. Taking into account, in addition, the comments by UNICEF in document E/CN.4/1989/WG.1/CRP.1 concerning the word "wishes", the Working Group may wish to delete article 7 and add a new paragraph 3 to article 7a reading:

*"(c) The views of the child shall be given due weight in accordance with his or her age and maturity."*

# E.     Second reading (1988-1989)

## 1.     Proposal submitted to the Working Group at second reading

### (a)     German Democratic Republic

*For the text of this proposal, see paragraph 269 in section 2 below.*

## 2.　　Discussion and adoption at second reading

*The following is taken from the 1989 report of the Working Group to the Commission on Human Rights (E/CN.4/1989/48, paras. 268 to 279).*

268.　　The Working Group had before it article 7a as adopted at first reading (E/CN.4/1989/WG.1/WP.2):

"1.　　The child shall have the right to freedom of expression; this right shall include freedom to seek, receive and impart information and ideas of all kinds, regardless of frontiers, either orally, in writing or in print, in the form of art, or through any other media of the child's choice.

2.　　The exercise of this right may be subject to certain restrictions, but these shall only be such as are provided by law and are necessary:

(a)　　for respect of the rights and reputations of others; or

(b)　　for the protection of national security or of public order (*ordre public*), or of public health or morals."

269.　　The Chairman declared that since article 7 had been kept the suggestions made by UNICEF and the Secretariat (E/CN.4/1989/WG.1/WP.2) for its deletion and its addition under article 7a as paragraph 2 (c), were not retained and that the only proposal of amendment came from the German Democratic Republic in E/CN.4/1989/WG.1/WP.39, reading as follows:

"Add the following phrase to paragraph 2b (amendments [in italics])

(b)　　for the protection of national security or of public order (*ordre public*), or of public health or morals, *or the spiritual and moral well-being of the child;* or"

270.　　The delegation of the German Democratic Republic took the floor in order to point out that article 7a stemmed from article 19 of the International Covenant on Civil and Political Rights and that this amendment was in view of the addition of article 20 of the Covenant. He added that the purpose was to cover certain dangers of violent information disseminated by the mass media.

271.　　The representative of China declared her support for the amendment.

272.　　The delegate of the United States of America reminded the Working Group that this article had been adopted the previous year and that he could not agree with the amendment since such extra restrictions of freedom of expression were to be avoided; and that this restriction did not appear anywhere in the International Covenant on Civil and Political Rights and it would thus be unfair to impose it on children alone. Further, this article also covered the right of children to expression and such a restriction could be used as an excuse to curtail this right. He added that the paternalistic flavour of the amendment was against the spirit of the convention.

273.　　The delegate of Portugal declared that the amendment was superfluous since article 5 bis on the parents' rights and duties already covered the issue of the guidance of children, not to mention the Preamble as well as article 16 concerning the purposes of education.

274.　　The observer for Australia objected to the amendment on the same grounds and drew attention to national legislation that already protects children (by, for example, film classification). The Australian delegate declared that if the amendment was accepted then the following should be added: "... or, in the case of received information."

275.　　The delegation of Poland declared that the proposal of the German Democratic Republic deserved attention.

276.　　The representative of Sweden objected to the proposal and warned against the undermining of the existing standards.

277.    The delegations of Canada and Argentina stated that the matter was already dealt with under article 9, and the latter proposed the creation of a special drafting group.

278.    The delegate of the German Democratic Republic declared it would not insist on the amendment.

279.    The suggested revision contained in document E/CN.4/1989/WG.1/WP.2 to substitute the word "or" in subparagraph 2 (a) of the article for the word "and" was agreed to and the Working Group went on to adopt article 7a to read as follows:

"1.    The child shall have the right to freedom of expression; this right shall include freedom to seek, receive and impart information and ideas of all kinds, regardless of frontiers, either orally, in writing or in print, in the form of art, or through any other media of the child's choice.

2.    The exercise of this right may be subject to certain restrictions, but these shall only be such as are provided by law and are necessary:

(a)    for respect of the rights or reputations of others; or

(b)    for the protection of national security or of public order (*ordre public*), or of public health or morals."

# Article 14 (Freedom of thought, conscience and religion)

## A.    Final text adopted by the General Assembly (1989)

*The following text is that approved by the General Assembly in its resolution 44/25 of 20 November 1989.*

1.        States Parties shall respect the right of the child to freedom of thought, conscience and religion.

2.        States Parties shall respect the rights and duties of the parents and, when applicable, legal guardians, to provide direction to the child in the exercise of his or her right in a manner consistent with the evolving capacities of the child.

3.        Freedom to manifest one's religion or beliefs may be subject only to such limitations as are prescribed by law and are necessary to protect public safety, order, health or morals, or the fundamental rights and freedoms of others.

## B.    First Polish draft convention and comments (1978)

*Neither the first Polish draft nor the views received on it (see document E/CN.4/1324 and Corr.1 and Add.1-5) addressed the issues raised in article 14 of the Convention.*

## C.    First reading (1979-1988)

*The issues raised under article 14 were discussed by the Working Group in 1983 and the text was adopted in 1984. This article was referred to as article 7 bis throughout the first and second readings.*

### 1.    Proposal submitted to the Working Group (1982)

**(a)    United States of America**

*For the text of this proposal, see paragraph 52 in section 2 below.*

### 2.    Discussion in the Working Group (1983)

*The following is taken from the 1983 report of the Working Group to the Commission on Human Rights (E/CN.4/1983/62, paras. 52-57).*

52.        The representative of the United States reintroduced a proposal he had made in 1982 (E/1982/12/Add.1, part C, para. 118). The proposal read as follows:

"1.        The States Parties to the present Convention shall ensure that the child has the right to freedom of thought, conscience and religion, including the freedom to have or to adopt a religion or belief of his choice, and freedom, either individually or in community with others and in public or private, to manifest his religion or belief in worship, observance, practice and teaching.

2.        The States Parties to the present Convention shall ensure that no child is subject to coercion which would impair his freedom to have or to adopt a religion or belief of his choice.

3.        The States Parties to the present Convention shall ensure that the child's freedom to manifest his religion or beliefs may be subject only to such limitations as are prescribed by law and are necessary to protect public safety, order, health, or morals or the fundamental rights and freedoms of others.

4.        The States Parties to the present Convention shall ensure that the child has:

(a)     the freedom to worship or assemble with others in connection with his religion or belief;

(b)     the freedom to make, to acquire and to use to an adequate extent the necessary articles and materials related to the rites or customs of a religion or belief;

(c)     the freedom to observe days of rest and to celebrate holidays and ceremonies in accordance with the precepts of his religion or belief; and

(d)     the freedom to establish and maintain communications with individuals and communities in matters of religion and belief at the national and international levels."

53.     Several speakers supported the idea of including in the draft convention a specific provision on the right of the child to freedom of thought, conscience and religion, as well as access to religious education. It was also said that the formulation on the matter which is contained in other international instruments could also be used in the draft convention. Reference was made to the Declaration on the Elimination of All Forms of Intolerance on Religion or Belief and to paragraph 4 of article 18 of the International Covenant on Civil and Political Rights.

54.     Several other speakers were of the opinion that a specific provision on religious education and the right to practise religion was not necessary in the draft convention, since the matter was already covered by other proposals. Reference was made in this connection to the proposals contained in the draft convention submitted by Poland (E/CN.4/1349).

55.     Although not necessarily opposed to the inclusion of an article on religion in the draft convention, some speakers expressed doubts as to whether it should be the responsibility of the State to ensure that the child has the right to freedom of thought, conscience and religion. In many countries, it was noted, a child follows the religion of his parents and does not generally make a choice of his own. It was also observed that the right to practise religion had to be applied within the limits permitted by public order, safety and morals.

56.     No agreement was reached as regards the adoption of the United States proposal as article 7 bis of the draft convention.

57.     The representative of the United States submitted a revised version of his proposal. As revised, the text reads:

"1.     The States Parties to the present Convention shall ensure that the child has the right to freedom of thought, conscience and religion, including the right to have a religion or whatever belief of his choice, and freedom, either individually or in community with others and in public or private, to manifest, in a manner not incompatible with public order and morals, his religion or belief in worship, observance, practice and teaching.

2.     The States Parties shall ensure that no child is subject to coercion which would impair his freedom to have a religion or belief of his choice and shall ensure that every child shall enjoy the right to have access to education in the matter of religion or belief in accordance with the wishes of his parents or, as the case may be, legal guardians, and shall not be compelled to receive teaching on religion or belief against the wishes of his parents or legal guardians.

3.     The States Parties to the present Convention undertake to have respect for the liberty of parents and, when applicable, legal guardians to ensure the religious and moral education of their children in conformity with their own convictions."

# 3. Proposals submitted to the Working Group (1984)

## (a)    Canada

*For the text of this proposal, see paragraph 13 in section 4 below.*

## (b)    Denmark, Finland, Norway and Sweden

*For the text of this proposal, see paragraph 13 in section 4 below.*

# 4. Discussion and adoption by the Working Group (1984)

*The following is taken from the 1984 report of the Working Group to the Commission on Human Rights (E/CN.4/1984/71, paras. 13-33).*

13.    There were three texts for consideration by the Working Group to be taken as the basis for discussion. Firstly, there was the amended text, submitted in 1983, of an original United States proposal made in 1982, as set out in paragraph 57 of document E/CN.4/1983/62. Secondly, the delegation of Canada proposed the following text:

> "The States Parties to the present Convention undertake to ensure the freedom of thought, conscience and religion of the child in accordance with the Universal Declaration of Human Rights and other international instruments that relate to this freedom and subject to the authority of the parents or legal guardian to provide direction to the child in the exercise of this freedom in a manner consistent with the evolving capacities of the child and not incompatible with public order and morals."

Thirdly, the representative of Sweden introduced the following text elaborated by the delegations of Denmark, Finland, Norway and his own:

> "1.    The States Parties to the present Convention shall ensure to the child the right to freedom of thought, conscience and religion.
>
> 2.    These rights shall include in particular the right to have or to adopt a religion or whatsoever belief of his choice, and freedom, either individually or in community with others and in public or private, to manifest his religion or belief, and the right to have unimpeded access to education in the matter of religion and belief of his choice.
>
> 3.    The States Parties shall, subject to the evolving capacities of the child, respect the wishes, freedoms and rights of the parents or legal guardians in the exercise of these rights of the child and shall ensure the freedom to manifest religion or belief, in a manner not incompatible with public safety, order, health and morals."

14.    The representative of the Ukrainian SSR accepted the Canadian proposal which he considered constituted a common denominator of the views presented by delegations at the Group's 1983 session.

15.    The representative of the Holy See expressed his hesitancy with regard to the various proposals notwithstanding their individual merits. The Canadian text was particularly appreciated due to its conciseness, but his delegation did not think that the right of the child to have or to choose a religion or belief was explicit enough. The United States proposal, although acceptable, did not meet with his delegation's full approval because the right of the child was not sufficiently affirmed in relation to the right of the parents to give the child a religion or a philosophical belief and to educate him therein. His delegation made similar observations with regard to the Scandinavian text, although it had some positive aspects, because the relationship of rights and the respect for the family environment were not adequately acknowledged and emphasized.

16.    A lengthy debate followed regarding the choice of the text to be utilized as a basis for discussion. The representatives of the Netherlands and the Ukrainian SSR suggested that a compromise text be elaborated after consultations, and the delegations of Canada and Sweden joined them in this suggestion. The Chairman therefore requested that a new draft be prepared by an informal open-ended working party, and it was so decided.

17.    The draft was introduced by the delegation of the United Kingdom and read as follows:

"1.    The States Parties to the present Convention shall recognize the right of the child to freedom of thought, conscience and religion in accordance with the principles of the Universal Declaration of Human Rights, the Declaration on the Elimination of All Forms of Intolerance and of Discrimination Based on Religion or Belief, and the International Covenant on Civil and Political Rights, and of other relevant international instruments.

2.    These rights shall include in particular the right to have or to adopt a religion or whatsoever belief of his choice, and freedom, either individually or in community with others and in public or private to manifest his religion or belief, in conformity with public safety, order, health and morals.

3.    This right is subject to the authority of the parents or legal guardians to provide direction to the child in the exercise of this right in a manner consistent with the evolving capacities of the child.

4.    The States Parties to the present Convention undertake to have respect of the liberty of the child and his parents, or, when applicable, legal guardians, to ensure the religious and moral education of the child."

This consolidated text was generally considered to be a useful basis for discussion.

*Paragraph 1*

18.    Many delegations viewed the enumeration of international instruments as unnecessary. Some suggested that reference be made to the Universal Declaration of Human Rights only, while others proposed adding the phrase "and other relevant international instruments". The representatives of the Federal Republic of Germany and of the German Democratic Republic wished that at least a reference to the International Covenant on Civil and Political Rights be included in the text, while the delegation of the Islamic Republic of Iran requested a reference to the International Convention on the Suppression and Punishment of the Crime of Apartheid.

19.    The representative of the United States proposed adding the phrase "and ensure" in the first line of paragraph 1, after the word "recognize". Some delegations found difficulty in accepting this proposal, if account was to be taken of the separation of Church and State in many countries, and preferred to keep the word "recognize".

20.    The United Kingdom delegation suggested that the word "recognize" should be replaced by the word "ensure", and several delegations agreed with that proposal. The United States representative expressed her preference for the words "shall ensure", and explained that if the right of freedom to unimpeded religious beliefs was ensured, that did not mean that the State would be obliged to provide religious education; she therefore agreed with the United Kingdom proposal.

21.    The opinion of the Group was divided among those who supported the inclusion of the word "ensure" and those who wished to retain the word "recognize". Finally, the representative of the Islamic Republic of Iran proposed that the words "and respect" be added after the word "recognize".

22.    The representative of the Holy See drew the attention of the Working Group to the fact that the Holy See used the words "to promote respect" in its "Charte des Droits de la Famille" of 22 October 1983. The representative of Australia then suggested that the word "recognize" be replaced by the word "respect", and

that proposal found acceptance among most delegations, including those of the United Kingdom and the United States which preferred that wording.

23.      The representative of the Netherlands expressed his belief that there should be no enumeration of international instruments and that consequently the first paragraph should end with the word "religion". Many delegations were sympathetic to his proposal and the Working Group proceeded to agree to paragraph 1 as amended.

*Paragraph 2*

24.      The representative of the Ukrainian SSR drew the attention of the Group to the fact that paragraph 2 began with the words "These rights", which should be amended to read "This right"; this amendment was accepted. The delegation of the United States suggested the insertion after the word "choice", of the phrase "and to be free from coercion which would impair his freedom in this respect". After the words "to manifest his religion or belief", the United States delegation requested the inclusion of the phrase "subject only to such limitations as are prescribed by law and are necessary to protect the" instead of "in conformity with". The delegation of the Ukrainian SSR was in favour of that amendment.

25.      The United States delegation also proposed that the phrase "and the right to have unimpeded access to and freedom from coercion with respect to education in the matter of religion or belief" be added at the end of the paragraph. The delegation of Australia suggested that the last proposal made by the representative of the United States be amended to read "and the right to have access to education in the matter of religion or belief".

26.      With respect to a query from the representative of the Ukrainian SSR as to whether such a reference to access to a right would create a precedent requiring a similar insertion in subsequent articles, the representative of the United States said that it would not, because it was only necessary to ensure access to a right, in addition to the right itself, in cases where it was particularly relevant to the right to protect access to it, as the Working Group had considered was the case in 1983 with regard to article 12.

27.      The delegation of the Netherlands proposed replacing the word "right" in the first line by the word "freedom". The Working Group was also reminded of the Ukrainian SSR proposal to begin the paragraph with the expression "This right". The delegation of the Netherlands also proposed the deletion of the word "the" between the words "to protect" and "public safety", and the placing of a comma between the phrases "in public or private" and "to manifest his religion". The representative of the United States then withdrew her first amendment to paragraph 2, namely the insertion of the phrase "and to be free from coercion which would impair his freedom in this respect".

28.      The Working Group agreed to the second paragraph as amended.

*Paragraph 3*

29.      The representative of Finland proposed that the word "authority" in the first line of the paragraph be replaced by the phrase "rights and duties", and this proposal was found acceptable by a majority of delegations. The United States delegation proposed that in the first line the phrase "This right is subject to" be replaced by the words "The States Parties shall respect".

30.      The representative of the Netherlands suggested that the word "or" between "parents" and "legal guardians" be replaced by the phrase "and, where applicable,". The United States delegation proposed that the words "this right" between the words "exercise of" and "in a manner" be amended to read "his right". All these amendments were accepted by the Working Group which agreed to paragraph 3.

*Paragraph 4*

31.      The representative of Canada proposed that the words "to the present Convention undertake to have" be replaced by the words "shall equally" in the first line of the paragraph and that the word "for" be

deleted between the words "respect" and "the liberty of the child". The delegation of the United States suggested that the word "or" between the words "parents" and "when applicable" be replaced by the word "and"; it also proposed the addition of the phrase ", and unimpeded access thereto, in conformity with their own convictions" at the end of the paragraph. The representative of Finland proposed that the phrase "when applicable" should read "where applicable".

32.      All the amendments mentioned above met with the acceptance of most delegations with the exception of the proposed addition at the end of the sentence made by the United States delegation. The representative of the United States therefore withdrew part of the proposed phrase leaving only the words "in conformity with their own convictions".

33.      The delegation of the Netherlands considered that if the United States representative was referring to the convictions of the child, then such a phrase was unnecessary. The United States representative explained that the phrase was meant to make it clear that the education was to be in conformity with both the parents' and the child's convictions, in order to provide a buffer for the family and to prevent a religious belief and education from being foisted on the child, possibly by State interference. The delegation of Finland then pointed out that another possibility would be a reference to "convictions of their choice", and both the delegations of the Netherlands and the United States accepted the Finnish proposal. Accordingly the Working Group agreed to paragraph 4 as amended and adopted article 7 bis.

## 5.      Comment submitted to the Working Group (1986)

### (a)      Bangladesh

*The following comment regarding article 7 bis (present article 14) is contained in a paper submitted by the Permanent Representative of Bangladesh to the United Nations Office at Geneva with the request that the paper be annexed to the report of the Working Group. For the complete text, including general comments on the draft convention, see document E/CN.4/1986/39, annex IV.*

Article 7 (bis) appears to run counter to the traditions of the major religious systems of the world and in particular to Islam. It appears to infringe upon the sanctioned practice of a child being reared in the religion of his parents. We believe that the article as presently drafted will give rise to considerable difficulties in application and appears also to be in conflict with article 8.

## 6.      Comment submitted to the Working Group (1987)

### (a)      Morocco

*The following is taken from the 1987 report of the Working Group to the Commission on Human Rights (E/CN.4/1987/25, para. 2).*

2.      [...] By a note verbale of 30 January 1987, the Permanent Representative of Morocco asked that their observations on the draft convention be brought to the attention of the Working Group; those observations were contained in E/CN.4/1987/WG.1/WP.35.

*The following is taken from document E/CN.4/1987/WG.1/WP.35.*

Article 7 bis - *Choice of religion*

On the question of religion, the rule adopted in Moroccan legislation is that the child shall follow the religion of his father. In this case, the child does not have to choose his religion, as the religion of the State is Islam. Islam guarantees freedom of worship to members of other faiths.

## 7. Related discussion in the Working Group (1987)

*The following is taken from the 1987 report of the Working Group to the Commission on Human Rights (E/CN.4/1987/25, paras. 100-110).*

100.     The Working Group had before it the following proposal by the delegations of Australia and the United States for an article 5 bis:

> "To help the child enjoy the rights enumerated in this Convention, States Parties undertake to protect the family as the natural and fundamental unit of society. Parents or legal guardians shall enjoy the primary rights and responsibilities for the care, upbringing and development of the child, having due regard for the importance of allowing the child to develop the skills and knowledge required for an independent adulthood."

101.     The representative of the United States explained that his country attached great importance to the family as the natural and fundamental group unit of society. He explained that the family should be explicitly protected, with language similar to that contained in paragraph 1 of articles 10 and 23, respectively, of the International Covenants on Economic, Social and Cultural Rights, and Civil and Political Rights, and that such protection should be included in the draft convention. The United States representative requested that the article under consideration by the Group be included early in the draft convention as article 5 bis, in order to emphasize its importance and relationship to all the other rights contained in the draft convention.

102.     During the debate, the attention of the Working Group was drawn to the possible overlap of the proposal with the already existing articles in the draft convention and in the International Covenants on Civil and Political Rights and on Economic, Social and Cultural Rights.

103.     Some delegations specifically drew the attention of the Working Group to the fact that the proposal did not introduce any new element, as compared to paragraph 3 of article 7 bis of the draft convention.

104.     The delegation of Canada indicated that it would support such a provision - already included in articles 7 bis and 15 - to the extent that the proposed article 5 bis would deal with the parental responsibility in the exercise of its rights over the child, with due regard for the evolving capacities of the child and for the child's need to mature into an independent adulthood. However, the observer for Canada concluded that as the concept was already included in the aforementioned articles 7 bis and 15, it would be possible that on the second reading of the draft convention, a generally applicable article could be developed from the - by that time - adopted limited provisions. The delegation of Finland agreed with the suggestions made by the observer for Canada.

105.     The observer for the Netherlands suggested that the latter part of the proposal by the American and Australian delegations be combined with paragraph 3 of article 7 bis in the following manner:

> "The States Parties to the present Convention shall respect the rights and duties of the parents and, where applicable, legal guardians, to provide direction to the child in the exercise of his rights enumerated in this Convention in a manner consistent with the evolving capacities of the child, having due regard for the importance of allowing the child to develop the skills and knowledge required for an independent adulthood."

106.     The observer for Canada supported the revised proposal put forward by the delegation of the Netherlands. However, with respect to that part of the original proposal, which was based on the protection given to the family under article 23 of the International Covenant on Civil and Political Rights, the Canadian delegation had expressed concern that because article 23 was intended to protect the family from the State, incorporation of such a provision in a convention on the rights of the child must also ensure that the rights of the child would not be left solely to the wishes of the family, without any protection whatsoever from the State; in other words, in protecting the family from the State, the family must not be given arbitrary control over the child. Any protection from the State given to the family must be equally balanced with the protection of the child within the family.

107.     The representative of Austria, while agreeing with the insertion of a separate article along those lines strongly supported the first sentence of the original proposal feeling that, although it appeared in the Covenants, it would be regrettable if it did not also appear in the draft convention.

108.     The Chairman then suggested keeping the first sentence, as it appeared in the original proposal, with the following modifications: to add the words "to the present Convention" between "States Parties" and "undertake" and the words "and assist" between "protect" and "the family". The delegations of Austria and the United States were amenable to the insertion of the above-mentioned words as proposed by the Chairman.

109.     The representative of Australia said that the revised proposal by the delegation of the Netherlands was a good one and therefore should be included in the draft convention, and that during the second reading, references that would appear to be a duplication of already existing texts of the draft convention would be struck out. In addition, he proposed to introduce the words "within the family" between "to provide" and "direction to the child".

110.     After some further exchange of views and after listening to the opinion put forward by the delegation of Finland to the effect that the discussions on this question should be postponed until the second reading of the draft convention, the Chairman proceeded to adjourn the debate with the request that a new proposal for an article 5 bis be prepared.

## 8.     Text as adopted at first reading

*The following is taken from document E/CN.4/1988/WG.1/WP.1/Rev.1.*

*Article 7 bis*

1.     The States Parties to the present Convention shall respect the right of the child to freedom of thought, conscience and religion.

2.     This right shall include in particular the freedom to have or to adopt a religion or whatsoever belief of his choice and freedom, either individually or in community with others and in public or private, to manifest his religion or belief, subject only to such limitations as are prescribed by law and are necessary to protect public safety, order, health and morals; and the right to have access to education in the matter of religion or belief.

3.     The States Parties shall respect the rights and duties of the parents and, where applicable, legal guardians, to provide direction to the child in the exercise of his right in a manner consistent with the evolving capacities of the child.

4.     The States Parties shall equally respect the liberty of the child and his parents and, where applicable, legal guardians, to ensure that religious and moral education of the child in conformity with convictions of their choice.

## D.     Technical review (1988)

### 1.     Comment by the United Nations Educational, Scientific and Cultural Organization (UNESCO)

*The following is taken from document E/CN.4/1989/WG.1/CRP.1, page 22.*

In paragraph 2 of this article, the expression "the freedom to have or to adopt a religion" should be replaced by "the freedom to have or not to have, to adopt or not to adopt a religion", and the expression "to manifest his religion or belief" should be replaced by "to manifest or not to manifest religion or belief".

In the English version, paragraphs 3 and 4 of article 7 bis "where" should be replaced by "when".

## 2.  Comment by the United Nations Children's Fund (UNICEF)

*The following is taken from document E/CN.4/1989/WG.1/CRP.1, pages 22-23.*

*Paragraph 1*

This paragraph reads as follows:

> "The States Parties to the present Convention shall respect the right of the child to freedom of thought, conscience and religion".

It is modelled after the first sentence in paragraph 1 of article 18 of the International Covenant on Civil and Political Rights which states that:

> "Everyone shall have the right to freedom of thought, conscience and religion."

The difference between the two is that under the Covenant (article 2, paragraph 1 and article 18, paragraph 1, read in conjunction) States Parties undertake to "respect and ensure" the right, whereas the draft convention (article *4, paragraph 1* and article *7 bis, paragraph 1*, read in conjunction) obligates States Parties only to "respect and extend" the right. The latter formulation, unlike the former, imposes no obligation to take affirmative action to ensure the right, or to protect the child from violations of his or her rights by non-State entities.

This discrepancy could be resolved either by amending article *4, paragraph 1*, as proposed above, or by adding the words "and ensure" after the word "respect" in article *7 bis, paragraph 1*. For the sake of consistency, consideration might be given to making both amendments.

*Paragraph 2*

A comma should be inserted after the word "choice" (in line 2 of the English text).

For the most part, this provision is modelled after article 18, paragraph 1, of the International Covenant on Civil and Political Rights and article 1, paragraph 1, of the Declaration on the Elimination of All Forms of Intolerance and of Discrimination Based on Religion or Belief. The principal difference is that each of those instruments includes the words "in worship, observance, practice and teaching" after the phrase "to manifest his religion or belief". The *travaux préparatoires* of the draft convention do not indicate any reason for their omission from this paragraph and the Working Group may wish to consider whether they should be inserted.

In order to ensure consistency with the International Covenant on Civil and Political Rights (article 18, paragraph 3) the limitations clause should read in part:

> "necessary to protect public safety, order, health, *or* morals, *or the fundamental rights and freedoms of others*; and..."

*Gender neutrality*

Paragraph 2. This could be reformulated as follows:

> "This right shall include in particular the freedom to have or to adopt a religion or whatsoever belief of *the child's* choice, and freedom, either individually or in community with others and in public or private, to manifest *that* religion or belief..."

Paragraph 3. The middle part of the paragraph could read:

> "...to provide direction to the child in the exercise of his *or her* rights..."

Paragraph 4. The first part of the paragraph could read:

> "The States Parties shall equally respect the liberty of the child and his *or her* parents...".

### 3. Additional comments and clarifications by the Secretariat

*The following is taken from document E/CN.4/1989/WG.1/CRP.1/Add.1, page 6.*

17.     As in article 4, the reference in paragraph 3 to "legal guardians" does not reflect the listing made in article 5 bis. The Working Group may therefore wish, in accordance also with language used in, for example, article 8, paragraphs 1 and 2, to change this phrase to read *"guardians"*.

## E.     Second reading (1988-1989)

### 1.     Proposals submitted to the Working Group at second reading

**(a)     Algeria, Egypt, Iraq, Jordan, Kuwait, Libyan Arab Jamahiriya, Morocco, Oman, Pakistan and Tunisia**

*The following text is taken from document E/CN.4/1989/WG.1/WP.4.*

*Article 7 bis*

1.     Paragraphs 1 and 2 should be combined to read as follows:

"The States parties to the present Convention shall respect the right of the child to freedom of thought, conscience and religion, as well as his right to have access to education in the matter of religion or belief, subject only to such limitations as are prescribed by national laws and legislation and are necessary to protect public safety, order, health and morals".

2.     Paragraphs 3 and 4 remain unchanged.

**(b)     Mexico**

*The following text is taken from document E/CN.4/1989/WG.1/WP.28.*

*Article 7 bis, paragraph 4:*

Delete.

### 2.     Discussion and adoption at second reading

*The following is taken from the 1989 report of the Working Group to the Commission on Human Rights (E/CN.4/1989/48, paras. 16 and 280 to 291).*

*General debate*

[...]

16.     The observer for Egypt referred to the seminar on the rights of the child that had been held at Alexandria in November 1988, stating that its main recommendations were: (a) that the United Nations Working Group on the question of a convention on the rights of the child should bear in mind during the second reading the fact that articles 7 bis and 11 were incompatible with the legal systems of several countries and should take the concern of those countries into account; (b) that the Working Group should give closer attention in the draft convention to encouraging the mental and spiritual education of the child; (c) that the Egyptian Ministry of Justice should be requested to revise the country's laws - if and where necessary - to bring them into line with the future convention on the rights of the child.

[...]

*Article 14* (Article 7 bis)

280.     The Working Group had before it a proposal (E/CN.4/1989/WG.1/WP.68) submitted by the drafting group on article 7 bis composed of Bangladesh, China, the Holy See, Mexico, Morocco, the Netherlands and Poland, which were joined by the delegations of the United States of America, the Union of Soviet Socialist Republics, Argentina, Algeria, Egypt, Tunisia and two representatives of non-governmental organizations. The proposal read as follows:

"[The States Parties to the present Convention shall respect the right of the Child to freedom of thought, conscience and religion].

1.      The States shall respect the right and duties of the parents and, when applicable, legal guardians, to provide direction to the child in the exercise of his right in a manner consistent with the evolving capacities of the child.

2.      The States Parties shall equally respect the liberty of the parents and when applicable legal guardians, to ensure the religious and moral education of the child in conformity with their own conviction [of their choice].

[3.      Freedom to manifest one's religion or beliefs may be subject only to such limitations as are prescribed by law and are necessary to protect public safety, order, health, or morals or the fundamental rights and freedoms of others.]

[4.      No restrictions may be placed on the exercise of these rights other than those imposed in conformity with [national] laws and legislation and which are necessary to protect public safety, public order, health and morals [and the fundamental rights and freedom of others]]".

281.     In introducing this proposal, the observer for Morocco, acting as a coordinator of the drafting group, indicated that, despite all the efforts undertaken, the drafting group had been unable to reconcile the various views and positions of delegations.

282.     The Chairman drew the attention of the Working Group to the fact that paragraph 2 of article 7 bis as proposed by the drafting group (E/CN.4/1989/WG.1/WP.68) was identical to paragraph 3 of article 7 bis as adopted at first reading.

283.     Having made some editorial and gender neutrality revisions, the Working Group then adopted paragraph 2 of article 7 bis reading as follows:

"2.      States Parties shall respect the rights and duties of the parents and, when applicable, legal guardians, to provide direction to the child in the exercise of his or her right in a manner consistent with the evolving capacities of the child."

284.     The observer for Finland stated that when adopting paragraph 2 of article 7 bis it was the understanding of his delegation that article 7 as already adopted was also applicable in religious matters. The Chairman stated that since article 7 was a general provision it applied to all matters affecting the child, including religious matters, and associated himself with the interpretation expressed by the observer for Finland.

285.     With regard to other paragraphs of article 7 bis the opinions of the delegations were divided. On the one hand it was argued that the text of article 7 bis had been already agreed upon during the first reading and therefore it should be used as a basis for consideration of all other issues involved. It was stressed by some participants that the Working Group should not engage in establishing standards lower than those already set, nor should it detract from the International Covenants and other basic human rights instruments. The view was expressed that the formulations proposed in document E/CN.4/1989/WG.1/WP.68 undercut certain rights and freedoms established in the International Covenant on Civil and Political Rights and the Universal Declaration of Human Rights.

286.     According to another approach, it was only on the basis of the text in document E/CN.4/1989/WG.1/WP.68 that any discussion could be productive. It was indicated in this connection that the drafting group had proposed alternative formulations which better reflected the position of those who could not accept any provision giving the child a freedom to choose and change his or her religion or belief.

287.     In the discussion that followed some delegations proposed to merge paragraphs 1 and 5 of the text contained in document E/CN.4/1989/WG.1/WP.68. Another idea was to delete article 7 bis altogether. It was emphasized by some speakers that in the final analysis article 7 bis should reflect all legal systems and all models of social development. One participant urged that all attempts to impose one's position upon other delegations should be abandoned as contrary to the principal task of the Working Group which was to elaborate a universally acceptable legal document.

288.     Observing that a consensus on the various proposals was not possible, the Chairman suggested that only paragraphs 1 and 4 of document E/CN.4/1989/WG.1/WP.68 which did not contain any new or controversial provisions, be retained in article 7 bis, in addition to its paragraph 2 as adopted earlier. The Working Group agreed with this proposal and adopted article 7 bis reading as follows:

> "1.     States Parties shall respect the right of the child to freedom of thought, conscience and religion.
>
> 2.     States Parties shall respect the rights and duties of the parents and, when applicable, legal guardians, to provide direction to the child in the exercise of his or her right in a manner consistent with the evolving capacities of the child.
>
> 3.     Freedom to manifest one's religion or beliefs may be subject only to such limitations as are prescribed by law and are necessary to protect public safety, order, health, or morals or the fundamental rights and freedoms of others."

289.     Following the adoption of article 7 bis the observer for Sweden stated that his delegation had joined in the consensus on the understanding that the right to freedom of thought, conscience and religion, as laid down in article 18 of the International Covenant on Civil and Political Rights, should include freedom to have or to adopt a religion or belief of one's choice, and freedom to manifest one's religion or belief in worship, observance, practice and teaching.

290.     The observer for the Holy See stated with regard to article 7 bis after its adoption that "the right of parents to give their child a religious and moral education in conformity with their personal beliefs forms part of the right to manifest one's religion and this right of religious and moral education must be respected by States".

291.     The representative of Italy stated that her delegation associated itself with the declaration made by the observer for the Holy See.

# Article 15 (Freedom of association and peaceful assembly)

## A.    Final text adopted by the General Assembly (1989)

*The following text is that approved by the General Assembly in its resolution 44/25 of 20 November 1989.*

> 1.    States Parties recognize the rights of the child to freedom of association and to freedom of peaceful assembly.
>
> 2.    No restrictions may be placed on the exercise of these rights other than those imposed in conformity with the law and which are necessary in a democratic society in the interests of national security or public safety, public order (*ordre public*), the protection of public health or morals or the protection of the rights and freedoms of others.

## B.    First Polish draft convention and comments (1978)

*Neither the first Polish draft nor the views received on it (see document E/CN.4/1324 and Corr.1 and Add.1-5) addressed the issues raised in article 15 of the Convention.*

## C.    First reading (1979-1988)

*Issues raised under article 15 were first discussed at the Working Group in 1986 and a text was adopted at the 1988 session. This article was referred to as article 16 bis in 1985, 18 quater in 1986 and 7 ter thereafter.*

### 1.    Proposal submitted to the Working Group (1985)

**(a)    United States of America**

*The following text is taken from the 1985 report of the Working Group to the Commission on Human Rights (E/CN.4/1985/64, annex II, p. 3).*

> *Article 16 bis*
>
> The States Parties to the present Convention shall ensure that the child shall enjoy civil and political rights and freedoms in public life to the fullest extent commensurate with his age including in particular, freedom from arbitrary governmental interference with privacy, family, home or correspondence; the right to petition for redress of grievances; and, subject only to such reasonable restrictions provided by law as are necessary for respect of the rights and legally protected interests of others or for the protection of national security, public safety and order, or public health and morals, freedom of association and expression; and the right of peaceful assembly.

### 2.    Proposal submitted to the Working Group (1986)

**(a)    United States of America**

*For the text of this proposal, see paragraph 84 in section 3 below.*

### 3.    Discussion in the Working Group (1986)

*The following is taken from the 1986 report of the Working Group to the Commission on Human Rights (E/CN.4/1986/39, paras. 84 to 87).*

> 84.    The Working Group had before it the following revised proposal by the delegation of the United States for an article 18 quater:

"1.        States Parties to the present Convention recognize the rights of the child to freedom of association with others, to peaceful assembly, and to be protected by law against arbitrary or unlawful interference with his privacy, family, home or correspondence.

2.        States Parties shall respect and guarantee these rights, and shall not place any restrictions on their exercise, except as provided in paragraph 3 of this article. In no case shall a child be subjected to incarceration or other confinement for the legitimate exercise of these rights or other rights recognized in this Convention.

3.        The exercise of the right to freedom of association and the right to peaceful assembly may be subject to those restrictions provided by law which are consistent with the international obligations of a State Party and which are necessary in a democratic society in the interests of national security, public safety, public order (*ordre public*), the protection of public health or morals or the protection of the rights and freedoms of others.

4.        Nothing in this article shall be interpreted as limiting or otherwise affecting the authority, rights or responsibilities of a parent or other legal guardian of the child."

85.        While the delegations of Australia and Canada expressed their support for the inclusion of the United States proposal in the draft convention, the representative of the USSR stated that he was totally opposed to it and the representatives of Algeria, China, Iraq and Poland said that it would be difficult for them to accept the proposal.

86.        The delegation of Bangladesh proposed two amendments to paragraph 1, namely, to delete the words "with others" and to replace the words "be protected" by the words "the protection".

87.        The Working Group postponed consideration of this article until its next session.

## 4.        Proposal submitted to the Working Group (1987)

### (a)        United States of America

*For the text of this proposal, see paragraph 111 in section 5 below.*

## 5.        Discussion in the Working Group (1987)

*The following is taken from the 1987 report of the Working Group to the Commission on Human Rights (E/CN.4/1987/25, paras. 111 to 118).*

111.        The Working Group had before it the following revised proposal, submitted by the delegation of the United States, of a text that had been put forward by the representative of the United States during the Working Group's 1986 session:

"1.        States Parties to the present Convention recognize the rights of the child to freedom of expression, freedom of association and freedom of peaceful assembly.

2.        States Parties recognize the right of the child not to be subjected to arbitrary or unlawful interference with his or her privacy, family, home or correspondence.

3.        The exercise of the rights to freedom of expression, association and peaceful assembly shall be subject only to those restrictions which are provided by law and which are necessary in a democratic society in the interests of national security, public order ("*ordre public*"), the protection of public health and morals or the protection of the rights and freedoms of others.

4.        In no case shall a child be subjected to incarceration or other confinement for the legitimate exercise of these rights or other rights recognized in this Convention.

5.    This article shall not be interpreted as affecting the lawful rights and duties of parents or legal guardians, which should be exercised in a manner consistent with the evolving capacities of the child."

112.    The representative of the United States said that the protection of children's civil and political rights was of fundamental importance to his country, particularly because the "child", as defined in the draft convention, included adolescents who had often acquired the skills needed to participate fully and effectively in society. He noted that the draft convention already protected certain other fundamental rights, including the right to freedom of religion. He also explained that the rights in the draft article were universally accepted and were contained in the Universal Declaration of Human Rights and in the International Covenant on Civil and Political Rights.

113.    The Chairman suggested that the proposal submitted by the representative of the United States could carry the number 7 ter, and this suggestion met with the agreement of the American delegation.

114.    A lengthy discussion ensued dealing with the merits of such a proposal. During this general discussion, some delegations made observations concerning different aspects of the proposal. For example, the representative of the United Kingdom said, inter alia, that already existent international instruments dealt with certain parts of the proposal, and suggested that the language in which the draft article was worded called for some clarification. The delegation of Australia, although generally supporting the proposal, raised some questions remarking among other things that there appeared to be confusion about the freedoms of association and expression and that of privacy, as well as that the proposal made no provision whatsoever for the evolving sense of responsibility of children.

115.    The delegation of Norway, in supporting the American proposal, shared the concern of the Australian delegation that there was a need for a general provision dealing with the evolving capacities of the child. The observer for Canada indicated her support for the proposal put forward by the United States representative and her wish that the principle set out in paragraph 5 of draft article 7 ter be dealt with in a comprehensive manner in a general article. The representative of Argentina, although in general favourable to the draft article, voiced the same concerns as other delegations regarding its paragraph 5, and found that there was much to be clarified in the proposal being considered by the Working Group.

116.    The representative of the USSR indicated that he was not in a position to support draft article 7 ter as it stood, and considered that the draft convention should deal with new issues and not reproduce provisions already existing in international instruments. He raised the question as to why the proposal focused on certain civil and political rights and bypassed others, suggesting to break down the proposed article and proceed to separate the civil from the political rights in an approach that would not be selective, yet fully consistent with the provisions of the International Covenant on Civil and Political Rights.

117.    The Chinese delegation was not in a position to accept the United States proposal. It was of the opinion that the freedoms of association, peaceful assembly and privacy could not be enjoyed by children in the same way as they are enjoyed by adults because the intellect of a child was not as developed as that of an adult, and therefore a child could only engage in activities commensurate with its intellect. The observer for Sweden indicated her support for the text tabled by the delegation of the United States, but called for a separate article on the evolving capacities of the child.

118.    The Chairman voiced his hope that the representative of the United States would propose a revised text for article 7 ter and that in doing so would take into account the Working Group's observations. The delegation of the United States accepted the Chairman's suggestion to consider the comments made by other delegations and to resubmit article 7 ter for consideration by the Working Group at its 1988 session. It stated that in doing so, it was its understanding that the proposal would be considered early in the Working Group's deliberations.

## 6. Proposals submitted to the Working Group (1988)

### (a) United States of America

*For the text of this proposal, see paragraph 35 in section 7 below.*

### (b) NGO Ad Hoc Group *(see annex III (B) for participating organizations)*

*The following is taken from document E/CN.4/1988/WG.1/WP.2, page 15.*

> 1. States parties to the present Convention recognize the rights of the child to freedom of association and freedom of peaceful assembly.
>
> 2. The exercise of these rights shall be subject only to those restrictions which are provided by law and which are necessary in a democratic society in the interests of national security, public order (*ordre public*), the protection of public health and morals or the protection of the rights and freedoms of others.

## 7. Discussion and adoption by the Working Group

*The following is taken from the 1988 report of the Working Group to the Commission on Human Rights (E/CN.4/1988/28, paras. 35 to 38 and 47 to 54).*

> *Article 7a (Freedom of expression and information)*
>
> 35. The Working Group had before it a proposal submitted by the United States of America on civil and political rights of the child (E/CN.4/1988/WG.1/WP.18) which read as follows:
>
> > [...]
> >
> > "III NEW ARTICLE 7 ter (FREEDOM OF ASSOCIATION, PEACEFUL ASSEMBLY)
> >
> > 1. The States Parties to the present Convention recognize the right of the child to freedom of association and freedom of peaceful assembly.
> >
> > 2. No restrictions may be placed on the exercise of this right other than those imposed in conformity with the law and which are necessary in a democratic society in the interests of national security or public safety, public order (*ordre public*), the protection of public health or morals or the protection of the rights and freedoms of others.
> >
> > 3. States Parties shall respect the rights and duties of parents and, where applicable, legal guardians, to provide direction to the child in the exercise of these rights in a manner consistent with the evolving capacities of the child."
> >
> > [...]
>
> 36. In introducing that proposal, the representative of the United States of America stated that children not only had the right to expect certain benefits from their Governments; they also had civil and political rights to protect them from abusive action of their Governments. These rights are largely the same as those enjoyed by adults, although it is generally recognized that children do not have the right to vote. While children might need direction and guidance from parents or legal guardians in the exercise of these rights, this does not affect the content of the rights themselves. The United States proposal was intended to complete the process already begun by the Working Group of incorporating provisions from the International Covenant on Civil and Political Rights into the draft convention. The proposal reflects the recognition contained in the International Covenant that the ability of all individuals to exercise civil and political rights is not absolute, but is subject to certain limited restrictions that may be imposed by States. The proposal was designed to incorporate into the draft convention the right to freedom of expression, the right to freedom of association and to peaceful assembly, and certain privacy rights as elaborated in the International Covenant.

The representative of the United States reminded the Working Group that these rights protect children from action of the State, and would not affect the legitimate rights of parents or legal guardians to provide direction and guidance to children.

37.	The idea of including civil and political rights in the draft convention to reinforce the protection of children was strongly supported by several participants. However, the legitimate rights of parents and tutors should be safeguarded, the balance between rights of children and rights of the family should be preserved and the wording of the article should be in line with the Covenants.

38.	The view was expressed that, if parents should be protected from States, the child should be protected from parents. The following additional paragraph was thus proposed for insertion in article 7 quater:

> "States Parties to the present Convention shall respect the right of the child to the protection of law against such interference or attacks."

[...]

*Article 7 ter (Freedom of association and freedom of peaceful assembly)*

47.	The representative of the United States of America stated that, in his delegation's proposal (see paragraph 35 above), freedom of association and freedom of peaceful assembly were combined in one article, even though the International Covenant on Civil and Political Rights treated them separately. The separate treatment in the International Covenant was necessary to address issues raised by the right of adults to join trade unions. The draft convention need not address such issues, although it should be recognized that older children have the right to join trade unions. States retained their authority to restrict this right in article 7 ter, paragraph 2. He indicated that he would not insist on paragraph 3 if article 5 bis were adopted.

*Paragraph 1*

48.	It was observed that freedom of association and of assembly did not mean any kind of associations or organizations, such as trade unions; this freedom should be commensurate with the age, maturity and level of development of the child, as stated in article 7 in relation to the child's right to express opinions, the wishes of the child being given due weight in accordance with his age and maturity. The representative of China therefore proposed the following amended text for article 7 ter, paragraph 1:

> "The States Parties to the present Convention recognize, in accordance with the child's age and maturity, his or her right to freedom of association and freedom of peaceful assembly."

49.	Several participants supported the inclusion of freedom of association and of freedom of peaceful assembly which was recognized by the International Covenant on Civil and Political Rights.

50.	Many participants indicated their preference for retaining article 7 ter, paragraph 1, as it stood, and said that they would agree to take up the Chinese concerns in article 7 ter, paragraph 3. The view was expressed that, in the exercise of the right to freedom of peaceful assembly, the age of the child was not important and the parents could take him with them, while in all countries, for the exercise of the right to freedom of association, there were specific age restrictions by law, for example, in the field of employment or admission to a trade union.

51.	The Working Group adopted article 7 ter, paragraph 1 (see paragraph 54 below).

*Paragraph 2*

52.	The discussion on paragraph 2 (see paragraph 35 above) focused on the proposal to delete the word "morals", and to insert the words "or the promotion of the best interests of the child" after the word "order". The view was expressed that that proposal was not acceptable since it would impose new restrictions on freedom of association which were incompatible with article 22, paragraph 2, of the International Covenant on Civil and Political Rights. It was based on the assumption that the child was acting against its best interests, while he was only exercising his rights. In a spirit of compromise proposals were made: (a) to add, at the end of paragraph 2, the words "or where the exercise of these rights would be (manifestly) contrary to the best interests of the child"; (b) to add, at the end of paragraph 2 or paragraph 3, the words "in order to promote the best interests of the child".

53.     One speaker stated that in her country, parents and legal guardians had the right to guide children, while other social organs, both governmental and non-governmental were also involved in guiding children. She therefore proposed to insert in paragraph 3, the words "social organs" after the word "guardians". She also stated that children's rights should be better protected, and that, because of their age and level of maturity, they needed guidance from adults. Another speaker was of the view that children could act contrary to their interests, particularly in the case of children without adequate maturity. These comments were supported by the observer for Egypt.

54.     Finally, a consensus was reached on paragraph 2 as proposed by the United States of America. The adopted article 7 ter reads as follows:

> "1.     The States Parties to the present Convention recognize the rights of the child to freedom of association and to freedom of peaceful assembly.
>
> 2.     No restrictions may be placed on the exercise of these rights other than those imposed in conformity with the law and which are necessary in a democratic society in the interests of national security or public safety, public order (*ordre public*), the protection of public health or morals or the protection of the rights and freedoms of others."

## 8.     Text as adopted at first reading

*The following is taken from document E/CN.4/1988/WG.1/WP.1/Rev.1.*

*Article 7 ter*

1.     The States Parties to the present Convention recognize the rights of the child to freedom of association and to freedom of peaceful assembly.

2.     No restrictions may be placed on the exercise of these rights other than those imposed in conformity with the law and which are necessary in a democratic society in the interests of national security or public safety, public order (*ordre public*), the protection of public health or morals or the protection of the rights and freedoms of others.

# D.     Technical review (1988)

## 1.     Comment by the International Labour Organization (ILO)

*The following is taken from document E/CN.4/1989/WG.1/CRP.1, page 24.*

Regarding article 7 ter, it would appear from the relevant discussion (paragraphs 47-50 of the Report of the Working Group (E/CN.4/1988/28)) that the right of *older children* to join trade unions is also contemplated, but rather as an accessory aspect, and therefore not expressly mentioned as in article 22 of the International Covenant on Civil and Political Rights. Also, different from article 22 of the Covenant, the draft convention does not provide that the child "*shall have*" the right to freedom of association but "*recognizes*" this right of the child (the reservations of *paragraph 2* of article 7 ter are, however, substantially the same as the corresponding provisions of paragraph 2 of article 22 of the [Covenant]).

This difference in treatment, admittedly justified as regards the right of association in general of the child, may cause difficulties as regards the right to form and join trade unions of older, working children, specifically children who have reached or are above the *general minimum age* for admission to employment but are still under 18 years, therefore still a "child" according to article 1 of the draft convention. Under the International

Labour Organization's *Minimum Age Convention, 1973 (No. 138)*, the general minimum age for employment is fixed as not lower than 15 years (14 for developing countries). Such "children", if they are in employment, must be regarded as *workers* and consequently enjoy the trade union rights laid down in the Covenants and in the ILO's *Freedom of Association and Protection of the Right to Organize Convention, 1948 (No. 87)*, the latter being expressly referred to in the saving clauses of article 8, paragraph 3, and article 22, paragraph 3, respectively of the Covenant on Economic, Social and Cultural Rights and of the Covenant on Civil and Political Rights. (In this connection, see also comments on article 21.)

## 2.    Additional comments and clarifications by the Secretariat

*The following is taken from document E/CN.4/1989/WG.1/CRP.1/Add.1, paragraph 18.*

18.    Noting the comments by the ILO (document E/CN.4/1989/WG.1/CRP.1) and comparing article 7 ter with articles 21 and 22 of the International Covenant on Civil and Political Rights, the Working Group, for reasons of consistency, may wish to modify paragraph 1 of article 7 ter to read:

"*The child shall have the right* to freedom of association and to freedom of assembly."

# E.    Second reading (1988-1989)

## 1.    Discussion and adoption at second reading

*The following is taken from the 1989 report of the Working Group to the Commission on Human Rights (E/CN.4/1989/48, paras. 292 to 295).*

292.    The Working Group had before it article 7 ter as adopted at first reading (E/CN.4/1989/WG.1/WP.2):

"1.    The States Parties to the present Convention recognize the rights of the child to freedom of association and to freedom of peaceful assembly.

2.    No restrictions may be placed on the exercise of these rights other than those imposed in conformity with the law and which are necessary in a democratic society in the interests of national security or public safety, public order (*ordre public*), the protection of public health or morals or the protection of the rights and freedoms of others."

293.    The Chairman drew attention to the amendment proposed by the International Labour Organization as it appears in E/CN.4/1989/WG.1/WP.2, p. 35. The representative of the ILO pointed out that it was the Legal Counsel and not the ILO which sponsored the amendment but that the ILO would support it because it used the same wording as article 22 of the International Covenant on Civil and Political Rights. She then stated that while article 7 ter reproduced in its paragraph 2 the terms of paragraph 2 of article 22 of the Covenant, it did not contain a clause similar to paragraph 3 of this article, which safeguarded the obligations arising from the ILO Convention on Freedom of Association (No. 87), 1948. In order to avoid any conflict, the ILO would favour the adoption of a general clause safeguarding more clearly than the present article 21 the rights recognized in other international instruments. Such a clause had been proposed by Finland at the first reading.

294.    The representative of Venezuela expressed her support for this safeguard clause.

295.    The Chairman declared that the safeguard clause would be discussed under article 21 and the Working Group proceeded to adopt article 7 ter as follows:

"1.    States Parties recognize the rights of the child to freedom of association and to freedom of peaceful assembly.

2.      No restrictions may be placed on the exercise of these rights other than those imposed in conformity with the law and which are necessary in a democratic society in the interests of national security or public safety, public order (*ordre public*), the protection of public health or morals or the protection of the rights and freedoms of others."

# Article 16 (Protection of privacy)

## A.    Final text adopted by the General Assembly (1989)

*The following text is that approved by the General Assembly in its resolution 44/25 of 20 November 1989.*

> 1.        No child shall be subjected to arbitrary or unlawful interference with his or her privacy, family, home or correspondence, nor to unlawful attacks on his or her honour and reputation.
>
> 2.        The child has the right to the protection of the law against such interference or attacks.

## B.    First Polish draft convention and comments (1978)

*Neither the first Polish draft nor the views received on it (see document E/CN.4/1324 and Corr.1 and Add.1-5) addressed the issues raised in article 16 of the Convention.*

## C.    First reading (1979-1988)

*The issues raised under article 16 were first discussed at the Working Group in 1983 and a text was adopted in 1988. This article was referred to as article 7 quater throughout the first and second readings.*

### 1.    Proposal submitted to the Working Group (1982)

#### (a)    United States of America

*For the text of this proposal, see paragraph 42 in section 3 below.*

### 2.    Proposal submitted to the Working Group (1983)

#### (a)    United States of America

*The following is taken from document E/CN.4/1983/WG.1/WP.30.*

> 6 quater (formerly 6 ter)
>
> "The States Parties to the present Convention shall ensure that the child enjoys legal protection from arbitrary or unlawful interference by government authorities with his family or home."

### 3.    Discussion in the Working Group (1983)

*The following is taken from the 1983 report of the Working Group to the Commission on Human Rights (E/CN.4/1983/62, paras.  42 to 44).*

> 42.        The representative of the United States reintroduced a proposal he made in 1982 according to which the draft convention should contain a provision ensuring the right of the child not to be subjected to arbitrary or unlawful interference by government authorities. The proposal, which was previously designated article 6 ter reads as follows (E/1982/12/Add.1, part C, para. 118).
>
> > "The States Parties to the present Convention shall ensure that the child and his parents are not subjected to arbitrary or unlawful interference with their privacy, family, home or correspondence."
>
> 43.        For some speakers, the inclusion of such provision was not necessary. In their opinion, the fulfilment of the child's basic needs was a more urgent matter.
>
> 44.        No agreement was reached. The proposal was not, therefore, adopted.

## 4. Proposal submitted to the Working Group (1985)

### (a)　United States of America

*The following text is taken from the 1985 report of the Working Group to the Commission on Human Rights (E/CN.4/1985/64, annex II, p. 3).*

> *Article 16 bis*
>
> The States Parties to the present Convention shall ensure that the child shall enjoy civil and political rights and freedoms in public life to the fullest extent commensurate with his age including in particular, freedom from arbitrary governmental interference with privacy, family, home or correspondence; the right to petition for redress of grievances; and, subject only to such reasonable restrictions provided by law as are necessary for respect of the rights and legally protected interests of others or for the protection of national security, public safety and order, or public health and morals, freedom of association and expression; and the right of peaceful assembly.

## 5. Proposal submitted to the Working Group (1986)

### (a)　United States of America

*For the text of this proposal, see paragraph 84 in section 6 below.*

## 6. Discussion in the Working Group (1986)

*The following is taken from the 1986 report of the Working Group to the Commission on Human Rights (E/CN.4/1986/39, paras. 84 to 87).*

> 84.　The Working Group had before it the following revised proposal by the delegation of the United States for an article 18 quater:
>
> > "1.　States Parties to the present Convention recognize the rights of the child to freedom of association with others, to peaceful assembly, and to be protected by law against arbitrary or unlawful interference with his privacy, family, home or correspondence.
> >
> > 2.　States Parties shall respect and guarantee these rights, and shall not place any restrictions on their exercise, except as provided in paragraph 3 of this article. In no case shall a child be subjected to incarceration or other confinement for the legitimate exercise of these rights or other rights recognized in this Convention.
> >
> > 3.　The exercise of the right to freedom of association and the right to peaceful assembly may be subject to those restrictions provided by law which are consistent with the international obligations of a State Party and which are necessary in a democratic society in the interests of national security, public safety, public order (*ordre public*), the protection of public health or morals or the protection of the rights and freedoms of others.
> >
> > 4.　Nothing in this article shall be interpreted as limiting or otherwise affecting the authority, rights or responsibilities of a parent or other legal guardian of the child."
>
> 85.　While the delegations of Australia and Canada expressed their support for the inclusion of the United States proposal in the draft convention, the representative of the USSR stated that he was totally opposed to it and the representatives of Algeria, China, Iraq and Poland said that it would be difficult for them to accept the proposal.
>
> 86.　The delegation of Bangladesh proposed two amendments to paragraph 1, namely, to delete the words "with others" and to replace the words "be protected" by the words "the protection".

87.     The Working Group postponed consideration of this article until its next session.

## 7.      Proposal submitted to the Working Group (1987)

### (a)      United States of America

*For the text of this proposal, see paragraph 111 in section 8 below.*

## 8.      Discussion in the Working Group (1987)

*The following is taken from the 1987 report of the Working Group to the Commission on Human Rights (E/CN.4/1987/25, paras. 111 to 118).*

111.     The Working Group had before it the following revised proposal, submitted by the delegation of the United States, of a text that had been put forward by the representative of the United States during the Working Group's 1986 session:

> "1.      States Parties to the present Convention recognize the rights of the child to freedom of expression, freedom of association and freedom of peaceful assembly.
>
> 2.      States Parties recognize the right of the child not to be subjected to arbitrary or unlawful interference with his or her privacy, family, home or correspondence.
>
> 3.      The exercise of the rights to freedom of expression, association and peaceful assembly shall be subject only to those restrictions which are provided by law and which are necessary in a democratic society in the interests of national security, public order ("*ordre public*"), the protection of public health and morals or the protection of the rights and freedoms of others.
>
> 4.      In no case shall a child be subjected to incarceration or other confinement for the legitimate exercise of these rights or other rights recognized in this Convention.
>
> 5.      This article shall not be interpreted as affecting the lawful rights and duties of parents or legal guardians, which should be exercised in a manner consistent with the evolving capacities of the child."

112.     The representative of the United States said that the protection of children's civil and political rights was of fundamental importance to his country, particularly because the "child", as defined in the draft convention, included adolescents who had often acquired the skills needed to participate fully and effectively in society. He noted that the draft convention already protected certain other fundamental rights, including the right to freedom of religion. He also explained that the rights in the draft article were universally accepted and were contained in the Universal Declaration of Human Rights and in the International Covenant on Civil and Political Rights.

113.     The Chairman suggested that the proposal submitted by the representative of the United States could carry the number 7 ter, and this suggestion met with the agreement of the American delegation.

114.     A lengthy discussion ensued dealing with the merits of such a proposal. During this general discussion, some delegations made observations concerning different aspects of the proposal. For example, the representative of the United Kingdom said, inter alia, that already existent international instruments dealt with certain parts of the proposal, and suggested that the language in which the draft article was worded called for some clarification. The delegation of Australia, although generally supporting the proposal, raised some questions remarking among other things that there appeared to be confusion about the freedoms of association and expression and that of privacy, as well as that the proposal made no provision whatsoever for the evolving sense of responsibility of children.

115.	The delegation of Norway, in supporting the American proposal, shared the concern of the Australian delegation that there was a need for a general provision dealing with the evolving capacities of the child. The observer for Canada indicated her support for the proposal put forward by the United States representative and her wish that the principle set out in paragraph 5 of draft article 7 ter be dealt with in a comprehensive manner in a general article. The representative of Argentina, although in general favourable to the draft article, voiced the same concerns as other delegations regarding its paragraph 5, and found that there was much to be clarified in the proposal being considered by the Working Group.

116.	The representative of the USSR indicated that he was not in a position to support draft article 7 ter as it stood, and considered that the draft convention should deal with new issues and not reproduce provisions already existing in international instruments. He raised the question as to why the proposal focused on certain civil and political rights and bypassed others, suggesting to break down the proposed article and proceed to separate the civil from the political rights in an approach that would not be selective, yet fully consistent with the provisions of the International Covenant on Civil and Political Rights.

117.	The Chinese delegation was not in a position to accept the United States proposal. It was of the opinion that the freedoms of association, peaceful assembly and privacy could not be enjoyed by children in the same way as they are enjoyed by adults because the intellect of a child was not as developed as that of an adult, and therefore a child could only engage in activities commensurate with its intellect. The observer for Sweden indicated her support for the text tabled by the delegation of the United States, but called for a separate article on the evolving capacities of the child.

118.	The Chairman voiced his hope that the representative of the United States would propose a revised text for article 7 ter and that in doing so would take into account the Working Group's observations. The delegation of the United States accepted the Chairman's suggestion to consider the comments made by other delegations and to resubmit article 7 ter for consideration by the Working Group at its 1988 session. It stated that in doing so, it was its understanding that the proposal would be considered early in the Working Group's deliberations.

## 9.	Proposals submitted to the Working Group (1988)

### (a)	United States of America

*For the text of this proposal, see paragraph 35 in section 10 below.*

### (b)	NGO Ad Hoc Group *(see annex III (B) for participating organizations)*
*The following is taken from document E/CN.4/1988/WG.1/WP.2, page 11.*

Every child has the right to respect for his or her privacy, family, home and correspondence.

## 10.	Discussion and adoption by the Working Group (1988)

*The following is taken from the 1988 report of the Working Group to the Commission on Human Rights (E/CN.4/1988/28, paras. 35 to 38 and 55 to 59).*

Article 7a (Freedom of expression and information)

35.	The Working Group had before it a proposal submitted by the United States of America on civil and political rights of the child (E/CN.4/1988/WG.1/WP.18) which read as follows:

	[...]

	"IV. NEW ARTICLE 7 QUATER (RIGHT TO PRIVACY)

The States Parties to the present Convention recognize the right of the child not to be subjected to arbitrary or unlawful interference with his or her right to privacy, family, home or correspondence, nor to unlawful attacks on his or her honour and reputation."

36. In introducing that proposal, the representative of the United States of America stated that children not only had the right to expect certain benefits from their Governments; they also had civil and political rights to protect them from abusive action of their Governments. These rights are largely the same as those enjoyed by adults, although it is generally recognized that children do not have the right to vote. While children might need direction and guidance from parents or legal guardians in the exercise of these rights, this does not affect the content of the rights themselves. The United States proposal was intended to complete the process already begun by the Working Group of incorporating provisions from the International Covenant on Civil and Political Rights into the draft convention. The proposal reflects the recognition contained in the International Covenant that the ability of all individuals to exercise civil and political rights is not absolute, but is subject to certain limited restrictions that may be imposed by States. The proposal was designed to incorporate into the draft convention the right to freedom of expression, the right to freedom of association and to peaceful assembly, and certain privacy rights as elaborated in the International Covenant. The representative of the United States reminded the Working Group that these rights protect children from action of the State, and would not affect the legitimate rights of parents or legal guardians to provide direction and guidance to children.

37. The idea of including civil and political rights in the draft convention to reinforce the protection of children was strongly supported by several participants. However, the legitimate rights of parents and tutors should be safeguarded, the balance between rights of children and rights of the family should be preserved and the wording of the article should be in line with the Covenants.

38. The view was expressed that, if parents should be protected from States, the child should be protected from parents. The following additional paragraph was thus proposed for insertion in article 7 quater:

"States Parties to the present Convention shall respect the right of the child to the protection of law against such interference or attacks."

[...]

*Article 7 quater (Privacy, honour, reputation)*

55. The proposed article 7 quarter (see paragraph 35 above) related to the right of the child to privacy, family, home or correspondence, and as orally revised by the representative of the United States of America would contain a second paragraph to read as follows:

"1. The States Parties to the present Convention recognize the right of the child not to be subjected to arbitrary or unlawful interference with his or her right to privacy, family, home or correspondence, nor to unlawful attacks on his or her honour and reputation.

2. States Parties recognize the child's right to protection of the law against such interference or attacks."

56. The view was expressed that article 17 of the International Covenant on Civil and Political Rights could not be applied to the draft convention. It was proposed to delete the word "arbitrary" which was vague and subjective; to replace "the right to privacy" by "the right to personal freedom"; and to delete the words "right to" before the word "privacy" since in article 17 of the International Covenant on Civil and Political Rights mention was made only of privacy but no right to privacy. The right to privacy might, to some extent, impair the relationship between the parents and the child.

57.     Reference was made to the guidelines laid down in paragraph 4 of General Assembly resolution 41/120 entitled "Setting international standards in the field of human rights" and it was argued that the draft convention should be in conformity with the provisions of the Covenants.

58.     The Working Group finally reached a consensus on the retention of the word "arbitrary" and the deletion of the words "right to" before "privacy" and adopted paragraph 2 as proposed by the United States of America. Article 7 quater as adopted read as follows:

> "1.     The States Parties to the present Convention recognize the right of the child not to be subjected to arbitrary or unlawful interference with his or her privacy, family, home or correspondence, nor to unlawful attacks on his or her honour and reputation.
>
> 2.     The child has the right to the protection of the law against such interference or attacks."

59.     One representative expressed its concern at the piecemeal transfer of provisions from other legal instruments to the convention on the rights of the child as in the case of article 7 quater as adopted since, depending upon the way it was applied, it might have repercussions on the right of parents to guide and educate their children and, consequently, have repercussions on the family, the basis of society. She recalled that the law concerning minor children was nowadays an independent branch of the law and it should provide specific guidance to the Working Group.

## 11.     Text as adopted at first reading

*The following is taken from document E/CN.4/1988/WG.1/WP.1/Rev.1.*

### Article 7 quater

1.     The States Parties to the present Convention recognize the right of the child not to be subjected to arbitrary or unlawful interference with his or her privacy, family, home or correspondence, nor to unlawful attacks on his or her honour and reputation.

2.     The child has the right to the protection of the law against such interference or attacks.

## D.     Technical review (1988)

### 1.     Additional comments and clarifications by the Secretariat

*The following is taken from document E/CN.4/1989/WG.1/CRP.1/Add.1, paragraph 19.*

> 19.     In order to ensure the conformity of this article with article 17 of the International Covenant on Civil and Political Rights, the Working Group may wish to modify paragraph 1 to read:
>
> *"The child shall not be subjected ..."*

## E.     Second reading (1988-1989)

### 1.     Discussion and adoption at second reading

*The following is taken from the 1989 report of the Working Group to the Commission on Human Rights (E/CN.4/1989/48, paras. 296 to 303).*

> 296.     The Working Group had before it article 7 quater as adopted at first reading (E/CN.4/1989/WG.1/WP.2):

"1.	The States Parties to the present Convention recognize the right of the child not to be subjected to arbitrary or unlawful interference with his or her privacy, family, home or correspondence, nor to unlawful attacks on his or her honour and reputation.

2.	The child has the right to the protection of the law against such interference or attacks."

297.	The Chairman stated that no major amendments were proposed except for the small change suggested by the Secretariat in E/CN.4/1989/WG.1/WP.2, and according to which the first paragraph would start as follows:

"1.	The child shall not be subjected to arbitrary … etc."

298.	The observer for Australia agreed with the change.

299.	The delegation of the Federal Republic of Germany suggested that "No child shall be …" would be closer to the Covenant.

300.	The Chairman agreed and article 7 quater was adopted by the Working Group to read as follows:

"1.	No child shall be subjected to arbitrary or unlawful interference with his or her privacy, family, home or correspondence, nor to unlawful attacks on his or her honour and reputation.

2.	The child has the right to the protection of the law against such interference or attacks."

301.	Following the adoption of article 7 quater, the delegate of Venezuela stated that articles 7, 7 bis, 7 ter, 7 quater needed a safeguard clause concerning the exercise of those rights as subject to national legislation, since this latter would best protect the interests of children.

302.	The representatives of the United States of America, Sweden and Portugal expressed their opposition to such a clause.

303.	The delegation of Morocco endorsed the Venezuelan position and reserved its right to discuss the issue under article 21.

# Article 17 (Access to appropriate information)

## A.    Final text adopted by the General Assembly (1989)

*The following text is that approved by the General Assembly in its resolution 44/25 of 20 November 1989.*

States Parties recognize the important function performed by the mass media and shall ensure that the child has access to information and material from a diversity of national and international sources, especially those aimed at the promotion of his or her social, spiritual and moral well-being and physical and mental health. To this end, States Parties shall:

(a)    Encourage the mass media to disseminate information and material of social and cultural benefit to the child and in accordance with the spirit of article 29;

(b)    Encourage international cooperation in the production, exchange and dissemination of such information and material from a diversity of cultural, national and international sources;

(c)    Encourage the production and dissemination of children's books;

(d)    Encourage the mass media to have particular regard to the linguistic needs of the child who belongs to a minority group or who is indigenous;

(e)    Encourage the development of appropriate guidelines for the protection of the child from information and material injurious to his or her well-being, bearing in mind the provisions of articles 13 and 18.

## B.    First Polish draft convention and comments (1978)

*Neither the first Polish draft nor the views received on it (see document E/CN.4/1324 and Corr.1 and Add.1-5) addressed the issues raised in article 17 of the Convention.*

## C.    First reading (1979-1988)

*The text of article 17, which was based on article 9 of the revised Polish draft, was discussed at the Working Group in 1981 and 1982 and a text was adopted in 1984. An additional subparagraph was adopted in 1987. This article was referred to as article 9 throughout the first and second readings.*

### 1.    Revised Polish draft (1979)

*The following text is taken from Commission on Human Rights document E/CN.4/1349, which was reissued for technical reasons.*

*Article 9*

"Parents, guardians, State organs and social organizations shall protect the child against any harmful influence that mass media, and in particular the radio, film, television, printed materials and exhibitions, on account of their contents, may exert on his mental and moral development."

### 2.    Proposals submitted to the Working Group (1981)

#### (a)    Australia

*For the text of this proposal, see paragraph 122 in section 3 below.*

#### (b)    Holy See

*For the text of this proposal, see paragraph 118 in section 3 below.*

**(c)    Norway**

*For the text of this proposal, see paragraph 117 in section 3 below.*

## 3.    Discussion in the Working Group (1981)

*The following is taken from paragraphs 116-124 of the 1981 report of the Working Group to the Commission on Human Rights (E/CN.4/L.1575), which is reproduced in paragraph 289 of the 1981 report of the Commission on Human Rights (E/CN.4/1475).*

116.    Article 9 of the revised Polish draft read as follows:

"Parents, guardians, State organs and social organizations shall protect the child against any harmful influence that mass media, and in particular the radio, film, television, printed materials and exhibitions, on account of their contents, may exert on his mental and moral development."

117.    The delegation of Norway proposed that the word "film" in the [second] line of the paragraph be replaced by the phrase "recorded vision or sound".

118.    The observer of the Holy See suggested the insertion of the words "spiritual and social" in the [third] line between the words "moral" and "development".

119.    Differing views were expressed regarding the extent to which States parties should ensure the protection of the child against any harmful influence that mass media, and in particular radio, film, television, printed materials and exhibitions, on account of their contents, might exert on his mental and moral development.

120.    One speaker felt that the mass media does more good than harm and therefore the article should be phrased in a positive way, rather than in terms of protecting children from the mass media. States parties should ensure freedom of information, so that children can take advantage of a diversity of opinion concerning all matters. The speaker also stated that his delegation would urge deletion of the article unless it could be reformulated to take a positive approach, acknowledging the educational role of the mass media, the need for reciprocity in the free flow of information across international borders, and the importance of guaranteeing children access to information from a diversity of sources.

121.    Some delegations agreed with what had been advocated by that speaker, while another speaker pointed out that protecting the child from harmful influences of the mass media deserved special treatment by the Working Group. Also, the idea was put forward that it was necessary to recognize liberty, diversity and free circulation of information, as well as reciprocity of information between the States parties. Some other delegations supported the text of article 9 of the revised draft convention and indicated that in the Polish draft there was no question of limiting the freedom of information but only of the protection of children from the harmful influences of the mass media.

122.    The representative of Australia proposed that article 9 of the revised Polish draft should be replaced by the following text:

"States parties to the present Convention shall assure to the child the right to protection from exploitation and abuse. To this end, States parties shall encourage parents and guardians to provide their children with appropriate protection from written, printed or recorded material injurious to the health or morals of children and shall encourage the mass media to follow guidelines consistent with its responsibilities."

The representative of Australia observed that the proposal had been submitted not as a result of consultations but to facilitate further discussion of the issues raised in article 9.

123.     The Working Group, however, was unable further to consider article 9 for lack of time.

124.     Before finishing its work, several delegations expressed the view that the Working Group had made a very positive contribution towards the next phase of the drafting of the draft convention on the rights of the child, and thanked the delegation of Poland for the draft that was contained in document E/CN.4/1349 which had proved a most useful basis for discussion.

## 4.     Modified proposal submitted by Poland (1982)

*For the text of the proposal, for article 9 (present article 17), see paragraph 34 in section 6 below.*

## 5.     Proposals submitted to the Working Group (1982)

### (a)     Australia

*For the text of this proposal, see paragraph 35 in section 6 below.*

### (b)     Joint NGO proposal

*(Co-sponsors: International Council of Women, Friends World Committee for Consultation, International Association of Penal Law, International Catholic Child Bureau, International Catholic Union of the Press, International Commission of Jurists, International Council of Jewish Women, International Federation of Women in Legal Careers, International Federation of Women Lawyers and the World Jewish Congress). The following text is taken from document E/CN.4/1982/WG.1/WP.1, paragraph 3.*

States parties to the present Convention shall assure to the child the right to protection from exploitation and abuse. To this end, States parties shall encourage parents and guardians to provide their children with appropriate protection from written, printed or recorded material injurious to the health, morals, or spiritual and social development of children and shall encourage the mass media to follow guidelines consistent with its responsibilities.

## 6.     Discussion in the Working Group (1982)

*The following is taken from the 1982 report of the Working Group to the Commission on Human Rights (E/CN.4/1982/30/Add.1, paras. 34 to 41).*

34.     Article 9 of the revised Polish draft read as follows:

"Parents, guardians, State organs and social organizations shall protect the child against any harmful influence that mass media, and in particular the radio, film, television, printed materials and exhibitions, on account of their contents, may exert on his mental and moral development."

35.     The representative of Australia submitted a revised proposal as noted hereunder:

"States Parties shall encourage mass media agencies to develop special programmes for the benefit of children and to design guidelines, consistent with the right to freedom of expression, to protect the child from written, printed or recorded material injurious to his physical or mental health and development, bearing in mind also that in accordance with article 8, the primary responsibility for such protection rests with the parents or guardians of the child."

36.     The representative of the Union of Soviet Socialist Republics and a number of other delegations supported draft article 9 proposed by Poland; however, some delegations objected to that draft article. Then, the representative of the Union of Soviet Socialist Republics proposed as a compromise the following text for article 9 as contained in document A/C.3/36/6:

"1.     The States Parties to the present Convention shall encourage opinion-making quarters to disseminate information which promotes the upbringing of children in the spirit of the principles as laid down in article 16.

2.     The States Parties shall also encourage parents and guardians to provide their children with appropriate protection if, on account of its contents, the disseminated information might negatively affect the physical and moral development of the child."

37.     In the view of some representatives, the mass media does far more good than harm and therefore the article should be phrased in positive terms, rather than in terms seeking to protect children from the mass media. These representatives urged deletion of the article unless it could be reformulated in such a way as to take a positive approach to the question, acknowledging the need for reciprocity in the free flow of information across international borders and the importance of guaranteeing children access to information from a diversity of sources. In addition, the educational role of the mass media and the dangers of government censorship were emphasized. The attention of the Group was also drawn to the problem of child neglect and abuse, as well as of negligence and cruelty to children. It was stressed that such problems should be dealt with in the elaboration of the convention. Other speakers stressed the idea that the States Parties to the convention should have the obligation to protect children against any harmful influence that the contents of mass media may exert on their mental and moral development.

38.     It was further stated that the article under consideration should be formulated in a more positive way and that the right of the child to protection from exploitation and abuse should be dealt with by the Group later on.

39.     One representative, while acknowledging the educational role of the mass media, emphasized the fact that information must not exert a negative influence on the child, and pointed out that the question of protecting the child from the harmful influences of the mass media in such matters as apartheid, racist theories and ideologies and the like deserved special treatment by the Working Group. He also suggested that the Group should prepare a separate article concerning child abuse.

40.     The observer of the Holy See again proposed that the words "spiritual and social" should be introduced between the words "moral" and "development" in the revised Polish draft of article 9.

41.     The Working Group postponed to its next session consideration of article 9.

## 7.     Proposals submitted to the Working Group (1983)

### (a)     United States of America

*For the text of this proposal, see paragraph 53 in section 9 below.*

### (b)     Baha'i International Community

*The following text is taken from document E/CN.4/1983/WG.1/WP.2.*

*Article 9*

In order to ensure to the child enjoyment of the benefits of mass communication systems, the States Parties to the present Convention shall:

(a)     encourage mass media agencies to disseminate information designed to promote the health and welfare of the child and the upbringing of the child in the spirit of article 17;

(b)     encourage mass media agencies to disseminate material of social and cultural benefit to the child and, as appropriate, to develop and disseminate programmes designed to support, supplement or enhance existing programmes of education and introduce new programmes designed to expand educational opportunities for the child;

(c)	encourage mass media agencies to disseminate their child-oriented programmes not only in the official language(s) of the State but also in the language(s) of the State's minority and indigenous groups;

(d)	encourage international cooperation in the production, exchange and dissemination of child-oriented material from a diversity of cultural and national sources;

(e)	encourage mass media agencies to develop guidelines to protect the child from written, printed, audio or visual material injurious to his physical or mental health or to his social, spiritual or moral well-being, bearing in mind that, in accordance with article 8, the primary responsibility for such protection rests with the parents or guardians of the child.

## 8.	Proposals submitted to the Working Group (1984)

### (a)	Finland

*The following text is taken from document E/CN.4/1984/WG.1/WP.14.*

*Introduction of article 9*

The States Parties recognize the important function performed by the mass media and shall take any necessary steps to ensure that the child has access to information and material from a diversity of sources aimed at the promoting of his social, spiritual and moral well-being and physical and mental health. To this end, the States Parties to the present Convention shall:

### (b)	Ukrainian SSR

*For the text of this proposal, see paragraph 55 in section 9 below.*

### (c)	United States of America

*For the text of this proposal, see paragraph 53 in section 9 below.*

### (d)	NGO Ad Hoc Group *(see annex III (B) for participating organizations)*

*The following text, which was made available to the Working Group in 1984, is taken from document E/CN.4/1985/ WG.1/WP.1.*

This is a slightly amended version of the proposal submitted by the Baha'i International Community in E/ CN.4/1983/WG.1/WP.2:

In order to ensure to the child the right to hold opinions without interference, and to enjoy the benefits of mass communication systems, the States Parties to the present Convention shall:

(a)	encourage mass media agencies to disseminate information designed to promote the health and welfare of the child and the upbringing of the child in the spirit of [proposed] article 17;

(b)	encourage mass media agencies to disseminate material of social and cultural benefit to the child and, as appropriate, to develop and disseminate programmes designed to support, supplement or enhance existing programmes of education and introduce new programmes designed to expand educational opportunities for the child;

(c)	encourage mass media agencies to disseminate their child-oriented programmes not only in the official language(s) of the State but also in the language(s) of the State's minority groups and indigenous peoples;

(d)     encourage international cooperation in the production, exchange and dissemination of child-oriented material from a diversity of cultural, national and international sources;

(e)     encourage mass media agencies to develop guidelines to protect the child from written, printed, audio or visual material injurious to his physical or mental health or to his social, spiritual or moral well-being, bearing in mind that, in accordance with article 8 the primary responsibility for such protection rests with the parents or guardians of the child.

## 9.     Discussion and adoption by the Working Group (1984)

*The following is taken from the 1984 report of the Working Group to the Commission on Human Rights (E/CN.4/1984/71, paras. 51 to 79).*

51.     The Polish delegation submitted article 9 as contained in document A/C.3/36/6, which read as follows:

"1.     The States Parties to the present Convention shall encourage opinion-making quarters to disseminate information which promotes the upbringing of children in the spirit of the principles as laid down in article 16.

2.     The States Parties shall also encourage parents and guardians to provide their children with appropriate protection if, on account of its contents, the disseminated information might negatively affect the physical and moral development of the child."

In addition, proposals submitted by the Baha'i International Community in 1983 and by the Informal NGO Ad Hoc Group on the Drafting of the Convention were brought to the attention of the Working Group.

52.     Some delegations shared the view that the original Polish proposal stressed some negative aspects of the mass media and should not be used as the basis for discussion, while other delegations deemed the texts put forward by the non-governmental organizations too detailed for the purposes of discussion.

53.     The representative of the United States, in retabling a proposal from 1983, stated that that proposal recognized the educational function of the mass media and that it would be consistent with both the public and private sector of a country. It read as follows:

"Recognizing the important educational function performed by the mass media, States Parties shall ensure that the child has access to information from a diversity of sources, in particular by not impeding the free flow of information across international borders and the availability of such information, as well as by assuring freedom of expression and opinion for all."

Further, the representative of the United States stated that any article on this subject should take into account the concerns of States where the private sector was involved in the mass media and it was not possible or desirable for the State to ensure or guarantee anything in that field. The United States proposal stressed, however, that the State should and could guarantee the free flow of information.

54.     Following the suggestion of several delegations and the Chairman's request that a compromise text be elaborated after consultations, an open, informal working party [consisting of Canada, France, Netherlands, Poland, Ukrainian SSR, United Kingdom, United States of America and Baha'i International Community] prepared, for use as a basis for discussion, a redrafted proposal that attempted to consolidate many delegations' views. This proposal was submitted by the representative of Canada and read as follows:

"Recognizing the important function performed by the mass media and the need to ensure that the child has access to information and material from a diversity of sources aimed at the promoting of his social, spiritual and moral well-being and physical and mental health, the States Parties to the present Convention shall:

(a)      Encourage the mass media agencies to disseminate information of social and cultural benefit to the child and in accordance with the spirit of the article 16;

(b)      Encourage international cooperation in the production, exchange and dissemination of such information and shall not impede the free flow of information across international borders;

(c)      Encourage the mass media agencies to have particular regard to the linguistic needs of minority groups;

(d)      Encourage the development of voluntary guidelines for the protection of the child from material potentially injurious to his well-being bearing in mind that the primary responsibility for such protection rests with the parents or guardians of the child."

55.      The representative of the Ukrainian SSR introduced another proposal which read as follows:

"1.      The States Parties to the present Convention shall use their governmental bodies and encourage private mass media agencies to develop and disseminate information designed to promote the health and welfare of the child, his social and cultural upbringing. Information shall be produced and disseminated in both the official language(s) of the State and the language(s) of the State's minority groups and indigenous peoples.

2.      The States Parties shall encourage international cooperation in the production, exchange and dissemination of information from different cultural, national and international sources compatible with the ideals of peace, humanism, liberty and international solidarity and all other ideals promoting international understanding and cooperation.

3.      The States Parties shall also encourage all those concerned with the care of the child, to protect him from material injuries to his physical or mental health or to his social, spiritual or moral well-being."

56.      After an exchange of views, it was agreed that the proposed redraft by the informal working party would be used as the basis for discussion.

*Introductory part*

57.      The introductory part of the article reminded the representative of Finland more of a preambular paragraph and consequently he suggested the following amendments: the sentence should begin with the words "The States Parties recognize", the words "the need" should be replaced by "shall take the necessary steps", and the sentence should end with the word "health". Further, the words "the States Parties to the present Convention shall" should be replaced by the words "To this end the States Parties to this Convention shall". The delegation of the United States requested that the words "the need to" should be replaced by the word "shall".

*Subparagraph (a)*

58.      The Working Group proceeded to consider subparagraph (a) which was provisionally agreed to with a reference to article 16 of the revised Polish draft.

*Subparagraph (b)*

59.      As the Group went on to subparagraph (b), the representative of the Ukrainian SSR proposed inserting the phrase "compatible with the ideals of peace, humanism, liberty and international solidarity and all other ideals promoting international understanding and cooperation" after the phrase "free flow of information", as contained in the amendment proposed by his delegation, and the deletion of the words "across international borders". The delegation of the United Kingdom suggested the addition of the word "such" between the words "free flow of" and "information", and his proposal met with the approval of many delegations.

60.    The delegation of the Union of Soviet Socialist Republics then requested, in a spirit of compromise, that subparagraph (b) be deleted and that subparagraph (d) of the text of the Informal NGO Ad Hoc Group be used instead. The proposed new text was as follows:

> "Encourage international cooperation in the production, exchange and dissemination of child-oriented material from a diversity of cultural, national and international sources."

61.    The Canadian delegation agreed with the above text with the exception of the words "child-oriented material". The representative of the United States rejected the proposal put forward by the delegation of the Union of Soviet Socialist Republics but suggested the insertion in subparagraph (b) of the informal working party's redraft of the words "for this purpose" between "information and" and "shall not impede" in order to relate the concept concerning the free flow of information more closely to international cooperation.

62.    The representative of the United Kingdom suggested that the word "child-oriented" be replaced by "such" in the text proposed by the delegation of the Union of Soviet Socialist Republics, and the Canadian delegation agreed to this proposal. The Australian delegation proposed that the phrase should read "such information and material". For the purpose of consistency the representative of Canada suggested the introduction of the words "and material" in subparagraph (a) as well as subparagraph (b).

63.    The United States delegation subsequently proposed that, in subparagraph (b) of the informal working party's redraft, the word "facilitate" should replace the words "not impede", or that the word "facilitate" should appear in brackets. The representative of the United States also proposed including the idea in the introductory part of the article with the following opening line: "The States Parties recognize the importance of the mass media and the free flow of information across international borders and shall ensure", and indicated that, if the Working Group accepted her suggestion, she would not insist on having the word "facilitate" retained in subparagraph (b). In the course of the exchange of views that ensued, the delegation of Australia proposed replacing the phrase following "dissemination of such information" by the words "and shall use their best endeavours to facilitate the free flow of such information across international borders".

64.    With regard to the question of the free flow of information across international borders, delegations continued to manifest divergent views. Some delegations deemed it a question worthy of separate consideration while still others saw its inclusion as a recognition of the importance of the concept of free flow of information.

65.    Pursuant to the Chairman's request that the delegations of the Ukrainian SSR and the United States engage in consultations to produce a compromise text, a consensus was reached between the two delegations with regard to the introductory part and subparagraph (b). The compromise proposal read as follows:

> "The States Parties recognize the important function performed by the mass media and shall ensure that the child has access to information and material from a diversity of international and national sources, including those aimed at the promoting of his social, spiritual and moral well-being and physical and mental health. To this end, the States Parties to the present Convention shall:
>
> > [...]
> >
> > (b)    Encourage international cooperation in the production, exchange and dissemination of such information and material from a diversity of cultural, national and international sources."

The United States delegation stated that the words "international and national" had been added before "sources" as well as "including those" after "sources" and that it had been agreed to delete "and shall not impede the free flow of information across international borders", and requested that the compromise proposal be accepted as drafted.

66.    The Chairman suggested the addition of the words "to the present Convention" after "States Parties" in the first line of the text and their deletion in the following sentence; the representative of Canada supported this suggestion.

67.     The representative of the United Kingdom requested that the sequence of the words "international and national" be reversed and the delegations of the Netherlands and the Ukrainian SSR supported his request. The Working Group agreed to the text of the introductory part and subparagraph (b).

*Subparagraph (c)*

68.     The Canadian delegation requested that, if there was to be a clause with the expression "minority groups" in subparagraph (c), the words "or indigenous peoples" be added to it, explaining that indigenous peoples disliked being referred to as "minority groups". Some speakers questioned the appropriateness of the word "peoples" as opposed to "populations"; reference was made to the terminology used by the Sub-Commission on Prevention of Discrimination and Protection of Minorities, namely "indigenous populations", and the Group agreed on the use of the word "populations".

69.     The representative of the Netherlands proposed the insertion of the expression "the child belonging to" between the words "linguistic needs of" and "minority groups", and the representative of the United Kingdom suggested that "or" should replace "and" after the words "minority group". The delegation of Australia then proposed that the phrase being discussed should read: "the linguistic needs of the child who belongs to a minority group or an indigenous population". With these amendments, subparagraph (c) was provisionally agreed to by the Working Group.

*Subparagraph (d)*

70.     The representative of Canada reminded the Group that subparagraph (d) was based on subparagraph (e) of the text of the Informal NGO Ad Hoc Group, and that it was intended to encourage the development of guidelines to protect the child but without any indication as to who would develop them. The delegation of Australia suggested the insertion of the words "information and" between the phrases "protection of the child from" and "material potentially injurious" as well as the addition at the end of this subparagraph of the phrase "or any other person who has the care of the child".

71.     The representative of the Ukrainian SSR, although agreeing with the inclusion of the subparagraph under consideration in article 9, believed that the phrase after "well-being" was superfluous and accordingly recommended its deletion, so that the subparagraph would end with the word "well-being". In this connection, the delegation of the Netherlands explained that the phrase following "well-being", namely "bearing in mind that the primary responsibility for such protection rests with the parents or guardians of the child", was fully in line with article 8 of the draft convention already adopted some time ago.

72.     The representative of the Ukrainian SSR then proposed placing the following phrase after "well-being": "bearing in mind that the responsibility rests on all those concerned with the care of the child". The Canadian delegation suggested ending the subparagraph with the word "well-being" as had been previously recommended by the Ukrainian SSR delegation. The United States delegation proposed adding the phrase "in accordance with article 8" after "well-being" and ending subparagraph (d) in that way. The Swedish delegation suggested adding the words "and physical and mental health" after the word "well-being".

73.     The representative of the Union of Soviet Socialist Republics agreed with the proposal made by the delegation of the United States but objected to the word "voluntary" qualifying "guidelines" and suggested its deletion.

74.     The Chairman then suggested that the subparagraph should end with the phrase "well-being and physical and mental health", but the representative of the United Kingdom pointed out that anything injurious to a child's physical and mental health would be injurious to his well-being also. The Swedish amendment was consequently withdrawn.

75.     Furthermore, the delegation of the United Kingdom proposed that the words "voluntary guidelines" in the first line should be replaced by the phrase "appropriate guidelines and codes of conduct"; the representatives of Finland and the Union of Soviet Socialist Republics supported the United Kingdom amendment.

76.      The representative of the United States did not agree with the inclusion of "codes of conduct" and suggested that the Group might consider deleting "voluntary" and leaving only "guidelines". The delegation of Canada proposed instead replacing "voluntary" by "appropriate" and eliminating reference to "codes of conduct". Many delegations supported the Canadian proposal and the delegation of the United Kingdom withdrew its amendment regarding the inclusion of "codes of conduct".

77.      Returning to the question whether subparagraph (d) should end with the word "well-being", the representative of France stated that, although the word "well-being" was sufficient, she would also wish to see a reference to article 8 in subparagraph (d). This proposal, which met with the support of many delegations, was reinforced by the representative of Canada who referred again to the United States proposal that such reference should read "in accordance with article 8".

78.      After an exchange of views regarding the best wording for the reference to article 8 at the end of the subparagraph, the Chairman suggested the expression "bearing in mind the provisions of article 8". The Group accepted the Chairman's proposal and subparagraph (d) was provisionally agreed to.

79.      The Working Group adopted article 9 as a whole.

## 10.      Proposal submitted to the Working Group (1987)

### (a)      International Board on Books for Young People

*For the text of this proposal, see paragraph 21 in section 11 below.*

## 11.      Discussion and adoption by the Working Group (1987)

*The following is taken from the 1987 report of the Working Group to the Commission on Human Rights (E/CN.4/1987/25, paras. 21 to 23).*

21.      For the consideration of this article, the Working Group had before it a proposal submitted by the International Board on Books for Young People, for a new subparagraph (c), whereby the present (c) becomes (d) and the present (d) becomes (e), which read:

> "Encourage, at all levels, literacy and the reading habit through children's book production and dissemination, as well as the habit of storytelling."

22.      The representative of Austria was in agreement with the basic idea of the proposal submitted by that non-governmental organization and suggested that it should be put forward in legal terms. Accordingly, he submitted the following proposal:

> "Encourage the production and dissemination of children's books."

23.      The delegations of France, Italy and the Netherlands supported the above-mentioned proposal and the Working Group adopted it by consensus.

## 12.      Text as adopted at first reading

*The following is taken from document E/CN.4/1988/WG.1/WP.1/Rev.1.*

*Article 9*

The States Parties to the present Convention recognize the important function performed by the mass media and shall ensure that the child has access to information and material from a diversity of national and international sources, including those aimed at the promoting of his social, spiritual and moral well-being and physical and mental health. To this end, the States Parties shall:

(a)      Encourage the mass media agencies to disseminate information and material of social and cultural benefit to the child and in accordance with the spirit of article 16;

(b)     Encourage international cooperation in the production, exchange and dissemination of such information and material from a diversity of cultural, national and international sources;

(c)     Encourage the production and dissemination of children's books;

(d)     Encourage the mass media agencies to have particular regard to the linguistic needs of the child who belongs to a minority group or an indigenous population;

(e)     Encourage the development of appropriate guidelines for the protection of the child from information and material potentially injurious to his well-being bearing in mind the provisions of article 8.

# D.  Technical review (1988)

## 1.     Comment by the United Nations Educational, Scientific and Cultural Organization (UNESCO)

*The following is taken from document E/CN.4/1989/WG.1/CRP.1, page 25.*

In paragraph (c) the following text should be added after the end of the present phrase:

"in particular promoting the ideals of the United Nations Charter."

## 2.     Comment by the United Nations Children's Fund (UNICEF)

*The following is taken from document E/CN.4/1989/WG.1/CRP.1, page 25.*

*Gender neutrality*

The middle part of the first paragraph could read:

"... including those aimed at [ ] promoting the social, spiritual and moral well-being and physical and mental health *of children* ..."

## 3.     Additional comments and clarifications by the Secretariat

*The following is taken from document E/CN.4/1989/WG.1/CRP.1/Add.1, paragraphs 20-21.*

20.     It may be pointed out that the use of the term "mass media agencies" in subparagraphs (a) and (d) may be more restrictive than was the intention of that provision inasmuch as the word "agencies" may exclude some significant sources and means of information and material of social and cultural benefit. The Working Group may wish to consider the possibility of deleting the word "agencies" in the two subparagraphs and employ instead the term *"mass media"* which would be consistent with frequent references in resolutions, including the Declaration on Fundamental Principles concerning the Contribution of the Mass Media to Strengthening Peace and International Understanding, to the Promotion of Human Rights and to Countering Racialism, Apartheid and Incitement to War, proclaimed by the General Conference of UNESCO at its twentieth session in Paris, on 28 November 1978.

21.     As to subparagraph (e), a conflict may arise with regard to the provisions of article 7a of the draft convention and, by extension, with article 19 of the International Covenant on Civil and Political Rights inasmuch as "The protection of the child from information ... potentially injurious" introduces an additional restriction to those listed in the above-mentioned articles. In order to meet this concern, the Working Group may wish to consider the possibility of deleting the word "potentially" and adding at the end of the subparagraph a reference to article 7a so that this part of the subparagraph would read:

"... the protection of the child from information and material injurious to his or her well-being having in mind the provisions of articles *7a and* 8."

# E.    Second reading (1988-1989)

## 1.    Proposals submitted to the Working Group at second reading

### (a)    Turkey

*The following is taken from document E/CN.4/1989/WG.1/WP.42.*

Article 9 paragraph (d)

Delete the paragraph.

### (b)    Venezuela

*For the text of this proposal, see paragraph 320 in section 2 below.*

### (c)    Latin American meeting

*By note verbale to the Centre for Human Rights, the Permanent Mission of Argentina requested that the report and recommendations of the Latin American meeting [of NGOs] in support of the United Nations draft convention on the rights of the child be circulated as an official information document at the Working Group. The meeting took place in Buenos Aires from 29 September to 2 October 1988. The following is taken from document E/CN.4/1989/WG.1/WP.1.*

Article 9: ... physical and mental health, granting priority to a society's right to its own cultural identity. The States parties recognize the importance of mass media in formal and informal education; therefore, the policies that govern the use of mass media should adjust their approach, methods and contents to the above principles when minors have access to the messages of the media.

To this end, the States parties shall:

1.    Encourage and promote the development of programmes for education, training and updating of knowledge through mass media.

2.    Check that messages of mass media to which a minor has access:

(a)    Do not disseminate attitudes that justify crime or violence, including the promotion of the use of warlike toys;

(b)    Do not encourage any type of addiction such as alcoholism, drug addiction, tobacco consumption or any other that could affect the minor's physical and mental health;

(c)    Do not disseminate advertisements aimed at minors since they do not have an adult's possibility of choice.

## 2.    Discussion and adoption at second reading

*The following is taken from the 1989 report of the Working Group to the Commission on Human Rights (E/CN.4/1989/48, paras. 320 to 332).*

320.    The representative of Venezuela proposed the following paragraph (E/CN.4/1989/WG.1/WP.40):

"Any problem in which a child is involved shall be of a CONFIDENTIAL NATURE, for the fundamental purpose of sparing the child publicity which might be harmful in his or her future contacts with society, so that the child's full social and individual development may become a reality."

The Chairman established a drafting group composed of representatives of countries which had introduced proposals: Venezuela, Turkey, United States of America and Yugoslavia.

321.    The representative of the United States of America, acting as coordinator of a drafting group composed also of Turkey, Venezuela and Yugoslavia, informed the participants of the results of the work of this group in connection with various proposals made in regard to article 9, including those contained in E/CN.4/1989/WG.1/WP.2, E/CN.4/1989/WG.1/WP.40 and E/CN.4/1989/WG.1/WP.42.

322.    In summarizing the outcome of the consultations held so far, the representative of the United States of America indicated that there were four basic proposals which should be now concentrated upon by the Working Group. One of the proposals, which the drafting group deemed unacceptable, sought to delete subparagraphs (a) to (e) of article 9 altogether. Another approach was that the original text of article 9 as adopted at first reading should be retained. One more suggestion was made to the effect that a new subparagraph (f) should be added to article 9 in which the idea of a strict confidentiality of any matter involving children was to be fixed. Finally, a proposal was also made to amend subparagraph (d) of article 9 by replacing the expression "indigenous population" by some alternative wording such as "indigenous people", "indigenous child" or "who is indigenous".

323.    In the discussion that followed most of the participants expressed their desire not to depart from the language and basic provisions of article 9 as approved in the first reading, and no support was given to the proposal to delete all subparagraphs of the article.

324.    With regard to the proposed changes of language of subparagraph (d), some speakers said they could not agree with the expression "indigenous people" but would be eventually ready to accept some other formulations. The proposal to replace the words "an indigenous population" by the words "who is indigenous" seemed to receive the greatest support.

325.    With respect to the proposed addition of a new subparagraph on confidentiality (E/CN.4/1989/WG.1/WP.40), several participants expressed the view that this matter did not belong to article 9 and it was therefore not appropriate to discuss it in connection with this article, the whole thrust of which was aimed rather at the spread of information than at its limitation. It was said in this connection that this proposal might be very well received somewhere else in the convention, especially in its article 19.

326.    The representative of Venezuela said she was under instructions from her Government to seek the inclusion of the proposed amendment on confidentiality to the draft convention since it was regarded as extremely important for the due protection of children. She would nevertheless agree not to insist on its inclusion into article 9 if she could be absolutely certain that this matter of confidentiality would be dealt with under articles 10, 11, 18 and 19 and be accordingly reflected therein.

327.    The representative of the German Democratic Republic proposed to delete the words "including those" in the introductory part of article 9. While most speakers did not oppose this amendment, one participant said that he would be reluctant to agree with this deletion since it would then change the whole meaning of the article and would give it a more restrictive character. The Working Group consequently accepted a compromise suggestion of the representative of the Netherlands who proposed to replace the word "including" by the word "especially".

328.    With regard to the amendment of UNESCO (E/CN.4/1989/WG.1/CRP.1) seeking to add the words "in particular promoting the ideals of the United Nations Charter" at the end of subparagraph (c), two delegations voiced their support for this proposal. However, more delegations opposed this amendment stating that this concern had been already covered in article 16 as well as in the introductory part of this same article which contained a reference to "international sources" of information. Portugal stated that children needed different books, taking into account their recreational and cultural needs.

329.    The observer for Turkey stated that, since the introductory part of article 9 dealt adequately with the right of children to receive information through mass media, there was no need for the subparagraphs

in article 9, and that it should not be the role of this convention to give detailed guidance as to what the States Parties should do in implementing the article. He then drew the attention of the Working Group to subparagraph (d) which mentioned "minority group" and "indigenous population". Since a consensus definition of these concepts had not been reached despite the efforts being deployed in international forums, he said the subparagraph would be non-applicable. He said it would be practical to delete all subparagraphs and leave article 9 only with its introductory part. If this was not acceptable, subparagraph (d) which was, in his view, not only useless but non-applicable as well, should be deleted.

330.     The representative of Venezuela orally proposed three amendments to subparagraphs (a), (c) and (e) which were subsequently recognized by the Working Group as having a purely linguistic character and relating to the Spanish version only.

331.     The Working Group then adopted article 9, as revised and amended, reading as follows:

"States Parties recognize the important function performed by the mass media and shall ensure that the child has access to information and material from a diversity of national and international sources, especially those aimed at the promotion of his or her social, spiritual and moral well-being and physical and mental health. To this end, States Parties shall:

(a)     Encourage the mass media to disseminate information and material of social and cultural benefit to the child and in accordance with the spirit of article 16;

(b)     Encourage international cooperation in the production, exchange and dissemination of such information and material from a diversity of cultural, national and international sources;

(c)     Encourage the production and dissemination of children's books;

(d)     Encourage the mass media to have particular regard to the linguistic needs of the child who belongs to a minority group or who is indigenous;

(e)     Encourage the development of appropriate guidelines for the protection of the child from information and material injurious to his or her well-being bearing in mind the provisions of articles 7a and 8."

332.     The observer for Turkey, upon the adoption of article 9, further stated that the article was adopted with subparagraph (d) making reference to terms upon which there were no agreed definitions. Reiterating his delegation's view, he said there would be no alternative by States Parties but to interpret, under the circumstances, these terms according to their national law. Therefore, such a reservation might be felt necessary if and when the draft convention would be open to signature.